# Second BlackboxNLP Workshop on Analyzing and Interpreting Neural Networks for NLP at ACL 2019

Florence, Italy
1 August 2019

ISBN: 978-1-5108-9109-8

**Printed from e-media with permission by:**

Curran Associates, Inc.
57 Morehouse Lane
Red Hook, NY  12571

**Some format issues inherent in the e-media version may also appear in this print version.**




Printed by Curran Associates, Inc. (2019)

For permission requests, please contact the Association for Computational Linguistics
at the address below.

Association for Computational Linguistics
209 N. Eighth Street
Stroudsburg, Pennsylvania 18360

Phone:   1-570-476-8006
Fax:       1-570-476-0860

acl@aclweb.org

**Additional copies of this publication are available from:**

Curran Associates, Inc.
57 Morehouse Lane
Red Hook, NY 12571 USA
Phone:  845-758-0400
Fax:      845-758-2633
Email:   curran@proceedings.com
Web:     www.proceedings.com

ACL 2019

# The BlackboxNLP Workshop on Analyzing and Interpreting Neural Networks for NLP at ACL 2019

## Proceedings of the Second Workshop

August 1, 2019
Florence, Italy

Sponsored by:

Google facebook Microsoft

# Introduction

BlackboxNLP is the workshop on analyzing and interpreting neural networks for NLP. In the last few years, neural networks have rapidly become a central component in NLP systems. The improvement in accuracy and performance brought by the introduction of neural networks has typically come at the cost of our understanding of the system: How do we assess what the representations and computations are that the network learns? The goal of this workshop is to bring together people who are attempting to peek inside the neural network black box, taking inspiration from machine learning, psychology, linguistics, and neuroscience.

In this second edition of the workshop, hosted by the 2019 Annual Meeting of the Association of Computational Linguistics in Florence, Italy, we accepted 29 archival papers and 16 extended abstracts. We hope this workshop continues to bring together ideas and stimulating new ways of building methods and resources for the analysis and understanding of the inner-dynamics of neural networks for NLP.

BlackboxNLP would not have been possible without the dedication of its program committee. We would like to thank them for their invaluable effort in providing timely and high-quality reviews on a short notice. We are also grateful to our invited speakers for contributing to our program. Finally, we are very thankful to our sponsors, Google, Facebook and Mircrosoft for supporting the workshop.

Tal Linzen, Grzegorz Chrupała, Yonatan Belinkov and Dieuwke Hupkes

**Organizers:**

Tal Linzen, Johns Hopkins University
Grzegorz Chrupała, Tilburg University
Yonatan Belinkov, Harvard University and MIT
Dieuwke Hupkes, ILLC, University of Amsterdam


**Program Committee:**

Samira Abnar
Željko Agić
Afra Alishahi
Antonios Anastasopoulos
Niranjan Balasubramanian
Joost Bastings
Lisa Beinborn
Laurent Besacier
Or Biran
Samuel R. Bowman
Stergios Chatzikyriakidis
Miryam de Lhoneux
Ewan Dunbar
Jacob Eisenstein
Allyson Ettinger
Antske Fokkens
Robert Frank
Richard Futrell
Sharon Goldwater
Kristina Gulordava
David Harwath
Germán Kruszewski
Yair Lakretz
Shalom Lappin
Jindřich Libovický
Nelson F. Liu
Pranava Madhyastha
David Mareček
Paola Merlo
Raymond Mooney
Sebastian Padó
Yves Peirsman
Adam Poliak
Rudolf Rosa
Carolyn Rose
Hassan Sajjad
Wojciech Samek
Naomi Saphra
Rico Sennrich

Pia Sommerauer
György Szaszák
Francesca Toni
Adina Williams
Roberto Zamparelli
Fabio Massimo Zanzotto
Willem Zuidema

# Table of Contents

# Conference Program

**August 1**

**9:00–9:10**     **Opening remarks**

**9:15–10:00**     **Keynote speaker 1: Arianna Bisazza**

**10:00–11:15**     **Poster session 1**

*Transcoding Compositionally: Using Attention to Find More Generalizable Solutions*
Kris Korrel, Dieuwke Hupkes, Verna Dankers and Elia Bruni

*Sentiment Analysis Is Not Solved! Assessing and Probing Sentiment Classification*
Jeremy Barnes, Lilja Øvrelid and Erik Velldal

*Second-order Co-occurrence Sensitivity of Skip-Gram with Negative Sampling*
Dominik Schlechtweg, Cennet Oguz and Sabine Schulte im Walde

*Can Neural Networks Understand Monotonicity Reasoning?*
Hitomi Yanaka, Koji Mineshima, Daisuke Bekki, Kentaro Inui, Satoshi Sekine, Lasha Abzianidze and Johan Bos

*Multi-Granular Text Encoding for Self-Explaining Categorization*
Zhiguo Wang, Yue Zhang, Mo Yu, Wei Zhang, Lin Pan, Linfeng Song, Kun Xu and Yousef El-Kurdi

*The Meaning of "Most" for Visual Question Answering Models*
Alexander Kuhnle and Ann Copestake

*Do Human Rationales Improve Machine Explanations?*
Julia Strout, Ye Zhang and Raymond Mooney

*Analyzing the Structure of Attention in a Transformer Language Model*
Jesse Vig and Yonatan Belinkov

*Detecting Political Bias in News Articles Using Headline Attention*
Rama Rohit Reddy Gangula, Suma Reddy Duggenpudi and Radhika Mamidi

**11:15–12:30**  **Oral presentations 1 (5 x 15 minutes)**

*Character Eyes: Seeing Language through Character-Level Taggers*
Yuval Pinter, Marc Marone and Jacob Eisenstein

*Faithful Multimodal Explanation for Visual Question Answering*
Jialin Wu and Raymond Mooney

*Evaluating Recurrent Neural Network Explanations*
Leila Arras, Ahmed Osman, Klaus-Robert Müller and Wojciech Samek

*On the Realization of Compositionality in Neural Networks*
Joris Baan, Jana Leible, Mitja Nikolaus, David Rau, Dennis Ulmer, Tim Baumgärtner, Dieuwke Hupkes and Elia Bruni

*Learning the Dyck Language with Attention-based Seq2Seq Models*
Xiang Yu, Ngoc Thang Vu and Jonas Kuhn

**12:30–14:00**  *Lunch*

**14:00–14:50**  **Keynote speaker 2: Michael F. Bonner**

**14:50–16:00**  **Poster session 2**

*Modeling Paths for Explainable Knowledge Base Completion*
Josua Stadelmaier and Sebastian Padó

*Probing Word and Sentence Embeddings for Long-distance Dependencies Effects in French and English*
Paola Merlo

*Derivational Morphological Relations in Word Embeddings*
Tomáš Musil, Jonáš Vidra and David Mareček

# Transcoding compositionally: using attention to find more generalizable solutions


**Kris Korrel**
University of Amsterdam
kris.korrel@gmail.com

**Dieuwke Hupkes**
University of Amsterdam
d.hupkes@uva.nl

**Verna Dankers**
University of Amsterdam
verna.dankers@gmail.com

**Elia Bruni**
Universitat Pompeu Fabra
elia.bruni@gmail.com



## Abstract

While sequence-to-sequence models have shown remarkable generalization power across several natural language tasks, their construct of solutions are argued to be less compositional than human-like generalization. In this paper, we present seq2attn, a new architecture that is specifically designed to exploit attention to find compositional patterns in the input. In seq2attn, the two standard components of an encoder-decoder model are connected via a *transcoder*, that modulates the information flow between them. We show that seq2attn can successfully generalize, without requiring any additional supervision, on two tasks which are specifically constructed to challenge the compositional skills of neural networks. The solutions found by the model are highly interpretable, allowing easy analysis of both the types of solutions that are found and potential causes for mistakes. We exploit this opportunity to introduce a new paradigm to test compositionality that studies the extent to which a model *overgeneralizes* when confronted with exceptions. We show that seq2attn exhibits such overgeneralization to a larger degree than a standard sequence-to-sequence model.


## 1 Introduction

In recent years, deep artificial neural networks have been at the root of many successes in a wide variety of AI tasks, including sequential tasks, for which encoder-decoder models are the de facto standard (Cho et al., 2014; Sutskever et al., 2014). These successes have also caused a renewed interest in the types of solutions that they learn (Linzen et al., 2018) and, in particular, have prompted the question: to what extent can their high accuracy be taken as evidence that they in fact understood the task they are modeling. A number of recent studies argues that it cannot, when 'understanding the task' is explained as understanding the im-

plicit rules by which it is governed (e.g., Johnson et al., 2017; Lake and Baroni, 2018; Liška et al., 2018; Feng et al., 2018; Ravfogel et al., 2018). More specifically, they argue that rather than understanding those implicit rules and being able to compositionally apply them, RNN models exploit biases in the data that are unrelated to the underlying system. While the latter strategy is remarkably effective when large amounts of training data are available, the lack of understanding of the actual task leads to sample inefficiency, inability to transfer knowledge between tasks and difficulty to generalize to sequences that are drawn from the same rule space, but differ distributionally from the training data. Furthermore, the use of such strategies, which deviate largely from human approaches, that are typically compositional (Lake et al., 2015), makes it difficult to understand what a model does and when it may make a mistake.

In this work, we propose a new component that aims to address this particular weakness of seq2seq models. This component, which is a recurrent attention module that can be integrated in any form of encoder-decoder model, modulates the information flow from encoder to decoder. We test our module, which we dub *seq2attn*, in a recurrent encoder-decoder model. Using two tasks that are designed such that their accuracy reflects directly whether the underlying rule-based system is learned – the lookup table task (Liška et al., 2018) and SCAN (Lake and Baroni, 2018; Loula et al., 2018) – we show that seq2attn strongly encourages rule-based behaviour, which is easily interpreted by studying the attention patterns generated by the module. Additionally, we propose a new testing paradigm based on *overgeneralization*, that can be used to gain more insights in the biases of a model which cannot be inferred from task success alone.




*Proceedings of the Second BlackboxNLP Workshop on Analyzing and Interpreting Neural Networks for NLP*, pages 1–11
Florence, Italy, August 1, 2019. ©2019 Association for Computational Linguistics

## 2   Related Work

### 2.1   Compositional datasets

The ability to learn and compositionally apply
symbolic rules is considered to be an important
prerequisite for understanding and modeling natural language. While (gated) recurrent neural networks are in principle capable of modeling compositional systems (e.g., Gers and Schmidhuber,
2001; Rodriguez, 2001), whether they in fact do
so when trained on large amounts of data to perform natural language processing tasks remains an
open question. Some positive results in this direction have been presented (e.g., Hupkes et al.,
2018b), but a number of recent papers have argued that, rather than understanding the underlying compositional structure of a problem, RNNs
rely on heuristics and exploit biases in the data.
Particularly relevant to the current work are the
studies of Lake and Baroni (2018) and Liška et al.
(2018), who both present data sets specifically designed to reflect compositionality in their task accuracy. Using their compositional tests, they show
that vanilla seq2seq models do not readily generalize to solutions that exhibit an understanding of
the underlying rule system of the tasks.

### 2.2   Models

Some recent approaches attack the lack of compositional behaviour of RNNs by designing models that have compositionality explicitly built in,
for instance by equiping architectures with a series of specialized modules and a controller that
composes them (e.g., Andreas et al., 2016; Johnson et al., 2017). In this work, instead, we focus
on inducing compositional solutions in RNN models, that are less rigid and generally require fewer
supervision.

Our method draws inspiration from the work on
compositional learning of Hupkes et al. (2018a).
The authors introduce the concept of *Attentive
Guidance*, a training signal given to the attention
mechanism of a seq2seq model to induce more
compositional solutions. While they convincingly
show that seq2seq models with attention can in
fact implement such solutions (see Baan et al.
(2019) for an in-depth analysis), their model requires attention annotation of the training data,
which may not always be available. In this work,
we address this problem by designing a model that
still aims to be compositional through the attention mechanism, but instead learns these patterns

fully automatically, obtaining similar or even improved performance without the need of extra supervision.

Another line of work which exploits attention
as a regularization technique is proposed by Hudson and Manning (2018), who introduce the Memory, Attention and Composition (MAC) cell. The
MAC cell consists of three components, whose
communication within one cell is restricted to using attention. An important limitation of the MAC
cell is that the number of reasoning steps needs
to be specified in advance. Our model, as vanilla
seq2seq models, doesn't suffer from this limitation.

## 3   Model

We propose *seq2attn*, a novel attention-centric
module that connects the encoder and decoder of a
seq2seq model.[1] The core component of seq2attn
is the transcoder: a recurrent module that modulates the information flow between encoder and
decoder by generating *sparse* attention vectors using separate *keys* and *values*. Below, we demonstrate and test how seq2attn can be used in combination with a vanilla encoder-decoder architecture.

### 3.1   Encoder

In our tests, we assume a standard recurrent encoder, that, given an input sequence $\{x_1, \ldots, x_N\}$
and an embedding layer $\mathcal{E}^{enc}$, generates a sequence of outputs and hidden states:

$$\mathbf{x}_t^{enc} = \mathcal{E}^{enc}(x_t) \tag{1}$$

$$\mathbf{y}_t^{enc}, \mathbf{h}_t^{enc} = \mathcal{S}^{enc}(\mathbf{x}_t^{enc}, \mathbf{h}_{t-1}^{enc}) \tag{2}$$

$\mathcal{S}$ is a recurrent state transition model, such as a
vanilla RNN, LSTM or GRU.

### 3.2   Transcoder

The transcoder is initialized with $\mathbf{h}_0^{trans} = \mathbf{h}_N^{enc}$
and uses the hidden states of the encoder to com-
pute context vectors $\mathbf{c}_t$ that will be passed to the
decoder.

The input to the transcoder is the embedded output of te decoder (Eq. 11):

$$\mathbf{x}_t^{trans} = \mathcal{E}^{trans}(\hat{y}_{t-1}) \tag{3}$$

$$\mathbf{y}_t^{trans}, \mathbf{h}_t^{trans} = \mathcal{S}^{trans}(\mathbf{x}_t^{trans}, \mathbf{h}_{t-1}^{trans}) \tag{4}$$

---

[1]We will make our code available upon publication.

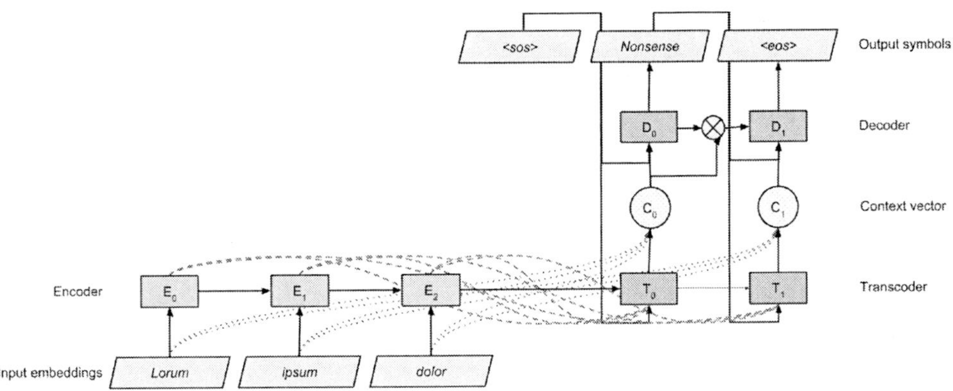



Figure 1: Schematic of the seq2attn architecture. The input sequence is processed by the encoder (E), after which the transcoder (T) generates context vectors, which are weighted means over the input embeddings.

The transcoder state is then used to query the hidden states of the encoder. The resulting scores are normalized using the Softmax function:

$$\alpha_t(s) = \boldsymbol{v}_a^\top \cdot ReLU(\boldsymbol{W}_a \cdot [\mathbf{h}_t^{enc}; \mathbf{h}_{t-1}^{trans}]) \quad (5)$$

$$\pi_t(s) = \frac{\exp \alpha_t(s)}{\sum_{i=1}^{N} \exp \alpha_t(i)} \quad (6)$$

Using the Softmax distribution often results in distributed vectors that attend to many input symbols at the same time, while an ideal compositional attention vector only focuses on the relevant parts of the input. To force the transcoder to be more selective in the information it selects, we use Gumbel-Softmax, which allows us to draw from the categorical distribution computed in Eq. 6, with continuous relaxation (Jang et al., 2017; Maddison et al., 2016). The Straight-Through estimator is then used as a biased gradient estimator of the $\arg\max$ operator:

$$\tilde{\mathbf{a}}_t(s) = \frac{\exp \frac{\log \pi_t(s) + g_s}{\tau}}{\sum_{i=1}^{N} \exp \frac{\log \pi_t(i) + g_i}{\tau}} \quad (7)$$

$$\mathbf{a}_t = \tilde{\mathbf{a}}_t - \hat{\mathbf{a}}_t + \text{one\_hot}(\arg\max(\tilde{\mathbf{a}}_t)) \quad (8)$$

The temperature $\tau$ can be interpreted as a measure of uncertainty. $\hat{\mathbf{a}}_t$ is a copy of $\tilde{\mathbf{a}}_t$ which we do not backpropagate through. At inference time the stochasticity of Gumbel-Softmax is not needed, and $\arg\max$ is used as activation function.

The resulting attention weights are used to compute the context vectors that will be passed to the decoder:

$$\mathbf{c}_t = \sum_{i=1}^{N} \mathbf{a}_t(i) \cdot \mathbf{x}_i^{enc} \quad (9)$$

Crucially, the context vector represents a weighted average of the *input embeddings* of the encoder, while the weights $\mathbf{a}_t(i)$ are depending on the *hidden states* of the encoder, thus introducing a separation between attention *keys* and *values* (similar to, e.g., Mino et al., 2017; Vaswani et al., 2017).

### 3.3 Decoder

The decoder of a seq2seq model is commonly initialized with the final hidden state of the encoder. However, as this state vector encodes the entire input sequence, this type of initialization does not urge compositional behavior of the decoder. When seq2attn is used, the decoder should be initialized with a fixed, *learned* initialization vector. In combination with using input embeddings as attention values (Eq. 9), this restricts the decoder to work only with disentangled representations of the input sequence, which encourages it to learn and process the individual meaning of all input symbols.

To model outputs, the decoder uses the context vector $\mathbf{c}_t$, its own embedded output (identical to Eq. 3) and a vector $\mathbf{h}_{t-1}^{dec}$ that integrates the current decoder hidden state with the context vector:

$$\mathbf{y}_t^{dec}, \tilde{\mathbf{h}}_t^{dec} = \mathcal{S}^{dec}([\mathbf{c}_t; \mathcal{E}^{trans}(\hat{y}_{t-1})], \mathbf{h}_{t-1}^{dec}) \quad (10)$$

$$\hat{y}_t = \arg\max(\text{Softmax}(\mathbf{y}_t^{dec})) \quad (11)$$

Where $\mathbf{h}_{t-1}^{dec}$ is computed using an element-wise multiplication of the context vector with the previous hidden state of the decoder:

$$\mathbf{h}_{t-1}^{dec} = \tilde{\mathbf{h}}_{t-1}^{dec} \odot \mathbf{c}_t \quad (12)$$

This way of integrating the context vector with the decoder, which we call *full focus*, makes the output of the decoder at decoding step $t$ more directly dependent on the current context vector $c_t$.

|          | held-out inputs | held-out compositions | held-out tables |
|----------|-----------------|-----------------------|-----------------|
| Baseline | $38.25 \pm 0.04$ | $43.28 \pm 0.09$ | $7.86 \pm 0.02$ |
| Seq2attn | **$100 \pm 0.00$** | **$100 \pm 0.00$** | **$100 \pm 0.00$** |

Table 1: Average sequence accuracies and standard deviations of the baseline and seq2attn models on all lookup tables test sets.

## 4 Test Case 1: Lookup tables

Our first test-case is the lookup table task introduced by Liška et al. (2018).

### 4.1 Task

The core of the *lookup table composition* domain consists in sequentially applying simple lookup table functions. The functions to be applied are bijective mappings from the set of all $n$-bit bitstrings onto itself. Following Liška et al. (2018), we focus on 3-bit strings, resulting in $2^3 = 8$ possible inputs and outputs. We create 8 random table lookup functions, to which we refer with the names t1, t2, ..., t8. Given the simplicity of the functions, the main challenge of the task resides in inferring that the input sequences should be treated *compositionally*, rather than considered as a whole.

We borrow the setup presented in Hupkes et al. (2018a), which differs slightly from the setup as it was originally presented. In this setup, a typical input output example could be 001 t1 t2 → 001 010 111. Computing the output for this example requires the sequential application of t1 to 001, and then t2 to the intermediate result. Since two tables are to be applied in succession, we refer to such an examples as a *binary composition*, as opposed to a *unary composition* in which only one function has to be applied on the input. The input bitstring and all intermediate outputs are included in the target output sequence.

Liška et al. (2018) train models on all 8 inputs for unary compositions and on 6 out of 8 input bitstrings of all binary compositions. The remaining 2 *held-out inputs* are used to test for generalization. Following Hupkes et al. (2018a), we do not include all 64 binary compositions in the training set, but leave out some for testing. In particular, we create one test set that contains all binary compositions containing t7 or t8, which are thus only seen in the training set as unary compositions. We call this condition *held-out tables*. Of the remaining binary compositions, that contain only functions in $\{t1, \ldots, t6\}$, 8 randomly

|              | held-out inputs | held-out compositions | held-out tables |
|--------------|-----------------|-----------------------|-----------------|
| Baseline+G   | $34.17 \pm 8.25$ | $38.54 \pm 12.39$ | $8.16 \pm 3.57$ |
| Baseline+E   | $82.50 \pm 12.42$ | $85.42 \pm 12.39$ | $31.08 \pm 7.85$ |
| Baseline+F   | $85.83 \pm 16.50$ | $91.67 \pm 11.79$ | $30.03 \pm 16.12$ |
| Baseline+T   | $43.33 \pm 12.30$ | $47.40 \pm 15.33$ | $3.99 \pm 2.70$ |
| Baseline+GE  | $82.50 \pm 12.42$ | $83.85 \pm 7.48$ | $30.21 \pm 3.32$ |
| Baseline+GF  | $69.17 \pm 21.25$ | $76.04 \pm 13.28$ | $4.69 \pm 1.47$ |
| Baseline+GT  | $32.50 \pm 8.90$ | $45.31 \pm 10.13$ | $1.56 \pm 1.53$ |
| Baseline+EF  | $85.00 \pm 9.35$ | $82.29 \pm 18.46$ | $24.13 \pm 2.99$ |
| Baseline+ET  | **$100.00 \pm 0.00$** | **$100.00 \pm 0.00$** | $41.49 \pm 3.30$ |
| Baseline+FT  | $68.33 \pm 21.44$ | $71.88 \pm 23.00$ | $19.44 \pm 19.06$ |
| Baseline+GEF | $74.17 \pm 36.53$ | $72.40 \pm 37.94$ | $37.33 \pm 22.10$ |
| Baseline+GET | $97.50 \pm 3.54$ | $98.44 \pm 1.28$ | $24.31 \pm 17.87$ |
| Baseline+GFT | $90.83 \pm 3.12$ | $91.15 \pm 3.21$ | $28.30 \pm 7.23$ |
| Baseline+EFT | $66.67 \pm 47.14$ | $66.67 \pm 47.14$ | $66.67 \pm 47.14$ |
| Seq2attn     | **$100.00 \pm 0.00$** | **$100.00 \pm 0.00$** | **$100.00 \pm 0.00$** |

Table 2: Mean sequence accuracies and standard deviation on the lookup tables task of a baseline seq2seq model with additional components of seq2attn. **G**=Gumbel-Softmax, **E**=embeddings as attention values, **F**=full focus, **T**=transcoder.

selected compositions are held out from the train set for all inputs, which form the *held-out compositions* test set. Lastly, we remove 2 of the 8 inputs for each binary composition independently to form the *held-out inputs* test set, which is similar to the generalization condition presented by Liška et al. (2018).

### 4.2 Results

We first compare the seq2attn architecture to a standard seq2seq model with an attention mechanism on generalization to new test examples. We establish the optimal parameters for both models using a grid search over a separate validation set. Our search includes the type of RNN cell ($\{$GRU, LSTM$\}$), the embedding and RNN sizes ($\{32, 64, 128, 256, 512, 1024\}$) and the dropout rate ($\{0, 0.2, 0.5\}$). The results are summarized in Table 3. The mini-batch size (1) and optimizer (Adam with default parameters (Kingma and Ba, 2014)) are fixed. We train 10 models with the optimal parameters and report mean sequence accuracy. For simplicity we will henceforth simply refer to this as the accuracy.

Our experiments confirm the findings previously presented by Hupkes et al. (2018a) and Liška et al. (2018): Vanilla seq2seq models do not find generalizing solutions for the lookup table task (Table 1, first row). Seq2attn, on the other hand, generalizes perfectly to data outside the training distribution. This first test confirms our hypothesized compositional bias of seq2attn.

### 4.3 Ablation Study

The difference between a traditional seq2seq and the seq2attn model can be summarized as the use of (i) a transcoder, (ii) the Gumbel-Softmax activation for the attention vector, (iii) using input embeddings as attention values and (iv) using full focus. To assess the contributions of these components, we take the seq2attn model with optimal hyper-parameters as a base model, and increasingly ablate components. The results of this study (Table 2) indicate that, while some of the components of seq2attn cause an increase in accuracy on their own, no subset of them can match the performance of the full seq2attn model.

### 4.4 Attention patterns

As the modeled output of the decoder is highly dictated by the context vectors that it receives, we can gain insights into the types of solutions the models are forming by studying their attention vectors. As illustrated in Figure 2, seq2attn learns to generate a "correct" attention trace, attending to the right input at the right time. Contrastingly, the baseline fails to capture a systematic pattern and produces a diffused attention instead or attends to irrelevant inputs, indicating that it does not utilize the attention mechanism to its full advantage.

### 4.5 Overgeneralization

The results for the lookup tables task indicate that seq2attn performs much better than the baseline on data containing held-out inputs, tables and compositions. The model is thus better able to infer the compositional rules underlying the data. To further explore seq2attn's bias towards compositionality, we test its behaviour when confronted with *uncompositional* examples, that do not adhere to the previously mentioned rules. Where a model unaware of the underlying task structure would have little problems learning such exceptions – or in fact, would not realise that they are exceptions – a model with a strong compositional bias may sometimes wrongly assume the exceptions also adhere to the underlying system, and *overgeneralize* an inferred rule. The extent to which a model overgeneralizes can thus be seen as a proxy for the strength of its compositional bias. Whether overgeneralization is actually preferentiable behavior is depend on the task to be solved.

In the proposed setup, a small number of training instances are assigned adapted output targets.

We call these instances *exceptions*. The target output sequences of the exceptions are changed such that they can only be learned through memorization. For the lookup table task, we adapt the training set such that one composition, t1 t2, is an exception to the general rules for three out of the eight existing input bitstrings. In the target output, the third bitstring is replaced with a randomly selected bitstring, thus changing the application of table t2 in this context. Both the three adapted samples and the other five unadapted samples for t1 t2 are included in the training set.

While training a model, we monitor the output sequences generated for these exceptions. The accuracy on the original targets is reported to identify whether the model is processing the exceptions compositionally despite being exposed to the adapted targets in the training set, i.e., whether the model is overgeneralizing.

Figure 3 displays the accuracy on the *original* targets of all eight inputs in composition t1 t2 over the first 30 training epochs. While both the baseline and seq2attn learn to memorize the three exceptions, only seq2attn shows a strong bias to treat the inputs compositionally before memorizing the adapted targets. The performance goes as high up as 8/8 between the fifth and fifteenth epoch for differently initialized models, before dropping to 5/8. This indicates that the rules are learned before the adapted instances are memorized as exceptions to these rules.

## 5 Test Case 2: SCAN

While the lookup table task provides an excellent test case to evaluate the compositional abilities of a neural network model, its simplicity limits the conclusions that can be drawn about the usability of seq2attn in more challenging domains. In this section, we evaluate seq2attn on *SCAN* (Lake and Baroni, 2018), a task involving mapping navigational commands to sequences of output actions.

### 5.1 Task

The input commands of the SCAN task are composed of a small set of predefined atomic commands (*jump*, *walk*, *run* and *look*), modifiers (*twice*, *thrice*, *around*, *opposite*, *left* and *right*) and conjunctions (*after* and *and*) that are combined via a limited context free grammar, such that there are no ambiguities. An example input is *jump after walk left twice*, where the learn-

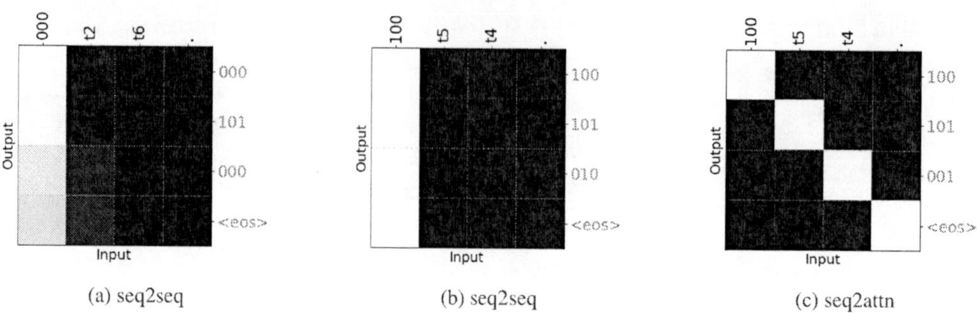

(a) seq2seq          (b) seq2seq          (c) seq2attn

Figure 2: Examples of modeled attention patterns on held-out input examples of the lookup tables domain.

|  | Baseline | Seq2attn |
|---|---|---|
| Lookup tables | 128, 512, 1, GRU, 0.5 | 256, 256, 1, GRU, 0.5 |
| SCAN | 200, 200, 2, LSTM, 0.5 | 512, 512, 1, GRU, 0.5 |

Table 3: Hyperparameters (embedding dimensions, RNN dimensions, RNN layers, RNN type, dropout rate) used for both the seq2seq baseline and seq2attn model for both tasks.

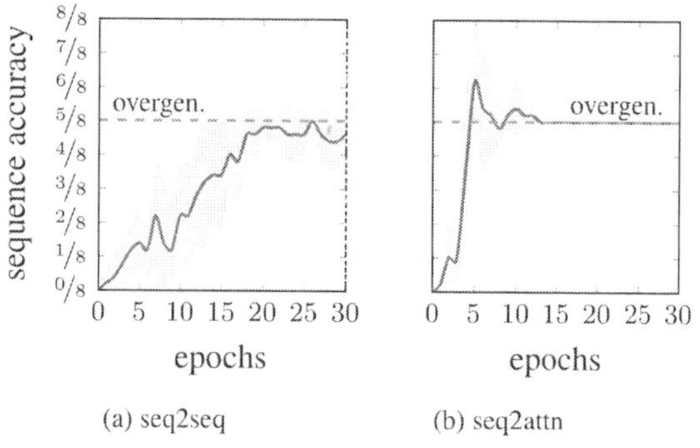

(a) seq2seq        (b) seq2attn

Figure 3: Average accuracies on *original targets* for the eight inputs in composition t1 t2. As three of these compositions are exceptions, we refer to accuracy higher than $5/8$ as overgeneralization. The 95% confidence interval is indicated.

ing agent has to mentally perform these actions in a 2-dimensional grid and output the sequence of actions it takes: "I_TURN_LEFT  I_WALK  I_TURN_LEFT  I_WALK  I_JUMP". For full details of the data set and experiments, we refer to Lake and Baroni (2018).

Lake and Baroni use three different train-test distributions of the total of 20.910 examples. They show that vanilla seq2seq models are able to almost perfectly generalize when the data is randomly split in a training and testing set, but that they are unfit for generalizing to longer test sequences and for one-shot learning to commands seen only in their atomic form. Later, Loula et al. (2018) proposed a new set of experiments based on the same task, which they argue are better suited for assessing systematic compositionality. We focus on experiments 2 and 3 of their paper.

Experiment 2 contains four different train-test distributions as there are four primitive commands involved. For all four conditions, the test set is the same. This test set consists of all examples that contain "jump around right" in their input sequences. The first condition, which is called **0 fillers**, contains no subsequences of the form "*primitive* around right" in the training set, where *primitive* is either of the four primitives "jump", "look", "run" or "walk". This condition should thus test whether a model can induce a compositional understanding of "jump around right" by showing those symbols ("jump", "around" and "right") only in different contexts. The next three conditions, **1 filler**, **2 fillers** and **3 fillers**, are considered increasingly easier. They retain the same test set, but increasingly add more examples to the train set of the template "*primitive* around right". **1 filler** adds all examples of this template where *primitive* is "look". **2 fillers** and **3 fillers** add "walk" and "run" respectively.

As Loula et al. (2018) observed a great difference in performance between the **0 fillers** and **1 filler** conditions, they zoom in on these conditions in experiment 3. The **0 fillers** condition contains 0 examples with the subsequence "*primitive* around right" in the training set. The **1 filler** condition contains 1.100 of those, namely all examples which contain the subsequence "look around right". In experiment 3, they test a more smooth and dense transition from the **0 fillers** condition

6

to the **1 filler** conditions. They accomplish this by taking the training set of the **0 fillers** condition and adding respectively 1, 2, 4, 8, 16, 32, 64, 128, 256, 512 and 1024 extra examples containing the subsequence "look around right", resulting in 11 new training sets. The test set is again the same as in experiment 2.

## 5.2 Results

We compare a baseline seq2seq to the seq2attn architecture on these two tasks. First, we perform a grid search using a random split of the data to find the optimal parameters for seq2attn. The results of this are summarized in Table 3. As a baseline, we used the model which Lake and Baroni (2018) found to be overall best performing, which is a seq2seq model with 2-layer LSTMs, 200 hidden units per layer and a dropout rate of 0.5. For comparison to the seq2attn model, we also added an attention mechanism, which was missing in the original model. For all reported results we ran these models 10 times with random weight initialization. Since experiments 2 and 3 by Loula et al. (2018) do not have validation sets for early stopping, we ran all models for 50 epochs.

Firstly, we confirm the findings of Lake and Baroni (2018) and Loula et al. (2018) (see Fig. 4, left). A vanilla seq2seq with attention is able to perform analogical generalization (95.19% accuracy): it requires examples of **1 filler** only to generalize to other fillers of the same template. On the other hand, it is not able to apply "right" and "around" to a primitive verb in a productive way, when they were never seen together (0.26% accuracy, **0 fillers** condition). When we look at seq2attn, we notice how not only it is able to perform analogical generalization (94.32% accuracy, **1 filler**) but, to a certain extent, it is also able to generalize productively in the **0 fillers** condition (36.23% accuracy).

In Figure 4 (right) we report the results for experiment 3 of Loula et al. (2018) where we consider the **0 fillers** condition of Experiment 2 and progressively add extra training examples from **1 filler**. As Loula et al. (2018) observed, performance of a seq2seq model ramps up as more samples are injected in the training set. Yet, the fact that performance increases gradually and takes long to peak (at 512 examples) suggests that rather than systematically understanding the rule, the model is piling up evidence for a very spe-

cific pattern. The situation is quite different for the seq2attn model, whose performance spikes much earlier, reaching a plateau at 16 examples already. Interestingly, the performance peak is also at 512, but with an improvement of just over 5 percentage points over 16 examples vs. approximately 50 percentage points improvement in the case of baseline. Seq2attn seems then to show evidence for an opposite interpretation, namely for a network that, to a certain extent, is able to induce the compositional rules. A property that is often linked to sample efficiency (Lake and Baroni, 2018).

## 5.3 Analysis

In Figure 5, we now look at some attention patterns for the **0 fillers** condition. While baseline models emit sparser and more informative attentional patterns here than in the lookup table task, they still are locally diffused and, more importantly, do not maintain a systematic input-output alignment, which suggests that the models are not understanding the rules of the task, but use a pattern matching strategy instead. On the contrary, seq2attn shows always fully sparse, one-hot attention patterns. Figure 5c shows how the model usually aligns outputs to their respective primitive commands or directions in the input sequence, e.g., "I_JUMP" aligns to "jump", and "I_TURN_RIGHT" aligns to "right". A modifier like "opposite" is used as an indicator to repeat the last modeled directional action.

Seq2attn reaches an accuracy of 36.23% on the **0 fillers** condition, which still leaves room for improvement. However, the attentional patterns quickly show the main cause of error. Figure 5b shows how the model outputs "I_TURN_LEFT" instead of "I_TURN_RIGHT" whenever it attends to the input "around". Whenever the model does attend to "right", as is the expected, optimal behavior, the output is correct. This behavior can be easily explained by analyzing the data that the model was trained on. The input "around" has only been encountered within the context "*primitive* around left" during training. Thus, within this context, "around" and "left" could be used synonymically by the transcoder to communicate to the decoder to output "I_TURN_LEFT". The great majority of errors on this task by seq2attn have the same cause. Although seq2attn still does not perfectly solve the task, contrary to a standard seq2seq model, it provides an immediate under-

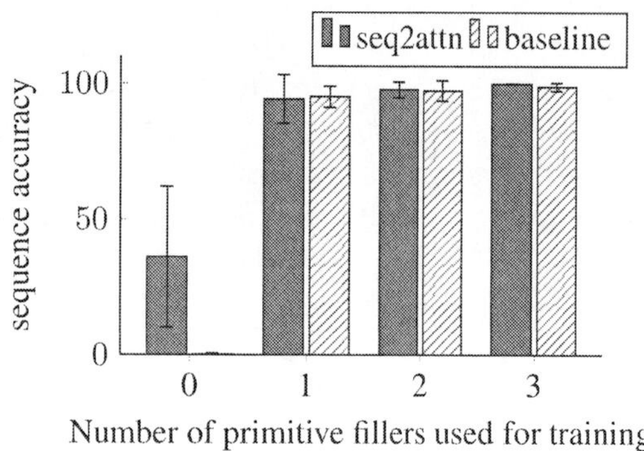
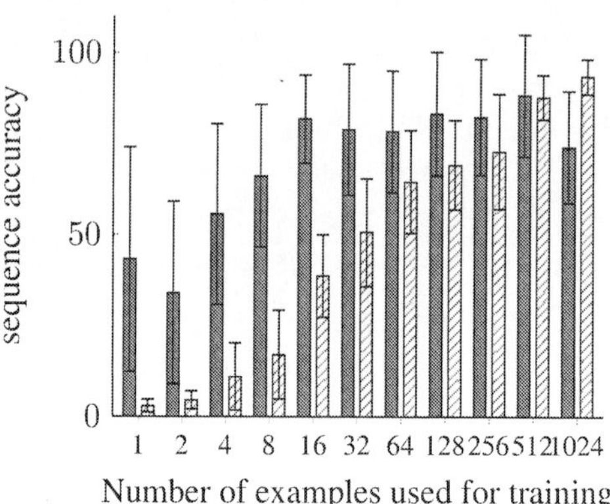

Figure 4: Mean sequence accuracies on experiment 2 (left) and 3 (right) of Loula et al. (2018). The bootstrapped 95% confidence intervals are indicated with error bars.

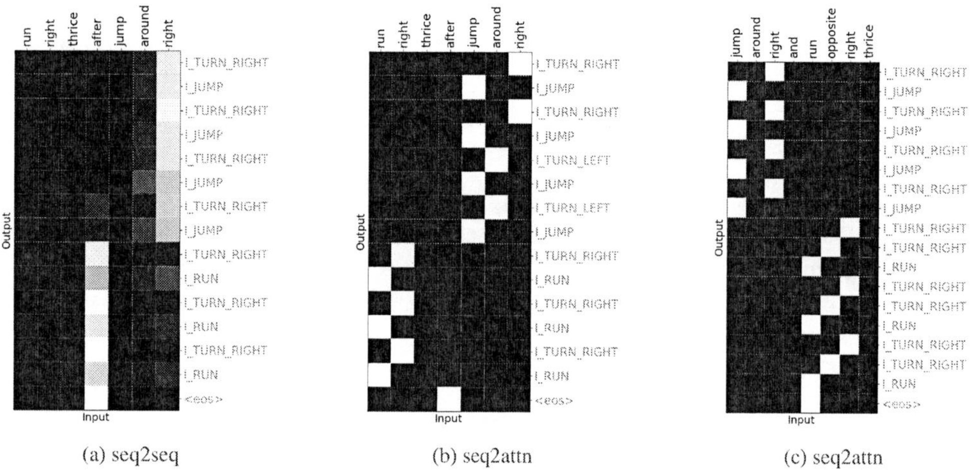

(a) seq2seq

(b) seq2attn

(c) seq2attn

Figure 5: Examples of attention patterns on the **0 fillers** condition. Seq2attn models the output incorrectly when the attention pattern is incorrect.

standing of the root of this.

## 5.4 Overgeneralization

To assess seq2attn's overgeneralization abilities for the SCAN task, we repeated experiment 3. In addition to gradually adding samples indicating the correct interpretation of "*primitive* around right", we also added a single exception for "jump around right" to the training set. The target for this sequence, originally consisting of four repetitions of "I_TURN_RIGHT I_JUMP", was modified to consist of only two repetitions.

For all conditions of experiment 3, we added the exception to the training set, trained multiple randomly initialized models, and monitored the output sequences generated for this exception over the course of training. In Figure 6, we visualize the distribution over the adapted and original targets for the conditions with 4 and 512 filler samples respectively. Note that the models have implicit and explicit evidence for the correct application of the rules for "*primitive* around right": explicit evidence through training examples containing "look around right" subsequences, and implicit evidence through training samples including "around" or "right" seen in different contexts.

Both models exhibit overgeneralization behavior for SCAN. Generally, overgeneralization occurs at the start of the training process and precedes memorization of the adapted target. However, the baseline model needs a substantially larger amount of explicit evidence to overgeneralize as much as the seq2attn model. The condition where 512 filler samples are included illustrates that the tendency to overgeneralize does not necessarily relate to the overall task performance.

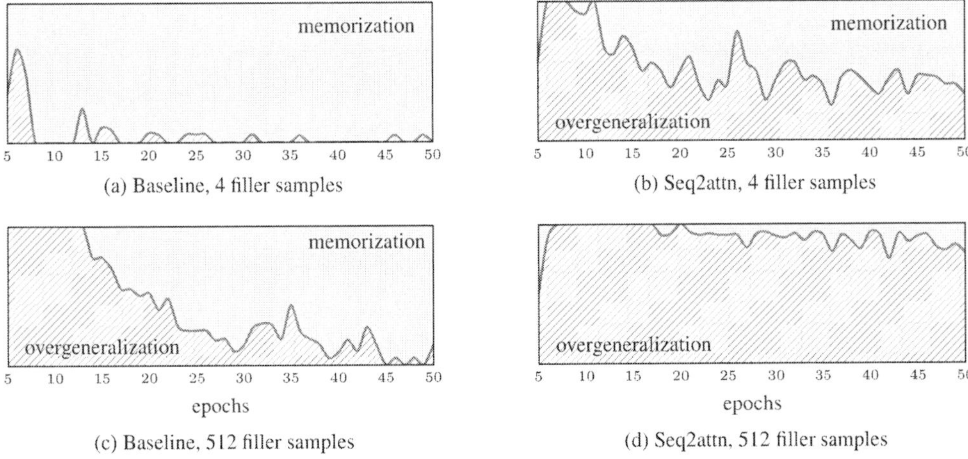

(a) Baseline, 4 filler samples      (b) Seq2attn, 4 filler samples

(c) Baseline, 512 filler samples      (d) Seq2attn, 512 filler samples

Figure 6: Mean sequence accuracy on the *original target* of "jump around right" of multiple models as training progresses. The distribution was normalized for cases in which the output emitted was neither the original or the adapted target.

For this condition, seq2attn and the baseline yield similar sequence accuracies in the original setup of experiment 3 (see Figure 6), but seq2attn overgeneralizes more frequently, indicating that seq2attn has a stronger compositional bias.

## 6 Discussion

In search for a neural network architecture that exhibits a bias towards systematic generalization, we introduced **seq2attn**, a recurrent attention-centric module that controls the information flow from encoder to decoder. We installed this module in a standard recurrent encoder-decoder architecture. To quantify its capabilities in terms of systematic compositionality, we tested the model on the lookup table and SCAN tasks.

On both tasks, we see significant improvements compared to a standard recurrent seq2seq model, providing evidence for a compositional bias in the system. Furthermore, because the architecture relies heavily on its attention mechanism, its solutions can more easily be interpreted by looking at the generated attention patterns. This provides opportunities for analyzing what the model has learned as well as for detecting potential biases in the training set.

Although on the considered tasks, which are specifically designed to evaluate compositionality, seq2attn leads to clear improvements, its contribution could not have been observed when considering a task for which the test accuracy is not directly linked to compositionality, such as nat-ural language modeling and translation. We argue that, for those cases, additional assessment methods are needed to compare the compositional skills of different models. We propose one such method, which involves monitoring to what extent a model *overgeneralizes*. We show how a model with seq2attn, for both tasks, has a greater tendency to overgeneralize than the baseline.

A possible limitation of the design of seq2attn is that the flow of information from transcoder to decoder is very rigid. Possible solutions could be found in the use of less skewed activations than the Gumbel-Softmax such as Sparsemax (Martins and Astudillo, 2016), or allowing the transcoder to communicate multiple embeddings using adaptive computation time (Graves, 2016).

Importantly, seq2attn is not tied to a particular type of seq2seq architecture. In future work, we plan to install it into other popular seq2seq architectures such as convolutional seq2seq (Gehring et al., 2017) and Transformer models (Vaswani et al., 2017).

## Acknowledgements

We are grateful to Kristina Gulordava for ideas and feedback. DH is funded by the Netherlands Organization for Scientific Research (NWO), through a Gravitation Grant 024.001.006 to the Language in Interaction Consortium. EB is funded by the European Union's Horizon 2020 research and innovation program under the Marie Sklodowska-Curie grant agreement No 790369 (MAGIC).

## References

Jacob Andreas, Dan Klein, and Sergey Levine. 2016. Modular multitask reinforcement learning with policy sketches. *arXiv preprint arXiv:1611.01796*.

Joris Baan, Jana Leible, Nikolaus Mitja, Rau David, Ulmer Dennis, Tim Baumgrtner, Dieuwke Hupkes, and Elia Bruni. 2019. On the realization of compositionality in neural networks. *BlackboxNLP 2019, ACL*.

Kyunghyun Cho, Bart van Merriënboer, Caglar Gulcehre, Fethi Bougares Holger Schwenk, and Yoshua Bengio. 2014. Learning phrase representations using RNN encoder–decoder for statistical machine translation. In *Proceedings of the 2014 Conference on Empirical Methods in Natural Language Processing (EMNLP)*, page 17241734. Association for Computational Linguistics.

Shi Feng, Eric Wallace, Alvin Grissom II, Mohit Iyyer, Pedro Rodriguez, and Jordan Boyd-Graber. 2018. Pathologies of neural models make interpretations difficult. In *Proceedings of the 2018 Conference on Empirical Methods in Natural Language Processing*, pages 3719–3728. Association for Computational Linguistics.

Jonas Gehring, Michael Auli, David Grangier, Denis Yarats, and Yann N Dauphin. 2017. Convolutional sequence to sequence learning. *arXiv preprint arXiv:1705.03122*.

Felix A Gers and Jürgen Schmidhuber. 2001. LSTM recurrent networks learn simple context-free and context-sensitive languages. *Neural Networks, IEEE Transactions on*, 12(6):1333–1340.

Alex Graves. 2016. Adaptive computation time for recurrent neural networks. *arXiv preprint arXiv:1603.08983*.

Drew A Hudson and Christopher D Manning. 2018. Compositional attention networks for machine reasoning. *arXiv preprint arXiv:1803.03067*.

Dieuwke Hupkes, Anand Singh, Kris Korrel, German Kruszewski, and Elia Bruni. 2018a. Learning compositionally through attentive guidance. *arXiv preprint arXiv:1805.09657*.

Dieuwke Hupkes, Sara Veldhoen, and Willem Zuidema. 2018b. Visualisation and 'diagnostic classifiers' reveal how recurrent and recursive neural networks process hierarchical structure. *Journal of Artificial Intelligence Research*, 61:907–926.

Eric Jang, Shixiang Gu, and Ben Poole. 2017. Categorical reparameterization with gumbel-softmax. In *Proceedings of the International Conference on Learning Representations (ICLR2017)*.

Justin Johnson, Bharath Hariharan, Laurens van der Maaten, Li Fei-Fei, C Lawrence Zitnick, and Ross Girshick. 2017. Clevr: A diagnostic dataset for compositional language and elementary visual reasoning. In *Computer Vision and Pattern Recognition (CVPR), 2017 IEEE Conference on*, pages 1988–1997. IEEE.

Diederik P Kingma and Jimmy Ba. 2014. Adam: A method for stochastic optimization. *arXiv preprint arXiv:1412.6980*.

Brenden Lake and Marco Baroni. 2018. Generalization without systematicity: On the compositional skills of sequence-to-sequence recurrent networks. In *International Conference on Machine Learning*, pages 2879–2888.

Brenden M Lake, Ruslan Salakhutdinov, and Joshua B Tenenbaum. 2015. Human-level concept learning through probabilistic program induction. *Science*, 350(6266):1332–1338.

Tal Linzen, Grzegorz Chrupała, and Afra Alishahi, editors. 2018. *Proceedings of the 2018 EMNLP Workshop BlackboxNLP: Analyzing and Interpreting Neural Networks for NLP*. Association for Computational Linguistics.

Adam Liška, Germán Kruszewski, and Marco Baroni. 2018. Memorize or generalize? searching for a compositional rnn in a haystack. *arXiv preprint arXiv:1802.06467*.

João Loula, Marco Baroni, and Brenden M Lake. 2018. Rearranging the familiar: Testing compositional generalization in recurrent networks. *arXiv preprint arXiv:1807.07545*.

Chris J Maddison, Andriy Mnih, and Yee Whye Teh. 2016. The concrete distribution: A continuous relaxation of discrete random variables. In *Proceedings of the International Conference on Learning Representations (ICLR2017)*.

Andre Martins and Ramon Astudillo. 2016. From softmax to sparsemax: A sparse model of attention and multi-label classification. In *International Conference on Machine Learning*, pages 1614–1623.

Hideya Mino, Masao Utiyama, Eiichiro Sumita, and Takenobu Tokunaga. 2017. Key-value attention mechanism for neural machine translation. In *Proceedings of the Eighth International Joint Conference on Natural Language Processing (Volume 2: Short Papers)*, volume 2, pages 290–295.

Shauli Ravfogel, Yoav Goldberg, and Francis Tyers. 2018. Can lstm learn to capture agreement? the case of basque. In *Proceedings of the 2018 EMNLP Workshop BlackboxNLP: Analyzing and Interpreting Neural Networks for NLP*, pages 98–107.

Paul Rodriguez. 2001. Simple recurrent networks learn context-free and context-sensitive languages by counting. *Neural computation*, 13(9):2093–118.

Ilya Sutskever, Oriol Vinyals, and Quoc V Le. 2014. Sequence to sequence learning with neural networks. In *Advances in neural information processing systems*, pages 3104–3112.

Ashish Vaswani, Noam Shazeer, Niki Parmar, Jakob Uszkoreit, Llion Jones, Aidan N Gomez, Łukasz Kaiser, and Illia Polosukhin. 2017. Attention is all you need. In *Advances in Neural Information Processing Systems*, pages 5998–6008.

# Sentiment analysis is not solved!
## Assessing and probing sentiment classification


**Jeremy Barnes, Lilja Øvrelid, Erik Velldal**

University of Oslo
{jeremycb,liljao,erikve}@ifi.uio.no



## Abstract

Neural methods for sentiment analysis have led to quantitative improvements over previous approaches, but these advances are not always accompanied with a thorough analysis of the qualitative differences. Therefore, it is not clear what outstanding conceptual challenges for sentiment analysis remain. In this work, we attempt to discover what challenges still prove a problem for sentiment classifiers for English and to provide a challenging dataset. We collect the subset of sentences that an (oracle) ensemble of state-of-the-art sentiment classifiers misclassify and then annotate them for 18 linguistic and paralinguistic phenomena, such as negation, sarcasm, modality, etc.[1] Finally, we provide a case study that demonstrates the usefulness of the dataset to probe the performance of a given sentiment classifier with respect to linguistic phenomena.


## 1 Introduction

Over the last 15 years, approaches to sentiment analysis which concentrated on creating and curating sentiment lexicons (Turney, 2002; Liu et al., 2005) or used n-grams for classification (Pang et al., 2002) have been replaced by models that are able to exploit compositionality (Socher et al., 2013; Irsoy and Cardie, 2014) or implicitly learn relations between tokens (Peters et al., 2018; Howard and Ruder, 2018; Devlin et al., 2018). These neural models push the state of the art to over 90% accuracy on binary sentence-level sentiment analysis.

Although these methods show a quantitative improvement over previous approaches, they are not often accompanied with a thorough analysis of the qualitative differences. This has led to the current situation, where we are aware of quantitative, but not qualitative differences between state-of-the-art

sentiment classifiers. It also means that we are not aware of the outstanding conceptual challenges that we still face in sentiment analysis.

In this work, we attempt to discover what conceptual challenges still prove a problem for all state-of-the-art sentiment methods for English. To do so, we train and test three state-of-the-art machine learning classifiers (BERT, ELMo, and a BiLSTM) as well as a bag-of-words classifier on six sentence-level sentiment datasets available for English. We then collect the subset of sentences that all models misclassify and annotate them for 18 linguistic and paralinguistic phenomena, such as negation, sarcasm, modality or world knowledge. We present this new data as a challenging dataset for future research in sentiment analysis, which enables probing the problems that sentiment classifiers still face in more depth.

Specifically, the contributions of this work are:

- the creation of a challenging sentiment dataset from previously available data,

- the annotation of errors in this dataset for 18 linguistic and paralinguistic phenomena,

- a thorough analysis of the dataset,

- and finally presenting a practical use-case demonstrating how the dataset can be used to probe the particular types of errors made by a new model.

The rest of the paper is organized into related work (Section 2), a description of the experimental setup (Section 3), a brief description of the dataset (Section 4), an in-depth analysis (Section 5), a case-study that demonstrates the usefulness of the dataset (Section 6), and finally a conclusion (Section 7).

---

[1]The dataset is available at https://github.com/ltgoslo/assessing_and_probing_sentiment.

12


*Proceedings of the Second BlackboxNLP Workshop on Analyzing and Interpreting Neural Networks for NLP*, pages 12–23
Florence, Italy, August 1, 2019. ©2019 Association for Computational Linguistics

## 2   Related work

Neural networks are now ubiquitous in NLP tasks, often giving state-of-the-art results. However, they are known for being "black boxes" which are not easily interpretable. Recent interest in interpreting these methods has led to new lines of research which attempt to discover what linguistic phenomena neural networks are able to learn (Linzen et al., 2016; Gulordava et al., 2018; Conneau et al., 2018), how robust neural networks are to perturbations in input data (Ribeiro et al., 2018; Ebrahimi et al., 2018; Schluter and Varab, 2018), and what biases they propagate (Park et al., 2018; Zhao et al., 2018; Kiritchenko and Mohammad, 2018).

Specifically within the task of sentiment analysis, certain linguistic phenomena are known to be challenging. Negation is one of the aspects of language that most clearly affects expressions of sentiment and that has been studied widely within sentiment analysis (see Wiegand et al. (2010) for an early survey). The difficulties of resolving negation for sentiment analysis include determining negation scope (Hogenboom et al., 2011; Lapponi et al., 2012; Reitan et al., 2015), and semantic composition (Wilson et al., 2005; Choi and Cardie, 2008; Kiritchenko and Mohammad, 2016).

Verbal polarity shifters have also been studied. Schulder et al. (2018) annotate verbal shifters at the sense-level. They conclude that, although individual negation words are more frequent in the Amazon Product Review Data corpus, the overall frequency of negation words and shifters is likely similar. This suggests that there is a Zipfian tail of shifters which are not often handled within sentiment analysis.

Furthermore, the linguistic phenomenon of modality has also been shown to be problematic. Both Narayanan et al. (2009) and Liu et al. (2014) explore the effect of modality on sentiment classification and find that explicitly modeling certain modalities improves classification results. They advocate for a divide-and-conquer approach, which would address the various realizations of modality individually. Benamara et al. (2012) perform linguistic experiments using native speakers concerning the effects of both negation and modality on opinions, and similarly find that the type of negation and modality determines the final interpretation of polarity.

The sentiment models inspected in these analyses, however, were lexicon- and word- and n-

| Label | MPQA | OP. | Sem. | SST | Ta. | Th. |
|---|---|---|---|---|---|---|
| ++ | — | 379 | — | 1,852 | — | — |
| + | 193 | 879 | 3,499 | 3,111 | 923 | 2,727 |
| 0 | 527 | — | 4,478 | 2,242 | 1,419 | 1,779 |
| − | 413 | 399 | 1,310 | 3,140 | 1,320 | 1,828 |
| − − | — | 74 | — | 1,510 | — | — |
| Total | 1,133 | 1,731 | 9,287 | 11,855 | 3,662 | 6,334 |

Table 1: Statistics for the sentence-level annotations in each dataset.

gram-based models. It is not clear that neural networks have the same weaknesses, as they have been shown to deal with compositionality and long-distance dependencies to some degree (Socher et al., 2013; Linzen et al., 2016). Additionally, authors did not attempt to discover from the data what phenomena were present that could affect sentiment. In the current paper we aim to provide a systematic analysis of error types found across a range of datasets, domains and classifiers.

## 3   Experimental setup

In these experiments, we test three state-of-the-art models for sentence-level sentiment classification. We choose to focus on sentence-level classification for three reasons: 1) sentence-level classification is a popular and useful task, 2) there is a large amount of high-quality annotated data available, and 3) annotation of linguistic phenomena is easier at sentence-level than document-level. It is also likely that most phenomena that occur at sentence-level, *e. g.*, negation, comparative sentiment, or modality, will transfer to other sentiment tasks.

### 3.1   Datasets

In order to discover a subset of sentences that all state-of-the-art models are unable to correctly predict, we collect six English-language datasets previously annotated for sentence-level sentiment from five domains (news wire, hotel reviews, movie reviews, twitter, and micro-blogs). Table 1 shows the statistics for each of the datasets.

**MPQA**   The Multi-perspective Question Answer (MPQA) Opinion Corpus (Wilson et al., 2005) provides contextual polarity annotations for English news documents from world press. The annotations are private state frames, which include annotations for text anchor, source, target, and attitude type, among others. We extract sentiment labeled sentences by taking only those sentences that have sentiment annotations. Additionally, we remove sentences that contain both positive and negative sentiment. This leaves a three-class (positive, neutral, negative) sentence-level dataset.

**OpeNER** The Open Polarity Enhanced Named Entity Recognition (OpeNER) sentiment datasets (Agerri et al., 2013) contain hotel reviews annotated for 4-class (strong positive, positive, negative, strong negative) sentiment classification. We take the English dataset, where self-attention networks give state-of-the-art results (Ambartsoumian and Popowich, 2018).

**SemEval** The SemEval 2013 tweet classification dataset (Nakov et al., 2013) contains tweets collected and annotated for three-class (positive, neutral, negative) sentiment. The state-of-the-art model is a Convolutional Network (Severyn and Moschitti, 2015).

**Stanford Sentiment Treebank** The Stanford Sentiment Treebank (Socher et al., 2013) contains 11,855 English sentences from movie reviews which have been annotated at each node of a constituency parse tree. Contextualized word representations combined with a bi-attentive sentiment network currently give state-of-the-art results (Peters et al., 2018).

**Täckström dataset** The Täckström dataset (Täckström and McDonald, 2011) contains product reviews which have been annotated at both document- and sentence-level for three-class sentiment, although the sentence-level annotations also have a "not relevant" label. We keep the sentence-level annotations, which gives 3,662 sentences annotated for three-class sentiment.

**Thelwall dataset** The Thelwall dataset derives from datasets provided with SentiStrength[2] (Thelwall et al., 2010). It contains microblogs annotated for both positive and negative sentiment on a scale from 1 to 5. We map these to single sentiment labels such that sentences which are clearly positive ($pos >= 3$ and $neg < 3$) are given the positive label, clearly negative sentences ($pos < 3$ and $neg >= 3$) the negative label, and clearly neutral sentences ($3 < pos > 2$ and $3 < neg > 2$) the neutral. We discard all other sentences, which finally leaves 6,334 annotated sentences.

### 3.2 Models

In order to gain an idea of what errors most models suffer from, we test three state-of-the-art models on the datasets. Additionally, we use a bag-of-words model as it is a strong baseline for text classification. For the SINGLE setup, we train all models on the training and development data for each dataset and test on the corresponding test set, therefore avoiding domain problems.

**BERT** The BERT model (Devlin et al., 2018) is a bidirectional transformer that is pretrained on two tasks: 1) a cloze-like language modeling task and 2) a binary next-sentence prediction task. It is pretrained on 330 million words from the BooksCorpus (Zhu et al., 2015) and English Wikipedia. We fine-tune the available pretrained model[3] on each sentiment dataset.

**ELMo** We use the bi-attentive classification network[4] from Peters et al. (2018). The network uses both word embeddings, as well as creating character-based embeddings from a character-level CNN-BiLSTM network. The word representations are first passed through a feedforward layer, and then through a sequence-to-sequence network with biattention. This new representation of the text is combined with the original representation and passed through another sequence-to-sequence network. Finally, a max, min, mean and self-attention pool representation is created from this last sequence. For classification, these features are sent to a maxout layer.

**BiLSTM** Bidirectional long short-term memory (BiLSTM) networks have shown to be strong baselines for sentiment tasks (Tai et al., 2015; Barnes et al., 2017). We implement a single-layered BiLSTM which takes pretrained skipgram embeddings as input, creates a sentence representation by concatenating the final hidden layer of both left and right LSTMs, and then passes this representation to a softmax layer for classification. Additionally, dropout serves as a regularizer.

**Bag-of-Words classifier** Finally, bag-of-words classifiers are strong baselines for sentiment and when combined with other features can still give

---



[3]https://github.com/google-research/bert
[4]https://s3-us-west-2.amazonaws.com/allennlp/models/sst-5-elmo-biattentive-classification-network-2018.09.04.tar.gz

state-of-the-art results for sentiment tasks (Moham-mad et al., 2013). Therefore, we train a Linear SVM on a bag-of-words representation of the training sentences.

### 3.3 Model performance

Table 2 shows the accuracy of the models on the six tasks. Both methods that use pretrained language model classifiers (ELMo and BERT) are the best performing models, with an average of 11.8 difference between the language model classifiers and standard models (BOW and BILSTM). The error rates range between 8.3 on OpeNER and 20.5 on SST (see Table 3), indicating that there are differences in difficulty of datasets due to domain and annotation characteristics.

Additional experiments on a MERGED setup, where the labels from OpeNER and SST are mapped to the three-class setup, and a single model is trained on the concatenation of the training sets from all datasets, indicate that no clear performance gain is achieved. We therefore prefer to avoid the problem of domain differences and keep only the original results.

## 4 Challenging dataset

We create a challenging dataset by collecting the subset of test sentences that *all* of the sentiment systems predicted incorrectly (statistics are shown in Table 3). After removing sentences with incorrect gold labels, there are a total of 836 sentences in the dataset, with a similar number of positive, neutral, and negative labels and fewer strong labels. This is expected, as only two datasets have strong labels.

Furthermore, the main sources of examples are the SemEval task (249), Stanford Sentiment Treebank (452) and Thelwall datasets (215), while the Täckström dataset (129), MPQA (39) and OpeNER (29) contribute much less. This is a result of both dataset size and difficulty.

## 5 Dataset analysis

In order to give a clearer view of the data found in the dataset, we annotate these instances using 19 linguistic and paralinguistic labels. While most of these come from previous attempts to qualitatively analyze sentiment classifiers (Hu and Liu, 2004; Das and Chen, 2007; Pang and Lee, 2008; Socher et al., 2013; Barnes et al., 2018), others (incorrect label, no sentiment, morphology) emerged

during the error annotation process. We further chose to manually annotate for the polarity of the sentence irrespective of the gold label in order to be able to locate possible annotation errors during our analysis. The annotation scheme and (manually constructed) examples of each label are shown in Table 6. Note that we did not limit the number of labels that the annotator could assign to each sentence and in principle they should assign all suitable labels during annotation.

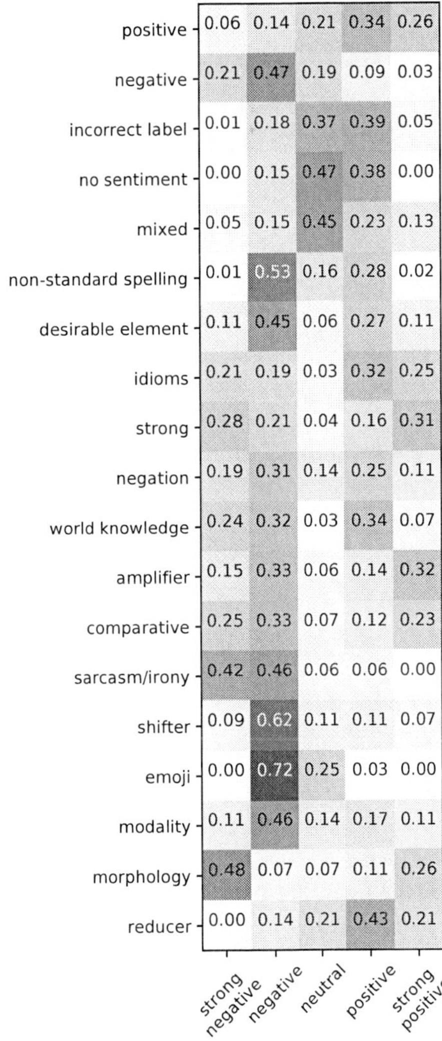

Figure 1: Distribution of labels across error categories.

An initial analysis of the errors shown in Table 5 and Figure 1 reveals that the most common errors come from the no-sentiment (214), mixed category

|  |  | MPQA | OpeNER | SemEval | SST | Täckström | Thelwall |
|---|---|---|---|---|---|---|---|
| Single | BOW | 40.9 | 69.7 | 62.3 | 50.9 | 46.0 | 53.5 |
|  | BiLSTM | 48.7 | 71.5 | 58.0 | 37.5 | 45.0 | 52.0 |
|  | ELMo | 61.0 | 82.1 | 71.9 | 51.3 | 53.1 | 59.1 |
|  | BERT | **62.3** | **84.2** | **75.1** | **53.0** | **60.2** | **63.9** |

Table 2: Accuracy of models on the sentiment datasets, where a different classifier is trained for each dataset.

| Label | MPQA | OpeNER | SemEval | SST | Täckström | Thelwall | Total |
|---|---|---|---|---|---|---|---|
| ++ | — | 8 | — | 87 | — | — | 95 |
| + | 16 | 9 | 59 | 49 | 46 | 9 | 188 |
| 0 | 1 | — | 45 | 75 | 31 | 48 | 200 |
| — | 16 | 2 | 47 | 51 | 18 | 116 | 250 |
| — — | — | 4 | — | 99 | — | — | 103 |
| Total | 33 | 23 | 151 | 361 | 95 | 173 | **836** |
| % of original | 14.5 | 6.6 | 6.4 | 16.3 | 12.9 | 13.6 | 11.7 |
| avg. length | 25.0 | 13.4 | 19.0 | 19.9 | 23.4 | 17.5 | 19.7 |

Table 3: Statistics of dataset, including the number of sentences from each dataset and for each label, the percentage of the original dataset kept in the dataset, and average length (in tokens) of sentences.

(185), non-standard spelling and hashtags (180), desirable elements (144), and the strong label (122).

The distribution of errors across labels (strong negative: 106, negative: 299, neutral: 303, positive: 296, strong positive: 109) compared to the gold distribution (strong negative: 294, negative: 1742, neutral: 2249, positive: 2402, strong positive: 475) shows that the strong negative is the most difficult and least common class, while positive is the easiest to classify. In the following we briefly discuss the error categories, also showing examples for each.

**Mixed Polarity**  The largest set of errors, with 185 sentences labeled, are what we refer to as "mixed" polarity sentences. These are sentences where two differing polarities are expressed, either towards two separate entities, or towards the same entity. While the first can be solved by a more fine-grained approach (aspect-level or targeted sentiment), the second is more difficult and is often considered a category of its own (Shamma et al., 2009; Saif et al., 2013; Kenyon-Dean et al., 2018).

| Strong Positive | It was **spot on**. |
|---|---|
| Positive | They're **on a roll**. |
| Neutral | It's a bit **hit-or-miss**. |
| Negative | I'm **pulling my hair out**. |
| Strong Negative | Madonna **can't act a lick**. |

Table 4: Examples of idioms.

An analysis of the mixed category errors reveals that while most of the examples are in the "neutral" category (45%), the other 55% are annotated as having mostly positive or negative sentiment. This is a confusing situation for both annotators and sentiment classifiers, and a direct product of performing sentence-level classification rather than aspect-level. Nearly a third of the errors contain "but" clauses, which could be correctly classified by splitting them.

A more problematic situation is found among nearly 20% of the examples (34), where the annotator found the original label to be completely incorrect.[5]

**Non-standard spelling**  Most errors in this category (180 total) are labeled either negative (49%) or positive (29%), with almost no strong positive or strong negative, which comes mainly from the fact that the noisier datasets do not contain the strong labels.

Around a third of the examples contain hashtags that clearly express the sentiment of the whole sentence, e. g., "#imtiredof this SNOW and COLD weather!!!". This indicates the need to properly deal with hashtags in order to correctly classify sentiment.

**Idioms**  Table 4 presents some examples of sentiment-bearing idioms that are taken from the challenge data set. In this category, errors (132

| label | # examples |
| --- | --- |
| incorrect label | **277** |
| no sentiment | **214** |
| mixed | **185** |
| non-standard spelling | **180** |
| desirable element | **144** |
| idioms | 132 |
| strong | 122 |
| negation | 97 |
| world knowledge | 81 |
| amplifier | 79 |
| comparative | 68 |
| sarcasm/irony | 58 |
| shifter | 50 |
| emoji | 46 |
| modality | 38 |
| morphology | 31 |
| reducer | 13 |

Table 5: Number of labels for each category in annotation study. **Bold** numbers indicate the five most frequent sources of errors. The total number of labels does not sum to the number of sentences in the dataset, as each sentence can have multiple labels.

sentences labeled) are spread relatively uniformly across labels. Learning these correctly from sentence-level annotations is unlikely, especially because they are seldom found repeatedly, even in a training corpus of decent size. Therefore, incorporating idiomatic information from external data sources may be necessary to improve the classification of sentences within this category.

**Strong Labels** This category (122 total) is particularly difficult for sentiment classifiers for several reasons. First, strong negative sentiment is often expressed in an understated or ironic manner. For example, "Better at putting you to sleep than a sound machine."

For strong positive examples in the dataset, there is often difficult vocabulary and morphologically creative uses of language, *e. g.*, "It is a kickass , dense sci-fi action thriller hybrid that delivers and then some.", while strong negative examples often contain sarcasm or non-standard spelling, *e. g.*, "All prints of this film should be sent to and buried on Pluto.".

**Negation** Negation, which accounts for 97 errors, directly affects the classification of polar sentence (Wiegand et al., 2010). Therefore, we look at the differences between correctly and incorrectly classified sentences containing negation, by analyzing 100 correctly and incorrectly classified sentences containing negation.

From our analysis, there is no specific negator that is more difficult to resolve regarding its effect on sentiment classification.

We also perform an analysis of negation scope under the assumption that when a negator occurs farther from its negated element, it is more difficult for the sentiment classifier to correctly resolve the negation. Let $d$ be the distance between the negator $n$ and the relevant sentiment element $se$, such that $d = |ind(se) - ind(n)|$ where the function $ind$ calculates the index of a token in a sentence. We find that the incorrectly classified examples have an average $d$ of 2.7, while the correctly classified examples had 2.5. This seems to rule out a problem of negation scope as the underlying difference.

High-level or clausal negation occurs when the negator negates a full clause, rather than an adjective or noun phrase, *e. g.*, "I don't think it is a particularly interesting film". In the dataset this phenomenon is found more prevalently in the incorrectly classified examples (8%) versus the correctly classified examples (3%), but does not occur often in absolute terms.

The main source of difference regarding correctly classifying examples involving negation seems to be irrelevant negation. Irrelevant negation refers to cases where a sentence contains a negation but where the sentiment-bearing expression is not within the scope of negation. In our data, there is a strong difference in the distribution of irrelevant negation in correctly and incorrectly classified examples (80% vs. 25%, respectively), suggesting that sentiment classifiers learn to ignore most occurrences of negation.

**World Knowledge** Examples from the dataset where world knowledge is necessary to correctly classify a sentence (81 sentences) include comparisons with entities commonly associated with positive or negative polarity, *e. g.*, "Elicits more groans from the audience than Jar Jar Binks, Scrappy Doo and Scooby Dumb, all wrapped up into one.", analogies, *e. g.*, "Adam Sandler is to Gary Cooper what a gnat is to a racehorse.", or rating scales, *e. g.*, "10/10 overall".

This category is also highly correlated with sarcasm and irony. In fact, irony is often defined as "violating expectations" (Hao and Veale, 2010),

| positive | "It was good." |
| negative | "It was bad." |
| negation | "It was not good." |
| strong | "It was incredible." |
| amplifier | "It was really good." |
| reducer | "It was kind of bad." |
| desirable element | "It had a pool." |
| comparative | "It was better than the first hotel." |
| shifter | "They denied him the scholarship" |
| modality | "I would have loved the room if it been bigger." |
| world knowledge | "It was 2 minutes from the beach." vs. "It was 2 hours from the beach." |
| morphology | "It was un-fricking-believable." |
| non-standard spelling | "It was awesoooome." |
| idioms | "It's not my cup of tea." |
| sarcasm/irony | "I love it when people yell at me first thing in the morning." |
| emoji | ":)" |
| no sentiment | "The president will hold a talk tomorrow." |
| mixed | "The plot was nice, but a little slow." |
| incorrect label | Any clearly incorrect label. |

Table 6: Categories and examples for error annotation guidelines.

which presupposes that we possess a world knowledge containing expectations of a situation.

**Amplified**  Amplifiers occur mainly in negative and strong positive examples, such as "It's an awfully derivative story." Most of the amplified sentences found in the dataset (71/79) contain amplifiers other than "very", such as "super", "incredibly", or "so".

**Comparative**  Comparative sentiment, with 68 errors, is known to be difficult (Hu and Liu, 2004; Liu, 2012), as it is necessary to determine which entity is on which side of the inequality. Sentences like "Will probably stay in the shadow of its two older, more accessible Qatsi siblings" are difficult for sentiment classifiers that do not model this phenomenon explicitly.

**Sarcasm/Irony**  Sarcasm and irony (58 errors), which are often treated separately from sentiment analysis (Filatova, 2012; Barbieri et al., 2014), are present mainly in negative and strong negative examples in the dataset. Correctly capturing sarcasm and irony is necessary to classify some negative and strong negative examples, e. g., "If Melville is creatively a great whale, this film is canned tuna."

**Shifters**  Shifters (50 errors), such as "abandon", "lessen", or "reject" are less common within the dataset, but normally move positive polarity words towards a more negative sentiment. The most common shifter is the word "miss", used as in "We miss the quirky amazement that used to come along for an integral part of the ride."

**Emoji**  While the models handle most occurrences of emojis well, they falter more on the negative examples (46 errors). More than half of the examples in the dataset present positive emoji with a negative gold label, such as "Pricess Leia is going to be gutted! :-)."

**Modality**  None of the state-of-the-art sentiment systems deals explicitly with modality (38 total errors). While in many of the examples modality does not express a different sentiment than the same sentence without modality, in the dataset there are examples that do, e. g., "Still, I thought it could have been more."

**Morphology**  While not the most prominent label (31 errors), the examples in the dataset that contain morphological features that effect sentiment are normally strong positive or strong negative. This most often contains creative use of English morphology, e. g., "It was fan-freakin-tastic!" or "It's hyper-cliched".

**Reducers**  Reducers (13 errors), such as "kind of", "less", or "all that" cooccur with both positive and negative polar words within the dataset, and

| label | Sent. | Phrases | Rel. Imp. |
| --- | --- | --- | --- |
| overall | 23.0 | 31.1 | 10.5 |
| positive | 19.0 | **26.9** | 9.8% |
| negative | 23.1 | **35.0** | 15.5% |
| mixed | 21.2 | **26.5** | 6.7% |
| no-sentiment | 37.6 | **42.6** | 8.1% |
| non-strd spelling | 40.3 | **43.5** | 3.8% |
| desirable | 25.7 | **28.7** | 4.0% |
| idioms | 13.7 | **23.1** | 11.0% |
| strong | 15.5 | **23.7** | 9.7% |
| negation | 23.9 | **38.6** | 19.3% |
| world know. | 14.9 | **21.6** | 19.6% |
| amplified | 13.9 | **31.9** | 20.9% |
| comparative | 11.7 | **13.3** | 1.8% |
| irony | **20.8** | 18.8 | -2.5% |
| shifters | **33.3** | 24.4 | -11.8% |
| emoji | 33.3 | **50.0** | 25.0% |
| modality | 20 | **22.9** | 3.6% |
| morphology | **18.5** | 18.5 | 0% |
| reduced | 7.7 | **23.1** | 16.7% |

Table 7: Per category accuracy and relative improvement (last column) of BERT model trained on SST sentences (8,544) and SST phrases (155,019).

tend to lead to positive or neutral sentiment, *e. g.*, "It was a lot less hassle."

## 6 Case study: Training with phrase-level annotations

As a case study for the usage of the dataset presented here, we evaluate a model that has access to more compositional information. Besides having sentence-level annotations, the SST dataset also contains annotations for each phrase in a constituency tree, which gives a considerable amount more training data, specifically 155,019 annotated phrases vs. 8,544 annotated sentences. It has been claimed that this data allows models to learn more compositionality (Socher et al., 2013). Therefore, we fine-tune the best performing model (BERT) on this data and test on our dataset. The BERT model trained on phrases achieves 55.1 accuracy on the SST dataset, versus 53.0 for the model trained only on sentence-level annotations.

Table 7 shows that the model trained on the SST phrases performs overall much better than the model trained on SST sentences[6] on the dataset. Using the error annotations in the challenge data set, we find that results improve greatly on the sentences which contain the labels negation, world knowledge, amplified, emoji, and reduced, while performing worse on irony, shifters and equally on morphology. This analysis seems to indicate that phrase-level annotations help primarily with learning compositional sentiment (negation, amplified, reduced), while other phenomena, such as irony or morphology do not receive improvements. This confirms that training on the phrase-level annotations improves a sentiment model's ability to classify compositional sentiment, while also demonstrating the usefulness of our dataset for introspection.

## 7 Conclusion and future work

In this paper, we tested three state-of-the-art sentiment classifiers and a baseline bag-of-words classifier on six English sentence-level sentiment datasets. We gathered the sentences that all methods misclassified in order to create a dataset. Additionally, we performed a fine-grained annotation of error types in order to provide insight into the kinds of problems sentiment classifiers have. We will release both the code and the annotated data with the hope that future research will utilize this resource to probe sentiment classifiers for qualitative differences, rather than rely only on quantitative scores, which often obscure the plentiful challenges that still exist.

Many of the phenomena found in the dataset, *e. g.*, negation or modality, have been discussed in depth in (Liu, 2012). However, the dataset that resulted from this work demonstrates that modern neural methods still fail on many examples of these phenomena. Additionally, our dataset enables a quick analysis of qualitative differences between models, probing their performance with respect to the linguistic and paralinguistic categories of errors.

Additionally, many of the findings from this paper are likely to vary to a degree for other languages, due to typological differences, as well as differences in available training data. The annotation method proposed in this paper, however,

---

[6]It is important to realize that the SST-sentence model has 0 accuracy on the subset of the dataset taken from the SST dataset, but not on the sentences taken from the other datasets.

should enable the creation of similar analyses and datasets in other languages.

We expect that this approach to creating a dataset is also easily transferable to other tasks which are affected by linguistic or paralinguistic phenomena, such as hate speech detection or sarcasm detection. It would be more useful to have some knowledge of the phenomena that could affect the task beforehand, but a careful error analysis can also lead to insights which can be translated into annotation labels.

Regarding ways of moving forward, there are already many sources of data for the linguistic phenomena we have analyzed in this work, ranging from datasets annotated for negation (Morante and Blanco, 2012; Liu et al., 2018), irony (Van Hee et al., 2018), emoji (Barbieri et al., 2018), as well as datasets for idioms (Muzny and Zettlemoyer, 2013) and their relationship with sentiment (Jochim et al., 2018). We believe that discovering ways to explicitly incorporate this available information into state-of-the-art sentiment models may provide a way to improve current approaches. Multi-task learning (Caruana, 1993) and transfer learning (Peters et al., 2018; Devlin et al., 2018; Howard and Ruder, 2018) have shown promise in this respect, but have not been exploited for improving sentiment classification with regards to these specific phenomena.

## Acknowledgements

This work has been carried out as part of the SANT project, funded by the Research Council of Norway (grant number 270908).

## References

Rodrigo Agerri, Montse Cuadros, Sean Gaines, and German Rigau. 2013. OpeNER: Open polarity enhanced named entity recognition. *Sociedad Española para el Procesamiento del Lenguaje Natural*, 51(Septiembre):215–218.

Artaches Ambartsoumian and Fred Popowich. 2018. Self-attention: A better building block for sentiment analysis neural network classifiers. In *Proceedings of the 9th Workshop on Computational Approaches to Subjectivity, Sentiment and Social Media Analysis*, pages 130–139.

Francesco Barbieri, Jose Camacho-Collados, Francesco Ronzano, Luis Espinosa Anke, Miguel Ballesteros, Valerio Basile, Viviana Patti, and Horacio Saggion. 2018. SemEval 2018 task 2: Multilingual emoji prediction. In *Proceedings of The 12th International Workshop on Semantic Evaluation*, pages 24–33, New Orleans, Louisiana.

Francesco Barbieri, Horacio Saggion, and Francesco Ronzano. 2014. Modelling sarcasm in twitter, a novel approach. In *Proceedings of the 5th Workshop on Computational Approaches to Subjectivity, Sentiment and Social Media Analysis*, pages 50–58.

Jeremy Barnes, Toni Badia, and Patrik Lambert. 2018. MultiBooked: A Corpus of Basque and Catalan Hotel Reviews Annotated for Aspect-level Sentiment Classification. In *Proceedings of the Eleventh International Conference on Language Resources and Evaluation (LREC 2018)*, Miyazaki, Japan.

Jeremy Barnes, Roman Klinger, and Sabine Schulte im Walde. 2017. Assessing state-of-the-art sentiment models on state-of-the-art sentiment datasets. In *Proceedings of the 8th Workshop on Computational Approaches to Subjectivity, Sentiment and Social Media Analysis*, pages 2–12, Copenhagen, Denmark.

Farah Benamara, Baptiste Chardon, Yannick Mathieu, Vladimir Popescu, and Nicholas Asher. 2012. How do negation and modality impact on opinions? In *Proceedings of the Workshop on Extra-Propositional Aspects of Meaning in Computational Linguistics*, pages 10–18.

Richard Caruana. 1993. Multitask learning: A knowledge-based source of inductive bias. In *Proceedings of the Tenth International Conference on Machine Learning*, pages 41–48. Morgan Kaufmann.

Yejin Choi and Claire Cardie. 2008. Learning with compositional semantics as structural inference for subsentential sentiment analysis. In *Proceedings of the 2008 Conference on Empirical Methods in Natural Language Processing*, pages 793–801.

Alexis Conneau, Germán Kruszewski, Guillaume Lample, Loïc Barrault, and Marco Baroni. 2018. What you can cram into a single \\$&!#* vector: Probing sentence embeddings for linguistic properties. In *Proceedings of the 56th Annual Meeting of the Association for Computational Linguistics (Volume 1: Long Papers)*, pages 2126–2136.

Sanjiv R. Das and Mike Y. Chen. 2007. Yahoo! for amazon: Sentiment extraction from small talk on the web. *Management Science*, 53(9):1375–1388.

Jacob Devlin, Ming-Wei Chang, Kenton Lee, and Kristina Toutanova. 2018. Bert: Pre-training of deep bidirectional transformers for language understanding. *CoRR*, abs/1810.04805.

Javid Ebrahimi, Anyi Rao, Daniel Lowd, and Dejing Dou. 2018. Hotflip: White-box adversarial examples for text classification. In *Proceedings of the 56th Annual Meeting of the Association for Computational Linguistics (Volume 2: Short Papers)*, pages 31–36.

Elena Filatova. 2012. Irony and sarcasm: Corpus generation and analysis using crowdsourcing. In *Proceedings of the Eight International Conference on Language Resources and Evaluation (LREC'12)*, Istanbul, Turkey.

Kristina Gulordava, Piotr Bojanowski, Edouard Grave, Tal Linzen, and Marco Baroni. 2018. Colorless green recurrent networks dream hierarchically. In *Proceedings of the 2018 Conference of the North American Chapter of the Association for Computational Linguistics: Human Language Technologies, Volume 1 (Long Papers)*, pages 1195–1205.

Yanfen Hao and Tony Veale. 2010. An ironic fist in a velvet glove: Creative mis-representation in the construction of ironic similes. *Minds and Machines*, 20(4):635–650.

A. Hogenboom, P. Van Iterson, B. Heerschop, F. Frasincar, and U. Kaymak. 2011. Determining negation scope and strength in sentiment analysis. pages 2589–2594.

Jeremy Howard and Sebastian Ruder. 2018. Universal language model fine-tuning for text classification. In *Proceedings of the 56th Annual Meeting of the Association for Computational Linguistics (Volume 1: Long Papers)*, pages 328–339.

Minqing Hu and Bing Liu. 2004. Mining opinion features in customer reviews. In *Proceedings of the 10th ACM SIGKDD International Conference on Knowledge Discovery and Data Mining (KDD 2004)*, pages 168–177.

Ozan Irsoy and Claire Cardie. 2014. Deep recursive neural networks for compositionality in language. In *Advances in Neural Information Processing Systems*, volume 3, pages 2096–2104.

Charles Jochim, Francesca Bonin, Roy Bar-Haim, and Noam Slonim. 2018. SLIDE - a sentiment lexicon of common idioms. In *Proceedings of the 11th Language Resources and Evaluation Conference*, Miyazaki, Japan.

Kian Kenyon-Dean, Eisha Ahmed, Scott Fujimoto, Jeremy Georges-Filteau, Christopher Glasz, Barleen Kaur, Auguste Lalande, Shruti Bhanderi, Robert Belfer, Nirmal Kanagasabai, Roman Sarrazingendron, Rohit Verma, and Derek Ruths. 2018. Sentiment analysis: It's complicated! In *Proceedings of the 2018 Conference of the North American Chapter of the Association for Computational Linguistics: Human Language Technologies, Volume 1 (Long Papers)*, pages 1886–1895.

Svetlana Kiritchenko and Saif Mohammad. 2016. The effect of negators, modals, and degree adverbs on sentiment composition. In *Proceedings of the 7th Workshop on Computational Approaches to Subjectivity, Sentiment and Social Media Analysis*, pages 43–52.

Svetlana Kiritchenko and Saif Mohammad. 2018. Examining gender and race bias in two hundred sentiment analysis systems. In *Proceedings of the Seventh Joint Conference on Lexical and Computational Semantics*, pages 43–53.

Emanuele Lapponi, Jonathon Read, and Lilja Øvrelid. 2012. Representing and resolving negation for sentiment analysis. In *Proceedings of the 2012 IEEE 12th International Conference on Data Mining Workshops*, ICDMW '12, pages 687–692, Washington, DC, USA.

Tal Linzen, Emmanuel Dupoux, and Yoav Goldberg. 2016. Assessing the ability of lstms to learn syntax-sensitive dependencies. *Transactions of the Association for Computational Linguistics*, 4:521–535.

Bing Liu. 2012. Sentiment analysis and opinion mining. *Synthesis Lectures on Human Language Technologies*, 5(1):1–167.

Bing Liu, Minqing Hu, and Junsheng Cheng. 2005. Opinion Observer: Analyzing and comparing opinions on the web. In *Proceedings of the 14th international World Wide Web conference (WWW-2005)*, Chiba Japan.

Qianchu Liu, Federico Fancellu, and Bonnie Webber. 2018. NegPar: A parallel corpus annotated for negation. In *Proceedings of the Eleventh International Conference on Language Resources and Evaluation (LREC 2018)*, Miyazaki, Japan.

Yang Liu, Xiaohui Yu, Bing Liu, and Zhongshuai Chen. 2014. Sentence-level sentiment analysis in the presence of modalities. In *Computational Linguistics and Intelligent Text Processing*, pages 1–16, Berlin, Heidelberg. Springer Berlin Heidelberg.

Saif M. Mohammad, Svetlana Kiritchenko, and Xiaodan Zhu. 2013. Nrc-canada: Building the state-of-the-art in sentiment analysis of tweets. In *Proceedings of the seventh international workshop on Semantic Evaluation Exercises (SemEval-2013)*.

Roser Morante and Eduardo Blanco. 2012. *SEM 2012 shared task: Resolving the scope and focus of negation. In **SEM 2012: The First Joint Conference on Lexical and Computational Semantics – Volume 1: Proceedings of the main conference and the shared task, and Volume 2: Proceedings of the Sixth International Workshop on Semantic Evaluation (SemEval 2012)*, pages 265–274, Montréal, Canada.

Grace Muzny and Luke Zettlemoyer. 2013. Automatic idiom identification in Wiktionary. In *Proceedings of the 2013 Conference on Empirical Methods in Natural Language Processing*, pages 1417–1421, Seattle, Washington, USA.

Preslav Nakov, Sara Rosenthal, Zornitsa Kozareva, Veselin Stoyanov, Alan Ritter, and Theresa Wilson. 2013. Semeval-2013 task 2: Sentiment analysis in twitter. In *Second Joint Conference on Lexical and*

Computational Semantics (*SEM), Volume 2: Proceedings of the Seventh International Workshop on Semantic Evaluation (SemEval 2013).

Ramanathan Narayanan, Bing Liu, and Alok Choudhary. 2009. Sentiment analysis of conditional sentences. In *Proceedings of the 2009 Conference on Empirical Methods in Natural Language Processing*, pages 180–189.

Bo Pang and Lillian Lee. 2008. Opinion mining and sentiment analysis. *Foundations and trends in information retrieval*, 2(1-2):1–135.

Bo Pang, Lillian Lee, and Shivakumar Vaithyanathan. 2002. Thumbs up? sentiment classification using machine learning techniques. In *Proceedings of the 2002 Conference on Empirical Methods in Natural Language Processing*, pages 79–86.

Ji Ho Park, Jamin Shin, and Pascale Fung. 2018. Reducing gender bias in abusive language detection. In *Proceedings of the 2018 Conference on Empirical Methods in Natural Language Processing*, pages 2799–2804.

Matthew Peters, Mark Neumann, Mohit Iyyer, Matt Gardner, Christopher Clark, Kenton Lee, and Luke Zettlemoyer. 2018. Deep contextualized word representations. In *Proceedings of the 2018 Conference of the North American Chapter of the Association for Computational Linguistics: Human Language Technologies, Volume 1 (Long Papers)*, pages 2227–2237.

Johan Reitan, Jørgen Faret, Björn Gambäck, and Lars Bungum. 2015. Negation scope detection for twitter sentiment analysis. In *Proceedings of the 6th Workshop on Computational Approaches to Subjectivity, Sentiment and Social Media Analysis*, pages 99–108.

Marco Tulio Ribeiro, Sameer Singh, and Carlos Guestrin. 2018. Semantically equivalent adversarial rules for debugging nlp models. In *Proceedings of the 56th Annual Meeting of the Association for Computational Linguistics (Volume 1: Long Papers)*, pages 856–865.

Hassan Saif, Miriam Fernández, Yulan He, and Harith Alani. 2013. Evaluation datasets for twitter sentiment analysis: A survey and a new dataset, the sts-gold. In *1st Interantional Workshop on Emotion and Sentiment in Social and Expressive Media: Approaches and Perspectives from AI (ESSEM 2013)*, Turin, Italy.

Natalie Schluter and Daniel Varab. 2018. When data permutations are pathological: the case of neural natural language inference. In *Proceedings of the 2018 Conference on Empirical Methods in Natural Language Processing*, pages 4935–4939.

Marc Schulder, Michael Wiegand, Josef Ruppenhofer, and Stephanie Køser. 2018. Introducing a Lexicon of Verbal Polarity Shifters for English. In *Proceedings of the Eleventh International Conference on*

Language Resources and Evaluation (LREC 2018), Miyazaki, Japan.

Aliaksei Severyn and Alessandro Moschitti. 2015. Unitn: Training deep convolutional neural network for twitter sentiment classification. In *Proceedings of the 9th International Workshop on Semantic Evaluation (SemEval 2015)*, pages 464–469.

David A. Shamma, Lyndon Kennedy, and Elizabeth F. Churchill. 2009. Tweet the debates: Understanding community annotation of uncollected sources. In *Proceedings of the First SIGMM Workshop on Social Media*, WSM '09, pages 3–10, New York, NY, USA.

Richard Socher, Alex Perelygin, Jy Wu, Jason Chuang, Chris Manning, Andrew Ng, and Chris Potts. 2013. Recursive deep models for semantic compositionality over a sentiment treebank. *Proceedings of the 2013 Conference on Empirical Methods in Natural Language Processing*, pages 1631–1642.

Oscar Täckström and Ryan McDonald. 2011. Semi-supervised latent variable models for sentence-level sentiment analysis. In *Proceedings of the 49th Annual Meeting of the Association for Computational Linguistics: Human Language Technologies*, pages 569–574.

Kai Sheng Tai, Richard Socher, and Christopher D Manning. 2015. Improved semantic representations From tree-structured long short-term memory networks. *Association for Computational Linguistics 2015 Conference*, pages 1556–1566.

Mike Thelwall, Kevin Buckley, Georgios Paltoglou, Di Cai, and Arvid Kappas. 2010. Sentiment strength detection in short informal text. *Journal of the American Society for Information Science and Technology*, 61(12):2544–2558.

Peter Turney. 2002. Thumbs up or thumbs down? semantic orientation applied to unsupervised classification of reviews. In *Proceedings of the 40th Annual Meeting of the Association for Computational Linguistics*.

Cynthia Van Hee, Els Lefever, and Veronique Hoste. 2018. SemEval-2018 task 3: Irony detection in English tweets. In *Proceedings of The 12th International Workshop on Semantic Evaluation*, pages 39–50, New Orleans, Louisiana.

Michael Wiegand, Alexandra Balahur, Benjamin Roth, Dietrich Klakow, and Andrés Montoyo. 2010. A survey on the role of negation in sentiment analysis. In *Proceedings of the Workshop on Negation and Speculation in Natural Language Processing*, pages 60–68.

Theresa Wilson, Janyce Wiebe, and Paul Hoffmann. 2005. Recognizing contextual polarity in phrase-level sentiment analysis. In *Proceedings of Human Language Technology Conference and Conference on Empirical Methods in Natural Language Processing*.

Jieyu Zhao, Yichao Zhou, Zeyu Li, Wei Wang, and Kai-Wei Chang. 2018. Learning gender-neutral word embeddings. In *Proceedings of the 2018 Conference on Empirical Methods in Natural Language Processing*, pages 4847–4853.

Yukun Zhu, Ryan Kiros, Rich Zemel, Ruslan Salakhutdinov, Raquel Urtasun, Antonio Torralba, and Sanja Fidler. 2015. Aligning books and movies: Towards story-like visual explanations by watching movies and reading books. In *The IEEE International Conference on Computer Vision (ICCV)*.

# Second-order Co-occurrence Sensitivity of Skip-Gram with Negative Sampling


**Dominik Schlechtweg, Cennet Oguz, Sabine Schulte im Walde**
Institute for Natural Language Processing, University of Stuttgart
`{schlecdk,oguzct,schulte}@ims.uni-stuttgart.de`



## Abstract

We simulate first- and second-order context overlap and show that Skip-Gram with Negative Sampling is similar to Singular Value Decomposition in capturing second-order co-occurrence information, while Pointwise Mutual Information is agnostic to it. We support the results with an empirical study finding that the models react differently when provided with additional second-order information. Our findings reveal a basic property of Skip-Gram with Negative Sampling and point towards an explanation of its success on a variety of tasks.


## 1 Introduction

The idea of second-order co-occurrence vectors was introduced by Schütze (1998) for word sense discrimination and has since then been extended and applied to a variety of tasks (Lemaire and Denhiere, 2006; Islam and Inkpen, 2006; Schulte im Walde, 2010; Zhuang et al., 2018). The basic idea is to represent a word $w$ not by a vector of the counts of context words it directly co-occurs with, but instead by a count vector of the context words of the context words, i.e., the second-order context words of $w$. These second-order vectors are supposed to be less sparse and more robust than first-order vectors (Schütze, 1998). Moreover, capturing second-order co-occurrence information can be seen as a way of generalization. To see this, cf. examples (1) and (2) inspired by Schütze and Pedersen (1993).

(1)  As far as the Soviet Communist **Party** and the Comintern were concerned ...

(2)  ... this is precisely the approach taken by the British **Government**.

The nouns *Party* and *Government* have similar meanings in these contexts, although they have little contextual overlap: A frequent topic in the British corpus used by Schütze and Pedersen is the Communist Party of the Soviet Union, but governments are rarely qualified as communist in the corpus. Hence, there is little overlap in first-order context words of *Party* and *Government*. However, their context words *Communist* and *British* in turn have a greater overlap, because they are frequently used to qualify the same nouns from the political domain, as in *Communist authorities* and *British authorities*. Hence, although *Party* and *Government* may have no first-order context overlap, they do have second-order context overlap. According to Schütze and Pedersen, capturing this information corresponds to the generalization "occurring with a political adjective."

While most traditional count-based vector learning techniques such as raw count vectors or Point-wise Mutual Information (PPMI) do not capture second-order co-occurrence information, truncated Singular Value Decomposition (SVD) has been shown to do so. Regarding the more recently developed embeddings based on shallow neural networks, such as Skip-Gram with Negative Sampling (SGNS), it is presently unknown whether they capture higher-order co-occurrence information. So far, this question has been neglected as a research topic, although the answer is crucial to explain performance differences: Levy et al. (2015) show that SGNS performs similarly to SVD and differently from PPMI across semantic similarity data sets. If SGNS captures second-order co-occurrence information, this provides a possible explanation for the observed performance differences.

We examine this question in two experiments: (i) We create an artificial data set with target words displaying context overlap in different orders of co-occurrence and show that SGNS behaves similarly to SVD in capturing second-order co-occurrence information. The experiment supplies additional and striking evidence to prior




*Proceedings of the Second BlackboxNLP Workshop on Analyzing and Interpreting Neural Networks for NLP*, pages 24–30
Florence, Italy, August 1, 2019. ©2019 Association for Computational Linguistics

work on SVD and introduces a method to further investigate questions more precisely than done before. (ii) We transfer second-order context information to the first-order level in a small corpus and test the models' reaction on a standard evaluation data set when provided with the additional information. We find that SGNS and SVD, already capturing second-order information, do not benefit, whereas PPMI benefits.

## 2 Related Work

An early connection between second-order context information and generalization can be found in Schütze and Pedersen (1993). The authors claim that SVD is able to generalize by using second-order context information as described above. Later work supports this claim and indicates that SVD even captures information from higher orders of co-occurrence (Landauer et al., 1998; Kontostathis and Pottenger, 2002; Newo Kenmogne, 2005; Kontostathis and Pottenger, 2006).

Since then, second-order co-occurrence information has mainly been exploited for traditional count-based vector learning techniques with different aims. Schütze (1998) had used second-order vectors for word sense clustering. Various studies model synonymy or semantic similarity (Edmonds, 1997; Islam and Inkpen, 2006; Lemaire and Denhiere, 2006) indicating that second-order co-occurrence plays an important role for these tasks.

The only works we are aware of exploring second-order information for word embeddings are Newman-Griffis and Fosler-Lussier (2017) learning embeddings from nearest-neighbor graphs and Zhuang et al. (2018) indicating that a specific type of word embeddings may benefit from second-order information. However, no study investigated the question whether SGNS or other word embeddings already capture higher-order co-occurrence information, which may make the integration of second-order information superfluous.

## 3 Semantic Vector Spaces

We compare SGNS to two traditional count-based vector space learning techniques: PPMI and SVD, where the former does not capture second-order information while the latter does. All methods are based on the concept of semantic vector spaces:

A semantic vector space constructed from a corpus $C$ with vocabulary $V$ is a matrix $M$, where each row vector represents a word $w$ in the vocabulary $V$ reflecting its co-occurrence statistics (Turney and Pantel, 2010).

**Positive Pointwise Mutual Information (PPMI).** For PPMI representations, we first construct a high-dimensional and sparse co-occurrence matrix $M$. The value of each matrix cell $M_{i,j}$ represents the number of co-occurrences of the word $w_i$ and the context $c_j$, $\#(w_i, c_j)$. Then, the co-occurrence counts in each matrix cell $M_{i,j}$ are weighted by the smoothed and shifted positive mutual information of target $w_i$ and context $c_j$ reflecting their degree of association. The values of the transformed matrix are

$$M_{i,j}^{\text{PPMI}} = \max \left\{ \log \left( \frac{\#(w_i, c_j) \sum_c \#(c)^\alpha}{\#(w_i)\#(c_j)^\alpha} \right) - \log(k), 0 \right\},$$

where $k > 1$ is a prior on the probability of observing an actual occurrence of $(w_i, c_j)$ and $0 < \alpha < 1$ is a smoothing parameter reducing PPMI's bias towards rare words (Levy and Goldberg, 2014; Levy et al., 2015). To our knowledge PPMI representations have never been claimed to capture higher-order co-occurrence information.

**Singular Value Decomposition (SVD).** Truncated Singular Value Decomposition is an algebraic algorithm finding the optimal rank $d$ factorization of matrix $M$ with respect to L2 loss (Eckart and Young, 1936).[1] It is used to obtain low-dimensional approximations of the PPMI representations by factorizing $M^{\text{PPMI}}$ into the product of the three matrices $U\Sigma V^\top$. We keep only the top $d$ elements of $\Sigma$ and obtain

$$M^{\text{SVD}} = U_d \Sigma_d^p,$$

where $p$ is an eigenvalue weighting parameter (Levy et al., 2015). Ignoring $V$ for $M^{\text{SVD}}$ reduces dimensionality while preserving the dot-products between rows. While it is not clear whether SVD generalizes better than other models in general (Gamallo and Bordag, 2011), its sensitivity to higher orders of co-occurrence has been shown empirically and mathematically (Kontostathis and Pottenger, 2002; Newo Kenmogne, 2005; Kontostathis and Pottenger, 2006). Kontostathis and Pottenger (2006) prove that the ex-

---

[1] We use 'SVD' to refer to the particular application of the algebraic method described.

istence of a non-zero value in a truncated term-to-term co-occurrence matrix follows directly from the existence of a higher-order co-occurrence in the full matrix. They also show that there is an empirical correlation between the magnitude of the value and the number of higher-order co-occurrences found for the particular term pair.

**Skip-Gram with Negative Sampling (SGNS).** SGNS differs from the above techniques in that it directly represents each word $w \in V$ and each context $c \in V$ as a $d$-dimensional vector by implicitly factorizing $M = WC^\top$ when solving

$$\arg\max_\theta \sum_{(w,c)\in D} \log \sigma(v_c \cdot v_w) + \sum_{(w,c)\in D'} \log \sigma(-v_c \cdot v_w),$$

where $\sigma(x) = \frac{1}{1+e^{-x}}$, $D$ is the set of all observed word-context pairs and $D'$ is the set of randomly generated negative samples (Mikolov et al., 2013a,b; Goldberg and Levy, 2014). The optimized parameters $\theta$ are $v_{c_i} = C_{i*}$ and $v_{w_i} = W_{i*}$ for $w, c \in V$, $i \in 1, ..., d$. $D'$ is obtained by drawing $k$ contexts from the empirical unigram distribution $P(c) = \frac{\#(c)}{|D|}$ for each observation of $(w, c)$, cf. Levy et al. (2015). The final SGNS matrix is given by

$$M^{\text{SGNS}} = W.$$

Levy and Goldberg (2014) relate SGNS to SVD by showing that under specific assumptions their learning objectives have the same global optimum. However, it is unknown whether SGNS is also similar to SVD in capturing higher-order co-occurrence information. The model architecture suggests that this is possible: consider the two context vectors $\vec{c_1}, \vec{c_2}$ in $C$ of two words having large context overlap (e.g. the vectors for *Communist* and *British*). $\vec{c_1}, \vec{c_2}$ will be similar, because the dot product with the same target vectors in $W$ will be maximized (as $\vec{c_1}, \vec{c_2}$ frequently occur as contexts of the same target words). If $\vec{c_1}, \vec{c_2}$ are then in turn each used to maximize the dot product with two different new target vectors (e.g. the vectors for *Party* and *Government*), these also tend to be similar.

**Model Training.** For both experiments we use the implementation of Levy et al. (2015), allowing us to train all models on extracted word-context pairs instead of the corpus directly. We follow previous work in setting the hyper-parameters (Levy et al., 2015). For PPMI we set $\alpha = .75$ and $k = 5$.

We set the number of dimensions $d$ for SVD and SGNS to 300. SGNS is trained with 5 negative samples, 5 epochs and without subsampling. For SVD we set $p = 0$.

**Similarity Measure.** For all methods we measure similarity between word vectors with Cosine Distance (CD), where low CD means high similarity. CD is based on cosine similarity, $cos(\vec{x}, \vec{y})$, which measures the cosine of the angle between two non-zero vectors $\vec{x}, \vec{y}$ with equal magnitudes (Salton and McGill, 1983). CD is then defined as

$$CD(\vec{x}, \vec{y}) = 1 - cos(\vec{x}, \vec{y}).$$

## 4 Experiment 1: Simulating second-order context overlap

In order to see whether SGNS captures second-order co-occurrence information, we artificially simulate context overlap for first- and second-order co-occurrence separately. This allows us to simulate clear cases of overlap controlling for confounding factors which are present in empirical data. We generate target-context pairs in such a way that specific target words have either context word overlap in first-order co-occurrence, or by contrast in second order. We compare the behavior of PPMI, SVD and SGNS on three groups of such target words (see Table 1):

**first-order overlap (1ST):** Target words $T$ occurring with the *same* context words $C1$ in the first order, while in the second order all context words from $C1$ have distinct context words $C2$.

**2nd-order overlap (2ND):** Target words $T$ occurring with *distinct* context words $C1$ in the first order, while all context words from $C1$ have the same context words $C2$.

**no overlap (NONE):** Target words $T$ occurring with distinct context words $C1$ in the first order and also all context words in $C1$ have distinct context words $C2$.

As an example, consider the column 2ND in Table 1. The target words $T$ are $a$ and $b$. Each has distinct context words: $a$ occurs only with $c, d \in C1$, while b occurs only with $e, f \in C1$. However, the first-order context words $c, d, e, f \in C1$ do have context overlap: $c, d, e, f$ occur all with $u, v \in C2$, i.e., they have the same second-order context words.

For each group we generate 10 target words ($T$). Per target word, each of $C1$, $C2$ is constructed by first generating 1000 context words $C$, assigning a sampling probability from a lognormal distribution to each context word in $C$ and then sampling 1000 times from $C$.[2] For the 1ST-group, the set of context words $C$ will be shared across target words, meaning that they have a context word overlap. For the target words in the 2ND-group this will not be the case, but instead their first-order context words ($C1$) will have context overlap (see Table 1). In this way, we simulate context overlap in first vs. second order. For the target words in the NONE-group, $C$ will instead be completely disjunct in both orders. Because co-occurrence is symmetric (if $a$ occurs with $c$, $c$ also occurs with $a$), for each pair ($a$,$c$) generated by the above-described process, we also add the reverse pair ($c$,$a$). To make sure that the pairs from the different groups (1ST, 2ND, NONE) do not interfere with each other, each string generated for a group is unique to the group. Finally, we mix and randomly shuffle the pairs from all groups. In this way, we generate 10 x 1000 x 1000 x 2 target-context pairs for each group: 10 target words occurring with 1000 context words in $C1$ where each in turn occurs with 1000 context words in $C2$, plus each of these pairs reversed.[3]

Our main hypothesis is that SGNS and SVD will predict target words from the 2ND-group to be more similar on average than target words from the NONE-group (although both groups have no first-order context overlap), while PPMI will predict similar averages for both groups.

**Results.** Figure 1 shows the average cosine distance between the target words in each of the three target word groups with context overlap in different orders (1ST, 2ND and NONE). As expected, PPMI predicts the target words without contextual overlap in any order (NONE) to be orthogonal to each other (1.0). Further, PPMI is sensitive to first-order overlap, but not at all to second-order overlap (0.51 vs. 1.0). SVD also predicts orthogonality for the NONE-group (1.0) and shows sensitivity to first-order overlap (0.34), but is extremely

| order | 1ST | 2ND | NONE |
|---|---|---|---|
| C1 | a c | a c | a c |
| | a d | a d | a d |
| | b c | b e | b e |
| | b d | b f | b f |
| C2 | c u | c u | c u |
| | c v | c v | c v |
| | d w | d u | d w |
| | d x | d v | d x |

Table 1: Artificial co-occurrence pairs with context overlap in different orders of co-occurrence (1ST, 2ND and NONE). $C1$ and $C2$ give co-occurrence in first and second order respectively. For each pair (a,c) shown above we also add the reverse pair (c,a).

sensitive to second-order overlap: it predicts the target words in 2ND to be perfectly similar to each other (0.0), notwithstanding the fact that they have no first-order context word overlap. SGNS shows a similar behavior, although its vectors are distributed more densely: target words in NONE are predicted to be least similar (0.79), while target words in 1ST are more similar (0.11) and in 2ND they are predicted to be completely similar (0.0).

We further hypothesize that the fact that for SGNS and SVD the average cosine distance in 1ST is higher than in 2ND is related to our choice to make the context words $C1$ of the target words in 1ST dissimilar to each other by assigning completely distinct context words $C2$ (see Table 1). We test this hypothesis by creating a second artificial set of target-context pairs completely parallel to the above-described set with the only difference that 1ST has additional context overlap in $C2$. On these targets words with overlap in both orders we find that PPMI makes similar predictions (0.56) as before, while for SVD and SGNS predictions drop to 0.0, confirming our hypothesis.

**Discussion.** SGNS and SVD capture second-order co-occurrence information. Notably, they are more sensitive to the similarity of context words than to the words themselves (2ND vs. 1ST), which means that they abstract over mere co-occurrence with specific context words and take into account the co-occurrence structure of these words in the second order (and potentially higher orders). PPMI does not have this property and only measures context overlap in first order.

---

[2] By sampling from a lognormal distribution we aim to approximate the empirical frequency distribution of context words. Context words receive probabilities by randomly sampling 1000 values from $f(x) = \frac{1}{x\sqrt{2\pi}} \exp\left(-\frac{\log(x)^2}{2}\right)$ and normalizing them to a probability distribution.

[3] Find the code generating the artificial pairs under: https://github.com/Garrafao/SecondOrder.

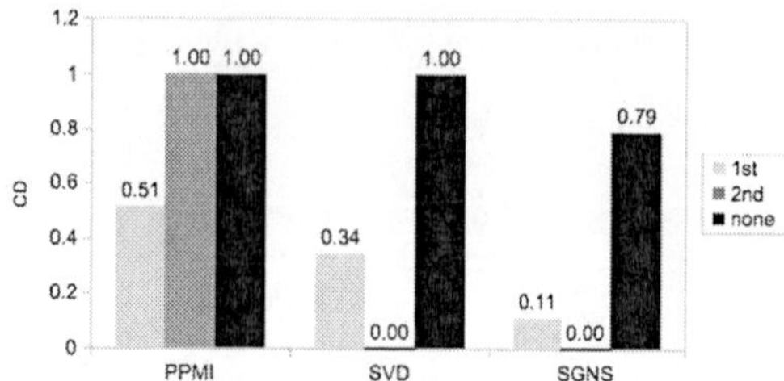

Figure 1: Results of simulation experiment. Values give average cosine distances across target words with different levels of context overlap. Pair-wise differences between group means (except PPMI 2ND vs. NONE) are statistically significant according to a two-sample bootstrap test ($p < 0.001$, adjusted through Bonferroni correction for 9 tests, two-tailed).

## 5 Experiment 2: Propagating second-order co-occurrence information

We now propagate second-order information to the first-order level by extracting second-order word-context pairs and adding them to the first-order pairs. We hypothesize that the additional second-order information will impact PPMI representations positively and stronger than SVD and SGNS, because we saw that the latter already capture second-order information. We reckon that the additional information is beneficial for PPMI in two ways: (i) it helps to generalize as described in (1) and (2), and (ii) it overcomes data sparsity for low-frequency words. Note that these two aspects are often highly related: with only a limited amount of data available it is more likely that similar words do not have exactly the same, but still similar context words. Generalization then helps to overcome sparsity.

**Corpus.** We use ukWaC (Baroni et al., 2009), a $> 1$B token web-crawled corpus of English. The corpus provides part-of-speech tagging and lemmatization. We keep only the lemmas which are tagged as nouns, adjectives or verbs. In order to assure we have low-frequency words in the test data, we create a small corpus by randomly choosing 1M sentences and shuffling them. The final corpus contains roughly 10M tokens. Under these sparse conditions we expect to observe

strong effects on model performance highlighting the differences between the models.

### 5.1 Pair Extraction

We first extract first-order word-context pairs by iterating over all sentences and extracting one word context pair $(w,c)$ for each token $w$ and each context word $c$ surrounding $w$ in a symmetric window of size 5 (BASE pairs). Then, we extract additional second-order pairs in the following way: For each word type $t$ in the corpus, we build a second-order vector $\vec{v}$ by summing over all of $t$'s first-order context token count vectors (Schütze, 1998). Then we randomly sample $n$ second-order context tokens from $\vec{v}$ (with replacement) where each context type $c_i$ has a sampling probability of $\frac{\vec{v}_i}{\sum_{j=1} \vec{v}_j}$ and $\vec{v}_i$ is $\vec{v}$'s $i$th entry. We then exclude all sampled context tokens $c = t$.[4]

We extract second-order pairs only for words below a specific co-occurrence frequency threshold $f$ to test the impact on sparse words separately. We experiment with $f \in \{2k,20k,200k\}$. We set $n$ globally to 200% of $t$'s co-occurrence frequency to add a substantial amount of information. For each of the second-order pairs we add the reverse pair $(c,w)$. Finally, the respective second-order pairs are combined with the base pairs and randomly shuffled. In this way, we generate roughly 22/99/218M (2/20/200k) second-order pairs from 57M base pairs. Then we train each model on each of the combined pair files separately.

### 5.2 Results

We evaluate the obtained vector spaces on Word-Sim353 (Finkelstein et al., 2002), a standard human similarity judgment data set, by measuring the Spearman correlation of the cosine similarity for target word pairs with human judgments. The results are shown in Figure 2. As we can see, the models show different reactions to the additional second-order information: PPMI is the only model benefiting (in one case), while SVD and SGNS never benefit from the additional information and are always impacted negatively. The strongest negative impact can be observed for SVD (-0.17). PPMI shows a clear improvement with rather low-frequency words (20k). Adding second-order information for high-frequency words (200k) has a strong negative impact for PPMI and SVD.

---

[4]Find the code under: `https://github.com/Garrafao/SecondOrder`.

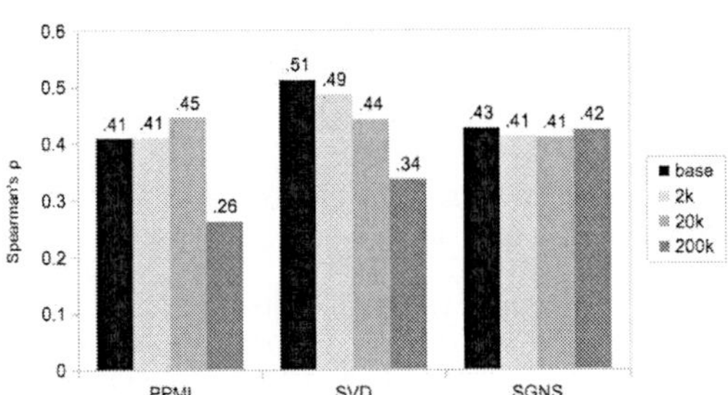

Figure 2: Results of experiment 2. Values give correlation (Spearman's $\rho$) of model predictions with human similarity judgments.

**Discussion.** The different reactions of PPMI vs. SVD and SGNS partly confirm our hypothesis which was based on the findings in experiment 1: only PPMI benefits from additional second-order information. However, we did not expect the observed negative impacts, especially the strong performance drop for SVD. Moreover, it is notable that SVD on the base pairs shows a much higher performance (0.51) than SGNS and PPMI (0.43, 0.41), which is not the case in less sparse conditions (Levy et al., 2015). This indicates that SVD makes much better use of the available information and overcomes data sparsity in this way. It remains for future research to determine how much the exploitation of higher-order co-occurrence information contributes to this clear performance advantage.

## 6   Conclusion

We showed that SGNS captures second-order co-occurrence information, a property it shares with SVD and distinguishes it from PPMI. We further tested the reaction of the models when provided with additional second-order information, expecting that only PPMI would benefit. We find this confirmed, but also observe unexpectedly strong negative impacts on SVD by the supposedly redundant information. In general, SVD turns out to have strong performance advantages over PPMI and SGNS in the sparse experimental conditions we created.

Our findings are relevant for a variety of algorithms relying on the SGNS architecture (i.a. Grover and Leskovec, 2016; Bamler and Mandt,

2017). Future work will look into the relationship between the second-order sensitivity of SVD and SGNS and their high performances across tasks. In addition, we aim to use the introduced method of generating artificial context overlap to see which higher orders of co-occurrence SVD, SGNS and other embedding types (Pennington et al., 2014; Peters et al., 2018; Athiwaratkun et al., 2018) capture. Because the aim of the study was only to test the second-order sensitivity of different models, we did not focus on finding the best way to provide this information. Given the results for PPMI, however, developing a smoother way to provide second-order information to models seems to be a promising starting point for further research.

## Acknowledgments

The first author was supported by the Konrad Adenauer Foundation and the CRETA center funded by the German Ministry for Education and Research (BMBF) during the conduct of this study. We thank Agnieszka Falenska, Sascha Schlechtweg and the anonymous reviewers for their valuable comments.

## References

Ben Athiwaratkun, Andrew Gordon Wilson, and Anima Anandkumar. 2018. Probabilistic fasttext for multi-sense word embeddings. In *Proceedings of the 56th Annual Meeting of the Association for Computational Linguistics*, pages 1–11, Melbourne, Australia.

Robert Bamler and Stephan Mandt. 2017. Dynamic word embeddings. In *Proceedings of the 34th International Conference on Machine Learning*, volume 70, pages 380–389, Sydney, Australia.

Marco Baroni, Silvia Bernardini, Adriano Ferraresi, and Eros Zanchetta. 2009. The wacky wide web: A collection of very large linguistically processed web-crawled corpora. *Language Resources and Evaluation*, 43(3):209–226.

Carl Eckart and Gale Young. 1936. The approximation of one matrix by another of lower rank. *Psychometrika*, 1:211–218.

Philip Edmonds. 1997. Choosing the word most typical in context using a lexical co-occurrence network. In *Proceedings of the 8th Conference of the European Chapter of the Association for Computational Linguistics*, pages 507–509.

Lev Finkelstein, Evgeniy Gabrilovich, Yossi Matias, Ehud Rivlin, Zach Solan, Gadi Wolfman, and Eytan Ruppin. 2002. Placing search in context: The concept revisited. *ACM Transactions on Information Systems*, 20(1):116–131.

Pablo Gamallo and Stefan Bordag. 2011. Is singular value decomposition useful for word similarity extraction? *Language Resources and Evaluation*, 45(2):95–119.

Yoav Goldberg and Omer Levy. 2014. Word2vec Explained: Deriving Mikolov et al.'s negative-sampling word-embedding method. *CoRR*, abs/1402.3722.

Aditya Grover and Jure Leskovec. 2016. Node2vec: Scalable feature learning for networks. In *Proceedings of the 22nd ACM SIGKDD International Conference on Knowledge Discovery and Data Mining*, pages 855–864, San Francisco, California, USA.

Aminul Islam and Diana Inkpen. 2006. Second order co-occurrence pmi for determining the semantic similarity of words. In *Proceedings of the 5th International Conference on Language Resources and Evaluation*, pages 1033–1038, Genoa, Italy.

April Kontostathis and William M. Pottenger. 2002. Detecting patterns in the LSI term-term matrix. In *Proceedings of the Workshop on Foundations of Data Mining and Discovery*.

April Kontostathis and William M. Pottenger. 2006. A framework for understanding latent semantic indexing LSI performance. *Information Processing & Management*, 42(1):56–73.

Thomas K Landauer, Peter W Foltz, and Darrell Laham. 1998. An introduction to latent semantic analysis. *Discourse Processes*, 25(2-3):259–284.

Benoit Lemaire and Guy Denhiere. 2006. Effects of high-order co-occurrences on word semantic similarity. *Current Psychology Letters – Behaviour, Brain and Cognition*, 18(1).

Omer Levy and Yoav Goldberg. 2014. Neural word embedding as implicit matrix factorization. In *Proceedings of the 27th International Conference on Neural Information Processing Systems*, pages 2177–2185, Montreal, Canada.

Omer Levy, Yoav Goldberg, and Ido Dagan. 2015. Improving distributional similarity with lessons learned from word embeddings. *Transactions of the Association for Computational Linguistics*, 3:211–225.

Tomas Mikolov, Kai Chen, Greg Corrado, and Jeffrey Dean. 2013a. Efficient estimation of word representations in vector space. In *Proceedings of the International Conference on Learning Representations*.

Tomas Mikolov, Ilya Sutskever, Kai Chen, Greg Corrado, and Jeffrey Dean. 2013b. Distributed representations of words and phrases and their compositionality. In *Proceedings of the Neural Information Processing Systems Conference*.

Denis Newman-Griffis and Eric Fosler-Lussier. 2017. Second-order word embeddings from nearest neighbor topological features. *arXiv preprint arXiv:1705.08488*.

Regis Newo Kenmogne. 2005. Understanding LSI via the truncated term-term matrix. Master's thesis, Universität des Saarlandes, Saarbrücken.

Jeffrey Pennington, Richard Socher, and Christopher Manning. 2014. Glove: Global vectors for word representation. In *Proceedings of the 2014 Conference on Empirical Methods in Natural Language Processing*, pages 1532–1543, Doha, Qatar.

Matthew Peters, Mark Neumann, Mohit Iyyer, Matt Gardner, Christopher Clark, Kenton Lee, and Luke Zettlemoyer. 2018. Deep contextualized word representations. In *Proceedings of the 2018 Conference of the North American Chapter of the Association for Computational Linguistics: Human Language Technologies*, pages 2227–2237, New Orleans, LA, USA.

Gerard Salton and Michael J McGill. 1983. *Introduction to Modern Information Retrieval*. McGraw - Hill Book Company, New York.

Sabine Schulte im Walde. 2010. Comparing computational approaches to selectional preferences: Second-order co-occurrence vs. latent semantic clusters. In *Proceedings of the 7th International Conference on Language Resources and Evaluation*, pages 1381–1388, Valletta, Malta.

Hinrich Schütze. 1998. Automatic word sense discrimination. *Computational Linguistics*, 24(1):97–123.

Hinrich Schütze and Jan Pedersen. 1993. A vector model for syntagmatic and paradigmatic relatedness. In *Proceedings of the 9th Annual Conference of the UW Centre for the New OED and Text Research*, pages 104–113, Oxford, UK.

Peter D Turney and Patrick Pantel. 2010. From frequency to meaning: Vector space models of semantics. *Journal of Artificial Intelligence Research*, 37:141–188.

Yimeng Zhuang, Jinghui Xie, Yinhe Zheng, and Xuan Zhu. 2018. Quantifying context overlap for training word embeddings. In *Proceedings of the 2018 Conference on Empirical Methods in Natural Language Processing*, pages 587–593.

# Can neural networks understand monotonicity reasoning?

**Hitomi Yanaka**[1,2]**, Koji Mineshima**[2]**, Daisuke Bekki**[2]**,
Kentaro Inui**[1,3]**, Satoshi Sekine**[1]**, Lasha Abzianidze**[4]**, and Johan Bos**[4]
[1]RIKEN, [2]Ochanomizu University, [3]Tohoku University, Japan
[4]University of Groningen, Netherlands
{hitomi.yanaka, satoshi.sekine}@riken.jp,
mineshima.koji@ocha.ac.jp, bekki@is.ocha.ac.jp,
inui@ecei.tohoku.ac.jp, {l.abzianidze, johan.bos}@rug.nl

## Abstract

Monotonicity reasoning is one of the important reasoning skills for any intelligent natural language inference (NLI) model in that it requires the ability to capture the interaction between lexical and syntactic structures. Since no test set has been developed for monotonicity reasoning with wide coverage, it is still unclear whether neural models can perform monotonicity reasoning in a proper way. To investigate this issue, we introduce the Monotonicity Entailment Dataset (MED). Performance by state-of-the-art NLI models on the new test set is substantially worse, under 55%, especially on downward reasoning. In addition, analysis using a monotonicity-driven data augmentation method showed that these models might be limited in their generalization ability in upward and downward reasoning.

## 1 Introduction

Natural language inference (NLI), also known as recognizing textual entailment (RTE), has been proposed as a benchmark task for natural language understanding. Given a premise $P$ and a hypothesis $H$, the task is to determine whether the premise semantically entails the hypothesis (Dagan et al., 2013). A number of recent works attempt to test and analyze what type of inferences an NLI model may be performing, focusing on various types of lexical inferences (Glockner et al., 2018; Naik et al., 2018; Poliak et al., 2018) and logical inferences (Bowman et al., 2015b; Evans et al., 2018).

Concerning logical inferences, monotonicity reasoning (van Benthem, 1983; Icard and Moss, 2014), which is a type of reasoning based on word replacement, requires the ability to capture the interaction between lexical and syntactic structures. Consider examples in (1) and (2).

(1)    a.   ***All*** [ *workers* ↓] [*joined for a French dinner* ↑]

      b.   *All workers joined for a <u>dinner</u>*

      c.   *All <u>new workers</u> joined for a French dinner*

(2)    a.   ***Not all*** [<u>*new workers*</u> ↑] *joined for a dinner*

      b.   ***Not all*** <u>*workers*</u> *joined for a dinner*

A context is **upward entailing** (shown by [... ↑]) that allows an inference from (1a) to (1b), where *French dinner* is replaced by a more general concept *dinner*. On the other hand, a **downward entailing** context (shown by [... ↓]) allows an inference from (1a) to (1c), where *workers* is replaced by a more specific concept *new workers*. Interestingly, the direction of monotonicity can be reversed again by embedding yet another downward entailing context (e.g., *not* in (2)), as witness the fact that (2a) entails (2b). To properly handle both directions of monotonicity, NLI models must detect monotonicity operators (e.g., *all*, *not*) and their arguments from the syntactic structure.

For previous datasets containing monotonicity inference problems, FraCaS (Cooper et al., 1994) and the GLUE diagnostic dataset (Wang et al., 2019) are manually-curated datasets for testing a wide range of linguistic phenomena. However, monotonicity problems are limited to very small sizes (FraCaS: 37/346 examples and GLUE: 93/1650 examples). The limited syntactic patterns and vocabularies in previous test sets are obstacles in accurately evaluating NLI models on monotonicity reasoning.

To tackle this issue, we present a new evaluation dataset[1] that covers a wide range of monotonicity reasoning that was created by crowdsourcing and collected from linguistics publications (Section 3). Compared with manual or automatic construction, we can collect naturally-occurring examples by crowdsourcing and well-designed ones from linguistics publications. To enable the evaluation of

---

[1]The dataset will be made publicly available at https://github.com/verypluming/MED.



*Proceedings of the Second BlackboxNLP Workshop on Analyzing and Interpreting Neural Networks for NLP*, pages 31–40
Florence, Italy, August 1, 2019. ©2019 Association for Computational Linguistics

skills required for monotonicity reasoning, we annotate each example in our dataset with linguistic tags associated with monotonicity reasoning.

We measure the performance of state-of-the-art NLI models on monotonicity reasoning and investigate their generalization ability in upward and downward reasoning (Section 4). The results show that all models trained with SNLI (Bowman et al., 2015b) and MultiNLI (Williams et al., 2018) perform worse on downward inferences than on upward inferences.

In addition, we analyzed the performance of models trained with an automatically created monotonicity dataset, HELP (Yanaka et al., 2019). The analysis with monotonicity data augmentation shows that models tend to perform better in the same direction of monotonicity with the training set, while they perform worse in the opposite direction. This indicates that the accuracy on monotonicity reasoning depends solely on the majority direction in the training set, and models might lack the ability to capture the structural relations between monotonicity operators and their arguments.

## 2  Monotonicity

As an example of a monotonicity inference, consider the example with the determiner *every* in (3); here the premise $P$ entails the hypothesis $H$.

(3)  $P$: *Every* [NP *person* ↓] [VP *bought a movie ticket* ↑]
     $H$: *Every young person bought a ticket*

*Every* is downward entailing in the first argument (NP) and upward entailing in the second argument (VP), and thus the term *person* can be more specific by adding modifiers (*person* ⊒ *young person*), replacing it with its hyponym (*person* ⊒ *spectator*), or adding conjunction (*person* ⊒ *person and alien*). On the other hand, the term *buy a ticket* can be more general by removing modifiers (*bought a movie ticket* ⊑ *bought a ticket*), replacing it with its hypernym (*bought a movie ticket* ⊑ *bought a show ticket*), or adding disjunction (*bought a movie ticket* ⊑ *bought or sold a movie ticket*). Table 1 shows determiners modeled as binary operators and their polarities with respect to the first and second arguments.

There are various types of downward operators, not limited to determiners (see Table 2). As shown in (4), if a propositional object is embedded in a downward monotonic context (e.g., *when*), the polarity of words over its scope can be reversed.

| Determiners | First argument | Second argument |
|---|---|---|
| *every, each, all* | downward | upward |
| *some, a, a few, many, several*, proper noun | upward | upward |
| *any, no, few, at most X, fewer than X, less than X* | downward | downward |
| *the, both, most, this, that* | non-monotone | upward |
| *exactly* | non-monotone | non-monotone |

Table 1: Determiners and their polarities.

| Category | Examples |
|---|---|
| determiners | *every, all, any, few, no* |
| negation | *not, n't, never* |
| verbs | *deny, prohibit, avoid* |
| nouns | *absence of, lack of, prohibition* |
| adverbs | *scarcely, hardly, rarely, seldom* |
| prepositions | *without, except, but* |
| conditionals | *if, when, in case that, provided that, unless* |

Table 2: Examples of downward operators.

(4)  $P$: *When* [every [NP *young person* ↑] [VP *bought a ticket* ↓]], [*that shop was open*]
     $H$: *When* [every [NP *person*] [VP *bought a movie ticket*]], [*that shop was open*]

Thus, the polarity (↑ and ↓), where the replacement with more general (specific) phrases licenses entailment, needs to be determined by the interaction of monotonicity properties and syntactic structures; polarity of each constituent is calculated based on a monotonicity operator of functional expressions (e.g., *every*, *when*) and their function-term relations.

## 3  Dataset

### 3.1  Human-oriented dataset

To create monotonicity inference problems, we should satisfy three requirements: (a) detect the monotonicity operators and their arguments; (b) based on the syntactic structure, induce the polarity of the argument positions; and (c) replace the phrase in the argument position with a more general or specific phrase in natural and various ways (e.g., by using lexical knowledge or logical connectives). For (a) and (b), we first conduct polarity computation on a syntactic structure for each sentence, and then select premises involving upward/downward expressions.

For (c), we use crowdsourcing to narrow or broaden the arguments. The motivation for using crowdsourcing is to collect naturally alike monotonicity inference problems that include various expressions. One problem here is that it is un-

**1. Premise Selection**

Every *spectator*↓ *buys*↑ *a ticket*↑

**2. Hypothesis Creation Task**

| | |
|---|---|
| Question: | Make the underlined part more specific in 3 ways. |
| Text: | *Every spectator buys a ticket* |
| Answer: | *female spectator, spectator and buyer, spectator younger than me* |

**3. Validation Task**

| | |
|---|---|
| Question: | Is the hypothesis true under any situation described in the premise? |
| Premise: | *Every spectator buys a ticket* |
| Hypothesis: | *Every female spectator buys a ticket* |
| Answer: | ✓ yes  ☐ unknown  ☐ unnatural |

**Resulting data**

| Premise | Hypothesis | Gold | |
|---|---|---|---|
| *Every spectator buys a ticket* | *Every female spectator buys a ticket* | E | swap |
| *Every female spectator buys a ticket* | *Every spectator buys a ticket* | NE | |

Figure 1: Overview of our human-oriented dataset creation. E: entailment, NE: non-entailment.

clear how to instruct workers to create monotonicity inference problems without knowledge of natural language syntax and semantics. We must make tasks simple for workers to comprehend and provide sound judgements. Moreover, recent studies (Gururangan et al., 2018; Poliak et al., 2018; Tsuchiya, 2018) point out that previous crowdsourced datasets, such as SNLI (Bowman et al., 2015a) and MultiNLI (Williams et al., 2018), include hidden biases. As these previous datasets are motivated by approximated entailments, workers are asked to freely write hypotheses given a premise, which does not strictly restrict them to creating logically complex inferences.

Taking these concerns into consideration, we designed two-step tasks to be performed via crowdsourcing for creating a monotonicity test set; (i) a hypothesis creation task and (ii) a validation task. The task (i) is to create a hypothesis by making some polarized part of an original sentence more specific. Instead of writing a complete sentence from scratch, workers are asked to rewrite only a relatively short sentence. By restricting workers to rewrite only a polarized part, we can effectively collect monotonicity inference examples. The task (ii) is to annotate an entailment label for the premise-hypothesis pair generated in (i). Figure 1 summarizes the overview of our human-oriented dataset creation. We used the crowdsourcing platform Figure Eight for both tasks.

### 3.1.1 Premise collection

As a resource, we use declarative sentences with more than five tokens from the Parallel Meaning Bank (PMB) (Abzianidze et al., 2017). The PMB contains syntactically correct sentences an-notated with its syntactic category in Combinatory Categorial Grammar (CCG; Steedman, 2000) format, which is suitable for our purpose. To get a whole CCG derivation tree, we parse each sentence by the state-of-the-art CCG parser, depccg (Yoshikawa et al., 2017). Then, we add a polarity to every constituent of the CCG tree by the polarity computation system ccg2mono (Hu and Moss, 2018) and make the polarized part a blank field.

We ran a trial rephrasing task on 500 examples and detected 17 expressions that were too general and thus difficult to rephrase them in a natural way (e.g., *every one*, *no time*). We removed examples involving such expressions. To collect more downward inference examples, we select examples involving determiners in Table 1 and downward operators in Table 2. As a result, we selected 1,485 examples involving expressions having arguments with upward monotonicity and 1,982 examples involving expressions having arguments with downward monotonicity.

### 3.1.2 Hypothesis creation

We present crowdworkers with a sentence whose polarized part is underlined, and ask them to replace the underlined part with more specific phrases in three different ways. In the instructions, we showed examples rephrased in various ways: by adding modifiers, by adding conjunction phrases, and by replacing a word with its hyponyms.

Workers were paid US$0.05 for each set of substitutions, and each set was assigned to three workers. To remove low-quality examples, we set the minimum time it should take to complete each set to 200 seconds. The entry in our task was restricted to workers from native speaking English countries. 128 workers contributed to the task, and we created 15,339 hypotheses (7,179 upward examples and 8,160 downward examples).

### 3.1.3 Validation

The gold label of each premise-hypothesis pair created in the previous task is automatically determined by monotonicity calculus. That is, a downward inference pair is labeled as *entailment*, while an upward inference pair is labeled as *non-entailment*.

However, workers sometimes provided some ungrammatical or unnatural sentences such as the case where a rephrased phrase does not satisfy the selectional restrictions (e.g., original: *Tom doesn't live in Boston*, rephrased: *Tom doesn't live in yes*), making it difficult to judge their entailment relations. Thus, we performed an annotation task to ensure accurate labeling of gold labels. We asked workers about the entailment relation of each premise-hypothesis pair as well as how natural it is.

Worker comprehension of an entailment relation directly affects the quality of inference problems. To avoid worker misunderstandings, we showed workers the following definitions of labels and five examples for each label:

1. *entailment*: the case where the hypothesis is true under any situation that the premise describes.

2. *non-entailment*: the case where the hypothesis is not always true under a situation that the premise describes.

3. *unnatural*: the case where either the premise and/or the hypothesis is ungrammatical or does not make sense.

Workers were paid US$0.04 for each question, and each question was assigned to three workers. To collect high-quality annotation results, we imposed ten test questions on each worker, and removed workers who gave more than three wrong answers. We also set the minimum time it should take to complete each question to 200 seconds. 1,237 workers contributed to this task, and we annotated gold labels of 15,339 premise-hypothesis pairs.

Table 3 shows the numbers of cases where answers matched gold labels automatically determined by monotonicity calculus. This table shows that there exist inference pairs whose labels are difficult even for humans to determine; there are 3,354 premise-hypothesis pairs whose gold labels as annotated by polarity computations match with those answered by all workers. We selected these naturalistic monotonicity inference pairs for the candidates of the final test set.

To make the distribution of gold labels symmetric, we checked these pairs to determine if we can swap the premise and the hypothesis, reverse their gold labels, and create another monotonicity inference pair. In some cases, shown below, the gold label cannot be reversed if we swap the premise and the hypothesis.

|  | Upward /cases(%) | Downward /cases(%) | Total /cases(%) |
|---|---|---|---|
| 3 labels match | 1,069 (7.0) | 2,285 (14.9) | 3,354 (21.9) |
| 2 labels match | 1,814 (11.8) | 2,301 (15.0) | 4,115 (26.8) |
| 1 labels match | 2,295 (15.0) | 1,915 (12.5) | 4,210 (27.5) |
| no match | 1,998 (27.8) | 1,652 (10.8) | 3,650 (37.8) |

Table 3: Numbers of cases where answers matched automatically determined gold labels.

**(a) Replacement with synonyms** In (5), *child* and *kid* are not hyponyms but synonyms, and the premise $P$ and the hypothesis $H$ are paraphrases.

(5)   $P$:  *Tom is no longer a child*
       $H$:  *Tom is no longer a kid*

These cases are not strict downward inference problems, in the sense that a phrase is not replaced by its hyponym/hypernym.

**(b) Non-constituents** Consider the example (6).

(6)   $P$:  *The moon has no atmosphere*
       $H$:  *The moon has no atmosphere, and the gravity force is too low*

The hypothesis $H$ was created by asking workers to make *atmosphere* in the premise $P$ more specific. However, the additional phrase *and the gravity force is too low* does not form constituents with *atmosphere*. Thus, such examples are not strict downward monotone inferences.

In such cases as (a) and (b), we do not swap the premise and the hypothesis. In the end, we collected 4,068 examples from crowdsourced datasets.

## 3.2 Linguistics-oriented dataset

We also collect monotonicity inference problems from previous manually curated datasets and linguistics publications. The motivation is that previous linguistics publications related to monotonicity reasoning are expected to contain well-designed inference problems, which might be challenging problems for NLI models.

We collected 1,184 examples from 11 linguistics publications (Barwise and Cooper, 1981; Hoeksema, 1986; Heim and Kratzer, 1998; Bonevac et al., 1999; Fyodorov et al., 2003; Geurts, 2003; Geurts and van der Slik, 2005; Zamansky et al., 2006; Szabolcsi et al., 2008; Winter, 2016; Denic et al., 2019). Regarding previous manually-curated datasets, we collected 93 examples for monotonicity reasoning from the GLUE diagnostic dataset, and 37 single-premise problems from FraCaS.

| Genre | Tags | Premise | Hypothesis | Gold |
|---|---|---|---|---|
| Crowd | up | *There is a cat on the chair* | *There is a cat sleeping on the chair* | NE |
| | up:cond | *If you heard her speak English, you would take her for a native American* | *If you heard her speak English, you would take her for an American* | E |
| | up:rev:conj | *Dogs and cats have all the good qualities of people without at the same time possessing their weaknesses* | *Dogs have all the good qualities of people without at the same time possessing their weaknesses* | E |
| | up:lex | *He approached the boy reading a magazine* | *He approached the boy reading a book* | E |
| | down:lex | *Tom hardly ever listens to music* | *Tom hardly ever listens to rock 'n' roll* | E |
| | down:conj | *You don't like love stories and sad endings* | *You don't like love stories* | NE |
| | down:cond | *If it is fine tomorrow, we'll go on a picnic* | *If it is fine tomorrow in the field, we'll go on a picnic* | E |
| | down | *I never had a girlfriend before* | *I never had a girlfriend taller than me before* | E |
| Paper | up:rev | *Every cook who is not a tall man ran* | *Every cook who is not a man ran* | E |
| | up:disj | *Every man sang* | *Every man sang or danced* | E |
| | up:lex:rev | *None of the sopranos sang with fewer than three of the tenors* | *None of the sopranos sang with fewer than three of the male singers* | E |
| | non | *Exactly one man ran quickly* | *Exactly one man ran* | NE |
| | down | *At most three elephants are blue* | *At most three elephants are navy blue* | E |

Table 4: Examples in the MED dataset. Crowd: problems collected through crowdsourcing, Paper: problems collected from linguistics publications, up: upward monotone, down: downward monotone, non: non-monotone, cond: condisionals, rev: reverse, conj: conjunction, disj: disjunction, lex: lexical knowledge, E: entailment, NE: non-entailment.

| Type | Label | Crowd | Paper | Total |
|---|---|---|---|---|
| Upward (1,820) | Entailment | 323 | 305 | 628 |
| | Non-entailment | 893 | 299 | 1,192 |
| Downward (3,270) | Entailment | 1,871 | 201 | 2,072 |
| | Non-entailment | 979 | 219 | 1,198 |
| Non-monotone (292) | Entailment | 0 | 15 | 15 |
| | Non-entailment | 2 | 275 | 277 |
| Total | | 4,068 | 1,314 | 5,382 |

Table 5: Statistics for the MED dataset.

Both the GLUE diagnostic dataset and FraCaS categorize problems by their types of monotonicity reasoning, but we found that each dataset has different classification criteria.[2] Thus, following GLUE, we reclassified problems into three types of monotone reasoning (upward, downward, and non-monotone) by checking if they include (i) the target monotonicity operator in both the premise and the hypothesis and (ii) the phrase replacement in its argument position. In the GLUE diagnostic dataset, there are several problems whose gold labels are *contradiction*. We regard them as *non-entailment* in that the premise does not semantically entail the hypothesis.

### 3.3 Statistics

We merged the human-oriented dataset created via crowdsourcing and the linguistics-oriented dataset created from linguistics publications to create the current version of the monotonicity entailment dataset (MED). Table 4 shows some examples from the MED dataset. We can see that our dataset contains various phrase replacements (e.g., conjunction, relative clauses, and comparatives). Table 5 reports the statistics of the MED dataset, including 5,382 premise-hypothesis pairs (1,820 upward examples, 3,270 downward examples, and 292 non-monotone examples). Regarding non-monotone problems, gold labels are always *non-entailment*, whether a hypothesis is more specific or general than its premise, and thus almost all non-monotone problems are labeled as *non-entailment*.[3] The size of the word vocabulary in the MED dataset is 4,023, and overlap ratios of vocabulary with previous standard NLI datasets is 95% with MultiNLI and 90% with SNLI.

We assigned a set of annotation tags for linguistic phenomena to each example in the test set. These tags allow us to analyze how well models perform on each linguistic phenomenon related to monotonicity reasoning. We defined 6 tags (see Table 4 for examples):

1. *lexical knowledge* (2,073 examples): inference problems that require lexical relations (i.e., hypernyms, hyponyms, or synonyms)

2. *reverse* (240 examples): inference problems where a propositional object is embedded in a downward environment more than once

3. *conjunction* (283 examples): inference problems that include the phrase replacement by adding conjunction (*and*) to the hypothesis

---

[2] FraCaS categorizes each problem by whether its replacement broadens an argument (upward monotone) or narrows it (downward monotone).

[3] 15 non-monotone problems which include the replacement with synonyms are labeled as *entailment*.

4. *disjunction* (254 examples): inference problems that include the phrase replacement by adding disjunction (*or*) to the hypothesis

5. *conditionals* (149 examples): inference problems that include conditionals (e.g., *if, when, unless*) in the hypothesis [4]

6. *negative polarity items* (NPIs) (338 examples): inference problems that include NPIs (e.g., *any, ever, at all, anything, anyone, anymore, anyhow, anywhere*) in the hypothesis

## 4 Results and Discussion

### 4.1 Baselines

To test the difficulty of our dataset, we checked the majority class label and the accuracies of five state-of-the-art NLI models adopting different approaches: BiMPM (Bilateral Multi-Perspective Matching Model; Wang et al., 2017), ESIM (Enhanced Sequential Inference Model; Chen et al., 2017), Decomposable Attention Model (Parikh et al., 2016), KIM (Knowledge-based Inference Model; Chen et al., 2018), and BERT (Bidirectional Encoder Representations from Transformers model; Devlin et al., 2019). Regarding BERT, we checked the performance of a model pretrained on Wikipedia and BookCorpus for language modeling and trained with SNLI and MultiNLI. For other models, we checked the performance trained with SNLI. In agreement with our dataset, we regarded the prediction label *contradiction* as *non-entailment*.

Table 6 shows that the accuracies of all models were better on upward inferences, in accordance with the reported results of the GLUE leaderboard. The overall accuracy of each model was low. In particular, all models underperformed the majority baseline on downward inferences, despite some models having rich lexical knowledge from a knowledge base (KIM) or pretraining (BERT). This indicates that downward inferences are difficult to perform even with the expansion of lexical knowledge. In addition, it is interesting to see that if a model performed better on upward inferences, it performed worse on downward inferences. We will investigate these results in detail below.

---

[4] *When*-clauses can have temporal and non-temporal interpretations (Moens and Steedman, 1988). We assign the conditional tag to those cases where *when* is interchangeable with *if*, thus excluding those cases where *when*-clauses have temporal episodic interpretation (e.g., *When she came back from the trip, she bought a gift*).

| Model | Train | Upward | Downward | Non | All |
|---|---|---|---|---|---|
| Majority | | 65.5 | 63.3 | 99.3 | 50.4 |
| BiMPM | SNLI | 53.5 | **57.6** | 27.4 | **54.6** |
| ESIM | SNLI | 71.1 | 45.2 | 41.8 | 53.8 |
| DeComp | SNLI | 66.1 | 42.1 | **64.4** | 51.4 |
| KIM | SNLI | 78.8 | 30.3 | 53.1 | 48.0 |
| BERT | SNLI | 50.1 | 46.8 | 7.5 | 45.8 |
| BERT | MNLI | **82.7** | 22.8 | 52.7 | 44.7 |

Table 6: Accuracies (%) for different models and training datasets.

| Training set | Upward | Downward | Non | All |
|---|---|---|---|---|
| MNLI | **82.7** | 22.8 | 52.7 | 44.7 |
| MNLI–Hyp | 34.3 | 18.3 | 31.5 | 24.4 |
| MNLI+HELP | 76.0 | **70.3** | **59.9** | **71.6** |
| MNLI+HELP–Hyp | 61.3 | 30.5 | 34.9 | 41.1 |

Table 7: Evaluation results on types of monotonicity reasoning. –Hyp: Hypothesis-only model.

### 4.2 Data augmentation for analysis

To explore whether the performance of models on monotonicity reasoning depends on the training set or the model themselves, we conducted further analysis performed by data augmentation with the automatically generated monotonicity dataset HELP (Yanaka et al., 2019). HELP contains 36K monotonicity inference examples (7,784 upward examples, 21,192 downward examples, and 1,105 non-monotone examples). The size of the HELP word vocabulary is 15K, and the overlap ratio of vocabulary between HELP and MED is 15.2%.

We trained BERT on MultiNLI only and on MultiNLI augmented with HELP, and compared their performance. Following Poliak et al. (2018), we also checked the performance of a hypothesis-only model trained with each training set to test whether our test set contains undesired biases.

#### 4.2.1 Effects of data augmentation

Table 7 shows that the performance of BERT with the hypothesis-only training set dropped around 10-40% as compared with the one with the premise-hypothesis training set, even if we use the data augmentation technique. This indicates that the MED test set does not allow models to predict from hypotheses alone. Data augmentation by HELP improved the overall accuracy to 71.6%, but there is still room for improvement. In addition, while adding HELP increased the accuracy on downward inferences, it slightly decreased accuracy on upward inferences. The size of down-

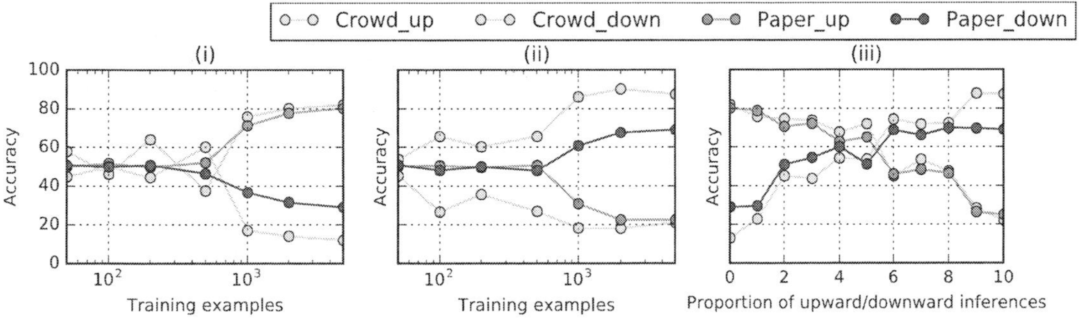



Figure 2: Accuracy throughout training BERT (i) with only upward examples and (ii) with only downward examples. We checked the accuracy at sizes [50, 100, 200, 500, 1000, 2000, 5000] for each direction. (iii) Performance on different ratios of upward/downward training sets. The total size of the training sets was 5,000 examples.

ward examples in HELP is much larger than that of upward examples. This might improve accuracy on downward inferences, but might decrease accuracy on upward inferences.

To investigate the relationship between accuracy on upward inferences and downward inferences, we checked the performance throughout training BERT with only upward and downward inference examples in HELP (Figure 2 (i), (ii)). These two figures show that, as the size of the upward training set increased, BERT performed better on upward inferences but worse on downward inferences, and vice versa.

Figure 2 (iii) shows performance on a different ratio of upward and downward inference training sets. When downward inference examples constitute more than half of the training set, accuracies on upward and downward inferences were reversed. As the ratio of downward inferences increased, BERT performed much worse on upward inferences. This indicates that a training set in one direction (upward or downward entailing) of monotonicity might be harmful to models when learning the opposite direction of monotonicity.

Previous work using HELP (Yanaka et al., 2019) reported that the BERT trained with MultiNLI and HELP containing both upward and downward inferences improved accuracy on both directions of monotonicity. MultiNLI rarely comes from downward inferences (see Section 4.3), and its size is large enough to be immune to the side-effects of downward inference examples in HELP. This indicates that MultiNLI might act as a *buffer* against side-effects of the monotonicity-driven data augmentation technique.

| Genre | | −HELP | +HELP | △ |
|---|---|---|---|---|
| Crowd | Up | 87.1 | 83.6 | −3.5 |
| | Down | 21.2 | 70.3 | +49.1 |
| | Non | 100.0 | 100.0 | ±0.0 |
| | All | 40.9 | 74.3 | +33.4 |
| Paper | Up | 74.5 | 60.8 | −13.7 |
| | Down | 33.8 | 69.5 | +35.7 |
| | Non | 52.4 | 59.7 | +7.3 |
| | All | 56.6 | 63.3 | +6.7 |

Table 8: Evaluation results by genre. Paper: problems collected from linguistics publications, Crowd: problems via crowdsourcing.

### 4.2.2 Linguistics-oriented versus human-oriented

Table 8 shows the evaluation results by genre. This result shows that inference problems collected from linguistics publications are more challenging than crowdsourced inference problems, even if we add HELP to training sets. As shown in Figure 2, the change in performance on problems from linguistics publications is milder than that on problems from crowdsourcing. This result also indicates the difficulty of problems from linguistics publications. Regarding non-monotone problems collected via crowdsourcing, there are very few non-monotone problems, so accuracy is 100%. Adding non-monotone problems to our test set is left for future work.

### 4.2.3 Linguistic phenomena

Table 9 shows the evaluation results by type of linguistic phenomenon. While accuracy on problems involving NPIs and conditionals was improved on both upward and downward inferences, accuracy on problems involving conjunction and disjunction was improved on only one direction. In addition, it is interesting to see that the change in

| Tag | | | −HELP | +HELP | △ |
|---|---|---|---|---|---|
| Up | Lexical | (743) | 81.0 | 70.8 | −10.2 |
| | non-Lexical | (1,077) | 84.1 | 79.6 | −4.5 |
| | NPIs | (64) | 20.3 | 35.9 | +15.6 |
| | Conditionals | (29) | 51.7 | 62.1 | +9.4 |
| | Conjunction | (175) | 94.3 | 88.0 | −6.3 |
| | Disjunction | (96) | 4.2 | 32.3 | +28.1 |
| | Reverse | (240) | 74.2 | 28.7 | −45.5 |
| Down | Lexical | (477) | 46.1 | 64.6 | +18.5 |
| | non-Lexical | (2,793) | 18.8 | 71.2 | +52.4 |
| | NPIs | (266) | 44.0 | 60.2 | +16.2 |
| | Conditionals | (120) | 15.8 | 20.0 | +4.2 |
| | Conjunction | (106) | 24.5 | 40.6 | +16.1 |
| | Disjunction | (138) | 80.4 | 40.6 | −39.8 |
| Non | Lexical | (182) | 58.2 | 64.3 | +6.1 |
| | non-Lexical | (110) | 43.6 | 52.7 | +9.1 |
| | NPIs | (8) | 0.0 | 0.0 | ±0.0 |
| | Disjunction | (20) | 10.0 | 15.0 | +5.0 |

Table 9: Evaluation results by linguistic phenomenon type. (non-)Lexical: problems that (do not) require lexical relations. Numbers in parentheses are numbers of problems.

accuracy on conjunction was opposite to that on disjunction. Downward inference examples involving disjunction are similar to upward inference ones; that is, inferences from a sentence to a shorter sentence are valid (e.g., *Not many campers have had a sunburn or caught a cold* ⇒ *Not many campers have caught a cold*). Thus, these results were also caused by addition of downward inference examples. Also, accuracy on problems annotated with *reverse* tags was apparently better without HELP because all examples are upward inferences embedded in a downward environment twice.

Table 9 also shows that accuracy on conditionals was better on upward inferences than that on downward inferences. This indicates that BERT might fail to capture the monotonicity property that conditionals create a downward entailing context in their scope while they create an upward entailing context out of their scope.

Regarding lexical knowledge, the data augmentation technique improved the performance much better on downward inferences which do not require lexical knowledge. However, among the 394 problems for which all models provided wrong answers, 244 problems are non-lexical inference problems. This indicates that some non-lexical inference problems are more difficult than lexical inference problems, though accuracy on non-lexical inference problems was better than that on lexical inference problems.

## 4.3 Discussion

One of our findings is that there is a type of downward inferences to which every model fails to provide correct answers. One such example is concerned with the contrast between *few* and *a few*. Among 394 problems for which all models provided wrong answers, 148 downward inference problems were problems involving the downward monotonicity operator *few* such as in the following example:

(7)　*P*: *Few of the books had typical or marginal readers*
　　*H*: *Few of the books had some typical readers*

We transformed these downward inference problems to upward inference problems in two ways: (i) by replacing the downward operator *few* with the upward operator *a few*, and (ii) by removing the downward operator *few*. We tested BERT using these transformed test sets. The results showed that BERT predicted the same answers for the transformed test sets. This suggests that BERT does not understand the difference between the downward operator *few* and the upward operator *a few*.

The results of crowdsourcing tasks in Section 3.1.3 showed that some downward inferences can naturally be performed in human reasoning. However, we also found that the MultiNLI training set (Williams et al., 2018), which is one of the dataset created from naturally-occurring texts, contains only 77 downward inference problems, including the following one.[5]

(8)　*P*: *No racin' on the Range*
　　*H*: *No horse racing is allowed on the Range*

One possible reason why there are few downward inferences is that certain pragmatic factors can block people to draw a downward inference. For instance, in the case of the inference problem in (9), unless the added disjunct in *H*, i.e., *a small cat with green eyes*, is salient in the context, it would be difficult to draw the conclusion *H* from the premise *P*.

(9)　*P*: *I saw a dog*
　　*H*: *I saw a dog or a small cat with green eyes*

Such pragmatic factors would be one of the reasons why it is difficult to obtain downward inferences in naturally occurring texts.

---

[5]The MultiNLI training set has 1,700 inference problems where the downward entailing operators *no* and *never* occur in both the premise and the hypothesis, but most of them are not an instance of downward inferences.

## 5 Conclusion

We introduced a large monotonicity entailment dataset, called MED. To illustrate the usefulness of MED, we tested state-of-the-art NLI models, and found that performance on the new test set was substantially worse for all state-of-the-art NLI models. In addition, the accuracy on downward inferences was inversely proportional to the one on upward inferences.

An experiment with the data augmentation technique showed that accuracy on upward and downward inferences depends on the proportion of upward and downward inferences in the training set. This indicates that current neural models might have limitations on their generalization ability in monotonicity reasoning. We hope that the MED will be valuable for future research on more advanced models that are capable of monotonicity reasoning in a proper way.

## Acknowledgement

We thank our three anonymous reviewers for helpful suggestions. We are also grateful to Koki Washio, Masashi Yoshikawa, and Thomas McLachlan for helpful discussion.

## References

Lasha Abzianidze, Johannes Bjerva, Kilian Evang, Hessel Haagsma, Rik van Noord, Pierre Ludmann, Duc-Duy Nguyen, and Johan Bos. 2017. The Parallel Meaning Bank: Towards a multilingual corpus of translations annotated with compositional meaning representations. In *Proceedings of the 15th Conference of the European Chapter of the Association for Computational Linguistics (EACL-2017)*, pages 242–247.

Jon Barwise and Robin Cooper. 1981. Generalized quantifiers and natural language. *Linguistics and Philosophy*, 4:159–219.

Johan van Benthem. 1983. Determiners and logic. *Linguistics and Philosophy*, 6(4):447–478.

Daniel Bonevac, Nicholas M. Asher, and Robert C. Koons. 1999. *Logic, Sets, and Functions*. Kendall Hunt Publishing.

Samuel R. Bowman, Gabor Angeli, Christopher Potts, and Christopher D. Manning. 2015a. A large annotated corpus for learning natural language inference. In *Proceedings of the 2015 Conference on Empirical Methods in Natural Language Processing (EMNLP-2015)*, pages 632–642.

Samuel R. Bowman, Christopher Potts, and Christopher D. Manning. 2015b. Recursive neural networks can learn logical semantics. In *Proceedings of the 3rd Workshop on Continuous Vector Space Models and their Compositionality*, pages 12–21.

Qian Chen, Xiaodan Zhu, Zhen-Hua Ling, Diana Inkpen, and Si Wei. 2018. Neural natural language inference models enhanced with external knowledge. In *Proceedings of the 56th Annual Meeting of the Association for Computational Linguistics (ACL-2018)*, pages 2406–2417.

Qian Chen, Xiaodan Zhu, Zhen-Hua Ling, Si Wei, Hui Jiang, and Diana Inkpen. 2017. Enhanced lstm for natural language inference. In *Proceedings of the 55th Annual Meeting of the Association for Computational Linguistics (ACL-2017)*, pages 1657–1668.

Robin Cooper, Richard Crouch, Jan van Eijck, Chris Fox, Josef van Genabith, Jan Jaspers, Hans Kamp, Manfred Pinkal, Massimo Poesio, Stephen Pulman, et al. 1994. FraCaS–a framework for computational semantics. *Deliverable*, D6.

Ido Dagan, Dan Roth, Mark Sammons, and Fabio Massimo Zanzotto. 2013. *Recognizing Textual Entailment: Models and Applications*. Synthesis Lectures on Human Language Technologies. Morgan & Claypool Publishers.

Milica Denic, Vincent Homer, Daniel Rothschild, and Emmanuel Chemla. 2019. The influence of polarity items on inferential judgment. *Semantic Archive*, Archive/WY4OTMzO.

Jacob Devlin, Chang Ming-Wei, Lee Kenton, and Toutanova Kristina. 2019. BERT: Pre-training of deep bidirectional transformers for language understanding. In *Proceedings of the 2019 Conference of the North American Chapter of the Association for Computational Linguistics: Human Language Technologies (NAACLHLT-2019)*.

Richard Evans, David Saxton, David Amos, Pushmeet Kohli, and Edward Grefenstette. 2018. Can neural networks understand logical entailment? In *International Conference on Learning Representations (ICLR-2018)*.

Yaroslav Fyodorov, Yoad Winter, and Nissim Francez. 2003. Order-based inference in natural logic. *Logic Journal of the IGPL*, 11(4):385–416.

Bart Geurts. 2003. Reasoning with quantifiers. *Cognition*, 86:223–251.

Bart Geurts and Frans van der Slik. 2005. Monotonicity and processing load. *Journal of semantics*, 22(1):97–117.

Max Glockner, Vered Shwartz, and Yoav Goldberg. 2018. Breaking NLI systems with sentences that require simple lexical inferences. In *Proceedings of the 56th Annual Meeting of the Association for Computational Linguistics (ACL-2018)*, pages 650–655.

Suchin Gururangan, Swabha Swayamdipta, Omer Levy, Roy Schwartz, Samuel Bowman, and Noah A. Smith. 2018. Annotation artifacts in natural language inference data. In *Proceedings of the 2018 Conference of the North American Chapter of the Association for Computational Linguistics: Human Language Technologies (NAACLHLT-2018)*, pages 107–112.

Irene Heim and Angelika Kratzer. 1998. *Semantics in Generative Grammar*. Blackwell, Oxford.

Jack Hoeksema. 1986. Monotonicity phenomena in natural language. *Linguistic Analysis*, 16(1):25–40.

Hai Hu and Lawrence S. Moss. 2018. Polarity computations in flexible categorial grammar. In *Proceedings of the 7th Joint Conference on Lexical and Computational Semantics (*SEM-2018)*.

Thomas Icard and Lawrence Moss. 2014. Recent progress in monotonicity. *LILT*, 9(7):167–194.

Marc Moens and Mark Steedman. 1988. Temporal ontology and temporal reference. *Computational Linguistics*, 14(2):15–28.

Aakanksha Naik, Abhilasha Ravichander, Norman Sadeh, Carolyn Rose, and Graham Neubig. 2018. Stress test evaluation for natural language inference. In *Proceedings of the 27th International Conference on Computational Linguistics (ACL-2018)*, pages 2340–2353.

Ankur Parikh, Oscar Täckström, Dipanjan Das, and Jakob Uszkoreit. 2016. A decomposable attention model for natural language inference. In *Proceedings of the 2016 Conference on Empirical Methods in Natural Language Processing (EMNLP-2016)*, pages 2249–2255.

Adam Poliak, Jason Naradowsky, Aparajita Haldar, Rachel Rudinger, and Benjamin Van Durme. 2018. Hypothesis only baselines in natural language inference. In *Proceedings of the Seventh Joint Conference on Lexical and Computational Semantics (*SEM-2018)*, pages 180–191.

Mark Steedman. 2000. *The Syntactic Process*. MIT Press.

Anna Szabolcsi, Lewis Bott, and Brian McElree. 2008. The effect of negative polarity items on inference verification. *Journal of semantics*, 25(4):411–450.

Masatoshi Tsuchiya. 2018. Performance impact caused by hidden bias of training data for recognizing textual entailment. In *Proceedings of the 11th International Conference on Language Resources and Evaluation (LREC-2018)*.

Alex Wang, Amanpreet Singh, Julian Michael, Felix Hill, Omer Levy, and Samuel Bowman. 2019. GLUE: A multi-task benchmark and analysis platform for natural language understanding. In *Proceedings of the International Conference on Learning Representations (ICLR-2019)*.

Zhiguo Wang, Wael Hamza, and Radu Florian. 2017. Bilateral multi-perspective matching for natural language sentences. In *Proceedings of the 26th International Joint Conference on Artificial Intelligence (IJCAI-2017)*, pages 4144–4150.

Adina Williams, Nikita Nangia, and Samuel Bowman. 2018. A broad-coverage challenge corpus for sentence understanding through inference. In *Proceedings of the 2018 Conference of the North American Chapter of the Association for Computational Linguistics: Human Language Technologies (NAACLHLT-2018)*, pages 1112–1122.

Yoad Winter. 2016. *Elements of Formal Semantics: An Introduction to the Mathematical Theory of Meaning in Natural Language*. Edinburgh University Press.

Hitomi Yanaka, Koji Mineshima, Daisuke Bekki, Kentaro Inui, Satoshi Sekine, Lasha Abzianidze, and Johan Bos. 2019. HELP: A dataset for identifying shortcomings of neural models in monotonicity reasoning. In *Proceedings of the 8th Joint Conference on Lexical and Computational Semantics (*SEM-2019)*.

Masashi Yoshikawa, Hiroshi Noji, and Yuji Matsumoto. 2017. A* CCG parsing with a supertag and dependency factored model. In *Proceedings of the 55th Annual Meeting of the Association for Computational Linguistics (ACL-2017)*, pages 277–287.

Anna Zamansky, Nissim Francez, and Yoad Winter. 2006. A 'natural logic' inference system using the Lambek calculus. *Journal of Logic, Language and Information*, 15(3):273–295.

# Multi-Granular Text Encoding for Self-Explaining Categorization

**Zhiguo Wang[1], Yue Zhang[2], Mo Yu[1], Wei Zhang[1], Lin Pan[1]**
**Linfeng Song[3], Kun Xu[3], Yousef El-Kurdi[1]**
[1]IBM T.J. Watson Research Center, Yorktown Heights, NY 10598
[2]School of Engineering, Westlake University, China
[3]Tencent AI Lab
zgw.tomorrow@gmail.com

## Abstract

Self-explaining text categorization requires a classifier to make a prediction along with supporting evidence. A popular type of evidence is sub-sequences extracted from the input text which are sufficient for the classifier to make the prediction. In this work, we define multi-granular ngrams as basic units for explanation, and organize all ngrams into a hierarchical structure, so that shorter ngrams can be reused while computing longer ngrams. We leverage a tree-structured LSTM to learn a context-independent representation for each unit via parameter sharing. Experiments on medical disease classification show that our model is more accurate, efficient and compact than BiLSTM and CNN baselines. More importantly, our model can extract intuitive multi-granular evidence to support its predictions.

## 1 Introduction

Increasingly complex neural networks have achieved highly competitive results for many NLP tasks (Vaswani et al., 2017; Devlin et al., 2018), but they prevent human experts from understanding how and why a prediction is made. Understanding how a prediction is made can be very important for certain domains, such as the medical domain. Recent research has started to investigate models with self-explaining capability, i.e. extracting evidence to support their final predictions (Li et al., 2015; Lei et al., 2016; Lin et al., 2017; Mullenbach et al., 2018). For example, in order to make diagnoses based on the medical report in Table 1, the highlighted symptoms may be extracted as evidence.

Two methods have been proposed on *how to jointly provide highlights along with classification*. (1) an *extraction-based* method (Lei et al., 2016), which first extracts evidences from the original text and then makes a prediction solely based on the extracted evidences; (2) an *attention-based* method (Lin et al., 2017; Mullenbach et al., 2018), which leverages the self-attention mecha-

| |
|---|
| **Medical Report:** The patient was admitted to the Neurological Intensive Care Unit for close observation. She was begun on heparin anticoagulated carefully secondary to the petechial bleed . She started weaning from the vent the next day. She was started on Digoxin to control her rate and her Cardizem was held. She was started on antibiotics for possible aspiration pneumonia . Her chest x-ray showed retrocardiac effusion . She had some bleeding after nasogastric tube insertion . |
| **Diagnoses:** Cerebral artery occlusion; Unspecified essential hypertension; Atrial fibrillation; Diabetes mellitus. |

Table 1: A medical report snippet and its diagnoses.

nism to show the importance of basic units (words or ngrams) through their attention weights.

However, previous work has several limitations. Lin et al. (2017), for example, take single words as basic units, while meaningful information is usually carried by multi-word phrases. For instance, useful symptoms in Table 1, such as "bleeding after nasogastric tube insertion", are larger than a single word. Another issue of Lin et al. (2017) is that their attention model is applied on the representation vectors produced by an LSTM. Each LSTM output contains more than just the information of that position, thus the real range for the highlighted position is unclear. Mullenbach et al. (2018) defines all 4-grams of the input text as basic units and uses a convolutional layer to learn their representations, which still suffers from fixed-length highlighting. Thus the explainability of the model is limited. Lei et al. (2016) introduce a regularizer over the selected (single-word) positions to encourage the model to extract larger phrases. However, their method can not tell how much a selected unit contributes to the model's decision through a weight value.

In this paper, we study *what the meaningful units to highlight are*. We define multi-granular ngrams as basic units, so that all highlighted symptoms in Table 1 can be directly used for explaining the model. Different ngrams can have overlap. To improve the efficiency, we organize all



*Proceedings of the Second BlackboxNLP Workshop on Analyzing and Interpreting Neural Networks for NLP*, pages 41–45
Florence, Italy, August 1, 2019. ©2019 Association for Computational Linguistics

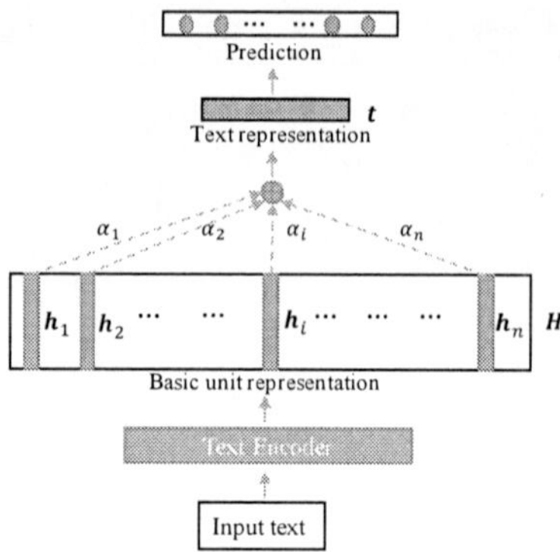

Figure 1: A generic architecture.

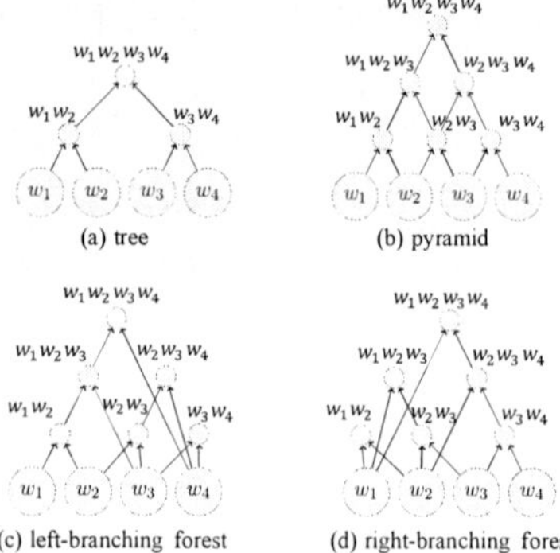

Figure 2: Structures for a sentence $w_1w_2w_3w_4$, where each node corresponds to a phrase or ngram.

ngrams into a hierarchical structure, such that the shorter ngram representations can be reused to construct longer ngram representations. Experiments on medical disease classification show that our model is more accurate, efficient and compact than BiLSTM and CNN baselines. Furthermore, our model can extract intuitive multi-granular evidence to support its predictions.

## 2  Generic architecture and baselines

Our work leverages the *attention-based* self-explaining method (Lin et al., 2017), as shown in Figure 1. First, our text encoder (§3) formulates an input text into a list of basic units, learning a vector representation for each, where the basic units can be words, phrases, or arbitrary ngrams. Then, the attention mechanism is leveraged over all basic units, and sums up all unit representations based on the attention weights $\{\alpha_1, ..., \alpha_n\}$. Eventually, the attention weight $\alpha_i$ will be used to reveal how important a basic unit $h_i$ is. The last prediction layer takes the fixed-length text representation $t$ as input, and makes the final prediction.

**Baselines**: We compare two types of baseline text encoders in Figure 1. (1) **Lin et al. (2017) (BiLSTM)**, which formulates single word positions as basic units, and computes the vector $h_i$ for the $i$-th word position with a BiLSTM; (2) **Extension of Mullenbach et al. (2018) (CNN)**. The original model in (Mullenbach et al., 2018) only utilizes 4-grams. Here we extend this model to take all unigrams, bigrams, and up to $n$-grams as the basic units.

For a fair comparison, both our approach and the baselines share the same architecture, and the only difference is the text encoder used.

## 3  Multi-granular text encoder

We propose the multi-granular text encoder to deal with drawbacks (as mentioned in the third paragraph of Section 1) of our baselines.

**Structural basic units**: We define basic units for the input text as multi-granular ngrams, organizing ngrams in four different ways. Taking a synthetic sentence $w_1w_2w_3w_4$ as the running example, we illustrate these structures in Figure 2 (a), (b), (c) and (d), respectively. The first is a tree structure (as shown in Figure 2(a)) that includes all phrases from a (binarized) constituent tree over the input text, where no cross-boundary phrases exists. The second type (as shown in Figure 2 (b,c,d)) includes all possible ngrams from the input text, which is a superset of the tree structure. In order to reuse representations of smaller ngrams while encoding bigger ngrams, all ngrams are organized into hierarchical structures in three different ways. First, inspired by Zhao et al. (2015), a pyramid structure is created for all ngrams as shown in Figure 2(b), where leaf nodes are unigrams of the input text, and higher level nodes correspond to higher-order ngrams. A disadvantage of the pyramid structure is that some lower level nodes may be used repeatedly while encoding higher level nodes, which may improperly augment the influence of the repeated units. For example, when encoding the trigram node "$w_1w_2w_3$", the unigram node "$w_2$" is used twice through two bigram nodes "$w_1w_2$" and "$w_2w_3$". To tackle this issue, a left-branching forest structure is constructed for all ngrams as shown in Figure 2(c), where ngrams with the same prefix are grouped together into a left-branching binary tree, and, in this arrangement, multiple trees construct a forest. Similarly, we construct a right-branching forest as shown in Figure 2(d).

**Encoding**: We leverage a tree-structured LSTM composition function (Tai et al., 2015; Zhu et al., 2015; Teng and Zhang, 2016) to compute node embeddings for all structures in Figure 2. Formally, the **state** of each node is represented as a pair of one hidden vector $h$ and one memory representation $c$, which are calculated by composing the node's label embedding $x$ and states of its left child $\langle h^l, c^l \rangle$ and right child $\langle h^r, c^r \rangle$ with gated functions:

$$i = \sigma(W^1 x + U_l^1 h^l + U_r^1 h^r + b^1) \tag{1}$$

$$f^l = \sigma(W^2 x + U_l^2 h^l + U_r^2 h^r + b^2) \tag{2}$$

$$f^r = \sigma(W^3 x + U_l^3 h^l + U_r^3 h^r + b^3) \tag{3}$$

$$o = \sigma(W^4 x + U_l^4 h^l + U_r^4 h^r + b^4) \tag{4}$$

$$u = \tanh(W^5 x + U_l^5 h^l + U_r^5 h^r + b^5) \tag{5}$$

$$c = i \odot u + f^l \odot h^l + f^r \odot h^r \tag{6}$$

$$h = o \odot \tanh(c) \tag{7}$$

where $\sigma$ is the sigmoid activation function, $\odot$ is the elementwise product, $i$ is the input gate, $f^l$ and $f^r$ are the forget gates for the left and right child respectively, and $o$ is the output gate. We set $x$ as the pre-trained word embedding for leaf nodes, and zero vectors for other nodes. The representations for all units (nodes) can be obtained by encoding each basic unit in a bottom-up order.

**Comparison with baselines** Our encoder is more efficient than CNN while encoding bigger ngrams, because it reuses representations of smaller ngrams. Furthermore, the same parameters are shared across all ngrams, which makes our encoder more compact, whereas the CNN baseline has to define different filters for different order of ngrams, so it requires much more parameters. Experiments show that using basic units up to 7-grams to construct the forest structure is good enough, which makes our encoder more efficient than BiLSTM. Since in our encoder, all ngrams with the same order can be computed in parallel, and the model needs at most 7 iterative steps along the depth dimension for representing a given text of arbitrary length.

## 4 Experiments

**Dataset**: We experiment on a public medical text classification dataset.[1] Each instance consists of a medical abstract with an average length of 207

<hr>

[1] https://github.com/SnehaVM/Medical-Text-Classification

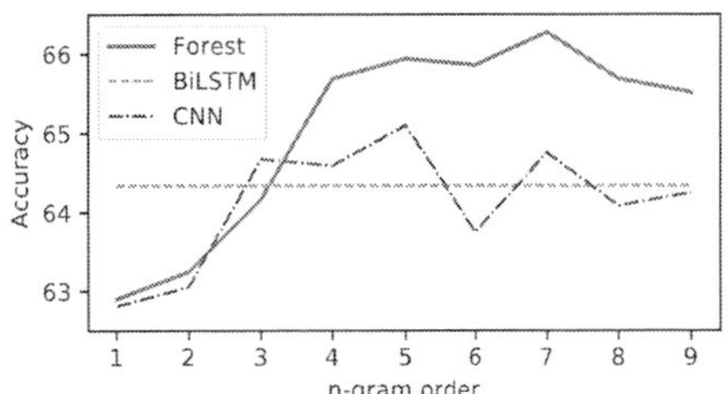

Figure 3: Influence of n-gram order.

| Model | Train Time | Eval Time | ACC | #Param. |
|---|---|---|---|---|
| CNN | 57.0 | 2.6 | 64.8 | 848,228 |
| BiLSTM | 92.1 | 4.6 | 64.5 | 147,928 |
| LeftForest | 30.3 | 1.4 | 66.2 | 168,228 |

Table 2: Efficiency evaluation.

tokens, and one label out of five categories indicating which disease this document is about. We randomly split the dataset into train/dev/test sets by 8:1:1 for each category, and end up with 11,216/1,442/1,444 instances for each set.

**Hyperparameters** We use the 300-dimensional GloVe word vectors pre-trained from the 840B Common Crawl corpus (Pennington et al., 2014), and set the hidden size as 100 for node embeddings. We apply dropout to every layer with a dropout ratio 0.2, and set the batch size as 50. We minimize the cross-entropy of the training set with the ADAM optimizer (Kingma and Ba, 2014), and set the learning rate is to 0.001. During training, the pre-trained word embeddings are not updated.

### 4.1 Properties of the multi-granular encoder

**Influence of the n-gram order**: For CNN and our *LeftForest* encoder, we vary the order of ngrams from 1 to 9, and plot results in Figure 3. For BiLSTM, we draw a horizontal line according to its performance, since the ngram order does not apply. When ngram order is less than 3, both CNN and *LeftForest* underperform BiLSTM. When ngram order is over 3, *LeftForest* outperforms both baselines. Therefore, in terms of accuracy, our multi-granular text encoder is more powerful than baselines.

**Efficiency**: We set ngram order as 7 for both CNN and our encoder. Table 2 shows the time cost (seconds) of one iteration over the training set and evaluation on the development set. BiLSTM is the slowest model, because it has to scan over the entire text sequentially. *LeftForest* is almost 2x faster than CNN, because *LeftForest* reuses lower-order ngrams while computing higher-order

| Model | Accuracy |
|---|---|
| BiLSTM | 62.7 |
| CNN | 62.5 |
| Tree | 63.8 |
| Pyramid | 63.7 |
| LeftForest | 64.6 |
| RightForest | 64.5 |
| BiForest | **65.2** |

Table 3: Test set results.

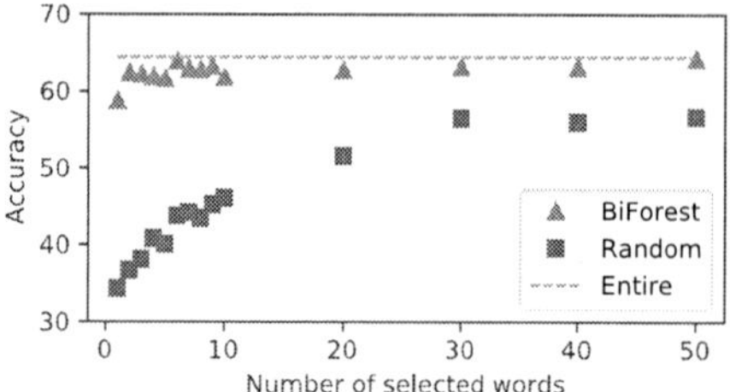

Figure 4: Effectiveness of the extracted evidence.

ngrams. This result reveals that our encoder is more efficient than baselines.

**Model size**: In Table 2, the last two columns show the accuracy and number of parameters for each model. *LeftForest* contains much less parameters than CNN, and it gives a better accuracy than BiLSTM with only a small amount of extra parameters. Therefore, our encoder is more compact.

## 4.2 Model performance

Table 3 lists the accuracy on the test set, where *BiForest* represents each ngram by concatenating representations of this ngram from both the *LeftForest* and the *RightForest* encoders. We get several interesting observations: (1) Our multi-granular text encoder outperforms both the CNN and BiLSTM baselines regardless of the structure used; (2) The *LeftForest* and *RightForest* encoders work better than the *Tree* encoder, which shows that representing texts with more ngrams is helpful than just using the non-overlapping phrases from a parse tree; (3) The *LeftForest* and *RightForest* encoders give better performance than the *Pyramid* encoder, which verifies the advantages of organizing ngrams with forest structures; (4) There is no significant difference between the *LeftForest* encoder and the *RightForest* encoder. However, by combining them, the *BiForest* encoder gets the best performance among all models, indicating that the *LeftForest* encoder and the *RightForest* encoder complement each other for better accuracy.

## 4.3 Analysis of explainability

**Qualitative analysis** The following text is a snippet of an example from the dev set. We leverage our *BiForest* model to extract ngrams whose attention scores are higher than 0.05, and use the bold font to highlight them. We extracted three ngrams as supporting evidence for its predicted category "nervous system diseases". Both the *spontaneous extradural spinal hematoma* and the *spinal arteriovenous malformation* are diseases related to the spinal cord, therefore they are good evidence to indicate the text is about "nervous system diseases".

**Snippet**: *Value of magnetic resonance imaging in **spontaneous extradural spinal hematoma** due to vascular malformation : case report . A case of spinal cord compression due to **spontaneous extradural spinal hematoma** is reported . A **spinal arteriovenous malformation** was suspected on the basis of magnetic resonance imaging. Early surgical exploration allowed a complete neurological recovery .*

**Quantitative analysis** For each instance in the training set and the dev set, we utilize the attention scores from *BiForest* to sort all ngrams, and create different copies of the training set and development set by only keeping the first $n$ important words. We then train and evaluate a BiLSTM model with the newly created dataset. We vary the number of words $n$ among $\{1, 2, 3, 4, 5, 6, 7, 8, 9, 10, 20, 30, 40, 50\}$, and show the corresponding accuracy with the green triangles in Figure 4. We define a *Random* baseline by randomly selecting a sub-sequence containing $n$ words, and plot its accuracy with blue squares in Figure 4. We also take a BiLSTM model trained with the entire texts as the upper bound (the horizontal line in Figure 4). When using only a single word for representing instances, single words extracted from our *BiForest* model are significantly more effective than randomly picked single words. When utilizing up to five extracted words from our *BiForest* model for representing each instance, we can obtain an accuracy very close to the upper bound. Therefore, the extracted evidence from our *BiForest* model are truly effective for representing the instance and its corresponding category.

## 5 Conclusion

We proposed a multi-granular text encoder for self-explaining text categorization. Comparing with the existing BiLSTM and CNN baselines, our

model is more accurate, efficient and compact. In
addition, our model can extract effective and intuitive evidence to support its predictions.

## References


Jacob Devlin, Ming-Wei Chang, Kenton Lee, and
Kristina Toutanova. 2018. Bert: Pre-training of deep
bidirectional transformers for language understanding. *arXiv preprint arXiv:1810.04805*.

Diederik Kingma and Jimmy Ba. 2014. Adam: A
method for stochastic optimization. *arXiv preprint
arXiv:1412.6980*.

Tao Lei, Regina Barzilay, and Tommi Jaakkola. 2016.
Rationalizing neural predictions. *arXiv preprint
arXiv:1606.04155*.

Jiwei Li, Xinlei Chen, Eduard Hovy, and Dan Jurafsky.
2015. Visualizing and understanding neural models
in nlp. *arXiv preprint arXiv:1506.01066*.

Zhouhan Lin, Minwei Feng, Cicero Nogueira dos Santos, Mo Yu, Bing Xiang, Bowen Zhou, and Yoshua
Bengio. 2017. A structured self-attentive sentence
embedding. *arXiv preprint arXiv:1703.03130*.

James Mullenbach, Sarah Wiegreffe, Jon Duke, Jimeng
Sun, and Jacob Eisenstein. 2018. Explainable prediction of medical codes from clinical text. *arXiv
preprint arXiv:1802.05695*.

Jeffrey Pennington, Richard Socher, and Christopher D
Manning. 2014. Glove: Global vectors for word
representation. In *EMNLP*.

Kai Sheng Tai, Richard Socher, and Christopher D
Manning. 2015. Improved semantic representations
from tree-structured long short-term memory networks. *arXiv preprint arXiv:1503.00075*.

Zhiyang Teng and Yue Zhang. 2016. Bidirectional
tree-structured lstm with head lexicalization. *arXiv
preprint arXiv:1611.06788*.

Ashish Vaswani, Noam Shazeer, Niki Parmar, Jakob
Uszkoreit, Llion Jones, Aidan N Gomez, Łukasz
Kaiser, and Illia Polosukhin. 2017. Attention is all
you need. In *Advances in Neural Information Processing Systems*, pages 6000–6010.

Han Zhao, Zhengdong Lu, and Pascal Poupart. 2015.
Self-adaptive hierarchical sentence model. In *IJCAI*,
pages 4069–4076.

Xiaodan Zhu, Parinaz Sobihani, and Hongyu Guo.
2015. Long short-term memory over recursive
structures. In *International Conference on Machine
Learning*, pages 1604–1612.

# The meaning of "most" for visual question answering models


**Alexander Kuhnle**
Department of Computer Science
and Technology
University of Cambridge
Cambridge, United Kingdom
aok25@cam.ac.uk

**Ann Copestake**
Department of Computer Science
and Technology
University of Cambridge
Cambridge, United Kingdom
aac10@cam.ac.uk



## Abstract

The correct interpretation of quantifier statements in the context of a visual scene requires non-trivial inference mechanisms. For the example of *"most"*, we discuss two strategies which rely on fundamentally different cognitive concepts. Our aim is to identify what strategy deep learning models for visual question answering learn when trained on such questions. To this end, we carefully design data to replicate experiments from psycholinguistics where the same question was investigated for humans. Focusing on the FiLM visual question answering model, our experiments indicate that a form of approximate number system emerges whose performance declines with more difficult scenes as predicted by Weber's law. Moreover, we identify confounding factors, like spatial arrangement of the scene, which impede the effectiveness of this system.


## 1 Introduction

Deep learning methods have been very successful in many natural language processing tasks, ranging from syntactic parsing to machine translation to image captioning. However, despite significantly raised performance scores on benchmark datasets, researchers increasingly worry about interpretability and indeed quality of model decisions. We see two distinct research endeavors here, one being more pragmatic, forward-oriented, and guided by the question *"Can a system solve this task?"*, the other being more analytic, reflective, and motivated by the question *"How does a system solve this task?"*. In other words, the former aspires to improve performance, while the latter aims to increase our understanding of deep learning models.

By 'understanding' here we mean observing a reasoning mechanism that, if not human-like, at least is cognitively plausible. This is by no

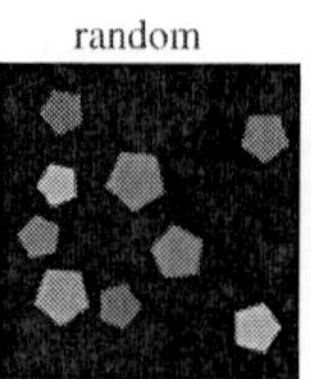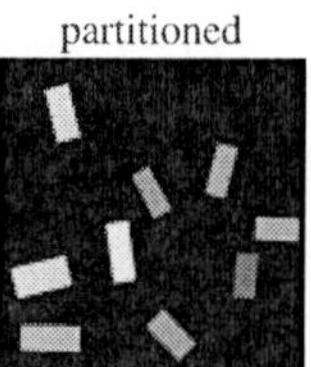


*"More than half the shapes are red shapes?"*

Figure 1: Three types of spatial arrangement of objects which may or may not affect the performance of a mechanism for verifying *"most"* statements. Going from left to right, a strategy based on pairing entities of each set and identifying the remainder presumably gets more difficult, while a strategy based on comparing set cardinalities does not.

means necessary for practically solving a task, however, we highlight two reasons why being able to explain model behavior is nonetheless important: On the one hand, cognitive plausibility increases confidence in the abilities of a system — one is generally more willing to rely on a reasonable than an incomprehensible mechanism. On the other hand, pointing out systematic shortcomings inspires systematic improvements and hence can guide progress. Moreover, particularly in the case of a human-centered domain like natural language, ultimately, some degree of comparability to human performance is indispensable.

In this paper we are inspired by experimental practice in psycholinguistics to shed light on the question how deep learning models for visual question answering (VQA) learn to interpret statements involving the quantifier *"most"*. We follow Pietroski et al. (2009) in designing abstract visual scenes where we control the ratio of the objects quantified over and their spatial arrangement, to identify whether VQA models exhibit a preferred strategy of verifying whether *"most"* applies. Figure 1 illustrates how visual scenes can be configured to favor one over another mechanism.




*Proceedings of the Second BlackboxNLP Workshop on Analyzing and Interpreting Neural Networks for NLP*, pages 46–55
Florence, Italy, August 1, 2019. ©2019 Association for Computational Linguistics

We want to emphasize the experimental approach and its difference to mainstream machine learning practice. For different verification strategies, conditions are identified that should or should not affect their performance, and test instances are designed accordingly. By comparing the accuracy of subjects on various instance patterns, predictions about a subject's performance for these mechanisms can be verified and the most likely explanation identified. Note that our advocated evaluation methodology is entirely extrinsic and does not constrain the system in any way (like requiring attention maps) or require a specific framework (like being probabilistic).

Psychology as a discipline has focused entirely on questions around how humans process situations and arrive at decisions, and consequently has the potential to inspire a lot of experiments (like ours) for investigating the same questions in the context of machine learning. Similar to psychology, we advocate the preference of an artificial experimentation environment which can be controlled in detail, over the importance of data originating from the real world, to arrive at more convincing and thus meaningful results.

It is less common recently to evaluate deep learning models on artificial data tailored to a specific problem, as opposed to big real-world datasets. However, artificial data has a history in deep learning of establishing new techniques – most prominently, LSTMs were introduced by showing their ability to handle various formal grammars (Gers and Schmidhuber, 2001) – and our higher-level goal with this paper is to demonstrate the potential for more informative evaluation of machine learning models in general. This is motivated by our belief that, in the long term, true progress can only be made if we do not just rely on the narrative of neural networks *"learning to understand/solve"* a task, but can actually confirm our theories experimentally. Taking inspiration from psychology seems particularly appropriate in the context of powerful deep learning models, which recently are not infrequently described by anthropomorphizing words like *"understanding"*, and compared to *"human-level"* performance.

## 2  The meaning of "most"

In this section we will discuss two mechanisms of interpreting *"most"* and introduce relevant cognitive concepts.

### 2.1  Generalized quantifiers and "most"

*"Most"* has a special status in linguistics due to the fact that it is the most prominent example of a quantifier whose semantics cannot be expressed in first-order logic, while other simple natural language quantifiers like *"some"*, *"every"* or *"no"* directly correspond to the quantifier primitives $\exists$ and $\forall$ (plus logical operators $\wedge$, $\vee$ and $\neg$). This situation is not just a matter of introducing further appropriate primitives, but requires a fundamental extension of the logic system and its expressivity.

In the following, by $x$ we denote an entity, $A$ and $B$ denote predicates (*"square"*, *"red"*), $A(x)$ is true if and only if $x$ satisfies $A$, and $S_A = \{x : A(x)\}$ is the corresponding set of entities satisfying this predicate (*"squares"*). Thus we can define the semantics of *"some"* and *"every"*:

$$\text{some}(A, B) \Leftrightarrow \exists x : A(x) \wedge B(x)$$
$$\text{every}(A, B) \Leftrightarrow \forall x : A(x) \Rightarrow B(x)$$

Importantly, these definitions do not involve the concept of set cardinality and indeed can be formulated without involving sets. This is not possible for *"most"*, which is commonly defined in one of the following ways:

$$\text{most}(A, B) \Leftrightarrow |S_{A \wedge B}| > 1/2 \cdot |A|$$
$$\Leftrightarrow |S_{A \wedge B}| > |S_{A \wedge \neg B}| \quad (1)$$

This makes *"most"* an example of a *generalized quantifier*, and in fact all generalized quantifiers can be defined in terms of cardinalities, indicating the apparent importance of a cardinality concept to human cognition.

### 2.2  Alternative characterization

There is another way to define *"most"* which uses the fact that whether two sets are equinumerous can be determined without a concept of cardinality, but based on the idea of a bijection:

$$A \leftrightarrow B :\Leftrightarrow \forall x : A(x) \Leftrightarrow B(x)$$
$$\Leftrightarrow |S_A| = |S_B|$$

The definition of equinumerosity can be generalized to *"more than"* (and, correspondingly, *"less than"*), which lets us define *"most"* as follows:

$$\text{most}(A, B) \Leftrightarrow \exists S \subsetneq S_{A \wedge B} : S \leftrightarrow S_{A \wedge \neg B} \quad (2)$$

Although, at a first glance, this definition looks similar to the one above, it can be seen as suggesting a different algorithmic approach to verifying *"most"*, as we will discuss below.

## 2.3 Two interpretation strategies

These two characterizations are of course truth-conditionally equivalent, that is, every situation in which one of them holds, the other holds, and vice versa. In particular, if we are just interested in solving a task involving *"most"* statements, we can be agnostic about which definition our system prefers. Nevertheless, the subtle differences between these two characterizations suggest different algorithmic mechanisms of verifying or falsifying such statements, meaning that a system processes a visual scene differently to come to the (same) conclusion about a statement's truth.

Characterization (1) represents the **cardinality-based strategy** of interpreting *"most"*:

1. Estimate the number of entities satisfying both predicates (*"red squares"*) and the number satisfying one predicate but not the other (*"non-red squares"*).

2. Compare these number estimates and check whether the former is greater than the latter.

We want to add that, actually, the two definitions in (1) already suggest a minor variation of this mechanism – see Hackl (2009) for a discussion on *"most"* versus *"more than half"*. However, we do not focus on this detail here, and assume the second variant in (1) to be 'strictly' simpler in the sense that both involve estimating and comparing cardinalities, but the first variant additionally involves the rather complex operation of halving one number estimates.

Characterization (2) utilizes the concept of a bijection, which is a comparatively simple pairing mechanism and as such could be imagined to be a primitive cognitive operation. This gives us the **pairing-based strategy** of verifying *"most"*:

1. Successively match entities satisfying both predicates (*"red squares"*) uniquely with entities satisfying one predicate but not the other (*"non-red squares"*).

2. The remaining entities are all of one type, so pick one and check whether it is of the first type (*"red square"*).

## 2.4 Cognitive implications

Finding evidence for one strategy over the other has substantial implications with respect to the 'cognitive abilities' of a neural network model. In particular, evidence for a cardinality-based processing of *"most"* suggests the existence of an **approximate number system** (ANS), which is able to simultaneously estimate the number of objects in two sets, and perform higher-level operations on the resulting number representations themselves, like the comparison operation here. Explicit counting would be an even more accurate mechanism here, but neither available to the subjects in the experiments of Pietroski et al. (2009) due to very short scene display time, nor likely to be learned by the 'one-glance' feed-forward-style neural network we evaluate in this work[1].

The ANS (see appendix in Lidz et al. (2011) for a summary) is an evolutionary comparatively old mechanism which is shared between many different species throughout the animal world. It emerges without explicit training and produces approximate representations of the number of objects of some type. They are approximate in the sense that their number judgment is not 'sharp', but resulting behavior exhibits variance – like interpreting *"most"* statements with a cardinality-based strategy, as described above. This variance follows **Weber's law** which states that the discriminability of two quantities is a function of their ratio[2]. The precision of the ANS is thus usually indicated by a characteristic value called **Weber fraction** which relates quantity and variance. The ANS of a typical adult human is often reported to have a Weber fraction of 1.14 or, more tangibly, it can distinguish a ratio of 7:8 with 75% accuracy. Finding evidence for the emergence of a similar system in deep neural networks indicates that these models can indeed learn more abstract concepts (approximate numbers) than mere superficial pattern matching (*"red squares"* etc).

---

[1] By *"one-glance feed-forward-style networks"* we refer to the predominant type of network architecture which, by design, consists of a fixed sequence of computation steps before arriving at a decision. In particular, such models do not have the ability to interact with their input dynamically depending on the complexity of an instance, or perform more general recursive computations beyond the fixed recurrent modules built into their design. Important for the discussion here is the fact that precise – in contrast to approximate or subitizing-style – counting is by definition a recursive ability, thus impossible to learn for such models.

[2] We want to emphasize that there is evidence for Weber's Law in a range of other approximate systems, some of them non-discrete and thus rendering a pairing-based strategy impossible. While this does not rule out such a strategy when observing performance decline as predicted by Weber's Law (which is probably not possible based on extrinsic evaluation alone), it strongly suggests that similar and thus non-pairing-based mechanisms are at work in all of these situations.

Both mechanisms to interpret *"most"* suggest conditions in which they should perform well or badly. For the cardinality-based one, the difference in numbers of the two sets in question is expected to be essential: smaller differences, or greater numbers for the same absolute difference, require more accurate number estimations and hence make this comparison harder, according to Weber's law. The pairing-based mechanism, on the other hand, is likely affected by the spatial arrangement of the objects in question: if the objects are more clustered within one set, pairing them with objects from the other set becomes harder. Importantly, these conditions are orthogonal, so each mechanism should not substantially be affected by the other condition, respectively. By constructing (artificial) scenes where one of the conditions dominates the configuration, and measuring the accuracy of being able to correctly interpret propositions involving *"most"*, the expected difficulties can be confirmed (or refuted) and thus indicate which mechanism is actually at work.

Using this methodology, Pietroski et al. (2009) show that humans exhibit a default strategy of interpreting *"most"*, at least when only given 200ms to look at the scene and hence having to rely on an immediate subconscious judgment. This strategy is based on the approximate number system and the cardinality-based mechanism. Moreover, the behavior is shown to be sub-optimal in some situations where humans would, in principle, be able to perform better if deviating from their default strategy. Since machine learning models are trained by optimizing parameters for the task at hand, it is far from obvious whether they learn a similarly stable default mechanism, or instead follow a potentially superior adaptive strategy depending on the situation. While the latter is likely more efficient in solving at least a narrowly defined task, the former would instead suggest that the system is able to acquire and utilize core concepts like an approximate number system.

We may speculate about the innate preference of modern network architectures for either of the strategies: Most of the visual processing is based on convolutions which, being an inherently local computation, we assume would favor the pairing-based strategy via locally matching and 'cancelling out' entities of the two predicates. On the other hand, the tensors resulting from the sequence of convolution operations are globally fused into a final embedding vector, which in turn would support the more globally aggregating cardinality-based strategy. However, the type of computations and representations learned by deep neural networks are poorly understood, making such speculations fallacious. We thus emphasize again that the higher-level motivation for this paper is to demonstrate how we need not rely on such speculative 'narratives', but can experimentally substantiate our claims.

## 3 Experimental setup

The setup in this paper closely resembles the psychological experiments conducted by Pietroski et al. (2009), but aimed at a state-of-the-art VQA model and its interpretation of *"most"*.

### 3.1 Training and evaluation data

We use the ShapeWorld framework (Kuhnle and Copestake, 2017) as starting point to generate appropriate data. ShapeWorld is a configurable generation system for abstract, visually grounded language data. A data point consists of an image, an accompanying caption, and an agreement value indicating whether the caption is true given the image. The underlying task, image caption agreement, essentially corresponds to yes/no questions and as such is a type of visual question answering. Internally, the system samples an abstract world description from which a semantic caption representation is extracted. Both are then turned into 'natural' (but still abstract) representations as image and natural language statement, respectively. The latter transformation is based on a semantic grammar formalism (see the paper for details).

We use the pre-implemented quantifier captioner component, both in its unrestricted version and one with available quantifiers restricted to *"more than half"* and *"less than half"*[3]. The former contains various additional (generalized) quantifiers (*"no"*, *"a/three quarter(s)"*, *"a/two third(s)"*, *"all"*) and numbers (ranging from *"zero"* to *"five"*), each in combination with a comparing modifier (*"less than"*, *"at most"*, *"exactly"*, *"at least"*, *"more than"*, *"not"*). We refer to the unrestricted version as Q-full, the other one

---

[3] We use these two instead of *"most"* since ShapeWorld generates them by default. The VQA model is trained from scratch on this data, so we do not expect any of the differences between *"most"* and *"more than half"* one observes with humans (Hackl, 2009) to matter.

Figure 2: Two example images with in-/correct captions, taken from the Q-full dataset (all quantifiers/numbers).

as Q-half. Figure 2 shows two images together with potential Q-full captions.

We also use the default world generator to produce training data (up to 15 randomly positioned objects, as seen in figure 2). However, all of the pre-implemented generator modules are too generic for our evaluation purposes, since they do not allow to control attributes and positioning of objects to the desired degree. We thus implemented our own custom generator module with the following functionality to produce test data.

**Attribute contrast:** For each instance, either the attribute 'shape' or 'color' is picked[4], and subsequently two values for this attribute and one value for the other is randomly chosen. This means that the only relevant difference between objects in every image is either one of two shape or color values (for instance, red vs blue squares, or red squares vs circles).

**Contrast ratios:** A list of valid ratios between the contrasted attributes can be specified, from which one will randomly be chosen per instance. For instance, a ratio of 2:3 means that there are 50% more objects with the second than the first attribute. We look at values close to 1:1, that is, 1:2, 2:3, 3:4, 4:5, etc. The increasing difficulty (for humans) resulting from closer ratios is illustrated in figure 3. Multiples of the smaller-valued ratios are also generated (e.g., 2:4 or 6:9), within the limit of up to 15 objects overall.

**Area-controlled (vs size-controlled):** If this option is set, object sizes are not chosen uniformly across the entire valid range, but size ranges for the two contrasting object types are adapted to the given contrast ratio and size of the chosen shape(s), so that both attributes cover the same image area on average. This means that the more numerous attribute will generally be represented by smaller objects, and the difference in covered area between, for instance, squares and triangles is taken into account.

While objects are still positioned randomly in the basic version of this new generator module, we define two modes which control this aspect as well. Figure 1 in the introduction illustrates the different modes.

**Partitioned positioning:** An angle is randomly chosen for each image, and objects of the contrasting attributes are consistently placed either on one side or the other.

**Paired positioning:** If there are objects of the contrasted attribute which are not yet paired, one of them is randomly chosen and the new object is placed next to it.

The captions of these evaluation instances are always of the form *"More/less than half the shapes are X"*. with *"X"* being the attribute in question, for instance, *"squares"* or *"red shapes"*. Note that this is an even more constrained captioner than the one used for Q-half. We also emphasize that, in contrast to this new evaluation generator module, the default generator configuration of the 'quantification' dataset pre-specified in ShapeWorld is used to generate the training instances in Q-half and Q-full. So these images generally contain many more than just two contrasted attributes, and ratios between attributes tend to be accordingly smaller. The examples in figure 2 are chosen to illustrate this fact: the second example contains a *"half"* statement with ratio 7:8, and the first contains one about a 0:4 ratio, while the image would also allow for a more 'interesting' 3:4 ratio (color of semicircles).

While we generally try to stay close to the experimental setup of Pietroski et al. (2009), in the following we point out some differences. Most importantly, instead of just using yellow and blue dots, we use all eight shapes and seven colors that ShapeWorld provides. This increases the visual variety of the instances and thus encourages the

---

[4]Note that we chose the examples in figures to always vary in color only, for clarity.

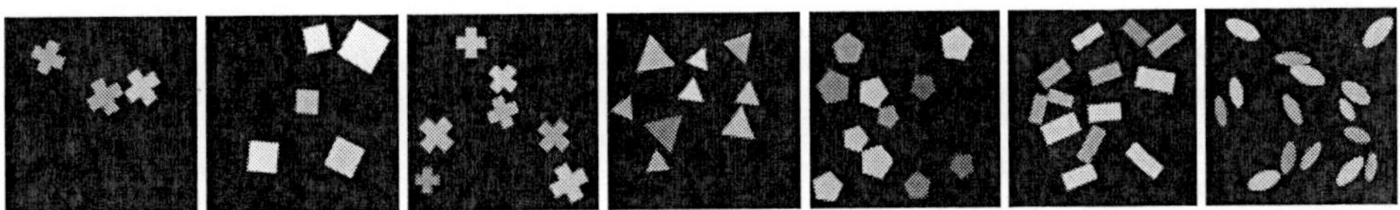

Figure 3: From left to right, the ratio between the two attributes is increasingly balanced.

system to actually learn the fact that shape and color are attributes that can be combined in any way, instead of just straightforward binary pattern matching. Note that the humans in the psychological experiments have learned language in even more complex situations, which we cannot hope to approximate here. Moreover, our data does not contain yes/no questions but true/false captions, and *"most"*-equivalent variations *"more/less than half"*. Since the model is trained from scratch on such data, this should not affect results.

We do not implement the 'column pairs mixed/sorted' modes since they would require comparatively big and mostly empty images, hence require bigger networks and might cause practical learning problems due to sparseness, which we do not want to address here. In contrast, our 'partitioned' mode is more difficult than the ones investigated by Pietroski et al. (2009), at least for a pairing-based mechanism.

## 3.2 Model

We focus on the FiLM model (Perez et al., 2018) here since it showed close-to-perfect accuracy on the CLEVR dataset (Johnson et al., 2017a). We interpret the ShapeWorld captions and agreement values as questions and answer, respectively. The image is processed using either a pre-trained CNN or a four-layer CNN trained from scratch on the task. The question is processed by a GRU. In a sequence of four residual blocks, the image information is processed with its features linearly modulated (scale, offset) conditioned on the processed question embedding. Finally, the classifier module produces the answer, true or false. We use the code made available by the authors of the FiLM model, without changing any parameters. The only aspect we adapt is the trainable four-layer CNN, which uses a kernel size of 3, batch normalization and a stride of 2 in the second and fourth layer.

We considered investigating other models as well: The PG+EE model (Johnson et al., 2017b) is openly available and achieved very good performance on CLEVR, however, it relies on the

'program tree' provided by CLEVR, and while there exists a basic conversion of ShapeWorld caption models to CLEVR program trees, first, the CLEVR-specific modules do not cover quantifiers like *"most"* and, second, these program trees encode the interpretation strategy, which would defeat the purpose of our investigation to analyze precisely this mechanism as learned from data. The RelationNet architecture (Santoro et al., 2017) explicitly implements a pairing-based mechanism and hence we considered its evaluation less interesting than FiLM. For similar reasons, we did not focus on the VQA model of Zhang et al. (2018), whose architecture includes an explicit counting component. While our aim is to investigate the strategy for understanding *"most"* learned from data, it would be interesting to examine in both cases whether their architectural prior does indeed have the expected effect. Finally, we only learned about the MAC model (Hudson and Manning, 2018) after we started this project and so decided to leave it for future work, but we definitely consider it one of the most interesting candidate models to evaluate, since its architecture does not suggest an obvious preference for either strategy.

## 3.3 Training details

The training set for both Q-full and Q-half consists of around 100k (25x 4096) images with 5 captions per image, so overall around 500k instances. The model is trained for 100k iterations with a batch size of 64. Training performance is measured on an additional validation set of 20k instances. Moreover, we produced 1024 instances for each of the overall 48 evaluation configurations, to investigate the trained model in more detail.

## 4 Results

**Training.** We train two versions of the FiLM model, with CNN trained from scratch on the task: one on the Q-full dataset which contains all available quantifier and number caption types, the other on the Q-half dataset which is restricted to captions involving the quantifier *"half"* only. Performance of the system over the course of the 100k training iterations is shown in figure 4. The two models, referred to by Q-full and Q-half below, learn to solve the task quasi-perfectly, with a final accuracy of 98.9% and 99.4% respectively. Not surprisingly, the system trained on the more diverse Q-full training set takes longer to reach this level of performance, but nevertheless plateaus after around 70k iterations.

For the sake of completeness, we also include the performance of other models in this figure, which failed to show clear improvement over the first 50k iterations. This includes the FiLM model with pre-trained instead of trainable CNN module (Q-full-pre, Q-half-pre), and an earlier trial on Q-half (Q-half-coll) where we did not constrain the data generation to not produce object collisions (the default in ShapeWorld is to allow up to 25% area overlap). We note, however, that we have not done any hyperparameter search which might alleviate these learning problems.

**Evaluation.** Table 5 presents a detailed breakdown of system performance on the evaluation settings. Before discussing the results in detail, we want to reiterate three key differences between the evaluation data and the training data:

- The visual scenes here do all exhibit close-to-balanced contrast ratios, while this is not the case for the training instances.

- The evaluation scenes only contain objects of two different attribute pairs, and consequently the numbers to compare are generally greater than in the training instances, where more attributes are likely present in a scene.

- Q-full contains not just statements involving *"half"* – in fact, a random sample of 100 images / 500 captions suggests that they constitute only around 8% of the dataset (and this includes combinations with modifiers beyond *"more/less than"*).

Considering that, the relatively high accuracy on test instances throughout indicates a remarkable degree of generalization.

**More balanced ratios.** The most consistent effect is that more balanced ratios of contrasted attributes cause performance to decrease. This is certainly affected by the tendency of the training data to not include many examples of almost balanced ratios. However, if this were the only rea-

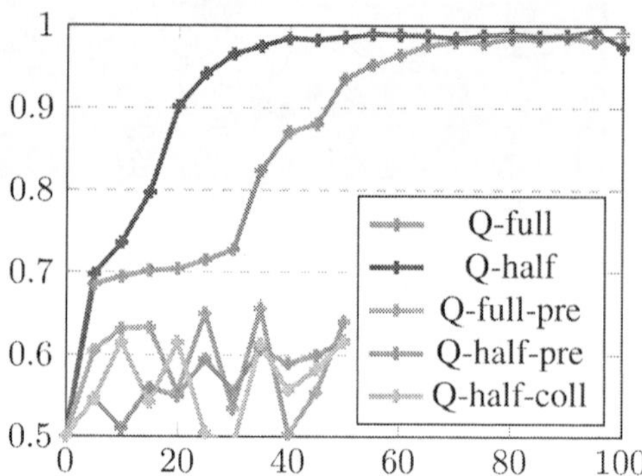

Figure 4: Training performance (iterations in 1000). *Q-full*: unconstrained dataset; *Q-half*: dataset restricted to *"less/more than half"*; *-pre*: using pre-trained CNN module; *-coll*: allowing object overlap.

son, one would expect a much more sudden and less uniformly linear decrease. More importantly, since Q-full generally contains fewer *"half"* statements, the decline should be more pronounced here. We do not observe either of these effects, and thus conclude that both models may actually have developed an approximate number system. This is further discussed at the end of this section.

**Random vs paired vs partitioned.** There is a clear negative effect of the partitioned configuration on performance for the model trained on Q-full, which suggests that the learned mechanism is not robust to a high degree of per-attribute clustering. This indicates at most a weak preference towards a pairing-based strategy for Q-full, though, since otherwise the model would not be expected to perform best on the random configuration. Interestingly, the results for Q-half even suggest slightly better performance on the area-controlled partitioned configuration. Overall, no clear preference for either the perfectly clustered partitioned or the perfectly mixed paired arrangement is apparent. We note, however, that the random mode instances are most similar to the random placement of objects in the training data, which might cause this effect.

**Size- vs area-controlled.** The performance in both cases is comparable, showing that the models do not (solely) learn to rely on comparing the overall covered area, which would only work well in the size-controlled mode. Nevertheless, we note a tendency for area-controlled instances to be somewhat more difficult in random and paired mode, more so for Q-half, which suggests that the

| train | mode | size-controlled | | | | | | | | area-controlled | | | | | | | |
|---|---|---|---|---|---|---|---|---|---|---|---|---|---|---|---|---|---|
| | | all | 1:2 | 2:3 | 3:4 | 4:5 | 5:6 | 6:7 | 7:8 | all | 1:2 | 2:3 | 3:4 | 4:5 | 5:6 | 6:7 | 7:8 |
| Q-full | random | 92 | 100 | 99 | 97 | 94 | 91 | 88 | 85 | 93 | 100 | 99 | 97 | 93 | 91 | 86 | 82 |
| | paired | 93 | 99 | 99 | 96 | 93 | 90 | 88 | 82 | 93 | 99 | 99 | 96 | 91 | 87 | 84 | 80 |
| | part. | 89 | 100 | 99 | 92 | 90 | 81 | 77 | 72 | 89 | 99 | 98 | 92 | 88 | 82 | 78 | 72 |
| Q-half | random | 92 | 100 | 100 | 98 | 93 | 88 | 88 | 87 | 93 | 100 | 100 | 97 | 92 | 86 | 85 | 82 |
| | paired | 92 | 100 | 100 | 96 | 90 | 86 | 84 | 79 | 92 | 100 | 99 | 96 | 87 | 84 | 79 | 76 |
| | part. | 91 | 100 | 99 | 96 | 86 | 83 | 83 | 80 | 91 | 100 | 99 | 94 | 89 | 83 | 83 | 80 |

Figure 5: Accuracy in percent of the models trained on Q-full and Q-half for the various evaluation configurations.

model(s) learn to use covered area as a feature to inform a correct decision in some cases.

**Q-full vs Q-half.** There seems to be a tendency of the system trained on Q-full to perform marginally better, except for the partitioned mode discussed before. The fact that this model performs at least on a par with the one trained on Q-half, while only seeing a fraction of directly relevant training captions, indicates that the learning process is not 'distracted' by the variety of captions, and indeed might profit from it.

**Ratios and Weber fraction.** We generated evaluation sets of even more balanced ratios (8:9, 9:10, 10:11, increasing the overall number of objects accordingly to 17/19/21), and in figure 6 plotted the accuracy of the Q-full model on increasingly balanced sets for all three spatial configuration modes, not controlling for area (which for greater numbers only has a negligible effect anyway). The figure also contains a diagram with accuracy plotted against ratio fraction, which is more common in the context of Weber's law. The characteristic Weber fraction can be read off directly as the ratio at which a subject is able to distinguish two values with 75% accuracy. We observe around 1.11 for random/paired and 1.16 for partitioned, which corresponds to 9:10 and 6:7 as closest integer ratios. These values are in the same region as the average human Weber fraction, which is often reported as being 1.14, or 7:8.

We emphasize that these curves align well with the trend predicted by Weber's law, even for the ratios with more than 15 objects overall, where such situations have never been encountered during training. All this strongly suggests that the model learns a mechanism similar to an ANS, which is able to produce representations that can (at least) be utilized for identifying the more numerous set. It can in particular be concluded that the system does not actually learn to explicitly count, since we would then not expect to observe such fuzziness characteristic to an ANS.

Moreover, since performance is affected somewhat by the partitioned and the area-controlled modes, the interpretation of *"most"* seems to be informed by other features as well. As we noted earlier, since the model is trained to optimize this task, an adaptive strategy is not unexpected. On the contrary, more surprising is the fact that an ANS-like system emerges as a dominating 'backbone' mechanism, with additional factors acting as less influential 'secondary' features.

## 5 Related work

Visual question answering (VQA) is the general task of answering questions about visual scenes. Since the introduction of the VQA Dataset (Antol et al., 2015), this dataset was widely used as evaluation benchmark for multimodal deep learning. It provides a shallow categorization of questions, including basic count questions, however, these categories are far too coarse for our purposes.

Motivated by various problems with the VQA Dataset (Goyal et al., 2017; Agrawal et al., 2016), a range of artificial abstract datasets have been introduced recently. CLEVR (Johnson et al., 2017a) consists of rendered images of geometric objects and questions generated based on templates, covering some abilities like number or attribute comparison in more detail, but still in a fixed categorization. NLVR (Suhr et al., 2017) contains crowd-sourced statements about abstract images, but does not sort them according to some criteria. Recently, the COG dataset (Yang et al., 2018) was introduced, which most explicitly focuses on replicating psychological experiments for deep learning models, hence most related to our work. However, their dataset does not contain any number or quantifier statements.

There is some work on investigating deep neural networks which look at numerosity from a more

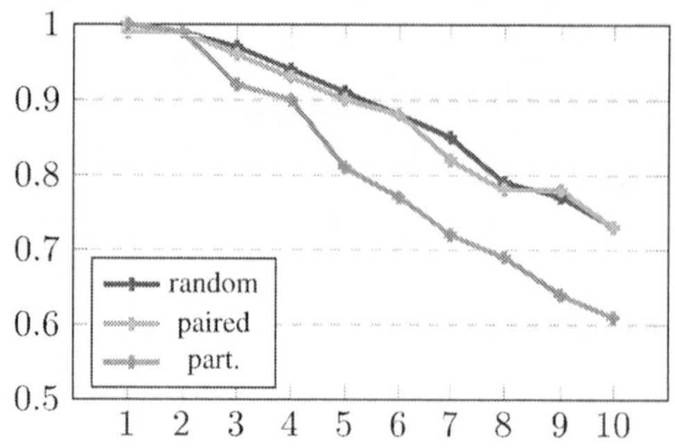 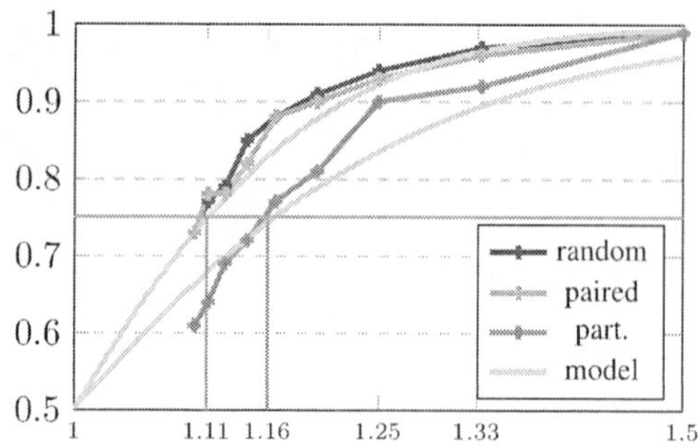

Figure 6: *Left:* Q-full model performance for increasingly balanced ratios (x-axis indicates ratio via n:n+1). *Right:* Performance as a function of the actual ratio fraction (n+1)/n, with Weber fraction (75%) highlighted.

psychologically inspired viewpoint. Stoianov and Zorzi (2012) find that visual numerosity emerges from unsupervised learning on abstract image data. Zhang et al. (2015) look at salient object subitizing in real-world images, formulated as a classification task over five classes ranging from "0" to "4 or more". In a more general number-per-category classification setup, Chattopadhyay et al. (2017) investigate different methods of obtaining counts per object category, including one which is inspired by subitizing. Moving beyond explicit number classification, (Zhang et al., 2018) recently introduced a dedicated counting module for visual question answering.

Other work looks at a similar classification task, but for proper quantifiers like "no", "few", "most", "all", first on abstract images of circles (Sorodoc et al., 2016), then on natural scenes (Sorodoc et al., 2018). Recently, Pezzelle et al. (2018) investigated a hierarchy of quantifier-related classification abilities, from comparatives via quantifiers like the ones above to fine-grained proportions. Wu et al. (2018), besides investigating precise numerosity via number classification as above, also look at approximate numerosity as binary greater/smaller decision, which closely corresponds to our experiments. However, on the one hand, their focus is on the subitizing ability, not the approximate number system. On the other hand, their experiments follow a different methodology in that they already train models on specifically designed datasets, while we deliberately leverage such targeted data only for evaluation.

On a methodological level, our proposal of inspiring experimental setup and evaluation practice for deep learning by cognitive psychology is in line with that of Ritter et al. (2017) and their shape bias investigation for modern vision architectures.

## 6  Conclusion

We identify two strategies of algorithmically interpreting *"most"* in a visual context, with different implications on cognitive concepts. Following experimental practice of similar investigations with humans in psycholinguistics, we design experiments and data to shed light on the question whether the state-of-the-art FiLM VQA model shows preference for one strategy over the other. Performance on various specifically designed instances does indeed indicate that a form of approximate number system is learned, which generalizes to more difficult scenes as predicted by Weber's law. The results further suggest that additional features influence the interpretation process, which are affected by the spatial arrangement and relative size of objects in a scene. There are many opportunities for future work from here, from strengthening the finding of an approximate number system and further analyzing confounding factors to investigating the relation to more explicit counting tasks.

### Acknowledgments

We thank the anonymous reviewers for their constructive feedback. AK is grateful for being supported by a Qualcomm Research Studentship and an EPSRC Doctoral Training Studentship.

## References

Aishwarya Agrawal, Dhruv Batra, and Devi Parikh. 2016. Analyzing the behavior of visual question answering models. In *Proceedings of the Conference on Empirical Methods in Natural Language Processing*, EMNLP 2016, pages 1955–1960.

Stanislaw Antol, Aishwarya Agrawal, Jiasen Lu, Margaret Mitchell, Dhruv Batra, C. Lawrence Zitnick, and Devi Parikh. 2015. VQA: Visual question answering. In *Proceedings of the IEEE International Conference on Computer Vision*, ICCV 2015.

Prithvijit Chattopadhyay, Ramakrishna Vedantam, Ramprasaath R. Selvaraju, Dhruv Batra, and Devi Parikh. 2017. Counting everyday objects in everyday scenes. In *Proceedings of the IEEE Conference on Computer Vision and Pattern Recognition*, CVPR 2017, pages 4428–4437.

Felix A. Gers and Jürgen Schmidhuber. 2001. LSTM recurrent networks learn simple context-free and context-sensitive languages. *Transactions on Neural Networks*, 12(6):1333–1340.

Yash Goyal, Tejas Khot, Douglas Summers-Stay, Dhruv Batra, and Devi Parikh. 2017. Making the V in VQA matter: Elevating the role of image understanding in Visual Question Answering. In *Proceedings of the IEEE Conference on Computer Vision and Pattern Recognition*, CVPR 2017, pages 6325–6334.

Martin Hackl. 2009. On the grammar and processing of proportional quantifiers: most versus more than half. *Natural Language Semantics*, 17(1):63–98.

Drew A. Hudson and Christopher D. Manning. 2018. Compositional attention networks for machine reasoning. In *Proceedings of the International Conference on Learning Representations*, ICLR 2018.

Justin Johnson, Bharath Hariharan, Laurens van der Maaten, Li Fei-Fei, C. Lawrence Zitnick, and Ross Girshick. 2017a. CLEVR: A diagnostic dataset for compositional language and elementary visual reasoning. In *Proceedings of the IEEE Conference on Computer Vision and Pattern Recognition*, CVPR 2017.

Justin Johnson, Bharath Hariharan, Laurens van der Maaten, Judy Hoffman, Li Fei-Fei, C Lawrence Zitnick, and Ross Girshick. 2017b. Inferring and executing programs for visual reasoning. In *Proceedings of the IEEE International Conference on Computer Vision*, ICCV 2017.

Alexander Kuhnle and Ann Copestake. 2017. Shape-World - A new test methodology for multimodal language understanding. *ArXiv e-prints 1704.04517*.

Jeffrey Lidz, Paul Pietroski, Justin Halberda, and Tim Hunter. 2011. Interface transparency and the psychosemantics of most. *Natural Language Semantics*, 19(3):227–256.

Ethan Perez, Florian Strub, Harm de Vries, Vincent Dumoulin, and Aaron C. Courville. 2018. FiLM: Visual reasoning with a general conditioning layer. In *AAAI*.

Sandro Pezzelle, Ionut-Teodor Sorodoc, and Raffaella Bernardi. 2018. Comparatives, quantifiers, proportions: A multi-task model for the learning of quantities from vision. In *Proceedings of the Conference of the North American Chapter of the Association for Computational Linguistics*, NAACL 2018.

Paul Pietroski, Jeffrey Lidz, Tim Hunter, and Justin Halberda. 2009. The meaning of 'most': Semantics, numerosity and psychology. *Mind and Language*, 24(5):554–585.

Samuel Ritter, David G. T. Barrett, Adam Santoro, and Matt M. Botvinick. 2017. Cognitive psychology for deep neural networks: A shape bias case study. In *Proceedings of the 34th International Conference on Machine Learning*, ICML 2017, pages 2940–2949.

Adam Santoro, David Raposo, David G. T. Barrett, Mateusz Malinowski, Razvan Pascanu, Peter Battaglia, and Timothy P. Lillicrap. 2017. A simple neural network module for relational reasoning. In *Proceedings of the Annual Conference on Neural Information Processing Systems*, NIPS 2017, pages 4974–4983.

Ionut Sorodoc, Angeliki Lazaridou, Gemma Boleda, Aurélie Herbelot, Sandro Pezzelle, and Raffaella Bernardi. 2016. "Look, some green circles!": Learning to quantify from images. In *Proceedings of the 5th Workshop on Vision and Language*, Berlin, Germany.

Ionut Sorodoc, Sandro Pezzelle, Aurélie Herbelot, Mariella Dimiccoli, and Raffaella Bernardi. 2018. Learning quantification from images: A structured neural architecture. *Natural Language Engineering*, page 130.

Ivilin Stoianov and Marco Zorzi. 2012. Emergence of a 'visual number sense' in hierarchical generative models. *Nature Neuroscience*, 15(194):194–196.

Alane Suhr, Mike Lewis, James Yeh, and Yoav Artzi. 2017. A corpus of natural language for visual reasoning. In *Proceedings of the 55th Annual Meeting of the Association for Computational Linguistics*, ACL 2017.

Xiaolin Wu, Xi Zhang, and Xiao Shu. 2018. On numerosity of deep convolutional neural networks. *ArXiv e-prints 1802.05160*.

Guangyu Robert Yang, Igor Ganichev, Xiao-Jing Wang, Jonathon Shlens, and David Sussillo. 2018. A dataset and architecture for visual reasoning with a working memory. *ArXiv e-prints 1803.06092*.

Jianming Zhang, Shuga Ma, Mehrnoosh Sameki, Stan Sclaroff, Margrit Betke, Zhe Lin, Xiaohui Shen, Brian Price, and Radomír Měch. 2015. Salient object subitizing. In *Proceedings of the IEEE Conference on Computer Vision and Pattern Recognition*, CVPR 2015.

Yan Zhang, Jonathon Hare, and Adam Prügel-Bennett. 2018. Learning to count objects in natural images for visual question answering. In *Proceedings of the International Conference on Learning Representations*, ICLR 2018.

# Do Human Rationales Improve Machine Explanations?

**Julia Strout, Ye Zhang and Raymond J. Mooney**
Department of Computer Science
University of Texas at Austin
{jstrout,yezhang,mooney}@cs.utexas.edu

## Abstract

Work on "learning with rationales" shows that humans providing explanations to a machine learning system can improve the system's predictive accuracy. However, this work has not been connected to work in "explainable AI" which concerns machines explaining their reasoning to humans. In this work, we show that learning with rationales can also improve the quality of the machine's explanations as evaluated by human judges. Specifically, we present experiments showing that, for CNN-based text classification, explanations generated using "supervised attention" are judged superior to explanations generated using normal unsupervised attention.

## 1 Introduction

Recently, the need for explainable artificial intelligence (XAI) has become a major concern due to the increased use of machine learning in automated decision making (Gunning, 2017; Aha, 2018). On the other hand, work on "learning with rationales" (Zaidan et al., 2007; Zhang et al., 2016) has shown that humans providing explanatory information supporting their supervised classification labels can improve the accuracy of machine learning. These human annotations that can explain classification labels are called *rationales*. In particular, for text categorization, humans select phrases or sentences from a document that most support their decision as rationales.

However, there is no work connecting "learning from rationales" with improving XAI, although they are clearly complementary problems.

**Contribution** We explore whether learning from human explanations actually improves a system's ability to explain its decisions to human users. Specifically, we show that for explanations for text classification in the form of selected passages that best support a decision, training on hu-

man rationales improves the quality of a system's explanations as judged by human evaluators.

Attention mechanisms (Bahdanau et al., 2015) have become standard practice in computer vision and text classification (Vaswani et al., 2017; Yang et al., 2016). In both computer vision and text-based tasks, learned attention weights have been shown through human evaluation to be useful explanations for a model's decisions (Park et al., 2018; Rocktäschel et al., 2015; Hermann et al., 2015; Xu et al., 2015); however, attention's explanatory power has come into question in recent work (Jain and Wallace, 2019), which we discuss in Section 2.

Traditional attention mechanisms are unsupervised; however, recent work has shown that supervising attention with human annotated rationales can improve learning for text classification based on Convolutional Neural Networks (CNNs) (Zhang et al., 2016). While this work alludes to improved explainability using supervised attention, it does not explicitly evaluate this claim. We extend this work by evaluating whether supervised attention using human rationales, rather than unsupervised attention, actually improves explanation. Explanations from both models are full sentences that the model has weighted as being most important to the document's final classification.

While automated evaluations of explanations (e.g. comparing them to human gold-standard explanations (Lei et al., 2016)) can be somewhat useful, we argue that because the goal of machine explanations is to help users, they should be directly evaluated by human judges. Machine explanations can be different from human ones, but still provide good justification for a decision (Das et al., 2017). This opinion is shared by other researchers in the area (Doshi-Velez, 2017), but human evaluation is often avoided due to the time required and difficulty of conducting human trials. We believe it is a

56

*Proceedings of the Second BlackboxNLP Workshop on Analyzing and Interpreting Neural Networks for NLP*, pages 56–62
Florence, Italy, August 1, 2019. ©2019 Association for Computational Linguistics

necessary element of explainability research, and in this work, we compare the explanations from the two models through human evaluation on Mechanical Turk and find that the model trained with human rationales is judged to generate explanations that better support its decisions.

## 2   Related Work

There is a growing body of research on explainable AI  (Koh and Liang, 2017; Ribeiro et al., 2016; Li et al., 2016; Hendricks et al., 2018), but it is not connected to work on learning with human rationales, which we review below.

As discussed above, Zhang et al. (2016) demonstrate increased predictive accuracy of CNN models augmented with human rationales. Here, we first reproduce their predictive results, and then focus on extracting and evaluating explanations from the models. Lei et al. (2016) present a model that extracts rationales for predictions without training on rationales. They compare their extracted rationales to human gold-standard ones through automated evaluations, i.e., precision and recall. Bao et al. (2018) extend this work by learning a mapping from the human rationales to continuous attention. They transfer this mapping to low resource target domains as an auxiliary training signal to improve classification accuracy in the target domain. They compare their learned attention with human rationales by calculating their cosine distance to the 'oracle' attention.

None of the above related work asks human users to evaluate the generated explanations. However, Nguyen (2018) does compare human and automatic evaluations of explanations. That work finds that human evaluation is moderately, but statistically significantly, correlated with the automatic metrics. However, it does not evaluate any explanations based on attention, nor do the explanations make use of any extra human supervision.

As mentioned above, there has also been some recent criticism of using attention as explanation (Jain and Wallace, 2019), due to a lack of correlation between the attention weights and gradient based methods which are more "faithful" to the model's reasoning. However, attention weights offer some insight into at least one point of internal representation in the model, and they also impact the training of the later features. Our contribution is to measure how useful these attention based explanations are to humans in understanding a model's decision as compared to a different model architecture that explicitly learns to predict which sentences make good explanations.

In this work, we have human judges evaluate both attention based machine explanations and machine explanations trained from human rationales, thus connecting learning from human explanations and machine explanations to humans.

## 3   Models and Dataset

### 3.1   Models

We replicate the work of Zhang et al. (2016) and use a CNN as our underlying baseline model for document classification. To model a document, each sentence is encoded as a sentence vector using a CNN, and then the document vector is formed by summing over the sentence vectors. We use two variations of this baseline model, a rationale-augmented CNN (*RA-CNN*) and an attention based CNN (*AT-CNN*) (Yang et al., 2016). RA-CNN is trained on both the document label and the rationale labels. In this model, the document vector is a weighted sum of the composite sentence vectors, where the weight is the probability of the sentence being a rationale. In AT-CNN, the document vector is still a weighted sum of sentence CNN vectors, but the weight is not learned from rationales. Rather, a trainable context vector is introduced from scratch. We calculate the interaction between this context vector and each sentence vector to induce attention weights over the sentences. The only difference between RA-CNN and AT-CNN is that RA-CNN relies on the human annotated rationales to learn the sentence weight at training time, while AT-CNN learns the sentence weight without utilizing any human rationales. For the details of these two models and training see  Zhang et al. (2016).

### 3.2   Explanations

At test time, each model can provide explanations for its classification decision by either choosing the sentences with the largest probability of being a rationale in RA-CNN or the sentences with the largest attention weights in AT-CNN. By comparing the quality of explanations output by the two models at test time, we can judge whether capitalizing on human explanations at training time can improve the machine explanations at test time.

### 3.3 Dataset

We evaluate the explanations for both models on the movie review dataset from Zaidan et al. (2007). It contains 1,000 positive reviews and 1,000 negative reviews where 900 of each are annotated with human rationales. Each review is a document consisting of 32 sentences on average, and each annotated document contains about 8 rationale sentences. We use the 1,800 annotated documents as the training set, and the remaining 200 documents without extra annotation as test. The human rationales are used as supervision in RA-CNN but not in AT-CNN.

### 3.4 Classification Accuracy

The classification accuracy of each model on the test set is summarized in Table 1. Since there is variance across multiple trials, we pick the best performing model across several trials for human evaluation of the explanations.

Table 1 reproduces Zhang et al. (2016)'s finding that providing human explanations to machines at training time (RA-CNN) improves predictive accuracy compared to learning explanations without human annotations (AT-CNN). Our results differ slightly from theirs in that our AT-CNN also outperforms the baseline Doc-CNN. We attribute this difference to possible slight variations in our implementation of AT-CNN.

Note there are other works on learning attention that could potentially increase the prediction accuracy (Lin et al., 2017; Devlin et al., 2018), but none of them are directly comparable to RA-CNN. We introduced the smallest difference (whether the sentence vector is trained using the rationale label) between AT-CNN and RA-CNN to make a fair comparison between their generated explanations.

The focus of this work is on evaluating explanations rather than predictive accuracy, so we turn our attention to the question: Does humans explaining themselves to machines improve machines explaining themselves to humans? We will explore this in the next section.

## 4 Explanation Evaluation Methods

We use Amazon Mechanical Turk (AMT) to evaluate the explanations from both AT-CNN and RA-CNN.

| Doc-CNN | AT-CNN | RA-CNN |
| --- | --- | --- |
| 86.00% | 88.50% | 90.00% |

Table 1: Classification accuracy for movie reviews.

### 4.1 HIT Design

Our Human Intelligence Task (HIT) shows a worker two copies of a test document along with the document's classification. Each copy of the document has a subset of sentences highlighted as explanations for the final classification. This subset is chosen as the 3 sentences with the largest weights from either AT-CNN's attention weights or RA-CNN's supervised weighting. We also evaluated a baseline model that selects 3 sentences at random. Given two randomly ordered documents, a worker must choose which document's highlighted sentences best support the overall classification. If the worker determines that both are equally supportive (or not supportive), then they can select 'equal'. We only show workers documents that were correctly classified by both models. This resulted in 166 documents from the 200 in the test set. An example from one HIT is in Appendix A.

### 4.2 Quality Control

In an effort to receive quality results from the crowd, we employ two strategies from crowdsourcing research: gold standard questions and majority voting (Hsueh et al., 2009; Eickhoff and de Vries, 2013). Gold standard questions are designed to weed out unreliable workers who either do not understand the goal of the task or are poor workers. If a worker gets the gold standard question wrong, then we assume that their other responses are untrustworthy and do not use them.

We also employ majority voting, which requires that at least two workers who pass the gold standard question agree on an answer. For greater than 90% of the test documents, a majority vote was found after having three workers perform the task. Less than 10% of the test documents required a fourth worker who passed the gold question to break a tie. We also chose to require the 'Master' qualification that AMT uses to designate the best workers on the platform.

## 5 Explanation Evaluation Results

Table 3 contains the results for comparing the top 3 explanations from AT-CNN to the top 3 explanations from RA-CNN for the 166 test documents

| Label | Rank | AT-CNN | RA-CNN |
|---|---|---|---|
| Pos | 1 | archer is also bound by the limits of new york society , which is as intrusive as any other in the world. | the performances are absolutely breathtaking. |
| | 2 | the marriage is one which will unite two very prestigious families , in a society where nothing is more important than the opinions of others . | there are a few deft touches of filmmaking that are simply outstanding , and joanne woodward' narration is exquisite. |
| | 3 | the supporting cast is also wonderful , with several characters so singular that they are indelible in one's memory . | the supporting cast is also wonderful , with several characters so singular that they are indelible in one's memory . |
| Neg | 1 | soon the three guys are dealing dope to raise funds , while avoiding the cops and rival dealer sampson simpson (clarence williams iii) . | it's just that the comic setups are obvious and the payoffs nearly all fall flat . |
| | 2 | only williams stands out (while still performing on the level of his humor-free comedy rocket man) , but that is because he's imprisoned throughout most of the film , giving a much needed change of pace (but mostly swapping one set of obvious gags for another) . | watching the film clean and sober , you are bound to recognize how truly awful it is . |
| | 3 | watching the film clean and sober , you are bound to recognize how truly awful it is . | the film would have been better off by sticking with the " rebel" tone it so eagerly tries to claim. |

Table 2: Top 3 explanations from both models for both a positive and negative correctly classified test document.

| RA-CNN | AT-CNN | Equal |
|---|---|---|
| 43.47% | 20.48% | 36.14% |

Table 3: AMT results comparing explanations from RA-CNN to AT-CNN. Workers were asked to choose which document's highlighted sentences were a better explanation for the final classification.

| AT-CNN | Random | Equal |
|---|---|---|
| 57.23% | 15.66% | 27.12% |

Table 4: AMT results comparing AT-CNN to the random baseline.

where the models each correctly classified the document. The statistics presented are the percentage of times reliable workers agreed that one model's explanations better supported the document's classification or were equal.

Overall, it is clear that RA-CNN is providing better explanations for the plurality of test documents (43.47%). The explanations are considered equal 36.14% of the time, and the remaining 20.48% of the documents were better explained by AT-CNN.

After seeing these results, we decided to run another baseline test to ensure that AT-CNN explanations are reasonable and can at least beat a weak baseline. The results from comparing AT-CNN explanations to randomly sampled sentences from the test document are in Table 4. From these results we can see that AT-CNN is beating the random baseline the majority of the time, demonstrating that attention, even without human supervision, can provide helpful explanations for a model's decision.

To further understand the differences between the explanations from AT-CNN and RA-CNN, we calculated statistics to find the amount of overlap in the top three explanatory sentences from each model. In 33.5% of the test documents, the models share no explanation sentences, in 43.1% they share one explanation sentence, in 22.2% they share two explanation sentences, and they share all three in 1.2%. When considering just the most highly weighted sentence, or top explanation, the models agree 18.6 % of the time. So while it is relatively rare for the models to produce the same top explanatory sentence, we chose to show humans three explanatory sentences per test document to provide insight even in those matching cases.

Table 2 contains the top 3 explanations from each model for two test documents. In both examples, AT-CNN extracts sentences that are more plot related and give less insight into the reviewer's opinion as compared to RA-CNN. These sentences are generally less helpful for understanding the classification of the movie review. In the second example, both models have identified a good explanatory sentence: "watching the film clean and sober, you are bound to recognize how truly awful it is." However, AT-CNN ranks it as less important than two sentences that primarily describe the plot of the film while RA-CNN only ranks another, equally explanatory sentence as more important.

An interesting future avenue for evaluation is to compare explanations from when the models make incorrect predictions. We found a trend in the explanations for test documents that both models misclassified where RA-CNN produced explanations that supported the misclassification while AT-CNN produced more explanations that supported the correct classification, despite the model's decision. While this analysis is too small scale to be conclusive, this raises the question for future work: Do we want our explanation systems to offer the best support for the chosen decision or would it be more beneficial if they provide an explanation that brings the decision into question?

## 6 Conclusion

This paper has demonstrated that training with human rationales improves explanations for a model's classification decisions as evaluated by human judges. We show that while an unsupervised attention based model does provide some valuable explanations, as proven in the experiments comparing to a random baseline, a supervised attention model that trains on human rationales outperforms those results.

## Acknowledgements

This research was supported by the DARPA XAI program through a grant from AFRL. The views and conclusions contained herein are those of the authors and should not be interpreted as necessarily representing the official policies or endorsements, either expressed or implied, of the U.S. Government.

## References

David Aha, editor. 2018. *Proceedings of the IJCAI Workshop on Explainable Artificial Intelligence.* Melbourne, Australia.

Dzmitry Bahdanau, Kyunghyun Cho, and Yoshua Bengio. 2015. Neural machine translation by jointly learning to align and translate. *International Conference on Learning Representations.*

Yujia Bao, Shiyu Chang, Mo Yu, and Regina Barzilay. 2018. Deriving machine attention from human rationales. In *Conference on Empirical Methods in Natural Language Processing.*

Abhishek Das, Harsh Agrawal, Larry Zitnick, Devi Parikh, and Dhruv Batra. 2017. Human attention in visual question answering: Do humans and deep networks look at the same regions? *Computer Vision and Image Understanding*, 163:90–100.

Jacob Devlin, Ming-Wei Chang, Kenton Lee, and Kristina Toutanova. 2018. Bert: Pre-training of deep bidirectional transformers for language understanding. *arXiv preprint arXiv:1810.04805.*

Been Doshi-Velez, Finale; Kim. 2017. Towards a rigorous science of interpretable machine learning. In *Spring Series on Challenges in Machine Learning: "Explainable and Interpretable Models in Computer Vision and Machine Learning".*

Carsten Eickhoff and Arjen P de Vries. 2013. Increasing cheat robustness of crowdsourcing tasks. *Information retrieval*, 16(2):121–137.

David Gunning. 2017. Explainable artificial intelligence (XAI). *Defense Advanced Research Projects Agency (DARPA).*

Lisa Anne Hendricks, Ronghang Hu, Trevor Darrell, and Zeynep Akata. 2018. Grounding visual explanations. In *European Conference of Computer Vision (ECCV).*

Karl Moritz Hermann, Tomas Kocisky, Edward Grefenstette, Lasse Espeholt, Will Kay, Mustafa Suleyman, and Phil Blunsom. 2015. Teaching machines to read and comprehend. In *Advances in Neural Information Processing Systems*, pages 1693–1701.

Pei-Yun Hsueh, Prem Melville, and Vikas Sindhwani. 2009. Data quality from crowdsourcing: A study of annotation selection criteria. In *Proceedings of the NAACL HLT 2009 Workshop on Active Learning for Natural Language Processing*, HLT '09, pages 27–35, Stroudsburg, PA, USA. Association for Computational Linguistics.

Sarthak Jain and Byron C. Wallace. 2019. Attention is not explanation. In *Proceedings of the 2019 North American Chapter of the Association for Computational Linguistics (NAACL).*

Pang Wei Koh and Percy Liang. 2017. Understanding black-box predictions via influence functions. In *34th International Conference on Machine Learning.*

Tao Lei, Regina Barzilay, and Tommi Jaakkola. 2016. Rationalizing neural predictions. In *Conference on Empirical Methods in Natural Language Processing.*

Jiwei Li, Xinlei Chen, Eduard Hovy, and Dan Jurafsky. 2016. Visualizing and understanding neural models in NLP. In *Proceedings of NAACL-HLT*, pages 681–691.

Zhouhan Lin, Minwei Feng, Cicero Nogueira dos Santos, Mo Yu, Bing Xiang, Bowen Zhou, and Yoshua Bengio. 2017. A structured self-attentive sentence embedding. In *International Conference on Learning Representations.*

Dong Nguyen. 2018. Comparing automatic and human evaluation of local explanations for text classification. In *Proceedings of the 2018 Conference of the North American Chapter of the Association for Computational Linguistics: Human Language Technologies, Volume 1 (Long Papers)*, pages 1069–1078.

Dong Huk Park, Lisa Anne Hendricks, Zeynep Akata, Anna Rohrbach, Bernt Schiele, Trevor Darrell, and Marcus Rohrbach. 2018. Multimodal explanations: Justifying decisions and pointing to the evidence. In *31st IEEE Conference on Computer Vision and Pattern Recognition*.

Marco Tulio Ribeiro, Sameer Singh, and Carlos Guestrin. 2016. Why should i trust you?: Explaining the predictions of any classifier. In *Proceedings of the 22nd ACM SIGKDD international conference on knowledge discovery and data mining*, pages 1135–1144. ACM.

Tim Rocktäschel, Edward Grefenstette, Karl Moritz Hermann, Tomáš Kočiský, and Phil Blunsom. 2015. Reasoning about entailment with neural attention. *arXiv preprint arXiv:1509.06664*.

Ashish Vaswani, Noam Shazeer, Niki Parmar, Jakob Uszkoreit, Llion Jones, Aidan N Gomez, Łukasz Kaiser, and Illia Polosukhin. 2017. Attention is all you need. In *Advances in Neural Information Processing Systems*, pages 5998–6008.

Kelvin Xu, Jimmy Ba, Ryan Kiros, Kyunghyun Cho, Aaron Courville, Ruslan Salakhudinov, Rich Zemel, and Yoshua Bengio. 2015. Show, attend and tell: Neural image caption generation with visual attention. In *International conference on machine learning*, pages 2048–2057.

Zichao Yang, Diyi Yang, Chris Dyer, Xiaodong He, Alex Smola, and Eduard Hovy. 2016. Hierarchical attention networks for document classification. In *Proceedings of the 2016 Conference of the North American Chapter of the Association for Computational Linguistics: Human Language Technologies*, pages 1480–1489.

Omar Zaidan, Jason Eisner, and Christine Piatko. 2007. Using annotator rationales to improve machine learning for text categorization. In *Human Language Technologies 2007: The Conference of the North American Chapter of the Association for Computational Linguistics: Proceedings of the Main Conference*, pages 260–267.

Ye Zhang, Iain Marshall, and Byron C Wallace. 2016. Rationale-augmented convolutional neural networks for text classification. In *Proceedings of the Conference on Empirical Methods in Natural Language Processing.*, volume 2016, page 795. NIH Public Access.

# A  Sample HIT

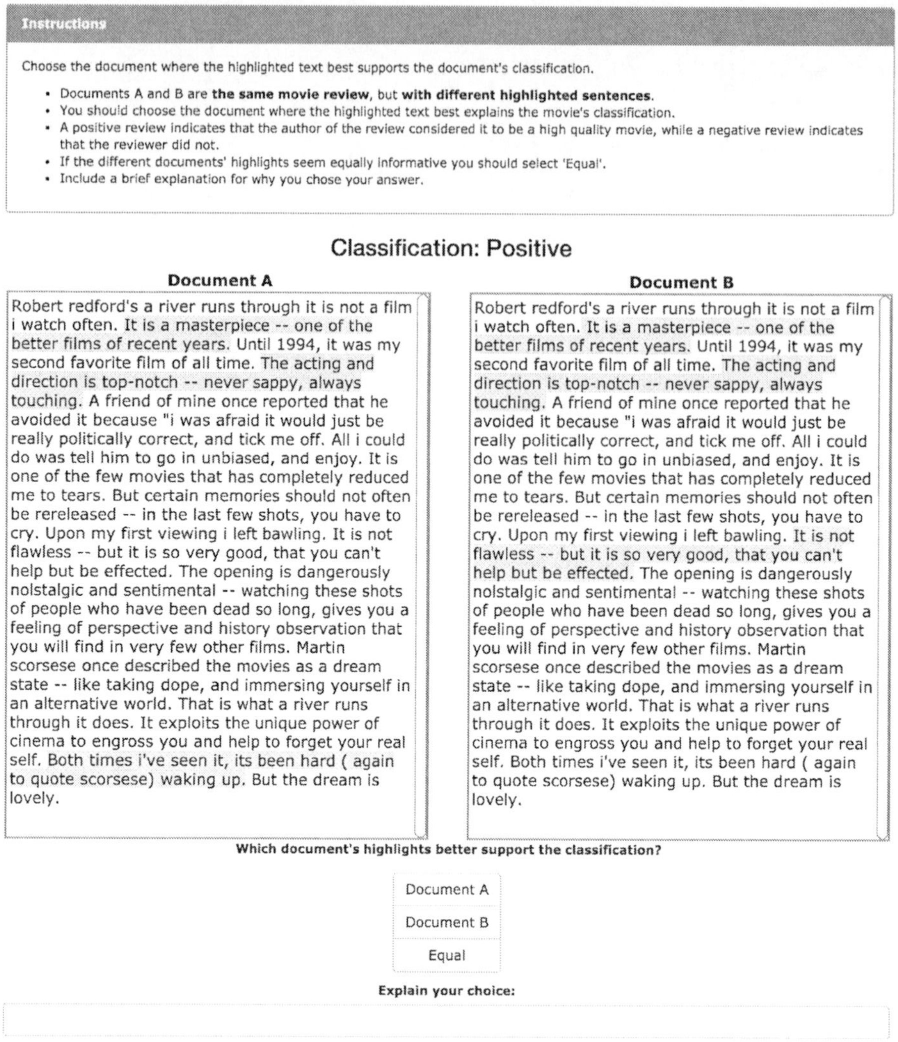

Figure 1: A sample HIT asking workers to compare two explanations for the same movie review.

# Analyzing the Structure of Attention in a Transformer Language Model


**Jesse Vig**
Palo Alto Research Center
Machine Learning and
Data Science Group
Interaction and Analytics Lab
Palo Alto, CA, USA
`jesse.vig@parc.com`

**Yonatan Belinkov**
Harvard John A. Paulson School of
Engineering and Applied Sciences and
MIT Computer Science and
Artificial Intelligence Laboratory
Cambridge, MA, USA
`belinkov@seas.harvard.edu`



## Abstract

The Transformer is a fully attention-based alternative to recurrent networks that has achieved state-of-the-art results across a range of NLP tasks. In this paper, we analyze the structure of attention in a Transformer language model, the GPT-2 small pretrained model. We visualize attention for individual instances and analyze the interaction between attention and syntax over a large corpus. We find that attention targets different parts of speech at different layer depths within the model, and that attention aligns with dependency relations most strongly in the middle layers. We also find that the deepest layers of the model capture the most distant relationships. Finally, we extract exemplar sentences that reveal highly specific patterns targeted by particular attention heads.


## 1 Introduction

Contextual word representations have recently been used to achieve state-of-the-art performance across a range of language understanding tasks (Peters et al., 2018; Radford et al., 2018; Devlin et al., 2018). These representations are obtained by optimizing a language modeling (or similar) objective on large amounts of text. The underlying architecture may be recurrent, as in ELMo (Peters et al., 2018), or based on multi-head self-attention, as in OpenAI's GPT (Radford et al., 2018) and BERT (Devlin et al., 2018), which are based on the Transformer (Vaswani et al., 2017). Recently, the GPT-2 model (Radford et al., 2019) outperformed other language models in a zero-shot setting, again based on self-attention.

An advantage of using attention is that it can help interpret the model by showing how the model attends to different parts of the input (Bahdanau et al., 2015; Belinkov and Glass, 2019). Various tools have been developed to visualize attention in NLP models, ranging from attention matrix heatmaps (Bahdanau et al., 2015; Rush et al., 2015; Rocktäschel et al., 2016) to bipartite graph representations (Liu et al., 2018; Lee et al., 2017; Strobelt et al., 2018). A visualization tool designed specifically for multi-head self-attention in the Transformer (Jones, 2017; Vaswani et al., 2018) was introduced in Vaswani et al. (2017).

We extend the work of Jones (2017), by visualizing attention in the Transformer at three levels of granularity: the attention-head level, the model level, and the neuron level. We also adapt the original encoder-decoder implementation to the decoder-only GPT-2 model, as well as the encoder-only BERT model.

In addition to visualizing attention for individual inputs to the model, we also analyze attention in aggregate over a large corpus to answer the following research questions:

- Does attention align with syntactic dependency relations?

- Which attention heads attend to which part-of-speech tags?

- How does attention capture long-distance relationships versus short-distance ones?

We apply our analysis to the GPT-2 small pretrained model. We find that attention follows dependency relations most strongly in the middle layers of the model, and that attention heads target particular parts of speech depending on layer depth. We also find that attention spans the greatest distance in the deepest layers, but varies significantly between heads. Finally, our method for extracting exemplar sentences yields many intuitive patterns.




*Proceedings of the Second BlackboxNLP Workshop on Analyzing and Interpreting Neural Networks for NLP*, pages 63–76
Florence, Italy, August 1, 2019. ©2019 Association for Computational Linguistics

## 2 Related Work

Recent work suggests that the Transformer implicitly encodes syntactic information such as dependency parse trees (Hewitt and Manning, 2019; Raganato and Tiedemann, 2018), anaphora (Voita et al., 2018), and subject-verb pairings (Goldberg, 2019; Wolf, 2019). Other work has shown that RNNs also capture syntax, and that deeper layers in the model capture increasingly high-level constructs (Blevins et al., 2018).

In contrast to past work that measure a model's syntactic knowledge through linguistic probing tasks, we directly compare the model's attention patterns to syntactic constructs such as dependency relations and part-of-speech tags. Raganato and Tiedemann (2018) also evaluated dependency trees induced from attention weights in a Transformer, but in the context of encoder-decoder translation models.

## 3 Transformer Architecture

**Stacked Decoder:** GPT-2 is a stacked decoder Transformer, which inputs a sequence of tokens and applies position and token embeddings followed by several decoder layers. Each layer applies multi-head self-attention (see below) in combination with a feedforward network, layer normalization, and residual connections. The GPT-2 small model has 12 layers and 12 heads.

**Self-Attention:** Given an input $x$, the self-attention mechanism assigns to each token $x_i$ a set of attention weights over the tokens in the input:

$$\text{Attn}(x_i) = (\alpha_{i,1}(x), \alpha_{i,2}(x), ..., \alpha_{i,i}(x)) \quad (1)$$

where $\alpha_{i,j}(x)$ is the attention that $x_i$ pays to $x_j$. The weights are positive and sum to one. Attention in GPT-2 is right-to-left, so $\alpha_{i,j}$ is defined only for $j \leq i$. In the multi-layer, multi-head setting, $\alpha$ is specific to a layer and head.

The attention weights $\alpha_{i,j}(x)$ are computed from the scaled dot-product of the *query vector* of $x_i$ and the *key vector* of $x_j$, followed by a softmax operation. The attention weights are then used to produce a weighted sum of value vectors:

$$\text{Attention}(Q, K, V) = \text{softmax}(\frac{QK^T}{\sqrt{d_k}})V \quad (2)$$

using query matrix $Q$, key matrix $K$, and value matrix $V$, where $d_k$ is the dimension of $K$. In a multi-head setting, the queries, keys, and values are linearly projected $h$ times, and the attention operation is performed in parallel for each representation, with the results concatenated.

## 4 Visualizing Individual Inputs

In this section, we present three visualizations of attention in the Transformer model: the attention-head view, the model view, and the neuron view. Source code and Jupyter notebooks are available at `https://github.com/jessevig/bertviz`, and a video demonstration can be found at `https://vimeo.com/339574955`. A more detailed discussion of the tool is provided in Vig (2019).

### 4.1 Attention-head View

The *attention-head view* (Figure 1) visualizes attention for one or more heads in a model layer. Self-attention is depicted as lines connecting the attending tokens (left) with the tokens being attended to (right). Colors identify the head(s), and line weight reflects the attention weight. This view closely follows the design of Jones (2017), but has been adapted to the GPT-2 model (shown in the figure) and BERT model (not shown).

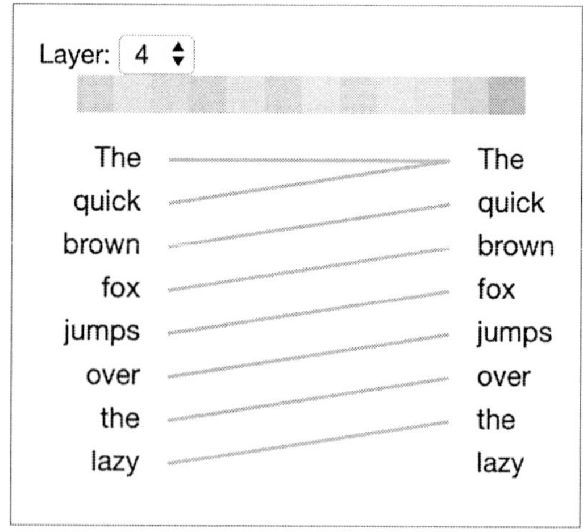


Figure 1: Attention-head view of GPT-2 for layer 4, head 11, which focuses attention on previous token.

This view helps focus on the role of specific attention heads. For instance, in the shown example, the chosen attention head attends primarily to the previous token position.

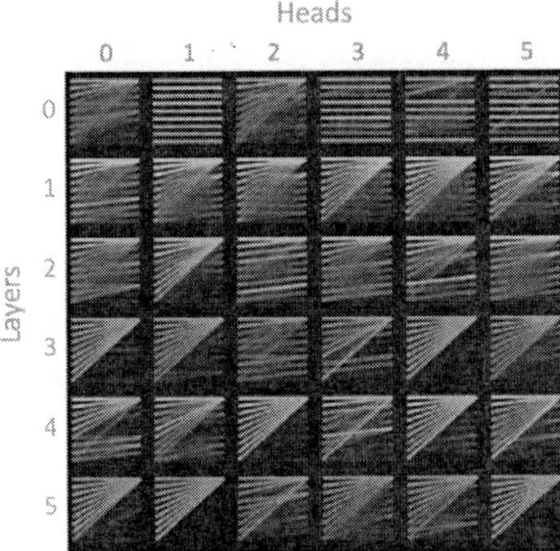

Figure 2: Model view of GPT-2, for same input as in Figure 1 (excludes layers 6–11 and heads 6–11).

## 4.2 Model View

The *model view* (Figure 2) visualizes attention across all of the model's layers and heads for a particular input. Attention heads are presented in tabular form, with rows representing layers and columns representing heads. Each head is shown in a thumbnail form that conveys the coarse shape of the attention pattern, following the *small multiples* design pattern (Tufte, 1990). Users may also click on any head to enlarge it and see the tokens.

This view facilitates the detection of coarse-grained differences between heads. For example, several heads in layer 0 share a horizontal-stripe pattern, indicating that tokens attend to the current position. Other heads have a triangular pattern, showing that they attend to the first token. In the deeper layers, some heads display a small number of highly defined lines, indicating that they are targeting specific relationships between tokens.

## 4.3 Neuron View

The *neuron view* (Figure 3) visualizes how individual neurons interact to produce attention. This view displays the queries and keys for each token, and demonstrates how attention is computed from the scaled dot product of these vectors. The element-wise product shows how specific neurons influence the dot product and hence attention.

Whereas the attention-head view and the model view show *what* attention patterns the model learns, the neuron view shows *how* the model forms these patterns. For example, it can help identify neurons responsible for specific attention patterns, as illustrated in Figure 3.

## 5 Analyzing Attention in Aggregate

In this section we explore the aggregate properties of attention across an entire corpus. We examine how attention interacts with syntax, and we compare long-distance versus short-distance relationships. We also extract exemplar sentences that reveal patterns targeted by each attention head.

### 5.1 Methods

#### 5.1.1 Part-of-Speech Tags

Past work suggests that attention heads in the Transformer may specialize in particular linguistic phenomena (Vaswani et al., 2017; Raganato and Tiedemann, 2018; Vig, 2019). We explore whether individual attention heads in GPT-2 target particular parts of speech. Specifically, we measure the proportion of total attention from a given head that focuses on tokens with a given part-of-speech tag, aggregated over a corpus:

$$
\mathrm{P}_\alpha(tag) = \frac{\sum\limits_{x \in X} \sum\limits_{i=1}^{|x|} \sum\limits_{j=1}^{i} \alpha_{i,j}(x) \cdot \mathbb{1}_{\mathrm{pos}(x_j)=tag}}{\sum\limits_{x \in X} \sum\limits_{i=1}^{|x|} \sum\limits_{j=1}^{i} \alpha_{i,j}(x)} \tag{3}
$$

where $tag$ is a part-of-speech tag, e.g., *NOUN*, $x$ is a sentence from the corpus $X$, $\alpha_{i,j}$ is the attention from $x_i$ to $x_j$ for the given head (see Section 3), and $\mathrm{pos}(x_j)$ is the part-of-speech tag of $x_j$. We also compute the share of attention directed *from* each part of speech in a similar fashion.

#### 5.1.2 Dependency Relations

Recent work shows that Transformers and recurrent models encode dependency relations (Hewitt and Manning, 2019; Raganato and Tiedemann, 2018; Liu et al., 2019). However, different models capture dependency relations at different layer depths. In a Transformer model, the middle layers were most predictive of dependencies (Liu et al., 2019; Tenney et al., 2019). Recurrent models were found to encode dependencies in lower layers for language models (Liu et al., 2019) and in deeper layers for translation models (Belinkov, 2018).

We analyze how attention aligns with dependency relations in GPT-2 by computing the proportion of attention that connects tokens that are also in a dependency relation with one another. We

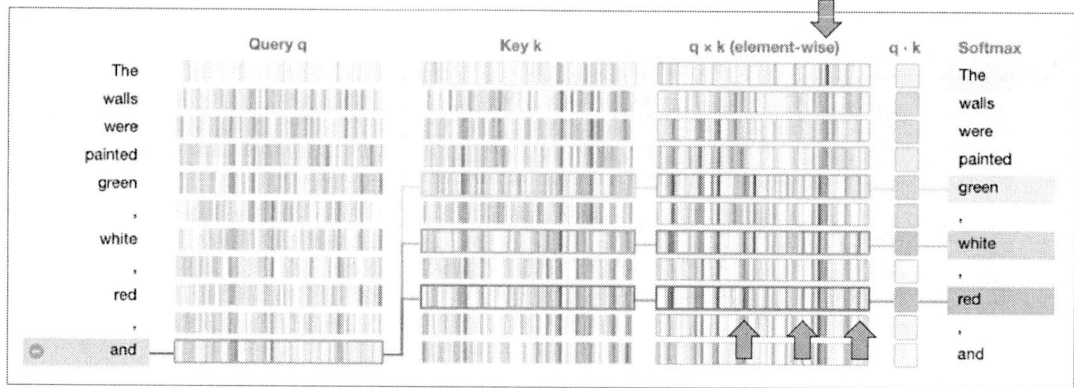

Figure 3: Neuron view for layer 8, head 6, which targets items in lists. Positive and negative values are colored blue and orange, respectively, and color saturation indicates magnitude. This view traces the computation of attention (Section 3) from the selected token on the left to each of the tokens on the right. Connecting lines are weighted based on attention between the respective tokens. The arrows (not in visualization) identify the neurons that most noticeably contribute to this attention pattern: the lower arrows point to neurons that contribute to attention towards list items, while the upper arrow identifies a neuron that helps focus attention on the first token in the sequence.

refer to this metric as *dependency alignment*:

$$\text{DepAl}_\alpha = \frac{\sum\limits_{x \in X} \sum\limits_{i=1}^{|x|} \sum\limits_{j=1}^{i} \alpha_{i,j}(x) dep(x_i, x_j)}{\sum\limits_{x \in X} \sum\limits_{i=1}^{|x|} \sum\limits_{j=1}^{i} \alpha_{i,j}(x)} \quad (4)$$

where $dep(x_i, x_j)$ is an indicator function that returns 1 if $x_i$ and $x_j$ are in a dependency relation and 0 otherwise. We run this analysis under three alternate formulations of dependency: (1) the attending token ($x_i$) is the parent in the dependency relation, (2) the token receiving attention ($x_j$) is the parent, and (3) either token is the parent.

We hypothesized that heads that focus attention based on position—for example, the head in Figure 1 that focuses on the previous token—would not align well with dependency relations, since they do not consider the content of the text. To distinguish between content-dependent and content-independent (position-based) heads, we define *attention variability*, which measures how attention varies over different inputs; high variability would suggest a content-dependent head, while low variability would indicate a content-independent head:

$$\text{Variability}_\alpha = \frac{\sum\limits_{x \in X} \sum\limits_{i=1}^{|x|} \sum\limits_{j=1}^{i} |\alpha_{i,j}(x) - \bar{\alpha}_{i,j}|}{2 \cdot \sum\limits_{x \in X} \sum\limits_{i=1}^{|x|} \sum\limits_{j=1}^{i} \alpha_{i,j}(x)} \quad (5)$$

where $\bar{\alpha}_{i,j}$ is the mean of $\alpha_{i,j}(x)$ over all $x \in X$.

Variability$_\alpha$ represents the mean absolute deviation[1] of $\alpha$ over $X$, scaled to the $[0, 1]$ interval.[2,3] Variability scores for three example attention heads are shown in Figure 4.

### 5.1.3 Attention Distance

Past work suggests that deeper layers in NLP models capture longer-distance relationships than lower layers (Belinkov, 2018; Raganato and Tiedemann, 2018). We test this hypothesis on GPT-2 by measuring the mean distance (in number of tokens) spanned by attention for each head. Specifically, we compute the average distance between token pairs in all sentences in the corpus, weighted by the attention between the tokens:

$$\bar{D}_\alpha = \frac{\sum\limits_{x \in X} \sum\limits_{i=1}^{|x|} \sum\limits_{j=1}^{i} \alpha_{i,j}(x) \cdot (i - j)}{\sum\limits_{x \in X} \sum\limits_{i=1}^{|x|} \sum\limits_{j=1}^{i} \alpha_{i,j}(x)} \quad (6)$$

We also explore whether heads with more dis-

---

[1] We considered using variance to measure attention variability; however, attention is sparse for many attention heads after filtering first-token attention (see Section 5.2.3), resulting in a very low variance (due to $\alpha_{i,j}(x) \approx 0$ and $\bar{\alpha}_{i,j} \approx 0$) for many content-sensitive attention heads. We did not use a probability distance measure, as attention values do not sum to one due to filtering first-token attention.

[2] The upper bound is 1 because the denominator is an upper bound on the numerator.

[3] When computing variability, we only include the first $N$ tokens ($N$=10) of each $x \in X$ to ensure a sufficient amount of data at each position $i$. The positional patterns appeared to be consistent across the entire sequence.

66

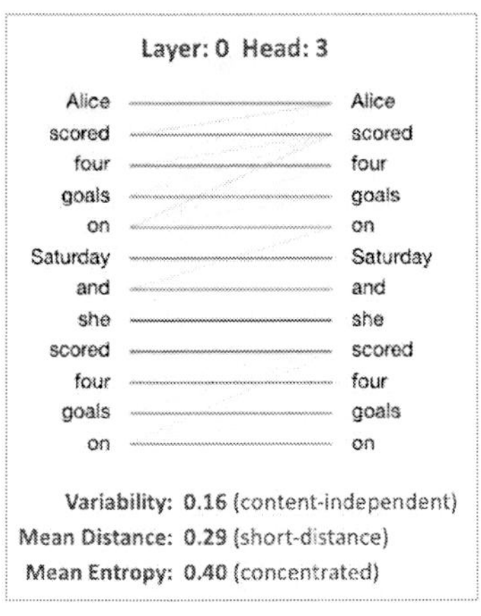


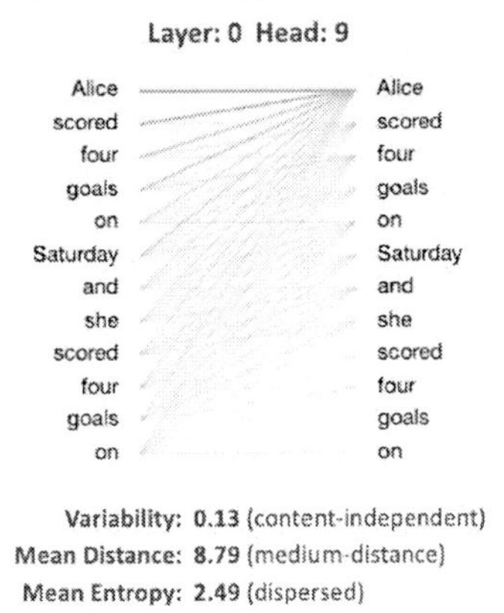


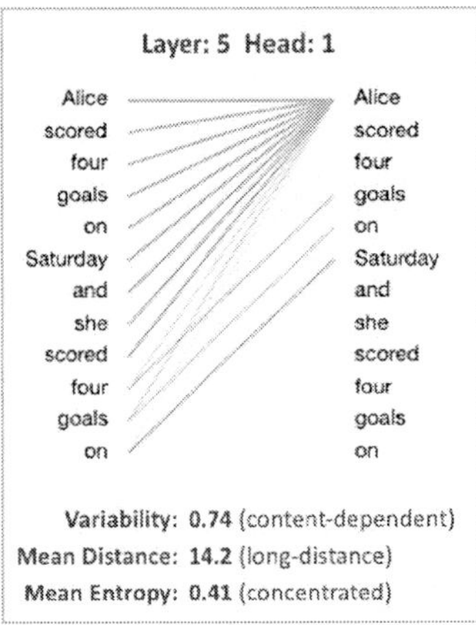


Figure 4: Attention heads in GPT-2 visualized for an example input sentence, along with aggregate metrics computed from all sentences in the corpus. Note that the average sentence length in the corpus is 27.7 tokens. **Left:** Focuses attention primarily on current token position. **Center:** Disperses attention roughly evenly across all previous tokens. **Right:** Focuses on words in repeated phrases.

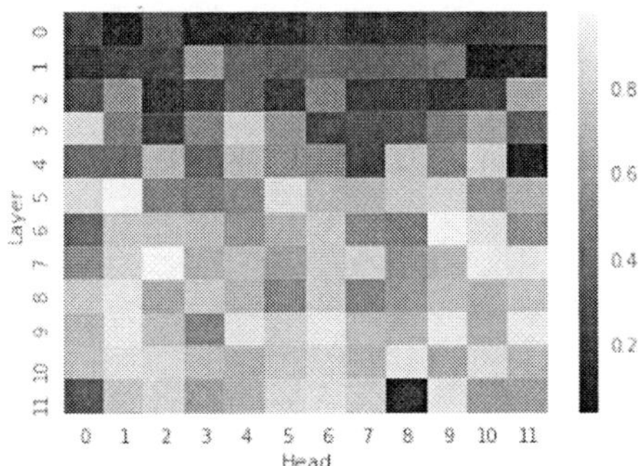

Figure 5: Proportion of attention focused on first token, broken out by layer and head.

persed attention patterns (Figure 4, center) tend to capture more distant relationships. We measure attention dispersion based on the entropy[4] of the attention distribution (Ghader and Monz, 2017):

$$\text{Entropy}_\alpha(x_i) = - \sum_{j=1}^{i} \alpha_{i,j}(x)\log(\alpha_{i,j}(x)) \quad (7)$$

Figure 4 shows the mean distance and entropy values for three example attention heads.

## 5.2 Experimental Setup

### 5.2.1 Dataset

We focused our analysis on text from English Wikipedia, which was not included in the training set for GPT-2. We first extracted 10,000 articles, and then sampled 100,000 sentences from these articles. For the qualitative analysis described later, we used the full dataset; for the quantitative analysis, we used a subset of 10,000 sentences.

### 5.2.2 Tools

We computed attention weights using the `pytorch-pretrained-BERT`[5] implementation of the GPT-2 small model. We extracted syntactic features using spaCy (Honnibal and Montani, 2017) and mapped the features from the spaCy-generated tokens to the corresponding tokens from the GPT-2 tokenizer.[6]

### 5.2.3 Filtering Null Attention

We excluded attention focused on the first token of each sentence from the analysis because it was not informative; other tokens appeared to focus on this token by default when no relevant tokens were found elsewhere in the sequence. On average, 57% of attention was directed to the first token. Some heads focused over 97% of attention to this token on average (Figure 5), which is consistent with recent work showing that individual attention heads may have little impact on overall performance (Voita et al., 2019; Michel et al., 2019). We refer to the attention directed to the first token as *null attention*.

---

[4]When computing entropy, we exclude attention to the first (null) token (see Section 5.2.3) and renormalize the remaining weights. We exclude tokens that focus over 90% of attention to the first token, to avoid a disproportionate influence from the remaining attention from these tokens.

[5]https://github.com/huggingface/pytorch-pretrained-BERT

[6]In cases where the GPT-2 tokenizer split a word into multiple pieces, we assigned the features to all word pieces.

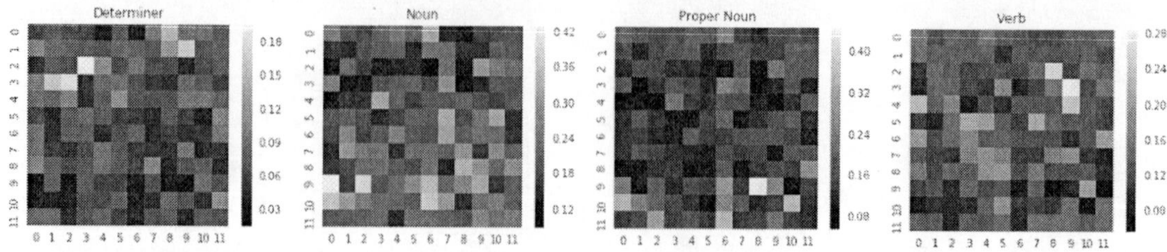

Figure 6: Each heatmap shows the proportion of total attention directed *to* the given part of speech, broken out by layer (vertical axis) and head (horizontal axis). Scales vary by tag. Results for all tags available in appendix.

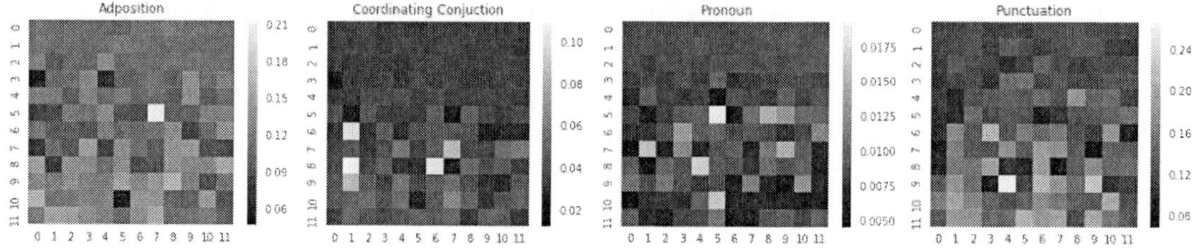

Figure 7: Each heatmap shows the proportion of total attention that originates *from* the given part of speech, broken out by layer (vertical axis) and head (horizontal axis). Scales vary by tag. Results for all tags available in appendix.

## 5.3 Results

### 5.3.1 Part-of-Speech Tags

Figure 6 shows the share of attention directed *to* various part-of-speech tags (Eq. 3) broken out by layer and head. Most tags are disproportionately targeted by one or more attention heads. For example, nouns receive 43% of attention in layer 9, head 0, compared to a mean of 21% over all heads. For 13 of 16 tags, a head exists with an attention share more than double the mean for the tag.

The attention heads that focus on a particular tag tend to cluster by layer depth. For example, the top five heads targeting proper nouns are all in the last three layers of the model. This may be due to several attention heads in the deeper layers focusing on named entities (see Section 5.4), which may require the broader context available in the deeper layers. In contrast, the top five heads targeting determiners—a lower-level construct—are all in the first four layers of the model. This is consistent with previous findings showing that deeper layers focus on higher-level properties (Blevins et al., 2018; Belinkov, 2018).

Figure 7 shows the proportion of attention directed *from* various parts of speech. The values appear to be roughly uniform in the initial layers of the model. The reason is that the heads in these layers pay little attention to the first (null) token (Figure 5), and therefore the remaining (non-null) attention weights sum to a value close to one. Thus, the net weight for each token in the weighted sum (Section 5.1.1) is close to one, and the proportion reduces to the frequency of the part of speech in the corpus.

Beyond the initial layers, attention heads specialize in focusing attention from particular part-of-speech tags. However, the effect is less pronounced compared to the tags receiving attention; for 7 out of 16 tags, there is a head that focuses attention from that tag with a frequency more than double the tag average. Many of these specialized heads also cluster by layer. For example, the top ten heads for focusing attention from punctuation are all in the last six layers.

### 5.3.2 Dependency Relations

Figure 8 shows the dependency alignment scores (Eq. 4) broken out by layer. Attention aligns with dependency relations most strongly in the middle layers, consistent with recent syntactic probing analyses (Liu et al., 2019; Tenney et al., 2019).

One possible explanation for the low alignment in the initial layers is that many heads in these layers focus attention based on position rather than content, according to the attention variability (Eq. 5) results in Figure 10. Figure 4 (left and center) shows two examples of position-focused heads from layer 0 that have relatively low dependency alignment[7] (0.04 and 0.10, respectively); the first

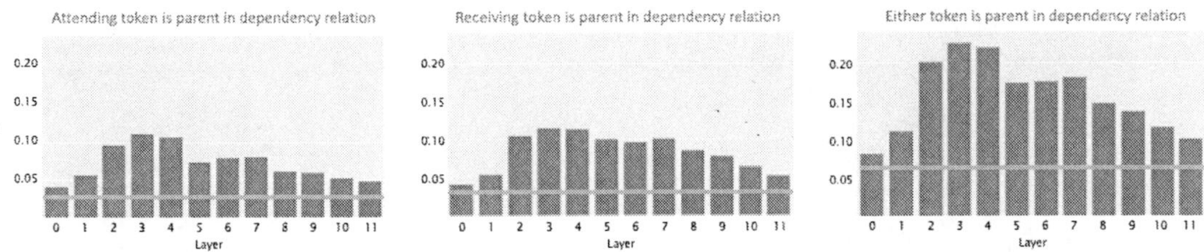

Figure 8: Proportion of attention that is aligned with dependency relations, aggregated by layer. The orange line shows the baseline proportion of token pairs that share a dependency relationship, independent of attention.

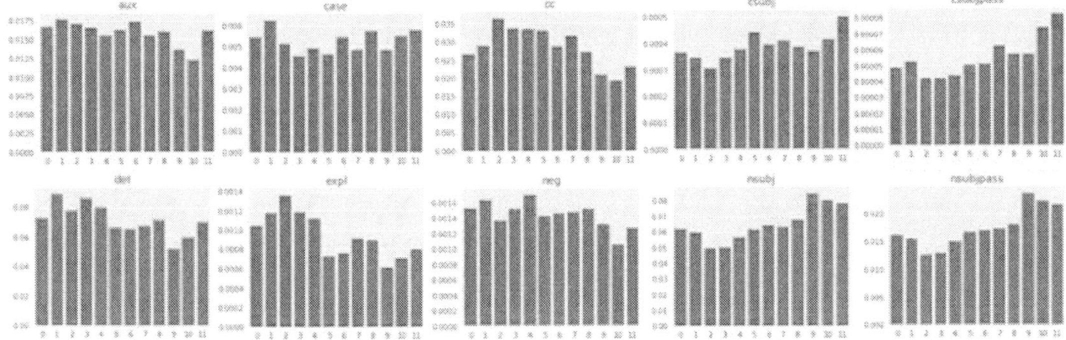

Figure 9: Proportion of attention directed to various dependency types, broken out by layer.

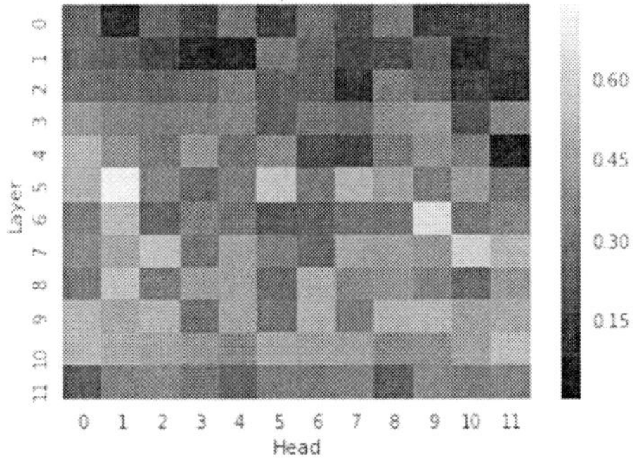

Figure 10: Attention variability by layer / head. High-values indicate content-dependent heads, and low values indicate content-independent (position-based) heads.

head focuses attention primarily on the current token position (which cannot be in a dependency relation with itself) and the second disperses attention roughly evenly, without regard to content.

An interesting counterexample is layer 4, head 11 (Figure 1), which has the highest dependency alignment out of all the heads (DepAl$_\alpha$ = $0.42)^7$ but is also the most position-focused (Variability$_\alpha$ = 0.004). This head focuses attention on the previous token, which in our corpus has a 42% chance of being in a dependency rela-

tion with the adjacent token. As we'll discuss in the next section, token distance is highly predictive of dependency relations.

One hypothesis for why attention diverges from dependency relations in the deeper layers is that several attention heads in these layers target very specific constructs (Tables 1 and 2) as opposed to more general dependency relations. The deepest layers also target longer-range relationships (see next section), whereas dependency relations span relatively short distances (3.89 tokens on average).

We also analyzed the specific dependency types of tokens receiving attention (Figure 9). Subjects (csubj, csubjpass, nsubj, nsubjpass) were targeted more in deeper layers, while auxiliaries (aux), conjunctions (cc), determiners (det), expletives (expl), and negations (neg) were targeted more in lower layers, consistent with previous findings (Belinkov, 2018). For some other dependency types, the interpretations were less clear.

### 5.3.3 Attention Distance

We found that attention distance (Eq. 6) is greatest in the deepest layers (Figure 11, right), confirming that these layers capture longer-distance relationships. Attention distance varies greatly across heads ($SD = 3.6$), even when the heads are in the same layer, due to the wide variation in attention structures (e.g., Figure 4 left and center).

---

$^7$Assuming relation may be in either direction.

69

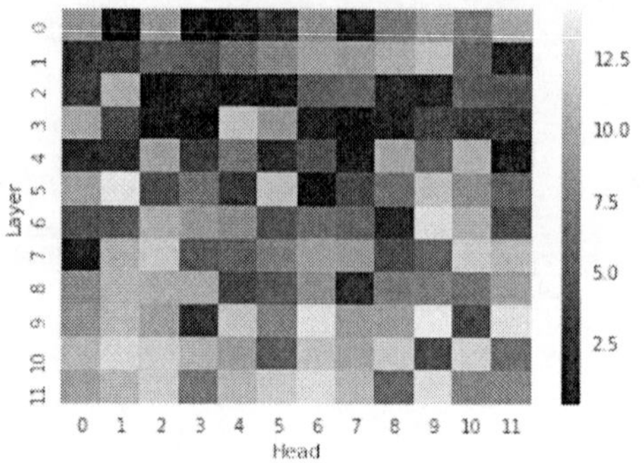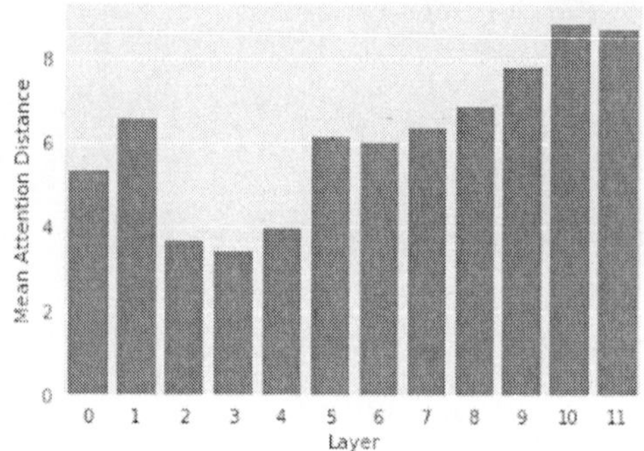

Figure 11: Mean attention distance by layer / head (left), and by layer (right).

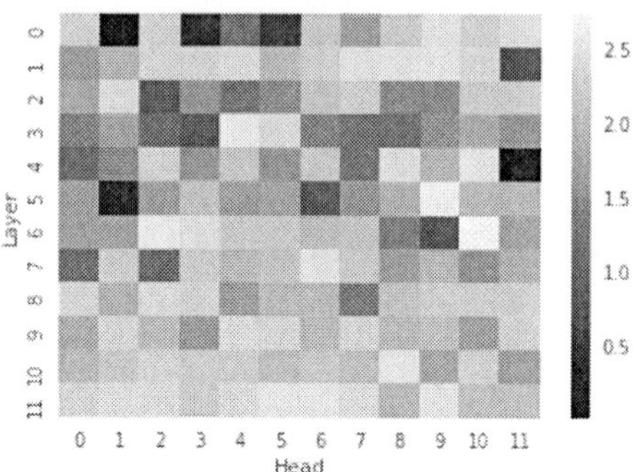

Figure 12: Mean attention entropy by layer / head. Higher values indicate more diffuse attention.

We also explored the relationship between attention distance and attention entropy (Eq. 7), which measures how diffuse an attention pattern is. Overall, we found a moderate correlation ($r = 0.61$, $p < 0.001$) between the two. As Figure 12 shows, many heads in layers 0 and 1 have high entropy (e.g., Figure 4, center), which may explain why these layers have a higher attention distance compared to layers 2–4.

One counterexample is layer 5, head 1 (Figure 4, right), which has the highest mean attention distance of any head (14.2), and one of the lowest mean entropy scores (0.41). This head concentrates attention on individual words in repeated phrases, which often occur far apart from one another.

We also explored how attention distance relates to dependency alignment. Across all heads, we found a negative correlation between the two quantities ($r = -0.73$, $p < 0.001$). This is consistent with the fact that the probability of two tokens sharing a dependency relation decreases as the distance between them increases[8]; for exam-

---

[8]This is true up to a distance of 18 tokens; 99.8% of dependency relations occur within this distance.

ple, the probability of being in a dependency relation is 0.42 for adjacent tokens, 0.07 for tokens at a distance of 5, and 0.02 for tokens at a distance of 10. The layers (2–4) in which attention spanned the shortest distance also had the highest dependency alignment.

## 5.4 Qualitative Analysis

To get a sense of the lexical patterns targeted by each attention head, we extracted exemplar sentences that most strongly induced attention in that head. Specifically, we ranked sentences by the maximum token-to-token attention weight within each sentence. Results for three attention heads are shown in Tables 1–3. We found other attention heads that detected entities (people, places, dates), passive verbs, acronyms, nicknames, paired punctuation, and other syntactic and semantic properties. Most heads captured multiple types of patterns.

## 6 Conclusion

In this paper, we analyzed the structure of attention in the GPT-2 Transformer language model. We found that many attention heads specialize in particular part-of-speech tags and that different tags are targeted at different layer depths. We also found that the deepest layers capture the most distant relationships, and that attention aligns most strongly with dependency relations in the middle layers where attention distance is lowest.

Our qualitative analysis revealed that the structure of attention is closely tied to the training objective; for GPT-2, which was trained using left-to-right language modeling, attention often focused on words most relevant to predicting the next token in the sequence. For future work, we would like to extend the analysis to other Transformer models such as BERT, which has a bidi-

| Rank | Sentence |
|---|---|
| 1 | The Australian search and rescue service is provided by Aus S AR , which is part of the Australian Maritime *Safety* Authority ( **AM** SA ). |
| 2 | In 1925 , Bapt ists worldwide formed the Baptist *World* Alliance ( **B** WA ). |
| 3 | The Oak dale D ump is listed as an Environmental Protection Agency Super fund site due to the contamination of residential drinking water wells with *volatile* organic compounds ( V OC s ) and heavy metals . |

Table 1: Exemplar sentences for layer 10, head 10, which focuses attention from acronyms to the associated phrase. The tokens with maximum attention are underlined; the attending token is bolded and the token receiving attention is italicized. It appears that attention is directed to the part of the phrase that would help the model choose the *next* word piece in the acronym (after the token paying attention), reflecting the language modeling objective.

| Rank | Sentence |
|---|---|
| 1 | After the two prototypes were completed , production began in Mar iet *ta* **,** Georgia , ... |
| 3 | The fictional character Sam Fisher of the Spl inter Cell video game series by Ubisoft was born in Tow *son* **,** as well as residing in a town house , as stated in the novel izations ... |
| 4 | Suicide bombers attack three hotels in Am *man* **,** Jordan , killing at least 60 people . |

Table 2: Exemplar sentences for layer 11, head 2, which focuses attention from commas to the preceding place name (or the last word piece thereof). The likely purpose of this attention head is to help the model choose the related place name that would follow the comma, e.g. the country or state in which the city is located.

| Rank | Sentence |
|---|---|
| 1 | With the United States isolation ist and Britain stout ly refusing to make the ” continental commitment ” to defend France on the same scale as in World War I , the *prospects* of Anglo - American assistance in another war with **Germany** appeared to be doubtful ... |
| 2 | The show did receive a somewhat favorable review from noted critic Gilbert Se ld es in the December 15 , 1962 TV Guide : ” The whole *notion* on which The Beverly Hill bill ies is **founded** is an encouragement to ignorance ... |
| 3 | he Arch im edes won significant market share in the education markets of the UK , Ireland , Australia and New Zealand ; the *success* of the Arch im edes in British **schools** was due partly to its predecessor the BBC Micro and later to the Comput ers for Schools scheme ... |

Table 3: Exemplar sentences for layer 11, head 10 which focuses attention from the end of a noun phrase to the head noun. In the first sentence, for example, the head noun is *prospects* and the remainder of the noun phrase is *of Anglo - American assistance in another war with* **Germany**. The purpose of this attention pattern is likely to predict the word (typically a verb) that follows the noun phrase, as the head noun is a strong predictor of this.

rectional architecture and is trained on both token-level and sentence-level tasks.

Although the Wikipedia sentences used in our analysis cover a diverse range of topics, they all follow a similar encyclopedic format and style. Further study is needed to determine how attention patterns manifest in other types of content, such as dialog scripts or song lyrics. We would also like to analyze attention patterns in text much longer than a single sentence, especially for new Transformer variants such as the Transformer-XL (Dai et al., 2019) and Sparse Transformer (Child et al., 2019), which can handle very long contexts.

We believe that interpreting a model based on attention is complementary to linguistic probing approaches (Section 2). While linguistic probing precisely quantifies the amount of information encoded in various components of the model, it requires training and evaluating a probing classifier. Analyzing attention is a simpler process that also produces human-interpretable descriptions of model behavior, though recent work casts doubt on its role in explaining individual predictions (Jain and Wallace, 2019). The results of our analyses were often consistent with those from probing approaches.

## 7 Acknowledgements

Y.B. was supported by the Harvard Mind, Brain, and Behavior Initiative.

## References

Dzmitry Bahdanau, Kyunghyun Cho, and Yoshua Bengio. 2015. Neural machine translation by jointly learning to align and translate. In *International Conference on Learning Representations (ICLR)*.

Yonatan Belinkov. 2018. *On Internal Language Representations in Deep Learning: An Analysis of Machine Translation and Speech Recognition*. Ph.D. thesis, Massachusetts Institute of Technology.

Yonatan Belinkov and James Glass. 2019. Analysis methods in neural language processing: A survey. *Transactions of the Association for Computational Linguistics*, 7:49–72.

Terra Blevins, Omer Levy, and Luke Zettlemoyer. 2018. Deep RNNs encode soft hierarchical syntax. *arXiv preprint arXiv:1805.04218*.

Rewon Child, Scott Gray, Alec Radford, and Ilya Sutskever. 2019. Generating long sequences with sparse transformers. *arXiv preprint arXiv:1904.10509*.

Zihang Dai, Zhilin Yang, Yiming Yang, Jaime G. Carbonell, Quoc V. Le, and Ruslan Salakhutdinov. 2019. Transformer-XL: Attentive language models beyond a fixed-length context.

Jacob Devlin, Ming-Wei Chang, Kenton Lee, and Kristina Toutanova. 2018. BERT: Pre-training of deep bidirectional transformers for language understanding. *arXiv preprint arXiv:1810.04805*.

Hamidreza Ghader and Christof Monz. 2017. What does attention in neural machine translation pay attention to? In *Proceedings of the Eighth International Joint Conference on Natural Language Processing (Volume 1: Long Papers)*, pages 30–39.

Yoav Goldberg. 2019. Assessing BERT's syntactic abilities. *arXiv preprint arXiv:1901.05287*.

John Hewitt and Christopher D. Manning. 2019. A structural probe for finding syntax in word representations. In *Proceedings of the Conference of the North American Chapter of the Association for Computational Linguistics: Human Language Technologies*.

Matthew Honnibal and Ines Montani. 2017. spaCy 2: Natural language understanding with Bloom embeddings, convolutional neural networks and incremental parsing. *To appear*.

Sarthak Jain and Byron C. Wallace. 2019. Attention is not explanation. *CoRR*, abs/1902.10186.

Llion Jones. 2017. Tensor2tensor transformer visualization. `https://github.com/tensorflow/tensor2tensor/tree/master/tensor2tensor/visualization`.

Jaesong Lee, Joong-Hwi Shin, and Jun-Seok Kim. 2017. Interactive visualization and manipulation of attention-based neural machine translation. In *Proceedings of the 2017 Conference on Empirical Methods in Natural Language Processing: System Demonstrations*.

Nelson F. Liu, Matt Gardner, Yonatan Belinkov, Matthew Peters, and Noah A. Smith. 2019. Linguistic knowledge and transferability of contextual representations. In *Proceedings of the 17th Annual Conference of the North American Chapter of the Association for Computational Linguistics: Human Language Technologies (NAACL-HLT)*.

Shusen Liu, Tao Li, Zhimin Li, Vivek Srikumar, Valerio Pascucci, and Peer-Timo Bremer. 2018. Visual interrogation of attention-based models for natural language inference and machine comprehension. In *Proceedings of the 2018 Conference on Empirical Methods in Natural Language Processing: System Demonstrations*.

Paul Michel, Omer Levy, and Graham Neubig. 2019. Are sixteen heads really better than one? *arXiv preprint arXiv:1905.10650*.

Matthew Peters, Mark Neumann, Mohit Iyyer, Matt Gardner, Christopher Clark, Kenton Lee, and Luke Zettlemoyer. 2018. Deep contextualized word representations. In *Proceedings of the 2018 Conference of the North American Chapter of the Association for Computational Linguistics: Human Language Technologies, Volume 1 (Long Papers)*, pages 2227–2237. Association for Computational Linguistics.

Alec Radford, Karthik Narasimhan, Tim Salimans, and Ilya Sutskever. 2018. Improving language understanding by generative pre-training. Technical report.

Alec Radford, Jeffrey Wu, Rewon Child, David Luan, Dario Amodei, and Ilya Sutskever. 2019. Language models are unsupervised multitask learners. Technical report.

Alessandro Raganato and Jörg Tiedemann. 2018. An analysis of encoder representations in Transformer-based machine translation. In *Proceedings of the 2018 EMNLP Workshop BlackboxNLP: Analyzing and Interpreting Neural Networks for NLP*, pages 287–297. Association for Computational Linguistics.

Tim Rocktäschel, Edward Grefenstette, Karl Moritz Hermann, Tomas Kocisky, and Phil Blunsom. 2016. Reasoning about entailment with neural attention. In *International Conference on Learning Representations (ICLR)*.

Alexander M. Rush, Sumit Chopra, and Jason Weston. 2015. A neural attention model for abstractive sentence summarization. In *Proceedings of the 2015 Conference on Empirical Methods in Natural Language Processing*.

H. Strobelt, S. Gehrmann, M. Behrisch, A. Perer, H. Pfister, and A. M. Rush. 2018. Seq2Seq-Vis: A Visual Debugging Tool for Sequence-to-Sequence Models. *ArXiv e-prints*.

Ian Tenney, Dipanjan Das, and Ellie Pavlick. 2019. BERT rediscovers the classical NLP pipeline. In *Proceedings of the Association for Computational Linguistics*.

Edward Tufte. 1990. *Envisioning Information*. Graphics Press, Cheshire, CT, USA.

Ashish Vaswani, Samy Bengio, Eugene Brevdo, Francois Chollet, Aidan N. Gomez, Stephan Gouws, Llion Jones, Łukasz Kaiser, Nal Kalchbrenner, Niki Parmar, Ryan Sepassi, Noam Shazeer, and Jakob Uszkoreit. 2018. Tensor2tensor for neural machine translation. *CoRR*, abs/1803.07416.

Ashish Vaswani, Noam Shazeer, Niki Parmar, Jakob Uszkoreit, Llion Jones, Aidan N Gomez, Ł ukasz Kaiser, and Illia Polosukhin. 2017. Attention is all you need. *arXiv preprint arXiv:1706.03762*.

Jesse Vig. 2019. A multiscale visualization of attention in the Transformer model. In *Proceedings of the Association for Computational Linguistics: System Demonstrations*.

Elena Voita, Pavel Serdyukov, Rico Sennrich, and Ivan Titov. 2018. Context-aware neural machine translation learns anaphora resolution. In *Proceedings of the 56th Annual Meeting of the Association for Computational Linguistics (Volume 1: Long Papers)*, pages 1264–1274. Association for Computational Linguistics.

Elena Voita, David Talbot, Fedor Moiseev, Rico Sennrich, and Ivan Titov. 2019. Analyzing multi-head self-attention: Specialized heads do the heavy lifting, the rest can be pruned. *arXiv preprint arXiv:1905.09418*.

Thomas Wolf. 2019. Some additional experiments extending the tech report "Assessing BERTs syntactic abilities" by Yoav Goldberg. Technical report.

# A   Appendix

Figures A.1 and A.2 shows the results from Figures 6 and 7 for the full set of part-of-speech tags.

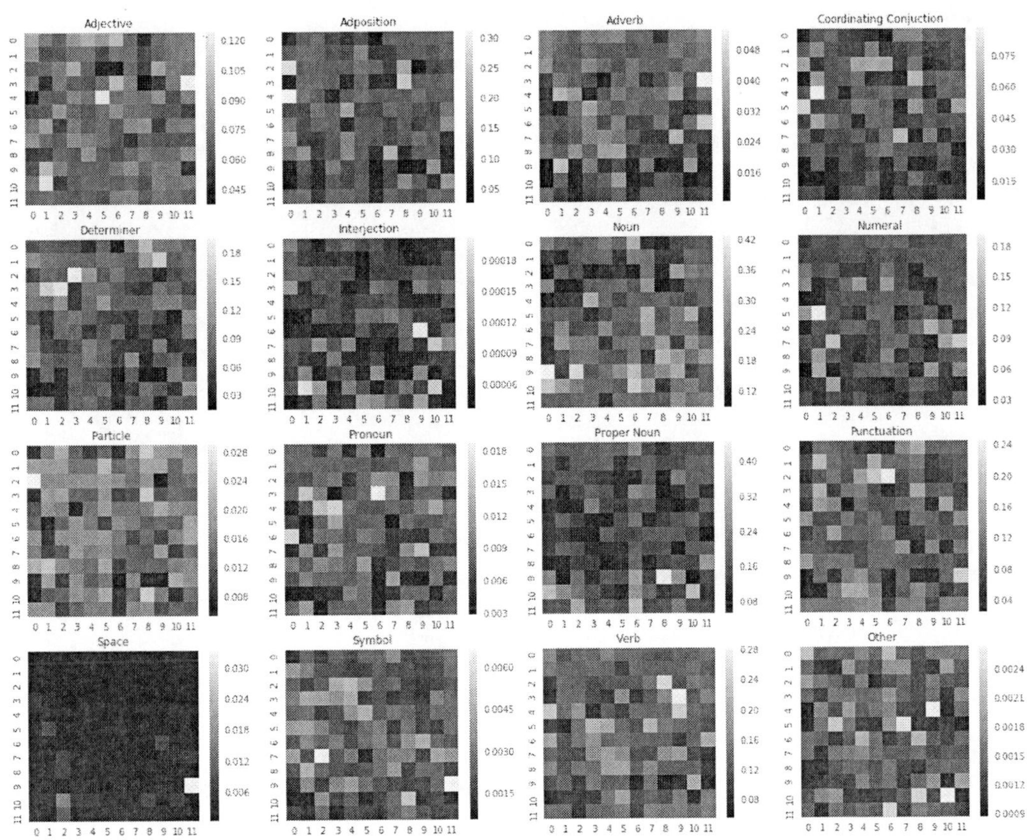

Figure A.1: Each heatmap shows the proportion of total attention directed *to* the given part of speech, broken out by layer (vertical axis) and head (horizontal axis).

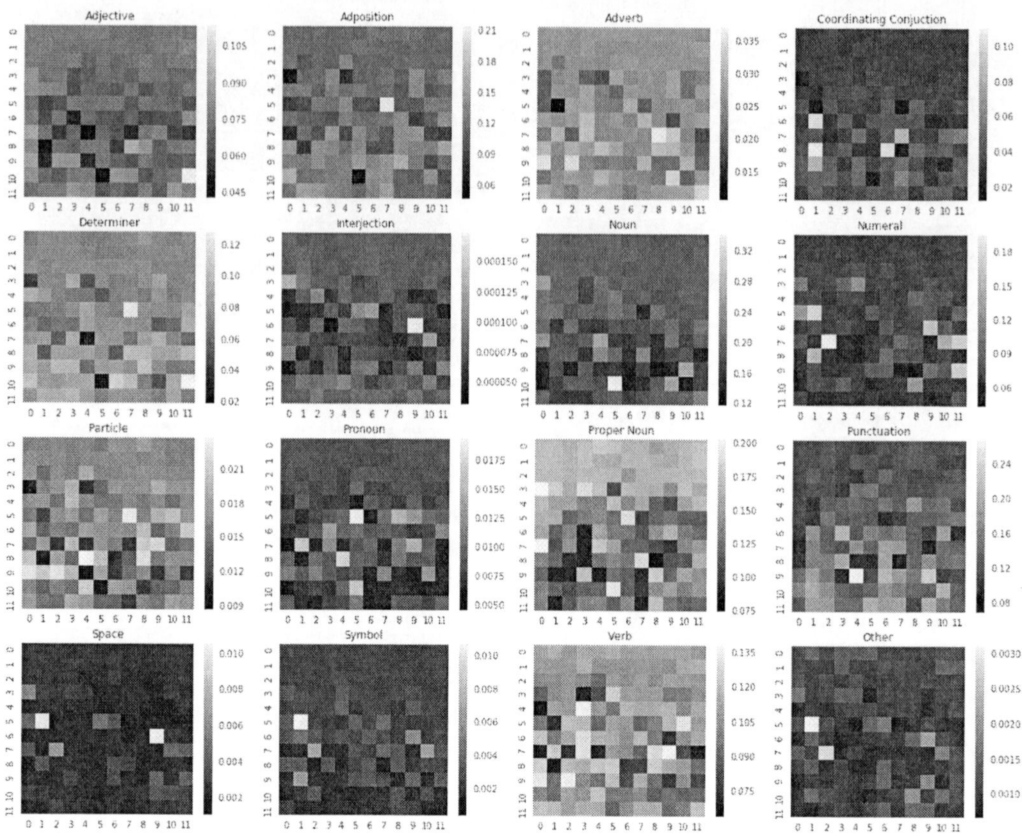

Figure A.2: Each heatmap shows the proportion of attention originating *from* the given part of speech, broken out by layer (vertical axis) and head (horizontal axis).

# Detecting Political Bias in News Articles Using Headline Attention


**Rama Rohit Reddy**
International Institute of
Information Technology,
Hyderabad
ramarohitreddy.g
@research.iiit.ac.in

**Suma Reddy Duggenpudi**
International Institute of
Information Technology,
Hyderabad
sumareddy.duggenpudi
@research.iiit.ac.in

**Radhika Mamidi**
International Institute of
Information Technology,
Hyderabad
radhika.mamidi
@iiit.ac.in



## Abstract

Language is a powerful tool which can be used to state the facts as well as express our views and perceptions. Most of the times, we find a subtle bias towards or against someone or something. When it comes to politics, media houses and journalists are known to create bias by shrewd means such as misinterpreting reality and distorting viewpoints towards some parties. This misinterpretation on a large scale can lead to the production of biased news and conspiracy theories. Automating bias detection in newspaper articles could be a good challenge for research in NLP.

We proposed a headline attention network for this bias detection. Our model has two distinctive characteristics: (i) it has a structure that mirrors a person's way of reading a news article (ii) it has attention mechanism applied on the article based on its headline, enabling it to attend to more critical content to predict bias. As the required datasets were not available, we created a dataset comprising of 1329 news articles collected from various Telugu newspapers and marked them for bias towards a particular political party. The experiments conducted on it demonstrated that our model outperforms various baseline methods by a substantial margin.


## 1 Introduction

News bias is a ubiquitous phenomenon, potentially present in most of the newspapers. The first step in challenging biased news is documenting bias. So detection of the inclination of a news article towards a political party has gained attention today. Such news articles are mostly selected and analyzed manually using a process called coding or theoretical frameworks like discourse analysis and content analysis. This analysis requires a lot of effort, concentration, attention to detail and is also time taking. Thus automating this bias detection in a news article could be very helpful and necessary for media verification.

Media bias can be observed and defined through various factors. In political domain, it ranges from selectively publishing articles to specifically choosing to highlight some events, parties and leaders. We also come across articles where bias can be detected by observing the unclear assumptions, loaded language, or lack of proper context. Especially during the election campaigning due to several unjust factors, media houses often align themselves either for or against some specific parties and instead of reporting just the content, they subtly add their stand towards it. This is usually reflected in the headline, and making the headline biased has an effect on the reader who reads the article after registering the headline subconsciously. As there was no dataset marked for political bias available in Telugu, we created a dataset comprising of 1329 news articles collected from various Telugu newspapers and annotated them for bias towards a political party. The bias is marked as None if the article is unbiased.

Telugu is an agglutinative Dravidian language spoken widely in two states of India namely Telangana and Andhra Pradesh. According to Ethnologue[1] list of most spoken languages worldwide, Telugu ranks fifteenth in the list, and a total of 85 million Telugu native speakers exist across the world. There are only 5 major political parties present in the two Telugu speaking states. We treat the problem of political bias detection as a classification problem. The political parties can be treated as labels and the goal will be to assign labels to each news article. Any news article deviating its reader from the original news towards a political party is considered biased. Traditional approaches of text classification represent

---

[1] https://www.ethnologue.com/statistics/size

77


*Proceedings of the Second BlackboxNLP Workshop on Analyzing and Interpreting Neural Networks for NLP*, pages 77–84
Florence, Italy, August 1, 2019. ©2019 Association for Computational Linguistics

documents with sparse lexical features, such as n-grams, and then use a linear model or kernel methods on this representation (Wang and Manning, 2012; Joachims, 1998). More recent approaches used deep learning, such as convolutional neural networks (Kalchbrenner et al., 2014) and recurrent neural networks based on long short-term memory (LSTM) (Hochreiter and Schmidhuber, 1997) to learn text representations.

Although neural-network based approaches have been quite effective, classification based only on articles or only on headlines may not give better results as articles may contain unnecessary extra information and headlines being short may not capture required information. So a combination of article and headline is required for better classification. In this paper, we test our hypothesis that classification can be improved by focusing on essential parts of news articles based on their headlines. Since headlines are designed to be short and catchy, journalists tend to exploit them to express their ideological view of the news stories and depending on these headlines the interpretation of the stories can change. So the intuition underlying our model is that bias in an article can be effectively found by focusing on essential parts of articles based on their headlines.

Our contributions in this paper are (i) The creation and annotation of a newspaper dataset for political bias detection, (ii) The proposal of a neural network architecture, the Headline Attention Network that is designed to capture the important parts of news article causing political bias by paying headline attention.Generally, readers first read the headlines and then go through the news article with those headlines in their mind. Thus attention is paid on news article with its headline in reader's mind. Headline Attention Networks are designed to do the same thing and find important parts that reflect bias in news articles. To illustrate, consider the example in Figure 1. In the figure, importance of each highlighted word in causing bias is directly proportional to the intensity of the blue colour in highlighting[2]. So focusing more on these words according to their importance would give better results rather than focusing on all words.The key difference to other neural networks is that our system focuses on the importance of headline for political bias detection in an article and discover which

sequence of tokens are relevant rather than simply filtering out. Our model outperforms various common classification architectures by a significant margin.

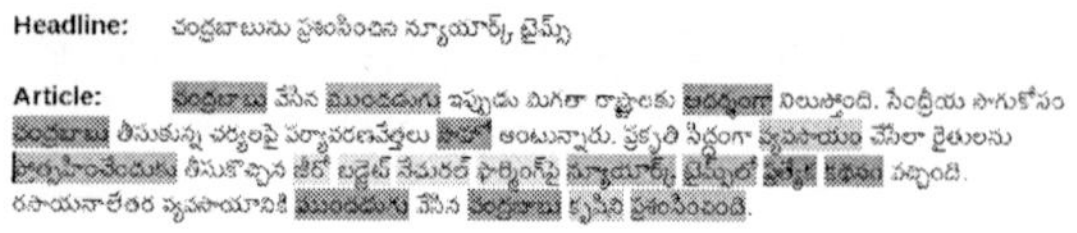

**Headline:** చంద్రబాబును ప్రశంసించిన న్యూయార్క్ టైమ్స్

**Article:** చంద్రబాబు చేసిన ముందడుగు ఇప్పుడు మిగిలా రాష్ట్రాలకు ఆదర్శంగా నిలుస్తుంది. సేంద్రియ సాగుకోసం చంద్రబాబు తీసుకున్న చర్యలపై పర్యావరణవేత్తలు హర్షం అంటున్నారు. ప్రకృతి సిద్ధంగా వ్యవసాయం చేసేలా రైతులను ప్రోత్సహించేందుకు తీసుకొచ్చిన జీరో బడ్జెట్ నేచురల్ ఫార్మింగ్‌పై న్యూయార్క్ టైమ్స్‌లో కూడా కథనం సర్యింది. రసాయనాలేతర వ్యవసాయానికి ముందడుగు చేసిన చంద్రబాబు కృషిని ప్రశంసించింది.

Figure 1: News article from the dataset. Bias towards "TDP"

## 2 Related Work

Identification and analysis of bias in news articles has led to extensive research in the fields of anthropology, discourse analysis, and media studies. (Sivandi and Dowlatabadi, 2015) used the headlines and leads of newspaper articles to detect bias in their complete linguistic approach to the problem.

(Iyyer et al., 2014) used recursive neural networks to detect political ideology.

(Rashkin et al., 2017) introduced a propagandists dataset focused propaganda news and presented a study on the language of news media in context of political fact checking.

(Recasens et al., 2013) conducted a study related to bias in the Wikipedia articles using logisitc regression.

Many industrial organizations are working in this space worldwide to fight disinformation. **First Draft News** is a project "to fight mis- and disinformation online" founded by 9 organizations brought together by the Google News Lab. **Full Fact** is a charity based in London to check and correct facts reported in the news. **CrossCheck** is a new initiative from Google Labs and First Draft to support truth and verification in Media.

In Telugu, a small amount of work is done on news data. (Mukku et al., 2016) apply ML techniques for Sentiment Analysis of Telugu news articles. (Gangula and Mamidi, 2018) performed multidomain sentiment analysis in Telugu.

## 3 Dataset

Our aim is to detect the bias of a newspaper article towards a particular political party. An article is said to be biased if it is inclined or prejudiced for or against a political party. We created a

---

[2]Translation, explanation and visualizations of Headline attention are given in Supplement Material

dataset[3] containing headline of the article, article and the political party towards which it is biased. We marked it with label "None" if it was unbiased. The statistics of the dataset is shown in Table 1.

Four annotators annotated each article in the dataset with one of the 5 parties namely BJP, TDP, Congress, TRS, YCP or as None if the article is unbiased. The annotators are native Telugu speakers with good proficiency in the language. While choosing annotators care was taken that they do not have any bias towards any party and have sufficient political knowledge. The following annotation guidelines were followed: Each article along with the headline was presented to the annotators. They were asked to read them just as they read newspapers. After reading, they were asked to annotate whether the article was subjectively biased towards or against a party or is unbiased. A Kappa score of 0.9 was achieved through multiple discussions.

Figure 6 presented in supplemental Material shows some of the examples from our dataset. We can see in the examples below that there is some inherent bias towards a party in the way a particular newspaper has reported. This could be due to several factors like the ownership of the media house, the present power of a party (ruling or opposition), and the ideology of the target group of readers that particular newspaper is catering to. Many a times, political parties themselves establish media houses and newspaper agencies to increase their outreach and glorify their party. This greatly contributes to bias in the published articles.

| Parties | Documents | Sentences | Words | avg #w in headline | avg #w in article |
|---|---|---|---|---|---|
| BJP | 182 | 2244 | 24863 | 4.13 | 132.48 |
| Congress | 82 | 1031 | 11410 | 4.06 | 135.08 |
| TRS | 151 | 1860 | 21685 | 4.09 | 139.52 |
| TDP | 361 | 3484 | 40495 | 3.86 | 108.3 |
| YCP | 335 | 1958 | 22370 | 3.79 | 62.98 |
| Unbiased | 218 | 1546 | 19245 | 4.09 | 65.14 |
| Total | 1329 | 12123 | 140068 | 3.95 | 98.3 |

Table 1: Data statistics: #w denotes the number of words per document

## 4 Headline Attention Networks

The overall architecture of the Headline Attention Network is shown in Figure 2. It consists of several parts: a headline encoder, an article encoder and a headline attention layer. We describe the details of these components below.



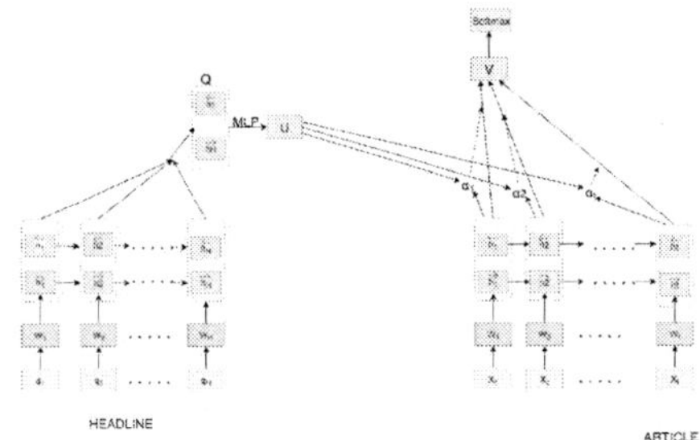

Figure 2: Headline Attention Network

### 4.1 Model

We focus on classifying a given article as biased towards one of the political parties in this work. Assume that the article has T words, $w_i$ with i $\in [1, T]$ represents the $i^{th}$ word in article and headline has H words, $q_i$ with i $\in [1, H]$ represents $i^{th}$ word in headline of the article. The proposed model projects the raw articles into a vector representation which can be used for classification. In the following, we will present this method of projection.

#### 4.1.1 Headline Encoder

Given the headline of an article with words $q_i$, i $\in [1, H]$, we first embed the words into vectors through an embedding matrix $W_e$, $x_i = W_e q_i$. We use a bidirectional LSTM to get contextual encoding of headline from both the directions. The bidirectional LSTM contains a forward LSTM $\overrightarrow{f}$ which reads headline from $q_1$ to $q_H$ and a backward LSTM $\overleftarrow{f}$ which reads headline from $q_H$ to $q_1$:

$$x_i = W_e q_i, i \in [1, H] \quad (1)$$

$$\overrightarrow{h_i} = \overrightarrow{LSTM}(x_i) i \in [1, H] \quad (2)$$

$$\overleftarrow{h_i} = \overleftarrow{LSTM}(x_i) i \in [H, 1] \quad (3)$$

We encode the headline of the article by concatenating the forward representation $\overrightarrow{h_H}$ and the backward representation $\overleftarrow{h_1}$, i.e, Q=$[\overleftarrow{h_1}, \overrightarrow{h_H}]$ is the representation of the article headline.

#### 4.1.2 Article Encoder

An article is nothing but a sequence of words. We embed these words into vectors and use bidirectional LSTM to get annotations of the words by summarizing information from both direction for words and therefore incorporating contextual information in the annotation. We encode article as:

$$x_i = W_e w_i, i \in [1, T] \quad (4)$$

$$\overrightarrow{h_i} = \overrightarrow{LSTM}(x_i), i \in [1, T] \qquad (5)$$

$$\overleftarrow{h_i} = \overleftarrow{LSTM}(x_i), i \in [T, 1] \qquad (6)$$

We concatenate $\overrightarrow{h_i}$ and $\overleftarrow{h_i}$ to get annotation of word $w_i$ i.e $h_i=[\overrightarrow{h_i},\overleftarrow{h_i}]$. $h_i$ summarizes the neighboring words around word $w_i$ but still focuses on word $w_i$.

### 4.1.3 Headline Attention Layer

Headline of a news article is very important to report news biased towards a political party as a reader generally reads headline first and then goes through the article with that headline in his mind i.e paying attention to article based on the headline. We introduce attention mechanism to extract words that contribute to political bias and form a vector representation v. Specifically,

$$u_i = tanh(W_w h_i + b_w) \qquad (7)$$

$$\alpha_i = \frac{exp(u_i^T.U)}{\sum_i exp(u_i^T.U)} \qquad (8)$$

$$v = \sum_i \alpha_i h_i \qquad (9)$$

We measure the importance of the word as the similarity of $u_i$ with U, the hidden representation of encoded headline representation Q and get a normalized importance $\alpha_i$ through a softmax function. After that we compute the representation of the news article as a weighted sum of the word annotations based on the weights. All of the above are learned during the training process.

### 4.1.4 Bias detection

The vector v is used to detect towards which political party the article is biased to as:

$$p = Softmax(W_c v + b_c) \qquad (10)$$

Training loss is the negative log likelihood of the correct labels:

$$L = -\sum_d Log(p_{di}) \qquad (11)$$

where i is the label of document d.

## 5 Experiments

All the experiments are carried out in a 5-fold cross validation scenario. As headlines express the ideological view of the news stories, in some cases only the headline would be sufficient to detect bias. So except for Headline Attention Networks, for all other baselines we divided dataset into three parts:

1. Only headline.

2. Only news article.

3. Concatenation of both headline and news article.

We compared how each of them differs in bias detection.

### 5.1 Baselines

We compare Headline Attention Networks with several baseline methods, including traditional approaches such as Naive Bayes, SVMs, CNNs, Branched CNNs, LSTMs and GRUs. Word embeddings are available for Telugu[4].

### 5.1.1 Naive Bayes

Naive Bayes classifier is used to classify documents using the following features.

**TFIDF** The TFIDF values of each word is used as features.

**Bag-of-means** The average word2vec (Mikolov et al., 2013) embedding is used as feature set.

### 5.1.2 SVMs

SVM-based classifier is used including following different features.

**TFIDF+Unigrams** The TFIDF values of bag of Unigrams is used as features.

**TFIDF+Bigrams** The TFIDF values of bag of Bigrams is used as features.

**AverageSG** The average word embeddings of each document is used as feature set.

### 5.1.3 Neural Network methods

We experimented with multiple neural network architectures like:

**CNNs** Word based neural network model like in (Kim, 2014) are used.

**Branched CNNs** Figure 3 shows the branched CNN architecture.

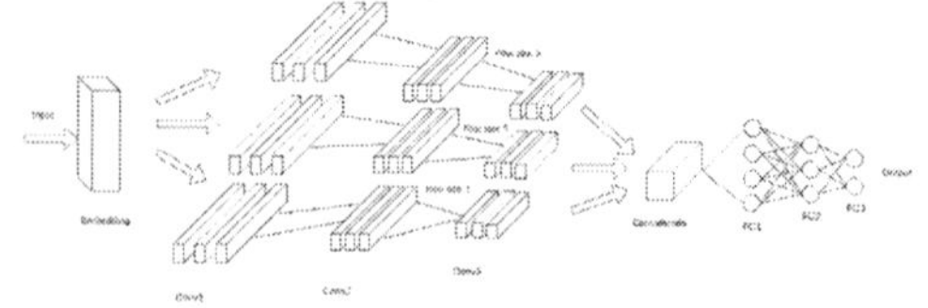

Figure 3: Branched CNN architecture

**LSTMs** and **GRU** based models like in (Wang et al., 2018) are used.

[4]https://bit.ly/2JQNYrw

| Methods | Only Headline | Only article | Concatenation of headline and article | Maximum |
|---|---|---|---|---|
| Naive Bayes+TFIDF+Unigrams | 39 | 58 | 59 | 59 |
| Naive Bayes+TFIDF+Bigrams | 29 | 32 | 33 | 33 |
| Naive Bayes+Bag-of-means | 49 | 63 | 63 | 63 |
| SVM+TFIDF+Unigrams | 41 | 69 | 69 | 69 |
| SVM+TFIDF+Bigrams | 55 | 76 | 71 | 76 |
| SVM+AverageSG | 57 | 69 | 66 | 69 |
| CNNs | 80 | 80.5 | 81.7 | 81.7 |
| Branched CNNs | 83.33 | 84.52 | 84.6 | 84.6 |
| LSTM | 84 | 85.25 | 85.32 | 85.32 |
| GRU | 81 | 82.7 | 82.7 | 82.7 |
| Headline Attention Network without attention layer | - | - | - | **85.25** |
| Headline Attention Network | - | - | - | **89.54** |

Table 2: Bias Detection Accuracy in percentage. Maximum is the best value among the three divisions of our dataset for baselines.

## 5.2 Results and analysis

The experimental results are shown in table 2. The results show that our model gives the best performance. Our model outperforms previous best baseline methods by 4.22%. From table 2 we can see that there is a significant improvement in neural network based methods compared to traditional methods. But involving the headline attention can significantly improve over them. As mentioned earlier, headlines are designed to be short and catchy so the journalists tend to exploit them to influence readers. Therefore, considering only the headlines also predicts bias with only a small difference in accuracy when compared to considering whole article. This can be clearly observed in table 2 in neural network methods. We can also observe that simply concatenating headline does not help much in bias prediction, instead attending to article with headline representation increases accuracy by a significant margin. Our Headline Attention Network outperforms all other models because it effectively finds out important words causing bias in a document.

## 6 Conclusion

In this paper, we proposed a headline attention mechanism for automatic detection of bias in news articles along with a manually annotated dataset to enable further research. Our model builds a vector for news article by aggregating important words obtained by paying attention based on headline representation. The experimental results demonstrate that our model significantly outperforms all the previous baseline models. Visualization of attention shows how headline attention effectively picks out words causing bias.

This model can also be extended to other sentiment based classification of texts such as blogs or online trending articles, which contains a title/headline and a body.

## Acknowledgments

We would like to thank Lalitha, Vaishnavi and other annotators for helping us with the dataset creation.

## References

Sreyasee Das Bhattacharjee, Ashit Talukder, and Bala Venkatram Balantrapu. 2017. Active learning based news veracity detection with feature weighting and deep-shallow fusion. In *2017 IEEE International Conference on Big Data, BigData 2017, Boston, MA, USA, December 11-14, 2017*, pages 556–565.

Ceren Budak, Sharad Goel, and Justin M. Rao. 2016. Fair and balanced? quantifying media bias through crowdsourced content analysis. 80:250–271.

Rama Rohit Reddy Gangula and Radhika Mamidi. 2018. Resource creation towards automated sentiment analysis in telugu (a low resource language) and integrating multiple domain sources to enhance sentiment prediction. In *Proceedings of the Eleventh International Conference on Language Resources and Evaluation, LREC 2018, Miyazaki, Japan, May 7-12, 2018*.

Sepp Hochreiter and Jürgen Schmidhuber. 1997. Unsupervised coding with LOCOCODE. In *Artificial Neural Networks - ICANN '97, 7th International Conference, Lausanne, Switzerland, October 8-10, 1997, Proceedings*, pages 655–660.

Nicholas Holtzman, J.P. Schott, Michael N Jones, David A Balota, and Tal Yarkoni. 2010. Exploring media bias with semantic analysis tools: Validation of the contrast analysis of semantic similarity (cass). 43:193–200.

Mohit Iyyer, Peter Enns, Jordan L. Boyd-Graber, and Philip Resnik. 2014. Political ideology detection using recursive neural networks. In *Proceedings of the 52nd Annual Meeting of the Association for Computational Linguistics, ACL 2014, June 22-27, 2014, Baltimore, MD, USA, Volume 1: Long Papers*, pages 1113–1122.

Thorsten Joachims. 1998. Text categorization with support vector machines: Learning with many relevant features. In *Machine Learning: ECML-98, 10th European Conference on Machine Learning, Chemnitz, Germany, April 21-23, 1998, Proceedings*, pages 137–142.

Nal Kalchbrenner, Edward Grefenstette, and Phil Blunsom. 2014. A convolutional neural network for modelling sentences. In *Proceedings of the 52nd Annual Meeting of the Association for Computational Linguistics, ACL 2014, June 22-27, 2014, Baltimore, MD, USA, Volume 1: Long Papers*, pages 655–665.

Yoon Kim. 2014. Convolutional neural networks for sentence classification. In *Proceedings of the 2014 Conference on Empirical Methods in Natural Language Processing, EMNLP 2014, October 25-29, 2014, Doha, Qatar, A meeting of SIGDAT, a Special Interest Group of the ACL*, pages 1746–1751.

Konstantina Lazaridou. 2016. Identifying political bias in news articles. *TCDL Bulletin*, 12(2).

Tomas Mikolov, Ilya Sutskever, Kai Chen, Gregory S. Corrado, and Jeffrey Dean. 2013. Distributed representations of words and phrases and their compositionality. In *Advances in Neural Information Processing Systems 26: 27th Annual Conference on Neural Information Processing Systems 2013. Proceedings of a meeting held December 5-8, 2013, Lake Tahoe, Nevada, United States.*, pages 3111–3119.

Sandeep Sricharan Mukku, Nurendra Choudhary, and Radhika Mamidi. 2016. Enhanced sentiment classification of telugu text using ML techniques. In *Proceedings of the 4th Workshop on Sentiment Analysis where AI meets Psychology (SAAIP 2016) co-located with 25th International Joint Conference on Artificial Intelligence (IJCAI 2016), New York City, USA, July 10, 2016.*, pages 29–34.

Hannah Rashkin, Eunsol Choi, Jin Yea Jang, Svitlana Volkova, and Yejin Choi. 2017. Truth of varying shades: Analyzing language in fake news and political fact-checking. In *Proceedings of the 2017 Conference on Empirical Methods in Natural Language Processing, EMNLP 2017, Copenhagen, Denmark, September 9-11, 2017*, pages 2931–2937.

Marta Recasens, Cristian Danescu-Niculescu-Mizil, and Dan Jurafsky. 2013. Linguistic models for analyzing and detecting biased language. In *Proceedings of the 51st Annual Meeting of the Association*

*for Computational Linguistics, ACL 2013, 4-9 August 2013, Sofia, Bulgaria, Volume 1: Long Papers*, pages 1650–1659.

Filipe Nunes Ribeiro, Lucas Henrique, Fabrício Benevenuto, Abhijnan Chakraborty, Juhi Kulshrestha, Mahmoudreza Babaei, and Krishna P. Gummadi. 2018. Media bias monitor: Quantifying biases of social media news outlets at large-scale. In *Proceedings of the Twelfth International Conference on Web and Social Media, ICWSM 2018, Stanford, California, USA, June 25-28, 2018.*, pages 290–299.

Rosa Sicilia, Stella Lo Giudice, Yulong Pei, Mykola Pechenizkiy, and Paolo Soda. 2017. Health-related rumour detection on twitter. In *2017 IEEE International Conference on Bioinformatics and Biomedicine, BIBM 2017, Kansas City, MO, USA, November 13-16, 2017*, pages 1599–1606.

Zohre Sivandi and Hamid Dowlatabadi. 2015. A critical discourse analysis on newspapers: The case study of nuclear program of iran. 4.

Jenq-Haur Wang, Ting-Wei Liu, Xiong Luo, and Long Wang. 2018. An LSTM approach to short text sentiment classification with word embeddings. In *Proceedings of the 30th Conference on Computational Linguistics and Speech Processing, ROCLING 2018, Hsinchu, Taiwan, October 4-5, 2018*, pages 214–223.

Sida I. Wang and Christopher D. Manning. 2012. Baselines and bigrams: Simple, good sentiment and topic classification. In *The 50th Annual Meeting of the Association for Computational Linguistics, Proceedings of the Conference, July 8-14, 2012, Jeju Island, Korea - Volume 2: Short Papers*, pages 90–94.

Zichao Yang, Diyi Yang, Chris Dyer, Xiaodong He, Alexander J. Smola, and Eduard H. Hovy. 2016. Hierarchical attention networks for document classification. In *NAACL HLT 2016, The 2016 Conference of the North American Chapter of the Association for Computational Linguistics: Human Language Technologies, San Diego California, USA, June 12-17, 2016*, pages 1480–1489.

Daniel Xiaodan Zhou, Paul Resnick, and Qiaozhu Mei. 2011. Classifying the political leaning of news articles and users from user votes. In *Proceedings of the Fifth International Conference on Weblogs and Social Media, Barcelona, Catalonia, Spain, July 17-21, 2011.*

# A  Supplemental Material

## A.1  Visualization of Headline Attention

Figure 4 and 5 show the visualization of our headline attention networks. Intensity of blue color denotes word weight.

Figures 4 and 5 shows that our model selects words with strong emphasis on a person or a political party. The darker the blue colour, it implies higher is its importance in predicting bias towards a party. Words with the darkest blue highlighting, such as YSRCP,Chandra Babu, People's leader are the most important ones as they refer to who/what the article is intending to inform about. So they are given more weight. The English translation of words in blue are "Chandra Babu", "progress", "inspiration", "strongest person on earth", "special", "encourage" etc. Our headline attention focuses most on "Chandra Babu" who is the chair person of the TDP political party and the other words are attended according to the intensity of praising.

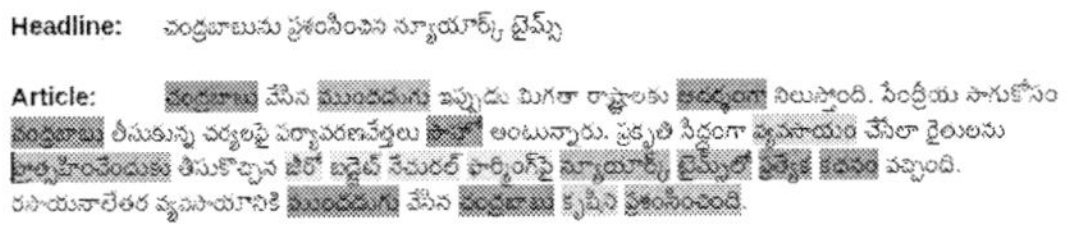

**Headline:** చంద్రబాబును ప్రశంసించిన న్యూయార్క్ టైమ్స్

**Article:** చంద్రబాబు చేసిన ముందడుగు ఇప్పుడు మిగతా రాష్ట్రాలకు ఆదర్శంగా నిలుస్తోంది. సేంద్రియ సాగుకోసం చంద్రబాబు తీసుకున్న చర్యలపై పర్యావరణవేత్తలు గ్రేట్ అంటున్నారు. ప్రకృతి సిద్ధంగా వ్యవసాయం చేసేలా రైతులను ప్రోత్సహించేందుకు తీసుకొచ్చిన జీరో బడ్జెట్ నేచురల్ ఫార్మింగ్‌పై న్యూయార్క్ టైమ్స్‌లో వ్యాస రచన వచ్చింది. రసాయనాలేతర వ్యవసాయానికి ముందడుగు వేసిన చంద్రబాబు కృషిని ప్రశంసించింది.

Figure 4: News article from the dataset. Bias towards "TDP"

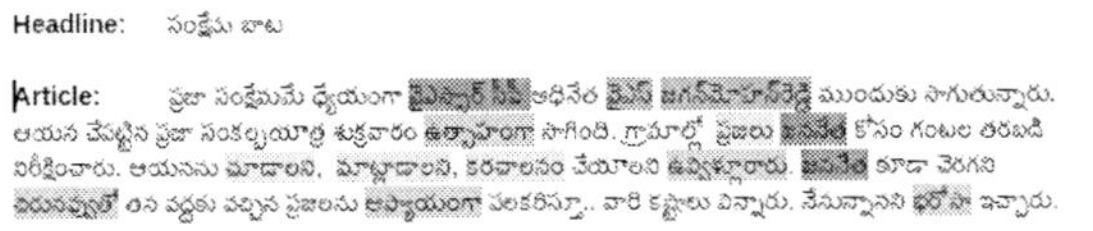

**Headline:** సంక్షేమ బాట

**Article:** ప్రజా సంక్షేమమే ధ్యేయంగా వైఎస్సార్ సీపీ అధినేత వైఎస్ జగన్‌మోహన్‌రెడ్డి ముందుకు సాగురున్నారు. ఆయన చేపట్టిన ప్రజా సంకల్పయాత్ర శుక్రవారం ఆర్భాటంగా సాగింది. గ్రామాల్లో ప్రజలు జగన్ కోసం గంటల తరబడి నిరీక్షించారు. ఆయనను చూడాలని, మాట్లాడాలని, కరచాలనం చేయాలని ఉవ్విళ్లూరారు. జగన్ కూడా చెరగని నవ్వుతో ఆన వద్దకు వచ్చిన ప్రజలను ఆత్మీయంగా పలకరిస్తూ.. వారి కష్టాలు విన్నారు. నేనున్నానని భరోసా ఇచ్చారు.

Figure 5: News article from the dataset. Bias towards "YCP"

Approximate translation of Figure 4:

Headline : Path of welfare

Article : On Friday, YSR Congress chief Jaganmohan Reddy carried out the fulfillment of people's desires successfully. The main goal of the walk is the welfare and betterment of the people of the state and people participated with a lot of excitement and offered immense support to the leader. The leader of the masses was given a warm welcome by the people, who have waited for hours just to see him. The people were very eager and enthusiastic to see him, meet him, greet him and to be addressed by him in the public talk that the leader addresses. The leader of masses, with a constant smile on his face, also greeted the people affectionately, spoke with them to find out about the current problems that they are facing and gave offered them to support and ensured that he is always with the people in any kind of need.

Approximate translation of Figure 5:

Headline : Chandra Babu Naidu praised by New York Times

Article : The step taken by Chandra Babu is now an inspiration for all other states. The measures taken by Chandra Babu regarding organic farming are exceptionally great and are getting great applauses from various environmentalists. New scheme called Zero Budget Natural Farming introduced by Chandra Babu mainly encourages the farmers to implement organic farming and techniques and are the main reason for the farmer to have hope on their life. The same has been even published in the New York Times. The effort put by Chandra Babu for encouraging farmers in chemical-free farming is truly appreciation worthy.

| *Headline* | Translated Headline | Article | Approximate Meaning | Political Bias |
|---|---|---|---|---|
| ఆంధ్రులకు భాజపా మోసం | BJP cheats Andhra pradesh | [illegible] | It is now evident for the whole nation to see how BJP has deceived all the Telugu people. Back in 2014, Narendra Modi himself promised that 10 year long special status to the state of Andhra Pradesh was on his agenda. And after assuring that all promises which were a part of the State Reformation Bill would be fulfilled, the party is showing its hypocrisy by not addressing even the smallest concerns of the nascent state of Andhra Pradesh. Chief Minister Siddaramaiah addressed the Telugu natives living in Karnataka in his open letter in which he empathised with them and urged them to teach the treacherous party a lesson. | BJP |
| వెనుకబడిన వర్గాల సంక్షేమమే తెదేపా లక్ష్యం | Goal of TDP is the betterment of backward communities | [illegible] | Right from the times when NTR was the Chief Minister to this date, TDP has always been a party which strives to succesfully implement various welfare schemes for the development of people, especially those belonging to the backward communities. When he was the Chief Minister, he introduced the Adarana scheme to financially aid the procurement of tools for every profession. Such meticulous planning and foresight on his part and determination of TDP will best serve the needs of people inspite of any crunch in the budget. Officials of the BC corporation further explained the details of the Adarana scheme, and expressed that this will definitely benefit handicraft workers and small scale industries the most. | TDP |
| తెదేపా గూండాల పార్టీ | TDP is the party of hooligans | [illegible] | TDP is full of hooligans, and the recent attack on BJP National Leader Amit Shah's convoy is an evidence for that. People from several parties slammed TDP for this attack. During a press meet, it was discussed that the other parties should come together and protest against this breach of democracy. TDP being the ruling party should ensure the safety of National leaders when they visit Andhra Pradesh and not itself raise attacks on them. Many leaders who attended the press meet expressed their concern that the police department hasn't taken any special measures eventhough the TDP leaders clearly threatened to oppose Amit Shah's visit. | TDP |

Figure 6: Examples of biased articles from our dataset.

# Testing the Generalization Power of Neural Network Models Across NLI Benchmarks


**Aarne Talman**
Department of Digital Humanities
University of Helsinki
Basement AI
aarne.talman@helsinki.fi

**Stergios Chatzikyriakidis**
Department of Philosophy, Linguistics and
Theory of Science, University of Gothenburg
Basement AI
stergios.chatzikyriakidis@gu.se



## Abstract

Neural network models have been very successful in natural language inference, with the best models reaching 90% accuracy in some benchmarks. However, the success of these models turns out to be largely benchmark specific. We show that models trained on a natural language inference dataset drawn from one benchmark fail to perform well in others, even if the notion of inference assumed in these benchmarks is the same or similar. We train six high performing neural network models on different datasets and show that each one of these has problems of generalizing when we replace the original test set with a test set taken from another corpus designed for the same task. In light of these results, we argue that most of the current neural network models are not able to generalize well in the task of natural language inference. We find that using large pre-trained language models helps with transfer learning when the datasets are similar enough. Our results also highlight that the current NLI datasets do not cover the different nuances of inference extensively enough.


## 1 Introduction

Natural Language Inference (NLI) has attracted considerable interest in the NLP community and, recently, a large number of neural network-based systems have been proposed to deal with the task. One can attempt a rough categorization of these systems into: a) sentence encoding systems, and b) other neural network systems. Both of them have been very successful, with the state of the art on the SNLI and MultiNLI datasets being 90.4%, which is our baseline with BERT (Devlin et al., 2019), and 86.7% (Devlin et al., 2019) respectively. However, a big question with respect to these systems is their ability to generalize outside the specific datasets they are trained and tested on. Recently, Glockner et al. (2018) have shown

that state-of-the-art NLI systems break considerably easily when, instead of tested on the original SNLI test set, they are tested on a test set which is constructed by taking premises from the training set and creating several hypotheses from them by changing at most one word within the premise. The results show a very significant drop in accuracy for three of the four systems. The system that was more difficult to break and had the least loss in accuracy was the system by Chen et al. (2018) which utilizes external knowledge taken from WordNet (Miller, 1995).

In this paper we show that NLI systems that have been very successful in specific NLI benchmarks, fail to generalize when trained on a specific NLI dataset and then these trained models are tested across test sets taken from different NLI benchmarks. The results we get are in line with Glockner et al. (2018), showing that the generalization capability of the individual NLI systems is very limited, but, what is more, they further show the only system that was less prone to breaking in Glockner et al. (2018), breaks too in the experiments we have conducted.

We train six different state-of-the-art models on three different NLI datasets and test these trained models on an NLI test set taken from another dataset designed for the same NLI task, namely for the task to identify for sentence pairs in the dataset if one sentence entails the other one, if they are in contradiction with each other or if they are neutral with respect to inferential relationship.

One would expect that if a model learns to correctly identify inferential relationships in one dataset, then it would also be able to do so in another dataset designed for the same task. Furthermore, two of the datasets, SNLI (Bowman et al., 2015) and MultiNLI (Williams et al., 2018), have been constructed using the same crowdsourcing approach and annotation instructions (Williams

85


*Proceedings of the Second BlackboxNLP Workshop on Analyzing and Interpreting Neural Networks for NLP*, pages 85–94
Florence, Italy, August 1, 2019. ©2019 Association for Computational Linguistics

et al., 2018), leading to datasets with the same or at least very similar definition of entailment. It is therefore reasonable to expect that transfer learning between these datasets is possible. As SICK (Marelli et al., 2014) dataset has been machine-constructed, a bigger difference in performance is expected.

In this paper we show that, contrary to our expectations, most models fail to generalize across the different datasets. However, our experiments also show that BERT (Devlin et al., 2019) performs much better than the other models in experiments between SNLI and MultiNLI. Nevertheless, even BERT fails when testing on SICK. In addition to the negative results, our experiments further highlight the power of pre-trained language models, like BERT, in NLI.

The negative results of this paper are significant for the NLP research community as well as to NLP practice as we would like our best models to not only to be able to perform well in a specific benchmark dataset, but rather capture the more general phenomenon this dataset is designed for. The main contribution of this paper is that it shows that most of the best performing neural network models for NLI fail in this regard. The second, and equally important, contribution is that our results highlight that the current NLI datasets do not capture the nuances of NLI extensively enough.

## 2   Related Work

The ability of NLI systems to generalize and related skepticism has been raised in a number of recent papers. Glockner et al. (2018) show that the generalization capabilities of state-of-the-art NLI systems, in cases where some kind of external lexical knowledge is needed, drops dramatically when the SNLI test set is replaced by a test set where the premise and the hypothesis are otherwise identical except for at most one word. The results show a very significant drop in accuracy. Kang et al. (2018) recognize the generalization problem that comes with training on datasets like SNLI, which tend to be *homogeneous* and with little linguistic variation. In this context, they propose to better train NLI models by making use of adversarial examples.

Multiple papers have reported hidden bias and annotation artifacts in the popular NLI datasets SNLI and MultiNLI allowing classification based on the hypothesis sentences alone (Tsuchiya,

2018; Gururangan et al., 2018; Poliak et al., 2018).

Wang et al. (2018) evaluate the robustness of NLI models using datasets where label preserving swapping operations have been applied, reporting significant performance drops compared to the results with the original dataset. In these experiments, like in the BreakingNLI experiment, the systems that seem to be performing the better, i.e. less prone to breaking, are the ones where some kind of external knowledge is used by the model (KIM by Chen et al., 2018 is one of those systems).

On a theoretical and methodological level, there is discussion on the nature of various NLI datasets, as well as the definition of what counts as NLI and what does not. For example, Chatzikyriakidis et al. (2017); Bernardy and Chatzikyriakidis (2019) present an overview of the most standard datasets for NLI and show that the definitions of inference in each of them are actually quite different, capturing only fragments of what seems to be a more general phenomenon.

Bowman et al. (2015) show that a simple LSTM model trained on the SNLI data fails when tested on SICK. However, their experiment is limited to this single architecture and dataset pair. Williams et al. (2018) show that different models that perform well on SNLI have lower accuracy on MultiNLI. However in their experiments they did not systematically test transfer learning between the two datasets, but instead used separate systems where the training and test data were drawn from the same corpora.[1]

## 3   Experimental Setup

In this section we describe the datasets and model architectures included in the experiments.

### 3.1   Data

We chose three different datasets for the experiments: SNLI, MultiNLI and SICK. All of them have been designed for NLI involving three-way classification with the labels *entailment*, *neutral* and *contradiction*. We did not include any datasets with two-way classification, e.g. SciTail (Khot et al., 2018). As SICK is a relatively small dataset with approximately only 10k sentence pairs, we did not use it as training data in any experiment.

---

[1]To be more precise, Williams et al. (2018) tested some transfer across datasets, but only between MultiNLI and SNLI.

| Train data | Test data | Size of the training set | Size of the test set |
| --- | --- | --- | --- |
| **SNLI** | **SNLI** | 550,152 | 10,000 |
| SNLI | MultiNLI | 550,152 | 20,000 |
| SNLI | SICK | 550,152 | 9,840 |
| **MultiNLI** | **MultiNLI** | 392,702 | 20,000 |
| MultiNLI | SNLI | 392,702 | 10,000 |
| MultiNLI | SICK | 392,702 | 9,840 |
| **SNLI + MultiNLI** | **SNLI** | 942,854 | 10,000 |
| SNLI + MultiNLI | SICK | 942,854 | 9,840 |

Table 1: Dataset combinations used in the experiments. The rows in bold are baseline experiments, where the test data comes from the same benchmark as the training and development data.

We also trained the models with a combined SNLI + MultiNLI training set.

For all the datasets we report the baseline performance where the training and test data are drawn from the same corpus. We then take these trained models and test them on a test set taken from another NLI corpus. For the case where the models are trained with SNLI + MultiNLI we report the baseline using the SNLI test data.[2] All the experimental combinations are listed in Table 1. Examples from the selected datasets are provided in Table 2. To be more precise, we vary three things: training dataset, model and testing dataset. We should qualify this though, since the three datasets we look at, can also be grouped by text domain/genre and type of data collection, with MultiNLI and SNLI using the same data collection style, and SNLI and SICK using roughly the same domain/genre. Hopefully, our set up will let us determine which of these factors matters the most.

We describe the source datasets in more detail below.

### SNLI

The Stanford Natural Language Inference (SNLI) corpus (Bowman et al., 2015) is a dataset of 570k human-written sentence pairs manually labeled with the labels entailment, contradiction, and neutral. The source for the premise sentences in SNLI were image captions taken from the Flickr30k corpus (Young et al., 2014).

### MultiNLI

The Multi-Genre Natural Language Inference (MultiNLI) corpus (Williams et al., 2018) consisting of 433k human-written sentence pairs labeled with entailment, contradiction and neutral.

MultiNLI contains sentence pairs from ten distinct genres of both written and spoken English. Only five genres are included in the training set. The development and test sets have been divided into matched and mismatched, where the former includes only sentences from the same genres as the training data, and the latter includes sentences from the remaining genres not present in the training data.

We used the matched development set (MultiNLI-m) for the experiments.[3] The MultiNLI dataset was annotated using very similar instructions as for the SNLI dataset.[4] Therefore we can assume that the definitions of entailment, contradiction and neutral is the same in these two datasets.

### SICK

SICK (Marelli et al., 2014) is a dataset that was originally constructed to test compositional distributional semantics (DS) models. The dataset contains 9,840 examples pertaining to logical inference (negation, conjunction, disjunction, apposition, relative clauses, etc.). The dataset was automatically constructed taking pairs of sentences from a random subset of the 8K ImageFlickr data set (Young et al., 2014) and the SemEval 2012 STS MSRVideo Description dataset (Agirre et al., 2012).

### 3.2 Model and Training Details

We perform experiments with six high-performing models covering the sentence encoding models,

---

[2] Here we could as well have selected MultiNLI test data. However the selection does not impact our findings.

[3] Here the choice between MultiNLI matched and mismatched does not make a difference to our experimental setup.

[4] The reason we are not saying "exactly the same" is because in some cases, as the authors report, "the prompts that surround each premise sentence during hypothesis collection are slightly tailored to fit the genre of that premise sentence".

| | **entailment** | |
|---|---|
| SICK | *A person, who is riding a bike, is wearing gear which is black* |
| | *A biker is wearing gear which is black* |
| SNLI | *A young family enjoys feeling ocean waves lap at their feet.* |
| | *A family is at the beach.* |
| MultiNLI | *Kal tangled both of Adrin's arms, keeping the blades far away.* |
| | *Adrin's arms were tangled, keeping his blades away from Kal.* |
| | **contradiction** | |
| SICK | *There is no man wearing a black helmet and pushing a bicycle* |
| | *One man is wearing a black helmet and pushing a bicycle* |
| SNLI | *A man with a tattoo on his arm staring to the side with vehicles and buildings behind him.* |
| | *A man with no tattoos is getting a massage.* |
| MultiNLI | *Also in Eustace Street is an information office and a cultural center for children, The Ark .* |
| | *The Ark, a cultural center for kids, is located in Joyce Street.* |
| | **neutral** | |
| SICK | *A little girl in a green coat and a boy holding a red sled are walking in the snow* |
| | *A child is wearing a coat and is carrying a red sled near a child in a green and black coat* |
| SNLI | *An old man with a package poses in front of an advertisement.* |
| | *A man poses in front of an ad for beer.* |
| MultiNLI | *Enthusiasm for Disney's Broadway production of The Lion King dwindles.* |
| | *The broadway production of The Lion King was amazing, but audiences are getting bored.* |

Table 2: Example sentence pairs from the three datasets.

cross-sentence attention models as well as fine-tuned pre-trained language models.

For sentence encoding models, we chose a simple one-layer bidirectional LSTM with max pooling (BiLSTM-max) with the hidden size of 600D per direction, used e.g. in InferSent (Conneau et al., 2017), and HBMP (Talman et al., 2018). For the other models, we have chosen ESIM (Chen et al., 2017), which includes cross-sentence attention, and KIM (Chen et al., 2018), which has cross-sentence attention and utilizes external knowledge. We also selected two model involving a pre-trained language model, namely ESIM + ELMo (Peters et al., 2018) and BERT (Devlin et al., 2019). KIM is particularly interesting in this context as it performed significantly better than other models in the Breaking NLI experiment conducted by Glockner et al. (2018). The success of pre-trained language models in multiple NLP tasks make ESIM + ELMo and BERT interesting additions to this experiment. Table 3 lists the different models used in the experiments.

For BiLSTM-max we used the Adam optimizer (Kingma and Ba, 2015), a learning rate of 5e-4 and batch size of 64. The learning rate was decreased by the factor of 0.2 after each epoch if the model did not improve. Dropout of 0.1 was used between the layers of the multi-layer perceptron classifier, except before the last layer.The BiLSTM-max models were initialized with pre-trained GloVe 840B word embeddings of size 300 dimensions (Pennington et al., 2014), which were fine-tuned during training. Our BiLSMT-max model was implemented in PyTorch.

For HBMP, ESIM, KIM and BERT we used the original implementations with the default settings and hyperparameter values as described in Talman et al. (2018), Chen et al. (2017), Chen et al. (2018) and Devlin et al. (2019) respectively. For BERT we used the uncased 768-dimensional model (BERT-base). For ESIM + ELMo we used the AllenNLP (Gardner et al., 2018) PyTorch implementation with the default settings and hyperparameter values.

## 4 Experimental Results

Table 4 contains all the experimental results.

Our experiments show that, while all of the six models perform well when the test set is drawn from the same corpus as the training and development set, accuracy is significantly lower when we test these trained models on a test set drawn from a separate NLI corpus, the average difference in accuracy being 24.9 points across all experiments.

Accuracy drops the most when a model is tested on SICK. The difference in this case is between 19.0-29.0 points when trained on MultiNLI, between 31.6-33.7 points when trained on SNLI and between 31.1-33.0 when trained on SNLI + MultiNLI. This was expected, as the method of constructing the sentence pairs was different, and hence there is too much difference in the kind of sentence pairs included in the training and test sets for transfer learning to work. However, the drop

| Model | Model type |
| --- | --- |
| BiLSTM-max (Conneau et al., 2017) | Sentence encoding |
| HBMP (Talman et al., 2018) | Sentence encoding |
| ESIM (Chen et al., 2017) | Cross-sentence attention |
| KIM (Chen et al., 2018) | Cross-sentence attention |
| ESIM + ELMo (Peters et al., 2018) | Pre-trained language model |
| BERT-base (Devlin et al., 2019) | Cross-sentence attention + pre-trained language model |

Table 3: Model architectures used in the experiments.

was more dramatic than expected.

The most surprising result was that the accuracy of all models drops significantly even when the models were trained on MultiNLI and tested on SNLI (3.6-11.1 points). This is surprising as both of these datasets have been constructed with a similar data collection method using the same definition of entailment, contradiction and neutral. The sentences included in SNLI are also much simpler compared to those in MultiNLI, as they are taken from the Flickr image captions. This might also explain why the difference in accuracy for all of the six models is lowest when the models are trained on MultiNLI and tested on SNLI. It is also very surprising that the model with the biggest difference in accuracy was ESIM + ELMo which includes a pre-trained ELMo language model. BERT performed significantly better than the other models in this experiment having an accuracy of 80.4% and only 3.6 point difference in accuracy.

The poor performance of most of the models with the MultiNLI-SNLI dataset pair is also very surprising given that neural network models do not seem to suffer a lot from introduction of new genres to the test set which were not included in the training set, as can be seen from the small difference in test accuracies for the matched and mismatched test sets (see e.g Williams et al., 2018). In a sense SNLI could be seen as a separate genre not included in MultiNLI. This raises the question if the SNLI and MultiNLI have e.g. different kinds of annotation artifacts, which makes transfer learning between these datasets more difficult.

All the models, except BERT, perform almost equally poorly across all the experiments. Both BiLSTM-max and HBMP have an average drop in accuracy of 24.4 points, while the average for KIM is 25.5 and for ESIM + ELMo 25.6. ESIM has the highest average difference of 27.0 points. In contrast to the findings of Glockner et al. (2018),

utilizing external knowledge did not improve the model's generalization capability, as KIM performed equally poorly across all dataset combinations.

Also including a pretrained ELMo language model did not improve the results significantly. The overall performance of BERT was significantly better than the other models, having the lowest average difference in accuracy of 22.5 points. Our baselines for SNLI (90.4%) and SNLI + MultiNLI (90.6%) outperform the previous state-of-the-art accuracy for SNLI (90.1%) by Kim et al. (2018).

To understand better the types of errors made by neural network models in NLI we looked at some example failure-pairs for selected models.[5] Tables 5 and 6 contain some randomly selected failure-pairs for two models: BERT and HBMP, and for three set-ups: SNLI→SICK, SNLI→MultiNLI and MultiNLI→SICK. We chose BERT as the current the state of the art NLI model. HBMP was selected as a high performing model in the sentence encoding model type. Although the listed sentence pairs represent just a small sample of the errors made by these models, they do include some interesting examples. First, it seems that SICK has a more narrow notion of contradiction – corresponding more to logical contradiction – compared to the contradiction in SNLI and MultiNLI, where especially in SNLI the sentences are contradictory if they describe a different state of affairs. This is evident in the sentence pair: *A young child is running outside over the fallen leaves* and *A young child is lying down on a gravel road that is covered with dead leaves*, which is predicted by BERT to be *contradiction* although the gold label is *neutral*. Another interesting example is the sentence pair: *A boat pear with people boarding and*

---

[5]More thorough error analysis of each of the models and set-up is out of scope of this work but we intend to address these in our future research.

| Train data | Test data | Test accuracy | Δ | Model |
|---|---|---|---|---|
| **SNLI** | **SNLI** | **86.1** | | **BiLSTM-max** (our baseline) |
| **SNLI** | **SNLI** | **86.6** | | **HBMP** (Talman et al., 2018) |
| **SNLI** | **SNLI** | **88.0** | | **ESIM** (Chen et al., 2017) |
| **SNLI** | **SNLI** | **88.6** | | **KIM** (Chen et al., 2018) |
| **SNLI** | **SNLI** | **88.6** | | **ESIM + ELMo** (Peters et al., 2018) |
| **SNLI** | **SNLI** | **90.4** | | **BERT-base** (Devlin et al., 2019) |
| SNLI | MultiNLI-m | 55.7* | -30.4 | BiLSTM-max |
| SNLI | MultiNLI-m | 56.3* | -30.3 | HBMP |
| SNLI | MultiNLI-m | 59.2* | -28.8 | ESIM |
| SNLI | MultiNLI-m | 61.7* | -26.9 | KIM |
| SNLI | MultiNLI-m | 64.2* | -24.4 | ESIM + ELMo |
| SNLI | MultiNLI-m | 75.5* | -14.9 | BERT-base |
| SNLI | SICK | 54.5 | -31.6 | BiLSTM-max |
| SNLI | SICK | 53.1 | -33.5 | HBMP |
| SNLI | SICK | 54.3 | -33.7 | ESIM |
| SNLI | SICK | 55.8 | -32.8 | KIM |
| SNLI | SICK | 56.7 | -31.9 | ESIM + ELMo |
| SNLI | SICK | 56.9 | -33.5 | BERT-base |
| **MultiNLI** | **MultiNLI-m** | **73.1*** | | **BiLSTM-max** |
| **MultiNLI** | **MultiNLI-m** | **73.2*** | | **HBMP** |
| **MultiNLI** | **MultiNLI-m** | **76.8*** | | **ESIM** |
| **MultiNLI** | **MultiNLI-m** | **77.3*** | | **KIM** |
| **MultiNLI** | **MultiNLI-m** | **80.2*** | | **ESIM + ELMo** |
| **MultiNLI** | **MultiNLI-m** | **84.0*** | | **BERT-base** |
| MultiNLI | SNLI | 63.8 | -9.3 | BiLSTM-max |
| MultiNLI | SNLI | 65.3 | -7.9 | HBMP |
| MultiNLI | SNLI | 66.4 | -10.4 | ESIM |
| MultiNLI | SNLI | 68.5 | -8.8 | KIM |
| MultiNLI | SNLI | 69.1 | -11.1 | ESIM + ELMo |
| MultiNLI | SNLI | 80.4 | -3.6 | BERT-base |
| MultiNLI | SICK | 54.1 | -19.0 | BiLSTM-max |
| MultiNLI | SICK | 54.1 | -19.1 | HBMP |
| MultiNLI | SICK | 47.9 | -28.9 | ESIM |
| MultiNLI | SICK | 50.9 | -26.4 | KIM |
| MultiNLI | SICK | 51.4 | -28.8 | ESIM + ELMo |
| MultiNLI | SICK | 55.0 | -29.0 | BERT-base |
| **SNLI + MultiNLI** | **SNLI** | **86.1** | | **BiLSTM-max** |
| **SNLI + MultiNLI** | **SNLI** | **86.1** | | **HBMP** |
| **SNLI + MultiNLI** | **SNLI** | **87.5** | | **ESIM** |
| **SNLI + MultiNLI** | **SNLI** | **86.2** | | **KIM** |
| **SNLI + MultiNLI** | **SNLI** | **88.8** | | **ESIM + ELMo** |
| **SNLI + MultiNLI** | **SNLI** | **90.6** | | **BERT-base** |
| SNLI + MultiNLI | SICK | 54.5 | -31.6 | BiLSTM-max |
| SNLI + MultiNLI | SICK | 55.0 | -31.1 | HBMP |
| SNLI + MultiNLI | SICK | 54.5 | -33.0 | ESIM |
| SNLI + MultiNLI | SICK | 54.6 | -31.6 | KIM |
| SNLI + MultiNLI | SICK | 57.1 | -31.7 | ESIM + ELMo |
| SNLI + MultiNLI | SICK | 59.1 | -31.5 | BERT-base |

Table 4: Test accuracies (%). For the baseline results (highlighted in bold) the training data and test data have been drawn from the same benchmark corpus. Δ is the difference between the test accuracy and the baseline accuracy for the same training set. Results marked with * are for the development set, as no annotated test set is openly available. Best scores with respect to accuracy and difference in accuracy are underlined.

*disembarking some boats.* and *people are boarding and disembarking some boats*, which is incorrectly predicted by BERT to be *contradiction* although it has been labeled as *entailment*. Here the two sentences describe the same event from different points of view: the first one describing a boat pear with some people on it and the second one describing the people directly. Interestingly the added information about the boat pear seems to confuse the model.

## 5 Discussion and Conclusion

In this paper we have shown that neural network models for NLI fail to generalize across different NLI benchmarks. We experimented with six state-of-the-art models covering sentence encoding approaches, cross-sentence attention models and pre-trained and fine-tuned language models. For all the systems, the accuracy drops between 3.6-33.7 points (the average drop being 24.9 points), when testing with a test set drawn from a separate corpus from that of the training data, as compared to when the test and training data are splits from the same corpus. Our findings, together with the previous negative findings, indicate that the state-of-the-art models fail to capture the semantics of NLI in a way that will enable them to generalize across different NLI situations.

The results highlight two issues to be taken into consideration: a) using datasets involving a fraction of what NLI is, will fail when tested in datasets that are testing for a slightly different definition of inference. This is evident when we move from the SNLI to the SICK dataset. b) NLI is to some extent genre/context dependent. Training on SNLI and testing on MultiNLI gives worse results than vice versa. This is particularly evident in the case of BERT. These results highlight that training on multiple genres helps. However, this help is still not enough given that, even in the case of training on MultiNLI (multi genre) and training on SNLI (single genre and same definition of inference with MultiNLI), accuracy drops significantly.

We also found that involving a large pre-trained language model helps with transfer learning when the datasets are similar enough, as is the case with SNLI and MultiNLI. Our results further corroborate the power of pre-trained and fine-tuned language models like BERT in NLI. However, not even BERT is able to generalize from SNLI and MultiNLI to SICK, possibly due to the difference between what kind of inference relations are contained in these datasets.

Our findings motivate us to look for novel neural network architectures and approaches that better capture the semantics on natural language inference beyond individual datasets. However, there seems to be a need to start with better constructed datasets, i.e. datasets that will not only capture fractions of what NLI is in reality. Better NLI systems need to be able to be more versatile on the types of inference they can recognize. Otherwise, we would be stuck with systems that can cover only some aspects of NLI. On a theoretical level, and in connection to the previous point, we need a better understanding of the range of phenomena NLI must be able to cover and focus our future endeavours for dataset construction towards this direction. In order to do this a more systematic study is needed on the different kinds of entailment relations NLI datasets need to include. Our future work will include a more systematic and broad-coverage analysis of the types of errors the models make and in what kinds of sentence-pairs they make successful predictions.

## Acknowledgments

The first author is supported by the FoTran project, funded by the European Research Council (ERC) under the European Unions Horizon 2020 research and innovation programme (grant agreement No 771113).

The first author also gratefully acknowledges the support of the Academy of Finland through project 314062 from the ICT 2023 call on Computation, Machine Learning and Artificial Intelligence.

The second author is supported by grant 2014-39 from the Swedish Research Council, which funds the Centre for Linguistic Theory and Studies in Probability (CLASP) in the Department of Philosophy, Linguistics, and Theory of Science at the University of Gothenburg.


## References


Eneko Agirre, Mona Diab, Daniel Cer, and Aitor Gonzalez-Agirre. 2012. Semeval-2012 task 6: A pilot on semantic textual similarity. In *Proceedings of the First Joint Conference on Lexical and Computational Semantics*.

Jean-Philippe Bernardy and Stergios Chatzikyriakidis. 2019. What kind of natural language inference are nlp systems learning: Is this enough? In *Proceedings of ICAART*.

Samuel R. Bowman, Gabor Angeli, Christopher Potts, and Christopher D. Manning. 2015. A large annotated corpus for learning natural language inference. In *Proceedings of EMNLP*.

Stergios Chatzikyriakidis, Robin Cooper, Simon Dobnik, and Staffan Larsson. 2017. An overview of natural language inference data collection: The way forward? In *Proceedings of the Computing Natural Language Inference Workshop*.

Qian Chen, Xiaodan Zhu, Zhen-Hua Ling, Diana Inkpen, and Si Wei. 2018. Neural natural language inference models enhanced with external knowledge. In *Proceedings of ACL*.

Qian Chen, Xiaodan Zhu, Zhen-Hua Ling, Si Wei, Hui Jiang, and Diana Inkpen. 2017. Enhanced lstm for natural language inference. In *ACL*.

Alexis Conneau, Douwe Kiela, Holger Schwenk, Loïc Barrault, and Antoine Bordes. 2017. Supervised learning of universal sentence representations from natural language inference data. In *Proceedings of EMNLP*.

Jacob Devlin, Ming-Wei Chang, Kenton Lee, and Kristina Toutanova. 2019. Bert: Pre-training of deep bidirectional transformers for language understanding. In *Proceedings of NAACL*.

Matt Gardner, Joel Grus, Mark Neumann, Oyvind Tafjord, Pradeep Dasigi, Nelson F. Liu, Matthew Peters, Michael Schmitz, and Luke S. Zettlemoyer. 2018. AllenNLP: A deep semantic natural language processing platform. In *ACL workshop for NLP Open Source Software*.

Max Glockner, Vered Shwartz, and Yoav Goldberg. 2018. Breaking nli systems with sentences that require simple lexical inferences. In *Proceedings of ACL*.

Suchin Gururangan, Swabha Swayamdipta, Omer Levy, Roy Schwartz, Samuel Bowman, and Noah A. Smith. 2018. Annotation artifacts in natural language inference data. In *Proceedings of NAACL*.

Dongyeop Kang, Tushar Khot, Ashish Sabharwal, and Eduard Hovy. 2018. Adversarial training for textual entailment with knowledge-guided examples. In *Proceedings of ACL*.

Tushar Khot, Ashish Sabharwal, and Peter Clark. 2018. Scitail: A textual entailment dataset from science question answering. In *Proceedings of AAAI*.

Seonhoon Kim, Jin-Hyuk Hong, Inho Kang, and Nojun Kwak. 2018. Semantic sentence matching with densely-connected recurrent and co-attentive information. *arXiv preprint arXiv:1805.11360*.

Diederik P. Kingma and Jimmy Ba. 2015. Adam: A method for stochastic optimization. In *Proceedings of ICLR*.

Marco Marelli, Stefano Menini, Marco Baroni, Luisa Bentivogli, Raffaella Bernardi, and Roberto Zamparelli. 2014. A sick cure for the evaluation of compositional distributional semantic models. In *Proceedings of LREC*.

George A. Miller. 1995. Wordnet: A lexical database for english. *Commun. ACM*, 38(11):39–41.

Jeffrey Pennington, Richard Socher, and Christopher D. Manning. 2014. Glove: Global vectors for word representation. In *Proceedings of EMNLP*.

Matthew E. Peters, Mark Neumann, Mohit Iyyer, Matt Gardner, Christopher Clark, Kenton Lee, and Luke Zettlemoyer. 2018. Deep contextualized word representations. In *Proceedings of NAACL*.

Adam Poliak, Jason Naradowsky, Aparajita Haldar, Rachel Rudinger, and Benjamin Van Durme. 2018. Hypothesis only baselines in natural language inference. In *Proceedings of the Seventh Joint Conference on Lexical and Computational Semantics*.

Aarne Talman, Anssi Yli-Jyrä, and Jörg Tiedemann. 2018. Natural language inference with hierarchical bilstm max pooling architecture. *arXiv preprint arXiv:1808.08762*.

Masatoshi Tsuchiya. 2018. Performance Impact Caused by Hidden Bias of Training Data for Recognizing Textual Entailment. In *Proceedings of LREC*.

Haohan Wang, Da Sun, and Eric P. Xing. 2018. What if we simply swap the two text fragments? a straightforward yet effective way to test the robustness of methods to confounding signals in nature language inference tasks. *arXiv preprint arXiv:1809.02719*.

Adina Williams, Nikita Nangia, and Samuel R. Bowman. 2018. A broad-coverage challenge corpus for sentence understanding through inference. In *Proceedings of NAACL*.

Peter Young, Alice Lai, Micah Hodosh, and Julia Hockenmaier. 2014. From image descriptions to visual denotations: New similarity metrics for semantic inference over event descriptions. *TACL*, 2:67–78.

| **BERT: SNLI → SICK** |
| --- |
| A young child is running outside over the fallen leaves |
| A young child is lying down on a gravel road that is covered with dead leaves |
| **Label:** neutral     **Prediction:** contradiction |
| The man is being knocked off of a horse |
| Someone is falling off a horse |
| **Label:** entailment     **Prediction:** contradiction |
| There is no one typing |
| Someone is typing on a keyboard |
| **Label:** contradiction     **Prediction:** neutral |
| The man in the purple hat is operating a camera that makes videos |
| There is no man with a camera studying the subject |
| **Label:** neutral     **Prediction:** contradiction |
| A woman is taking off a cloak, which is very large, and revealing an extravagant dress |
| A woman is putting on a cloak, which is very large, and concealing an extravagant dress |
| **Label:** contradiction     **Prediction:** neutral |
| **BERT: MultiNLI → SICK** |
| A cowboy is riding a horse and cornering a barrel |
| A cowgirl is riding a horse and corners a barrel |
| **Label:** neutral     **Prediction:** contradiction |
| A tan dog is jumping up and catching a tennis ball |
| A dog with a tan coat is jumping up and catching a tennis ball |
| **Label:** entailment     **Prediction:** neutral |
| The bunch of men are playing rugby on a muddy field |
| Some men are idling |
| **Label:** neutral     **Prediction:** contradiction |
| A blond child is going down a slide and throwing up his arms |
| A child with dark hair is going down a slide and throwing up his arms |
| **Label:** contradiction     **Prediction:** entailment |
| There is no person in bike gear standing steadily in front of the mountains |
| A group of people is equipped with protective gear |
| **Label:** neutral     **Prediction:** contradiction |
| **BERT: MultiNLI → SNLI** |
| A woman in a white wedding dress is being dressed and fitted by two other women. |
| A woman is being fitted for the first time. |
| **Label:** neutral     **Prediction:** contradiction |
| A boat pear with people boarding and disembarking some boats. |
| people are boarding and disembarking some boats |
| **Label:** entailment     **Prediction:** contradiction |
| Several men at a bar watch a sports game on the television. |
| The men are at a baseball game. |
| **Label:** contradiction     **Prediction:** entailment |
| A singer wearing a leather jacket performs on stage with dramatic lighting behind him. |
| a singer is on american idol |
| **Label:** neutral     **Prediction:** contradiction |
| A person rolls down a hill riding a wagon as another watches. |
| A person stares at an empty hill. |
| **Label:** contradiction     **Prediction:** neutral |

Table 5: Example failure-pairs for BERT.

**HBMP: SNLI → SICK**

a boy is sitting in a room and playing a piano by lamp light

a boy is playing a keyboard

**Label:** entailment      **Prediction:** contradiction

a woman is wearing ear protection and is firing a gun at an outdoor shooting range

a woman is shooting at target practices

**Label:** entailment      **Prediction:** neutral

a man in a purple hat isn't climbing a rocky wall with bare hands

a man in a purple hat is climbing a rocky wall with bare hands

**Label:** contradiction      **Prediction:** entailment

a cat is swinging on a fan

a cat is stuck on a moving ceiling fan

**Label:** neutral      **Prediction:** contradiction

a young boy is jumping and covering nearby wooden fence with grass

a young boy covered in grass is jumping near a wooden fence

**Label:** neutral      **Prediction:** entailment

**HBMP: MultiNLI → SICK**

two dogs are walking slowly through a park

two dogs are running quickly through a park

**Label:** neutral      **Prediction:** entailment

the woman is playing a guitar which is electric

the woman is playing an electric guitar

**Label:** entailment      **Prediction:** neutral

there is no man squatting in brush and taking a photograph

a man is crouching and holding a camera

**Label:** neutral      **Prediction:** contradiction

the snowboarder is jumping off a snowy hill

a snowboarder is jumping off the snow

**Label:** neutral      **Prediction:** entailment

the boy is sitting near the blue ocean

the boy is wading through the blue ocean

**Label:** contradiction      **Prediction:** neutral

**HBMP: MultiNLI → SNLI**

a man is holding a book standing in front of a chalkboard.

a person is in a classroom teaching.

**Label:** entailment      **Prediction:** contradiction

a woman with a pink purse walks down a crowded sidewalk.

a woman escapes a from a hostile enviroment

**Label:** neutral      **Prediction:** contradiction

a woman with a pink purse walks down a crowded sidewalk.

a woman escapes a from a hostile enviroment

**Label:** neutral      **Prediction:** contradiction

a person waterskiing in a river with a large wall in the background.

a dog waterskiing in a river with a large wall in the background.

**Label:** contradiction      **Prediction:** neutral

a man wearing a blue shirt and headphones around his neck raises his arm.

a man is raising his arm to get someones attention.

**Label:** neutral      **Prediction:** entailment

Table 6: Example failure-pairs for HBMP.

# Character Eyes: Seeing Language through Character-Level Taggers


**Yuval Pinter**
School of Interactive Computing
Georgia Institute of Technology
uvp@gatech.edu

**Marc Marone** [*]
Microsoft

mmarone6@gatech.edu

**Jacob Eisenstein**
Facebook AI Research

jacobeisenstein@fb.com



## Abstract

Character-level models have been used extensively in recent years in NLP tasks as both supplements and replacements for closed-vocabulary token-level word representations. In one popular architecture, character-level LSTMs are used to feed token representations into a sequence tagger predicting token-level annotations such as part-of-speech (POS) tags.

In this work, we examine the behavior of POS taggers across languages from the perspective of individual hidden units within the character LSTM. We aggregate the behavior of these units into language-level metrics which quantify the challenges that taggers face on languages with different morphological properties, and identify links between synthesis and affixation preference and emergent behavior of the hidden tagger layer. In a comparative experiment, we show how modifying the balance between forward and backward hidden units affects model arrangement and performance in these types of languages.


## 1   Introduction

Subword vector representations are now a standard part of neural architectures for natural language processing (e.g., Bojanowski et al., 2017; Peters et al., 2018).   In particular, character representations have been shown to handle out-of-vocabulary words in supervised tagging tasks (Ling et al., 2015; Lample et al., 2016). These advantages generalize across multiple languages, where morphological formation may differ greatly but the character composition of words remains a relatively reliable primitive (Plank et al., 2016).

While the advantages of character-level models are readily apparent, existing evaluation methods fail to explain the mechanism by which these models encode linguistic knowledge about morphology and orthography.  Different languages exhibit character-word correspondence in very different patterns, and yet the bi-directional LSTM appears to be, or is assumed to be, capable of capturing them all.  In large multilingual settings, it is not uncommon to tune hyperparameters on a handful of languages, and apply them to the rest (e.g., Pinter et al., 2017).

In this work, we challenge this implicit generalization.  We train character-based sequence taggers on a large selection of languages exhibiting various strategies for word formation, and subject the resulting models to a novel analysis of the behavior of individual units in the character-level Bi-LSTM hidden layer.  This reveals differences in the ability of the Bi-LSTM architecture to identify parts-of-speech, based on typological properties: hidden layers trained on agglutinative languages find more regularities on the character level than in fusional languages; languages that are suffix-heavy give a stronger signal to the backward-facing hidden units, and vice versa for prefix-heavy languages.  In short, character-level recurrent networks function differently depending on how each language expresses morphosyntactic properties in characters.

These empirical results motivate a novel Bi-LSTM architecture, in which the number of hidden units is unbalanced across the forward and backward directions.  We find empirical correspondence between the analytical findings above and performance of such unbalanced Bi-LSTM models, allowing us to translate the typological properties of a language into concrete recommendations for model selection. [1]

## 2   Related Work

Several recent papers attempt to explain neural network performance by investigating hidden state activation patterns on auxiliary or downstream

---


[*]Work done while at Georgia Institute of Technology.


[1]https://github.com/ruyimarone/character-eyes




*Proceedings of the Second BlackboxNLP Workshop on Analyzing and Interpreting Neural Networks for NLP*, pages 95–102
Florence, Italy, August 1, 2019. ©2019 Association for Computational Linguistics

tasks. On the word level, Linzen et al. (2016) trained LSTM language models, evaluated their performance on grammatical agreement detection, and analyzed activation patterns within specific hidden units. We build on this analysis strategy as we aggregate (character-) sequence activation patterns across all hidden units in a model into quantitative measures.

Substantial prior work exists on the character level as well (Karpathy et al., 2015; Vania and Lopez, 2017; Kementchedjhieva and Lopez, 2018; Gerz et al., 2018). Smith et al. (2018) examined the character component in multilingual parsing models empirically, comparing it to the contribution of POS embeddings and pre-trained embeddings. Chaudhary et al. (2018) leveraged cross-lingual character-level correspondence to train NER models for low-resource languages. Godin et al. (2018), compared CNN and LSTM character models on a type-level prediction task on three languages, using the post-network softmax values to see which models identify useful character sequences. Unlike their analysis, we examine a more applied token-level task (POS tagging), and focus on the hidden states within the LSTM model in order to analyze its raw view of word composition.

Our analysis assumes a characterization of unit roles, where each hidden unit is observed to have some specific function. Findings from Linzen et al. (2016) and others suggest that a single hidden unit can learn to track complex syntactic rules. Radford et al. (2017) found that a character-level language model can implicitly assign a single unit to track sentiment, without being directly supervised. Kementchedjhieva and Lopez (2018) also examined individual units in a character model and found complex behavior by inspecting activation patterns by hand. Most recently, Dalvi et al. (2019) performed post-hoc tuning of neurons trained in language model and machine translation components, and examined their ability to predict grammatical functions. Like them, we perform an aggregative analysis of individual units to reach measurable quantities of models at a whole, but apply our method to taggers trained directly on supervised grammatical tasks, and focus on cross-lingual variation as the main object of investigation.

| Language | Affix[†] | Morph synth[‡] | POS Accuracy % Dev | Test |
|---|---|---|---|---|
| Arabic | S | int | 96.11 | 95.93 |
| Bulgarian | S | fus | 97.91 | 97.80 |
| Coptic | p | agg | 92.54 | 92.51 |
| Danish | S | fus | 95.59 | 95.46 |
| Greek | S | fus | 96.13 | 96.46 |
| English | S | fus | 93.65 | 93.30 |
| Spanish | S | fus | 95.75 | 95.00 |
| Basque | = | agg | 92.99 | 92.43 |
| Persian | s | fus | 96.07 | 96.10 |
| Irish | = | fus | | 89.35 |
| Hebrew | s | int | 95.71 | 94.60 |
| Hindi | S | fus | 95.03 | 94.91 |
| Hungarian | S | agg | 94.14 | 92.00 |
| Indonesian | S | iso | 92.55 | 92.68 |
| Italian | S | fus | 96.82 | 96.95 |
| Latvian | s | fus | 94.70 | 93.09 |
| Russian | S | fus | 95.29 | 95.25 |
| Swedish | S | fus | 95.80 | 95.73 |
| Tamil | S | agg | 86.46 | 87.58 |
| Thai | ∅ | fus | 91.37 | |
| Turkish | S | agg | 92.08 | 92.48 |
| Ukrainian | S | fus | 95.68 | 95.26 |
| Vietnamese | ∅ | iso | 88.51 | 86.58 |
| Chinese | S | iso | 93.05 | 93.11 |

Table 1: Attributes and tagging accuracy by language (Irish and Thai do not have both dev and test sets). [†]Affixation: S/s is strongly/weakly suffixing; P/p is strongly/weakly prefixing; = is equally prefixing/suffixing; ∅ is little affixation. [‡]Morphological synthesis: agglutinative, fusional, introflexive, isolating.

## 3   Tagging Task

We train a set of LSTM tagging models, following the setup of Ling et al. (2015). A word representation trained from a character-level LSTM submodule is fed into a word-level bidirectional LSTM, with each word's hidden state subsequently fed into a two-layer perceptron producing tag scores, which are then softmaxed to produce a tagging distribution. For languages with additional morphosyntactic attribute tagging, we follow the architecture in Pinter et al. (2017) where the same word-level Bi-LSTM states are used to predict each attribute's value using its own perceptron+softmax scaffolding. In order to produce character models which would be as informative as possible to our subsequent analysis, we do not include word-level embeddings, pre-trained or otherwise, in our setup.

### 3.1   Language Selection

As our goal is to examine the relationship between character-level modeling and linguistic properties, we drove language selection based on two morphological properties deemed relevant to the architectural effects examined. All 24 datasets were obtained from Universal Dependencies (UD) version 2.3 (Nivre et al., 2018), and linguistic properties were found in the World Atlas of Language Structures (Bickel and Nichols, 2013; Dryer, 2013). The selected languages and their properties are presented in Table 1. We note that eleven of the 24 languages selected are not Indo-European.

**Affixation.** To evaluate the role of forward and backward units in a bidirectional model, we selected all languages available in UD which are not classified as either weakly or strongly suffixing in inflectional morphology (the vast majority of UD languages). This includes a single prefixing language (Coptic), two equally suffixing and prefixing languages (Basque and Irish), and two languages with little affixation (Thai and Vietnamese).

**Morphological Synthesis.** Linguistically functional features vary between being expressed as distinct tokens (isolating languages), detectable unique character substrings (agglutinative), fused together but still distinguishable from the stem (fusional), and non-linearly represented within the word form (introflexive). This property has previously been found to affect performance in character-level models (Pinter et al., 2017; Gerz et al., 2018; Chaudhary et al., 2018), and thus we select representatives of each group, including most available non-fusional languages.

### 3.2 Technical Setup

Most of our selected languages have only a single UD 2.3 treebank. For languages with multiple treebanks we selected the largest, except in the cases of Spanish and Indonesian, where we selected the GSD treebanks. The Irish IDT treebank has only a train and test split, so we used the test set for early stopping. The Thai PUD treebank only provided a single dataset with 1000 instances, which we shuffled and partitioned into a 850/150 split. Tokens were normalized to remove noisy data: tokens containing 'http' were replaced with 'URL' and tokens containing '@' were replaced with 'EMAIL'. This was most relevant (293 replacements) for the English treebank, which contained many long URLs.

**Hyperparameters.** For the initial bidirectional character-level LSTM, we used a total hidden state size of 128 (64 units in each direction). The character embedding size is set to 256, initialized using the method of Glorot and Bengio (2010). The word-level bidirectional LSTM has two layers and a hidden state size of 128, with 50% dropout applied in the style of Gal and Ghahramani (2016). Each attribute-prediction MLP has a single hidden layer that is the same size as the tagset size for that attribute, and includes a tanh nonlinearity. Models were trained for up to 80 epochs, and we select the model with the highest POS tagging accuracy on the dev set. Training used SGD with 0.9 momentum, and all models were implemented using DyNet 2.0 (Neubig et al., 2017).

### 3.3 Results

In our initial setup, we represent words using a concatenation of the final states from a bidirectional character-level LSTM with 64 forward and backward hidden units each. The results for POS tagging, presented in Table 1, are on par with similar models (Plank et al., 2016, for example) despite not including a word-level type embedding component. We attribute this success to our large character embedding size of 256, corroborating findings reported by Smith et al. (2018).

## 4 Analysis

We next analyze the models trained on the tagging task in an attempt to see how their character-level hidden states encode different manifestations of linguistic information. We suggest that individual hidden units in the character-level sequence model attune to track patterns in the words which would indicate their linguistic roles (POS and morphological properties), and so patterns in character-role regularity across typologically different languages would manifest themselves in an observable form at the individual unit activation level. This motivates us to devise metrics which would characterize languages through aggregation of individual unit behaviour.

### 4.1 Metrics

For each language, we run the character-level BiLSTM from the trained tagger on POS-unambiguous word types occurring frequently in the training set, grouped into their parts of speech.[2] This filtering was done in order to focus

---

[2] We used 8 as our frequency threshold, and define unambiguous forms as ones tagged at least 60% of the time with a single POS.

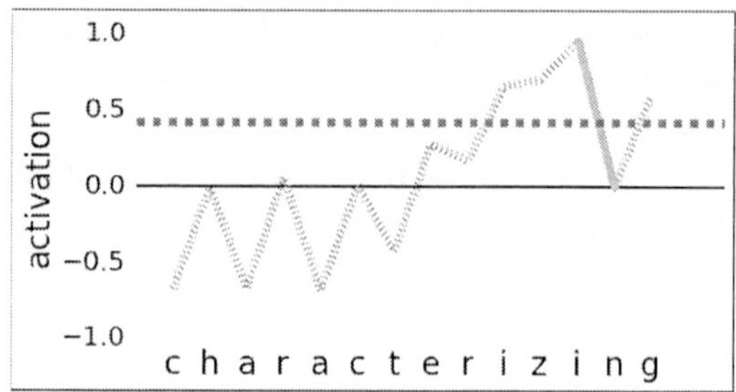


Figure 1: Activations of the English model's unit $42$ (forward) on the word *characterizing*. $b_{\mathrm{avg}|\cdot|}$ is 0.42, and $b_{\mathrm{mad}}$ is 0.96 (the drop from the second $i$ to $n$).

on the more consistent generalizations found by the taggers during training, as our goal is to qualify properties of languages.[3] On each word $w$, we observe each hidden unit $h_i$'s activation level (output) on each character $h_i^c$. We obtain a **base measure** $b(w, i)$ based on the activation pattern. For example, an *average absolute* base measure is defined as the average of absolute value activations:

$$b_{\mathrm{avg}|\cdot|}(w, i) = \frac{1}{|w|} \sum_{c=1}^{|w|} |h_i^c|.$$

The *max absolute diff* base measure is defined as:

$$b_{\mathrm{mad}}(w, i) = \max_{c=1}^{|w|-1} |h_i^{c+1} - h_i^c|.$$

Figure 1 demonstrates these two metrics for a sample (word, unit) pair, showing how the former captures the general level of activation the word caused on the unit, while the latter captures the local character pattern deemed most important by it. We intentionally did not consider metrics based on the final activation values, the direct signals used by the later layers in the model, as these bear no insight into the effect of a word's composition on the learned model.

Next, we derive a language-level metric for each hidden unit, based on the principle of Mutual Information (MI). The base metric's range ($[0, 1)$ for $b_{\mathrm{avg}|\cdot|}$, $[0, 2)$ for $b_{\mathrm{mad}}$) is divided into $B$ bins of equal size, and base activations from each word are summed across each of the $T$ POS tag categories[4], then normalized to produce a joint probability distribution. The mutual information is computed as:

$$\sum_{t=1}^{T} \sum_{b=1}^{B} P(t, b) [\ln P(t, b) - \ln P(t) - \ln P(b)],$$

and we call the resulting number the POS-Discrimination Index, or **PDI**. Intuitively, a higher PDI implies that the unit activates differently on words of different parts of speech, i.e. it is a better discriminator for the task.

At this point a language produces a set of $d_h$ PDI scores, one for each unit. We sort them from high to low, and define two language-level metrics: The **mass** is the sum of PDI values for all units, $\mathcal{M}(\mathcal{L}) := \sum_{i=1}^{d_h} \mathrm{PDI}(\mathcal{L}, i)$, intuitively meant to quantify the degree of success the model has in assigning hidden units to discriminate POS in this language. The **head forwardness** is the proportion of forward-directional units (under the sorted ordering) before the point at which half of the mass accumulates (in a random setup, this number would tend to 0.5):

$$\frac{\left| \left\{ k : \sum_{i=1}^{k} \mathrm{PDI}(\mathcal{L}, i) \leq \frac{\mathcal{M}(\mathcal{L})}{2} \wedge h_k \text{ is forward} \right\} \right|}{\left| \left\{ k : \sum_{i=1}^{k} \mathrm{PDI}(\mathcal{L}, i) \leq \frac{\mathcal{M}(\mathcal{L})}{2} \right\} \right|}$$

This metric aims to quantify the relative importance of forward and backward units in discriminating POS for $\mathcal{L}$. We use only the top units for the metric as a de-noising heuristic, under the assumption that all units end up with some minimal amount of mass even without performing a function.

### 4.2 PDI Patterns

The PDI patterns on the $b_{\mathrm{avg}|\cdot|}$ base measure with $B = 16$ bins on all 24 languages are presented in Table 2. We see that agglutinative languages, where we can expect a better discrimination signal to emerge from the consistently-formed morphemes, cluster mostly at the top of the PDI mass scale, suggesting more individual character-level units extract these signals successfully. Introflexive languages, where character sequences seldom correspond to useful indications of POS or morphosyntactic attributes, cluster towards the bottom.

We present the full unit-level PDI value distributions for Coptic, a prefixing agglutinative language, and English, a suffixing fusional language,

---


[3]This consideration also motivated our choice of UD data, which is tokenized to separate syntactic fusion such as Hebrew and Arabic function words, or Spanish *del*.

[4]We omit the following 'character-simple' part-of-speech tags: INTJ, NUM, PROPN, PUNCT, SYM, X.

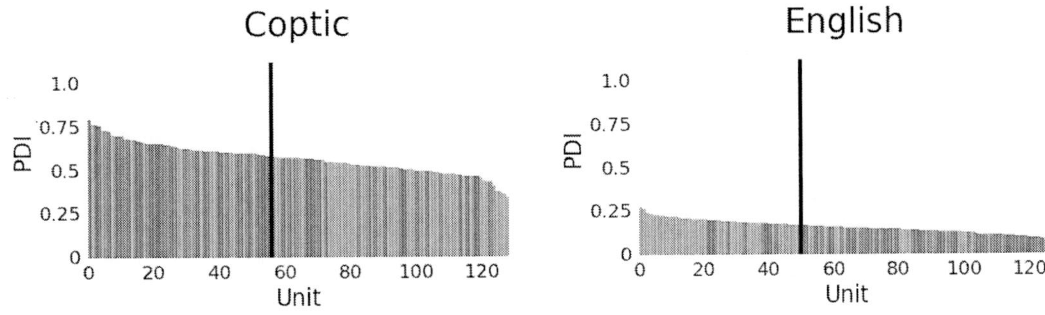


Figure 2: Distribution of PDI values ($b_{\mathrm{avg}|\cdot|}$) across hidden units in Coptic and English, shown in ordered PDI values from largest to smallest, with blue (orange) bars indicating forward (backward) units. The black line demarcates the median point of mass accumulation.

in Figure 2 (trends for $b_{\mathrm{mad}}$ are similar). Consistent with other agglutinative languages, Coptic's cumulative mass is very large ($\mathcal{M}(\mathrm{cop}) = 58.1$), suggesting the predictive qualities of the sequence-based LSTM allows good discrimination from the character signal, as one might expect from an agglutinative language. Conversely, $\mathcal{M}(\mathrm{eng}) = 16$, demonstrating the difficulty presented by fusional languages. The accumulation of 71% forward (80% backward) units in the head of the Coptic (English) value ranking suggests an interesting relationship between affixation and LSTM direction: LSTM units are likely to hone in on POS-indicative signals, which often occur as affixes, in the beginning of their run, causing activation values to rise (in absolute value) and stay large throughout the subsequent traversal of the stem. Unfortunately, since no other prefixing languages are available in UD, we were not able to pursue this hypothesis further.

| Language | Mass | Mass median index | % of forward units until median |
|---|---|---|---|
| **Tamil** | 71.0 | 55 | 49.1 |
| Irish | 62.0 | 56 | 42.9 |
| **Coptic** | 58.1 | 56 | 71.4 |
| **Hungarian** | 47.9 | 55 | 50.9 |
| Greek | 31.2 | 55 | 45.5 |
| **Turkish** | 30.1 | 54 | 57.4 |
| Russian | 25.9 | 54 | 40.7 |
| Thai | 25.9 | 55 | 47.3 |
| Ukrainian | 25.0 | 54 | 37.0 |
| Vietnamese | 24.2 | 55 | 36.4 |
| Chinese | 23.8 | 47 | 42.6 |
| Danish | 21.7 | 54 | 44.4 |
| Swedish | 20.8 | 53 | 34.0 |
| **Basque** | 20.6 | 51 | 64.7 |
| Indonesian | 20.3 | 45 | 71.1 |
| Latvian | 17.0 | 52 | 42.3 |
| Spanish | 16.1 | 45 | 33.3 |
| English | 16.0 | 50 | 20.0 |
| Bulgarian | 15.6 | 52 | 46.2 |
| Italian | 14.1 | 48 | 56.2 |
| *Arabic* | 12.6 | 46 | 58.7 |
| *Hebrew* | 11.4 | 51 | 74.5 |
| Persian | 10.3 | 50 | 46.0 |
| Hindi | 8.4 | 51 | 41.2 |

Table 2: PDI statistics for UD 2.3 models, $b_{\mathrm{avg}|\cdot|}$ metric, sorted by the mass metric (sum of PDIs). Agglutinative languages in **bold**, introflexive in *italics*.

## 4.3 Asymmetric Directionality

Based on these observations, we conduct a directionality balance study, where we vary the number of hidden units in the forward and backwards dimensions. In addition to the models analyzed above, which use 64 forward and 64 backward units (denoted hereafter 64/64), we trained models with imbalanced directionality (128/0, 96/32, 32/96, 0/128). We test the hypothesis that imbalanced models affect languages differently based on their linguistic properties and statistical metrics. We note that these settings do not maintain parameter set size: intra-direction transition operations are quadratic in that direction's hidden layer size, and so this adds a possible advantage in favor of direction-imbalanced models.

| Language Type | 128/0 | 96/32 | 64/64 (base) | 32/96 | 0/128 |
|---|---|---|---|---|---|
| *Inflectional Affixation Categories* | | | | | |
| S. suffix | **+0.22** | +0.07 | 94.50 | -0.06 | -0.02 |
| W. suffix | +0.26 | **+0.12** | 95.46 | -0.07 | -0.01 |
| Equal p/s | **+0.61** | +0.32 | 90.99 | -0.07 | +0.06 |
| Little aff. | -0.06 | -0.21 | 89.59 | -0.16 | -0.22 |
| W. prefix | **+0.52** | **+0.22** | 92.91 | **+0.40** | **+0.33** |
| *Morphological Synthesis Categories* | | | | | |
| Introflex. | **+0.17** | +0.05 | 95.87 | -0.06 | +0.01 |
| Fusional | **+0.22** | +0.07 | 94.95 | +0.01 | +0.06 |
| Agglutina. | **+0.59** | **+0.27** | 91.58 | -0.16 | -0.15 |
| Isolating | -0.14 | -0.13 | 91.15 | -0.15 | -0.13 |
| Overall | **+0.25** | **+0.08** | 93.85 | -0.05 | -0.01 |

Table 3: Imbalanced models' mean POS accuracy on UD development data (differences between three averaged random runs in all models; **boldfaced** when significant at $p < 0.05$ using a paired two-tailed $t$-test).

The results for this study are presented in Table 3 as averages for the language categories listed in Table 1 (the full, raw results are available in Table 4).

One trend which emerges is the preference of **agglutinative** languages for imbalanced models, whereas the other languages are little affected by this change. This could be explained by the increase in inter-unit interaction in the larger direction of an imbalanced model – contiguous character sequences consistently code reliable linguistic features in these languages. A second finding is the slight bias of suffixing languages towards more forward units and of the prefixing language to more backward units, indicating that hidden LSTM units are better in detecting formations close to their final state. Coupled with the findings regarding PDI mass distribution in the different directional units in § 4.2, we suggest that a subtle relation exists between morphological information and model directionality: units which end their run on the affix are more important for detecting the POS signal, so having more of them helps the model. We also note the stability of isolating and little-affixing languages to directionality balance, possibly owing to the relatively small significance of contiguous character sequences in detecting word role. Lastly, we point out that the compromise *sesquidirectional* models 96/32 and 32/96 did not tend to stand out significantly on our tested language categories, suggesting there is no substantial middle-ground between the two popular techniques of unidirectional and bidirectional

| Language | 128/0 | 96/32 | 64/64 | 32/96 | 0/128 |
|---|---|---|---|---|---|
| Arabic | 96.29 | 96.08 | 96.06 | 96.09 | 96.16 |
| Bulgarian | 97.95 | 97.86 | 97.84 | 97.74 | 97.71 |
| Coptic | 93.10 | 92.80 | 92.58 | 92.98 | 92.91 |
| Danish | 95.93 | 95.68 | 95.61 | 95.60 | 95.70 |
| Greek | 96.19 | 96.07 | 96.01 | 96.00 | 95.93 |
| English | 93.86 | 93.74 | 93.65 | 93.80 | 93.87 |
| Spanish | 95.74 | 95.63 | 95.64 | 95.64 | 95.77 |
| Basque | 93.52 | 93.13 | 92.89 | 92.59 | 92.90 |
| Persian | 96.31 | 96.20 | 96.11 | 96.02 | 96.20 |
| Irish | 89.54 | 89.35 | 88.95 | 89.11 | 89.07 |
| Hebrew | 95.76 | 95.72 | 95.60 | 95.50 | 95.57 |
| Hindi | 95.35 | 95.22 | 95.12 | 95.11 | 95.25 |
| Hungarian | 94.25 | 94.29 | 94.20 | 93.97 | 94.00 |
| Indonesian | 92.42 | 92.34 | 92.49 | 92.53 | 92.55 |
| Italian | 97.00 | 96.78 | 96.87 | 96.88 | 97.01 |
| Latvian | 95.10 | 94.84 | 94.69 | 94.58 | 94.61 |
| Russian | 95.51 | 95.39 | 95.32 | 95.31 | 95.36 |
| Swedish | 95.93 | 95.69 | 95.64 | 95.52 | 95.85 |
| Tamil | 87.54 | 87.28 | 86.88 | 86.28 | 85.99 |
| Thai | 91.52 | 91.27 | 91.38 | 91.47 | 91.32 |
| Turkish | 93.14 | 92.45 | 92.06 | 92.03 | 92.09 |
| Ukrainian | 95.72 | 95.76 | 95.63 | 95.68 | 95.66 |
| Vietnamese | 87.98 | 87.92 | 88.23 | 87.83 | 87.85 |
| Chinese | 93.01 | 93.17 | 93.12 | 93.03 | 93.04 |

Table 4: Full scores for the directionality balance experiment, each point averaged over three random seed runs.

LSTMs.

## 5 Conclusion

While character-level Bi-LSTM models compute meaningful word representations across many languages, the way they do it depends on each language's typological properties. These observations can guide model selection: for example, in agglutinative languages we observe a strong preference for a single direction of analysis, motivating the use of unidirectional character-level LSTMs for at least this type of language. In future work, we plan to introduce further control into our metrics by incorporating dataset attributes such as tag distribution and number of instances, as well as learning-related properties like convergence rate and effect of initialization.

## Acknowledgments

We would like to thank Sebastian Mielke, anonymous reviewers from NAACL and BlackboxNLP, and the members of the Computational Linguistics lab at Georgia Tech for their valuable notes. YP is a Bloomberg Data Science PhD Fellow. MM's work was funded by the Georgia Tech Undergraduate Research Opportunities Program.

## References

Balthasar Bickel and Johanna Nichols. 2013. Fusion of selected inflectional formatives. In Matthew S. Dryer and Martin Haspelmath, editors, *The World Atlas of Language Structures Online*. Max Planck Institute for Evolutionary Anthropology, Leipzig.

Piotr Bojanowski, Edouard Grave, Armand Joulin, and Tomas Mikolov. 2017. Enriching word vectors with subword information. *Transactions of the Association of Computational Linguistics*, 5(1):135–146.

Aditi Chaudhary, Chunting Zhou, Lori Levin, Graham Neubig, David R Mortensen, and Jaime Carbonell. 2018. Adapting word embeddings to new languages with morphological and phonological subword representations. In *Proceedings of the 2018 Conference on Empirical Methods in Natural Language Processing*, pages 3285–3295.

Fahim Dalvi, Nadir Durrani, Hassan Sajjad, Yonatan Belinkov, D Anthony Bau, and James Glass. 2019. What is one grain of sand in the desert? analyzing individual neurons in deep nlp models. In *Proceedings of the 32th AAAI Conference on Artificial Intelligence*.

Matthew S. Dryer. 2013. Prefixing vs. suffixing in inflectional morphology. In Matthew S. Dryer and Martin Haspelmath, editors, *The World Atlas of Language Structures Online*. Max Planck Institute for Evolutionary Anthropology, Leipzig.

Yarin Gal and Zoubin Ghahramani. 2016. A theoretically grounded application of dropout in recurrent neural networks. In D. D. Lee, M. Sugiyama, U. V. Luxburg, I. Guyon, and R. Garnett, editors, *Advances in Neural Information Processing Systems 29*, pages 1019–1027. Curran Associates, Inc.

Daniela Gerz, Ivan Vulić, Edoardo Maria Ponti, Jason Naradowsky, Roi Reichart, and Anna Korhonen. 2018. Language modeling for morphologically rich languages: Character-aware modeling for word-level prediction. *Transactions of the Association of Computational Linguistics*, 6:451–465.

Xavier Glorot and Yoshua Bengio. 2010. Understanding the difficulty of training deep feedforward neural networks. In *Proceedings of the thirteenth international conference on artificial intelligence and statistics*, pages 249–256.

Fréderic Godin, Kris Demuynck, Joni Dambre, Wesley De Neve, and Thomas Demeester. 2018. Explaining character-aware neural networks for word-level prediction: Do they discover linguistic rules? In *Proceedings of the 2018 Conference on Empirical Methods in Natural Language Processing*, pages 3275–3284.

Andrej Karpathy, Justin Johnson, and Li Fei-Fei. 2015. Visualizing and understanding recurrent networks. *arXiv preprint arXiv:1506.02078*.

Yova Kementchedjhieva and Adam Lopez. 2018. 'indicatements' that character language models learn english morpho-syntactic units and regularities. In *Proceedings of the 2018 EMNLP Workshop BlackboxNLP: Analyzing and Interpreting Neural Networks for NLP*, pages 145–153.

Guillaume Lample, Miguel Ballesteros, Sandeep Subramanian, Kazuya Kawakami, and Chris Dyer. 2016. Neural architectures for named entity recognition. In *Proceedings of NAACL-HLT*, pages 260–270.

Wang Ling, Tiago Luís, Luís Marujo, Ramón Fernandez Astudillo, Silvio Amir, Chris Dyer, Alan W Black, and Isabel Trancoso. 2015. Finding function in form: Compositional character models for open vocabulary word representation. In *Proceedings of the 2015 Conference on Empirical Methods in Natural Language Processing*.

Tal Linzen, Emmanuel Dupoux, and Yoav Goldberg. 2016. Assessing the ability of lstms to learn syntax-sensitive dependencies. *Transactions of the Association of Computational Linguistics*, 4(1):521–535.

Graham Neubig, Chris Dyer, Yoav Goldberg, Austin Matthews, Waleed Ammar, Antonios Anastasopoulos, Miguel Ballesteros, David Chiang, Daniel Clothiaux, Trevor Cohn, Kevin Duh, Manaal Faruqui, Cynthia Gan, Dan Garrette, Yangfeng Ji, Lingpeng Kong, Adhiguna Kuncoro, Gaurav Kumar, Chaitanya Malaviya, Paul Michel, Yusuke Oda, Matthew Richardson, Naomi Saphra, Swabha Swayamdipta, and Pengcheng Yin. 2017. Dynet: The dynamic neural network toolkit. *arXiv preprint arXiv:1701.03980*.

Joakim Nivre et al. 2018. Universal dependencies 2.3. LINDAT/CLARIN digital library at the Institute of Formal and Applied Linguistics (ÚFAL), Faculty of Mathematics and Physics, Charles University.

Matthew Peters, Mark Neumann, Mohit Iyyer, Matt Gardner, Christopher Clark, Kenton Lee, and Luke Zettlemoyer. 2018. Deep contextualized word representations. In *Proceedings of the 2018 Conference of the North American Chapter of the Association for Computational Linguistics: Human Language Technologies, Volume 1 (Long Papers)*, volume 1, pages 2227–2237.

Yuval Pinter, Robert Guthrie, and Jacob Eisenstein. 2017. Mimicking Word Embeddings using Subword RNNs. In *Proceedings of the 2017 Conference on Empirical Methods in Natural Language Processing*, pages 102–112.

Barbara Plank, Anders Søgaard, and Yoav Goldberg. 2016. Multilingual part-of-speech tagging with bidirectional long short-term memory models and auxiliary loss. In *Proceedings of the 54th Annual Meeting of the Association for Computational Linguistics (Volume 2: Short Papers)*, pages 412–418. Association for Computational Linguistics.

Alec Radford, Rafal Jozefowicz, and Ilya Sutskever. 2017. Learning to generate reviews and discovering sentiment. *arXiv preprint arXiv:1704.01444*.

Aaron Smith, Miryam de Lhoneux, Sara Stymne, and Joakim Nivre. 2018. An investigation of the interactions between pre-trained word embeddings, character models and pos tags in dependency parsing. In *Proceedings of the 2018 Conference on Empirical Methods in Natural Language Processing*, pages 2711–2720.

Clara Vania and Adam Lopez. 2017. From characters to words to in between: Do we capture morphology? In *Proceedings of the 55th Annual Meeting of the Association for Computational Linguistics (Volume 1: Long Papers)*, volume 1, pages 2016–2027.

# Faithful Multimodal Explanation for Visual Question Answering


**Jialin Wu**
Department of Computer Science
University of Texas at Austin
jialinwu@cs.utexas.edu

**Raymond J. Mooney**
Department of Computer Science
University of Texas at Austin
mooney@cs.utexas.edu



## Abstract

AI systems' ability to explain their reasoning is critical to their utility and trustworthiness. Deep neural networks have enabled significant progress on many challenging problems such as visual question answering (VQA). However, most of them are opaque black boxes with limited explanatory capability. This paper presents a novel approach to developing a high-performing VQA system that can elucidate its answers with integrated textual and visual explanations that faithfully reflect important aspects of its underlying reasoning process while capturing the style of comprehensible human explanations. Extensive experimental evaluation demonstrates the advantages of this approach compared to competing methods using both automated metrics and human evaluation.


## 1 Introduction

Deep neural networks have made significant progress on visual question answering (VQA), the challenging AI problem of answering natural-language questions about an image (Antol et al., 2015). However successful systems (Fukui et al., 2016; Anderson et al., 2018; Yang et al., 2016; Wu et al., 2018a; Jiang et al., 2018) based on deep neural networks are difficult to comprehend because of many layers of abstraction and a large number of parameters. This makes it hard to develop user trust. Partly due to the opacity of current deep models, there has been a recent resurgence of interest in *explainable AI*, systems that can explain their reasoning to human users. In particular, there has been some recent development of explainable VQA systems (Selvaraju et al., 2017; Park et al., 2018; Hendricks et al., 2016, 2018).

One approach to explainable VQA is to generate *visual explanations*, which highlight image regions that most contributed to the system's answer, as determined by attention mechanisms (Lu

Figure 1: Example of our multimodal explanation. It highlights relevant image regions together with a textual explanation with corresponding words in the same color.

et al., 2016) or gradient analysis (Selvaraju et al., 2017). However, such simple visualizations do not explain *how* these regions support the answer. An alternate approach is to generate a *textual explanation*, a natural-language sentence that provides reasons for the answer. Some recent work has generated textual explanations for VQA by training a recurrent neural network (RNN) to directly mimic examples of human explanations (Hendricks et al., 2016; Park et al., 2018). A *multimodal* approach that integrates *both* a visual and textual explanation provides the advantages of both. Words and phrases in the text can point to relevant regions in the image. An illustrative explanation generated by our system is shown in Figure. 1.

Recent research on such multimodal VQA explanation is presented in (Park et al., 2018) that employs a form of "post hoc justification" that does not truly follow and reflect the system's actual processing. We believe that explanations should more faithfully reflect the actual processing of the underlying system in order to provide users with a deeper understanding of the system, increasing trust for the right reasons, rather than




*Proceedings of the Second BlackboxNLP Workshop on Analyzing and Interpreting Neural Networks for NLP*, pages 103–112
Florence, Italy, August 1, 2019. ©2019 Association for Computational Linguistics

trying to simply convince them of the system's reliability (Bilgic and Mooney, 2005). In order to be faithful, the textual explanation generator should focus on the set of objects that contribute to the predicted answers, and receive proper supervision from only the gold standard explanations that are consistent with the actual VQA reasoning process. Towards this end, our explanation module directly uses the VQA-attended features and is trained to only generate human explanations that can be traced back to the relevant object set using a gradient-based method called GradCAM (Selvaraju et al., 2017). To enforce local faithfulness, we also align the gradient-based visual explanations generated by the textual explanation module and the VQA module during training.

In addition, our explanations provide direct links between terms in the textual explanation and segmented items in the image, as shown in Figure 1. The result is a nice synthesis of a faithful explanation that highlights concepts actually used to compute the answer and a comprehensible, human-like, linguistic explanation. Below we describe the details of our approach and present extensive experimental results on the VQA-X (Park et al., 2018) dataset that demonstrates the advantages of our approach compared to prior work using this data (Park et al., 2018) in terms of both automated metrics and human evaluation. Further, in order to evaluate the faithfulness, we design two metrics: (1) We first measure the degree of similarity between the highlighted image segments in our textual explanations and the influential segments determined by the LIME explainer (Ribeiro et al., 2016); (2) we also measure the consistency between the gradient-based visual explanation (Selvaraju et al., 2017) of the predicted answer and the generated textual explanation.

## 2   Related Work

In this section, we review related work including visual and textual explanation generation and VQA.

### 2.1   VQA

Answering visual questions (Antol et al., 2015) has been widely investigated in both the NLP and computer vision communities. Most VQA models (Fukui et al., 2016; Lu et al., 2016) embed images using a CNN and questions using an RNN and then use these embeddings to train an answer classifier to predict answers from a pre-extracted set. Attention mechanisms are frequently applied to recognize important visual features and filter out irrelevant parts. A recent advance is the use of the Bottom-Up-Top-Down (Up-Down) attention mechanism (Anderson et al., 2018) that attends over high-level objects instead of convolutional features to avoid emphasis on irrelevant portions of the image. We adopt this mechanism, but replace object detection (Ren et al., 2015) with segmentation (Hu et al., 2018) to obtain more precise object boundaries.

### 2.2   Visual Explanation

A number of approaches have been proposed to visually explain decisions made by vision systems by highlighting relevant image regions. Grad-CAM (Selvaraju et al., 2017) analyzes the gradient space to find visual regions that most affect the decision. Attention mechanisms in VQA models can also be directly used to determine highly-attended regions and generate visual explanations. Unlike conventional visual explanations, ours highlight segmented objects that are linked to words in an accompanying textual explanation, thereby focusing on more precise regions and filtering out noisy attention weights.

### 2.3   Textual and Multimodal Explanation

Visual explanations highlight key image regions behind the decision, however, they do not explain the reasoning process and crucial relationships between the highlighted regions. Therefore, there has been some work on generating textual explanations for decisions made by visual classifiers (Hendricks et al., 2016). As mentioned in the introduction, there has also been some work on multimodal explanations that link textual and visual explanations (Park et al., 2018). A recent extension of this work (Hendricks et al., 2018) first generates multiple textual explanations and then filters out those that could not be grounded in the image. We argue that a good explanation should focus on referencing visual objects that actually influenced the system's decision, therefore generating more faithful explanations.

## 3   Approach

Our goal is to generate more faithful multimodal explanations that specifically include the segmented objects in the image that are the focus of

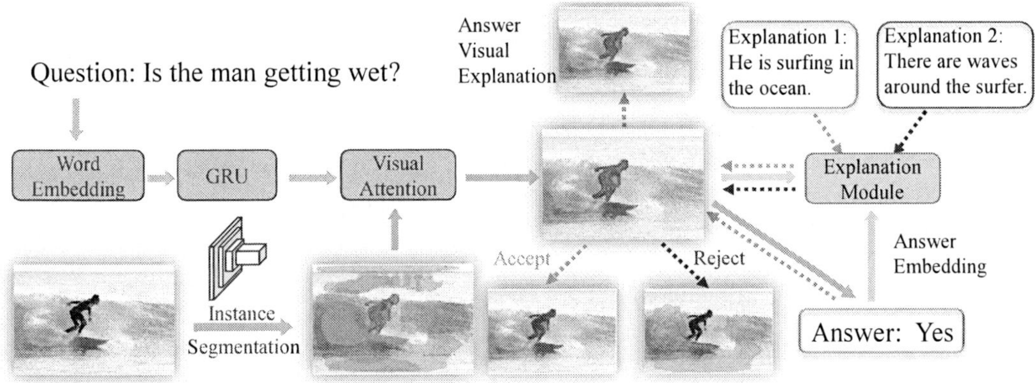



Figure 2: Model overview: We first segment the image and then predict the answer for the visual question with a pretrained VQA module. Then, we learn to embed the question, answer, and the VQA-attended features to generate textual explanations. During training, we only use the faithful human explanation whose gradient-based visual explanation is consistent with that of the predicted answer. In the example, our explanation module is only trained to generate "Explanation 1" and further enforces the consistency between this explanation and the predicted answer. "Explanation 2" is filtered out since its visual explanation is mainly focused on the waves and is not consistent with VQA module's focus on the surfer. Dashed arrows denote gradients, gray and yellow arrows denote fixed and trainable parameters, respectively. The three smaller images denote the visual explanations for the predicted answer and the two textual explanations.

the VQA module. Figure 2 illustrates our model's pipeline in the training phase, consisting of the VQA module (Section 3.2), and textual explanation module (Section 3.4). We first segment the objects in the image and predict the answer using the VQA module, which has an attention mechanism over those objects. Next, the explanation module is trained to generate textual explanations conditioned on the question, answer, and VQA-attended features. To faithfully train the explanation module, we filter out human textual explanations whose gradient-based visual explanation is not consistent with that of the predicted answer. For example, in Figure 2 "Explanation 1" is accepted as the textual explanation since it is mainly focused on the surfer and "Explanation 2" is rejected. For the consistent textual explanations, we also train the explanation module to align its visual explanation with the predicted answer's to enforce local faithfulness.

## 3.1 Notation

We use $f$ to denote the fully-connected $fc$ layers of the neural network, and these $fc$ layers do not share parameters. We notate the sigmoid functions as $\sigma$. The subscript $i$ indexes the elements of the segmented object sets from images. Bold letters denote vectors, overlining $\bar{\cdot}$ denotes averaging, and $[\cdot, \cdot]$ denotes concatenation.

## 3.2 VQA Module

We base our VQA module on Up-Down (Anderson et al., 2018) with some modifications. First, we replace the two-branch gated *tanh* answer classifier with single *fc* layers with Leaky ReLU activation (Maas et al., 2013). In order to ground the explanations in more precise visual regions, we use instance segmentation (Hu et al., 2018) to segment objects in over 3,000 categories. Specifically, we extract at most the top $V < 80$ objects in terms of segmentation scores and concatenate each object's *fc6* representation in the bounding box classification branch and *mask_fcn[1-4]* features in the mask generation branch to form a 2048-d vector. This results in an image feature set $\mathbf{V}$ containing $V$ 2048-d vectors $\mathbf{v}_i$ for each image. We encode each question as the last hidden state $\mathbf{q}$ of a gated recurrent unit (GRU) with 512 hidden units. We learn visual attention over all the segments $\boldsymbol{\alpha}^{vqa} \in \mathbb{R}^V$, and use the attended visual features $\mathbf{v}_i^q$ together with the question embedding to produce a joint representation $\mathbf{h}$. Then the model predicts the logits $\mathbf{s}^{vqa}$ for each answer candidate using a 2-layer $fc$ networks, which is passed through a sigmoid function to compute the final probabilities. For the detailed network architecture, please refer to (Anderson et al., 2018). The parameters in the VQA module are fixed during the training of the explanation module.

### 3.3 Question and Answer Embedding for Explanation Generation

As suggested in (Park et al., 2018), we also encode questions and answers as input features to the explanation module. In particular, we regard the normalized answer prediction output as a multinomial distribution, and sample one answer from this distribution at each time step. We re-embed it as a one-hot vector $\mathbf{a}_s = \text{one-hot}(\text{multinomial}(s))$.

$$\mathbf{u}_i = \mathbf{v}_i^q \odot f(\mathbf{a}_s) \odot f(\mathbf{q}) \tag{1}$$

Next, we element-wise multiply the embedding of $\mathbf{q}$ and $\mathbf{a}_s$ with $\mathbf{v}_i^q$ to compute the joint representation $\mathbf{u}_i$. Note that $\mathbf{u}$ faithfully represents the focus of the VQA process, in that it is directly derived from the VQA-attended features.

### 3.4 Explanation Generation

In this section, we describe the Explanation Module depicted by the yellow box in Figure. 2. The explanation module has a two-layer-LSTM architecture whose first layer produces an attention over the $\mathbf{u}_i$, and whose second layer learns a representation for predicting the next word using the first layer's features.

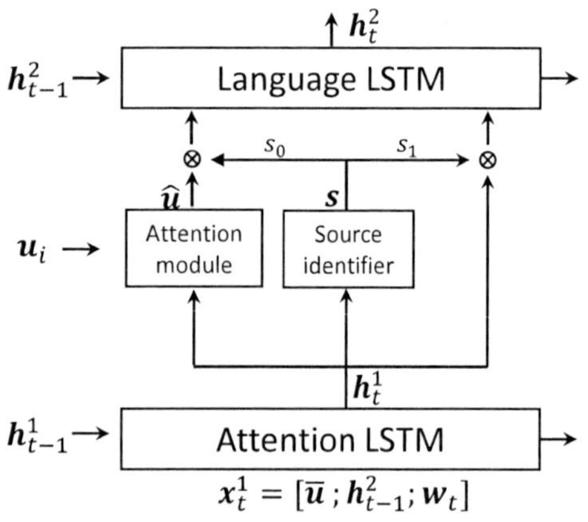


Figure 3: Overview of the explanation module.

In particular, the first visual attention LSTM takes the concatenation $\mathbf{x}_t^1$ of the second language LSTM's previous output $\mathbf{h}_{t-1}^2$, the average pooling of $\mathbf{u}_i$, and the previous words' embedding as input and produces the hidden presentation $\mathbf{h}_t^1$. Then, an attention mechanism re-weights the image feature $\mathbf{u}_i$ using the generated $\mathbf{h}_t^1$ as input shown in Eq. 2. For the detailed structure, please refer to (Ander-

son et al., 2018).

$$a_{i,t} = f(tanh(f(\mathbf{u}_i) + f(\mathbf{h}_t^1))) \tag{2}$$
$$\boldsymbol{\alpha}_t = softmax(\boldsymbol{\alpha}_t) \tag{3}$$

For the purpose of faithfully grounding the generated explanation in the image, we argue that the generator should be able to determine if the next word should be based on image content attended to by the VQA system or on learned linguistic content. To achieve this, we introduce a "source identifier" to balance the total amount of attention paid to the visual features $\mathbf{u}_i$ and the recurrent hidden representation $\mathbf{h}_t^1$ at each time step. In particular, given the output $\mathbf{h}_t^1$ from the attention LSTM and the average pooling $\overline{\mathbf{u}}_i$ over $\mathbf{u}_i$, we train a $fc$ layer to produce a 2-d output $\mathbf{s} = \sigma(f([\mathbf{h}_t^1, \overline{\mathbf{u}}_i])) = (s_0, s_1)$ that identifies which source the current generated word should be based on (*i.e.* $s_0$ for the output of the attention LSTM[1] and $s_1$ for the attended image features).

$$\mathbf{s} = \sigma(f([\mathbf{h}_t^1, \overline{\mathbf{u}}_i])) \tag{4}$$

We use the following approach to obtain training labels $\hat{\mathbf{s}}$ for the source identifier. For each visual features $\mathbf{u}_i$, we assign label 1 (indicating the use of attended visual information) when there exists a segmentation $\mathbf{u}_i$ whose cosine similarity between its category name's GloVe representation and the current generated word's GloVe representation is above 0.6. Given the labeled data, we train the source identifier using cross entropy loss $\mathcal{L}_s$ as shown in Eq. 5:

$$\mathcal{L}_s = -(\sum_{j=0}^{1} \hat{s}_j \log s_j + (1 - \hat{s}_j) \log(1 - s_j)) \tag{5}$$

where the $\hat{s}_0, \hat{s}_1$ are the aforementioned labels.

Next, we concatenate the re-weighted $\mathbf{h}_t^1$ and $\overline{\mathbf{u}}_i$ with the output of the source identifier as the input $\mathbf{x}_t^2 = [\mathbf{h}_t^1 s_0, \overline{\mathbf{u}}_i s_1]$ for the language LSTM. For more detail on the language LSTM structure, please refer to (Anderson et al., 2018).

With the hidden states $\mathbf{h}_t^2$ in the Language LSTM, the output word's probability is computed

---

[1] We tried to directly use the source weights $s_0$ in the language LSTM's hidden representation $\mathbf{h}_{t-1}^2$ and found that using $\mathbf{h}_t^1$ works better. The reason is that directly constraining $\mathbf{h}_{t-1}^2$ makes the language LSTM forget the previously encoded content and prevents it from learning long term dependencies.

using Eq. 6:

$$p(y_t|y_{1:t-1}) = softmax(f(\mathbf{h}_t^2)) \qquad (6)$$

where $y_t$ denotes the $t$-th word in the explanation $\mathbf{y}$ and $y_{1:t-1}$ denotes the first $t-1$ words.

**Faithful Explanation Supervision.** Directly collecting faithful textual explanations is infeasible because it would require an annotation process where workers provide explanations based on the attended VQA features. Instead, we design an online algorithm that automatically filters unfaithful explanations from the human ones in the VQA-X data (Park et al., 2018) based on the idea that a proper explanation should focus on the same set of objects as the VQA module and be locally faithful. As recent research suggested that gradient-based methods more faithfully present the models' decision making process (Zhang et al., 2018; Wu et al., 2018b; Wu and Mooney, 2019; Jain and Wallace, 2019), we define a faithfulness score $\mathcal{S}_f$ as the cosine similarity between the Grad-CAM (Selvaraju et al., 2017) visual explanation vectors of the textual explanation and the predicted answer as shown in Eq. 7:

$$\mathcal{S}_f(\mathbf{y}) = cos(g(s_{pred}^{vqa}, \mathbf{v}^q), g(\log p(\mathbf{y}), \mathbf{v}^q)) \quad (7)$$

where $g$ denotes the Grad-CAM operation and the result is a vector of length $|V|$ indicating the contribution of each segmented object. $s_{pred}^{vqa}$ is the logit for the predicted answer.

Then, we filter out the explanations in the training set whose faithfulness scores are less than $\xi \max(0.02\, it, 1)$, where $\xi$ is a threshold and the $\max(0.02\, it, 1)$ term is used to jump-start the randomly initialized explanation module. For example, during training, we only accept "Explanation 1" in Figure 2 because the visual explanations of the predicted answer and the textual explanation are consistent and reject "Explanation 2".

Since the VQA-X dataset only has explanations for the correct answers, we also discard the explanations when the predicted answers are wrong. With the remaining human explanations, we minimize the cross-entropy loss $\mathcal{L}_{XE}$ in Eq. 8:

$$\mathcal{L}_{XE} = \sum_{t=1}^{T} \log(p(y_t|y_{1:t-1})) \qquad (8)$$

To enforce local faithfulness, we further align these two gradient vectors using cosine distance $\mathcal{L}_f = 1 - \mathcal{S}_f$.

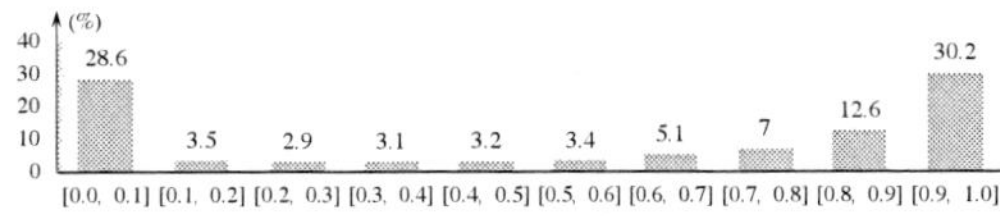


Figure 4: The distribution of explanations' faithfulness scores in the last epoch during training.

In Figure 4, we report the distribution of the explanations' faithfulness scores $\mathcal{S}_f$ in the last epoch during training ($\xi$ is set to 0.3). We observe that about 30% of the human explanations in the training set cannot be traced back to similar image segments that highly contribute to the predicted answer using our trained explanation module. These textual explanations cannot be seen as faithful either because the explanations themselves are not faithful or because the explanation module fails to develop the correct mappings between the textual explanations and the VQA-attended features. There are only a small fraction of the explanations whose faithfulness scores are in the interval of [0.1, 0.6] indicating that there is a clear boundary between whether or not an explanation is deemed faithful according to our metric.

### 3.5 Training

We pre-train the VQA module on the entire VQA v2 training set for 15 epochs using the Adam optimizer (Kingma and Ba, 2014) with a learning rate of 0.001. After that, the parameters in the VQA module are frozen. Our VQA module is capable of achieving 82.9% and 80.3% in the VQA-X train and test split respectively. and 63.5% in the VQA v2 validation set which is comparable to the baseline Up-Down model (63.2%) (Anderson et al., 2018). Note that VQA performance is not the focus of this work, and our experimental evaluation focuses on the generated explanations. Finally, we train the explanation module using the human explanations in the VQA-X dataset (Park et al., 2018) filtered for faithfulness. VQA-X contains 29,459 question answer pairs and each pair is associated with a human explanation. We train to minimize the joint loss $\mathcal{L}$ (Eq. 9), and $\xi$ is empirically set to 0.3. We ran the Adam optimizer for 25 epochs with a batch size of 128. The learning rate for training the explanation module is initialized to 5e-4 and decays by a factor of 0.8 every three epochs.

$$\mathcal{L} = \mathcal{L}_{XE} + \mathcal{L}_s + \mathcal{L}_f \qquad (9)$$

| | $\mathcal{L}_s$ | $\mathcal{F}$ | $\mathcal{L}_f$ | # Expl. | Textual | | | | | Visual |
| | | | | | B-4 | M | R-L | C | S | EMD |
|---|---|---|---|---|---|---|---|---|---|---|
| PJ-X (Park et al., 2018) | | | | 29K | 19.5 | 18.2 | 43.7 | 71.3 | 15.1 | 2.64 |
| Ours (Justification) | | | | 29K | 23.5 | 19.0 | 46.2 | 81.2 | 17.2 | 2.46 |
| Ours (Justification) | ✓ | | | 29K | 24.4 | 19.5 | 47.4 | 88.8 | 17.9 | 2.41 |
| Ours (Justification) | ✓ | | | 15K | 24.1 | 18.6 | 46.2 | 83.4 | 16.2 | 2.59 |
| Ours (Explanation) | ✓ | ✓ | | 15K | 24.7 | 19.2 | 47.0 | 85.1 | 16.6 | 2.56 |
| Ours (Explanation) | ✓ | ✓ | ✓ | 15K | **25.1** | **19.7** | **48.2** | **86.7** | **17.2** | **2.52** |

Table 1: Explanation evaluation results, the top half shows results using the entire train set and the bottom half shows results using about 15K explanations. $\mathcal{F}$ denotes whether to filter out the unfaithful training explanations. With $\mathcal{F}$, the 15K explanations are the remaining explanation and without $\mathcal{F}$, the 15K explanations are randomly sampled from train set. $\mathcal{L}_s$, $\mathcal{L}_f$ denote the losses of the source identifier and the faithful gradient alignment, respectively. B-4, M, R-L, C and S are short hand for BLEU-4, METEOR, ROUGE-L, CIDEr and SPICE, respectively.

## 3.6 Multimodal Explanation Generation

As a last step, we link words in the generated textual explanation to image segments in order to generate the final multimodal explanation. To determine which words to link, we extract all common nouns whose source identifier weight $s_1$ in Eq. 4 exceeds 0.5. We then link them to the segmented object with the highest attention weight $\alpha_t$ in Eq. 2 when that corresponding output word $y_t$ was generated, but only if this weight is greater than 0.2.[2]

## 4 Experimental Evaluation

This section experimentally evaluates both the textual and visual aspects of our multimodal explanations, including comparisons to competing methods and ablations that study the impact of the various components of our overall system. Finally, we present metrics and evaluation for the faithfulness of our explanations.

## 4.1 Textual Explanation Evaluation

Similar to (Park et al., 2018), we first evaluate our textual explanations using automated metrics by comparing them to the gold-standard human explanations in the VQA-X test data using standard sentence-comparison metrics: BLEU-4 (Papineni et al., 2002), METEOR (Banerjee and Lavie, 2005), ROUGE-L (Lin, 2004), CIDEr (Vedantam et al., 2015) and SPICE (Anderson et al., 2016). Table 1 reports our performance, including ablations. In particular, "Justification" denotes training on the entire or randomly sampled VQA-X dataset and "Explanation" denotes

training only on the remaining faithful explanations. We outperform the current state-of-the-art PJ-X model (Park et al., 2018) on all automated metrics by a clear margin with only about half the explanation training data. This indicates that constructing explanations that faithfully reflect the VQA process can actually generate explanations that match human explanations better than just training to directly match human explanations, possibly by avoiding over-fitting and focusing more on important aspects of the test images.

## 4.2 Multimodal Explanation Evaluation

In this section, we present the evaluations of our model on both visual and multimodal aspects.

**Automated Evaluation:** As in previous work (Selvaraju et al., 2017; Park et al., 2018), we first used Earth Mover Distance (EMD) (Pele and Werman, 2008) to compare the image regions highlighted in our explanation to image regions highlighted by human judges. In order to fairly compare to prior results, we resize all the images in the entire test split to $14 \times 14$ and adjust the segmentation in the images accordingly using bi-linear interpolation. Next, we sum up the multiplication of attention values and source identifiers' values in Eq. 2 over time ($t$) and assign the accumulated attention weight to each corresponding segmentation region. We then normalize attention weights over the $14 \times 14$ resized images to sum to 1, and finally compute the EMD between the normalized attentions and the ground truth.

As shown in the Visual results in Table 1, our approach matches human attention maps more

---

[2]Due to duplicated segments, we use a lower threshold.

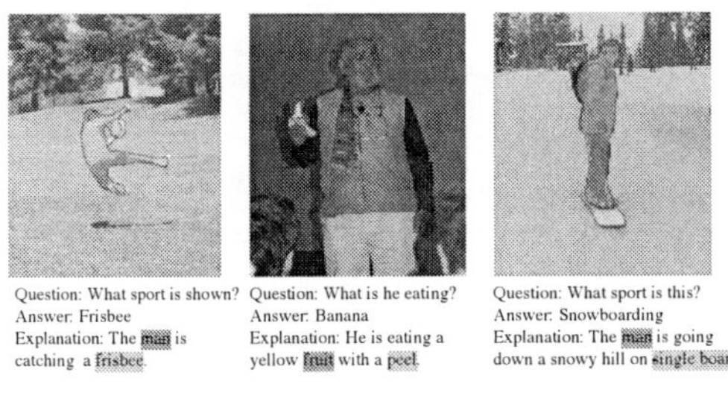

Question: What sport is shown? Answer: Frisbee Explanation: The man is catching a frisbee.

Question: What is he eating? Answer: Banana Explanation: He is eating a yellow fruit with a peel.

Question: What sport is this? Answer: Snowboarding Explanation: The man is going down a snowy hill on single board.

Figure 5: Sample positively-rated explanations.

closely than PJ-X (Park et al., 2018). We attribute this improvement to the following reasons. First, our approach uses detailed image segmentation which avoids focusing on background and is much more precise than bounding-box detection. Second, our visual explanation is focused by textual explanation where the segmented visual objects must be linked to specific words in the textual explanation. Therefore, the risk of attending to unnecessary objects in the images is significantly reduced. As a result, we filter out most of the noisy attention in a purely visual explanation like that in PJ-X.

**Human Evaluation:** We also asked AMT workers to evaluate our final multimodal explanations that link words in the textual explanation directly to segments in the image. Specifically, we randomly selected 1,000 correctly answered question and asked workers " How well do the highlighted image regions support the answer to the question?" and provided them a Likert-scale set of possible answers: "Very supportive", "Supportive", "Neutral", 'Unsupportive" and "Completely unsupportive". The second task was to evaluate the quality of the links between words and image regions in the explanations. We asked workers "How well do the colored image segments highlight the appropriate regions for the corresponding colored words in the explanation?" with the Like-scale choices: "Very Well", "Well", "Neutral", "Not Well", "Poorly". We assign five questions in each AMT HIT with one "validation" item to control the HIT's qualities.

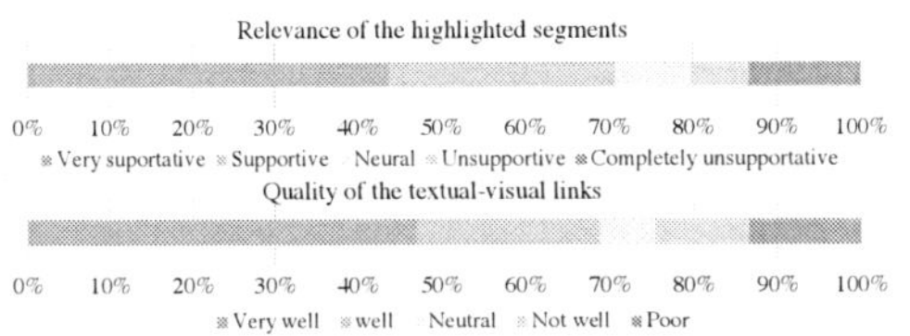

Figure 6: Human evaluation results.

As shown in Figure 6, in both cases, about 70% of the evaluations are positive and about 45% of them are strongly positive. This indicates that our multimodal explanations provide good connections among visual explanations, textual explanations, and the VQA process. Figure 5 presents some sample positively-rated multimodal explanations.

### 4.3 Faithfulness Evaluation

In this section, we measure the faithfulness of our explanations, i.e. how well they reflect the underlying VQA system's reasoning. First, we measured how many words in a generated explanation are actually linked to a visual segmentation in the image. We analyzed the explanations from 1,000 correctly answered questions from the test data. On average, our model is able to link 1.6 words in an explanation to an image segment, indicating that the textual explanation is actually grounded in objects detected by our VQA system.

**Faithfulness Evaluation using LIME.** We use the model-agnostic explainer LIME (Ribeiro et al., 2016) to determine the segmented objects that most influenced a particular answer, and measure how well the objects referenced in our explanation match these influential segments. We regard all the detected visual segments as the "interpretable" units used by LIME to explain decisions. Using these interpretable units, LIME applies LASSO with the regularization path (Efron et al., 2004) to learn a linear model of the local decision boundary around the example to be explained. In particular, we collect 256 points around the example by randomly blinding each segment's features with a probability of $0.4$. The highly weighted features in this model are claimed to provide a faithful explanation of the decision on this example (Ribeiro et al., 2016). The complexity of the explanation is controlled by the number of units, $K$, that can be used in this linear model. Using the coefficients $\mathbf{w}$ of LIME's weighted linear model, we compare the object segments selected by LIME to the set of objects that are actually linked to words in our explanations. Specifically, we define our faithfulness metric as:

$$score = \frac{\sum_{i=1}^{|V|} |w_i| \max_{j \in \mathcal{L}} cos(\mathbf{v}_i, \mathbf{v}_j)}{\sum_{i=1}^{|V|} |w_i|} \quad (10)$$

where $\mathbf{v}_i$ denotes the visual feature of the $i$-th segmented object and the $\mathcal{L}$ denotes the set of explanation-linked objects. For each object in the LIME explanation, it finds the closest object in our explanation and multiplies its LIME weight by this similarity. The normalized sum of these matches is used to measure the similarity of the two explanations.

We collect all correctly answered questions in the VQA-X test set, and Table 2 reports the average score for their explanations using models trained on 15K training explanations with different numbers of interpretable units $K$. The influential objects recognized by LIME match objects that are linked to words in our explanations with an average cosine similarity around 0.7. This indicates that the explanations are faithfully making reference to visual segmentations that actually influenced the decision of the underlying VQA system. Also, we observe that training with faithful human explanation outperforms purely mimicking human explanations in terms of our faithful metric, and further enforcing the local faithfulness achieves a better result.

|  | K = 1 | K = 2 | K = 3 |
|---|---|---|---|
| Ours (Random) | 0.588 | 0.601 | 0.574 |
| Ours (Filtered) | 0.636 | 0.651 | 0.643 |
| Ours (Filtered+$\mathcal{L}_f$) | **0.686** | **0.705** | **0.678** |

Table 2: Evaluation of LIME-based faithfulness scores for different numbers of interpretable units $K$ using 15K training explanations. "Random" means the training explanations are randomly sampled from the train set, and "Filtered" means the models are trained using the remaining faithful explanations.

**Faithfulness Evaluation using Grad-CAM.** We also evaluated the consistency between the Grad-CAM visual explanation vectors from the textual explanation and the predicted answer using the faithful score $S_f$ defined in Eq. 7. Table 3 reports the results from using filtered verses randomly sampled explanations for training. We observe that with faithful human explanations, the average faithfulness evaluation score increases 7% over training with randomly sampled explanations. Moreover, with the faithfulness loss $\mathcal{L}_f$, the model can better align the visual explanation for the textual explanation with that for the predicted answer, leading to a further 11% increase.

We also report the distribution of the generated explanations' cosine similarity between their visual explanation and the visual explanation of the

|  | # Expl. | Average $S_f$ |
|---|---|---|
| Ours (Random) | 15K | 0.38 |
| Ours (Filtered) | 15K | 0.45 |
| Ours (Filtered+$\mathcal{L}_f$) | 15K | **0.56** |

Table 3: Average faithfulness evaluation score using different explanations models. "Random" means the training explanations are randomly sampled from the train set, and "Filtered" means the models are trained using the remaining faithful explanations.

answers in Figure 7. The fraction of the faithfulness scores between the interval [0.0, 0.1] is significantly decreased by over 17% when using the faithful human explanations for supervision and further enforcing the local faithfulness with the faithfulness loss, $\mathcal{L}_f$.

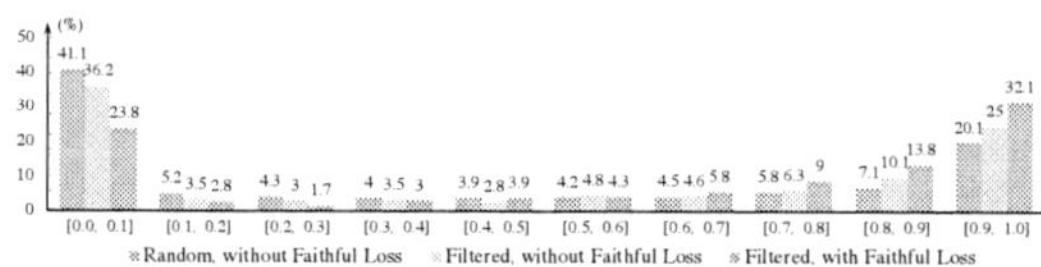


Figure 7: The distribution of explanations' cosine similarity between the visual explanation of the textual explanation and the predicted answer.

## 5 Conclusion and Future Work

This paper has presented a new approach to generating multimodal explanations for visual question answering systems that aims to more faithfully represent the reasoning of the underlying VQA system while maintaining the style of human explanations. The approach generates textual explanations with words linked to relevant image regions actually attended to by the underlying VQA system. Experimental evaluations of both the textual and visual aspects of the explanations using both automated metrics and crowdsourced human judgments were presented that demonstrate the advantages of this approach compared to a previously-published competing method. In the future, we would like to incorporate more information from the VQA networks into the explanations. In particular, we would like to integrate *network dissection* (Bau et al., 2017) to allow recognizable concepts in the learned hidden-layer representations to be included in explanations.

## Acknowledgement

This research was supported by the DARPA XAI program under a grant from AFRL.

## References

Peter Anderson, Basura Fernando, Mark Johnson, and Stephen Gould. 2016. Spice: Semantic Propositional image caption evaluation. In *European Conference on Computer Vision*, pages 382–398.

Peter Anderson, Xiaodong He, Chris Buehler, Damien Teney, Mark Johnson, Stephen Gould, and Lei Zhang. 2018. Bottom-Up and Top-Down Attention for Image Captioning and Visual Question Answering. In *Proceedings of the IEEE Conference on Computer Vision and Pattern Recognition*, volume 3, page 6.

Stanislaw Antol, Aishwarya Agrawal, Jiasen Lu, Margaret Mitchell, Dhruv Batra, C Lawrence Zitnick, and Devi Parikh. 2015. VQA: Visual question answering. In *Proceedings of the IEEE International Conference on Computer Vision*, pages 2425–2433.

Satanjeev Banerjee and Alon Lavie. 2005. Meteor: An Automatic Metric for MT Evaluation with Improved Correlation with Human Judgments. In *Proceedings of the ACL workshop on intrinsic and extrinsic evaluation measures for machine translation and/or summarization*, pages 65–72.

David Bau, Bolei Zhou, Aditya Khosla, Aude Oliva, and Antonio Torralba. 2017. Network Dissection: Quantifying Interpretability of Deep Visual Representations. In *Proceedings of the IEEE Conference on Computer Vision and Pattern Recognition*.

Mustafa Bilgic and Raymond Mooney. 2005. Explaining Recommendations: Satisfaction vs. Promotion. In *Proceedings of Beyond Personalization 2005: A Workshop on the Next Stage of Recommender Systems Research at the 2005 International Conference on Intelligent User Interfaces*.

Bradley Efron, Trevor Hastie, Iain Johnstone, Robert Tibshirani, et al. 2004. Least angle regression. *The Annals of statistics*, 32(2):407–499.

Akira Fukui, Dong Huk Park, Daylen Yang, Anna Rohrbach, Trevor Darrell, and Marcus Rohrbach. 2016. Multimodal Compact Bilinear Pooling for Visual Question Answering and Visual Grounding. In *Proceedings of the 2016 Empirical Methods on Natural Language Processing*.

Lisa Anne Hendricks, Zeynep Akata, Marcus Rohrbach, Jeff Donahue, Bernt Schiele, and Trevor Darrell. 2016. Generating Visual Explanations. In *European Conference on Computer Vision*, pages 3–19. Springer.

Lisa Anne Hendricks, Ronghang Hu, Trevor Darrell, and Zeynep Akata. 2018. Grounding Visual Explanations. *arXiv preprint arXiv:1807.09685*.

Ronghang Hu, Piotr Dollár, Kaiming He, Trevor Darrell, and Ross Girshick. 2018. Learning to Segment Every Thing. In *Proceedings of the IEEE Conference on Computer Vision and Pattern Recognition*.

Sarthak Jain and Byron C Wallace. 2019. Attention is not explanation. *arXiv preprint arXiv:1902.10186*.

Yu Jiang, Vivek Natarajan, Xinlei Chen, Marcus Rohrbach, Dhruv Batra, and Devi Parikh. 2018. Pythia v0. 1: the winning entry to the vqa challenge 2018. *arXiv preprint arXiv:1807.09956*.

Diederik P Kingma and Jimmy Ba. 2014. Adam: A Method for Stochastic Optimization. *Proceedings of the 3rd International Conference on Learning Representations*.

Chin-Yew Lin. 2004. Rouge: A Package for Automatic Evaluation of Summaries. *Text Summarization Branches Out*.

Jiasen Lu, Jianwei Yang, Dhruv Batra, and Devi Parikh. 2016. Hierarchical Question-Image Coattention for Visual Question Answering. In *Advances In Neural Information Processing Systems*, pages 289–297.

Andrew L Maas, Awni Y Hannun, and Andrew Y Ng. 2013. Rectifier Nonlinearities Improve Neural Network Acoustic Models. In *International Conference on Machine Learning*, volume 30, page 3.

Kishore Papineni, Salim Roukos, Todd Ward, and Wei-Jing Zhu. 2002. Bleu: A Method for Automatic Evaluation of Machine Translation. In *Proceedings of the 40th Annual Meeting on Association for Computational Linguistics*, ACL '02, pages 311–318, Stroudsburg, PA, USA. Association for Computational Linguistics.

Dong Huk Park, Lisa Anne Hendricks, Zeynep Akata, Anna Rohrbach, Bernt Schiele, Trevor Darrell, and Marcus Rohrbach. 2018. Multimodal Explanations: Justifying Decisions and Pointing to the Evidence. In *Proceedings of the IEEE conference on computer vision and pattern recognition*.

Ofir Pele and Michael Werman. 2008. A Linear Time Histogram Metric for Improved Sift Matching. In *Computer Vision–ECCV 2008*, pages 495–508. Springer.

Shaoqing Ren, Kaiming He, Ross Girshick, and Jian Sun. 2015. Faster R-CNN: Towards Real-time Object Detection with Region Proposal Networks. pages 91–99.

Marco Tulio Ribeiro, Sameer Singh, and Carlos Guestrin. 2016. Why should i trust you?: Explaining the predictions of any classifier. In *Proceedings of the 22nd ACM SIGKDD international conference on knowledge discovery and data mining*, pages 1135–1144. ACM.

Ramprasaath R Selvaraju, Michael Cogswell, Abhishek Das, Ramakrishna Vedantam, Devi Parikh, and Dhruv Batra. 2017. Grad-cam: Visual Explanations from Deep Networks via Gradient-Based Localization. In *Proceedings of the IEEE International Conference on Computer Vision*.

Ramakrishna Vedantam, C Lawrence Zitnick, and Devi Parikh. 2015. Cider: Consensus-Based Image Description Evaluation. In *Proceedings of the IEEE Conference on Computer Vision and Pattern Recognition*, pages 4566–4575.

Jialin Wu, Zeyuan Hu, and Raymond J Mooney. 2018a. Joint image captioning and question answering. *arXiv preprint arXiv:1805.08389*.

Jialin Wu, Dai Li, Yu Yang, Chandrajit Bajaj, and Xiangyang Ji. 2018b. Dynamic Filtering with Large Sampling Field for Convnets. *ECCV*.

Jialin Wu and Raymond J Mooney. 2019. Self-critical reasoning for robust visual question answering. *arXiv preprint arXiv:1905.09998*.

Zichao Yang, Xiaodong He, Jianfeng Gao, Li Deng, and Alex Smola. 2016. Stacked attention networks for image question answering. In *Proceedings of the IEEE Conference on Computer Vision and Pattern Recognition*, pages 21–29.

Jianming Zhang, Sarah Adel Bargal, Zhe Lin, Jonathan Brandt, Xiaohui Shen, and Stan Sclaroff. 2018. Top-down neural attention by excitation backprop. *International Journal of Computer Vision*, 126(10):1084–1102.

# Evaluating Recurrent Neural Network Explanations

**Leila Arras[1], Ahmed Osman[1], Klaus-Robert Müller[2,3,4], and Wojciech Samek[1]**

[1]Machine Learning Group, Fraunhofer Heinrich Hertz Institute, Berlin, Germany
[2]Machine Learning Group, Technische Universität Berlin, Berlin, Germany
[3]Department of Brain and Cognitive Engineering, Korea University, Seoul, Korea
[4]Max Planck Institute for Informatics, Saarbrücken, Germany
`{leila.arras, wojciech.samek}@hhi.fraunhofer.de`

## Abstract

Recently, several methods have been proposed to explain the predictions of recurrent neural networks (RNNs), in particular of LSTMs. The goal of these methods is to understand the network's decisions by assigning to each input variable, e.g., a word, a *relevance* indicating to which extent it contributed to a particular prediction. In previous works, some of these methods were not yet compared to one another, or were evaluated only qualitatively. We close this gap by systematically and quantitatively comparing these methods in different settings, namely (1) a toy arithmetic task which we use as a sanity check, (2) a five-class sentiment prediction of movie reviews, and besides (3) we explore the usefulness of word relevances to build sentence-level representations. Lastly, using the method that performed best in our experiments, we show how specific linguistic phenomena such as the negation in sentiment analysis reflect in terms of relevance patterns, and how the relevance visualization can help to understand the misclassification of individual samples.

## 1 Introduction

Recurrent neural networks such as LSTMs (Hochreiter and Schmidhuber, 1997) are a standard building block for understanding and generating text data in NLP. They find usage in pure NLP applications, such as abstractive summarization (Chopra et al., 2016), machine translation (Bahdanau et al., 2015), textual entailment (Rocktäschel et al., 2016); as well as in multimodal tasks involving NLP, such as image captioning (Karpathy and Fei-Fei, 2015), visual question answering (Xu and Saenko, 2016) or lip reading (Chung et al., 2017).

As these models become more and more widespread due to their predictive performance, there is also a need to understand *why* they took

a particular decision, i.e., when the input is a sequence of words: *which* words are determinant for the final decision? This information is crucial to unmask "Clever Hans" predictors (Lapuschkin et al., 2019), and to allow for transparency of the decision-making process (EU-GDPR, 2016).

Early works on *explaining* neural network predictions include Baehrens et al. (2010); Zeiler and Fergus (2014); Simonyan et al. (2014); Springenberg et al. (2015); Bach et al. (2015); Alain and Bengio (2017), with several works focusing on explaining the decisions of convolutional neural networks (CNNs) for image recognition. More recently, this topic found a growing interest within NLP, amongst others to explain the decisions of general CNN classifiers (Arras et al., 2017a; Jacovi et al., 2018), and more particularly to explain the predictions of recurrent neural networks (Li et al., 2016, 2017; Arras et al., 2017b; Ding et al., 2017; Murdoch et al., 2018; Poerner et al., 2018).

In this work, we focus on RNN explanation methods that are solely based on a trained neural network model and a single test data point[1]. Thus, methods that use additional information, such as training data statistics, sampling, or are optimization-based (Ribeiro et al., 2016; Lundberg and Lee, 2017; Chen et al., 2018) are out of our scope. Among the methods we consider, we note that the method of Murdoch et al. (2018) was not yet compared against Arras et al. (2017b); Ding et al. (2017); and that the method of Ding et al. (2017) was validated only visually. Moreover, to the best of our knowledge, no recurrent neural network explanation method was tested so far on a toy problem where the *ground truth* rele-

---

[1]These methods are deterministic, and are essentially based on a *decomposition* of the model's current prediction. Thereby they intend to reflect the *sole* model's "point of view" on the test data point, and hence are not meant to provide an averaged, smoothed or denoised explanation of the prediction by additionally exploiting the data's distribution.



*Proceedings of the Second BlackboxNLP Workshop on Analyzing and Interpreting Neural Networks for NLP*, pages 113–126
Florence, Italy, August 1, 2019. ©2019 Association for Computational Linguistics

vance value is known.

Therefore our contributions are the following: we evaluate and compare the aforementioned methods, using two different experimental setups, thereby we assess basic properties and differences between the explanation methods. Along-the-way we purposely adapted a simple toy task, to serve as a testbed for recurrent neural networks explanations. Lastly, we explore how word relevances can be used to build sentence-level representations, and demonstrate how the relevance visualization can help to understand the (mis-)classification of selected samples w.r.t. semantic composition.

## 2  Explaining Recurrent Neural Network Predictions

First, let us settle some notations. We suppose given a trained recurrent neural network based model, which has learned some scalar-valued prediction function $f_c(\cdot)$, for each class $c$ of a classification problem. Further, we denote by $\mathbf{x} = (\boldsymbol{x_1}, \boldsymbol{x_2}, ..., \boldsymbol{x_T})$ an unseen input data point, where $\boldsymbol{x_t}$ represents the $t$-th input vector of dimension $D$, within the input sequence $\mathbf{x}$ of length $T$. In NLP, the vectors $\boldsymbol{x_t}$ are typically word embeddings, and $\mathbf{x}$ may be a sentence.

Now, we are interested in methods that can explain the network's prediction $f_c(\mathbf{x})$ for the input $\mathbf{x}$, and for a chosen *target* class $c$, by assigning a scalar relevance value to each input variable or word. This relevance is meant to quantify the variable's or word's importance *for* or *against* a model's prediction *towards* the class $c$. We denote by $R_{x_i}$ (index $i$) the relevance of a *single* variable. This means $x_i$ stands for any arbitrary input variable $x_{t,d}$ representing the $d$-th dimension, $d \in \{1, ..., D\}$, of an input vector $\boldsymbol{x_t}$. Further, we refer to $R_{\boldsymbol{x_t}}$ (index $t$) to designate the relevance value of an *entire* input vector or word $\boldsymbol{x_t}$. Note that, for most methods, one can obtain a word-level relevance value by simply summing up the relevances over the word embedding dimensions, i.e. $R_{\boldsymbol{x_t}} = \sum_{d \in \{1,...,D\}} R_{x_{t,d}}$.

### 2.1  Gradient-based explanation

One standard approach to obtain relevances is based on partial derivatives of the prediction function: $R_{x_i} = \left| \frac{\partial f_c}{\partial x_i}(\mathbf{x}) \right|$, or $R_{x_i} = \left( \frac{\partial f_c}{\partial x_i}(\mathbf{x}) \right)^2$ (Dimopoulos et al., 1995; Gevrey et al., 2003; Simonyan et al., 2014; Li et al., 2016).

In NLP this technique was employed to visualize the relevance of single input variables in RNNs for sentiment classification (Li et al., 2016). We use the latter formulation of relevance and denote it as *Gradient*. With this definition the relevance of an entire word is simply the squared $L_2$-norm of the prediction function's gradient w.r.t. the word embedding, i.e. $R_{\boldsymbol{x_t}} = \|\nabla_{\boldsymbol{x_t}} f_c(\mathbf{x})\|_2^2$.

A slight variation of this approach uses partial derivatives multiplied by the variable's value, i.e. $R_{x_i} = \frac{\partial f_c}{\partial x_i}(\mathbf{x}) \cdot x_i$. Hence, the word relevance is a dot product between prediction function gradient and word embedding: $R_{\boldsymbol{x_t}} = (\nabla_{\boldsymbol{x_t}} f_c(\mathbf{x}))^T \boldsymbol{x_t}$ (Denil et al., 2015). We refer to this variant as *Gradient×Input*.

Both variants are general and can be applied to any neural network. They are computationally efficient and require one forward and backward pass through the net.

### 2.2  Occlusion-based explanation

Another method to assign relevances to single variables, or entire words, is by occluding them in the input, and tracking the difference in the network's prediction w.r.t. a prediction on the original unmodified input (Zeiler and Fergus, 2014; Li et al., 2017). In computer vision the occlusion is performed by replacing an image region with a grey or zero-valued square (Zeiler and Fergus, 2014). In NLP word vectors, or single of its components, are replaced by zero; in the case of recurrent neural networks, the technique was applied to identify important words for sentiment analysis (Li et al., 2017).

Practically, the relevance can be computed in two ways: in terms of prediction function differences, or in the case of a classification problem, using a difference of probabilities, i.e. $R_{x_i} = f_c(\mathbf{x}) - f_c(\mathbf{x}_{|x_i=0})$, or $R_{x_i} = P_c(\mathbf{x}) - P_c(\mathbf{x}_{|x_i=0})$, where $P_c(\cdot) = \frac{\exp f_c(\cdot)}{\sum_k \exp f_k(\cdot)}$. We refer to the former as *Occlusion*$_{\text{f-diff}}$, and to the latter as *Occlusion*$_{\text{P-diff}}$. Both variants can also be used to estimate the relevance of an entire word, in this case the corresponding word embedding is set to zero in the input. This type of explanation is computationally expensive and requires $T$ forward passes through the network to determine one relevance value per word in the input sequence $\mathbf{x}$.

A slight variation of the above approach uses word omission (similarly to Kádár et al., 2017) instead of occlusion. On a morphosyntactic agreement experiment (see Poerner et al., 2018), omission was shown to deliver inferior results, therefore we consider only occlusion-based relevance.

### 2.3 Layer-wise relevance propagation

A general method to determine input space relevances based on a backward decomposition of the neural network prediction function is layer-wise relevance propagation (LRP) (Bach et al., 2015). It was originally proposed to explain feed-forward neural networks such as convolutional neural networks (Bach et al., 2015; Lapuschkin et al., 2016), and was recently extended to recurrent neural networks (Arras et al., 2017b; Ding et al., 2017; Arjona-Medina et al., 2018).

LRP consists in a standard forward pass, followed by a specific backward pass which is defined for each type of layer of a neural network by dedicated propagation rules. Via this backward pass, each neuron in the network gets assigned a relevance, starting with the output neuron whose relevance is set to the prediction function's value, i.e. to $f_c(\mathbf{x})$. Each LRP propagation rule redistributes iteratively, layer-by-layer, the relevance from higher-layer neurons to lower-layer neurons, and verifies a relevance conservation property[2]. These rules were initially proposed in Bach et al. (2015) and were subsequently justified by Deep Taylor decomposition (Montavon et al., 2017) for deep ReLU nets.

In practice, for a linear layer of the form $z_j = \sum_i z_i w_{ij} + b_j$ , and given the relevances of the output neurons $R_j$, the input neurons' relevances $R_i$ are computed through the following summation: $R_i = \sum_j \frac{z_i \cdot w_{ij}}{z_j + \epsilon \cdot sign(z_j)} \cdot R_j$ , where $\epsilon$ is a stabilizer (small positive number); this rule is commonly referred as $\epsilon$-LRP or $\epsilon$-rule[3]. With this redistribution the relevance is conserved, up to the relevance assigned to the bias and "absorbed" by the stabilizer.

Further, for an element-wise nonlinear activation layer, the output neurons' relevances are redistributed identically onto the input neurons.

In addition to the above rules, in the case of a multiplicative layer of the form $z_j = z_g \cdot z_s$, Arras et al. (2017b) proposed to redistribute zero relevance to the *gate* (the neuron that is sigmoid

activated) i.e. $R_g = 0$, and assign all the relevance to the remaining *signal* neuron (which is usually tanh activated) i.e. $R_s = R_j$. We call this LRP variant *LRP-all*, which stands for "signal-take-all" redistribution. An alternative rule was proposed in Ding et al. (2017); Arjona-Medina et al. (2018), where the output neuron's relevance $R_j$ is redistributed onto the input neurons via: $R_g = \frac{z_g}{z_g + z_s} R_j$ and $R_s = \frac{z_s}{z_g + z_s} R_j$. We refer to this variant as *LRP-prop*, for "proportional" redistribution. We also consider two other variants. The first one uses absolute values instead: $R_g = \frac{|z_g|}{|z_g| + |z_s|} R_j$ and $R_s = \frac{|z_s|}{|z_g| + |z_s|} R_j$, we call it *LRP-abs*. The second uses equal redistribution: $R_g = R_s = 0.5 \cdot R_j$ (Arjona-Medina et al., 2018), we denote it as *LRP-half*. We further add a stabilizing term to the denominator of the *LRP-prop* and *LRP-abs* formulas, it has the form $\epsilon \cdot sign(z_g + z_s)$ in the first case, and simply $\epsilon$ in the latter.

Since the relevance can be computed in one forward and backward pass, the LRP method is efficient. Besides, it is general as it can be applied to any neural network made of the above layers: it was applied successfully to CNNs, LSTMs, GRUs, and QRNNs (Poerner et al., 2018; Yang et al., 2018)[4].

### 2.4 Contextual Decomposition

Another method, specific to LSTMs, is contextual decomposition (*CD*) (Murdoch et al., 2018). It is based on a *linearization* of the activation functions that enables to decompose the LSTM forward pass by distinguishing between two contributions: those made by a chosen contiguous subsequence (a word or a phrase) within the input sequence $\mathbf{x}$, and those made by the remaining part of the input. This decomposition results in a final hidden state vector $h_T$ (see the Appendix for a full specification of the LSTM architecture) that can be rewritten as a sum of two vectors: $\beta_T$ and $\gamma_T$, where the former corresponds to the contribution from the "relevant" part of interest, and the latter stems from the "irrelevant" part. When the LSTM is followed by a linear output layer of the form $w_c^T h_T + b_c$ for class $c$, then the relevance of a given word (or phrase) and for the *target* class $c$, is given by the dot product: $w_c^T \beta_T$.

---

[2]Methods based on a similar conservation principle include contribution propagation (Landecker et al., 2013), Deep Taylor decomposition (Montavon et al., 2017), and DeepLIFT (Shrikumar et al., 2017).

[3]Such a rule was employed by previous works with recurrent neural networks (Arras et al., 2017b; Ding et al., 2017; Arjona-Medina et al., 2018), although there exist also other LRP rules for linear layers (see e.g. Montavon et al., 2018)

[4]Note that in the present work we apply LRP to *standard* LSTMs, though Arjona-Medina et al. (2018) showed that some LRP rules for product layers can benefit from simultaneously adapting the LSTM architecture.

| Method | Relevance Formulation | Redistributed Quantity ($\sum_i R_{x_i}$) | Complexity |
|---|---|---|---|
| Gradient | $R_{x_i} = \left(\frac{\partial f_c}{\partial x_i}(\mathbf{x})\right)^2$ | $\|\nabla_{\mathbf{x}} f_c(\mathbf{x})\|_2^2$ | $\Theta(2 \cdot T)$ |
| Gradient$\times$Input | $R_{x_i} = \frac{\partial f_c}{\partial x_i}(\mathbf{x}) \cdot x_i$ | $(\nabla_{\mathbf{x}} f_c(\mathbf{x}))^T \mathbf{x}$ | $\Theta(2 \cdot T)$ |
| Occlusion | $R_{x_i} = f_c(\mathbf{x}) - f_c(\mathbf{x}_{|x_i=0})$ | - | $\Theta(T^2)$ |
| LRP | backward decomposition of the neurons' relevance | $f_c(\mathbf{x})$ | $\Theta(2 \cdot T)$ |
| CD | linearization of the activation functions | $f_c(\mathbf{x})$ | $\Theta(T^2)$ |

Table 1: Overview of the considered explanation methods. The last column indicates the computational complexity to obtain one relevance value per input vector, or word, where $T$ is the length of the input sequence.

The method is computationally expensive as it requires $T$ forward passes through the LSTM to compute one relevance value per word. Although it was recently extended to CNNs (Singh et al., 2019; Godin et al., 2018), it is yet not clear how to compute the *CD* relevance in other recurrent architectures, or in networks with multi-modal inputs.

See Table 1 for an overview of the explanation methods considered in the present work.

## 2.5 Methods not considered

Other methods to compute relevances include Integrated Gradients (Sundararajan et al., 2017). It was previously compared against *CD* in Murdoch et al. (2018), and against the LRP variant of Arras et al. (2017b) in Poerner et al. (2018), where in both cases it was shown to deliver inferior results. Another method is DeepLIFT (Shrikumar et al., 2017), however, according to its authors, DeepLIFT was not designed for multiplicative connections, and its extension to recurrent networks remains an open question[5]. For a comparative study of explanation methods with a main focus on feed-forward nets, see Ancona et al. (2018)[6]. For a broad evaluation of explanations, including several recurrent architectures, we refer to Poerner et al. (2018). Note that the latter didn't include the *CD* method of Murdoch et al. (2018), and the LRP variant of Ding et al. (2017), which we compare here.

## 3 Evaluating Explanations

### 3.1 Previous work

How to generally and objectively evaluate explanations, without resorting to *ad-hoc* evaluation procedures that are domain and task specific, is still active research (Alishahi et al., 2019; Belinkov and Glass, 2019).

In computer vision, it has become common practice to conduct a perturbation analysis (Bach et al., 2015; Samek et al., 2017; Shrikumar et al., 2017; Lundberg and Lee, 2017; Ancona et al., 2018; Chen et al., 2018; Morcos et al., 2018): hereby a few pixels in an image are perturbated (e.g. set to zero or blurred) according to their relevance (most relevant or least relevant pixels are perturbated first), and then the impact on the network's prediction is measured. The higher the impact, the more accurate is the relevance.

Other studies explored in which way relevances are consistent or helpful w.r.t. human judgment (Ribeiro et al., 2016; Lundberg and Lee, 2017; Nguyen, 2018). Some other works relied solely on the visual inspection of a few selected relevance heatmaps (Li et al., 2016; Sundararajan et al., 2017; Ding et al., 2017).

In NLP, Murdoch et al. (2018) proposed to measure the correlation between word relevances obtained on an LSTM, and the word importance scores obtained from a linear Bag-of-Words. However, the latter model ignores the word ordering and context, which the LSTM can take into account, hence this type of evaluation is not adequate[7]. Other evaluations in NLP are task specific. For example Poerner et al. (2018) use the subject-verb agreement task proposed by Linzen et al. (2016), where the goal is to predict a verb's

---

[5] Though Poerner et al. (2018) showed that, when using only the Rescale rule of DeepLIFT, and combining it with the product rule proposed in Arras et al. (2017b), then the resulting explanations perform on-par with the LRP method of Arras et al. (2017b)

[6] Note that in order to redistribute the relevance through product layers, Ancona et al. (2018) simply relied on standard gradient backpropagation. Such a redistribution scheme is not appropriate for methods such as LRP, since it violates the relevance conservation property, hence their results for recurrent nets are not conclusive.

[7] The same way Murdoch et al. (2018) try to "match" phrase-level relevances with n-gram linear classifier scores or human annotated phrases, but again this might be misleading, since the latter scores or annotations ignore the whole sentence context.

number, and use the relevances to verify that the most relevant word is indeed the correct subject (or a noun with the predicted number).

Other studies include an evaluation on a synthetic task: Yang et al. (2018) generated random sequences of MNIST digits and train an LSTM to predict if a sequence contains zero digits or not, and verify that the explanation indeed assigns a high relevance to the zero digits' positions.

A further approach uses randomization of the model weights and data as sanity checks (Adebayo et al., 2018) to verify that the explanations are indeed dependent on the model and data. Lastly, some evaluations are "indirect" and use relevances to solve a broader task, e.g. to build document-level representations (Arras et al., 2017a), or to redistribute predicted rewards in reinforcement learning (Arjona-Medina et al., 2018).

### 3.2   Toy Arithmetic Task

As a first evaluation, we ask the following question: if we add two numbers within an input sequence, can we recover from the relevance the true input values? This amounts to consider the adding problem (Hochreiter and Schmidhuber, 1996), which is typically used to test the long-range capabilities of recurrent models (Martens and Sutskever, 2011; Le et al., 2015). We use it here to test the faithfulness of explanations. To that end, we define a setup similar to Hochreiter and Schmidhuber (1996), but without *explicit* markers to identify the sequence start and end, and the two numbers to be added. Our idea is that, in general, it is not clear what the ground truth relevance for a marker should be, and we want only the relevant numbers in the input sequence to get a non-zero relevance. Hence, we represent the input sequence $\mathbf{x} = (x_1, x_2, ..., x_T)$ of length $T$, with two-dimensional input vectors as:

$$\begin{pmatrix} 0 & 0 & 0 & n_a & 0 & 0 & 0 & n_b & 0 & 0 & 0 \\ n_1 & ... & n_{a-1} & 0 & n_{a+1} & ... & n_{b-1} & 0 & n_{b+1} & ... & n_T \end{pmatrix}$$

where the non-zero entries $n_t$ are random real numbers, and the two relevant positions $a$ and $b$ are sampled uniformly among $\{1, ..., T\}$ with $a < b$.

More specifically, we consider two tasks that can be solved by an LSTM model with a hidden layer of size *one* (followed by a linear output layer with no bias[8]): the *addition* of signed numbers ($n_t$

is sampled uniformly from $[-1, -0.5] \cup [0.5, 1.0]$) and the *subtraction* of positive numbers ($n_t$ is sampled uniformly from $[0.5, 1.0]$[9]). In the former case the target output $y$ is $n_a + n_b$, in the latter it is $n_a - n_b$. During training we minimize Mean Squared Error (MSE). To ensure that train/val/test sets do not overlap we use 10000 sequences with lengths $T \in \{4, ..., 10\}$ for training, 2500 sequences with $T \in \{11, 12\}$ for validation, and 2500 sequences with $T \in \{13, 14\}$ as test set. For each task we train 50 LSTMs with a validation MSE $< 10^{-4}$, the resulting test MSE is $< 10^{-4}$.

Then, given the model's predicted output $y_{\text{pred}}$, we compute one relevance value $R_{x_t}$ per input vector $x_t$ (for the occlusion method we compute only $Occlusion_{\text{f-diff}}$ since the task is a regression; we also don't report *Gradient* results since it performs poorly). Finally, we track the correlation between the relevances and the two input numbers $n_a$ and $n_b$. We also track the portion of relevance assigned to the relevant time steps, compared to the relevance for all time steps. Lastly, we calculate the "MSE" between the relevances for the relevant positions $a$ and $b$ and the model's output. Our results are compiled in Table 2.

Interestingly, we note that on the addition task several methods perform well and produce a relevance that correlates perfectly with the input numbers: *Gradient×Input*, *Occlusion*, *LRP-all* and *CD* (they are highlighted in bold in the Table). They further assign all the relevance to the time steps $a$ and $b$ and almost no relevance to the rest of the input; and present a relevance that sum up to the predicted output. However, on subtraction, only *Gradient×Input* and *LRP-all* present a correlation of near one with $n_a$, and of near minus one with $n_b$. Likewise these methods assign only relevance to the relevant positions, and redistribute the predicted output entirely onto these positions.

The main difference between our addition and subtraction tasks, is that the former requires only summing up the first dimension of the input vectors and can be solved by a Bag-of-Words approach (i.e. by ignoring the ordering of the inputs), while our subtraction task is truly *sequential* and requires the LSTM model to remember which number arrived first, and which number arrived second, via exploiting the gating mechanism.

Since in NLP several applications require the

---

[8]We omit the output layer bias since all considered explanation methods ignore it in the relevance computation, and we want to explain the "full" prediction function's value.

[9]We avoid small numbers by using 0.5 as a minimum magnitude only to simplify learning, since otherwise this would encourage the model weights to grow rapidly.

| | $\rho(R_{x_a}, n_a)$ (in %) | $\rho(R_{x_b}, n_b)$ (in %) | $E[\frac{|R_{x_a}|+|R_{x_b}|}{\sum_t |R_{x_t}|}]$ (in %) | $E[((R_{x_a} + R_{x_b}) - y_{\text{pred}})^2]$ ("MSE") |
|---|---|---|---|---|
| **Toy Task Addition** | | | | |
| Gradient $\times$ Input | **99.960** (0.017) | **99.954** (0.019) | **99.68** (0.53) | **24.10$^{-4}$** (8.10$^{-4}$) |
| Occlusion | **99.990** (0.004) | **99.990** (0.004) | **99.82** (0.27) | **20.10$^{-5}$** (8.10$^{-5}$) |
| LRP-prop | 0.785 (3.619) | 10.111 (12.362) | 18.14 (4.23) | 1.3 (1.0) |
| LRP-abs | 7.002 (6.224) | 12.410 (17.440) | 18.01 (4.48) | 1.3 (1.0) |
| LRP-half | 29.035 (9.478) | 51.460 (19.939) | 54.09 (17.53) | 1.1 (0.3) |
| LRP-all | **99.995** (0.002) | **99.995** (0.002) | **99.95** (0.05) | **2.10$^{-6}$** (4.10$^{-6}$) |
| CD | **99.997** (0.002) | **99.997** (0.002) | **99.92** (0.06) | **4.10$^{-5}$** (12.10$^{-5}$) |
| **Toy Task Subtraction** | | | | |
| Gradient $\times$ Input | **97.9** (1.6) | **-98.8** (0.6) | **98.3** (0.6) | **6.10$^{-4}$** (4.10$^{-4}$) |
| Occlusion | 99.0 (2.0) | -69.0 (19.1) | 25.4 (16.8) | 0.05 (0.08) |
| LRP-prop | 3.1 (4.8) | -8.4 (18.9) | 15.0 (2.4) | 0.04 (0.02) |
| LRP-abs | 1.2 (7.6) | -23.0 (11.1) | 15.1 (1.6) | 0.04 (0.002) |
| LRP-half | 7.7 (15.3) | -28.9 (6.4) | 42.3 (8.3) | 0.05 (0.06) |
| LRP-all | **98.5** (3.5) | **-99.3** (1.3) | **99.3** (0.6) | **8.10$^{-4}$** (25.10$^{-4}$) |
| CD | -25.9 (39.1) | -50.0 (29.2) | 49.4 (26.1) | 0.05 (0.05) |

Table 2: Statistics of the relevance w.r.t. the input numbers $n_a$ and $n_b$ and the predicted output $y_{\text{pred}}$, on toy arithmetic tasks. $\rho$ denotes the correlation and $E$ the mean. Each statistic is computed over 2500 test data points. Reported are the mean (and standard deviation in parenthesis) over 50 trained LSTM models.

word *ordering* to be taken into account to accurately capture a sentence's meaning (e.g. in sentiment analysis or in machine translation), our experiment, albeit being an abstract numerical task, is pertinent and can serve as a first sanity check to check whether the relevance can reflect the *ordering* and the *value* of the input vectors.

Hence we view our toy task as a minimal and unambiguous test (which besides being sequential, also exhibits a linear input-output relationship) that acts as a necessary (though not sufficient) requirement for a recurrent neural network explanation method to be trustworthy in a more complex setup, where the ground truth relevance is less clear.

For the *Occlusion* method, the unreliability is probably due to the fact that the neural network has always seen two "relevant" input numbers in the input sequence during training, and therefore gets confused when one of these inputs is missing at the time of the relevance computation ("out-of-sample" effect). For *CD*, the weakness may come from the saturation of the activations, in particular of the gates, which makes their linearization induced by the *CD* decomposition inaccurate.

### 3.3   5-Class Sentiment Prediction

As a sentiment analysis dataset, we use the Stanford Sentiment Treebank (Socher et al., 2013) which contains labels (very negative $--$, negative $-$, neutral 0, positive $+$, very positive $++$) for resp. 8544/1101/2210 train/val/test sentences and their constituent phrases. As a classifier we employ the bidirectional LSTM from Li et al.

(2016)[10], which achieves 82.9% binary, resp. 46.3% five-class, accuracy on full sentences.

**Perturbation Experiment**. In order to evaluate the *selectivity* of word relevances, we perform a perturbation experiment aka "pixel-flipping" in computer vision (Bach et al., 2015; Samek et al., 2017), i.e. we remove words from the input sentences according to their relevance, and track the impact on the classification performance. A similar experiment has been conducted in previous NLP studies (Arras et al., 2016; Nguyen, 2018; Chen et al., 2018); and besides, such type of experiment can be seen as the input space pendant of *ablation*, which is commonly used to identify "relevant" intermediate neurons, e.g. in Lakretz et al. (2019). For our experiment we retain test sentences with a length $\geq$ 10 words (i.e. 1849 sentences), and remove 1, 2, and 3 words per sentence[11], according to their relevance obtained on the original sentence with the *true* class as the *target* class. Our results are reported in Table 3. Note that we distinguish between sentences that are initially correctly classified, and those that are initially falsely classified by the LSTM model. Further, in order to condense the "ablation" results in a single number per method, we compute the accuracy decrease (resp. increase) *proportionally* to two cases: i) random removal, and ii) removal ac-

---


[10]https://github.com/jiweil/Visualizing-and-Understanding-Neural-Models-in-NLP

[11]In order to remove a word we simply discard it from the input sentence and concatenate the remaining parts. We also tried setting the word embeddings to zero, which gave us similar results.

| Accuracy Change (in %) | random | Grad. | Grad.×Input | LRP-prop | LRP-abs | LRP-half | LRP-all | CD | Occlusion$_{\text{f-diff}}$ | Occlusion$_{\text{P-diff}}$ |
|---|---|---|---|---|---|---|---|---|---|---|
| decreasing order (std<16) | 0 | 35 | 66 | 15 | -1 | -3 | **97** | **92** | **96** | **100** |
| increasing order (std<5) | 0 | -18 | 31 | 11 | -1 | 3 | **49** | **36** | **50** | **100** |

Table 3: Average change in accuracy when removing up to 3 words per sentence, either in *decreasing* order of their relevance (starting with correctly classified sentences), or in *increasing* order of their relevance (starting with falsely classified sentences). In both cases, the relevance is computed with the *true* class as the *target* class. Results are reported *proportionally* to the changes for i) random removal (0% change) and ii) removal based on *Occlusion*$_{\text{P-diff}}$ (100% change). For all methods, the higher the reported value the better. We boldface those methods that perform on-par with the occlusion-based relevances.

cording to *Occlusion*$_{\text{P-diff}}$. Our idea is that random removal is the least informative approach, while *Occlusion*$_{\text{P-diff}}$ is the most informative one, since the relevance for the latter is computed in a similar way to the perturbation experiment itself, i.e. by deleting words from the input and tracking the change in the classifier's prediction. Thus, with this normalization, we expect the accuracy change (in %) to be mainly rescaled to the range $[0, 100]$.

When removing words in decreasing order of their relevance, we observe that *LRP-all* and *CD* perform on-par with the occlusion-based relevance, with near 100% accuracy change, followed by *Gradient×Input* which performs only 66%.

When removing words in increasing order of their relevance (which mainly corresponds to remove words with a negative relevance), *Occlusion*$_{\text{P-diff}}$ performs best, followed by *Occlusion*$_{\text{f-diff}}$ and *LRP-all* (both around 50%), then *CD* (36%). Unsurprisingly, *Gradient* performs worse than random, since its relevance is positive and thus low relevance is more likely to identify unimportant words for the classification (such as stop words), rather than identify words that *contradict* a decision, as noticed in Arras et al. (2017b). Lastly *Occlusion*$_{\text{f-diff}}$ is less informative than *Occlusion*$_{\text{P-diff}}$, since the former is not normalized by the classification scores for all classes.

This analysis revealed that methods such as *LRP-all* and *CD* can detect influential words supporting (resp. contradicting) a specific classification decision, although they were not tuned towards the perturbation criterion, as opposed to *Occlusion* (which can be seen as the brute force approach to determine the inputs the model is the most sensitive to), whereas gradient-based methods are less accurate in this respect. Remarkably *LRP-all* only require one forward and backward pass to provide this information.

**Sentence-Level Representations.** In addition to testing selectivity, we explore if the word rel-

evance can be leveraged to build sentence-level representations that present some regularities akin word2vec vectors. For this purpose we linearly combine word embeddings using their respective relevance as weighting[12]. For methods such as LRP and *Gradient×Input* that deliver also relevances for *single* variables, we perform an element-wise weighting, i.e. we construct the sentence representation as: $\sum_t R_{x_t} \odot x_t$. For every method we report the best performing variant from previous experiments, i.e. *Occlusion*$_{\text{P-diff}}$, *Gradient×Input*, *CD* and *LRP-all*. Additionally we report simple averaging of word embeddings (we call it *Avg*). Further, for LRP, we consider an element-wise reweighting of the last time step hidden layer $h_T$ by its relevance, since LRP delivers also a relevance for each intermediate neuron (we call it LRP $h_T$). We also tried using $h_T$ directly: this gave us a visualization similar to *Avg*. The resulting 2D whitened PCA projections of the test set sentences are shown in Fig. 1.

Qualitatively LRP delivers the most structured representations, although for all methods the first two PCA components explain most of the data variance. Intuitively it makes also sense that the neutral sentiment is located between the positive and negative sentiments, and that the very negative and very positive sentiments depart from their lower counterparts in the same vertical direction.

The advantage of having such regularities emerging via PCA projection, is that the sentence/phrase semantics might be investigated visually, without requiring any nonlinear dimensionality reduction like t-SNE (typically used to explore the representations learned by recurrent models, e.g. in Cho et al., 2014; Li et al., 2016). Such representations might also be useful in information retrieval settings, where one could retrieve simi-

---

[12]W.l.o.g. we use here the *true* class as the *target* class, since the classifier's 5-class performance is very low. In a practical use-case one would use the *predicted* class instead.

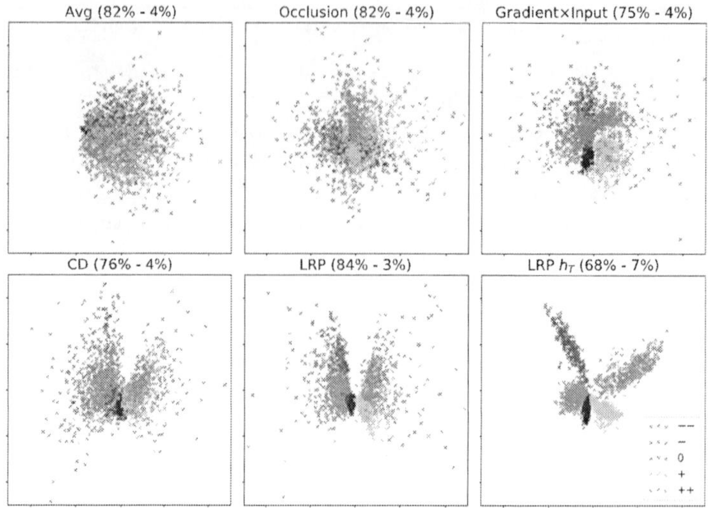


Figure 1: PCA projection of sentence-level representations built on top of word embeddings that were linearly combined using their respective relevance. *Avg* corresponds to simple averaging of word embeddings. For LRP $h_T$ the last time step hidden layer was reweighted by its relevance. In parenthesis we indicate the percentage of variance explained by the first two PCA components (those that are plotted) and by the third PCA component. The resulting representations were roughly ordered (row-wise) from less structured to more structured.

lar sentences/phrases by employing standard euclidean distance.

## 4 Interpreting Single Predictions

Next, we analyze single predictions using the same task and model as in Section 3.3, and illustrate the usefulness of relevance visualization with *LRP-all*, which is the method that performed well in both our previous quantitative experiments.

**Semantic Composition**. When dealing with real data, one typically has no ground truth relevance available. And the visual inspection of single relevance heatmaps can be counter-intuitive for two reasons: the relevance is not accurately reflecting the reasons for the classifier's decision (the explanation method is bad), or the classifier made an error (the classifier doesn't work as expected). In order to avoid the latter as much as possible, we automatically constructed bigram and trigram samples, which are built *solely* upon the classifier's predicted class, and visualize the resulting average relevance heatmaps for different types of semantic compositions in Table 4. For more details on how these samples were constructed we refer to the Appendix, note though that in our heatmaps the negation <not>, the intensifier <very> and the sentiment words act as placeholders for words with similar meanings, since the representative heatmaps were averaged over several samples. In these heatmaps one can see that, to transform a positive sentiment into a negative one, the negation is predominantly colored as red, while the sentiment word is highlighted in blue, which intuitively makes sense since the explanation is computed *towards* the negative sentiment, and in this context the negation is responsible for the sentiment prediction. For sentiment intensification, we note that the amplifier gets a relevance of the same sign as the amplified word, indicating the amplifier is *supporting* the prediction for the considered target class, but still has less importance for the decision than the sentiment word itself (deep red colored). Both previous identified patterns also reflect consistently in the case of a negated amplified positive sentiment.

**Understanding Misclassifications**. Lastly, we inspect heatmaps of misclassified sentences in Table 5. In sentence 1, according to the heatmap, the classifier didn't take the negation never into account, although it identified it correctly in sentence 1b. We postulate this is because of the strong sentiment assigned to fails that overshadowed the effect of never. In sentence 2, the classifier obviously couldn't grasp the meaning of the words preceding must-see. If we use a negation instead, we note that it's taken into account in the case of neither (2b), but not in the case of never (2c), which illustrates the complex dynamics in-

| Composition | Predicted | Heatmap | Relevance | | | # samples |
|---|---|---|---|---|---|---|
| 1. "negated positive sentiment" | — | <not> <good> | $2.5_{0.3}$ | $-1.4_{0.5}$ | | 213 |
| 2. "amplified positive sentiment" | ++ | <very> <good> | $1.1_{0.3}$ | $4.5_{0.7}$ | | 347 |
| 3. "amplified negative sentiment" | — — | <very> <bad> | $0.8_{0.2}$ | $4.3_{0.6}$ | | 173 |
| 4. "negated amplified positive sentiment" | — | <not> <very> <good> | $2.74_{0.54}$ | $-0.34_{0.17}$ | $-2.00_{0.40}$ | 1745 |

Table 4: Typical heatmaps for various types of semantic compositions (indicated in first column), computed with the *LRP-all* method. The LSTM's *predicted* class (second column) is used as the *target* class. The remaining columns contain the average heatmap (positive relevance is mapped to red, negative to blue, and the color intensity is normalized to the maximum absolute relevance), the corresponding word relevance mean (and std as subscript), and the number of bigrams (resp. trigrams) considered for each type of composition.

| Nº | Predicted | Heatmap |
|---|---|---|
| 1 | — — | it never fails to engage us . |
| 1a | + | engages us . |
| 1b | — | never engages us . |
| 1c | — — | fails to engage us . |
| 2 | ++ | ecks this one off your must-see list . |
| 2a | ++ | a must-see film . |
| 2b | — — | neither a must-see film . |
| 2c | ++ | never a must-see film . |

Table 5: Misclassified test sentences (1 and 2), and manually constructed sentences (1a-c, 2a-c). The LSTM's *predicted* class (second column) is used as the *target* class for the *LRP-all* heatmaps.

volved in semantic composition, and that the classifier might also exhibit a bias towards the types of constructions it was trained on, which might then feel more "probable" or "understandable" to him.

Besides, during our experimentations, we empirically found that the *LRP-all* explanations are more helpful when using the classifier's *predicted* class as the *target* class (rather than the sample's *true* class), which intuitively makes sense since it's the class the model is the most confident about. Therefore, to understand the classification of single samples, we generally recommend this setup.

## 5 Conclusion

In our experiments with standard LSTMs, we find that the LRP rule for multiplicative connections introduced in Arras et al. (2017b) performs consistently better than other recently proposed rules, such as the one from Ding et al. (2017). Further, our comparison using a 5-class sentiment prediction task highlighted that LRP is not equivalent to *Gradient×Input* (as sometimes inaccurately stated in the literature, e.g. in Shrikumar et al., 2017) and is more selective than the latter, which is consistent with findings of Poerner et al. (2018).

Indeed, the equivalence between *Gradient×Input* and LRP holds only if using the $\epsilon$-rule with no stabilizer ($\epsilon = 0$), and if the network contains *only* ReLU activations and max pooling as nonlinearities (Kindermans et al., 2016; Shrikumar et al., 2016). When using other LRP rules, or if the network contains other activations or product nonlinearities (such as this is the case for LSTMs), then the equivalence does not hold (see Montavon et al. (2018) for a broader discussion).

Besides, we discovered that a few methods such as Occlusion (Li et al., 2017) and CD (Murdoch et al., 2018) are not reliable and get inconsistent results on a simple toy task using an LSTM with only *one* hidden unit.

In the future, we expect decomposition-based methods such as LRP to be further useful to analyze character-level models, to explore the role of single word embedding dimensions, and to discover important hidden layer neurons. Compared to attention weights (such as Bahdanau et al., 2015; Xu et al., 2015; Osman and Samek, 2019), decomposition-based explanations take into account all intermediate layers of the neural network model, and can be related to a specific class.

## Acknowledgments

We thank Grégoire Montavon for helpful discussions. This work was supported by the German Federal Ministry for Education and Research through the Berlin Big Data Centre (01IS14013A), the Berlin Center for Machine Learning (01IS18037I) and the TraMeExCo project (01IS18056A). Partial funding by DFG is acknowledged (EXC 2046/1, project-ID: 390685689). This work was also supported by the Information & Communications Technology Planning & Evaluation (IITP) grant funded by the Korea government (No. 2017-0-00451).

## References

Julius Adebayo, Justin Gilmer, Michael Muelly, Ian Goodfellow, Moritz Hardt, and Been Kim. 2018. Sanity Checks for Saliency Maps. In *Advances in Neural Information Processing Systems 31 (NIPS)*, pages 9505–9515.

Guillaume Alain and Yoshua Bengio. 2017. Understanding intermediate layers using linear classifier probes. In *International Conference on Learning Representations - Workshop track (ICLR)*.

Afra Alishahi, Grzegorz Chrupala, and Tal Linzen. 2019. Analyzing and Interpreting Neural Networks for NLP: A Report on the First BlackboxNLP Workshop. *arXiv:1904.04063*. Version 1.

Marco Ancona, Enea Ceolini, Cengiz Öztireli, and Markus Gross. 2018. Towards better understanding of gradient-based attribution methods for deep neural networks. In *International Conference on Learning Representations (ICLR)*.

Jose A. Arjona-Medina, Michael Gillhofer, Michael Widrich, Thomas Unterthiner, Johannes Brandstetter, and Sepp Hochreiter. 2018. RUDDER: Return Decomposition for Delayed Rewards. *arXiv:1806.07857*. Version 2.

Leila Arras, Franziska Horn, Grégoire Montavon, Klaus-Robert Müller, and Wojciech Samek. 2016. Explaining Predictions of Non-Linear Classifiers in NLP. In *Proceedings of the 2016 ACL Workshop on Representation Learning for NLP (Rep4NLP)*, pages 1–7. Association for Computational Linguistics.

Leila Arras, Franziska Horn, Grégoire Montavon, Klaus-Robert Müller, and Wojciech Samek. 2017a. "What is relevant in a text document?": An interpretable machine learning approach. *PLoS ONE*, 12(8):e0181142.

Leila Arras, Grégoire Montavon, Klaus-Robert Müller, and Wojciech Samek. 2017b. Explaining Recurrent Neural Network Predictions in Sentiment Analysis. In *Proceedings of the 2017 EMNLP Workshop on Computational Approaches to Subjectivity, Sentiment and Social Media Analysis (WASSA)*, pages 159–168. Association for Computational Linguistics.

Sebastian Bach, Alexander Binder, Grégoire Montavon, Frederick Klauschen, Klaus-Robert Müller, and Wojciech Samek. 2015. On Pixel-Wise Explanations for Non-Linear Classifier Decisions by Layer-Wise Relevance Propagation. *PLoS ONE*, 10(7):e0130140.

David Baehrens, Timon Schroeter, Stefan Harmeling, Motoaki Kawanabe, Katja Hansen, and Klaus-Robert Müller. 2010. How to Explain Individual Classification Decisions. *Journal of Machine Learning Research (JMLR)*, 11:1803–1831.

Dzmitry Bahdanau, Kyunghyun Cho, and Yoshua Bengio. 2015. Neural Machine Translation by Jointly Learning to Align and Translate. In *International Conference on Learning Representations (ICLR)*.

Yonatan Belinkov and James Glass. 2019. Analysis Methods in Neural Language Processing: A Survey. *Transactions of the Association for Computational Linguistics*, 7:49–72.

Jianbo Chen, Le Song, Martin Wainwright, and Michael Jordan. 2018. Learning to Explain: An Information-Theoretic Perspective on Model Interpretation. In *Proceedings of the 35th International Conference on Machine Learning (ICML)*, pages 883–892.

Kyunghyun Cho, Bart van Merrienboer, Caglar Gulcehre, Dzmitry Bahdanau, Fethi Bougares, Holger Schwenk, and Yoshua Bengio. 2014. Learning Phrase Representations using RNN Encoder-Decoder for Statistical Machine Translation. In *Proceedings of the 2014 Conference on Empirical Methods in Natural Language Processing (EMNLP)*, pages 1724–1734. Association for Computational Linguistics.

Sumit Chopra, Michael Auli, and Alexander M. Rush. 2016. Abstractive Sentence Summarization with Attentive Recurrent Neural Networks. In *Proceedings of the 2016 Conference of the North American Chapter of the Association for Computational Linguistics: Human Language Technologies (NAACL-HLT)*, pages 93–98. Association for Computational Linguistics.

Joon Son Chung, Andrew Senior, Oriol Vinyals, and Andrew Zisserman. 2017. Lip Reading Sentences in the Wild. In *IEEE Conference on Computer Vision and Pattern Recognition (CVPR)*, pages 3444–3453.

Misha Denil, Alban Demiraj, and Nando de Freitas. 2015. Extraction of Salient Sentences from Labelled Documents. *arXiv:1412.6815*. Version 2.

Yannis Dimopoulos, Paul Bourret, and Sovan Lek. 1995. Use of some sensitivity criteria for choosing networks with good generalization ability. *Neural Processing Letters*, 2(6):1–4.

Yanzhuo Ding, Yang Liu, Huanbo Luan, and Maosong Sun. 2017. Visualizing and Understanding Neural Machine Translation. In *Proceedings of the 55th Annual Meeting of the Association for Computational Linguistics (ACL)*, pages 1150–1159. Association for Computational Linguistics.

EU-GDPR. 2016. Regulation (EU) 2016/679 of the European Parliament and of the Council of 27 April 2016 on the protection of natural persons with regard to the processing of personal data and on the free movement of such data, and repealing Directive 95/46/EC (General Data Protection Regulation). *Official Journal of the European Union L 119*, 59:1–88.

Tamar Fraenkel and Yaacov Schul. 2008. The meaning of negated adjectives. *Intercultural Pragmatics*, 5(4):517–540.

Felix A. Gers, Jürgen Schmidhuber, and Fred Cummins. 1999. Learning to Forget: Continual Prediction with LSTM. In *International Conference on Artificial Neural Networks (ICANN)*, volume 2, pages 850–855.

Muriel Gevrey, Ioannis Dimopoulos, and Sovan Lek. 2003. Review and comparison of methods to study the contribution of variables in artificial neural network models. *Ecological Modelling*, 160(3):249–264.

Fréderic Godin, Kris Demuynck, Joni Dambre, Wesley De Neve, and Thomas Demeester. 2018. Explaining Character-Aware Neural Networks for Word-Level Prediction: Do They Discover Linguistic Rules? In *Proceedings of the 2018 Conference on Empirical Methods in Natural Language Processing(EMNLP)*, pages 3275–3284. Association for Computational Linguistics.

Klaus Greff, Rupesh K. Srivastava, Jan Koutník, Bas R. Steunebrink, and Jürgen Schmidhuber. 2017. LSTM: A Search Space Odyssey. *IEEE Transactions on Neural Networks and Learning Systems*, 28(10):2222–2232.

Sepp Hochreiter and Jürgen Schmidhuber. 1996. LSTM can Solve Hard Long Time Lag Problems. In *Advances in Neural Information Processing Systems 9 (NIPS)*, pages 473–479.

Sepp Hochreiter and Jürgen Schmidhuber. 1997. Long Short-Term Memory. *Neural Computation*, 9(8):1735–1780.

Alon Jacovi, Oren Sar Shalom, and Yoav Goldberg. 2018. Understanding Convolutional Neural Networks for Text Classification. In *Proceedings of the 2018 EMNLP Workshop BlackboxNLP: Analyzing and Interpreting Neural Networks for NLP*, pages 56–65. Association for Computational Linguistics.

Ákos Kádár, Grzegorz Chrupala, and Afra Alishahi. 2017. Representation of Linguistic Form and Function in Recurrent Neural Networks. *Computational Linguistics*, 43(4):761–780.

Andrej Karpathy and Li Fei-Fei. 2015. Deep visual-semantic alignments for generating image descriptions. In *IEEE Conference on Computer Vision and Pattern Recognition (CVPR)*, pages 3128–3137.

Pieter-Jan Kindermans, Kristof Schütt, Klaus-Robert Müller, and Sven Dähne. 2016. Investigating the influence of noise and distractors on the interpretation of neural networks. *arXiv:1611.07270*. Version 1.

Yair Lakretz, Germán Kruszewski, Théo Desbordes, Dieuwke Hupkes, Stanislas Dehaene, and Marco Baroni. 2019. The Emergence of Number and Syntax Units in LSTM Language Models. In *Proceedings of the 2019 Conference of the North American Chapter of the Association for Computational Linguistics: Human Language Technologies (NAACL-HLT)*, pages 11–20. Association for Computational Linguistics.

Will Landecker, Michael D. Thomure, Luís M. A. Bettencourt, Melanie Mitchell, Garrett T. Kenyon, and Steven P. Brumby. 2013. Interpreting Individual Classifications of Hierarchical Networks. In *IEEE Symposium on Computational Intelligence and Data Mining (CIDM)*, pages 32–38.

Sebastian Lapuschkin, Alexander Binder, Grégoire Montavon, Klaus-Robert Müller, and Wojciech Samek. 2016. Analyzing Classifiers: Fisher Vectors and Deep Neural Networks. In *IEEE Conference on Computer Vision and Pattern Recognition (CVPR)*, pages 2912–2920.

Sebastian Lapuschkin, Stephan Wäldchen, Alexander Binder, Grégoire Montavon, Wojciech Samek, and Klaus-Robert Müller. 2019. Unmasking Clever Hans Predictors and Assessing What Machines Really Learn. *Nature Communications*, 10:1096.

Quoc V. Le, Navdeep Jaitly, and Geoffrey E. Hinton. 2015. A Simple Way to Initialize Recurrent Networks of Rectified Linear Units. arXiv:1504.00941. Version 2.

Jiwei Li, Xinlei Chen, Eduard Hovy, and Dan Jurafsky. 2016. Visualizing and Understanding Neural Models in NLP. In *Proceedings of the 2016 Conference of the North American Chapter of the Association for Computational Linguistics: Human Language Technologies (NAACL-HLT)*, pages 681–691. Association for Computational Linguistics.

Jiwei Li, Will Monroe, and Dan Jurafsky. 2017. Understanding Neural Networks through Representation Erasure. arXiv:1612.08220. Version 3.

Tal Linzen, Emmanuel Dupoux, and Yoav Goldberg. 2016. Assessing the Ability of LSTMs to Learn Syntax-Sensitive Dependencies. *Transactions of the Association for Computational Linguistics*, 4:521–535.

Scott M. Lundberg and Su-In Lee. 2017. A Unified Approach to Interpreting Model Predictions. In *Advances in Neural Information Processing Systems 30 (NIPS)*, pages 4765–4774.

James Martens and Ilya Sutskever. 2011. Learning Recurrent Neural Networks with Hessian-Free Optimization. In *Proceedings of the 28th International Conference on Machine Learning (ICML)*, pages 1033–1040.

Grégoire Montavon, Sebastian Lapuschkin, Alexander Binder, Wojciech Samek, and Klaus-Robert Müller. 2017. Explaining nonlinear classification decisions with deep Taylor decomposition. *Pattern Recognition*, 65:211–222.

Grégoire Montavon, Wojciech Samek, and Klaus-Robert Müller. 2018. Methods for interpreting and understanding deep neural network. *Digital Signal Processing*, 73:1–15.

Ari S. Morcos, David G.T. Barrett, Neil C. Rabinowitz, and Matthew Botvinick. 2018. On the importance of single directions for generalization. In *International Conference on Learning Representations (ICLR)*.

W. James Murdoch, Peter J. Liu, and Bin Yu. 2018. Beyond Word Importance: Contextual Decomposition to Extract Interactions from LSTMs. In *International Conference on Learning Representations (ICLR)*.

Dong Nguyen. 2018. Comparing Automatic and Human Evaluation of Local Explanations for Text Classification. In *Proceedings of the 2018 Conference of the North American Chapter of the Association for Computational Linguistics: Human Language Technologies (NAACL-HLT)*, pages 1069–1078. Association for Computational Linguistics.

Ahmed Osman and Wojciech Samek. 2019. DRAU: Dual Recurrent Attention Units for Visual Question Answering. *Computer Vision and Image Understanding*.

Nina Poerner, Hinrich Schütze, and Benjamin Roth. 2018. Evaluating neural network explanation methods using hybrid documents and morphosyntactic agreement. In *Proceedings of the 56th Annual Meeting of the Association for Computational Linguistics (ACL)*, pages 340–350. Association for Computational Linguistics.

Marco Tulio Ribeiro, Sameer Singh, and Carlos Guestrin. 2016. "Why Should I Trust You?": Explaining the Predictions of Any Classifier. In *Proceedings of the 22nd ACM SIGKDD International Conference on Knowledge Discovery and Data Mining*, pages 1135–1144.

Tim Rocktäschel, Edward Grefenstette, Karl Moritz Hermann, Tomas Kocisky, and Phil Blunsom. 2016. Reasoning about Entailment with Neural Attention. In *International Conference on Learning Representations (ICLR)*.

Wojciech Samek, Alexander Binder, Grégoire Montavon, Sebastian Lapuschkin, and Klaus-Robert Müller. 2017. Evaluating the Visualization of what a Deep Neural Network has learned. *IEEE Transactions on Neural Networks and Learning Systems*, 28(11):2660–2673.

Mike Schuster and Kuldip K. Paliwal. 1997. Bidirectional Recurrent Neural Networks. *IEEE Transactions on Signal Processing*, 45(11):2673–2681.

Avanti Shrikumar, Peyton Greenside, and Anshul Kundaje. 2017. Learning Important Features Through Propagating Activation Differences. In *Proceedings of the 34th International Conference on Machine Learning (ICML)*, pages 3145–3153.

Avanti Shrikumar, Peyton Greenside, Anna Shcherbina, and Anshul Kundaje. 2016. Not Just A Black Box: Interpretable Deep Learning by Propagating Activation Differences. *1605.01713*. Version 1.

Karen Simonyan, Andrea Vedaldi, and Andrew Zisserman. 2014. Deep Inside Convolutional Networks: Visualising Image Classification Models and Saliency Maps. In *International Conference on Learning Representations - Workshop track (ICLR)*.

Chandan Singh, W. James Murdoch, and Bin Yu. 2019. Hierarchical interpretations for neural network predictions. In *International Conference on Learning Representations (ICLR)*.

Richard Socher, Alex Perelygin, Jean Y. Wu, Jason Chuang, Christopher D. Manning, Andrew Y. Ng, and Christopher Potts. 2013. Recursive Deep Models for Semantic Compositionality Over a Sentiment Treebank. In *Proceedings of the 2013 Conference on Empirical Methods in Natural Language Processing (EMNLP)*, pages 1631–1642. Association for Computational Linguistics.

Jost T. Springenberg, Alexey Dosovitskiy, Thomas Brox, and Martin Riedmiller. 2015. Striving for Simplicity: The All Convolutional Net. In *International Conference on Learning Representations - Workshop track (ICLR)*.

Florian Strohm and Roman Klinger. 2018. An Empirical Analysis of the Role of Amplifiers, Downtoners, and Negations in Emotion Classification in Microblogs. In *IEEE International Conference on Data Science and Advanced Analytics (DSAA)*, pages 673–681.

Mukund Sundararajan, Ankur Taly, and Qiqi Yan. 2017. Axiomatic Attribution for Deep Networks. In *Proceedings of the 34th International Conference on Machine Learning (ICML)*, pages 3319–3328.

Huijuan Xu and Kate Saenko. 2016. Ask, Attend and Answer: Exploring Question-Guided Spatial Attention for Visual Question Answering. In *Computer Vision - ECCV 2016*, pages 451–466.

Kelvin Xu, Jimmy Ba, Ryan Kiros, Kyunghyun Cho, Aaron Courville, Ruslan Salakhutdinov, Richard Zemel, and Yoshua Bengio. 2015. Show, Attend and Tell: Neural Image Caption Generation with Visual Attention. In *Proceedings of the 32nd International Conference on Machine Learning (ICML)*, pages 2048–2057.

Yinchong Yang, Volker Tresp, Marius Wunderle, and Peter A. Fasching. 2018. Explaining Therapy Predictions with Layer-Wise Relevance Propagation in Neural Networks. In *IEEE International Conference on Healthcare Informatics (ICHI)*, pages 152–162.

Matthew D. Zeiler and Rob Fergus. 2014. Visualizing and Understanding Convolutional Networks. In *Computer Vision - ECCV 2014*, pages 818–833.

## A Appendix

### A.1 Long-Short Term Memory (LSTM) model

All LSTMs used in the present work have the following recurrence form (Hochreiter and Schmidhuber, 1997; Gers et al., 1999), which is also the most commonly used in the literature (Greff et al., 2017):

$$i_t = \texttt{sigm}\left(W_i\, h_{t-1} + U_i\, x_t + b_i\right)$$

$$f_t = \texttt{sigm}\left(W_f\, h_{t-1} + U_f\, x_t + b_f\right)$$

$$o_t = \texttt{sigm}\left(W_o\, h_{t-1} + U_o\, x_t + b_o\right)$$

$$g_t = \texttt{tanh}\left(W_g\, h_{t-1} + U_g\, x_t + b_g\right)$$

$$c_t = f_t \odot c_{t-1} + i_t \odot g_t$$

$$h_t = o_t \odot \texttt{tanh}(c_t)$$

where $\mathbf{x} = (x_1, x_2, ..., x_T)$ is the input sequence, $\texttt{sigm}$ and $\texttt{tanh}$ are element-wise activations, and $\odot$ is an element-wise multiplication. The matrices $W$'s, $U$'s, and vectors $b$'s are connection weights and biases, and the initial states $h_0$ and $c_0$ are set to zero. The resulting last time step hidden vector $h_T$ is ultimately fed to a fully-connected linear output layer yielding a prediction vector $\boldsymbol{f}(\mathbf{x})$, with one entry $f_c(\mathbf{x})$ per class.

The bidirectional LSTM (Schuster and Paliwal, 1997) we use for the sentiment prediction task, is a concatenation of two separate LSTM models as described above, each of them taking a different sequence of word embedding vectors as input. One LSTM takes as input the words in their original order, as they appear in the input sentence/phrase. The other LSTM takes as input the same word sequence but in *reversed* order. Each of these LSTMs yields a final hidden vector, say $h_T^{\rightarrow}$ and $h_T^{\leftarrow}$. The concatenation of these two vectors is then fed to a fully-connected linear output layer, retrieving one prediction score $f_c(\mathbf{x})$ per class.

### A.2 Layer-wise Relevance Propagation (LRP) implementation

We employ the code released by the authors (Arras et al., 2017b) (`https://github.com/ArrasL/LRP_for_LSTM`), and adapt it to work with different LRP product rule variants.

In the toy task experiments, we didn't find it necessary to add any stabilizing term for numerical stability (therefore we use $\epsilon = 0$ for all LRP

rules). In the sentiment analysis experiments, we use $\epsilon = 0.001$ (except for the *LRP-prop* variant where we use $\epsilon = 0.2$, we tried the following values: [0.001, 0.01, 0.1, 0.2, 0.3, 0.4, 1.0] and took the lowest one to achieve numerical stability).

### A.3 Contextual Decomposition (CD) implementation

We employ the code released by the authors (Murdoch et al., 2018) (`https://github.com/jamie-murdoch/ContextualDecomposition`), and adapt it to work with a bidirectional LSTM. We also made a slight modification w.r.t. the author's latest available version (commit e6575aa from March 30, 2018). In particular in file `sent_util.py` we changed line 125 to: `if i>=start and i<stop`, to exclude the stop index, and call the function CD with the arguments `start=k` and `stop=k+1` to compute the relevance of the k-th input vector, or word, in the input sequence. This consistently led to better results for the *CD* method in all our experiments.

### A.4 Toy task setup

As an LSTM model we consider a unidirectional LSTM with a hidden layer of size one (i.e. with one memory cell $c_t$), followed by a linear output layer with no bias. Since the input is two-dimensional, this results in an LSTM model with 17 learnable parameters. The weights are randomly initialized with the uniform distribution $U(-1.0, 1.0)$, and biases are initialized to zero. We train the model with Pytorch's LBFGS optimizer, with an initial learning rate of 0.002, for 1000 optimizer steps, and reduce the learning rate by a factor of 0.95 if the error doesn't decrease within 10 steps. We also clip the gradient norm to 5.0. With this setting around 1/2 of the trained models on addition and 1/3 of the models for subtraction converged to a good solution with a validation MSE $< 10^{-4}$.

### A.5 Semantic composition: generation of representative samples

In a first step, we build a list of words with a positive sentiment $(+)$, resp. a negative sentiment $(-)$, as identified by the bidirectional LSTM model. To that end, we predict the class of each word contained in the model's vocabulary, and select for each sentiment a list of 50 words with the highest prediction scores. This way we try to ensure that the considered sentiment words are clearly identified by the model as being from the positive sentiment (+), resp. the negative sentiment (−) class.

In a second step, we build a list of negations and amplifiers. To that end, we start by considering the same lists of 39 negations and 69 amplifiers as in Strohm and Klinger (2018), from which we retain only those that are classified as neutral (class 0) by the LSTM model, which leaves us with a list of 8 negations and 29 amplifiers. This way we discard modifiers that are *biased* towards a specific sentiment, since our goal is to analyze the compositional effect of modifiers.

Then, for each type of considered semantic composition (see Table 4), we generate bigrams resp. trigrams by using the previously defined lists of modifiers and sentiment words.

For compositions of type 1 ("negation of positive sentiment"), we note that among the constructed bigrams 60% are classified as negative (−) by the LSTM model, 26% are predicted as neutral (0), and for the remaining 14% of bigrams the negation is not identified correctly and the corresponding bigram is classified as positive (+). In order to remove negations that are ambiguous to the classifier, we retain only those negations which in at least 40% of the cases predict the bigram as negative. These negations are: ['neither', 'never', 'nobody', 'none', 'nor']. Then we average the results over all bigrams classified as negative (−).

For compositions of type 2 and 3 we proceed similarly. For type 2 compositions ("amplification of positive sentiment"), we note that 29% of the constructed bigrams are classified as very positive (++), and for type 3 compositions ("amplification of negative sentiment"), 24% are predicted as very negative (−−), while the remaining bigrams are of the same class as the original sentiment word (thus the amplification is not identified by the classifier). Here again we retain only unambiguous modifiers, which in at least 40% of the cases amplified the corresponding sentiment. The resulting amplifiers are: ['completely', 'deeply', 'entirely', 'extremely', 'highly', 'insanely', 'purely', 'really', 'so', 'thoroughly', 'utterly', 'very'] for type 2 compositions; and ['completely', 'entirely', 'extremely', 'highly', 'really', 'thoroughly', 'utterly'] for type 3 compositions. Then we average the results over the corresponding bigrams which are predicted as very positive (++), resp. very negative (−−).

For type 4 compositions ("negation of amplified positive sentiment"), we construct all possible trigrams with the initial lists of negations, amplifiers and positive sentiment words. We keep for the final averaging of the results only those trigrams where both the effect of the amplifier, and of the negation are correctly identified by the LSTM model. To this end we classify the corresponding bigram formed by combining the amplifier with the positive sentiment word, and keep the corresponding sample if this bigram is predicted as very positive (++). Then we average the results over trigrams predicted as negative (−) (this amounts to finally retain 1745 trigrams).

We also tried to investigate the following composition: "negation of negative sentiment", similarly to compositions of type 1. However, we found that only 1% of the constructed bigrams are classified as neutral (0), and that the remaining bigrams are classified as negative (−) (81%) or even very negative (−−) (18%). This means, in most cases, negating a negative sentiment doesn't change the classifier's prediction, i.e. the negation is not detected by the LSTM model. Therefore we did not retain this type of composition for constructing representative heatmaps. That the impact of negation is not symmetric across different sentiments was also observed in previous works (Socher et al., 2013; Li et al., 2016), and is probably due to the fact that some type of semantic compositions are more frequent than others in the training data (and more generally, in natural language) (Fraenkel and Schul, 2008).

# On the Realization of Compositionality in Neural Networks


Joris Baan[1], Jana Leible[1], Mitja Nikolaus[2], David Rau[1], Dennis Ulmer[1],
Tim Baumgärtner[1], Dieuwke Hupkes[1,*] and Elia Bruni[3,*]

```
{joris.baan,jana.leible,david.rau,dennis.ulmer}@student.uva.nl
               mitja.nikolaus@posteo.de
               baumgaertner.t@gmail.com
                   d.hupkes@uva.nl
                elia.bruni@gmail.com
```

[1]University of Amsterdam, [2]University of Tübingen, [3]Universitat Pompeu Fabra



## Abstract

We present a detailed comparison of two types of sequence to sequence models trained to conduct a compositional task. The models are architecturally identical at inference time, but differ in the way that they are trained: our *baseline* model is trained with a task-success signal only, while the other model receives additional supervision on its attention mechanism (Attentive Guidance), which has shown to be an effective method for encouraging more compositional solutions (Hupkes et al., 2019). We first confirm that the models with attentive guidance indeed infer more compositional solutions than the baseline, by training them on the lookup table task presented by Liška et al. (2019). We then do an in-depth analysis of the *structural* differences between the two model types, focusing in particular on the organisation of the parameter space and the hidden layer activations and find noticeable differences in both these aspects. Guided networks focus more on the components of the input rather than the sequence as a whole and develop small functional groups of neurons with specific purposes that use their gates more selectively. Results from parameter heat maps, component swapping and graph analysis also indicate that guided networks exhibit a more modular structure with a small number of specialized, strongly connected neurons.


## 1 Introduction

Sequence to sequence models (seq2seqs), a subset of neural networks that use sequences as input and output, have enjoyed great success in many NLP tasks such as machine translation (Bahdanau et al., 2015) and speech recognition (Graves et al.,

2013). Even though these feats indicate excellent generalization capabilities, the way seq2seqs generalize has found to be different from how humans do. In particular, seq2seqs lack of compositional understanding: the ability to construct new representations by combining familiar primitive components (e.g. Szabó, 2012). Humans, instead, heavily rely on compositionality to learn complex functional structure efficiently (Schulz et al., 2016). Once the primitive components are understood, a possibly infinite amount of novel combinations can be made, which allows for large scale generalization from a limited amount of examples (Fodor, 1975). For instance, sentences consist of words, which in turn consist of characters constructed from strokes.

Recently, Liška et al. (2019) have shown how seq2seqs can produce many different fits on the training data using stochastic gradient descent, but rarely, if ever, find a compositional solution. The authors introduce a new data set called the **lookup table** task, which tests for out of distribution generalization. This data set will be discussed in more detail in Section 2.1.

As a remedy, Hupkes et al. (2019) proposed Attentive Guidance (AG), a training technique which encourages seq2seqs to encode a more compositional solution without changing their internal architecture. AG provides additional information about the structure of the input sequence by supervising the attention mechanism of a model. As a result, the model is able to find what are the basic components of the lookup table task and how to combine them in a compositional manner.

Thanks to this work, we are now in the unique position of having a compositional (from now on *AG*) and non-compositional (from now on *base-*

---

* Shared senior authorship

127


*Proceedings of the Second BlackboxNLP Workshop on Analyzing and Interpreting Neural Networks for NLP*, pages 127–137
Florence, Italy, August 1, 2019. ©2019 Association for Computational Linguistics

*line*) model that have identical architectures, but implement very different approaches to the same task. In this paper, we compare those two models and aim to find structural differences between the way they organise their weights and form their representations, that could be indicative of compositional solutions. In particular:

- We show, through inspection of the parameter space and activations, that individual neurons in the AG model show a degree of specialization with respect to specific inputs that is unseen in baseline models.

- We demonstrate, by substituting parts of both models with the corresponding component of its counterpart, which model sections contribute most to the observed compositional behavior in AG models.

These differences confirm the findings of Hupkes et al. (2019) that seq2seqs do not necessarily require big architectural adjustments to handle compositionality, since a network with identical architecture is capable of finding such a solution. Furthermore, these findings could be exploited to inform architectural changes in models, such that their priors to infer compositional solutions increase even when they are not provided explicit additional feedback on the compositional structure of the data.

## 2  Setup

In our experiments, we compare vanilla seq2seq with models that are trained with AG. Below, we briefly discuss both setups and the data we use for our experiments.

### 2.1  Task

For our experiments, we use the lookup table composition task proposed by Liška et al. (2019), which was created to test the compositional abilities of neural networks. In this task, atomic lookup tables are created as to define a unique mapping from one binary string to another binary string of the same length. These atomic tables are then applied sequentially to a binary input string and yield a binary string. To give an example: if $t1(001) = 110$ and $t2(110) = 001$, then the function $(t1 \circ t2)(001) = 001$ can be computed as a composition of $t1$ and $t2$. See Table 1 for a more comprehensive example.

Following Hupkes et al. (2019), we generate eight atomic lookup tables with strings of length 3 and use them to produce all 64 possible length two compositions. This forms the basis of the dataset that all experiments were performed on. To test the model's ability of generalization on a more granular level, we compose four test sets with an increasing level of difficulty. For the first test set, we remove 2 out of 8 inputs for every composition (*heldout inputs*). For the second and third testset, we remove 8 random table compositions from the training set (*heldout compositions*), as well as all compositions that either contain $t7$ or $t8$ (*heldout tables*). Finally, we create a test set by removing all compositions that contain a combination of tables $t7$ and $t8$ from the training set (*new compositions*). The nature of the tasks requires the models to make use of the underlying compositionality. If this structure is not exploited, it is impossible to reliably find the correct solutions for the test data. For more details, we refer to Liška et al. (2019) and Hupkes et al. (2019).

| Atomic | Atomic | Composed |
|---|---|---|
| $t1$ | $t2$ | $t1 \circ t2$ |
| $000 \to 111$ | $000 \to 100$ | $000 \to 011$ |
| $001 \to 010$ | $001 \to 101$ | $001 \to 110$ |
| $010 \to 101$ | $010 \to 110$ | $010 \to 100$ |
| $\cdots$ | $\cdots$ | $\cdots$ |

Table 1: Example for atomic lookup tables ($t1$ and $t2$) of length 3 and a composition of length 2 ($t1 \circ t2$).

### 2.2  Baseline

The baseline model consists of an encoder-decoder architecture with an attention mechanism (Bahdanau et al., 2015) and Gated Recurrent Units (GRU)[1] (Cho et al., 2014).

GRUs compute the hidden activations $h_t$ based on the previous hidden state $h_{t-1}$ and the representation of the current input $x_t$ in the following way (biases were omitted for clarity):

$$z_t = \sigma(W_{iz}x_t + W_{hz}h_{t-1})$$
$$r_t = \sigma(W_{ir}x_t + W_{hr}h_{t-1})$$
$$\tilde{h}_t = \tanh(W_{ih}x_t + W_{hh}(r_t \circ h_{t-1}))$$
$$h_t = (1 - z_t) \cdot h_{t-1} + z_t \cdot \tilde{h}_t,$$

---

[1] We also trained models with Long-Short Term Memory units (Hochreiter and Schmidhuber, 1997) but found the results to be very similar and therefore decided to omit the latter from this work.

where we call $z_t$ and $r_t$ the activations of the *update gate* and *reset gate*, respectively.

### 2.3 Attentive Guidance

The AG model used in this work is identical to the baseline model in terms of architecture. The only difference occurs during the training procedure, where an additional loss term is enforced on the weights of the attention mechanism at decoding time step $t$ for input token $i$, $\hat{a}_{i,t}$:

$$\mathcal{L}_{\text{AG}} = \frac{1}{T} \Big( \sum_{t=1}^{T} \sum_{i=1}^{N} -a_{i,t} \log \hat{a}_{i,t} \Big),$$

where $\hat{a}_{i,t}$ denotes the target attention weights. The attention loss is computed with an additional set of labels, that express how the input should be segmented and in which order it should be processed. Hupkes et al. (2019) show that providing this additional supervision consistently improves the solutions found for the lookup table task: the guided models were found to have perfect generalization capabilities on the *heldout compositions* and *heldout inputs* and also perform well on *heldout tables* and *new compositions*. As inputs are supposed to be processed sequentially in our case, the target attention pattern is strictly monotonic, i.e. the target attention weights over the sequence are realized in a diagonal matrix.

### 2.4 Experiments

We train five baseline and AG models with the same hyperparameters and the Adam optimizer (Kingma and Ba, 2015). Given the small vocabulary, we use an embedding size of 16 and a hidden size to 512. All models were trained for a maximum of 100 epochs with an attention mechanism, determining attention weights by using a multi-layer perceptron. Models were selected by their best accuracy on a held-out set. A comprehensive list of model performances on the different sets can be found in the Appendix. The model implementations themselves stem from the `i-machine-think` codebase.[2]

In the following, we perform three different suits of experiments. Firstly, we examine the parameter space of both models (Section 3). Secondly, we take a closer look at the activations of single neurons and the GRU gates (Section 4).

Lastly, in Section 5, we perform two different ablation studies: we make components of one model interacting with the components of the other and we distill the network via strongly connected neurons.

## 3 Inspecting the Parameter Space

In this section, we look at the parameter space of the baseline and AG models. All discoveries regarding the parameter space were validated by comparing 5 runs of the same model class to make sure that observed differences can be ascribed to the differences in models and not different weight initializations.

### 3.1 Weight Inspection

To gain a better understanding of the organization of the weights, we generated weight heat maps with the y-axis representing the weights going from all neurons to one neuron of the next layer (incoming weights) and the x-axis the weights going from one neuron to all neurons of the next layer (outgoing weights). Neural networks are known to be good at distributing their weights rather than have strong spatial organization, which makes it interesting to see whether such heat maps would reveal any differences in the organization of weights between AG and baseline models [3].

The most striking difference between AG and baseline arises for the decoder embedding, as can be seen in Figure 1. The baseline model exhibits small weights whereas the AG model shows bigger weights in rows 2-10. Row number two is an exception, since it is equally strong for both networks. This might be explained by the fact that this row represents the start-of-sequence (SOS) token, which could be sending a stronger error signal for both models.

### 3.2 Neural Connectivity

Since the heat maps of the weight matrices for larger layers were hard to interpret, we explored a more intuitive visualization of the network's parameter space. We took neurons as nodes, and weights between neurons as edges. The thickness and color of an edge represents the magni-

---

[2]Available under `https://github.com/i-machine-think/machine`.

[3]Note that we do not normalize reported weights or activations by the activity of the 'pre-synaptic' neurons connected to it. This would be interesting to explore in future research, since a neuron's activation and the importance of its weight is in part dependant on the mean activation of its predecessors.

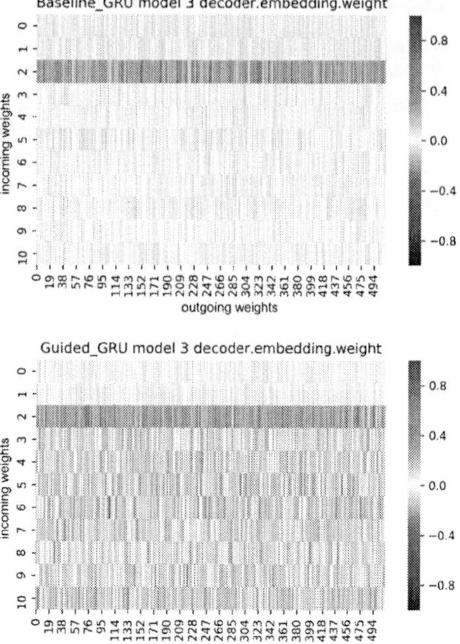


Figure 1: Heatmap of the decoder embedding weight values. Outgoing weights correspond to weights going from the embedding to one decoder output neuron, and incoming weights to all weights going from the embedding to all decoder output neurons. (Best viewed in color)

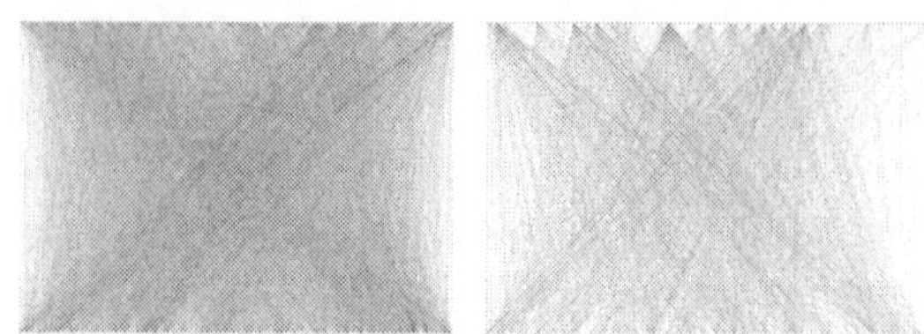

Left: baseline. Right: AG. Encoder update gates $W_{hz}$.

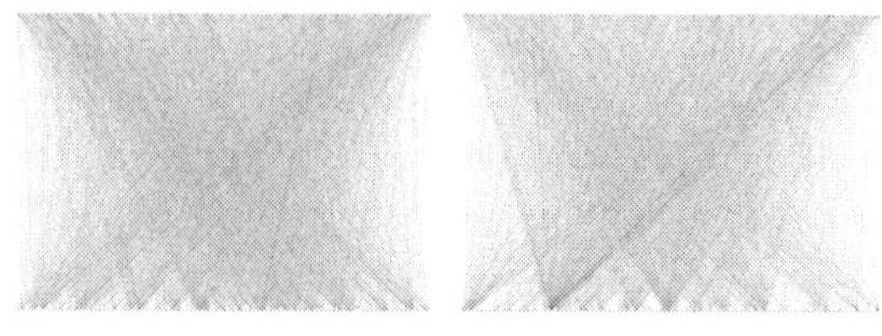

Left: baseline. Right: AG. Decoder update gates $W_{iz}$.

Figure 2: Visualization of weight matrices $W_{hz}$ of the encoder and $W_{iz}$ of the decoder. Weights going from the previous to the next layer are represented by lines going from bottom to the top. The color reflects the weight value, where blue denotes negative, red positive and white zero. (Best viewed in color)

tude of the weight. To prevent clutter, we applied thresholding to remove edges that corresponded to weak weights. For the encoder and decoder, we used a threshold of $\pm0.2$ and $\pm0.17$ respectively, which corresponds on average (between AG and vanilla models) to the strongest one percent of the weights.

The goal is to understand how the parameter space is structured and to see whether any differences between AG and baseline models can be found, for example, because of a stronger modularity, grouping or specialization of neurons in AG models.

Figure 2 depicts the update gate weights $W_{hz}$ of the encoder on the top and the weights $W_{iz}$ of the decoder at the bottom. The weights of the previous layer to the next are represented by edges going from bottom to top. The most striking difference is that the baseline weights seem much more cluttered, whereas the AG model exhibits a few distinct, strongly polar neurons - neurons whose weights are on average negative or positive. Neurons that have many strong connections occur in the top layer of the encoder of the AG model in

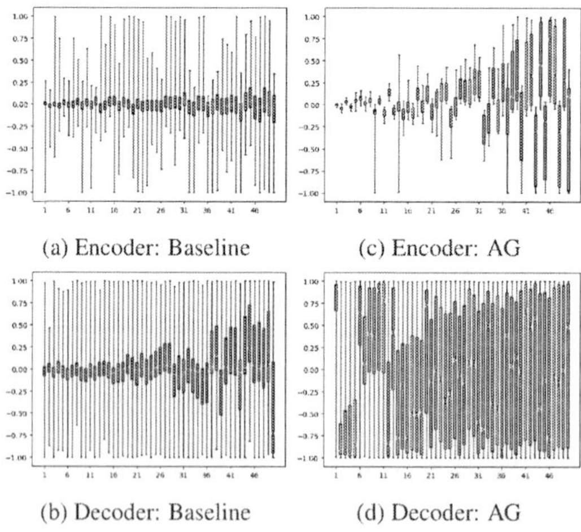



Figure 3: Distributions of activation values for 50 randomly sampled neurons for baseline (blue) and AG (orange) for both encoders (top) and decoders (bottom). Whiskers show the full range of the distribution. (Best viewed in color)

$W_{hz}$ and $W_{hr}$. Similarly, strong connected neurons can be found at the bottom layer of the AG's decoder in $W_{iz}$ and $W_{ir}$. The finding of highly connected neurons seems to further reinforce the hypothesis that AG models learn to specialize using fewer but more strongly connected neurons, which could help to learn a more modular solution.

Another interesting phenomenon that holds for both models can be observed by looking at the difference between update and reset gates of the same network (not shown here for the sake of space): The polarity of the neurons that are on average strongly positive or negative are inversely related. A possible explanation for this is that, when information from the current hidden state is to be retained, that same part is being reset in the previous hidden state.

## 4 Analyzing Activations

While analyzing the model weights gives us insight into the general trained structure of the model, analyzing activations lets us examine how the different model types respond to certain inputs. We thus try to identify groups of neurons that specialize to respond to certain inputs and provide further inside into the GRU's gating behavior.

### 4.1 Functional Groups

We hypothesize that solving the task compositionally is done by distinct groups of neurons in the network. Each group addresses different functionalities. For example, a group of units in the encoder could be responsible for representing the presence of the current table in the input sequence, as proposed in the previous section.

An indicator for this behavior can be seen in Figure 3, where we sampled 50 random neurons from the encoder and decoder of both models and tracked their activation values emitted over the samples in the test set. We can see that in contrast to the baseline, some neurons of the AG only produce activations in specific value ranges, which could be a hint for a potential specialization. The same can be found inside the AG's decoder, although most of the neurons sampled seem to cover the whole value range during processing.

To test this hypothesis, we analyze which hidden activations are crucial for correctly predicting the current table at a time step. The baseline model is expected to not be able to predict the presence

of single tables because it fails to see the tables as parts of a compositional task and instead memorizes the combinations it has encountered during training.

In a first experiment, we use diagnostic classification (DC, Hupkes et al., 2018), which consists in training linear classifiers on the hidden activations to predict a certain feature. In this case, we use the encoder's activations to predict the table in the input sequence of the corresponding time step. For example, if the input was '000 t1 t2', we trained the classifier to predict 't1' for the encoder activations of the second time step and to predict 't2' for the activations of the third time step. Similarly to the methodology of Dalvi et al. (2019), we subsequently added units to a set, depending on the absolute weight they were assigned in the diagnostic classifier.[4] After each addition, we re-calculated the accuracy for the prediction. This process was repeated until 95 % of the overall accuracy (with all units) is reached, the resulting subset of units forms the *functional group*.[5]

The results are shown in the first row of Table 2. All numbers are averaged over the five trained models. Some differences arise in the functional group size of the models: While for the baseline models on average 35 units are required to make a good prediction, the information is stored in only 2 units in the guided models.

To verify whether the units in the functional group are actually important units in the model, we further analyzed the strengths of the weights connected to each of the units. On average, 93% of the units in the functional group of the AG models can be found in the top 5% of the units with the strongest absolute weight values. We conclude that the units of the functional group are highly connected and thus very likely to play an essential role in the functionality of the model.

Assuming that the information of the current table being stored in the encoder activations is used by the decoder to perform according calculations, we expect that by using the gate activations of the

---

[4]However, unlike Dalvi et al. (2019), we do not use any regularization on the DC to contrast the different degrees to which information is distributed across neurons in the two model types.

[5]Applying the methods development by Lundberg and Lee (2017) seems to confirm the responsible neurons we found, but selects more neurons and gives less consistent results, which we trace back to the extensive approximations required and some model assumptions (e.g. feature independence) being violated.

| In | Model | Accuracy | #Units |
|---|---|---|---|
| $h_t^{\text{enc}}$ | BL | .93 (.98) | 35 |
| | AG | .98 (1.) | 2 |
| $z_t^{\text{dec}}$ | BL | .51 (.53) | 52 |
| | AG | .96 (1.) | 22.2 |
| $r_t^{\text{dec}}$ | BL | .50 (.52) | 44 |
| | AG | .96 (1.) | 20.8 |

Table 2: Performance of diagnostic classifiers for predicting the current input table with the hidden activations ($h_t^{\text{enc}}$) of the encoder, the input gate activations ($z_t^{\text{dec}}$) or the reset gate activations ($r_t^{\text{dec}}$) of the decoder of the baseline (BL) and Attentive Guidance (AG) model. The third column shows the accuracy when predicting using the functional group of units and in brackets the accuracy when using all units. The fourth column displays the average number of units in the functional group across different runs (which can be either hidden units or gate activations).

decoder it is also possible to predict the current input table. We use the same methodology as in the previous experiment, with the only difference that the inputs for the diagnostic classifier are the activations of the decoder gates. Results are shown in the second and third rows of Table 2. Using all gate activations of the update or the reset gate of GRUs, we are able to perfectly predict the current table in the guided models. With the baseline model, an accuracy of only around50 % is reached.[6] The size of the functional groups in the guided models is remarkably larger than with the encoder hidden activations, showing that the information is more distributed over the gates. This difference can be explained by the fact that the gates are not mainly representing information, but using represented information to perform calculations. Further, distribution of information across the gates is more likely because a gate activation affects only one hidden unit while a hidden layer activation can possibly affect all gates in the upcoming time step (Hupkes and Zuidema, 2017).

In another experiment, we aim to predict the current time step with the activations of the encoder.[7] We assume that counting is an essential part of solving the task in a compositional manner. The methodology is the same as in the previously described experiments. The result pattern

---

[6] Accuracy with a majority classifier for the task is 12.5 %.

[7] For example, if the input was '000 t1 t2', we trained the classifier to predict '0' for the encoder activations of the first time step, '1' for the encoder activations of the second time step and '2' for the activations of the third time step.

(cf. Table 3) can be compared to the first experiment: Using all units, it is possible to predict the time step with all models, but, in the guided attention models, the information is more concentrated in functional groups than units.

| In | Model | Accuracy | #Units |
|---|---|---|---|
| $h_t^{\text{enc}}$ | BL | .95 (.98) | 40 |
| | AG | 1.0 (1.0) | 2 |

Table 3: Performance of diagnostic classifiers for predicting the current time step with the hidden activations ($h_t$) of the encoder. The second column shows the accuracy when predicting using the functional group of units and in brackets the accuracy when using all units. The third column displays the number of units in the functional group.

These results, implying that some neurons specialize in tracking the current time step and reacting to distinct inputs, demonstrate that the AG model uses information about the current table in the decoder to perform operations in a compositional way (treating the tables as distinct parts). The baseline model does not show distinct activation patterns in the gates for specific tables.

## 4.2 Gating behavior

Based on the findings in previous section, we also expect the usage of reset and update gate to be significantly different for the two models under scrutiny. To study this, we use a technique introduced by Karpathy et al. (2015), that considers, for each gate in the network, the fraction of samples for which it is left-saturated (activation smaller than 0.1) or right-saturated (activation greater than 0.9), where being left-saturated corresponds to being closed and right-saturated to being open.

We show the results in Figure 4. The plots reveal a clear difference between the usage of gates in the baseline and the guided models. The guided models seem to be more distinct in their gate activation: Activations tend to stick to the axes. Values close to the diagonal mean that the respective gate is mostly saturated, values close to the axes reveal gates that are either saturated to one side or not saturated. Values in between, mostly seen in the baseline models, indicate gates that are rarely saturated.

The activation pattern of the update gates shows clear differences between the baseline and the AG models. In the baseline, they are mostly left saturated, which means that new information is rarely

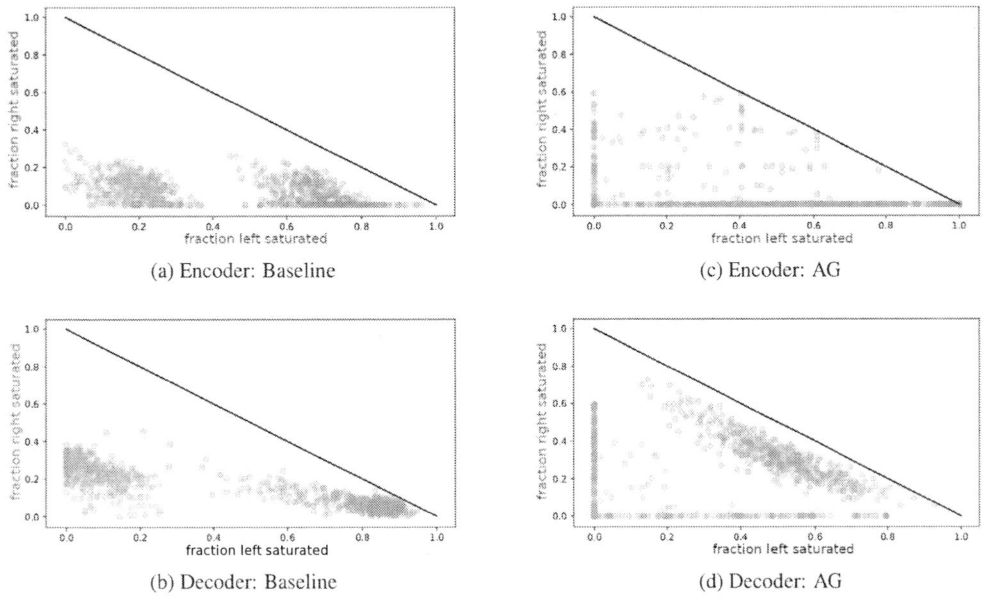

Figure 4: Gate activation plots for reset gate $r_t$ and update gate $z_t$. (Best viewed in color)

---

incorporated in the calculations, in both the encoder and decoder. In the encoder of the AG model, most gates are also only left-saturated, but there is a considerable amount of outliers which could be some units that are highly specialized to specific inputs. In the AG decoder, some gates are also often right-saturated, allowing for the intake of new information. One possible interpretation is that the gates in the AG decoder model selectively allow the relevant input for the current time step to be included in the calculations.

## 5  Ablation studies

In this section, we first swap components of both models and measure the effects on the models' performances to identify crucial model parts. We then check performance of the AG model when only its strongly connected neurons are used.

### 5.1  Component substitution

To understand to what extent specific components of a seq2seqs contribute to compositionality, we take components from one trained model and place them into the other model. We freeze the weights of the replaced component to prevent any re-learning, and retrain the resulting model using its original training procedure. We extract a total of eight different components. The entire encoder and decoder as well as embeddings, internal

GRU weights for input to hidden ($W_{ih}$), and recurrent hidden to hidden ($W_{hh}$) for both encoder and decoder. The experiment is twofold: components taken from a model trained with AG are placed into a baseline model and retrained without AG to examine whether a baseline can still learn a compositional solution. Additionally, components from a baseline model are placed into an AG model which is retrained with AG to examine whether the model can still learn a compositional solution without being able to adjust the parameters of the baseline component. We tune 16 models for each new component by retraining the remaining original parts for a maximum of 100 epochs, with a learning rate of 0.001 to allow for limited adjustment.

When retraining an AG model with a frozen baseline component, we expect the performance to drop when that component is important for a compositional solution, as the network is apparently unable to recover itself. Conversely, if a baseline model with a frozen component extracted from an AG model is retrained without AG and performs better, that component might contain weights organized in such a way that it forces the baseline model to retrain itself in a more compositional manner. Table 4 shows the results of substituting components on *new compositions*, which is considered the hardest compositional task. None of the baseline models given a frozen component from an AG model are able to retrain themselves such that they significantly increase performance. Thus, we left those results out of Table 4 for the sake of brevity.

For the AG models with frozen baseline components, the encoder embeddings seem irrelevant for a compositional solution: using baseline embeddings result in a similar score. The decoder embeddings, however, do seem to play a role, as indicated by a much lower score than the original AG model. This seems to be in line with the differences in heat maps shown earlier in Figure 1. Replacing the entire encoder results in a 80% drop in accuracy to 0.167. Interestingly, the encoder hidden to hidden ($W_{hh}$) weight can be replaced without as big a drop, and using the baseline input to hidden ($W_{ih}$) weights actually improves the accuracy. Finally, replacing the decoder's $W_{ih}$ weights drops the accuracy to around 0.6, but doing the same for the decoder's $W_{hh}$ weights again results in an unexpected increase to almost 0.9. This seems to indicate that the $W_{ih}$ weights of the decoder play an important role in a compositional fit, as the model is unable to recover itself when using baseline decoder $W_{ih}$ weights. The increase in performance after replacing either the encoder's $W_{ih}$ or the decoder's $W_{hh}$ implies that training with AG actually produces suboptimal weights for these components. Perhaps the use of a frozen baseline component in a model retrained with AG acts as some kind of regularization and incentivizes the remaining components of the model to become more compositional. Another explanation could be that the AG loss does not provide an appropriate signal for all components, and should thus not be backpropagated to all of them.

## 5.2 Neuron pruning

After showing in Section 4.1 that a few strongly connected neurons organized in functional groups carry out specific functions, we want to exhaust this observation and see if the model can still successfully solve the task by using **only** strongly connected neurons. We remove all weakly connected neurons, keeping only 5% of neurons with the biggest weights of the encoder and decoder of the trained AG models respectively. Distilling the network in this way results in a performance drop to 12.4% sequence accuracy on the new composi-

| Model | Component | Accuracy (NC) |
|---|---|---|
| AG | - | $.82 \pm .12$ |
| AG | Encoder | $.17 \pm .11$ |
| AG | Encoder Emb | $.75 \pm .09$ |
| AG | Encoder $W_{ih}$ | $.89 \pm .05$ |
| AG | Encoder $W_{hh}$ | $.79 \pm .12$ |
| AG | Decoder | $.12 \pm .05$ |
| AG | Decoder Emb | $.31 \pm .07$ |
| AG | Decoder $W_{ih}$ | $.60 \pm .08$ |
| AG | Decoder $W_{hh}$ | $.91 \pm .03$ |
| BL | - | $.01 \pm .02$ |
| BL | Encoder | $.02 \pm .02$ |
| BL | Decoder | $.02 \pm .02$ |

Table 4: Sequence accuracy on new compositions (NC). Accuracy is averaged over three models and depicted with its standard deviation. The model being retrained is specified the first column, the component taken from the opposite model and frozen specified in the second column.

tions task, averaged over all models. Re-training the network for 20 epochs fully restores the functionality and even yields better performance of 92.5% on average compared to the full network with 82.3%. We retrained the model using the same parameters as in the main training procedure (see Section 2.4).

The loss in performance that occurs when neurons are removed indicates that some functionality is distributed among weakly connected neurons. However, the fact that their functionality can be taken over by other neurons shows that weakly connected neurons do not play a crucial role.

We conclude that most of the neurons do not contribute to a compositional solution at all and therefore only an extremely small subset of all neurons of the AG model suffices to solve the task after retraining. Those neurons exhibit strong weights and are specialized in functional groups. Networks that find a compositional solution seem to rather form a small number of highly specialized neurons than distributing functionality over the whole network.

## 6 Conclusion

Thanks to Attentive Guidance, seq2seqs are able to generalize compositionally on the lookup table task when, without it, they cannot (Hupkes et al., 2019; Liška et al., 2019). In this paper, we presented an in-depth analysis of the differences between an attention-based sequence to sequence model trained with and without Attentive Guidance. Any identified differences can contribute to our understanding of what makes seq2seq better compositional learners and help with the design of a new generation of compositional learning architectures.

Our main finding is that guided networks have a more modular structure: small subsets of well-connected neurons are responsible for specific functions. Having specialized neurons could be crucial to a compositional solution. We have also shown via component substitutions how these neurons seem to play a more crucial part in specific model components like the encoder / decoder gates and decoder embeddings, while playing a negligible role in others.

Future research could focus on exploiting the findings about modularity and specialization of neurons to investigate whether similar compositional solutions can be achieved without the explicit use of Attentive Guidance, such as recently shown by Korrel et al. (2019) Additionally, it would be interesting to find out why models with fewer parameters cannot learn to solve the lookup table task (Hupkes et al., 2019), while we know from our distillation experiments that only 26 neurons in the encoder and decoder are needed to implement a perfect solution.

## Acknowledgements

DH is funded by the Netherlands Organization for Scientific Research (NWO), through a Gravitation Grant 024.001.006 to the Language in Interaction Consortium. EB is funded by the European Union's Horizon 2020 research and innovation program under the Marie Sklodowska-Curie grant agreement No 790369 (MAGIC).

## References

Dzmitry Bahdanau, Kyunghyun Cho, and Yoshua Bengio. 2015. Neural machine translation by jointly learning to align and translate. In *3rd International Conference on Learning Representations, ICLR 2015, San Diego, CA, USA, May 7-9, 2015, Conference Track Proceedings*.

Kyunghyun Cho, Bart van Merrienboer, Çaglar Gülçehre, Dzmitry Bahdanau, Fethi Bougares, Holger Schwenk, and Yoshua Bengio. 2014. Learning phrase representations using RNN encoder-decoder for statistical machine translation. In *Proceedings of the 2014 Conference on Empirical Methods in Natural Language Processing, EMNLP. Doha, Qatar*, pages 1724–1734.

Fahim Dalvi, Nadir Durrani, Hassan Sajjad, Yonatan Belinkov, Anthony Bau, and James Glass. 2019. What is one grain of sand in the desert? analyzing individual neurons in deep nlp models. In *Proceedings of the AAAI Conference on Artificial Intelligence AAAI. Honolulu, Hawaii, USA*.

Jerry A Fodor. 1975. *The language of thought*, volume 5. Harvard University Press.

Alex Graves, Abdel-rahman Mohamed, and Geoffrey Hinton. 2013. Speech recognition with deep recurrent neural networks. In *Acoustics, speech and signal processing (icassp), 2013 ieee international conference on*, pages 6645–6649. IEEE.

Sepp Hochreiter and Jürgen Schmidhuber. 1997. Long short-term memory. *Neural computation*, 9(8):1735–1780.

D. Hupkes and W. Zuidema. 2017. Diagnostic classification and symbolic guidance to understand and improve recurrent neural networks. Interpreting, explaining and visualizing deep learning. *NIPS2017*.

Dieuwke Hupkes, Anand Singh, Kris Korrel, German Kruszewski, and Elia Bruni. 2019. Learning compositionally through attentive guidance. In *20th International Conference on Computational Linguistics and Intelligent Text Processing (CICLing)*.

Dieuwke Hupkes, Sara Veldhoen, and Willem Zuidema. 2018. Visualisation and 'diagnostic classifiers' reveal how recurrent and recursive neural networks process hierarchical structure. *Journal of Artificial Intelligence Research*, 61:907–926.

Andrej Karpathy, Justin Johnson, and Li Fei-Fei. 2015. Visualizing and understanding recurrent networks. In *Proceedings of the International Conference on Learning Representations 2016*, pages 1–13.

Diederik P. Kingma and Jimmy Ba. 2015. Adam: A method for stochastic optimization. In *3rd International Conference on Learning Representations, ICLR. San Diego, CA, USA*.

Kris Korrel, Dieuwke Hupkes, Verna Dankers, and Elia Bruni. 2019. Transcoding compositionally: using attention to find more generalizable solutions. *BlackboxNLP 2019, ACL*.

Adam Liška, Germán Kruszewski, and Marco Baroni. 2019. Memorize or generalize? searching for a compositional rnn in a haystack. In *Proceedings of AEGAP (FAIM Joint Workshop on Architectures and Evaluation for Generality, Autonomy and Progress in AI)*.

Scott M Lundberg and Su-In Lee. 2017. A unified approach to interpreting model predictions. In *Advances in Neural Information Processing Systems*, pages 4768–4777.

Eric Schulz, Josh Tenenbaum, David K Duvenaud, Maarten Speekenbrink, and Samuel J Gershman. 2016. Probing the compositionality of intuitive functions. In *Advances in neural information processing systems*, pages 3729–3737.

Zoltan Szabó. 2012. The case for compositionality. *The Oxford handbook of compositionality*, 64:80.

# A  Model performances

Sequence accuracy for the increasingly difficult tasks heldout compositions (HC), heldout inputs (HI), heldout tables (HT) and new compositions (NC) of the baseline (Tab. 5) and the AG (Tab. 6) models.

| Run | HC | HI | HT | NC |
| --- | --- | --- | --- | --- |
| 1 | .25 | .20 | .04 | .00 |
| 2 | .16 | .20 | .06 | .00 |
| 3 | .25 | .23 | .04 | .03 |
| 4 | .22 | .23 | .03 | .03 |
| 5 | .23 | .20 | .07 | .06 |

Table 5: **Baseline** GRU models

| Run | HC | HI | HT | NC |
| --- | --- | --- | --- | --- |
| 1 | 1.0 | 1.0 | 0.85 | 0.69 |
| 2 | 1.0 | 1.0 | 0.98 | 0.97 |
| 3 | 1.0 | 1.0 | 0.88 | 0.81 |
| 4 | 1.0 | 1.0 | 0.98 | 0.97 |
| 5 | 1.0 | 1.0 | 0.94 | 0.91 |

Table 6: **Guided Attention** GRU models

# Learning the Dyck Language with Attention-based Seq2Seq Models

**Xiang Yu, Ngoc Thang Vu, Jonas Kuhn**
Institute for Natural Language Processing (IMS)
Universität Stuttgart, Germany
{xiangyu,thangvu,jonas}@ims.uni-stuttgart.de

## Abstract

The generalized Dyck language has been used to analyze the ability of Recurrent Neural Networks (RNNs) to learn context-free grammars (CFGs). Recent studies draw conflicting conclusions on their performance, especially regarding the generalizability of the models with respect to the depth of recursion. In this paper, we revisit several common models and experimental settings, discuss the potential problems of the tasks and analyses. Furthermore, we explore the use of attention mechanisms within the seq2seq framework to learn the Dyck language, which could compensate for the limited encoding ability of RNNs. Our findings reveal that attention mechanisms still cannot truly generalize over the recursion depth, although they perform much better than other models on the closing bracket tagging task. Moreover, this also suggests that this commonly used task is not sufficient to test a model's understanding of CFGs.

## 1 Introduction

The generalized Dyck language has been a testbed for several research on the ability of Recurrent Neural Networks (RNNs), in particular the Long Short-term Memory model (LSTM) (Hochreiter and Schmidhuber, 1997), to learn context-free grammars. It consists of strings with balanced pairs of brackets of different types, e.g., "[ < > ] [ ] < [ ] >". Recognizing the generalized Dyck language is considered to be more difficult than $a^n b^n$ as tested in Gers and Schmidhuber (2001), since it cannot be simply solved by counting. Rather, the model has to remember the sequence of different (unclosed) brackets.

Among the recent studies, Sennhauser and Berwick (2018) analyze the generalizability of LSTMs to learn the generalized Dyck language

with two pairs of brackets, and conclude that the model cannot learn the underlying grammar rules. In contrast, Skachkova et al. (2018) concludes that the LSTM can model the language quite well. Bernardy (2018) experiment with several variants of RNNs, and find that the LSTM works reasonably well on the given task, but fails to generalize to cases with deeper recursion.

All the aforementioned work explores the ability to "understand" context-free languages with some tagging task similar to language modeling. In these tasks, the RNN encodes a sequence, which is the prefix of a valid sequence in the language, and predicts the next possible token either for the last token or for every token. These probing tasks have one thing in common, namely they predict only one token, which does not necessarily close the whole sequence, and thus are not sufficient to prove that the model learns the whole sequence.

In this work, we show that a seq2seq model with attention mechanism not only solves the tagging task, but also generalizes well over unseen depths. While it appears to have "understood" the Dyck language, under closer inspection, it fails to complete deeper sequences and only closes the first several brackets correctly, which happens to be the evaluation metric of the tagging task.

## 2 Related Work

Modeling context-free grammars with RNNs is of great interest for natural language processing, since recursion is considered an essential characteristic of natural languages if not universal (Hauser et al., 2002). Several recent studies focus on the RNNs' ability to model deeper structural information against surface-level attractors (Linzen et al., 2016; Gulordava et al., 2018; Wilcox et al., 2018).

138

*Proceedings of the Second BlackboxNLP Workshop on Analyzing and Interpreting Neural Networks for NLP*, pages 138–146
Florence, Italy, August 1, 2019. ©2019 Association for Computational Linguistics

Instead of natural language data, where the correlation between structural and contextual/semantic information is difficult to avoid, many analyses with synthetic data have been conducted on RNNs since their invention, e.g., handling the XOR problem (Elman, 1990), the context-free language $a^n b^n$ and context-sensitive language $a^n b^n c^n$ (Gers and Schmidhuber, 2001; Weiss et al., 2018b), and extracting finite-state automata (Weiss et al., 2018a).

Among the context-free languages, the generalized Dyck language is a popular choice since it is simple enough in concept while expressive enough to represent all context-free languages (Chomsky and Schützenberger, 1963).

Skachkova et al. (2018) probes the recognition of the generalized Dyck language in two tasks. The first one is a language modeling task which predicts the next bracket in the actual generated data and measures the perplexity, which complicates the evaluation by introducing unnecessary non-determinism. The second task predicts the last closing bracket of a balanced Dyck word, which could be solved with a short-cut. One simply needs to keep a counter for the depth of the sequence, and record the most recent opening bracket each time the counter hits zero. The task is over-simplified by the fact that all the instances are balanced, thus there is no need to memorize anything deeper than the outmost bracket.

Bernardy (2018) and Sennhauser and Berwick (2018) both frame the task as predicting the next valid closing bracket at any position in a Dyck word, which is arguably more difficult to bypass. Both works also put much emphasis on the generalization over the depth. Comparing to Sennhauser and Berwick (2018), our tagger models, while not perfectly generalizable, perform well above chance level, and the discrepancy between training and testing performance is much smaller. But the general conclusion holds, the RNN-based taggers do not generalize well for the task. Bernardy (2018) reports better results, but they use much shorter sequences (less than 20) where the model has a chance to memorize instead of generalize.

With a different architecture, Deleu and Dureau (2016) uses a Neural Turing Machine (Graves et al., 2014) to recognize the Dyck language. They use the model as an acceptor for the original Dyck language with only one type of bracket pair, which

is much simpler both as a task and as a language. To solve this task, the model only needs to approximate a counter, and increment or decrement upon an opening or closing bracket. The LSTM's ability to approximate a counter machine is discussed in Weiss et al. (2018b).

While all these studies test the RNNs as acceptor (classifier) or transducer (tagger), we also test their ability to decode sequences, which is arguably a harder task.

## 3 Task and Models

The Dyck language consists of strings (a Dyck word) of equal number of opening and closing brackets, and the number of closing brackets is never more than the opening brackets in any prefix of the string (a Dyck prefix). The generalized Dyck language has more than one type of bracket pairs, where all pairs have to be balanced and no crossing of different pairs is allowed. Formally, the generalized Dyck language is defined as $D_P$ with $(o_i, c_i) \in P$, where $(o_i, c_i)$ are different bracket pairs. The language can be described by the following grammar:

$$S \rightarrow S\ S$$
$$S \rightarrow o_i\ S\ c_i$$
$$S \rightarrow o_i\ c_i$$

We adopt the commonly used tagging task, in which the model has to predict the next valid closing bracket given any Dyck prefix shorter than 100. Note that this differs from the language modeling task, since the target is not from the actual, stochastic dataset, but an unambiguous closing bracket. If the prefix is already a balanced Dyck word, then the target is a special symbol '$', which also makes it a recognition task for balanced Dyck words.

We compare four models with different architectures and different training objectives, but the main target is the same. All models have the same encoder architecture, a one-layer bidirectional LSTM with 50 hidden units, and only differ in the decoder.

The first model **tagger-last** predicts the target with a simple linear transformation from the LSTM state of the last token.

The second model **tagger-all** has exactly the same architecture, but it is trained to predict a closing bracket after every token in the sequence. The *last* predicted bracket is the main target for evaluation and comparison, while the rest can be viewed as an auxiliary task.

The third model **generator-simple** follows the common seq2seq architecture (Sutskever et al., 2014). It generates a sequence of closing brackets to eagerly complete the Dyck prefix into a balanced Dyck word, and the generation stops when the '$' symbol is predicted. For this model, the *first* generated bracket is the main target and the rest is the auxiliary task.

The fourth model **generator-attention** augments the decoder with the attention mechanism (Bahdanau et al., 2014). It uses the *general* variant of attention (Luong et al., 2015):

$$\text{score}\left(h_t, \overline{h}_s\right) = h_t^\top W_a \overline{h}_s$$

where $h_t$ denotes the decoder state, $\overline{h}_s$ denotes all encoder states, and $W_a$ is the model parameter.

All the models are trained with the Adam optimizer (Kingma and Ba, 2014) with the default parameters in the Dynet library (Neubig et al., 2017). The generator models are trained with the standard *teacher forcing* method, since there is only one correct target sequence and the model is evaluated on exact match.

No special tuning of hyperparameters is performed, and we do not use mini-batch or dropout, since the training is fast and stable enough.[1]

## 4 Experiments

### 4.1 Data

We largely adopt the experimental settings and terminologies in Sennhauser and Berwick (2018) for comparison.

The dataset we use in the experiment consists of 1 million instances, each one is a Dyck prefix of length up to 100 with two different types of brackets('[', ']' and '<', '>'). The instances are sampled proportional to their lengths, i.e., there are twice as many instances of length 20 as instances of length 10. We have a preference for longer sequences, since they represent the more difficult cases.

The instances are generated in the following procedure: Until the desired length is reached, generate a random opening bracket with a branching probability $p$ or a valid closing bracket with

---

[1]The code as well as the dataset are available at the first author's homepage.

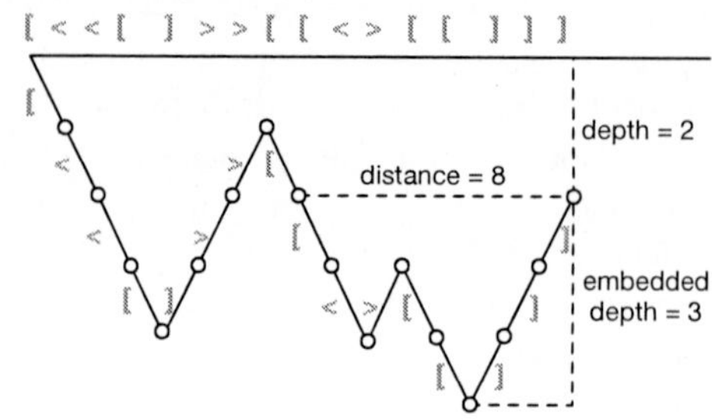



Figure 1: A visual representation of a Dyck prefix and the property values of the target token (the last ']').

probability $1 - p$. If the current sequence is balanced (no unclosed brackets), then generating a random opening bracket is the only option.

This generation procedure is similar to Skachkova et al. (2018), except that we do not stop generation once the sequence is balanced, instead we generate a new opening bracket and continue until the desired length is reached. Also, the generated sequence is not necessarily a Dyck word, but a prefix of it.

We adopt the following properties from Sennhauser and Berwick (2018) to describe the Dyck prefixes:

- *depth* is the number of unclosed brackets;

- *embedded depth* is the maximum depth between the target closing bracket and the corresponding opening bracket, which is also called the *relevant clause*;

- *distance* is the number of tokens in the relevant clause.

Intuitively, *embedded depth* correlates with *distance*, since the deeper the relevant clause, the longer the distance between the outermost brackets. Figure 1 illustrates an example of a Dyck prefix and the properties of the final target token.

The branching probability $p$ controls the distribution of the these properties in the samples, the higher its value, the deeper the string is likely to be. Figure 2 visualizes the distribution of each property value when selecting different $p$ in the generation. We choose $p = 0.5$ since it generates enough samples of reasonably high values of both depth and embedded depth/distance.

We ensure that all the instances are unique, mainly to avoid replicating shorter sequences.

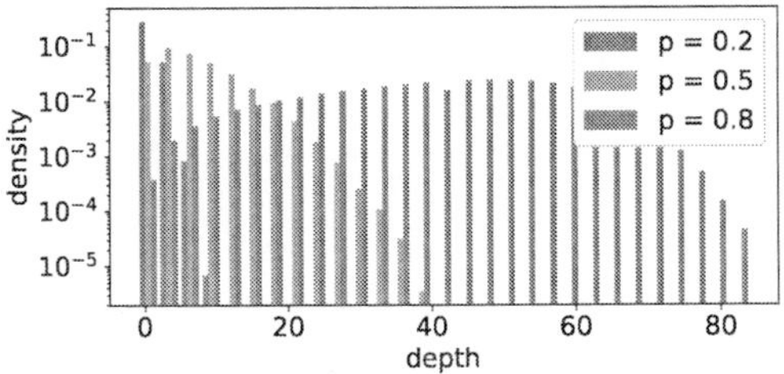

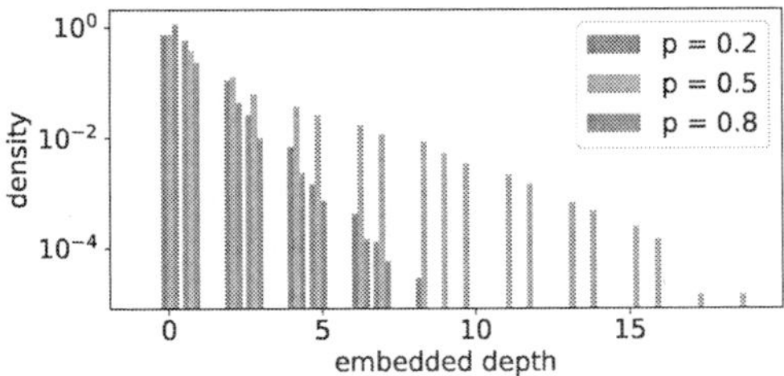

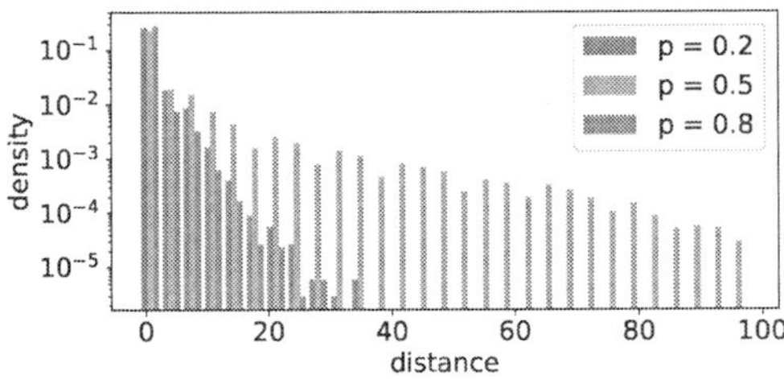

Figure 2: Distribution of depth, embedded depth, and distance of the dataset with different $p$ values. The plots are on logarithmic scales.

Generating identical longer sequences is practically impossible, since the number of generalized Dyck prefixes of length 100 is orders of magnitudes larger than the dataset[2].

The main target of an instance is the matching closing bracket given the prefix, and if the prefix is balanced, a special symbol '$' is the target. To avoid inflated results in the evaluation, we ignore the easy cases where the last token is an opening bracket, since the target is simply the corresponding closing bracket, and does not require further memory to make the correct prediction. However, we do not remove these cases from training, since it is still a correct behavior to learn, albeit very simple.

We split the dataset into training set and test set in different ways. In the in-domain setting, the dataset is equally split into training set and test set, and both sets have roughly the same distribution of

the property values. In the out-of-domain setting, where we test the generalization of the models, we sort the dataset by the respective maximum property values of the whole sequence, and train on the instances where the value is smaller than $\frac{1}{3}$ of the maximum in the dataset, i.e., we test the generalization on up to three times the training depth.

Note that the selection criteria is the *maximum* value over the whole sequence, not just of the final target. This is a much stricter condition than in Sennhauser and Berwick (2018), since the encoder would never see a training instance that is too deep at any step. For example in Figure 1, the target depth is 2, while the maximum depth is 5.

We test the models on the development set (a held-out portion of the training set) after every 10000 training steps, and stop training if the performance do not improve 5 times in a row. Most of the time, the training terminates before even iterating through the training data once.

Due to the stochastic nature of neural networks, we report the results of each model/condition from the average of 10 runs with different random seeds.

## 4.2 In-Domain Results

|  | target | all-tags | completion |
|---|---|---|---|
| tagger-last | 96.4% | 98.8% | - |
| tagger-all | 98.7% | 99.8% | - |
| gen-simple | 96.3% | - | 82.1% |
| gen-attn | 99.9% | - | 97.8% |

Table 1: Average accuracy of the models in different evaluations in the in-domain setting. In the three columns, **target** measures the accuracy of the main target, **all-tag** measures the average accuracy of predicting the next bracket for all tokens, **completion** measures the exact match of closing all the brackets. All results are averaged from 10 runs.

The average results of the in-domain experiments are shown in Table 1. All the models are evaluated on the main target of the same test set (the first column), and the tagger models are additionally evaluated on predicting the target for every token in the sequence (the second column).

Overall, all models perform reasonably well, while **tagger-all** performs better than **tagger-last** both for the main target and all targets. Although the training data is sufficient for all models, judged by the fact that they all stop training in one itera-

---

[2]The exact number is beyond the scope of this work, but a simple lower-bound would be the 50-th Catalan number (greater than $10^{27}$), which is the number of Dyck words of length 100 with only one pair of brackets.

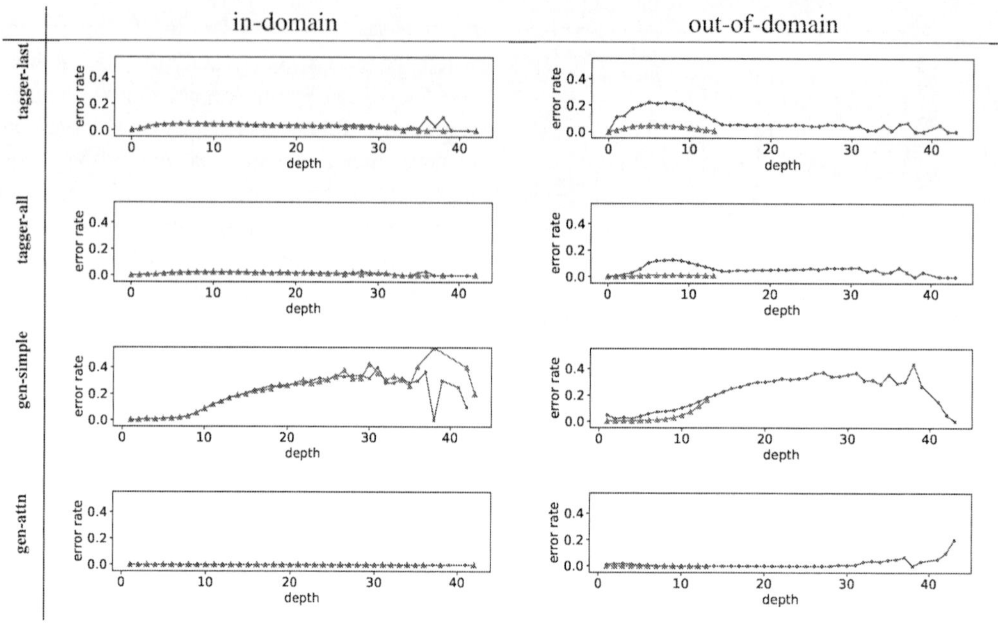

Figure 3: Errors of each model in the in-domain vs. out-of-domain setting for the **depth** property.

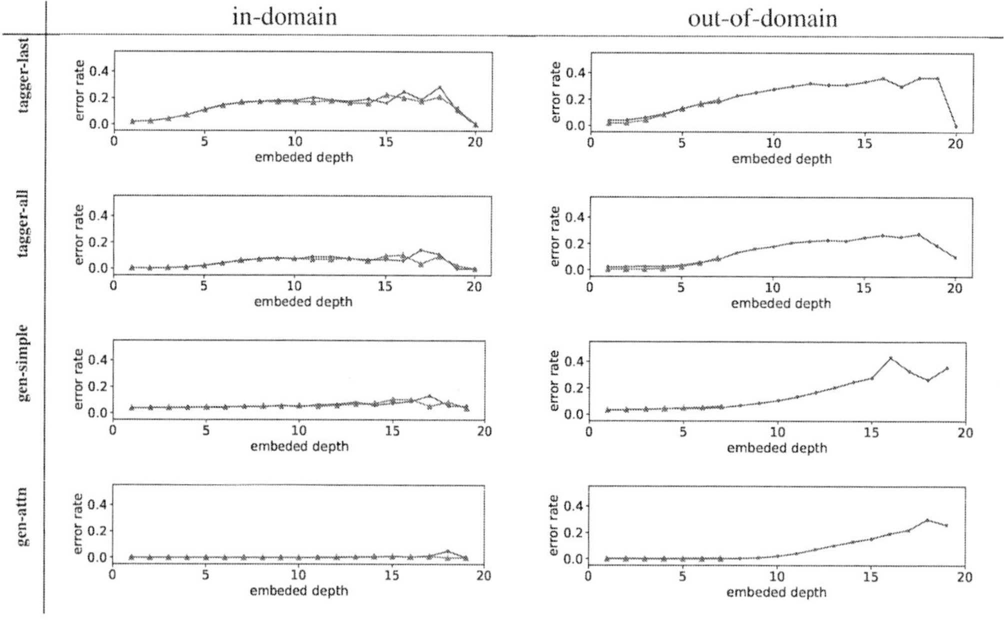

Figure 4: Errors of each model in the in-domain vs. out-of-domain setting for the **embedded depth** property.

tion, training on multiple targets in one sequence is still beneficial. We hypothesize that it is because predicting for all tokens in one sequence requires the model to encode the information more consistently. However, more experiments are needed to confirm the hypothesis. Both models have higher accuracies on all tags than the last tag, presumably because the average prefix depth and embedded depth on all tags are lower than that of the last tag, which are easier to predict.

The two generator models are evaluated on the accuracy of the main target as well as the exact match rate of the completion task (the third column), where the main target is the first prediction in the completion sequence. The **generator-simple** model performs on par with **tagger-last**. However, they tend to have different errors, as analyzed in in Section 4.3.

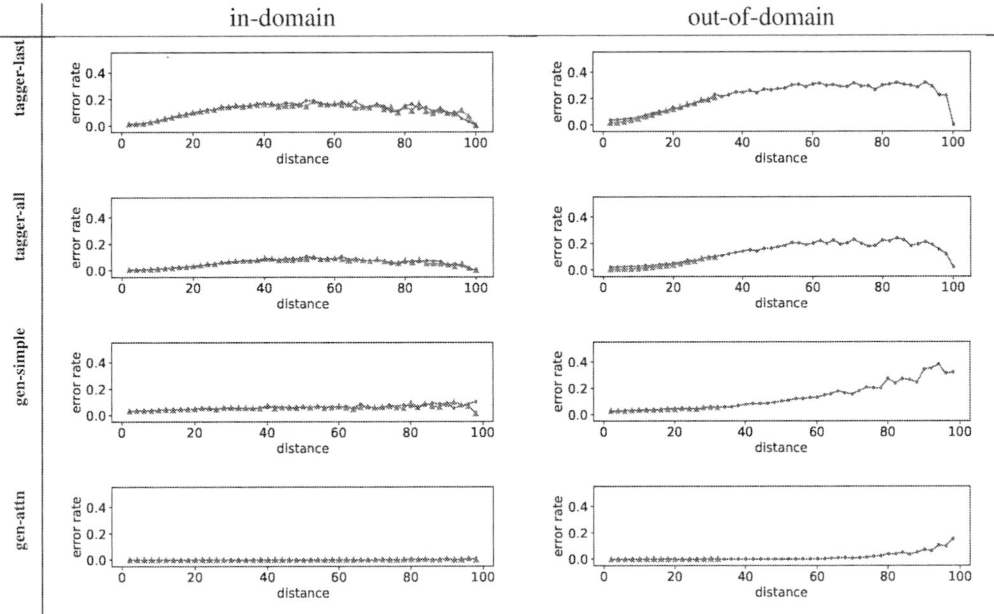

Figure 5: Errors of each model in the in-domain vs. out-of-domain setting for the **distance** property.

Finally, when the generator model is equipped with attention, it achieves almost perfect performance even for the exact completion.

### 4.3 Generalization

The detailed results of the four models in the in-domain vs. out-of-domain settings according to different properties (*depth*, *embedded depth*, and *distance*) are shown in Figure 3, 4, and 5, respectively. We remove the noisy points from the plot when there are less than 10 cases. The chance level of the error rate lies slightly over 0.5, since the two closing brackets are equiprobable and in about 10% of the case the target is '$' (a balanced Dyck word). In each group of plots, the ones on the left show the in-domain setting, on the right the out-of-domain setting. The four rows are the four models: **tagger-last**, **tagger-all**, **generator-simple**, and **generator-attention**. In each figure, the blue triangles are the training error rates, and the red dots the test error rates.

It is evident from the in-domain experiments on the left side of the plots that all the models generalize well in the in-domain setting (but not necessarily performing well), since the training errors (blue triangles) and test errors (red dots) align very closely. This means that all the models are not simply memorizing the training data.

The more interesting case is the out-of-domain condition, where we test the models on sequences up to three times as deep as the training data. Among the two weaker models, **generator-simple** is very sensitive to the *depth*, while **tagger-last** is more sensitive to the *embedded depth* and *distance*. This means that the two models are prone to different problems, although having comparable performance.

Note that in the out-of-domain setting for *depth*, the first three models have higher test error rate even for smaller depth. Recall that we split the dataset by the maximum depth of the sequence, while reporting the error by the depth of the current target, which means that they are tested on sequences that have deeper recursion at some point, and the encoder can not recover from it. The only exception is **generator-attention**, which is not affected by this situation. Furthermore, this model generalize well in all conditions.

### 4.4 Tasks Revisited

The different tasks of "understanding" the Dyck language also give rise to the question of what is exactly meant when stating that RNNs learn the language, and whether the task can sufficiently tests the claim. As mentioned before, some tasks are clearly flawed, since they can be reduced to the counting problem. For example, recognizing a Dyck word with only one type of brackets (Deleu and Dureau, 2016) only requires counting the depth. Similarly, completing the final bracket

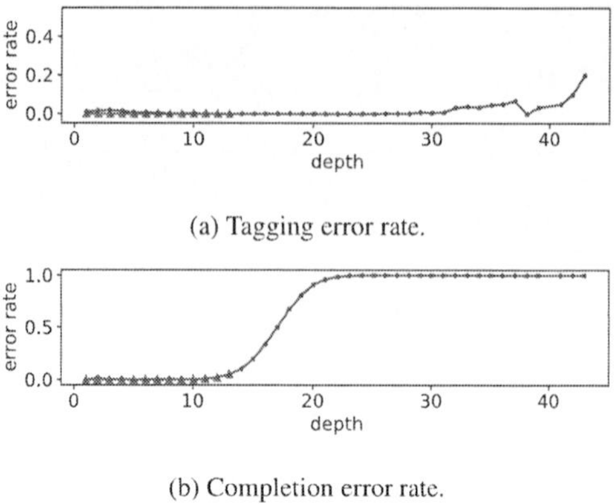

(a) Tagging error rate.

(b) Completion error rate.

Figure 6: Error rates of the tagging and completion tasks of the **generator-attention** model in the out-of-domain setting.

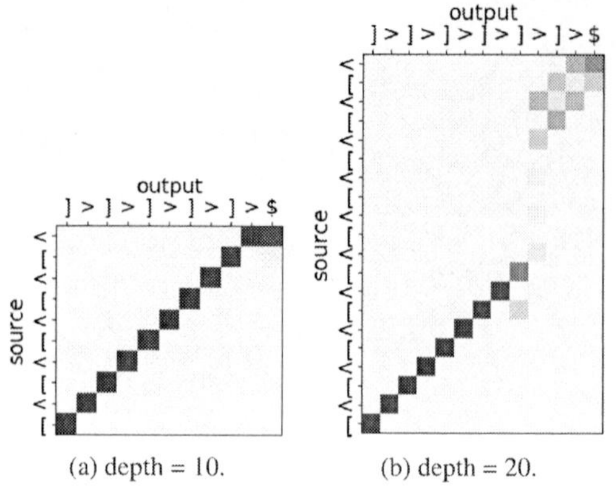

(a) depth = 10.      (b) depth = 20.

Figure 7: Attention matrices of a model trained on data with maximum depth of 10 and tested on sequences with depths of 10 and 20.

of a Dyck word (Skachkova et al., 2018) also only requires counting the depth and keeping track of the most recent opening bracket of depth 0.

In our tagging task, the **generator-simple** model performs very poorly when the depth is high. This is because the model has to memorize all the opening brackets, in order to generate the full closing sequences. Apparently, the RNN encoder alone is not capable of memorizing the whole sequence (even in the in-domain condition), and the noise in the memory causes the decoder unable to correctly predict even the first bracket, which is the main evaluation target.

The **generator-attention** model consistently performs better, since it avoids compressing the whole sequence into a fixed sized vector. Instead, it keeps all the input tokens as individual (contextualized) vectors, and use the attention mechanism to find out the corresponding opening bracket, and the decoder only needs to map the attended opening bracket into the corresponding closing one.

Figure 6 shows the tagging error rate and the completion (exact match) error rate of the same **generator-attention** model in the out-of-domain setting. The completion performance deteriorate very rapidly beyond the depth that the model is trained on, while the tagging performance seems quite stable. This contrast clearly demonstrates that the tagging task is inadequate to test the RNN's ability of modeling CFGs.

## 4.5 Attention

We have seen that even the best performing **generator-attention** model cannot generalize in the out-of-domain condition to complete the full closing bracket sequence, although it is able to predict the first bracket correctly.

To identify the problem, Figure 7 visualizes the attention matrices in the out-of-domain setting, in which we take a **generator-attention** model trained on the dataset with maximum depth of 10, and test on the sequences with depth of 10 and 20. While the attention alignment seems perfect for the sequence of depth 10, it gets blurry on a deeper sequence. The first 9 output brackets are still correctly aligned and predicted, the attention then jumps over to the beginning of the source and finishes the generation. This explains the sudden deterioration of completion performance in Figure 6b, since almost all instances that are too deep are closed prematurely.

This problem, however, is not manifested in the tagging task as in Figure 6a, since it only measures whether the first generated bracket is correct, while the generator only starts to make mistakes after a certain number of steps.

## 4.6 Equivalence Test

As human, while performing the tagging and completion tasks (as well as many other tasks mentioned before) on the generalized Dyck language, one can utilize an important property to simplify the task, namely the equivalence of different prefixes. For example, two prefixes "[ < < [ < < [ ] > >" and "[ < < [" are equivalent with respect to predicting the next closing bracket, since the closed clause is already irrelevant. An ideal composition model should also realize this fact and have the same or very

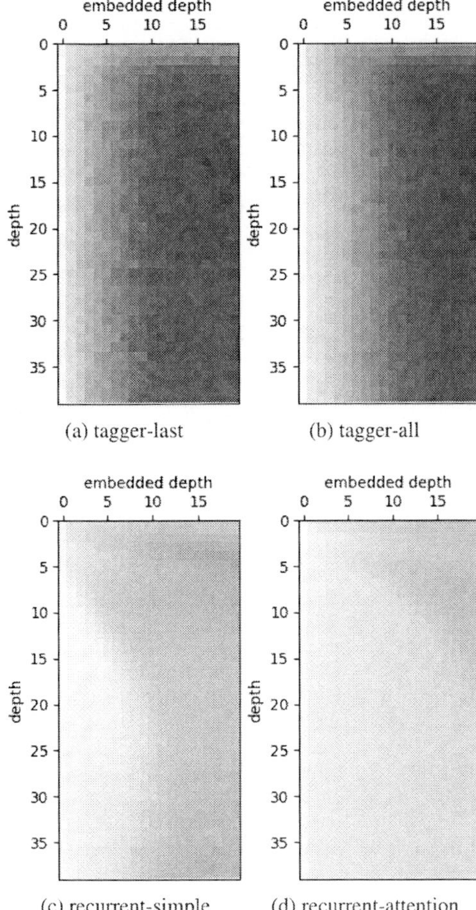

(a) tagger-last    (b) tagger-all

(c) recurrent-simple    (d) recurrent-attention

Figure 8: Equivalence test of four models.

similar representation for the two prefixes.

We thus design an experiment to test whether our different models are capable of realize such equivalence, and how well it holds under different conditions, namely the depth and embedded depth of the prefix. We construct the dataset by concatenating an open prefix ([ < < [) to a balanced clause (< < [ ] > >) of different lengths, and measure the L2-norm of the distance of the encoder LSTM states after reading the open prefix and the balanced clause. Ideally the two states should be very similar, thus the L2-distance close to 0. We randomly generate open prefixes up to length 40, and balanced clauses also up to 40, which correspond to the maximum depth of 40 and embedded depth of 20. We take the in-domain models which have been trained on instances up to these maximum values, but not necessarily the combination of both maximums. For each model, we plot the average L2-distance of 100 samples

for each combination.

Figure 8 shows the results, where lighter cells means two equivalent prefixes have more similar representations. Similar to the main task result, the **tagger-last** model shows the worst ability to capture the equivalence. Both tagger models are insensitive to the depth and sensitive to the embedded depth, which also agrees with the results in Figure 4.

The generator models clearly capture the equivalence better. However, we observe that the L2-distance at higher depth is slightly smaller, while Figure 3 has shown that **recurrent-simple** performs worse at higher depth. This suggests that the representation at deeper recursion may be similar but contains only noisy information, which requires further investigation in the future work.

## 5   Conclusion

In this work, we revisit the tasks based on the Dyck language to probe the ability and limitation of RNNs to encode context-free grammars.

We argue that the bracket tagging task is insufficient to prove the ability or expose the limitation of a model, while the bracket completion task has higher requirement as a test. Seq2seq models outperform the tagger models in the tagging task, but still fail to generalize in the completion task. The failure is especially apparent when visualizing the model's attention. We also conduct analysis on the RNN's representation of equivalent prefixes of different prefix depth and embedded depth.

Our results suggest that the RNNs can not truly model CFGs, even when powered by the attention mechanism. However, the seq2seq model with attention is still a good approximation and fully capable of dealing with recursions as deep as it is trained on.

As future work, we plan to further investigate the open questions in our experiments, especially regarding the attention alignment and equivalence test. Furthermore, the equivalence property could be used not only as a test for the representation, but also as an auxiliary task to enforce better encoding of the RNN.

## 6   Acknowledgments

This work was in part supported by funding from the Ministry of Science, Research and the Arts of the State of Baden-Württemberg (MWK), within the CLARIN-D research project.

## References

Dzmitry Bahdanau, Kyunghyun Cho, and Yoshua Bengio. 2014. Neural machine translation by jointly learning to align and translate. *arXiv preprint arXiv:1409.0473*.

Jean-Philippe Bernardy. 2018. Can recurrent neural networks learn nested recursion? *LiLT (Linguistic Issues in Language Technology)*, 16(1).

Noam Chomsky and Marcel P Schützenberger. 1963. The algebraic theory of context-free languages. In *Studies in Logic and the Foundations of Mathematics*, volume 35, pages 118–161. Elsevier.

Tristan Deleu and Joseph Dureau. 2016. Learning operations on a stack with neural turing machines. *arXiv preprint arXiv:1612.00827*.

Jeffrey L Elman. 1990. Finding structure in time. *Cognitive science*, 14(2):179–211.

Felix A Gers and E Schmidhuber. 2001. LSTM recurrent networks learn simple context-free and context-sensitive languages. *IEEE Transactions on Neural Networks*, 12(6):1333–1340.

Alex Graves, Greg Wayne, and Ivo Danihelka. 2014. Neural turing machines. *arXiv preprint arXiv:1410.5401*.

Kristina Gulordava, Piotr Bojanowski, Edouard Grave, Tal Linzen, and Marco Baroni. 2018. Colorless green recurrent networks dream hierarchically. In *Proceedings of the 2018 Conference of the North American Chapter of the Association for Computational Linguistics: Human Language Technologies, Volume 1 (Long Papers)*, pages 1195–1205, New Orleans, Louisiana. Association for Computational Linguistics.

Marc D Hauser, Noam Chomsky, and W Tecumseh Fitch. 2002. The faculty of language: what is it, who has it, and how did it evolve? *science*, 298(5598):1569–1579.

Sepp Hochreiter and Jürgen Schmidhuber. 1997. Long short-term memory. *Neural computation*, 9(8):1735–1780.

Diederik P Kingma and Jimmy Ba. 2014. Adam: A method for stochastic optimization. In *Proceedings of the 3rd International Conference on Learning Representations (ICLR)*.

Tal Linzen, Emmanuel Dupoux, and Yoav Goldberg. 2016. Assessing the ability of LSTMs to learn syntax-sensitive dependencies. *Transactions of the Association for Computational Linguistics*, 4:521–535.

Thang Luong, Hieu Pham, and Christopher D. Manning. 2015. Effective approaches to attention-based neural machine translation. In *Proceedings of the 2015 Conference on Empirical Methods in Natural Language Processing*, pages 1412–1421. Association for Computational Linguistics.

Graham Neubig, Chris Dyer, Yoav Goldberg, Austin Matthews, Waleed Ammar, Antonios Anastasopoulos, Miguel Ballesteros, David Chiang, Daniel Clothiaux, Trevor Cohn, Kevin Duh, Manaal Faruqui, Cynthia Gan, Dan Garrette, Yangfeng Ji, Lingpeng Kong, Adhiguna Kuncoro, Gaurav Kumar, Chaitanya Malaviya, Paul Michel, Yusuke Oda, Matthew Richardson, Naomi Saphra, Swabha Swayamdipta, and Pengcheng Yin. 2017. Dynet: The dynamic neural network toolkit. *arXiv preprint arXiv:1701.03980*.

Luzi Sennhauser and Robert Berwick. 2018. Evaluating the ability of lstms to learn context-free grammars. In *Proceedings of the 2018 EMNLP Workshop BlackboxNLP: Analyzing and Interpreting Neural Networks for NLP*, pages 115–124.

Natalia Skachkova, Thomas Trost, and Dietrich Klakow. 2018. Closing brackets with recurrent neural networks. In *Proceedings of the 2018 EMNLP Workshop BlackboxNLP: Analyzing and Interpreting Neural Networks for NLP*, pages 232–239.

Ilya Sutskever, Oriol Vinyals, and Quoc V Le. 2014. Sequence to sequence learning with neural networks. In *Advances in neural information processing systems*, pages 3104–3112.

Gail Weiss, Yoav Goldberg, and Eran Yahav. 2018a. Extracting automata from recurrent neural networks using queries and counterexamples. In *International Conference on Machine Learning*, pages 5244–5253.

Gail Weiss, Yoav Goldberg, and Eran Yahav. 2018b. On the practical computational power of finite precision rnns for language recognition. In *Proceedings of the 56th Annual Meeting of the Association for Computational Linguistics (Volume 2: Short Papers)*, volume 2, pages 740–745.

Ethan Wilcox, Roger Levy, Takashi Morita, and Richard Futrell. 2018. What do RNN Language Models Learn about Filler–Gap Dependencies? In *Proceedings of the 2018 EMNLP Workshop BlackboxNLP: Analyzing and Interpreting Neural Networks for NLP*, pages 211–221.

# Modeling Paths for Explainable Knowledge Base Completion

**Josua Stadelmaier** and **Sebastian Padó**
Institut für Maschinelle Sprachverarbeitung
University of Stuttgart, Germany
{josua.stadelmaier,sebastian.pado}@ims.uni-stuttgart.de

## Abstract

A common approach in knowledge base completion (KBC) is to learn representations for entities and relations in order to infer missing facts by generalizing existing ones. A shortcoming of standard models is that they do not *explain* their predictions to make them verifiable easily to human inspection.

In this paper, we propose the *context path model* (CPM) which generates explanations for new facts in KBC by providing sets of *context paths* as supporting evidence for these triples. For example, a new triple *(Theresa May, nationality, Britain)* may be explained by the path *(Theresa May, born in, Eastbourne, contained in, Britain)*. The CPM is formulated as a wrapper that can be applied on top of various existing KBC models. We evaluate it for the well-established TransE model. We observe that its performance remains very close despite the added complexity, and that most of the paths proposed as explanations provide meaningful evidence to assess the correctness.

## 1   Introduction

Knowledge bases (KBs), such as Freebase (Bollacker et al., 2008), Wikidata (Vrandečić and Krötzsch, 2014) or Yago (Suchanek et al., 2007), are structured representations of knowledge in form of entities and their respective relationships. For example, KBs can comprise facts about persons like their family relations and their occupation or facts about places like the region or country they are located in. A common application of knowledge bases is question answering systems (Bordes et al., 2014; Berant et al., 2013). KBs are also used by Google to better understand search queries, to present fact boxes and to provide explorative search suggestions (Steiner et al., 2012).

The major contemporary construction mode for KBs is collaborative, which is both a major advantage (as long as community interest persists, KBs grow over time) and a major shortcoming, since development is not directed. As a result, collaborative KBs tend to be *incomplete*. Min et al. (2013) show that in Freebase 93.8% of persons have no place of birth assigned and for 78.5% of persons, the nationality is missing. This motivates the task of knowledge base completion (KBC), i.e., the addition of correct but missing facts to existing KBs.

A common approach for KBC is to learn distributed representations for entities and relations that enable the generalization of existing connections in the KB to predict missing facts (Nickel et al., 2011; Bordes et al., 2013; Yang et al., 2015). A connection could be that the country of birth is highly correlated to the nationality of a given person. A fact about the country of birth could therefore be used as evidence when predicting a missing fact about the nationality. Such representation learning methods typically perform rather well and are simple to train. However, they crucially lack in the *explainability* that often comes with more symbolic systems: they do not justify the facts that they propose in a way that is transparent to human reviewers of the system output. Explainability of system outputs is increasingly recognized as an important component in the practical use of NLP, and more generally, AI systems (Holzinger et al., 2017; Ras et al., 2018; Ribeiro et al., 2018).

In this paper, we propose a new KBC model, the *Context Path Model* (CPM), which provides a *path-based explanation* for newly proposed facts. For example, the path $(e_1,$ *city of birth, contained by,* $e_2)$ states the country the person $e_1$ was born in. This path is informative to assess the correctness of the triple $(e_1,$ *nationality,* $e_2)$. To establish a relationship between facts and paths, the CPM explicitly includes the paths from the context of a fact $t$ into the estimation of $t$'s correctness. As part of this process, the CPM also estimates the paths' *rele-*



*Proceedings of the Second BlackboxNLP Workshop on Analyzing and Interpreting Neural Networks for NLP*, pages 147–157
Florence, Italy, August 1, 2019. ©2019 Association for Computational Linguistics

*vance* to identify those paths that provide the most convincing evidence for or against the correctness of the fact. The CPM is formulated as a wrapper that can be applied on top of various KBC models that learn a scoring function for individual facts.

We evaluate the CPM instantiated with the established TransE model as fact scorer on the FB15K dataset. We find that CPM, despite the added complexity, performs almost as well as vanilla TransE on scoring facts. The majority of paths assigned a high relevance for a given fact are either equivalent to the fact or provide strong evidence regarding its correctness.[1]

## 2 Background and Related Work

### 2.1 Knowledge Base Completion (KBC)

Knowledge bases are often formalized as a directed graph with labeled edges, here called knowledge graph. A knowledge graph $G$ is a set of $n$ facts, or edges, where each edge is defined as a triple $t$ of the form $(e_1, r, e_2)$ with entities $e_1$ and $e_2$ and relation $r$, $G = \{t_i\}_{i=1}^n$. We denote the set of entities as $E$ and the set of relations as $R$. The task of KBC can then be formalized as *assessing the correctness* of a triple $t \notin G$. As usual in studies of KBC, we concentrate on the case where $e_1$ and $e_2$ are known, i.e., we add edges, but not nodes, to the graph.

### 2.2 Representation Learning for KBC

An important current approach to KBC is to learn distributed representations (vectors, matrices, tensors) for entities and relations and define algebraic combination operations to score the correctness of novel triples $t = (e_1, r, e_2)$. This includes models like NTM (Socher et al., 2013), TransE (Bordes et al., 2013), Bilinear (Nickel et al., 2011) and Bilinear-diag (Yang et al., 2015).

For instance, TransE represents relations in the same vector space as entities and models relations as translation from $e_1$ to $e_2$. Given respective vector representations $e_1, e_2, r \in \mathbb{R}^d$, TransE predicts the entity that stands in relation $r$ to $e_1$ as $e_1 + r$. The representations are learned using a max-margin objective which minimizes the distance between $e_2$'s predicted and actual positions, $\|e_1 + r - e_2\|$, for correct facts, and maximizes it otherwise.

Research on novel neural architectures for KBC is ongoing. Schlichtkrull et al. (2018) replace sim-

ple embedding lookups by *Relational Graph Convolutional Networks* which are used as an encoder to learn globally optimized knowledge graph representations. Shen et al. (2017) propose a dynamic memory architecture that learns to perform inference and represents the current state of the art.

### 2.3 Modeling Paths for KBC

Several previous studies considered paths as information sources. Lao and Cohen (2010) use random walk probabilities for paths that connect $e_1$ and $e_2$ as features for scoring the correctness of facts $(e_1, r, e_2)$. Gardner et al. (2014) generalize the random walk approach with a relevance-based component. Unlike the "full" KBC models discussed above, however, these models do not represent entities as vectors, which prevents them from capturing entity specific information and from letting entities directly interact with relations.

Guu et al. (2015) show how vector space models like TransE (Bordes et al., 2013), Bilinear (Nickel et al., 2011) and Bilinear-diag (Yang et al., 2015) can be generalized to not only scoring the correctness of edges $t = (e_1, r, e_2)$ but also the correctness of paths $p = (e_1, r_1, ..., r_k, e_2)$. They propose a training objective that incorporates paths and demonstrate that it improves the performance of KBC models on predicting paths and on predicting single edges as well. In the case of TransE, the relations $r_1, ..., r_k$ of a path $p$ can be represented by their composition $r_p = r_1 + ... + r_k$. The distance computed by TransE can then be generalized to paths as $\|e_1 + r_p - e_2\|$. The objective proposed by Guu et al. encourages that $e_1 + r_p$ is learned to be close to the set of entities that are reached when traversing the knowledge graph over the edges $r_1, ..., r_k$, starting from $e_1$.

PTransE, proposed by Lin et al. (2015), assesses the correctness of $t$ by considering paths that connect $e_1$ and $e_2$ and assigns them scores that aim to indicate how reliable these paths are for estimating the correctness of $t$. They compute the reliability scores by using a heuristic called *path-constraint resource allocation*, which is based on the sizes of entity sets that can be reached by following the relations in a path step by step. They report improvements in the KBC task over the standard TransE model. This supports the idea of modeling paths explicitly to capture the context of a triple. A similar approach by Toutanova et al. (2016) is based on Bilinear-diag instead of TransE and comprises an

---

efficient algorithm to incorporate paths.

### 2.4 Providing Explanations for KBC

One possibility to provide explanations for KBC predictions is to generate logical rules. In the literature, these rules are often formalized as Horn rules (Gusmão et al., 2018) such as $(e_1, r_1, e_2) \wedge (e_2, r_2, e_3) \rightarrow (e_1, r_3, e_3)$. This rule claims that the path with the relation sequence $r_1, r_2$ between $e_1$ and $e_2$ implies the presence of the relation $r_3$ between the two entities.

Galárraga et al. (2013) propose the system AMIE which mines such rules. Their approach is to adapt association rule mining to incomplete knowledge bases. Rules are assigned confidence values that state how likely the conclusion of the rule is a correct triple. While this can be used to predict and explain new facts based on a single rule, there is no clear way of combining several rules that all have the same triple as conclusion. Furthermore, these rules only make a statement about triples that actually occur in the conclusion of a rule. The rules found by Galárraga et al. always have a positive conclusion and therefore cannot provide evidence for refuting triples. In contrast, representation learning can capture the characteristics of individual entities and can take arbitrary triples as input, provided that the involved entities and relations occur in the training set.

There are several studies that analyze learned representations of neural KBC models like TransE or Bilinear-diag to find Horn rules (Yang et al., 2015) or paths in the knowledge graph (Zhang et al., 2019). While similar in motivation to our model, these approaches share the disadvantage of using a pipeline approach: The rules or paths are extracted *post hoc* and cannot be used by the representation learning step to improve the consistency of its predictions, as would be desirable.

Xie et al. (2017) propose a neural KBC model that provides an alternative kind of explainability: it learns sparse attention vectors which capture abstract concepts shared by multiple relations. Due to the sparsity of attention vectors, the connections can be visualized and interpreted.

## 3 Context Path Model

As stated in the introduction, the main idea of our Context Path Model (CPM) is to capture the context of a triple $t = (e_1, r, e_2)$ in the shape of the paths surrounding $t$. The role of the paths is as a data source for estimating the correctness of $t$ as well as providing explanations for the estimate.

### 3.1 Motivation

Formally, we define a path of length k as a sequence of the form $(e_1, r_1, ..., r_k, e_2)$. Our fundamental intuition is that the correctness of triples and paths in their context can show different *degrees of correlation*, as the following examples illustrate.

**Example 1:** The triple $t_1 = (e_1, \textit{country of birth}, e_2)$ and the path $p_1 = (e_1, \textit{city of birth}, \textit{contained by}, e_2)$ are logically equivalent. Thus, any KBC model of correctness should assign the same score to $p_1$ and $t_1$: If a KB contains $p_1$, it should also contain $t_1$. Conversely, the absence of $p_1$ can be taken as evidence against $t_1$.

**Example 2:** The path $p_2 = (e_1, \textit{lived in country}, \textit{neighboring country}, e_2)$ has a weak connection with $t_1$: it is not unlikely to have lived in a country that adjoins the country of birth. However, as countries very often have several neighboring countries, $p_2$ cannot provide strong evidence either for or against the correctness of $t_1$.

We currently concentrate on cases of positive correlation, like Ex. 1, where either the presence of $p$ is evidence in favor of $t$, or the absence of $p$ is evidence against $t$. [2] Even though negative correlation (e.g., the presence of $p$ providing evidence against $t$) is in principle also informative, it is more difficult to capture empirically, since it requires learning exclusion relationships among paths.

### 3.2 Definition of the Context Path Model

To capture those connections, a KBC model needs to score the *correctness* of paths as well as determine their *relevance* as indicator for the correctness of triples $t$, that is, the strength of the correlation of the correctness scores of $p$ and $t$.

We denote the set of paths that are used to model the context of a triple $t$, its *context paths* as $P_t$ (see Section 3.4 for details). Based on $P_t$, the CPM estimates the correctness of $t$, $c(t, P_t)$, as follows:

$$c(t, P_t) = \sum_{p \in P_t} \frac{\rho(t, p)}{Z(t, P_t)} \cdot c(p), \qquad (1)$$

$$Z(t, P_t) = \sum_{p \in P_t} \rho(t, p). \qquad (2)$$

---

[2] Absence of paths from a KB is a weaker indicator than presence, since paths can be missing either because they are actually incorrect, or because at least one of its constituent edges are erroneously missing.

Thus, the correctness of a triple $t$ is a weighted average of the *correctness scores* $c(p)$ of its context paths, with the weights given by the normalized *relevance scores* $\rho(t, p)$ of paths $p$ for $t$, that is, the correlation between the correctness of $t$ and $p$.

Since we want $c(p)$ to be interpretable as the probability of $p$ being correct, we restrict the range of $c(p)$ to $[0, 1]$. We only require $\rho(t, p)$ to be non-negative, since the division by $Z(t, P_t)$ directly yields normalized relevance scores. The property of $c(p)$ being normalized carries over to $c(t, P_t)$ which also has a range of $[0, 1]$. Appropriate choices for $c(p)$ and $\rho(t, p)$ are discussed in the following subsubsections.

Applied to Ex. 1 from above, the path $p_1 = (e_1,$ *city of birth*, *contained by*, $e_2)$ should be assigned a high relevance score $\rho(t_1, p_1)$. If $p_1$ is correct, $c(p_1)$ should be close to 1. A high relevance score combined with a high correctness scores pushes $c(t_1, P_{t_1})$ towards 1. If $p_1$ is not correct, $c(p_1)$ should be close to 0. In this case a high relevance score is combined with a low correctness score, which pushes $c(t_1, P_{t_1})$ towards 0. Both effects match the intended meaning of $c(t_1, P_{t_1})$ to represent the correctness of $t_1$. In Ex. 2, the path $p_2$ has a low relevance for $t_1$ and should be assigned a low relevance score $\rho(t_1, p_2)$. Since correctness scores are restricted to $[0, 1]$, the effect of $c(p_2)$ on $c(t_1, P_{t_1})$ is small, whether $c(p_2)$ is high or low. This properly models that the correctness of $p_2$ has little effect on the correctness of $t_1$.

The CPM can serve as a source of explanations for its predictions by considering the context paths that have the highest relevance scores for a triple $t$. By normalizing relevance scores by $Z(t, P_t)$ (Equation 2), we obtain the normalized weight with which the correctness of a context path contributes to the correctness score of the triple. Furthermore, if $c(p) \approx 1$, $p$ represents evidence in favor of the correctness of $t$, and if $c(p) \approx 0$, $p$ is evidence against the correctness of $t$.

### 3.2.1 Estimating Context Paths Correctness

The first major parameter of the CPM is the context path correctness score $c(p)$, which is required to have two properties: It needs to be able to model paths and its output has to lie in $[0, 1]$. The first property is fulfilled by all *composable* KBC models like TransE (Bordes et al., 2013), Bilinear (Nickel et al., 2011) and Bilinear-diag (Yang et al., 2015), that is, models which can produce a functional representation $r_p$ for a path $p$ as a function of the

representation of its edges. Regarding the second property, models that are distance-based and do not directly fulfill it, can be adapted as follows. Since they are composable, we can compute the distance between the end of the path, $e_2$, and the path representation applied to the start of the path, as $dist(e_2, f(e_1, r_p))$, and map it to $[0, 1]$ via a logistic transformation $\sigma$ of the negated distance.

For the example of the TransE model (Bordes et al., 2014), the path representation is simply a translation defined by the addition of the relation vectors, $r_p = \sum_{r_i \in p} r_i$ and $f = \lambda x, y \,.\, x + y$. The correctness score for a path is then defined as a transformation of the distance:

$$c(p) = \sigma(-\|e_1 + r_p - e_2\|_2^2 + b_1^\mathsf{T} r_p) \qquad (3)$$

where $b_1 \in \mathbb{R}^d$ is a path-specific bias parameter. This model has $d \cdot (|R| + |E| + 1)$ parameters.

### 3.2.2 Estimating Context Path Relevance

The second major parameter of the CPM is the context path relevance score $\rho(t, p)$. To our knowledge, no such models have been proposed in the literature, so we propose a simple model which is again inspired by the translation-based TransE model. To estimate $\rho$ for a path $p = (e_1, r_1, ..., r_k, e_2)$ and a triple $t$, we represent the path as sequence of relations $r_1, ..., r_k$ in order to abstract away from the entities $e_1$ and $e_2$ and learn general regularities.[3] We represent each relation $r$ by one vector $a_r \in \mathbb{R}^d$ in order to recognize patterns in the compositional path representation $r_p$ that indicate how relevant the path $p$ is for the relation $r$. The exponential function is applied to obtain non-negative scores:

$$\rho(t, p) = \exp(a_r^\mathsf{T} r_p + b_2^\mathsf{T} r) \qquad (4)$$

where $b_2 \in \mathbb{R}^d$ is a bias parameter to enable relation specific scaling of $a_r^\mathsf{T} r_p$. This model has $d \cdot (|R| + 1)$ parameters.

### 3.3 Training the Context Path Model

We split the training process into two steps to first learn the parameters of $c(p)$ and then the parameters of $\rho(t, p)$. Learning $\rho(t, p)$ and $c(p)$ jointly could lead to $c(p)$ being influenced by the relevance of $p$ for $t$, which is undesirable since we want to guarantee that $c(p)$ is interpretable in terms of the correctness of $p$.

---

[3]We define $\rho$ as a generic function of $t$ and $p$ to indicate that extensions of the CPM could also make use of the entity representations.

**Training** $c(p)$. Following the training regimen of Guu et al. (2015), we first train $c(p)$ on the edges of the knowledge graph $G$ before training it on longer paths. This gives the model the opportunity to build up paths from meaningful edges.

We train $c(p)$ on a standard contrastive cross-entropy loss that provides a good fit for the probabilistic interpretation of $c(p)$ that we aim for:

$$-\sum_{p \in P} \frac{\log c(p)}{|P|} - \sum_{p' \in P'} \frac{\log(1 - c(p'))}{|P'|} \quad (5)$$

where $P$ is the set of correct paths and $P'$ a set of corrupted paths. For single edge training, we use $P = G$. In the subsequent path training, we sample a set of positive informative paths $P$ as described below in Section 3.4.

We also need to generate a set of negative samples $P'$, which we generate in the same way as Guu et al. (2015) by *type-matched corruption*– see Section 4.2 for a discussion. Given a path $p = (e_1, r_1, \ldots, r_k, e_2)$, let $\mathcal{F}(p)$ be the set of *final entities* of $p$ that can be reached when traversing $G$ via the relations $r_1, \ldots, r_k$ starting from $e_1$. We are guaranteed to corrupt $p$ if we replace $e_2$ with any entity $e_2' \notin \mathcal{F}(p)$ but matches the type of $r_k$, i.e., $e_2' \in D_2(r_k)$, with the *right domain* $D_2(r)$ defined as:

$$D_2(r) = \{e_2 \mid \exists e_1 : (e_1, r, e_2) \in G\} \quad (6)$$

Analogously, we define $\mathcal{I}(p)$ as the set of *initial entities* of $p$. We corrupt $e_1$ by replacing it with an entity in $D_1(r_1) \setminus \mathcal{I}(p)$, where $D_1(r)$ is the analogous *left domain* of $r$. In the case of TransE, the parameters to be updated are all $\boldsymbol{e}_i, \boldsymbol{r}_j$ as well as $\boldsymbol{b_1}$ (cf. Equation (3)).

**Training** $\rho(t, p)$. The relevance scores $\rho(t, p)$ use a similar cross-entropy loss based on $c(t, P_t)$:

$$-\sum_{t \in G} \frac{\log c(t, P_t)}{|G|} - \sum_{t' \in G'} \frac{\log(1 - c(t', P_{t'}))}{|G'|} \quad (7)$$

where $G$, the KB, is the set of correct triples and $G'$ is a set of triples with either $e_1$ or $e_2$ corrupted as above. The objective aims to assign correct triples a score of 1 and incorrect triples a score of 0, which, together with the fixed semantics of $c(p)$, encourages $\rho(t, p)$ to estimate the relevance of paths $p$ for $t$. Only the parameters of $\rho$, namely $\boldsymbol{a_r}$ and $\boldsymbol{b_2}$ (compare Equation (4)) are updated.

## 3.4 Selecting Context Paths

The final part of the Context Path Model (CPM) is the *selection of informative context paths*. Since the number of paths grows exponentially in the path length, it is infeasible to include all paths in the CPM. We now propose several criteria to limit the set of informative context paths $P_t$ for a given triple $t = (e_1, r, e_2)$ to keep the model tractable.

**Closed paths.** Paths that connect the two entities of a triple express a semantic relation between them. We therefore restrict paths to start with $e_1$ and end with $e_2$, i.e., to be closed paths.

**Limited length.** We limit path lengths to $k \leq 3$. This effectively reduces the number of potential paths and keeps the paths between $e_1$ and $e_2$ relatively easy to understand.

**Filtering redundant paths.** To be able to traverse edges of the knowledge graph in both directions, we need to add the inverse edge $(e_2, r^{-1}, e_1)$ for each edge $(e_1, r, e_2) \in G$ to the knowledge graph $G$. This has the unwanted consequence that we obtain *redundant* paths which comprise two successive, mutually inverse relations like $(e_1,$ *country of birth, contains, contains*$^{-1}, e_2)$ which is judged to be highly relevant for *country of birth* but for trivial reasons.

We consider the domains $D_1(r_i)$ and $D_2(r_i)$ (compare Equation (6)) to filter out trivial paths effectively. A path $(e_1, r_1, ..., r_k, e_2)$ is defined as trivial if $e_1$ occurs in any domain of $r_1, ..., r_k$ except $D_1(r_1)$ or $e_2$ in any domain except $D_2(r_k)$.

This general definition has the benefit of capturing cases of redundant paths caused by relations in the KB that are semantically, but not formally, inverses – such as the relations *contains* and *contained by*. It can also be too strict: E.g., the context path $p = (e_1,$ *mother of, mother of, $e_2$)* for the triple $t = (e_1,$ *grandmother of, $e_2$)* is excluded if the mother of $e_2$ participates in the relation *grandmother of*. This does however not pose a major problem in practice.

**Negative context paths.** The paths described so far can only be used by the CPM as positive evidence for the correctness of a triple. However, the CPM can also use incorrect (i.e., correctly absent) paths as negative evidence (i.e., as evidence that triples are incorrect). We now describe how such paths can be found.

| | | 14,951 |
|---|---|---|
| Entities | | 14,951 |
| Relations | | 1,345 |
| | Train | 483,142 |
| Triples | Validation | 50,000 |
| | Test | 59,071 |
| Paths of length 2 | Train | 3,110,893 |
| | Test | 81,124 |
| Paths of length 3 | Train | 3,711,317 |
| | Test | 101,717 |

Table 1: Statistics on the FB15K dataset

Assuming the first three criteria described above, let $P_r$ be the set of correct context paths corresponding to all triples $(e_1, r, e_2)$ for a fixed relation $r$. Let furthermore $S_r$ be the set of relation sequences occurring in paths $p = (e_1, r_1, ..., r_k, e_2) \in P_r$. We can then define the set of context paths $P_t$:

$$P_t = \{p \mid (r_1, ..., r_k) \in S_r \wedge \mathcal{I}(p) \cup \mathcal{F}(p) \neq \emptyset\} \quad (8)$$

In addition to the positive informative paths described so far, $P_t$ contains incorrect paths that connect $e_1$ and $e_2$ by corrupted relation sequences that conform to the criteria described above. The use of relation sequences that occur in context paths of other facts about the same relation makes it more likely that incorrect paths are relevant for $t$.

## 4 Experimental Evaluation

### 4.1 Dataset

We evaluate our approach on the FB15K dataset extracted by Bordes et al. (2013) from the FreeBase knowledge base. Table 1 shows the statistics of this dataset, including the number of context paths according to the definition in Section 3.4.

### 4.2 Experimental Setup

We instantiate the edge scoring model of CPM with the TransE model (Bordes et al., 2013), as shown in Eq. (3). We follow the two-step training regimen as described in Section 3.3. We train 100-dimensional vectors for all representations learned by the model (cf. Section 3.2). Optimization proceeds by applying the gradient-based optimizer Adam (Kingma and Ba, 2015) to minibatches of size 300. We use the learning rate of 0.001 for all parts of the model with the exception of $c(p)$ during path training, where we use 0.0001 based on performance on the validation set.

**Choice of negative samples.** Since KBs ideally contain only correct information, KBC methods generally need to generate incorrect samples synthetically. This is generally done by corrupting either the first entity $e_1$ or the last entity $e_2$ in a path $p$ to obtain negative samples $\mathcal{N}(p)$. Negative samples are used as parts of the ranking problems both at train time (cf. Section 3.3) and at test time. The generation of negative samples is therefore a crucial part of the experimental setup. Unfortunately, there is little consensus on the details of the process in the literature. We discuss the two major approaches below.

The first approach, *random corruption*, corrupts paths by replacing $e_1$ or $e_2$ by random entities from the KB (Bordes et al., 2013; Yang et al., 2015). The advantage of this approach is that a large number of negative samples can be generated easily – at the same time, most corrupted paths are arguably not particularly plausible confounders, as when a person is replaced by a country or a record. An alternative approach, *type-matched corruption* (Guu et al., 2015), employs only confounders seen with the same sequence of relations as the original entity (cf. Section 3.3 for a formal definition). This generally ensures that the confounders are plausible. On the downside, there are typically fewer such confounders.

For our study, we adopt the type-matching corruption setup, which we find more appropriate in the context of explainable KBC. For negative samples with incorrect types, the most natural reason for rejection is simply the domain mismatch, while the type-matching setting requires the models to capture fine-grained semantics within domains.

As a result, the evaluation numbers that we report are not directly comparable to numbers obtained with the random corruption approach, and tend to be higher. This is because the smaller numbers of negative samples lead to simpler ranking problems. The average size of $\mathcal{N}(t)$ for FB15k test triples $t$ is 1,738 in the type-matching setting and 29,543 in the setting without type-matching. As negative samples from the training can end up in $\mathcal{N}(t)$ for test triples $t$, the average number of unseen negative samples in $\mathcal{N}(t)$ is 765 in our setup.

We exclude negative samples that result in correct paths from the training or validation set. Similarly, context paths sampled for training or validation are excluded from the test set.

| Model | Training | H@10 | | MQ | |
|---|---|---|---|---|---|
| TransE | Edges | **90.2** | | **97.5** | |
| TransE | Paths | 84.2 | (-6.7%) | 97.1 | (-0.4%) |
| CPM | Paths | 83.1 | (-7.9%) | 96.7 | (-0.8%) |
| CPM$\backslash t$ | Paths | 80.0 | (-11.3%) | 96.2 | (-1.3%) |

Table 2: Results for Evaluation 1 (fact correctness). Numbers in brackets give relative deterioration compared to TransE (edge). CPM$\backslash t$ is the CPM ignoring all information about the target triple itself.

| | Edge training | | Path training | |
|---|---|---|---|---|
| Length | H@10 | MQ | H@10 | MQ |
| 1 | **90.2** | **97.5** | 84.2 | 97.1 |
| 2 | 73.4 | 94.1 | **82.7** | **97.5** |
| 3 | 54.0 | 89.0 | **64.4** | **93.3** |

Table 3: Results for Evaluation 2 (path correctness), varying path length and training regimen. Best results for each length shown in boldface.

## 4.3 Evaluation 1: Fact Correctness

We carry out three evaluations. We start with the traditional task of predicting individual facts (edges). We directly define the evaluation metrics for paths rather than facts for re-use in Evaluation 2 at the path level. The metrics apply to edges because they are paths of length 1.

**Evaluation metric.** We apply the commonly used ranking metric *hits at 10* (H@10), which is defined as the percentage of correct paths that are ranked within the top 10 of their respective negative samples. Additionally, we use the metric *mean quantile* (MQ), proposed by Guu et al. (2015), which computes the share of incorrect paths ranked lower than the correct path:

$$MQ = \frac{1}{|P|} \sum_{p \in P} \frac{|\{p' \in \mathcal{N}(p) \mid c(p') < c(p)\}|}{|\mathcal{N}(p)|} \quad (9)$$

In contrast to H@10, MQ accounts for the size of $\mathcal{N}(p)$. For $1 \leq |\mathcal{N}(p)| \leq 9$, H@10 always outputs 1. In the fact correctness evaluation, this is the case for 1.5% of used test facts. We exclude 1143 facts with $|\mathcal{N}(p)| = 0$ from the test set because both H@10 and MQ always output 1 in these cases.

**Results.** Table 2 presents the results of the ranking evaluation for fact prediction. We compare the full CPM model against TransE, the edge scorer "inside" our CPM (cf. Section 4.2), in both its edge-trained and path-trained versions[4] (cf. Section 3.3). We also consider CPM$\backslash t$, a variant of the CPM that excludes $t$ from $P_t$, that is, does not use any information about the predicted triple. This model examines to which degree the correctness of triples $t$ can be predicted purely on the basis of its KB context. This gives us four models to compare.

We find that the CPM performs somewhat worse than the best model overall, the edge-trained TransE, for both metrics: the drop is noticeable for H@10, and mild for MQ. We believe that the drop is primarily due to two factors: First, path training gives rise to a different optimization problem from edge training, which appears to be more difficult on the FB15K dataset.[5] In fact, as the second row shows, training the original TransE on paths leads to a comparable drop in H@10. Second, the bad results for CPM$\backslash t$, which are still substantially worse than for the plain CPM, indicate that, unsurprisingly, the most important source of information for the prediction of a single triple is the semantics of the triple itself. In other words, the contextual component that CPM adds does not provide additional support to single edge prediction at the technical level (we consider the produced justifications in the third evaluation).

In sum, CPM introduces a mild loss of quality in the prediction of individual facts. Given that the CPM has a more complex objective – modeling the correctness of facts/paths as well as modeling justifications – we see this nevertheless as a promising first evaluation result.

## 4.4 Evaluation 2: Path Correctness

The second evaluation concentrates on the CPM and its performance on the task it is designed for, namely predicting the correctness of longer paths. Table 3 shows results separated by path length (1 through 3). The results for path length 1 are, by definition, identical to the corresponding conditions in Evaluation 1, with an advantage for single-edge training. This effect reverses for the longer paths: while the edge-trained model loses substantially in quality because it fails to capture dependencies among edges, the path-trained model holds up well

---

[4]TransE can be seen as a special case of the CPM when all paths except for the triple itself are assigned a relevance of 0. The reported TransE scores are measured on the instantiation of $c(\cdot)$ with TransE.

[5]Path training appears to be beneficial on other datasets, as reported by Guu et al. (2015).

for longer paths. We see these results as validation of our choice of a path-based training regimen (Section 3.3).

### 4.5 Evaluation 3: Path Relevance

Our third evaluation focuses on relevance, that is, the relation between paths and the triples that they are supposed to provide evidence for or against. Since our goal is to use these paths as human-interpretable justifications for the triples, we perform a small annotation study of the CPM output.

**Dataset.** We manually select 24 relations for annotation whose relevance can arguably be judged without in-depth expertise of specific domains. The selected relations account for 13.2% of the facts in the test set. For each relation, we randomly sample two correct facts from the test set and obtain incorrect facts by corrupting either $e_1$ or $e_2$. This results in 48 positive and 48 negative facts. We furthermore exclude 17 triples for which no path (other than the trivial $t$ itself) was found with a normalized relevance score of at least 10%. For the remaining 79 triples, we annotate all paths with a normalized relevance score of at least 5% – again, with the exception of $t$ itself. We also do not consider paths with relations from the FB15K domains *dataworld* and *commons* because they encode only KB-specific meta information. This results in on average 2.45 context paths annotated per triple, accounting for 80% of the assigned relevance scores.

**Annotation.** As motivated in Section 3.1, the relevance of context paths $P_t$ describes how strongly their correctness is correlated with the correctness of $t$. In the annotation we distinguish between three levels (categories) of relevance:

1. **Equivalent:** The correctness of $p$ is logically equivalent to the correctness of $t$.

2. **Probable:** The path $p$ being correct makes the correctness of $t$ significantly more likely, or $p$ being incorrect makes the correctness of $t$ significantly less likely. However, $p$ provides no guarantee for the (in-)correctness of $t$.

3. **Unrelated:** The correctness of $p$ and $t$ are not strongly correlated. This class comprises all cases that are not in category 1 or 2.

**Qualitative Analysis.** Table 4 shows examples of the three annotated categories, both for positive cases (presence of $p$ supports $t$) and negative cases

(absence of $p$ casts doubt in $t$). Negative cases are marked with asterisks (*), and since all absent paths are corrupted versions of paths in the KB, the point of corruption is marked as well.

The 'equivalent' category shows two cases of equivalence between two Freebase relations – one positive (*profession* is supported by *people_with_profession*$^{-1}$) and one negative (*islands_in_group* is implausible if not accompanied by *island_group*$^{-1}$) – as well as one case of mutual entailment (the CAF has a football league iff there is a team that is a football team and plays in the CAF). The 'probable' category contains cases of defeasible inferences – e.g., Hindi is the most widely spoken language in India, but only by just over half of the population. The 'unrelated' category, finally, shows some paths that are largely irrelevant for their facts (e.g., someone is born in a place vs. someone often eats at a restaurant that uses the same currency as the birth place). The examples demonstrate that CPM is indeed capable of capturing meaningful relations between triples and the paths in its context.

**Quantitative Analysis.** Table 5 shows that just over half of all pairs we consider falls into the 'equivalent' category. These pairs are assigned a mean relevance of 0.47, and their share of the total sum of relevance scores is 72%. Another quarter of the annotated pairs falls into the 'probable' category, with a considerably lower mean relevance of 0.15, and a share of 15% of the relevance scores. The final quarter of pairs makes up the 'unrelated' category, with similar mean relevance and share of relevance scores.

We see this outcome as rather positive: about half of the paths identified by the CPM are equivalent to the triple in question, with another quarter providing probable evidence. Furthermore, the relevance scores manage very well to separate the 'equivalent' and 'probable' categories. The separation between 'probable' and 'unrelated' is weak, but may be due to our exclusion of the lowest-relevance paths from annotation (see above): these would arguably mostly be mostly 'unrelated' and thus decrease the mean relevance for this category.

## 5 Conclusion

This paper has considered the generation of explanations for predictions of facts in knowledge base completion (KBC). Our contribution is the *Context Path Model* (CPM), which provides explanations

| | Triple | Context path |
|---|---|---|
| **equivalent** | (*Jon Favreau*, *profession*, **Film director**) | (*Jon Favreau*, *people_with_profession*$^{-1}$, **Film director**) |
| | (**Football**, *leagues*, **Confed. of African Football**) | (**Football**, *teams*, **Zimbabwe national football team**, *league_participation/team*$^{-1}$, **Confed. of African Football**) |
| | *(**Hawaiian Islands**, *islands_in_group*, **Ireland**) | *(**Hawaiian Islands** [corrupted from: **British Isles**], *island_group*$^{-1}$, **Ireland**) |
| **probable** | (**Feroz Khan**, *languages*, **Hindi**) | (**Feroz Khan**, *nationality*, **India**, *countries_spoken_in*$^{-1}$, **Hindi**) |
| | (**Naval Postgraduate School**, *containedby*, **USA**) | (**Naval Postgraduate School**, *headquarters/state*, **California**, *representatives*, **Richard Nixon**, *nationality*, **USA**) |
| **unrelated** | (**Nashua**, *people_born_here*, **Mandy Moore**) | (**Nashua**, *currency*, **US Dollar**, *liabilities_in_currency*$^{-1}$, **Starbucks**, *eats_at*$^{-1}$, **Mandy Moore**) |
| | *(**Jared Harris**, *parents*, **Aaron Spelling**) | *(**Jared Harris**, *award_nominee*$^{-1}$, **Mad Men** [corrupted from **Beverly Hills, 90210**], *tv_program_creator*, **Aaron Spelling**) |

Table 4: Examples of triple–path pairs, with entities in boldface, and simplified freebase relations. Incorrect triples/paths marked with *, and point of corruption marked.

| Annotation category | equiv. | prob. | unrel. |
|---|---|---|---|
| Number of pairs | 98 | 49 | 47 |
| Share of pairs | 51% | 25% | 24% |
| Mean Relevance $\rho$ | 0.47 | 0.15 | 0.12 |
| Share of total $\sum \rho$ | 72% | 15% | 13% |

Table 5: Statistics for annotated triple–path pairs

by identifying context paths which are highly correlated with the fact: if the path is in the KB, then the triple should be as well; conversely, if the path is not in the KB, then the triple should not be either.

We demonstrate the usefulness of our model by instantiating its fact scorer with a simple but effective KBC model, TransE (Bordes et al., 2013). We find that the performance of the CPM is close to TransE, and manual evaluation confirms that most of the paths the model uses as explanation are meaningful and provide evidence for assessing the correctness of facts. This shows the potential of using paths as explanations for KBC predictions.

Beyond the KBC setting, the output of the CPM can also arguably be useful for a structural analysis of knowledge bases, for example the systematic identification of equivalences among relations or between relations and paths, to improve the consistency of the KB, e.g., by replacing equivalent paths by a canonical version.

The current study has three main limitations. First, we only apply the CPM to TransE. Future work should investigate the practical usefulness of the CPM for other composable KBC models like Bilinear-diag. Second, we use strong heuristics to limit the set of paths under consideration; future work should attempt to relax these. Third, the current CPM can only capture paths that are symmetrically (cor-)related with the fact in question, corresponding to strict or probabilistic entailment. A promising avenue for future work is to generalize the model to asymmetrical relations, i.e., find paths that represent (just) necessary or sufficient conditions for a fact, in order to enable a more comprehensive analysis of the inferential structures in KBs (Hitzler et al., 2009).

# References


Jonathan Berant, Andrew Chou, Roy Frostig, and Percy Liang. 2013. Semantic parsing on Freebase from question-answer pairs. In *Proceedings of the Conference on Empirical Methods in Natural Language Processing*, pages 1533–1544, Seattle, WA.

Kurt Bollacker, Colin Evans, Praveen Paritosh, Tim Sturge, and Jamie Taylor. 2008. Freebase: A collaboratively created graph database for structuring human knowledge. In *Proceedings of the ACM SIGMOD International Conference on Management of Data*, pages 1247–1250, Vancouver, Canada.

Antoine Bordes, Nicolas Usunier, Alberto Garcia-Duran, Jason Weston, and Oksana Yakhnenko. 2013. Translating embeddings for modeling multi-relational data. In *Proceedings of the International Conference on Neural Information Processing Systems*, pages 2787–2795.

Antoine Bordes, Jason Weston, and Nicolas Usunier. 2014. Open question answering with weakly supervised embedding models. In *Machine Learning and Knowledge Discovery in Databases*, pages 165–180. Springer.

Luis Antonio Galárraga, Christina Teflioudi, Katja Hose, and Fabian Suchanek. 2013. Amie: Association rule mining under incomplete evidence in ontological knowledge bases. In *Proceedings of the International Conference on World Wide Web*, pages 413–422, Rio de Janeiro, Brazil.

Matt Gardner, Partha Talukdar, Jayant Krishnamurthy, and Tom Mitchell. 2014. Incorporating vector space similarity in random walk inference over knowledge bases. In *Proceedings of the Conference on Empirical Methods in Natural Language Processing*, pages 397–406, Doha, Qatar.

Arthur Colombini Gusmão, Alvaro Henrique Chaim Correia, Glauber De Bona, and Fábio Gagliardi Cozman. 2018. Interpreting embedding models of knowledge bases: A pedagogical approach. In *Proceedings of the ICML Workshop on Human Interpretability in Machine Learning*.

Kelvin Guu, John Miller, and Percy Liang. 2015. Traversing knowledge graphs in vector space. In *Proceedings of the Conference on Empirical Methods in Natural Language Processing*, pages 318–327, Lisbon, Portugal.

Pascal Hitzler, Markus Krotzsch, and Sebastian Rudolph. 2009. *Foundations of semantic web technologies*. CRC Press.

Andreas Holzinger, Chris Biemann, Constantinos S. Pattichis, and Douglas B. Kell. 2017. What do we need to build explainable AI systems for the medical domain? *CoRR*, abs/1712.09923.

Diederik P. Kingma and Jimmy Ba. 2015. Adam: A method for stochastic optimization. In *Proceedings of the International Conference on Learning Representations*, San Diego, CA.

Ni Lao and William W. Cohen. 2010. Relational retrieval using a combination of path-constrained random walks. *Machine Learning*, 81(1):53–67.

Yankai Lin, Zhiyuan Liu, Huanbo Luan, Maosong Sun, Siwei Rao, and Song Liu. 2015. Modeling relation paths for representation learning of knowledge bases. In *Proceedings of the Conference on Empirical Methods in Natural Language Processing*, pages 705–714, Lisbon, Portugal.

Bonan Min, Ralph Grishman, Li Wan, Chang Wang, and David Gondek. 2013. Distant supervision for relation extraction with an incomplete knowledge base. In *Proceedings of the Conference of the North American Chapter of the Association for Computational Linguistics*, pages 777–782, Atlanta, GA.

Maximilian Nickel, Volker Tresp, and Hans-Peter Kriegel. 2011. A three-way model for collective learning on multi-relational data. In *Proceedings of the International Conference on Machine Learning*, pages 809–816, Bellevue, WA.

Gabriëlle Ras, Marcel van Gerven, and Pim Haselager. 2018. Explanation methods in deep learning: Users, values, concerns and challenges. In *Explainable and Interpretable Models in Computer Vision and Machine Learning*, pages 19–36. Springer.

Marco Tulio Ribeiro, Sameer Singh, and Carlos Guestrin. 2018. Anchors: High-precision model-agnostic explanations. In *Proceedings of the AAAI Conference on Artificial Intelligence*, New Orleans, LA.

Michael Schlichtkrull, Thomas N. Kipf, Peter Bloem, Rianne van den Berg, Ivan Titov, and Max Welling. 2018. Modeling relational data with graph convolutional networks. In *The Semantic Web*, pages 593–607. Springer.

Yelong Shen, Po-Sen Huang, Ming-Wei Chang, and Jianfeng Gao. 2017. Modeling large-scale structured relationships with shared memory for knowledge base completion. In *Proceedings of the 2nd Workshop on Representation Learning for NLP*, pages 57–68, Vancouver, Canada.

Richard Socher, Danqi Chen, Christopher D. Manning, and Andrew Y. Ng. 2013. Reasoning with neural tensor networks for knowledge base completion. In *Proceedings of the International Conference on Neural Information Processing Systems*, pages 926–934.

Thomas Steiner, Ruben Verborgh, Raphaël Troncy, Joaquim Gabarro, and Rik Van De Walle. 2012. Adding realtime coverage to the google knowledge graph. In *Proceedings of the International Semantic Web Conference*, pages 65–68.

Fabian M. Suchanek, Gjergji Kasneci, and Gerhard Weikum. 2007. Yago: A core of semantic knowledge. In *Proceedings of the 16th International Conference on World Wide Web*, pages 697–706, New York, NY.

Kristina Toutanova, Victoria Lin, Wen-tau Yih, Hoifung Poon, and Chris Quirk. 2016. Compositional learning of embeddings for relation paths in knowledge base and text. In *Proceedings of the Annual Meeting of the Association for Computational Linguistics*, pages 1434–1444, Berlin, Germany.

Denny Vrandečić and Markus Krötzsch. 2014. Wikidata: A free collaborative knowledge base. *Communications of the ACM*, 57:78–85.

Qizhe Xie, Xuezhe Ma, Zihang Dai, and Eduard Hovy. 2017. An interpretable knowledge transfer model for knowledge base completion. In *Proceedings of the Annual Meeting of the Association for Computational Linguistics*, pages 950–962, Vancouver, BC.

Bishan Yang, Wen-tau Yih, Xiaodong He, Jianfeng Gao, and Li Deng. 2015. Embedding entities and relations for learning and inference in knowledge bases. In *Proceedings of the International Conference on Learning Representations*, San Diego, CA.

Wen Zhang, Bibek Paudel, Wei Zhang, Abraham Bernstein, and Huajun Chen. 2019. Interaction embeddings for prediction and explanation in knowledge graphs. In *Proceedings of the ACM International Conference on Web Search and Data Mining*, pages 96–104.

# Probing word and sentence embeddings for long-distance dependencies effects in French and English

**Paola Merlo**
University of Geneva
`Paola.Merlo@unige.ch`

## Abstract

The recent wide-spread and strong interest in RNNs has spurred detailed investigations of the distributed representations they generate and specifically if they exhibit properties similar to those characterising human languages. Results are at present inconclusive. In this paper, we extend previous work on long-distance dependencies in three ways. We manipulate word embeddings to translate them in a space that is attuned to the linguistic properties under study. We extend the work to sentence embeddings and to new languages. We confirm previous negative results: word embeddings and sentence embeddings do not unequivocally encode fine-grained linguistic properties of long-distance dependencies.

## 1 Introduction

The recent wide-spread and strong interest in RNNs has spurred detailed investigations of the distributed representations they use, learn and generate and specifically if they exhibit properties similar to those characterising human languages. For a survey see Belinkov and Glass (2019).

Results are at present rather inconclusive on whether RNNs and the representations they learn have human-like properties. While many pieces of work seems to indicate that they do, some other pieces of work have mixed results, and a few appear to show that the representations of RNNs do not match those predicted by linguistic theory or human experiments. For example, one line of work aims to correlate RNN-induced representations to linguistic properties, namely the fact that subject-verb number agreement is structure-dependent. Initial work had shown RNNs do not really learn the structure-dependency of this construction (Linzen et al., 2016), but follow up work has shown that stronger techniques can yield more positive results (Gulordava et al., 2018), only to

be very promptly rebutted by work suggesting that the apparently positive results could be the artifact of a much simpler strategy, which takes advantage of the unnaturally simple structure of the examples and simply learns properties of the first word in the sentence (Kuncoro et al., 2018). Recent work by Lakretz et al. (2019), however, studies RNNs in more detail, looking at single neurons, and finds that individual neurons encode linguistically meaningful features very saliently and with behaviour over time that corresponds to the expected propagation of subject-verb number agreement information.

Similarly, probing different aspects of long-distance dependencies, so far divergent results have been reported on these constructions. While some experiments have shown that RNNs can learn the main descriptive properties of long-distance dependencies in English, for example the fact that they obey a uniqueness constraint (only one gap per filler) and also that they obey island constraints (Wilcox et al., 2018), work attempting to replicate finer-grained human judgments for French have failed to show a correlation with human behaviour (Merlo and Ackermann, 2018), while other work on English has found mixed results (Chowdhury and Zamparelli, 2018).

In this paper, we extend previous work on long-distance dependencies to tease apart the potential grounds for the different outcomes by making previous work more comparable. There are several differences between the pieces of work on long-distance dependencies mentioned above. First, the work that does not find a correspondence between the two sources of information being compared (Merlo and Ackermann, 2018) imposes a much stricter test of correspondence — total correlation— than the general effect reported in Wilcox et al. (2018). Secondly, the pieces of work vary in task: it is possible that word embed-



*Proceedings of the Second BlackboxNLP Workshop on Analyzing and Interpreting Neural Networks for NLP*, pages 158–172
Florence, Italy, August 1, 2019. ©2019 Association for Computational Linguistics

dings need to be used holistically in a prediction task similar to what humans solve to show a positive correlation. Finally, these pieces of work are on different languages.

Beside these differences in experimental setup, it is also possible that holistic representations such as word embeddings need to be transformed and translated into the right space to show correlations with human judgments. Specifically, word embeddings are a merger of the many levels of representation that we find in human languages: lexical, morphological, syntactic, semantic. It has been argued that post-processing transformations can tease apart syntactic aspects of distributed representations from semantic aspects (Artetxe et al., 2018).

Based on all these observation, we extend the work of Merlo and Ackermann (2018), which had found no correlation, along these lines. To preview, while we are able to get slightly better correlations to human judgments than those reported by Merlo and Ackermann (2018), the mixed results are confirmed: word embeddings and sentence embeddings, the representations produced by RNNs, do not unequivocally encode fine-grained linguistic properties of long-distance dependencies.

## 2 Intervention effects in human sentence processing

A core distinguishing property of human languages is the ability to interpret discontinuous elements as if they were a single element. These are called long-distance dependencies.

For example, sentence (1a) is an object-oriented restrictive relative clause, where the object of the verb phrase *annoying* is also the semantic recipient of the verb *smile*, connecting two distant elements. Long-distance dependencies are not all equally acceptable or even grammatical (for example, sentences (3a,b) and (4a,b) are not fully grammatical). A prominent explanation says that a long-distance dependency between two elements in a sentence is difficult, and often impossible, in the presence of an intervener (for example *speaker* in (1a)). An *intervener* is an element that is *similar* to the two elements that are in a long-distance relation, and structurally intervenes between the two, blocking the relation (Rizzi, 2004). Detailed investigations have shown that long-distance dependencies exhibit gradations of acceptability depend-

**Object Relatives**

(1a) Julie smiles to the **student** that the **speaker** has been seriously annoying from the beginning.

(1b) Julie smiles to the **students** that the **speaker** has been seriously annoying from the beginning.

(2a) Julie points out to the **student** that the **speaker** has been yawning frequently from the beginning.

(2b) Julie points out to the **students** that the **speaker** has been yawning frequently from the beginning.

**Weak islands**

(3a) **Which class** do you wonder **which student** liked?

(3b) **Which professor** do you wonder **which student** liked?

(4a) **What** do you wonder **who** liked?

(4b) **Who** do you wonder **who** liked?

Figure 1: The linguistic constructions and experimental materials, English version. (1) object relatives; (2) completives (experimental control, no long distance dependency), (a) number match, (b) number mismatch. (3) Lexically specified; (4) lexically bare; (a) animacy mismatch; (b) animacy match.

ing on properties of the intervener (Rizzi, 2004; Grillo, 2008; Friedmann et al., 2009). Franck et al. (2015); Villata and Franck (2016) concentrate on those features that are properties of words: *lexical restriction, number* and *animacy*. This is interesting for us as these are lexical features and therefore they can potentially be captured by word embeddings.

All else being equal, in complex question environments (weak islands, such as those shown in (3) and (4)), long-distance dependency involving a lexically restricted *wh*-phrase (*which class* or *which student*) is more acceptable than extraction of a bare *wh*-element (*who* or *what*), which is not very good.

Experiments on relative clauses also show that the morpho-syntactic feature *number* triggers intervention effects (Belletti et al., 2012; Bentea, 2016). So, for example, the sentence in (1b) is reported to be easier than the sentence in (1a), because the words *students* and *speaker* do not match in number. Completive sentences like those in (2), on the other hand, do not show any difference between (2a), where number matches, and (2b), where number does not match, as no long-distance dependency is at stake.

The status of a lexical-semantic feature such as *animacy* remains more controversial, but some recent studies show a clear effect of animacy as an intervention feature in *wh*-islands (Franck et al., 2015; Villata and Franck, 2016). So for example, (3a) is easier than (3b) and (4a) is easier than (4b) because the two *wh*-phrases do not match in animacy.

## 3 The human experiments

The psycholinguistic experiments that collected the experimental measures reflecting the acceptability or reading times of a sentence are described in Franck et al. (2015) and Villata and Franck (2016) and they are the same as those discussed in Merlo and Ackermann (2018). The initial experiments were done in French.[1] Figure 1 shows the English version of the kind of sentences that are used as stimuli in the experiments. The object relative clause experiment collected on-line reading times, manipulating the number (singular or plural) of the object of the relative clause as the intervening feature and the construction, with or without long-distance dependency. A speed-up effect in number mismatch configurations (plural object) was found in object relative clauses. The weak islands experiment collected off-line acceptability judgments, manipulating animacy and lexical restriction of the intervener. A clear effect of animacy match for lexically restricted phrases (less acceptable) and less so for bare *wh*-phrases was found.

Recall that, in Merlo and Ackermann (2018), it was found that similarity scores calculated on these experimental items using word embeddings do not correlate with experimental results. This lead to the conclusion that word embeddings do not encode relevant information related to the important notion of intervener. In the next two sections, we present our extensions to these results.

## 4 Divergent vectors for French

Artetxe et al. (2018) propose a post-processing vector transformation technique based on eigendecomposition that corresponds to calculating first, second, *nth*-order similarities. The basic intuition is that, for example, a second-order similarity is a similarity matrix of similarities. Instead of changing the similarity matrix, the word embeddings themselves are transformed, calculating first, second, *nth*-order similarities directly. These similarities are based on the tuning of a single parameter $\alpha$, the power of the matrix, to increase or decrease the similarity order. For example $\alpha = 0$ is first-order similarity, the similarity of two given words, $\alpha = 0.5$ is second-order similarity, the similarity of the context of two given words. Values of $\alpha$ can vary both positively and negatively. Intuitively, negative values are similarities of two given words as first, second, $n$-order contexts of other words. Artexte and colleagues argue that different-order similarities are related to different levels of linguistic representations, and certain values of the parameter move the vectors in a space where similarities are more syntactic (as in *sing, singing*), while other values of the parameter move the vectors in a space that is more semantic (as in *sing, chant*). They also distinguish a notion of similarity as analogy, such as the one exhibited by words like *car* and *automobile*, and relatedness, such as in *car* and *road*. Specifically, they claim that their results show that the notion of similarity represented in vectorial space can be decomposed into a more 'syntactic' notion of similarity and the notion of 'relatedness' of a more semantic flavour. They confirm these claims by better performance of the transformed vectors in different tasks of analogy and relatedness that tap into different notions of similarity.

We apply this eigendecomposition technique to our data, serching for the appropriate values of $\alpha$, to see if moving the vectors in a region of the space that corresponds better to syntactic similarity yields better correlations between word embeddings similarity scores and experimental results than found in Merlo and Ackermann (2018).

**Materials and Method** The language we use in this experiment is French. Recall that we want to calculate a correlation at the lexical level, as the notion of intervention is based on lexical properties. So we modify the word embeddings of the lexical items.

**List of words** We use all the words in the stimuli of the human experiments described above, including the fillers, to create an exact replication of the linguistic environment of the experiments. In

---

[1] We are very grateful to Sandra Villata and Julie Franck for sharing their stimuli and experimental results with us.

total, we have 388 unique words. We use only the words in the actual experimental stimuli for testing (96 words for object relatives and 128 words for weak islands). These are words shown in bold in Figure 1. For this experiment, in the case of lexically restricted weak islands, we only look at the head word; for example, for the phrase *which professor* we use *professor*.

**Vectors** For all these words, we extract vectors from preexisting trained vectors. We use Fasttext in its new version (Grave et al., 2018), as it is shown in Artetxe et al. (2018) that these vectors yield best results for their eigendecomposition technique. These publicly available vectors have been obtained on a 5-word window, for 300 resulting dimensions, on Wikipedia data using the skip-gram model described in Bojanowski et al. (2016).[2] In this model, every word is represented as an $n$-grams of characters, for $n$ between 3 and 6. Each $n$-gram is represented by a vector and the sum of these vectors forms the vector representing the given word.

**Transformation** We apply Artetxe et al. (2018)'s transformation to the word embeddings of the experimental items, for several values of $\alpha$, in the range $-1$ to 1.

**Calculation of results** We calculate correlations with experimental results. Specifically, we first calculate the cosine similarity between the transformed word embeddings of the head of the long-distance dependency and the intervening element (the words in bold in Figure 1). Then, we calculate a correlation between the obtained similarity scores and the experimental measures (mean acceptability judgments for weak islands and reaction times at the position of the verb for relative clauses).

**Results and discussion** Results for direct correlations are shown in Figure 2. The two panels show how the values of the Pearson correlations between the similarity scores of the transformed word embeddings and the experimental results vary with different values of $\alpha$. For example, the panel 2a indicates that the maximum correlation between the similarity scores of the word embeddings of the experimental items and the experimental scores are reached at $-0.50 > \alpha > -0.25$.

Overall, for values of $\alpha$ close to 0, the value of $\alpha$ indicating a direct correlation between the words

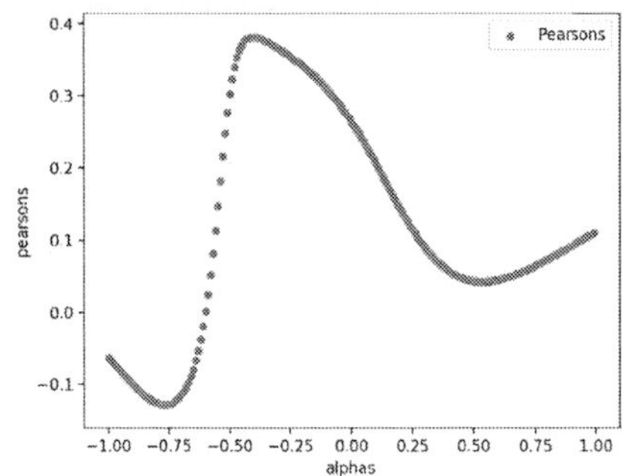

(a) Object relatives, number.

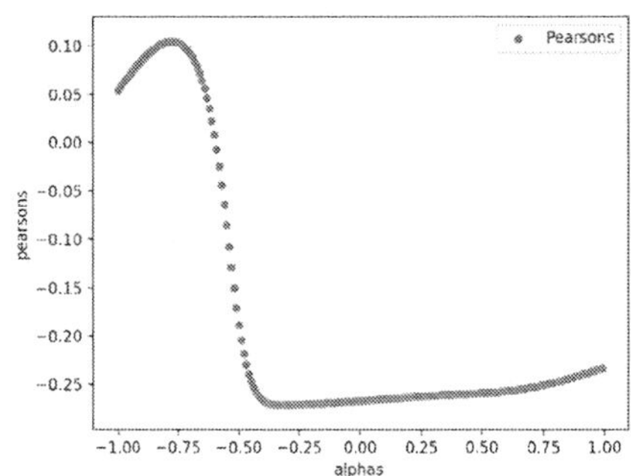

(b) Weak islands, animacy.

Figure 2: Pearson correlation (range of value of $\alpha$ for transformation: -1 to 1).

of interest, the correlation is very weak, positively for object relatives and the number feature and negatively for weak islands and the animacy feature.

The panel (a) shows how the correlations with the intervention effect of *number* vary with different values of $\alpha$. It shows a weak correlation reaching 0.4 for values of $\alpha$ between $-0.5$ and $-0.25$. This only weakly confirms Merlo and Ackermann (2018)'s results, showing there is some syntactic signal, although not sufficient to explain the experimental results. The panel (b) shows the correlations with the experiment testing the intervention effects of *animacy*. Here the correlation is even weaker, despite the transformation, as positive Pearson values never exceed 0.10 (and the strongest correlation is a negative $-0.25$), confirming Merlo and Ackermann (2018)'s results, even in this more propitious set up.

An interesting linguistic observation that is quite clear from the patterns of $\alpha$, is that both the feature *number*, more intuitively syntactic, and the feature *animacy*, whose status is ambiguous

---

[2]The French vectors are to be found here `https://fasttext.cc/docs/en/crawl-vectors.html`.

between syntax and semantics, find best correlations with human judgments in similar values of $\alpha$ (very small negatives). This indicates that animacy plays the role of a syntactic feature, in this context, analogously to what has been found in the human experiments.

Another striking feature of the results is the steep curve, in both panels, showing big changes as we move from the words of interest to words in the context. Finally, in both cases the best, but still weak, correlations are in a window of negative values. That is, we find the best correlation when the words in question are treated as context for other (unknown) words. In other words, human experimental results have the best correlation with (unknown) words whose paradigmatic context (the second-order context) is defined by the word embeddings. We can conjecture that this indicates that the words in the stimuli sentence (the words in bold in Figure 1), taken as a second-order context, define a lexical semantic field to which the experimental measures are sensitive.[3]

## 5 Prediction in weak islands and object relatives in French and English

While the previous experiments show that even transformed word embeddings do not encode fine-grained quantitative psycholinguistic measures, it is still possible that sentence embeddings can predict the coarser distinctions of qualitative acceptability judgments. Moving away from seeking direct correlations with experimental results to a prediction task that simply models acceptability judgments presents the added advantage that it is easily extended to new languages. The acceptability judgments in these constructions are easily established; in fact, in our case, they match exactly the judgments in French.

### 5.1 Materials and Method

**Sentences**  All French weak islands experimental stimuli used in the previous experiments were translated into English. The translations were literal. They were performed by a bilingual near-native speaker of English. They correspond to sentences established in the literature on weak islands in English.[4]

**Sentence embeddings**  We calculate sentence embeddings for all the sentences. Here, we follow the logic of probing tasks (Conneau et al., 2018). In this set up, single sentence embeddings are classified according to a single grammatical phenomenon. This technique allows the researchers to reach clear and conclusive insights into what information is encoded in the embeddings in a set-up that is agnostic of the architecture that has produced them. Our problem also meets other criteria that have been advocated for probing tasks, some formal and some more subjective. Namely, the domain of linguistic locality of the phenomenon we want to study is a single sentence (as opposed to multi-sentence tasks), and all the sentences are carefully controlled and matched to eliminate sentence length effects, for example.[5] Finally, we agree that probing tasks should address a set of linguistically interesting phenomena. From this standpoint, intervention effects in long-distance dependencies meet the requirement, as one of the core data paradigms definitional of human languages.

We use bag of vectors sentence embeddings for several reasons. First, our testing sentences are carefully constructed minimal pairs where the difference in grammaticality hinges on one lexical difference, which then has in turn syntactic repercussions. By using bag of vectors, we remain as close as possible to the lexical setting of the theoretical definition of intervention, We also differ only minimally from the previous experiment. Second, from a more practical standpoint, bag of vectors have been shown in general, and in probing tasks in particular, to have good performance. Notice also that the choice of not using more context-aware vector representations is voluntary. We want to test the predictive ability of a direct encoding of the linguistic notion of intervener, which is a lexical, non-contextualised notion.

We use BoVfastText,[6] which derives sentence representations by averaging the fastText embeddings of the words they contain.

**Classifiers**  We use a multi-layer perceptron, with four outputs, and two hidden layers of 50 and

---

[3]In future work, this conjecture could be verified by retrieving these unknown words and seeing if a direct correlation is confirmed.

[4]See supplementary materials for all the English datasets discussed in the paper.

[5] Differently from other probing tasks, we work here on a relatively small dataset, but in principle the sentences follow a specific structure that could be easily automated if more data needed to be tested. But the small amount of testing data already gives us an effect.

[6]https://fasttext.cc/docs/en/english-vectors.html

| Label | French | English |
|---|---|---|
| BareA | 0.151 | 0.485 |
| BareI | 0.909 | 0.156 |
| LexA | 0.788 | 0.273 |
| LexI | 0.303 | 0.091 |

(a) Weak islands (Bare= bare wh, Lex= lexically specified, A= animate, I= inanimate).

| Label | French | English |
|---|---|---|
| ORCsing | 0.250 | 0.417 |
| ORCplur | 0.125 | 0.375 |
| CMPsing | 0.291 | 0.291 |
| CMPplur | 0.500 | 0.292 |

(b) Object Relatives (CMP= completive).

Table 1: Percent accuracy predictions.

30 dimensions.[7] We run the training and testing in an $n$-fold cross-validation regime ($n = 33$ for weak islands and 24 for object relatives), where each quadruple of examples is used for testing.

**Dependent variable** We use accuracy as a measure of how much the information in the input embeddings supports the discrimination of the four sentence types in a categorical classifier. This measure is relevant under the assumption that the more acceptable sentences are more easily identified (discriminated from other classes) than less acceptable ones, because acceptable sentences better fit to the grammar. Less acceptable sentences do not fit or even do not belong to the grammar, and as such their classes are more easily confusable, given that the complement of a grammar does not necessarily have distinguishing structured characteristics. So we expect to see higher classification accuracy as the acceptability of the sentence increases.

### 5.2 Predictions and results

The accuracy prediction task corresponds to the structure of the human experiment.

In the materials on weak islands, we have four sentence types (BareA, BareI, LexA, LexI), shorthand for the four cases in which the stimuli had an animate (A) or inanimate (I) intervener and where the long-distance dependency was lexically specified (Lex) or bare (Bare).

Let Acc() be the accuracy of the prediction. Recall that animacy is the property that leads to intervention, and expected degraded performance, so we expect Acc(LexA) < Acc(LexI) and Acc(BareA) < Acc(BareI). Since we know that lexical specification improves acceptability, we expect Acc(LexA) > Acc(BareA) and Acc(LexI) > Acc(BareI).

We can see the results in Table 1, subtable 1a. For French, the prediction on the effect of animacy in the lexically specified case is confirmed, but the others are not. Furthermore, if we calculate the total interaction, we see that lexical specification makes these sentences easier to a greater extent than animacy makes them hard.[8] This result corroborates effects found in human experiments, which found a stronger effect of animacy than lexical specification (Franck et al., 2015; Villata and Franck, 2016). For English, we find that, given the same predictions as above, the prediction for the effect of animacy is confirmed both in bare *wh*-phrases and in lexicalised *wh*-phrases, but the others are not. A total interaction does not confirm the dominant effect of animacy, unlike French. [9]

For object relative clauses, it is a match in number of the relative head and the subject of the relative clause (both singular) that is expected to cause difficulty, compared to a mismatch. Object relative clauses are also compared to completives, where no differences should be found between the two items. So we expect, Acc(ORCsing) < Acc(ORCplur) and Acc(CMPsing) = Acc(CMPplur). Also, Acc(ORCsing) < Acc(CMPsing) and Acc(ORCplur) = Acc(CMPplur). We can see the results in Table 1, subtable 1b. For French, none of the predictions is confirmed, while for English the only confirmed prediction says that *number*, whether singular or plural should be roughly similar in completives, the control case.

More results of this same nature and reaching similar conclusions can be found in the Appendix, for both weak islands and object relative clauses in both English and French. The appendix shows results obtained with a Naive Bayes classifier, thereby also demonstrating that the negative effect is not due to the choice of classifier.

---

[7]Two larger hidden layers of 200 and 100 dimensions also gave similar results

[8](Acc(BareA) − Acc(BareI)) − (Acc(LexA) − Acc(LexI)), we find $(0.909 - 0.788) - (0.151 - 0.303) = 0.121 + 0.152 > 0$.

[9](Acc(BareA) − Acc(BareI)) − (Acc(LexA) − Acc(LexI)), we find $(0.156 - 0.273) - (0.485 - 0.091) == -0.117 - 0.394 < 0$.

# 6 Discussion and conclusions

These results prompt both scientific and methodological considerations. Scientifically, our results lead us to conclude that while current word embeddings encode some notion of similarity, as shown by many experiments on analogical tasks and textual and lexical similarity, they do not, however, encode the notion of similarity that has been shown to be at work in many human experiments and to be definitional in long-distance dependencies.

If our conclusions above are correct, our lack of replication of some of the theoretical predictions and human experiments adds one more discordant element to the complex debate of whether a narrow or broad definition of intervention best explains human judgments and linguistic facts, as discussed by Villata and Franck. The narrow notion of intervention is grammar-based, explains ungrammaticality, for example weak islands, and claims that only morpho-syntactic features are relevant to define intervention (Rizzi, 2004). So, the fact that word embeddings —usage-based representations of the lexical semantics of words— do not correlate with a grammar-based notion of similarity is to be expected, but the fact that object relative clauses where found to exhibit animacy effects in human experiments is not expected.

A broader notion of intervention is defined by cue-based memory based models: these are human sentence processing models that explain difficulty of otherwise grammatical sentences, such as object relatives (Van Dyke and McElree, 2006). In this framework, similarity can take any feature type into account and intervention is a kind of interference at retrieval in memory. This broader approach explains the experimental findings, but would have expected a correlation of word embeddings, which are fundamentally a semantic encoding of the word, with the experimental effects.

Methodologically, we might wonder about the sources of the fluctuation of results, both for long-distance dependence as reported here, and subject verb agreement as reported in other works mentioned in the introduction. Two explanations are possible: the methods are not sound, the fluctuations are to be expected. I very briefly explore both.

Consider the transformations we have applied in section 4. Word embeddings are a merger of many kinds of information and applying post-processing transformations has been argued to tease apart syntactic aspects of the encoding of the notion of similarity from semantic aspects. The notion of 'syntactic' and 'semantic' similarity used in previous work is itself vague and does not refer to any linguistic phenomenon that current linguistic theory (syntactic or semantic) would identify as belonging exclusively to one or other of these levels of representation. Trying to investigate RNN by claiming that certain constructions reflect syntax while other reflect semantics is therefore an ill-defined endeavour (Artetxe et al., 2018). All constructions have a syntax and a semantics and the investigation of what RNN learn can only be done by correlating the predictions of the syntactic or semantic *theory* involved in the construction. To prove this point further, consider the plots in Figure 3. Here, as an abstract exercise, the $\alpha$s have been varied on a much larger range of values than the more limited range of values reported in section 4. The interval of values in section 4 was chosen because it corresponds to previous proposals and because it is more easily interpretable. As it can be seen here, instead, the curves have a dramatic range of correlation values that do not seem to have any correspondence to anything we know about language. We would conclude here that Blackbox investigations must be driven by theory, or at least by precise expectations grounded in well-established linguistic facts, to become interpretable.

On the other hand, we are also at the beginning of this trend of Blackbox investigations. We submit here that these fluctuations are an effect known as the Proteus effect, fluctuations due to the fact that we are in the early stages of this promising avenue of research, due to the fast publishing rate and to the small size of the studies. The Proteus phenomenon—a term coined by Ioannidis and Trikalinos (2005)—describes the effect of rapidly alternating opposite research claims and extremely opposite refutations, particularly during the early accumulation of data. Meta-research and simulations show that first publication of results have a considerably higher chance of being inflated (Ioannidis, 2008), and that small studies have a higher chance of being false positives (Bertamini and Munafò, 2012). We submit, then, that the contradictory results are inevitable incongruities that will be resolved as more studies, large and small, accumulate on these same topics.

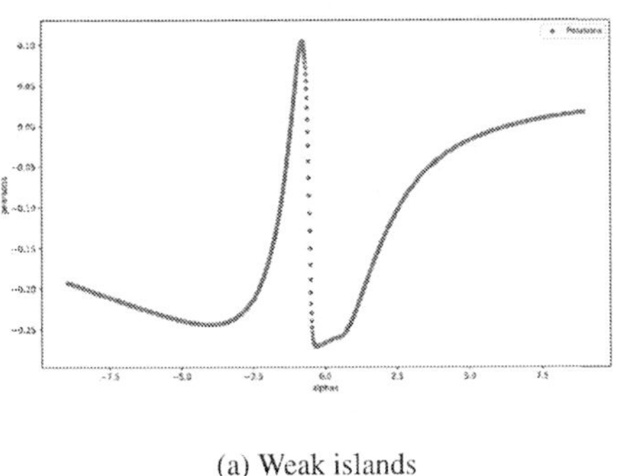
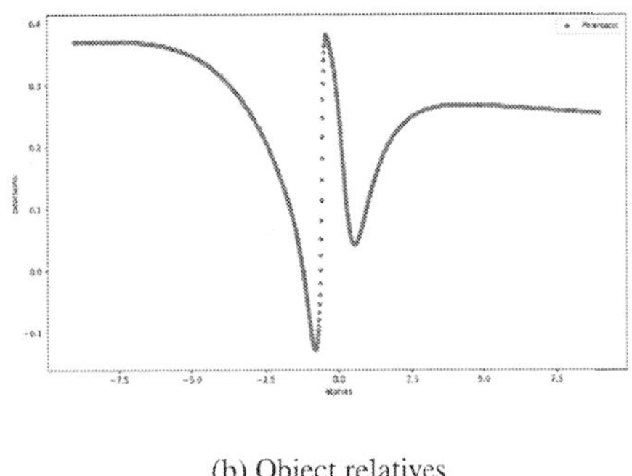

(a) Weak islands        (b) Object relatives

Figure 3: Pairwise correlation (range of value of alpha for transformation: -9 to 9).

## 7 Conclusions

In this work, we have extended previous work on long-distance dependencies applying new vector transformation techniques, extending the investigation to sentence embeddings and to new languages. We confirm previous negative results: word embeddings and sentence embeddings, the representations produced by RNNs, do not unequivocally encode fine-grained linguistic properties of long-distance dependencies. Future work, among many other avenues for extension, will investigate in more detail the limits of vector transformation techniques and extend the work to different vectorial encodings, to more constructions and to new languages.

## Acknowledgments

We thank Julie Franck and Sandra Villata for allowing the use of their French stimuli and their translation in English and Mikel Artexte for useful interactions. All remaining errors and opinions are our own.

## References


Mikel Artetxe, Gorka Labaka, Iñigo Lopez-Gazpio, and Eneko Agirre. 2018. Uncovering divergent linguistic information in word embeddings with lessons for intrinsic and extrinsic evaluation. In *Proceedings of the 22nd Conference on Computational Natural Language Learning, CoNLL 2018, Brussels, Belgium, October 31 - November 1, 2018*, pages 282–291.

Yonatan Belinkov and James Glass. 2019. Analysis methods in neural language processing: A survey. *Transaction of the ACL*, 7:49–72.

Adriana Belletti, Naama Friedmann, Dominique Brunato, and Luigi Rizzi. 2012. Does gender make a difference? Comparing the effect of gender on children's comprehension of relative clauses in Hebrew and Italian. *Lingua*, 122(10):1053–1069.

Anamaria Bentea. 2016. *Intervention effects in language acquisition: the comprehension of A-bar dependencies in French and Romanian.* Ph.D. thesis, University of Geneva.

Marco Bertamini and Marcus R. Munafò. 2012. Bite-size science and its undesired side effects. *Perspectives on Psychological Science*, 7:67–71.

Piotr Bojanowski, Edouard Grave, Armand Joulin, and Tomas Mikolov. 2016. Enriching word vectors with subword information. *CoRR*, abs/1607.04606.

Shammur Absar Chowdhury and Roberto Zamparelli. 2018. RNN simulations of grammaticality judgments on long-distance dependencies. In *Proceedings of the 27th International Conference on Computational Linguistics (COLING'18)*, pages 133–144. Association for Computational Linguistics.

Alexis Conneau, Germán Kruszewski, Guillaume Lample, Loïc Barrault, and Marco Baroni. 2018. What you can cram into a single \$&!#* vector: Probing sentence embeddings for linguistic properties. In *Proceedings of the 56th Annual Meeting of the Association for Computational Linguistics (Volume 1: Long Papers)*, pages 2126–2136. Association for Computational Linguistics.

Julie Franck, Saveria Colonna, and Luigi Rizzi. 2015. Task-dependency and structure dependency in number interference effects in sentence comprehension. *Frontiers in Psychology*, 6.

Naama Friedmann, Adriana Belletti, and Luigi Rizzi. 2009. Relativized relatives: Types of intervention in the acquisition of A-bar dependencies. *Lingua*, 119(1):67 – 88.

Edouard Grave, Piotr Bojanowski, Prakhar Gupta, Armand Joulin, and Tomas Mikolov. 2018. Learning word vectors for 157 languages. In *Proceedings of the International Conference on Language Resources and Evaluation (LREC 2018)*.

Nino Grillo. 2008. *Generalized minimality: Syntactic underspecification in Broca's aphasia*. Ph.D. thesis, University of Utrecht.

Kristina Gulordava, Piotr Bojanowski, Edouard Grave, Tal Linzen, and Marco Baroni. 2018. Colorless green recurrent networks dream hierarchically. In *Proceedings of the 2018 Conference of the North American Chapter of the Association for Computational Linguistics: Human Language Technologies, Volume 1 (Long Papers)*, pages 1195–1205. Association for Computational Linguistics.

John Ioannidis. 2008. Why most discovered true associations are inflated. *Epidemiology*, 19(5):640–648. Doi:10.1097/EDE.0b013e31818131e7.

John Ioannidis and Thomas A. Trikalinos. 2005. Early extreme contradictory estimates may appear in published research: The Proteus phenomenon in molecular genetics research and randomised trials. *Journal of Clinical Epidemiology*, pages 543–549.

Adhiguna Kuncoro, Chris Dyer, John Hale, and Phil Blunsom. 2018. The perils of natural behaviour tests for unnatural models: the case of number agreement. Poster at Learning Language in Humans and Machines (L2HM 2018).

Yair Lakretz, Germán Kruszewski, Theo Desbordes, Dieuwke Hupkes, Stanislas Dehaene, and Marco Baroni. 2019. The emergence of number and syntax units in LSTM language models. *CoRR*, abs/1903.07435.

Tal Linzen, Emmanuel Dupoux, and Yoav Goldberg. 2016. Assessing the ability of LSTMs to learn syntax-sensitive dependencies. *Transactions of the Association for Computational Linguistics*, 4:521–535.

Paola Merlo and Francesco Ackermann. 2018. Vectorial semantic spaces do not encode human judgments of intervention similarity. In *Proceedings of the 22nd Conference on Computational Natural Language Learning, CoNLL 2018, Brussels, Belgium, October 31 - November 1, 2018*, pages 392–401.

Luigi Rizzi. 2004. Locality and left periphery. In Adriana Belletti, editor, *The cartography of syntactic structures*, number 3 in Structures and beyond, pages 223–251. Oxford University Press, New York.

Julie A. Van Dyke and Brian McElree. 2006. Retrieval interference in sentence comprehension. *Journal of memory and language*, 55(2):157–166.

Sandra Villata and Julie Franck. 2016. Semantic similarity effects on weak islands acceptability. In *41st Incontro di Grammatica Generativa Conference*, Perugia, Italy. Https://archive-ouverte.unige.ch/unige:82418.


| Label | Precision | Recall | F-ratio |
|---|---|---|---|
| BareA | 0.257 | 0.625 | 0.365 |
| BareI | 0.196 | 0.350 | 0.252 |
| LexA | 0.454 | 0.062 | 0.110 |
| LexI | 0.238 | 0.065 | 0.102 |

(a) Weak Islands, English.

| Label | Precision | Recall | F-ratio |
|---|---|---|---|
| BareA | 0.707 | 0.854 | 0.773 |
| BareI | 0.410 | 0.854 | 0.555 |
| LexA | 0.181 | 0.054 | 0.084 |
| LexI | 0.340 | 0.205 | 0.256 |

(b) Weak Island, French

Table 2: Results for weak islands (Bare= bare wh, Lex= lexically specified, A= animate, I= inanimate).

Ethan Wilcox, Roger Levy, Takashi Morita, and Richard Futrell. 2018. What do rnn language models learn about filler–gap dependencies? In *Proceedings of the 2018 EMNLP Workshop BlackboxNLP: Analyzing and Interpreting Neural Networks for NLP*, pages 211–221. Association for Computational Linguistics.


## Appendix A: Comparing results across classifiers

As further demonstration of the fluctuating nature of the current results, we report here the same classification experiment reported above, but with a Naive Bayes classifier, and applied to both weak islands and object relative clauses. The classification results averaged over ten trials (same cross-validation settings as above) are shown in Table 2 and Table 3.

Recall that animacy is the property that leads to intervention in weak islands, and expected degraded performance, so we expect that Acc(LexA) < Acc(LexI) and Acc(BareA) < Acc(BareI). Furthermore, Acc(LexA) > Acc(BareA) and Acc(LexI) > Acc(BareI).

For object relative clauses, it is a match in number of the relative head and the subject of the relative clause (both singular) that is expected to cause difficulty, compared to a mismatch. Object relative clauses are also compared to completives, where no differences should be found between the two items. So we expect, Acc(ORCsg) < Acc(ORCpl) and Acc(CMPsg) = Acc(CMPpl). Also, Acc(ORCsg) < Acc(CMPsg) and Acc(ORCpl) = Acc(CMPpl).

Weak islands do not conform to expectations: For English, we can see that neither

| Label | Precision | Recall | F-ratio |
| --- | --- | --- | --- |
| CMPsg | 0.02 | 0.08 | 0.032 |
| CMPpl | 0.17 | 0.125 | 0.14 |
| ORCsg | 0.35 | 0.2 | 0.25 |
| ORCpl | 0.16 | 0.18 | 0.17 |

(a) Object relatives, English

| Label | Precision | Recall | F-ratio |
| --- | --- | --- | --- |
| CMPsg | 0.18 | 0.25 | 0.209 |
| CMPpl | 0.23 | 0.29 | 0.256 |
| ORCsg | 0.105 | 0.10 | 0.102 |
| ORCpl | 0.21 | 0.08 | 0.116 |

(b) Object relatives, French

Table 3: Results for object relatives.

Acc(LexA) < Acc(LexI) nor Acc(BareA) < Acc(BareI) are confirmed. Moreover, Acc(LexA) > Acc(BareA) is not confirmed and neither is Acc(LexI) > Acc(BareI). For French, we can see that Acc(LexA) < Acc(LexI) is confirmed, but Acc(BareA) < Acc(BareI) is not. Moreover, Acc(LexA) > Acc(BareA) is not confirmed and neither is Acc(LexI) > Acc(BareI).

For English Acc(ORCsg) < Acc(ORCpl) is not confirmed and Acc(CMPsg) = Acc(CMPpl) is also not confirmed as the difference is quite significant. Also, Acc(ORCsg) < Acc(CMPsg) is not confirmed but Acc(ORCpl) could be considered not very different from Acc(CMPpl) .

For French, Acc(ORCsg) < Acc(ORCpl) is not confirmed, but Acc(CMPsg) and Acc(CMPpl) are not very different Also, Acc(ORCsg) < Acc(CMPsg) is confirmed but Acc(ORCpl) is smaller than Acc(CMPpl).

## Appendix B: English sentences

**Weak Islands**

1. What model do you wonder what man painted?

2. Who do you wonder who painted?

3. What do you wonder who painted?

4. What landscape do you wonder what man painted?

5. What book do you wonder what student has forgotten?

6. What do you wonder who has forgotten?

7. What friend do you wonder what student has forgotten?

8. Who do you wonder who has forgotten?

9. Who do you wonder who has eaten?

10. What rooster do you wonder what fox has eaten?

11. What do you wonder who has eaten?

12. What cheese do you wonder what fox has eaten?

13. What trousers do you wonder what tailor has looked for?

14. What do wonder who has looked for?

15. Who do you wonder who has looked for?

16. What customer do you wonder what tailor has looked for?

17. Who do you wonder who was looking at?

18. What producer do you wonder what actor was looking at?

19. What do you wonder who was looking at?

20. What do you wonder what actor was looking at?

21. What do you wonder who has brought?

22. What bag do you wonder what traveller has brought?

23. What friend do you wonder what traveler has brought?

24. Who don ou wonder who has brought?

25. What professor do you wonder what student has appreciated?

26. Who do you wonder who has appreciated?

27. What do you wonder who has appreciated?

28. What course do you wonder what student has appreciated?

29. What exam do you wonder what intern has feared?

30. What do you wonder who has feared?

31. What doctor do you wonder what intern has feared?

32. Who do you wonder who has feared?

33. Who do you wonder who has heard?

34. What keeper do you wonder what animal has heard?

35. What noise do you wonder what animal has heard?

36. What do you wonder who has heard?

37. What number do you wonder what baby-sitter has kept?

38. What do you wonder who has kept?

39. Who do you wonder who has kept?

40. What baby do you wonder what baby-sitter has kept?

41. Who do you wonder who has regretted?

42. What colleague do you wonder what director has regretted?

43. What advice do you wonder what counsellor has regretted?

44. What do you wonder who has regretted?

45. What speech do you wonder what guest has listened to?

46. What do you wonder who has listened to?

47. What speaker do you wonder what guest has listened to?

48. Who do you wonder who has listened to?

49. Who do you wonder who has taken pictures of?

50. What model do you wonder what artist has taken pictures of?

51. What painting do you wonder what artist has taken pictures of?

52. What do you wonder who has taken pictures of?

53. What hat do you wonder what designer has chosen?

54. What do you wonder who has chosen?

55. What model do you wonder what designer has chosen?

56. Who do you wonder who has chosen?

57. What customer do you wonder what employee has been waiting for?

58. Who do you wonder who has been waiting for?

59. What do you wonder who has been waiting for?

60. What salary do you wonder what employee has been waiting for?

61. What do you wonder who has appreciated?

62. What gift do you wonder what winner has appreciated?

63. What athlete do you wonder what winner has appreciated?

64. Who don ou wonder who has appreciated?

65. What athlete do you wonder what winner has appreciated?

66. Who do you wonder who has appreciated?

67. What do you wonder who has appreciated?

68. What gift do you wonder what winner has appreciated?

69. What hero do you know what veteran had met?

70. Who do you know who has met?

71. What day ou know who has met?

72. What challenge do you know what veteran has met?

73. What necklace do you know what student has lost?

74. What do you know who has lost?

75. What friend do you know what student has lost?

76. Who do you know who has lost?

77. What actor do you know what viewer loved?

78. Who do you know who loved?

79. What movie do you know what viewer loved?

80. What do you know who loved?

81. What do you know who carried?

82. What suit do you know what singer carried?

83. What fan do you know what singer carried?

84. Who do you know who carried?

85. What bore do you know what pedestrian has found?

86. Who do you know who has found?

87. What do you know who has found?

88. What wallet do you know what pedestrian has found?

89. What do you know who has found?

90. Who do you know who has found?

91. What treasure do you know what child has found?

92. What friend do you know what child has found?

93. Who do you know who has abandoned?

94. What child do you know what man has abandoned?

95. What do you know who has abandoned?

96. What apartment do you know what man has abandoned?

97. What do you know who has filmed?

98. What documentary do you know what cameraman has filmed?

99. Who do you know who has filmed?

100. What actor do you know what cameraman has filmed?

101. What attacker dont you know what man has defeated?

102. Who dont you know who has defeated?

103. What cancer dont you know what man has defeated?

104. What dont you know who has defeated?

105. What dont you know who has kidnapped?

106. What evidence dont you know what kidnapper has concealed?

107. Who dont you know who has kidnapped?

108. What orphan dont you know what kidnapper has concealed?

109. Who dont you know who has left?

110. What friend dont you know what researcher has left?

111. What country dont you know what researcher has left?

112. What dont you know who has left?

113. What dont you know who has followed?

114. What studies dont you know what doctoral student has followed?

115. What intern dont you know what doctoral student has followed?

116. Who dont you know who has followed?

117. Who dont you know who has run over?

118. What pedestrian dont you know what driver has run over?

119. What bicycle dont you know what driver has run over?

120. What dont you know who has run over?

121. What difficulties dont you know what apprentice has met?

122. What dont you know who has met?

123. Who dont you know who has met?

124. What instructor dont you know what apprentice has met?

125. What criminal dont you know what lawyer denounced?

126. Who dont you know who denounced?

127. What dont you know who denounced?

128. What abuse dont you know what lawyer denounced?

129. What dont you know who decorated?

130. What banner dont you know what general decorated?

131. Who dont you know who decorated?

132. What lieutenant dont you know what general decorated?

**Object Relative Clauses**

1. Julia points out to the student that the speaker has been yawning frequently from the beginning.

2. Paul explains to the voter that the politician has been clearly lying since the elections.

3. Sebastian reveals to the patient that the tranquilliser has been acting progressively for a year.

4. Jerome points out to the prisoner that the warden sometimes comes into the courtyard.

5. Charles explains to the victim that the treatment is starting slowly but surely.

6. Benjamin reminds the teen-ager that the educator has been drinking frequently for a few years.

7. Bernard reminds the gamblers that the casino is closing unfortunately very soon.

8. Laura says to the shepherds that the sheep is bleeting stupidly after the shearing.

9. Peter announces to the candidates that the jury will deliberate firmly after the audition.

10. Mark repeats to the people that the unhappiness continues inevitably after the tragedy.

11. Claire reminds the workers that the fireplace has been smoking a lot since the works.

12. Patricia says to the customers that the hat is very pleasing because of the feathers.

13. Fred smiles to the child that the priest has been blessing happily after each service.

14. Lise speaks to the woman whose weight the diet is reducing surprisingly easily.

15. Giles speaks to the worker that the effort has been tiring inevitably with time.

16. Jack thinks of the owner that the stress has been aging prematurely despite the anti-anxiety medications.

17. Patrick thinks of the family that the holidays have been reuniting every year for ten days.

18. Louise smiles to the girl that the witch frightens on purpose for Halloween.

19. Aude is liked by the athletes that the massage relaxes always after the training.

20. Luke thinks of the girls that the seducer has been adressing assiduously for an hour.

21. Anne speaks to the actors that the audience has been applauding frantically after each show.

22. Joan speaks to the neighbours that the excursion has rarely enthused at the end of the year.

23. Joan calls the lawyers that the disappointment embitters inevitably after the trial.

24. Roland smiles to the offenders that the policeman has been investigating secretly for a month.

25. Julia smiles to the students that the speaker has been putting to sleep seriously from the beginning.

26. Paul thinks of the voters that the politician has been frankly disappointing since the elections.

27. Sebastian smiles to the patients that the tranquilliser has been weakening progressively for a year.

28. Jerome talks to the prisoners that the warden sometimes lets out into the courtyard.

29. Charles smiles to the victims that the treatment is curing slowly but surely.

30. Benjamin thinks of the teen-agers that the educator has been beating often for a few years.

31. Bernard reminds the gambler that the casino ruins unfortunately very fast.

32. Laura smiles to the shepherd that the sheep is following stupidly after the shearing.

33. Peter calls the candidate that the jury will firmly wait for after the audition.

34. Mark thinks of the people that the unhappiness unites inevitably after the tragedy.

35. Claire attracts the worker that the fireplace has blackened a lot since the works.

36. Patricia talks to the customer that the hat makes tall because of the feathers.

37. Fred tells the children that the priest has been leaving happily after each service.

38. Lise promises the women that the diet can be managed surprisingly easily.

39. Giles reminds the workers that the effort will double inevitably with time.

40. Jack explains the owners that stress arrives prematurely despite the anti-anxiety medications.

41. Patrick repeats to the families that the holidays last every year for ten days.

42. Louise repeats to the girls that the witch makes grimaces on purpose for Halloween.

43. Aude repeats to the athlete that the massage always begins after the training.

44. Luke tells the girl that the seducer has been chatting untiringly for an hour.

45. Anne reminds the actor that the audience has been laughing frantically after each show.

46. Joan reminds the neighbour that the excursion has rarely failed at the end of the year.

47. Joan reminds the lawyer that the disappointment remains inevitably after the trial.

48. Roland points out to the offender that the policeman has been intervening secretly for a month.

49. Julia points out to the students that the speaker has been yawning frequently from the beginning.

50. Paul explains to the voters that the politician has been clearly lying since the elections.

51. Sebastian reveals to the patients that the tranquilliser has been acting progressively for a year.

52. Jerome points out to the prisoners that the warden sometimes comes into the courtyard.

53. Charles explains to the victims that the treatment is starting slowly but surely.

54. Benjamin reminds the teen-agers that the educator has been drinking frequently for a few years.

55. Bernard reminds the gambler that the casino is closing unfortunately very soon.

56. Laura says to the shepherd that the sheep is bleeting stupidly after the shearing.

57. Peter announces to the candidate that the jury will deliberate firmly after the audition.

58. Mark repeats to the population that the unhappiness continues inevitably after the tragedy.

59. Claire reminds the worker that the fireplace has been smoking a lot since the works.

60. Patricia says to the customer that the hat is very pleasing because of the feathers.

61. Fred smiles to the children that the priest has been blessing happily after each service.

62. Lise speaks to the women whose weight the diet is reducing surprisingly easily.

63. Giles speaks to the workers that the effort has been tiring inevitably with time.

64. Jack thinks of the owners that the stress has been aging prematurely despite the anti-anxiety medications.

65. Patrick thinks of the families that the holidays have been reuniting every year for ten days.

66. Louise smiles to the girls that the witch frightens on purpose for Halloween.

67. Aude is liked by the athlete that the massage relaxes always after the training.

68. Luke thinks of the girl that the seducer has been adressing assiduously for an hour.

69. Anne speaks to the actor that the audience has been applauding frantically after each show.

70. Joan speaks to the neighbour that the excursion has rarely enthused at the end of the year.

71. Joan calls the lawyer that the disappointment embitters inevitably after the trial.

72. Roland smiles to the offender that the policeman has been investigating secretly for a month.

73. Julia smiles to the student that the speaker has been putting to sleep seriously from the beginning.

74. Paul thinks of the voter that the politician has been frankly disappointing since the elections.

75. Sebastian smiles to the patient that the tranquilliser has been weakening progressively for a year.

76. Jerome talks to the prisoner that the warden sometimes lets out into the courtyard.

77. Charles smiles to the victim that the treatment is curing slowly but surely.

78. Benjamin thinks of the teen-ager that the educator has been beating often for a few years.

79. Bernard reminds the gamblers that the casino ruins unfortunately very fast.

80. Laura smiles to the shepherds that the sheep is following stupidly after the shearing.

81. Peter calls the candidates that the jury will firmly wait for after the audition.

82. Mark thinks of the people that the unhappiness unites inevitably after the tragedy.

83. Claire attracts the workers that the fireplace has blackened a lot since the works.

84. Patricia talks to the customers that the hat makes tall because of the feathers.

85. Fred tells the child that the priest has been leaving happily after each service.

86. Lise promises the woman that the diet can be managed surprisingly easily.

87. Giles reminds the worker that the effort will double inevitably with time.

88. Jack explains the owner that stress arrives prematurely despite the anti-anxiety medications.

89. Patrick repeats to the family that the holidays last every year for ten days.

90. Louise repeats to the girl that the witch makes grimaces on purpose for Halloween.

91. Aude repeats to the athletes that the massage always begins after the training.

92. Luke tells the girls that the seducer has been chatting untiringly for an hour.

93. Anne reminds the actors that the audience has been laughing frantically after each show.

94. Joan reminds the neighbours that the excursion has rarely failed at the end of the year.

95. Joan reminds the lawyers that the disappointment remainsinevitably after the trial.

96. Roland points out to the offenders that the policeman has been intervening secretly for a month.

# Derivational Morphological Relations in Word Embeddings


**Tomáš Musil** and **Jonáš Vidra** and **David Mareček**
Charles University, Faculty of Mathematics and Physics
Institute of Formal and Applied Linguistics
Malostranské náměstí 25, 118 00 Prague, Czech Republic
`{musil,vidra,marecek}@ufal.mff.cuni.cz`



## Abstract

Derivation is a type of a word-formation process which creates new words from existing ones by adding, changing or deleting affixes. In this paper, we explore the potential of word embeddings to identify properties of word derivations in the morphologically rich Czech language. We extract derivational relations between pairs of words from DeriNet, a Czech lexical network, which organizes almost one million Czech lemmata into derivational trees. For each such pair, we compute the difference of the embeddings of the two words, and perform unsupervised clustering of the resulting vectors. Our results show that these clusters largely match manually annotated semantic categories of the derivational relations (e.g. the relation 'bake–baker' belongs to category 'actor', and a correct clustering puts it into the same cluster as 'govern–governor').


## 1 Introduction

Word embeddings are a way of representing discrete words in a continuous space. Embeddings are used in neural networks trained for various tasks, e.g. in neural machine translation (NMT), or can be pre-trained in various versions of language models to be used as continuous representations of words for other tasks. One of the most popular frameworks for training word embeddings is word2vec (Mikolov et al., 2013).

In this paper, we examine whether the word embeddings (trained on the whole words, not using any subword units or individual characters) capture derivational relations. We do this to better understand what different neural networks represent about words and to provide a base for further development of derivational networks.

Derivation is a type of word-formation process which creates new words from existing ones by

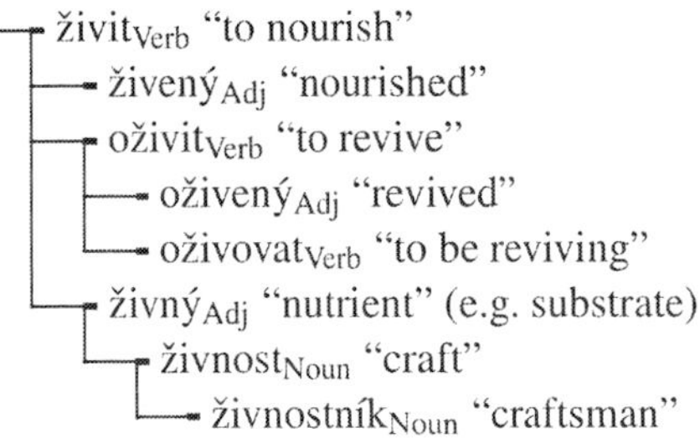


Figure 1: An excerpt from a derivational family rooted in the word "živit" (to nourish, to feed). Note that the word "oživený" (revived, rejuvenated), which can be derived from either "oživit" (to revive) or "živený" (nourished, fed), is arbitrarily connected only to the former, in order to simplify the derivational family to a rooted tree.

adding, changing or deleting affixes. For example, the word "collide" can be used as a base for deriving e.g. the words "collider" or "collision". The derived word "collision" can be, in turn, used as a base for "collisional".

Words derived from a single root create derivational families, which can be approximated by directed acyclic graphs or (with some loss of information) trees; see Figure 1 for an example.

Derivational relations have two sides: form-based and semantic. For a pair of words to be considered derivationally related, the two words must be related both by their phonological or orthographical forms and by their meaning.

## 2 Related work

We have not found any prior work aimed specifically at derivational relations in word embeddings.

Cotterell and Schütze (2018) present a model of the semantics and structure of derivationally complex words. Our work differs in that we are examining how are derivational relations represented in preexisting applications.

173


*Proceedings of the Second BlackboxNLP Workshop on Analyzing and Interpreting Neural Networks for NLP*, pages 173–180
Florence, Italy, August 1, 2019. ©2019 Association for Computational Linguistics

Gladkova et al. (2016) detect morphological and semantic relations (including some derivational relations) with word embeddings. Their approach is analogy-based and they conclude that their "experiments show that derivational and lexicographic relations remain a major challenge".

Gábor et al. (2017) explore vector spaces for semantic relations, using unsupervised clustering. They evaluate the clustering on 9 semantic relation classes. Our approach is similar, but we focus on derivational relations.

Soricut and Och (2015) use word embeddings to induce morphological segmentation in an unsupervised manner. Some of the relations between words that this approach implicitly uses are derivational.

## 3 Data

In this section, we describe the network of derivational relations and the corpora used in our experiments.

### 3.1 DeriNet

There are several large networks of derivational relations available for use in research, e.g. CELEX for Dutch, English and German (Baayen et al., 1995), Démonette for French (Hathout and Namer, 2014), DeriNet for Czech (Ševčíková and Žabokrtský, 2014) or DErivBase for German (Zeller et al., 2014). A more complete listing was published by Kyjánek (2018).

For our research, we chose to use the DeriNet-1.6 network mainly due to its large size – with over a million lemmata (citation forms), it is over three times larger than the second largest resource listed by Kyjánek (2018), DErivBase with 280,336 lemmata. Also, the authors are native speakers of Czech, which was necessary for the annotation of derivation classes (see Section 4 below). Large corpora are available for Czech (Bojar et al., 2016; Hnátková et al., 2014), which we need for training the word embeddings.

DeriNet is a network which approximates derivational families using trees – the lemmata it contains are annotated with a single derivational parent or nothing in case the word is either not derived or a parent has not been assigned yet. It contains 1,025,095 lemmata connected by 803,404 relations.

There is a fine line between derivation and inflection and in general, these processes are hard to separate from each other (see e.g. ten Hacken, 2014). Both change base words using affixes, but they differ in the type of the outcome: derivation creates new words, inflection only creates forms of the base word. DeriNet differentiates derivation from inflection the same way the Czech morphological tool MorphoDiTa (Straková et al., 2014) does – it considers the processes handled by the MorphoDiTa tool to be inflectional and other affixations derivational. This is in line with the Czech linguistic tradition (Dokulil et al., 1986), except perhaps for the handling of the two main borderline cases, whose categorization varies: negation (considered inflectional by us) and verbal aspect changes (considered derivational).

### 3.2 Word Embeddings

In our experiments, we compare the word embeddings obtained by the standard word2vec skip-gram model (Mikolov et al., 2013) with word embeddings learned when training three different neural machine translation (NMT) models (Sutskever et al., 2014; Bahdanau et al., 2015; Vaswani et al., 2017). The size of word embeddings is 512 for all the models.

NMT models are trained between English and Czech in both directions. We use the CzEng 1.6 parallel corpus (Bojar et al., 2016), section *c-fiction* (78 million tokens) and the Neural Monkey toolkit (Helcl et al., 2018)[1] for training the models. We experiment with three architectures:

- *RNN*: a simple recurrent neural (RNN) architecture (Sutskever et al., 2014) without attention mechanism, LSTM size 1,024

- *RNN+a*: RNN architecture with attention mechanism (Bahdanau et al., 2015), and

- *Transf.*: the Transformer (big) architecture (Vaswani et al., 2017) with 6 layers, hidden size 4,096 and 16 attention heads.

Unlike the standard setting in which embeddings of the source and the target words are shared in a common vector space, we use two separated dictionaries (each containing 25,000 word forms). We also do not use any kind of sub-word units. By this setting, we assure that the word vectors are not influenced by any other words that do not belong to the examined language. We extract the encoder word-embeddings from

---

[1]https://github.com/ufal/neuralmonkey

Czech-English NMT model and the decoder word-embeddings from the English-Czech model.

The word2vec system is trained on the Czech National Corpus (Hnátková et al., 2014), version *syn 4*, which has 4.6 billion tokens. It is a common practice (Mikolov et al., 2013) to normalize the resulting vectors, so that the length of each vector is equal to 1. We report results for both normalized and non-normalized vectors. In order to compare word2vec model with NMT models, we also train word2vec on the Czech part of the data used for training the NMT models.

All the word embeddings are trained on the word forms. To assign an embedding to the lemma from DeriNet, we simply select the embedding of the word form which is the same as the given lemma.

## 4 Annotation of Derivational Relations

The derivational relations in DeriNet are not labelled in any way. In this section, we describe a simple method of automatic division of relations into *derivation types* according to changes in prefixes and suffixes and then manual merging of these types into *derivation classes*.

When assigning a derivation type to a relation, we first identify the longest common substring of the two related words. For instance, for the relation "padat → padnout", the longest common substring is "pad". Then, we identify prefixes and suffixes using the '+' sign for addition and '-' sign for deletion. A sign after the string indicates a prefix and a sign before the string indicates a suffix. Our example "padat → padnout" would therefore belong to the derivation type "-at +nout", which means deleting the suffix "at" and adding the suffix "nout". Derivation type "na+" means to add the prefix "na", etc.

When applied on the DeriNet relations, we identified 5,371 derivation types in total. We selected only 71 most frequent types (only those that have at least 250 instances in DeriNet).[2] After that, two annotators[3] manually merged the 71 derivation types into 21 classes. The classes of derivations are listed in Table 1. The class *super+* contains derivations from nouns to nouns and from adjectives to adjectives. Except for insignificant

noise in the data, each of the rest of the classes contain only derivations for one POS pair.

The classes were designed in a way to separate different meanings of derivations where possible, and keep different types with the same meaning together (e.g. '+ová' and '-a +ová', which derive feminine surnames).

## 5 Unsupervised Clustering

We want to know whether and how the derivational relations are captured in the embedding space. We hypothetize that in that case *the differences between embedding vectors* for the words in a derivational relation would cluster according to the classes we defined.

We perform unsupervised clustering of such differences using three algorithms:

- **kmeans**: K-means algorithm (MacQueen, 1967),[4]
- **agg**: Hierarchical agglomerative clustering using Euclidean distance and Ward's linkage criterion (Joe H. Ward, 1963),[5]
- **agg (cos)**: The same hierarchical agglomerative clustering, but using cosine distance instead of Euclidean.

For each word pair $W_1$ and $W_2$, where $W_1$ is the derivational parent of $W_2$ and their embeddings $v_1$ and $v_2$, the clustering algorithm only gets the difference vector $d = v_2 - v_1$. The information about the word forms and their derivation type is only used in evaluation.

We evaluate the clustering quality by homogeneity (H), completeness (C) and V-measure (V) (Rosenberg and Hirschberg, 2007). These are entropy based methods, which can be compared across any number of clusters. Homogeneity is a measure of the ratio of instances of a single class pertaining to a single cluster. Completeness measures the ratio of the member of a given class that is assigned to the same cluster. V-measure is computed as the harmonic mean of homogeneity and completeness scores.

Following Gábor et al. (2017), we also report the accuracy (A) that would be achieved by the clustering if we assigned every cluster to the class that is most frequent in this cluster and then used the clustering as a classifier. The number of

---

[2] We count only such relations, for which both the lemmata occur at least 5 times in the Czech National Corpus.

[3] The annotators are both native speakers of Czech and they worked together in one shared document.

[4] We used standard Euclidean distance. The cosine distance does not work at all.

[5] We experiment also with other linking criteria, however, they performed much worse compared to the Ward's criterion.

| POS | class | syntactic change |
| --- | --- | --- |
| A→D | adjective→adverb | -ý +y, -í +ě, -ý +ě, -ý +e |
| A→N | designation | -ý +ec, -ý +ka |
| A→N | feature | -í +ost, -ý +ost |
| A→N | subject | -ký +tví |
| N→A | pertaining to | +ový, -a +ový, +ní, -a +ní, -ce +ční, +ný, +ský, -e +cký, -ka +cký |
| N→A | possessive | +ův, -a +in, -o +ův, -ek +kův, -a +ův |
| N→N | diminutization | +ek, -k +ček |
| N→N | instrument / scientist | -ie |
| N→N | man→woman | -a +ová, +ka, +ová, +vá, -ý +á, -ík +ice |
| N→N | man→woman / diminutization | -a +ka |
| N→N/A→A | super | super+ |
| N→V | noun→verb | +ovat |
| V→A | ability | +elný |
| V→A | acting | -it +ící, -ovat +ující, -t +jící |
| V→A | general property | -t +vý |
| V→A | patient | -t +ný, -it +ený, -it +ěný, -nout +lý, -t +lý, -out +utý |
| V→A | purpose | -t +cí |
| V→N | actor | +el, -t +č |
| V→N | nominalization | -t +ní, -at +ání, -it +ení, -it +ění, -out +utí, -ovat +ace |
| V→V | imperfectivization | -at +ávat, -it +ovat |
| V→V | perfectivization | -at +nout, do+, na+, o+, od+, po+, pro+, pře+, při+, roz+, u+, vy+, z+, za+ |

Table 1: Classes of Czech derivations.

| Method | cls | H | C | V | A |
|---|---|---|---|---|---|
| *normalized:* | | | | | |
| kmeans | 9 | 67.77 | 56.44 | **61.59** | **77.00** |
| agg | 10 | 62.30 | 52.88 | 57.20 | 72.81 |
| agg (cos) | 8 | 38.90 | 63.06 | 48.12 | 47.48 |
| *not normalized:* | | | | | |
| agg (cos) | 8 | 37.93 | 64.97 | 47.90 | 46.38 |
| agg | 9 | 41.19 | 39.92 | 40.54 | 50.09 |
| kmeans | 7 | 39.92 | 37.38 | 38.61 | 46.92 |

Table 2: Comparison of different clustering methods on differences of normalized and non-normalized word-vectors trained on Czech National Corpus and clustering into 21 clusters. The results are ordered according to V-measure.

| model | clust. | H | C | V | A |
|---|---|---|---|---|---|
| baseline | 15 | 3.79 | 2.70 | 3.15 | 30.82 |
| word2vec | 15 | 75.98 | 57.82 | **65.66** | 83.06 |
| baseline | 20 | 5.12 | 3.30 | 4.01 | 31.32 |
| word2vec | 20 | 77.00 | 54.04 | 63.50 | **84.26** |
| baseline | 21 | 5.31 | 3.37 | 4.12 | 30.87 |
| word2vec | 21 | 77.50 | 53.17 | 63.07 | 84.12 |
| baseline | 22 | 5.49 | 3.43 | 4.22 | 30.98 |
| word2vec | 22 | 77.07 | 52.15 | 62.20 | 83.97 |
| baseline | 25 | 6.13 | 3.68 | 4.60 | 31.41 |
| word2vec | 25 | 80.20 | 53.11 | 63.89 | 87.37 |

Table 3: Effect of number of clusters with K-means (averaged over 10 runs).

classes (cls) shows how many classes were assigned to at least one of the clusters.

## 6 Results

The results on the vectors trained on Czech National Corpus and comparison of normalized and non-normalized versions are summarized in Table 2. We can see that the normalization helps both clustering methods significantly. The best method, i.e. the K-means used on the normalized word vectors is used in the next experiments.

In Table 3, we examine the effect of the number of clusters on the clustering quality. We compare our models to the baseline, in which each derivation pair is assigned to a random cluster. The table shows that regardless of the number of clusters, the clustering on the word2vec embeddings performs better than the random baseline. It shows that as we allow the K-means algorithm to form more clusters, the homogeneity increases and the completeness decreases. The V-measure is highest

| model | cls | H | C | V | A |
|---|---|---|---|---|---|
| word2vec | 7.9 | 77.53 | 53.70 | **63.45** | **84.18** |
| RNN dec. | 6.8 | 73.09 | 52.20 | 60.89 | 83.70 |
| RNN+a enc. | 6.4 | 59.44 | 44.92 | 51.14 | 76.10 |
| Transf. enc. | 6.4 | 60.30 | 44.24 | 51.02 | 78.29 |
| RNN+a dec. | 6.8 | 60.94 | 40.25 | 48.48 | 76.40 |
| RNN enc. | 6.4 | 51.90 | 45.13 | 48.25 | 70.49 |
| Transf. dec. | 5.5 | 44.21 | 30.56 | 36.14 | 63.41 |
| baseline | 2.8 | 5.37 | 3.41 | 4.17 | 31.15 |
| POS baseline | 8 | 52.63 | 100.00 | **68.97** | 45.83 |

Table 4: Results on vectors learned by the NMT models compared to word2vec. K-means clustering with 21 clusters. The results are averaged over 10 independent runs.

with the lowest number of clusters. This may be because the clusters are of uneven size. The accuracy on the word2vec model embeddings is highest around the number of clusters that corresponds to the number of classes in the data.

Table 4 presents the results of clustering the differences of embedding vectors from NMT models. The *cls* columns shows how many different classes are assigned. Because some classes are more frequent than others, they may form the majority in multiple clusters. This is why random baseline assigns less than 3 different classes on average. We see that word2vec (trained on the Czech side of the parallel corpus) captures more information about derivations than NMT models. RNN models store more information in the embeddings if they do not utilize the attention mechanism. Even less information is stored in the embeddings by the Transformer architecture. This is probably because while in attention-less model the embedding is the only set of parameters directly associated with the given word, in the attention model the information can be split between embeddings and the attention weights. The transformer architecture with residual connections has even more parameters associated with a given word. Decoder in general stores more information about relation between words in the embeddings than encoder, presumably because it partially supplies the role of a language model.

We also evaluated clustering by POS tags (*POS baseline* in Table 4), where we created 8 clusters based on the POS tags of the parent and child words in the derivational relation. This clustering has a high V-measure, because its completeness is 100 % (the *super+* class is not present in the NMT data and for all the other classes it holds that each member of a class has the same parent-child POS tags pair). But it has lower accuracy than all the other models (except for the random baseline), showing that the unsupervised clustering does more than just clustering by POS.

The data naturally contains classes with significant differences in size. To prevent the small classes from being underrepresented, we also evaluated the clustering on a dataset, where the same number of derivation pairs was sampled from each class. Results for the experiment with classes of the same size are listed in Table 5. The results show that the classification does not rely only on changes of part-of-speech. Both *imperfectization* and *perfectivization* classses are classified well (97 % precision, 83 % recall and 93 % precision, 66 % recall respectively), even though they are both derivation from verbs to verbs. The only classes that have both precision and recall under 50 % are those being confused with *diminutization*: *man → woman* shares one common derivation type with *diminutization*, and the class *super*, which contains only the prefix "super" and is therefore opposite to *diminutization*, sharing the same semantic axis.

## 7 Conclusion

Our results show that word-level word embeddings capture information about semantic classes of derivational relations between words, despite not having any information about the orthography or morphological makeup of the words, and therefore not knowing about the formal relation between the words.

It is possible to cluster differences between embeddings in derivational relations, and the assigned clusters correspond to the semantic classes of the relations. The word2vec embeddings generally result in a better clustering than embeddings from the NMT models, and embeddings from the decoder of a plain RNN model perform better than those from NMT models with attention. All these methods outperform a random-assignment clustering baseline and POS clustering baseline.

## Acknowledgments

This work has been supported by the grant 18-02196S of the Czech Science Foundation. This study was supported by the Charles University Grant Agency (project No. 1176219). This research was partially supported by SVV project number 260 453. This work has been using language resources and tools developed, stored and distributed by the LINDAT/CLARIN project of the Ministry of Education, Youth and Sports of the Czech Republic (project LM2015071).

## References

R. Harald Baayen, Richard Piepenbrock, and Leon Gulikers. 1995. The CELEX lexical database (CD-ROM).

Dzmitry Bahdanau, Kyunghyun Cho, and Yoshua Bengio. 2015. Neural machine translation by jointly learning to align and translate. In *3rd International Conference on Learning Representations, ICLR 2015, San Diego*.

Ondřej Bojar, Ondřej Dušek, Tom Kocmi, Jindřich Libovický, Michal Novák, Martin Popel, Roman Sudarikov, and Dušan Variš. 2016. CzEng 1.6: Enlarged Czech-English Parallel Corpus with Processing Tools Dockered. In *Text, Speech, and Dialogue: 19th International Conference, TSD 2016*, number 9924 in Lecture Notes in Computer Science, pages 231–238, Cham / Heidelberg / New York / Dordrecht / London. Masaryk University, Springer International Publishing.

Ryan Cotterell and Hinrich Schütze. 2018. Joint semantic synthesis and morphological analysis of the derived word. *Transactions of the Association of Computational Linguistics*, 6:33–48.

Miloš Dokulil, Karel Horálek, Jiřina Hůrková, Miloslava Knappová, Jan Petr, and others. 1986. *Mluvnice češtiny (1)*, 1 edition. Academia, Prague, Czech Republic.

Kata Gábor, Haïfa Zargayouna, Isabelle Tellier, Davide Buscaldi, and Thierry Charnois. 2017. Exploring vector spaces for semantic relations. In *Proceedings of the 2017 Conference on Empirical Methods in Natural Language Processing*, pages 1814–1823.

Anna Gladkova, Aleksandr Drozd, and Satoshi Matsuoka. 2016. Analogy-based detection of morphological and semantic relations with word embeddings: what works and what doesn't. In *Proceedings of the NAACL Student Research Workshop*, pages 8–15.

Pius ten Hacken. 2014. *The Oxford Handbook of Derivational Morphology*, Oxford Handbooks in Linguistics, chapter Delineating Derivation and Inflection. Oxford University Press, Oxford, United Kingdom.

Nabil Hathout and Fiammetta Namer. 2014. Démonette, a French derivational morpho-semantic network. *Linguistic Issues in Language Technology (LiLT)*, 11:125–168.

| Derivation class | precision | recall |
| --- | --- | --- |
| ability | 70.71 | 68.96 |
| acting | 47.99 | 61.92 |
| actor | 63.03 | 60.00 |
| adjective→adverb | 87.72 | 28.00 |
| designation | 50.00 | 66.32 |
| diminutization | 24.09 | 42.40 |
| feature | 81.29 | 76.80 |
| general property | 63.22 | 69.84 |
| imperfectivization | 97.00 | 82.64 |
| instrument / scientist | 97.46 | 70.56 |
| man→woman | 98.01 | 62.96 |
| man→woman / diminutization | 34.88 | 47.52 |
| nominalization | 65.39 | 55.92 |
| noun→verb | 96.71 | 77.52 |
| patient | 47.20 | 51.92 |
| perfectivization | 92.85 | 66.48 |
| pertaining to | 36.85 | 52.88 |
| possessive | 65.29 | 78.24 |
| purpose | 52.33 | 31.44 |
| subject | 69.55 | 84.40 |
| super | 31.98 | 26.40 |

Table 5: Precision and recall for the derivation classes. We sampled 250 examples for each class from the data and clustered them with K-means on word2vec embeddings trained on the ČNK. Results presented here are averaged over 5 runs.


Jindřich Helcl, Jindřich Libovický, Tom Kocmi, Tomáš Musil, Ondřej Cífka, Dušan Variš, and Ondřej Bojar. 2018. Neural monkey: The current state and beyond. In *The 13th Conference of The Association for Machine Translation in the Americas, Vol. 1: MT Researchers' Track*, pages 168–176, Stroudsburg, PA, USA. The Association for Machine Translation in the Americas, The Association for Machine Translation in the Americas.

Milena Hnátková, Michal Kren, Pavel Procházka, and Hana Skoumalová. 2014. The syn-series corpora of written czech. In *LREC*, pages 160–164.

Jr. Joe H. Ward. 1963. Hierarchical grouping to optimize an objective function. 58(301):236–244.

Lukáš Kyjánek. 2018. Morphological resources of derivational word-formation relations. Technical Report TR-2018-61, Charles University, Faculty of Mathematics and Physics, Institute of Formal and Applied Linguistics, Prague, Czech Republic.

J. MacQueen. 1967. Some methods for classification and analysis of multivariate observations. In *Proceedings of the Fifth Berkeley Symposium on Mathematical Statistics and Probability, Volume 1: Statistics*, pages 281–297, Berkeley, Calif. University of California Press.

Tomas Mikolov, Kai Chen, Greg Corrado, and Jeffrey Dean. 2013. Efficient estimation of word representations in vector space. *arXiv preprint arXiv:1301.3781*.

Andrew Rosenberg and Julia Hirschberg. 2007. V-measure: A conditional entropy-based external cluster evaluation measure. In *Proceedings of the 2007 joint conference on empirical methods in natural language processing and computational natural language learning (EMNLP-CoNLL)*.

Magda Ševčíková and Zdeněk Žabokrtský. 2014. Word-formation network for Czech. In *Proceedings of the 9th International Conference on Language Resources and Evaluation (LREC 2014)*, pages 1087–1093, Reykjavík, Iceland. European Language Resources Association.

Radu Soricut and Franz Och. 2015. Unsupervised morphology induction using word embeddings. In *Proceedings of the 2015 Conference of the North American Chapter of the Association for Computational Linguistics: Human Language Technologies*, pages 1627–1637.

Jana Straková, Milan Straka, and Jan Hajič. 2014. Open-Source Tools for Morphology, Lemmatization, POS Tagging and Named Entity Recognition. In *Proceedings of 52nd Annual Meeting of the Association for Computational Linguistics: System Demonstrations*, pages 13–18, Baltimore, Maryland, USA. Association for Computational Linguistics.

Ilya Sutskever, Oriol Vinyals, and Quoc V Le. 2014.
Sequence to sequence learning with neural networks. In *Advances in neural information processing systems*, pages 3104–3112.

Ashish Vaswani, Noam Shazeer, Niki Parmar, Jakob
Uszkoreit, Llion Jones, Aidan N Gomez, Łukasz
Kaiser, and Illia Polosukhin. 2017. Attention is all
you need. In *Advances in Neural Information Processing Systems*, pages 5998–6008.

Britta Zeller, Sebastian Padó, and Jan Šnajder. 2014.
Towards semantic validation of a derivational lexicon. In *Proceedings of COLING 2014, the 25th International Conference on Computational Linguistics: Technical Papers*, pages 1728–1739. Dublin
City University and Association for Computational
Linguistics.

# Hierarchical Representation in Neural Language Models: Suppression and Recovery of Expectations

**Ethan Wilcox**[1], **Roger Levy**[2], and **Richard Futrell**[3]

[1]Department of Linguistics, Harvard University, `wilcoxeg@g.harvard.edu`
[2]Department of Brain and Cognitive Sciences, MIT, `rplevy@mit.edu`
[3]Department of Language Science, UC Irvine, `rfutrell@uci.edu`



## Abstract

Deep learning sequence models have led to a marked increase in performance for a range of Natural Language Processing tasks, but it remains an open question whether they are able to induce proper hierarchical generalizations for representing natural language from linear input alone. Work using artificial languages as training input has shown that LSTMs are capable of inducing the stack-like data structures required to represent context-free and certain mildly context-sensitive languages (Weiss et al., 2018)—formal language classes which correspond in theory to the hierarchical structures of natural language. Here we present a suite of experiments probing whether neural language models trained on linguistic data induce these stack-like data structures and deploy them while incrementally predicting words. We study two natural language phenomena: center embedding sentences and syntactic island constraints on the filler–gap dependency. In order to properly predict words in these structures, a model must be able to temporarily suppress certain expectations and then recover those expectations later, essentially pushing and popping these expectations on a stack. Our results provide evidence that models can successfully suppress and recover expectations in many cases, but do not fully recover their previous grammatical state.


## 1 Introduction

Deep learning sequence models such as RNNs (Elman, 1990; Hochreiter and Schmidhuber, 1997) have led to a marked increase in performance for a range of Natural Language Processing tasks (Jozefowicz et al., 2016; Dai et al., 2019), but it remains an open question whether they are able to induce hierarchical generalizations from linear input alone. Answering this question is important both for technical outcomes—models with explicit hierarchical structure show performance

gains, at least when training on relatively small datasets (Choe and Charniak, 2016; Dyer et al., 2016; Kuncoro et al., 2016)—and for the scientific aim of understanding what biases, learning objectives and training regimes led to human-like linguistic knowledge. Previous work has approached this question by either examining models' internal state (Weiss et al., 2018; Mareček and Rosa, 2018) or by studying model behavior (Elman, 1991; Linzen et al., 2016; Futrell et al., 2019; McCoy et al., 2018).

For this latter approach, much work has assessed sensitivity to hierarchy by examining whether the expectations associated with long-distance dependencies can be maintained even in the presence of intervening distractor words (Gulordava et al., 2018; Marvin and Linzen, 2018). For example, Linzen et al. (2016) fed RNNs with the prefix *The keys to the cabinet. . . .* If models assigned higher probability to the grammatical continuation *are* over the ungrammatical continuation *is*, they can be said to have learned the correct structural relationship between the subject and the verb, ignoring the syntactically-irrelevant singular distractor, *the cabinet*. Work in this paradigm has uncovered a complex pattern in terms of what specific hierarchical structures are and are not represented by neural language models.

At the same time, work using artificial languages as input has demonstrated that LSTMs are capable of inducing the data structures required to produce hierarchically-structured sequences. For example, Weiss et al. (2018) showed that LSTMs can learn to produce strings of the form $a^n b^n$, corresponding to context-free languages (Chomsky, 1956), and $a^n b^n c^n$, corresponding to mildly context-sensitive languages. Producing these strings requires a stack-like data structure where some number of *a*s are pushed onto the stack so that the same number of *b*s can be popped from




*Proceedings of the Second BlackboxNLP Workshop on Analyzing and Interpreting Neural Networks for NLP*, pages 181–190
Florence, Italy. August 1, 2019. ©2019 Association for Computational Linguistics

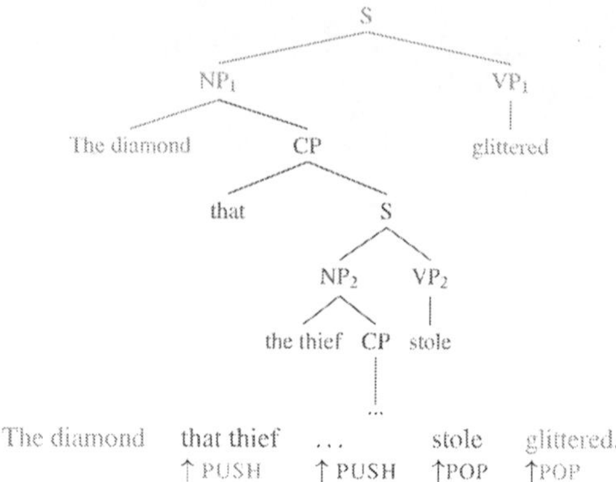



Figure 1: Anatomy of a center embedding sentence. At each point marked PUSH, comprehenders need to push the expectations generated by the subject noun onto a stack-like data structure, and suppress those expectations going forward. At the points marked POP, they must recover those expectations.

it. The hierarchical structures of natural language are widely believed to be mildly context-sensitive (Shieber, 1985; Weir, 1988; Seki et al., 1991; Joshi and Schabes, 1997; Kuhlmann, 2013), so this result shows that LSTMs are practically capable of inducing the proper data structures to handle the hierarchical structure of natural language.

What remains to be seen in a general way is that LSTMs induce and use these structures when trained on natural language input, rather than artificial language input. In this work, we present two suites of experiments that probe for evidence of hierarchical generalizations using two linguistic structures: **center embedding sentences** and **syntactic island constraints** on the filler–gap dependency. These structures exemplify context-free hierarchical structure in natural language. In order to correctly predict words in these structures, a model must use something like a stack data structure: certain expectations must be temporarily suppressed (pushed onto a stack), then recovered later at the right time and in the right order (popped from the stack in last-in-first-out order), as shown in Figure 1.

For both of these contexts we assess how well RNNs can suppress local expectations within intervening blocking-structures and recover expectations on the far side. Success at these tasks would provide evidence that models not only ignore intervening material, but modulate and recover local expectations based on relative location

within a syntactic structure.

**Center embeddings** are sentences in which a clause is embedded within the center of another clause, such that the expectations based on the external clause must be temporarily suppressed during the internal clause, and then recovered once the internal clause is complete. Such sentences were used as the original argument that natural language is not a regular language, but rather at least context-free (Chomsky, 1956). We find that neural language models can successfully suppress and recover expectations in sentences with two-layer embedding depth, but their accuracy depends on the particular lexical items used.

**Syntactic Islands** are structural configurations that block the filler–gap dependency, which is the dependency between a wh-word, such as *who* or *what*, and a gap, which is an empty syntactic position. Using controlled experimental material, we find that models are able to suppress expectations for gaps inside two island constructions and partially recover them on the far side. However, the recovered expectation is far weaker than in non-island sentences and only robust in one of the models tested. Together, both experiments provide new evidence that RNN language models can approximate a soft notion of hierarchy to drive predictions, suppressing local expectations in some contexts and reactivating them based on relative syntactic position.

Overall our results show that the LSTMs tested have learned an approximate stack-like data structure to predict natural language, but the deployment of this structure depends on the particular lexical items used, and the recovery of expectations is often imperfect, especially for structures requiring deep stacks.

## 2   Experimental Methodology

In this work, we adapt psycholinguistic experimental techniques for neural model assessment. In this paradigm, neural models are fed hand-crafted sentences designed to belie underlying network knowledge. Following standard practice in psycholinguistics, statistical significance is derived from linear mixed-effects models (Baayen et al., 2008), with sum-coded fixed-effect predictors and maximal random slope structure (Barr et al., 2013). This method permits us to factor out by-item variation and focus on differences in model behavior on materials differing only in the linguistic features of critical interest. [1]

## 2.1 Neural Models Tested

We study the behavior of two **LSTM** Language Models, one **Transformer** model and one baseline **N-gram** model, all trained on English text. The first LSTM is the "BIG LSTM+CNN Inputs" from (Jozefowicz et al., 2016), which we will refer to as the *Google Model*. It was trained on the One Billion Word benchmark (Chelba et al., 2013), with two hidden layers of 8196 per layer and uses Convolutional Neural Net (CNN) character embeddings as input. The second LSTM model is the best-performing LSTM presented in the supplementary materials of Gulordava et al. (2018), which we will refer to as the *Gulordava Model*. It is much smaller, with 650 hidden units per layer, and was trained on 90-million words of Wikipedia. The Google model is current state-of-the art for an LSTM model unenriched with structural supervision, and the Gulordava model has been assessed extensively (e.g. Gulordava et al. 2018; Futrell et al. 2018; Wilcox et al. 2018; Giulianelli et al. 2018). The transformer model used here is the one presented in Dai et al. (2019). It was trained on the Billion Word Benchmark and has 0.8 Billion parameters. The baseline is a 5-gram language model with Kneser-Ney smoothing, trained on the British National Corpus (Leech, 1992) using SLIRM V1.5.7 (Stolcke, 2002).

## 2.2 Dependent Measure: Surprisal

We assess model behavior by measuring the **surprisal values** RNN language models assign to each word in a given sentence. Surprisal is the inverse log probability of a word given its context:

$$S(x_i) = -\log_2 p(x_i|h_{i-1}),$$

In this case, $x_i$ is the current word and $h_{i-1}$ is the RNN's hidden state before processing $x_i$. The probability is calculated from the RNN's softmax layer, and the logarithm is taken in base 2 so that the surprisal is measured in bits. The surprisal at a certain word tells us the extent to which that word is expected under the language model's probability distribution. There is a strong tradition linking surprisal values derived from language models to psycholinguistic metrics, such as reading times in

humans (Hale, 2001; Levy, 2008; Smith and Levy, 2013; Goodkind and Bicknell, 2018).

## 3 Center Embeddings

In a center embedding sentence, the subject of a matrix (or main) clause is modified by an object-extracted relative clause. Because any Noun Phrase can serve as the host of a relative clause, the subject of the embedded relative clause can recursively serve as the start of a second center-embedding sentence, and so on *ad infinitum*, provided that there are an equal number of subjects and verbs, as in Example (1).

(1) The water [that the customer [that the waiter$_x$ disliked]$_y$ drank]$_z$ was cold.

Center embedding sentences exemplify the pattern $a^n b^n$, characteristic of context-free grammars, for natural language. However, the structure requires more than just counting: it is not sufficient that the number of verbs match the number of subjects, rather the *verbs must semantically and syntactically match* their appropriate subjects and objects. The verb *drank* is to be expected at the position marked $y$ in Example (1), but not at $x$ or $z$, because it corresponds to the subject *customer* and the object *water*. An incremental predictor must suppress an expectation for the word *drink* during the region containing $x$, and then recover this expectation at $y$.

To assess whether the RNN LMs tested could suppress expectations for verbs set up by subjects and activate them in the correct order, we created 40 test items following the template in (2).

(2) a. The diamond that the thief **stole**$_{VP1}$ **glittered**$_{VP2}$. [match, embedding]

   b. The diamond that the thief **glittered**$_{VP1}$ **stole**$_{VP2}$. [mismatch, embedding]

   c. The diamond that the thief in the black mask **stole**$_{VP1}$ **glittered**$_{VP2}$. [match, embedding-long]

   d. The diamond that the thief in the black mask **glittered**$_{VP1}$ **stole**$_{VP2}$. [mismatch, embedding-long]

   e. The thief **stole**$_{VP1}$ / The diamond **glittered**$_{VP2}$ [match, sentence]

   f. The thief **glittered**$_{VP1}$ / The diamond **stole**$_{VP2}$ [mismatch, sentence]

We use *plausibility match* of ordering effect to assess whether the model was linking the right subject with the right verb. For example, it is plausible that a diamond glitters and a thief steals, as

---

[1]Our studies were preregistered on `aspredicted.org`: To see the preregistrations go to `http://aspredicted.org/blind.php?x=X` where $X \in \{\text{uw873w}, \text{95gj46}\}$.

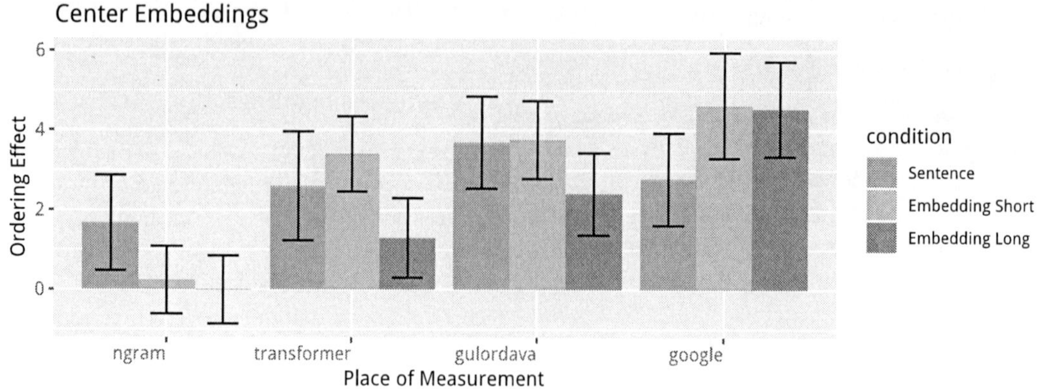


Figure 2: Model results for center embedding sentences. Higher values indicate stronger divergence between the ordering effect *match* and *mismatch* conditions, indicating that models have learned the proper subject-verb pairings for the center embedding construction.

in (2-a), but implausible that a thief glitters and a diamond steals as in (2-b). In our test sentences the matrix clause subject tended to be an inanimate entity that took an intransitive verb, and the relative clause subject tended to be an animate entity that took a transitive verb. For each item, we measure the strength of the models' expectation in terms of what we call the **ordering effect** at each verb: the surprisal in the [mismatch] condition minus the surprisal in the [match] condition. Our prediction is that if a model has learned the ordering restrictions imposed by the grammatical rules that govern English center embedding and uses these restrictions to appropriately guide predictions about upcoming words, the ordering effect should be at least as great in the two [embedding] conditions as in the [sentence] conditions. We report the summed ordering effect across the two VPs, which indicates the difference in surprisal between the two conditions due to specific order of the two verbs. As control sentences, we converted each item into a pair of simple subject-verb sentences with no embedding, as in (2-e)–(2-f). If the ordering effect for the control sentence conditions is not positive, it would call into question our selection of subject–verb pairs.

The results from this experiment can be seen in Figure 2, with the N-Gram model at left, the Transformer model center left and the two LSTM models at right. Error bars indicate 95% confidence intervals of across item means, with within-item means subtracted, as advocated in Masson and Loftus (2003). The baseline N-Gram model shows a positive ordering effect in the control *Sen-*

*tence* conditions, however the ordering effect is not significantly different from zero in the two *Embedding* conditions. For the Transformer and two LSTM models, the ordering effect is positive in the control *Sentence* conditions, as well as in the two critical *Embedding* conditions. Examining the contributions of the individual items themselves, we find that the surprisal difference at the second (matrix) verb is responsible for the majority of the effect. That is, given the context *The diamond that the thief* ... the continuations *stole* and *glittered* are equally likely. However, given the partially-saturated contexts in (3), the continuation *glittered* is much more likely in (3-a) than the continuation *stole* is in (3-b).

(3) a.  The diamond that the thief stole...

    b.  The diamond that the thief glittered...

It is this difference that drives the majority of the Ordering Effect for the LSTM and Transformer models. Crucially, this behavior is inconsistent with a linear approach to subject/verb plausibility match. If the models had learned only that a semantically plausible verb needed to follow a subject, then the order of the verbs should have no effect on surprisal. The positive ordering effect we see in the two *Embedding* conditions indicates the neural models have learned that the outer verb needs to be associated with the first subject: all three models exhibit a first-in-last-out approach to licensing consistent with stack-like representation.

Turning to differences between the three neural models: For the Gulordava and Transformer models the ordering effect is higher in the control *Sentence* and *Embedding Short* conditions than in the

*Embedding Long* conditions, although neither of the differences are significant. But for the Google model, the ordering effect is *larger* in the embedding conditions than in the control sentence condition. Although this increased effect size may at first glance be surprising, recall that in the embedding conditions, there is more preceding context than in the control-sentence condition that is available to predict both verbs—including both arguments of the transitive verb. This larger overall ordering effect in the embedding conditions suggests that the Google model, which is trained on an order of magnitude more data, may be more efficiently leveraging this additional preceding context. It remains an open question why the Transformer Model, which is trained on the same large dataset, is unable to leverage similar contextual cues and maintain equally strong verbal expectations across the relative clause modifier.

## 4 Filler–Gap Dependency Licensing

### 4.1 Measuring the Filler–Gap Dependency

In English, a range of linguistic structures—such as questions and relative clauses—are formed by inserting a wh-word and eliding (or *gapping*) subsequent material. For example, to turn the transitive sentence in (4-a) into a question, a filler ( *who*) is inserted at the beginning of the clause, and the material being questioned (the direct object) is gapped, which we represent using the underscores (these are for presentational purposes only and are not included in test items).

(4) a.  The count insulted the hostess yesterday.

    b.  **Who** did the count insult __ yesterday?

Crucially, the filler and the gap depend on each other, insofar as a filler word is illicit without a subsequent gap, and a gap is unlicensed without an upstream filler. Wilcox et al. (2018) established that the two LSTM language models tested here learn the filler–gap dependency insofar as they learn the $2 \times 2$ contingency between fillers and gaps. To assess this, for each of their test sentences they create four items following the four possible combinations of fillers and gaps, as in (5) (note that in these and subsequent examples the * indicates ungrammaticality).

(5) a.  I know that the count insulted the hostess yesterday. [–FILLER, -GAP]

    b.*I know who the count insulted the hostess yesterday. [+FILLER, -GAP]

    c.*I know that the count insulted __ yesterday. [–FILLER, +GAP]

    d.  I know who the count insulted __ yesterday. [+FILLER, +GAP]

Their logic is as follows: If the models are learning that gaps require fillers to be licensed, then the transition from an object-taking verb to a prepositional phrase that indicates a syntactic gap should be less surprising in the *presence* of an upstream, licensing filler. That is S([–FILLER, +GAP]) should be greater than S([+FILLER, +GAP]) in the post gap material "yesterday". We refer to this difference as the *+GAP wh-effect*, a large effect here indicates that the model has learned that gaps require fillers to be licensed. We measure the +GAP wh-effect in temporal adjuncts following the gap site, as in *yesterday* in (5).

Additionally, if the models are learning that fillers set up expectations for gaps, then a filled argument structure position such as a direct object should be less surprising in the *absence* of an upstream filler, a phenomena which is known in the psycholinguistics literature as the **filled gap effect**. That is, S([+FILLER, –GAP]) should be greater than S([–FILLER, –GAP]). We refer to this difference as a *-GAP wh-effect*, a large effect here indicates that models have learned that fillers set up expectations for gaps. We measure the -GAP wh-effect in the embedded verb direct object, e.g. at "the hostess" in (5).

Wilcox et al. (2018) sum differences into a single metric, the **wh-licensing interaction**, which they measure in a post-gap temporal adjunct. In this work, we eschew the wh-licensing and look instead at the two wh-effects in the +GAP and -GAP conditions. We do this for two reasons: First, collapsing all four surprisal values obfuscates which part of the contingency the models learn. It may be the case that the vast majority of the licensing interaction comes from surprisal differences in just one of the two conditions, a fact which would be hard to observe by studying the full interaction. Second, if upstream fillers set up expectations for empty argument structure positions, then the *filled gap effect* should be most noticeable on the object itself, not in a subsequent adjunct. Measuring the wh-effect separately for each condition allows us to take our measurement at the precise location where we would expect the effect to be the largest.

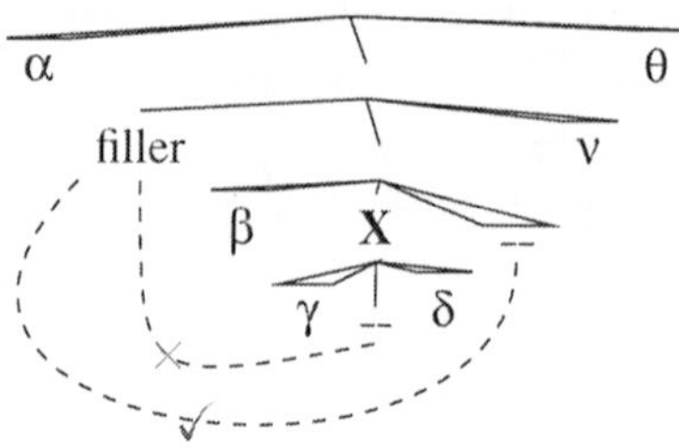

Figure 3: Island constraints and filling gaps across islands. If node **X** is an island, then a filler outside **X** cannot associate with a gap inside **X**, but it can associate with a filler on the far side of **X**. For our analyses, successful learning of an island constraint implies that we should *not* see wh-effects at the first part of the material δ immediately following the potential gap site, but we *should* see wh-effects in ν, following a licit gap site.

### 4.2 Licensing Over Syntactic Islands

In addition to basic filler–gap dependency licensing, Wilcox et al. (2018) and Wilcox et al. (2019a) argue that the RNNs tested show sensitivity to numerous **island effects** (although see Chowdhury and Zamparelli (2018) for a contrasting view). Islands are syntactic positions that locally block the filler–gap dependency (Ross, 1967). For example, fillers can associate with gaps located in object position of a matrix clause, as in (6-a), but not when the gap occurs within a relative clause, as in (6-b).

(6) a. Who did the hostess insult __ yesterday?

    b.*Who did the hostess insult [RC the count that knows __ ] yesterday?

Crucially, although islands block the fillers from associating with gaps within the island, they do not prohibit association between fillers and gaps that occur structurally to the right of the island, as shown in Figure 3.

Wilcox et al. (2019b) found that while large scale models are able to thread the $2 \times 2$ contingency between fillers and gaps into syntactically complex material–such as through numerous sentential embeddings—they do not thread the dependency into some island configurations. Inside of relative clauses and temporal adjuncts, for example, the presence or absence of an upstream filler has no effect on the relative surprisal of a gap, and the wh-licensing interaction drops to near zero.

However, model inability to thread the filler–gap dependency into island configurations provides only half of the evidence necessary to estab-lish that neural models are "learning" islands in a way meaningfully similar to humans. Island configurations act as blockers, but only for the duration of the island—the length of the relative clause or the temporal adjunct, for the two islands tested here. If RNNs learn islands as local contexts into which an outside filler cannot license a gap, they should recover their expectations for gaps following the island.

To assess whether models recover expectations for licit gaps following island configurations, we generated test sentences following the template in (7), featuring two well-studied islands: **adjunct islands** (7-b) and **complex noun phrase islands** (7-d). In these examples, the island portions of the sentences, in which gaps are not allowed, appear in boldface.

(7) a. I know who the count from the southern province talked very loudly with __ on the balcony. [object]

    b.*I know who , **after the count insulted __ on the balcony** , the hostess talked with the countess. [adjunct]

    c. I know who , **after insulting the hostess** , the count talked with __ on the balcony. [over-adjunct]

    d.*I know who **the count that insulted __ on the balcony** talked with the hostess. [cnp]

    e. I know who **the count that insulted the hostess** talked loudly with __ on the balcony. [over-cnp]

For each condition, we created a sentence template and seeded each region in the template with between three and seven examples. Permuting the examples, we generated thousands of candidate sentences, from which we sampled 100 at random and measured the wh-effect for the +GAP and −GAP conditions. If the models are sensitive to the island constraints, then we expect strong wh-effects in the grammatical [object] condition, but not in the ungrammatical [adjunct] and [complex noun phrase] ([cnp]) conditions. Furthermore, if models are able to recover expectations from gaps following the end of an island, we would expect strong wh-effects in the grammatical [over-adjunct] and [over-cnp] conditions.

The results from this experiment can be seen in Figure 4, with the wh-effect in the +GAP condition at left and the −GAP condition at right. The baseline N-Gram model showed wh-effects that were not significantly different from zero for all

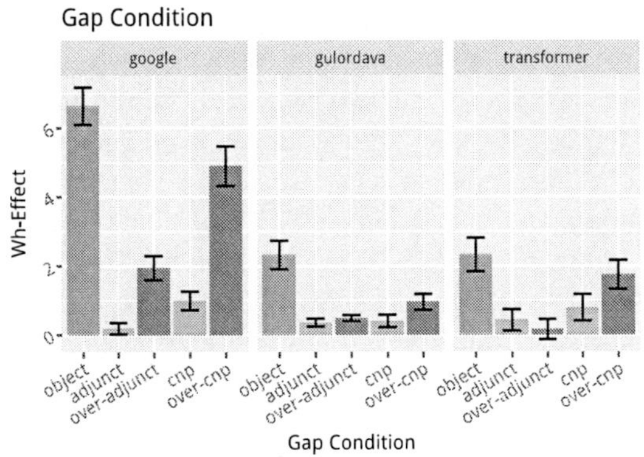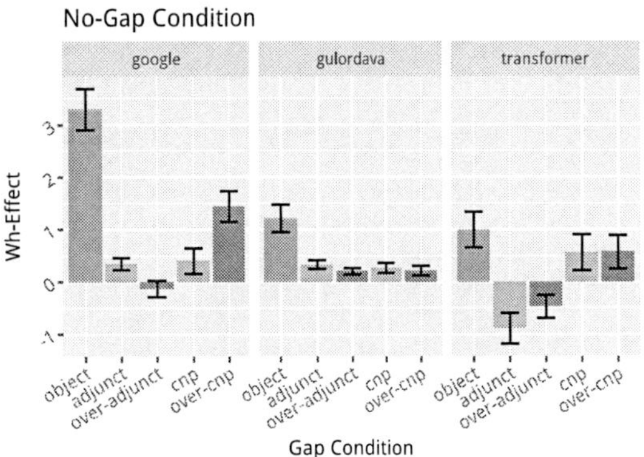

Figure 4: Model results for maintaining the filler–gap dependency over island constructions. Strong wh-effects are expected in the grammatical conditions (orange and blue), with reduced wh-effects in the island conditions (green).

conditions, and is not included in the graphs. Focusing on the +GAP condition at left, we see a strong wh-effect in the control *object* condition but a significant reduction of wh-effect in the *adjunct* and *cnp* conditions for all models ($p < 0.001$). In the grammatical *over-adjunct* and *over-cnp* we still see a significant reduction in wh-effect compared to the *object* condition ($p < 0.001$), but a significant increase in wh-effect relative to the corresponding island conditions in many cases. This recovery of expectations is significant for CNP Islands for all models ($p < 0.001$) and for the Adjunct Islands in the case of the Google model ($p < 0.001$). The results are especially striking for the Google Model: While the absence of an upstream filler induces only one more bit of surprisal at the gap site within an island, it induces between 2-5 more bits of surprisal when a gap occurs licitly downstream of an island.

Turning to the -GAP conditions at right, the results are more mixed. All three models show significantly more licensing interaction in the control *object* condition compared to the island conditions, except for the Transformer model in the case of CNP Islands. However, only the Google Model shows a significant recuperation of empty argument structure expectation in the *cnp* vs. *over-cnp* condition ($p < 0.001$). These results indicate that the three language models tested are able to bracket their expectations for gaps and regain them on the other side in the case of relative clauses. However, neither model does a good job of recovering the filled gap effect following an island, modulo complex noun phrase islands for the Google model.

### 4.3 Wh-Discharge Effects

The filler–gap dependency is constrained, insofar as fillers can license only one gap. Wilcox et al. (2018) found that RNN models were sensitive to this constraint, displaying a reduction in licensing interaction following a gap, if another gap existed upstream in the sentence as in (8-a). The presence of a filler sets up an expectation for a gap, which is discharged at the first gap site, and cannot participate in downstream licensing effects. However, if models are sensitive to the fact that gaps cannot licitly occur within islands (unless they are licensed within the island itself), the presence of a gap inside a relative clause or a temporal adjunct should not result in the discharge of gap expectation.

To assess whether gap discharge effects are mitigated when the first gap occurs inside of an island, we generated 100 examples following the process described in Section 4.2 and the template in (8). Following the results in Wilcox et al. (2018), section 3.3, we expect a slightly negative wh-effects in the *subject* condition. However, if gaps inside of islands do not discharge the wh-effect set up by a filler, we expect positive wh-effects in the *adjunct-discharge* and *cnp-discharge* conditions.

(8) a. I know who __ talked very loudly with __ on the balcony. [subject]

    b. I know who , after insulting __ , the count talked loudly with __ on the balcony. [adjunct-discharge]

    c. I know who the old man that insulted __ talked loudly with __ on the balcony. [cnp-discharge]

The results from this experiment can be seen in 5.

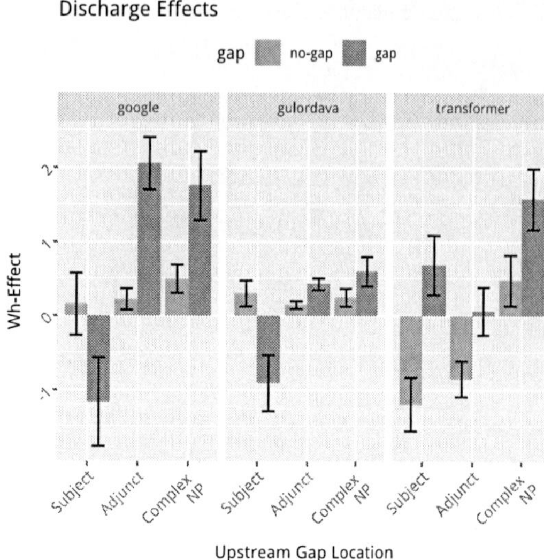


Figure 5: Discharge effects for gaps in Subject and Island positions. Strong Wh-Effects are expected in the Adjunct and ComplexNP conditions, with negative wh-effects in the Subject condition.

For the RNN models, In the –GAP cases, for both models there is no significant difference between the conditions. However, in the +GAP cases, there is a significant increase in wh-effect between the *subject* and *adjunct-discharge* and *cnp-discharge* conditions ($p < 0.001$ for both models). For the Transformer model, the *Adjunct* and *Subject* conditions pattern together, and there is a significant increase in Wh-Effect for the *Complex NP* condition, in both the +Gap and -Gap cases ($p < 0.001$).

These results conform to those found in 4.2: all models have a difficult time threading expectations for filled argument structure positions through syntactically-complex material. However, expectations surrounding gaps are clear, at least for the two LSTM models: When gaps occur inside of islands, they do not trigger the the same discharge effects as gaps in subject positions. Interestingly, this generalization seems to be less robust for the Transformer model, which demonstrates the correct behavior only for Complex NP islands. Overall, these results provide further evidence that the models are able to process the edge of a syntactic island, and recover expectations for gaps on the far side.

## 5    General Discussion and Conclusion

In this paper, we have provided new evidence that neural models can learn hierarchical generalizations from linear input alone. By adopting the psycholinguistic paradigm for RNN assessment, we have shown that two large-scale LSTM models and one Transformer modal can suppress and recover expectations set up by subject *Noun Phrases* and *fillers* within intervening blocking structures and recover those expectations on the far side of those syntactic blockers. This behavior corresponds to the idea of pushing and popping expectations in a stack-like data structure, which is required for proper incremental prediction of context-free languages.

However, the suppression and recovery of expectations is imperfect. For example, in the filler–gap dependency, we found that models only partially recover expectations for gaps on the far side of island structures, especially in the -GAP conditions, where no model was able to robustly recover *filled gap* expectations. Interestingly, the LSTM models tended to perform better than Transformer model, even when trained on orders of magnitude less data. These results indicate that the large number of parameters in the Transformer architecture may result in lower test-time perplexity, but may not necessarily result in more grammatical behavior, at least for the tightly-controlled syntactic test suites presented here. It may be that the smaller number of parameters in the LSTMs force the models to make more robust, and ultimately humanlike generalizations.

This work only assesses two model architectures. It is likely that neural models with a stronger structural bias, such as RNNGs (Dyer et al., 2016) or LSTMs enhanced with a structural bias as in Shen et al. (2018) would perform better on the tests presented here; testing these, and other models, will be the basis for future work.

## References

R Harald Baayen, Douglas J Davidson, and Douglas M Bates. 2008. Mixed-effects modeling with crossed random effects for subjects and items. *Journal of Memory and Language*, 59(4):390–412.

Dale J Barr, Roger Levy, Christoph Scheepers, and Harry J Tily. 2013. Random effects structure for confirmatory hypothesis testing: Keep it maximal. *Journal of Memory and Language*, 68(3):255–278.

Ciprian Chelba, Tomas Mikolov, Mike Schuster, Qi Ge, Thorsten Brants, Phillipp Koehn, and Tony Robinson. 2013. One billion word benchmark for measuring progress in statistical language modeling. *arXiv preprint arXiv:1312.3005*.

Doo Kok Choe and Eugene Charniak. 2016. Parsing as language modeling. In *Proceedings of the 2016 Conference on Empirical Methods in Natural Language Processing*, pages 2331–2336.

Noam Chomsky. 1956. Three models for the description of language. *IRE Transactions on Information Theory*, 2(3):113–124.

Shammur Absar Chowdhury and Roberto Zamparelli. 2018. Rnn simulations of grammaticality judgments on long-distance dependencies. In *Proceedings of the 27th International Conference on Computational Linguistics*, pages 133–144.

Zihang Dai, Zhilin Yang, Yiming Yang, William W Cohen, Jaime Carbonell, Quoc V Le, and Ruslan Salakhutdinov. 2019. Transformer-xl: Attentive language models beyond a fixed-length context. *arXiv preprint arXiv:1901.02860*.

Chris Dyer, Adhiguna Kuncoro, Miguel Ballesteros, and Noah A. Smith. 2016. Recurrent neural network grammars. In *Proc. of NAACL*.

Jeffrey L Elman. 1990. Finding structure in time. *Cognitive Science*, 14(2):179–211.

Jeffrey L Elman. 1991. Distributed representations, simple recurrent networks, and grammatical structure. *Machine learning*, 7(2-3):195–225.

Richard Futrell, Ethan Wilcox, Takashi Morita, and Roger Levy. 2018. Rnns as psycholinguistic subjects: Syntactic state and grammatical dependency. *arXiv preprint arXiv:1809.01329*.

Richard Futrell, Ethan Wilcox, Takashi Morita, Peng Qian, Miguel Ballesteros, and Roger Levy. 2019. Neural language models as psycholinguistic subjects: Representations of syntactic state. *arXiv preprint arXiv:1903.03260*.

Mario Giulianelli, Jack Harding, Florian Mohnert, Dieuwke Hupkes, and Willem Zuidema. 2018. Under the hood: Using diagnostic classifiers to investigate and improve how language models track agreement information. *arXiv preprint arXiv:1808.08079*.

Adam Goodkind and Klinton Bicknell. 2018. Predictive power of word surprisal for reading times is a linear function of language model quality. In *Proceedings of the 8th Workshop on Cognitive Modeling and Computational Linguistics (CMCL 2018)*, pages 10–18.

Kristina Gulordava, Piotr Bojanowski, Edouard Grave, Tal Linzen, and Marco Baroni. 2018. Colorless green recurrent networks dream hierarchically. *arXiv preprint arXiv:1803.11138*.

John Hale. 2001. A probabilistic earley parser as a psycholinguistic model. In *Proceedings of the second meeting of the North American Chapter of the Association for Computational Linguistics on Language technologies*, pages 1–8. Association for Computational Linguistics.

Sepp Hochreiter and Jürgen Schmidhuber. 1997. Long short-term memory. *Neural Computation*, 9(8):1735–1780.

Aravind K Joshi and Yves Schabes. 1997. Tree-adjoining grammars. In *Handbook of formal languages*, pages 69–123. Springer.

Rafal Jozefowicz, Oriol Vinyals, Mike Schuster, Noam Shazeer, and Yonghui Wu. 2016. Exploring the limits of language modeling. *arXiv*, 1602.02410.

Marco Kuhlmann. 2013. Mildly non-projective dependency grammar. *Computational Linguistics*, 39(2):355–387.

Adhiguna Kuncoro, Miguel Ballesteros, Lingpeng Kong, Chris Dyer, Graham Neubig, and Noah A Smith. 2016. What do recurrent neural network grammars learn about syntax? *arXiv preprint arXiv:1611.05774*.

Geoffrey Neil Leech. 1992. 100 million words of english: the british national corpus (bnc).

Roger Levy. 2008. Expectation-based syntactic comprehension. *Cognition*, 106(3):1126–1177.

Tal Linzen, Emmanuel Dupoux, and Yoav Goldberg. 2016. Assessing the ability of lstms to learn syntax-sensitive dependencies. *Transactions of the Association for Computational Linguistics*, 4:521–535.

David Mareček and Rudolf Rosa. 2018. Extracting syntactic trees from transformer encoder self-attentions. In *Proceedings of the 2018 EMNLP Workshop BlackboxNLP: Analyzing and Interpreting Neural Networks for NLP*, pages 347–349.

Rebecca Marvin and Tal Linzen. 2018. Targeted syntactic evaluation of language models. *arXiv preprint arXiv:1808.09031*.

Michael EJ Masson and Geoffrey R Loftus. 2003. Using confidence intervals for graphically based data interpretation. *Canadian Journal of Experimental Psychology/Revue canadienne de psychologie expérimentale*, 57(3):203.

R Thomas McCoy, Robert Frank, and Tal Linzen. 2018. Revisiting the poverty of the stimulus: hierarchical generalization without a hierarchical bias in recurrent neural networks. *arXiv preprint arXiv:1802.09091*.

John Robert Ross. 1967. Constraints on variables in syntax.

Hiroyuki Seki, Takashi Matsumura, Mamoru Fujii, and Tadao Kasami. 1991. On multiple context-free grammars. *Theoretical Computer Science*, 88(2):191–229.

Yikang Shen, Shawn Tan, Alessandro Sordoni, and Aaron Courville. 2018. Ordered neurons: Integrating tree structures into recurrent neural networks. *arXiv preprint arXiv:1810.09536*.

Stuart M Shieber. 1985. Evidence against the context-freeness of natural language. In *Philosophy, Language, and Artificial Intelligence*, pages 79–89. Springer.

Nathaniel J Smith and Roger Levy. 2013. The effect of word predictability on reading time is logarithmic. *Cognition*, 128(3):302–319.

Andreas Stolcke. 2002. Srilm-an extensible language modeling toolkit. In *Seventh international conference on spoken language processing*.

David Jeremy Weir. 1988. Characterizing mildly context-sensitive grammar formalisms.

Gail Weiss, Yoav Goldberg, and Eran Yahav. 2018. On the practical computational power of finite precision rnns for language recognition. *arXiv preprint arXiv:1805.04908*.

Ethan Wilcox, Roger Levy, and Richard Futrell. 2019a. What syntactic structures block dependencies in rnn language models? *arXiv preprint arXiv:1905.10431*.

Ethan Wilcox, Roger Levy, Takashi Morita, and Richard Futrell. 2018. What do rnn language models learn about filler-gap dependencies? *arXiv preprint arXiv:1809.00042*.

Ethan Wilcox, Peng Qian, Richard Futrell, Miguel Ballesteros, and Roger Levy. 2019b. Structural supervision improves learning of non-local grammatical dependencies. *arXiv preprint arXiv:1903.00943*.

# Blackbox meets blackbox: Representational Similarity and Stability Analysis of Neural Language Models and Brains

**Samira Abnar**     **Lisa Beinborn**     **Rochelle Choenni**     **Willem Zuidema**

Institute for Logic, Language and Computation
University of Amsterdam

`{abnar,l.beinborn}@uva.nl, rochelle.choenni@student.uva.nl, zuidema@uva.nl`

## Abstract

In this paper, we define and apply *representational stability analysis* (ReStA), an intuitive way of analyzing neural language models. ReStA is a variant of the popular *representational similarity analysis* (RSA) in cognitive neuroscience. While RSA can be used to compare representations in models, model components, and human brains, ReStA compares instances of the *same* model, while systematically varying single model parameter. Using ReStA, we study four recent and successful neural language models, and evaluate how sensitive their internal representations are to the amount of prior context. Using RSA, we perform a systematic study of how similar the representational spaces in the first and second (or higher) layers of these models are to each other and to patterns of activation in the human brain. Our results reveal surprisingly strong differences between language models, and give insights into where the *deep* linguistic processing, that integrates information over multiple sentences, is happening in these models. The combination of ReStA and RSA on models and brains allows us to start addressing the important question of what kind of linguistic processes we can hope to observe in fMRI brain imaging data. In particular, our results suggest that the data on story reading from Wehbe et al. (2014) contains a signal of *shallow* linguistic processing, but show no evidence on the more interesting *deep* linguistic processing.

## 1   Representational Similarity

Representational similarity analysis (RSA) is a technique which allows us to compare heterogeneous representational spaces (Laakso and Cottrell, 2000). It is very common in cognitive neuroscience because it allows researchers to study the relation between patterns of activation in the brain and representations of stimuli in a computational model (Kriegeskorte et al., 2008). The key idea is simple: instead of directly trying to map models to brains, we first construct two similarity matrices that record how similar brain responses are to each other for different stimuli, and how similar the computational model's representations for each stimulus are to each other. The representational similarity score is then defined as the similarity (typically: Pearson's correlation) of the two similarity matrices (or equivalently: the similarity of two distance matrices).

RSA can also be applied to deep learning models (Laakso and Cottrell, 2000; Dharmaretnam and Fyshe, 2018; Alvarez-Melis and Jaakkola, 2018; Wang et al., 2018; Chrupała and Alishahi, 2019). In this paper, we present a large-scale study and comparison of both neural language models and fMRI data from brain imaging experiments with human subjects, using RSA. However, we extend standard RSA using an approach we call *Representational Stability Analysis* (ReStA). The idea is again simple: we apply RSA to compare instances of the *same* model, while systematically varying a model parameter.

We focus on a single parameter: the length of the prior context presented to the model. Varying the amount of context allows us to quantify the degree of context-dependence of different neural language models, and different components of those models. If internal representations are similarly organized regardless of how much additional context is presented to the model, context-dependence is low. If, on the other hand, representations change with each additional amount of context included, context-dependence is high. Using this approach, we find intriguing differences between some recent, successful neural language models (GoogleLM, ELMO, BERT and the Universal Sentence Encoder; Table 1), and between the first and deeper layers of those models.

Context-dependence, in turn, gives us a handle on an important question in the research that tries



*Proceedings of the Second BlackboxNLP Workshop on Analyzing and Interpreting Neural Networks for NLP*, pages 191–203
Florence, Italy, August 1, 2019. ©2019 Association for Computational Linguistics

| Model | Objective | Corpus | Rep.Dim. | Architecture |
|---|---|---|---|---|
| GloVe (Pennington et al., 2014) | Predicting co-occurrence probabilities | Wikipedia | 300 | Bag of words |
| ELMO (Peters et al., 2018) | Bidirectional Language Modelling | 1B benchmark | 1,024 | BiLSTM |
| GoogleLM (Jozefowicz et al., 2016) | Language Modelling | 1B benchmark | 1,024 | LSTM |
| UniSentEnc. (Cer et al., 2018) | Skip-Thought/Classification | Variety of web sources / SNLI | 512 | Transformer Encoder |
| BERT (base) (Devlin et al., 2019) | Masked Language Modelling / Next Sent. Pred. | BooksCorpus / English Wikipedia | 768 | Transformer Encoder |

Table 1: Details of the third party computational models used in this paper, including a brief characterization of the optimization objective, the training corpus, and the dimensionality of representations we extract from them.

to link neural language models to brain activation: which aspects of language processing in the brain can we hope to observe in fMRI data using NLP and machine learning tools?

## 2 Bridging NLP Models and Neurolinguistics

An important motivation behind our work is to contribute to answering a big question in computational linguistics: how do we establish a relationship between NLP models and data on the human brain activation while they process language? Pioneering work of Mitchell et al. (2008) showed that techniques from distributional semantics could be used to predict and decode brain activation. In the decade since that paper, many efforts have been reported using brain data to evaluate computational models, or using NLP models to build predictive models of the human brain, or both (Murphy et al., 2012; Wehbe et al., 2014a; Ruan et al., 2016; Søgaard, 2016; Xu et al., 2016; Fyshe et al., 2014; Bingel et al., 2016; Bulat et al., 2017; Abnar et al., 2018; Pereira et al., 2018; Huth et al., 2016).

Most of that work is focused on lexical representations, reporting promising results for concrete nouns, presented in isolation. More recently researchers have tried to adapt the methodology to address words in context, in sentence and story processing tasks. Pereira et al. (2018), for instance, used a bag of words model of sentence meaning to decode sentences from brain activation. Wehbe et al. (2014b); Qian et al. (2016) use the internal states of LSTMs trained for language modelling for encoding. Jain and Huth (2018) report that the higher layers of the LSTM are better at predicting the activation of brain regions that are known for higher level language functions (a find-

ing seemingly at odds with results from section5).

In this effort, however, we run into a number of major conceptual, methodological and technical challenges. Most importantly: how do we determine what we are really observing in the brain data? Are we really seeing signatures of linguistic processes, or just neural correlates of general cognitive processes evoked by a correct understanding of the linguistic input? How do we adequately control for alternative explanations of the observed correlations? And how do we deal with the intricate temporal dynamics and the overwhelmingly high dimensionality of the brain, and the very indirect, delayed and/or coarse measurements that neuroimaging gives us of the processes in the brain? Merely demonstrating a correlation between two black boxes is clearly not sufficient.

We argue that experiments to find the model best correlated with brain activations should be accompanied by efforts for interpreting the internal representations and operations of the models. Applying ReStA for the prior context parameter gives us a way to roughly characterize the *depth* of linguistic processing in different language models and different components of these models. If a model component only tracks the lexical semantics of the current word, the representations it forms should not be sensitive to the amount of prior context. On the other hand, If a model component tracks long-distance syntactic dependen-

| Block | Words | Unique words | Sentences | Sent Length | Scans |
|---|---|---|---|---|---|
| 1 | 1583 | 553 | 115 | 11 | 326 |
| 2 | 1711 | 560 | 163 | 8 | 338 |
| 3 | 1411 | 461 | 134 | 8 | 265 |
| 4 | 1853 | 583 | 177 | 8 | 366 |

Table 2: Statistics of the Harry Potter dataset.

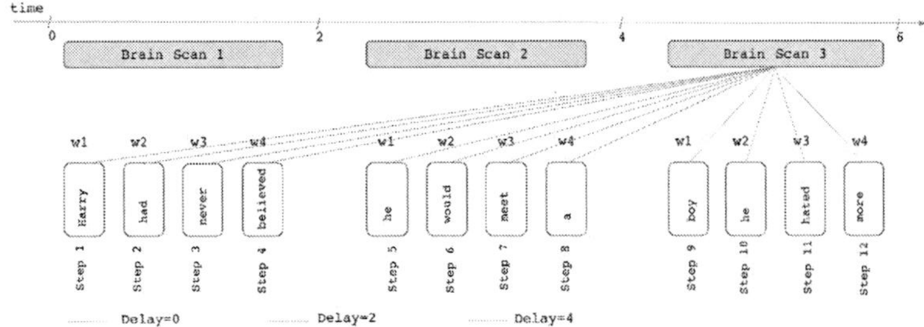


Figure 1: Alignment of the words in the story and the brain vectors. Each fMRI scan lasts for 2 seconds during which the subject is reading four words sequentially. Delay is the amount of time in seconds between the time the first of the four word is shown to the subject and when the fMRI scan is started to be taken.

cies, semantic polarity, named entities, topics or story arcs, resolves anaphora or builds up situation models, its representations will be different whenever different amounts of prior context are available. Hence, in this paper, we will interpret context-dependence as an imperfect but useful signature of deep linguistic processing.

## 3 Models and Data

In this section, we explain the language encoding models we study in our experiments and the dataset from which we get the language stimuli and their corresponding brain data.

### 3.1 Neural Language Models

We study language models with different architectures trained with different objective functions (see Table 1). As a word level embedding model, we use GloVe (Pennington et al., 2014). We consider a sentence as a bag of words and take the average of the GloVe embeddings.

We employ two high performing LSTM based language models: ELMO (Peters et al., 2018) and GoogleLM (Jozefowicz et al., 2016). Both of these models have two LSTM layers; however, ELMO uses bidirectional LSTM layers, whereas in the GoogleLM the LSTM layers are uni-directional. From these models, we take the internal states of each of the LSTM layers as two different representation spaces.

In our comparisons, we also use BERT and the Universal Sentence Encoder (UniSentEnc), as Transformer based models. BERT is trained on masked language modelling and next sentence prediction tasks (Devlin et al., 2019) while the Universal Sentence Encoder is trained on a different objective than language modelling. The parameters of this model are optimized with respect to different language tasks such that it can better encode the meaning of complete sentences. These two models do not have the recurrent inductive bias of LSTMs, and hence the representations they learn can be completely different.

To study how and where the models integrate information over time, we modify the amount of context provided to the models to obtain the contextualized word representations. We do this at the sentence level. Thus, for the context length of 0, we only feed the target words to the models; For context length 1 we feed all the previous words in the current sentence to the models. For context length $i$ where $i > 1$, in addition to the current sentence we feed all the words in the last $i$ sentences. We operate on the sentence level to feed the model with independently meaningful pieces of text.

From prior work, we expect a relation between the depth of the layers and the level of abstraction of their representations. We study this intuition here empirically by analyzing the different layers of the models, and we focus on the first and last layers. Note that the last layer corresponds to the second layer for the LSTM architectures, but to the 12th layer for Bert.

### 3.2 Brain Data

We compare the representations of our model to human brain activations captured while reading a story. We use the dataset by (Wehbe et al., 2014a) which consists of the fMRI scans of 8 participants reading chapter 9 of *Harry Potter and the Sorcerer's stone* (Rowling, 1998).[1]

The story was presented to the participants word

---

[1] The data is available at `http://www.cs.cmu.edu/~fmri/plosone/`. Further information on the preprocessing steps is described in the supplementary material.

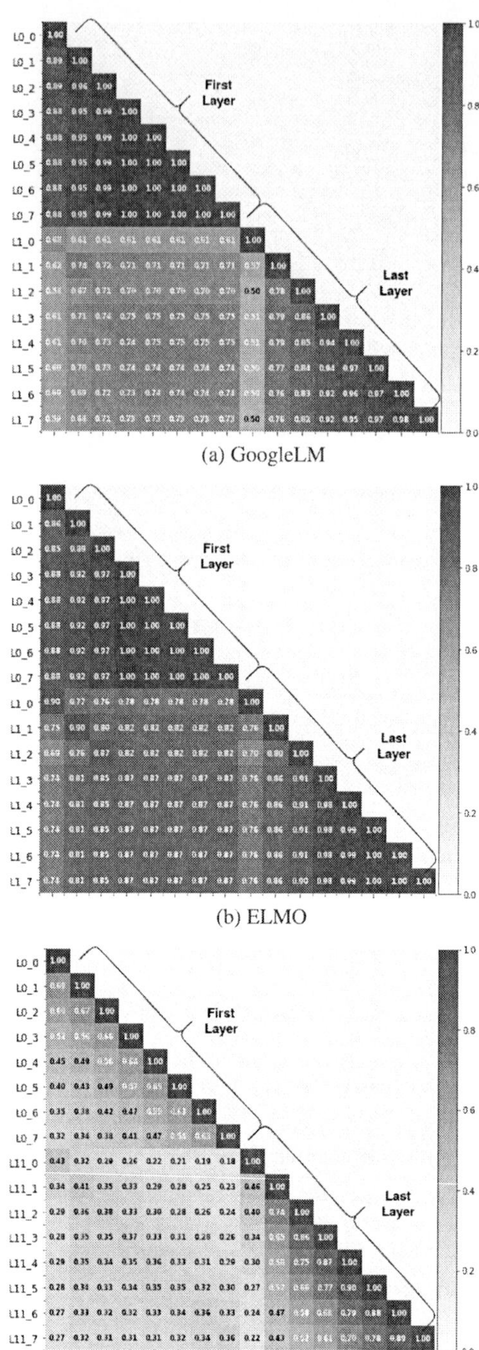

(a) GoogleLM

(b) ELMO

(c) BERT

Figure 2: RSA between different layers of each model given different context length in terms of number of previous sentences over the story words. In these plots, for example `L1_c3` means representation from layer 1, when the context length is 3 sentences including the current sentence. When $c = 0$, the model only sees the current words and when $c = 1$ the model sees current sentence up to the target word. Here darker means more similar. The values are averaged over the four story blocks and the standard deviation of all the values across the four blocks are below 0.002.

by word on a screen in four continuous blocks.[2] Each word was displayed for 0.5 seconds and an fMRI scan was taken every 2 seconds. Figure 1 visualizes an example for the beginning of the chapter. More detailed statistical information about the stimuli can be found in Table 2.

**Brain Regions** The fMRI data contains activation values for approximately 40,000 voxels per scan, each reflecting the oxygen usage (the "BOLD response") in approximately $3mm^3$ of brain tissue. To obtain the brain representations, we flatten the 3D fMRI images into vectors thereby ignoring the spatial relationships between the voxels. We do this either for the whole brain, or for specific regions separately. Not all of the scanned voxels are related to language processing, but the changes in activity might be associated with other cognitive processes like, for example, the noise perception in the scanner. A common reduction method is to restrict the brain response to voxels that fall within a pre-selected set of regions. In our analysis, we only include the voxels from the top $k$ regions that are most similar across different subjects given the same stimuli. We heuristically set the value of $k$ to 16 based on the distribution of the similarity scores.[3]

**Delay** An important point to consider when dealing with fMRI data is the hemodynamic response delay: from the time neurons start firing, it takes 4 to 6 seconds until the Bold response reaches its peak (Buckner, 1998). This means that from the time a stimulus is presented to a subject, it takes approximately 5 seconds before we can observe its response in the fMRI scan of the brain. We account for this delay by varying the alignment between stimuli and scans. If we apply a delay of 0 seconds, scan 3 in the example would be applied to the sequence *boy he hated more*, Figure 1. With a delay of 2 seconds, it is aligned to the previous stimulus *he would meet a* and a delay of 4 would result in alignment with *Harry had never believed*.

---

[2]The story chapter is split into four almost equal length blocks, each reflecting approximately 12 minutes of measurements. Each block is presented to the participant in one continuous trial, and experimental blocks are separated by pauses for the subjects.

[3]We sort the brain regions based on their cross-subject similarities for different stimuli and pick a threshold value based when there is a relatively big jump in the similarity scores.

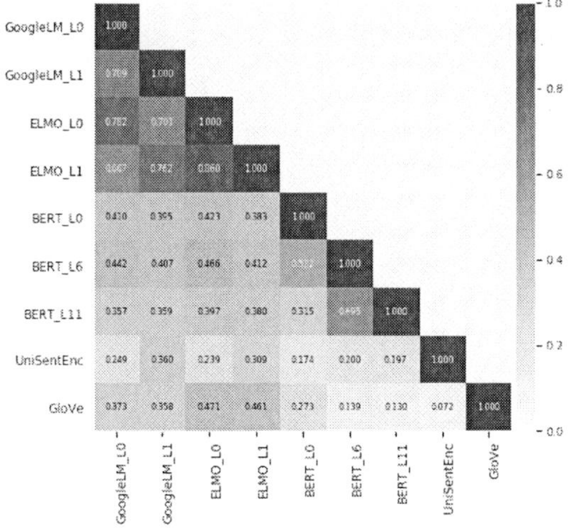

Figure 3: RSA across models

## 4 Analyzing Neural Language Models

In this section, we present the results of applying ReStA, Representational Stability Analysis, to three different language encoding models, GoogleLM, ELMO and BERT. We investigate what type of information is captured in the learned representations without making any explicit assumptions. Next, we apply standard RSA to, first, investigate the relations between different components of the language encoding models, and second to study the alignment of these components with the activity patterns in the human brain.[4]

### 4.1 Representational Stability Analysis

We define the *Representational Stability* as the similarity between the representations obtained from a model, when a single condition is changed, i.e. increase in context length. We use RSA to measure the similarity between the representational spaces. And to compute *RSA* we use *cosine* similarity to measure the intra-space similarities and use *Pearson* correlation to quantify the similarities across representational spaces.

In Figure 2 the representations of the different layers given different context lengths are compared for GoogleLM, ELMO and BERT. The values under the diagonal of these plots indicate the ReStA when the varying condition is context length. This is measured as $RSA(L_{k-c_i}, L_{k-c_j})$, where $k$ is the layer id and $c_i$ and $c_j$ are differ-



ent conditions which in this case indicate different context lengths. We have depicted the trends of how the ReStA changes for different context length in Figures 4a and 4b.

**Effect of depth** As we can see in Figure 2 and more clearly in Figure 5, for the LSTM based models, we observe a higher degree of similarity between the two layers ($\sim 0.75$ and $\sim 0.80$) compared to BERT ($\sim 0.35$). This can be partly explained by the higher number of layers in BERT, i.e the first and last layer are further apart. Moreover, the relation between the first and last layers is almost the same for all context lengths and for all these three models the two layers are most similar when provided with the same amount of context.

**Context sensitivity** Next, we analyse the sensitivity of different layers of each model to context length. In Figures 4a and 2, we see that for both LSTM based models, GoogleLM and ELMO, the first layer, $L0$, is less sensitive to the changes in the context length compared to the last layer, $L1$, i.e. the representations are not affected anymore by increasing the context length to more than 3 sentences. A hierarchical encoding mechanism, where the first layer is responsible for encoding the local context and the second(last) layer is encoding more global information, can justify these results.

We can see in Figure 4a, that the sensitivity to the context length is more significant in the Transformer based models compared to LSTM based models. In these models, the difference in the representations at different context lengths does not fade away as the context length increases but the rate of the changes becomes constant. As illustrated in Figures 4a and 2c we observe that in BERT, regardless of the current context length, adding more context leads to different representations. In addition, in this model, the representations from the first layer, $L0$ are more context-dependent than those from the last layer, $L11$. Since in self-attention layers, there is a direct connection between the representations at different positions, the higher degree of sensitivity to context length is not surprising. This is evidence that, for computing the representations of each position in the input, the representations from all positions, no matter how far they are, are in fact taken into account. We speculate that the last layer of BERT is less sensitive to context could be that in higher

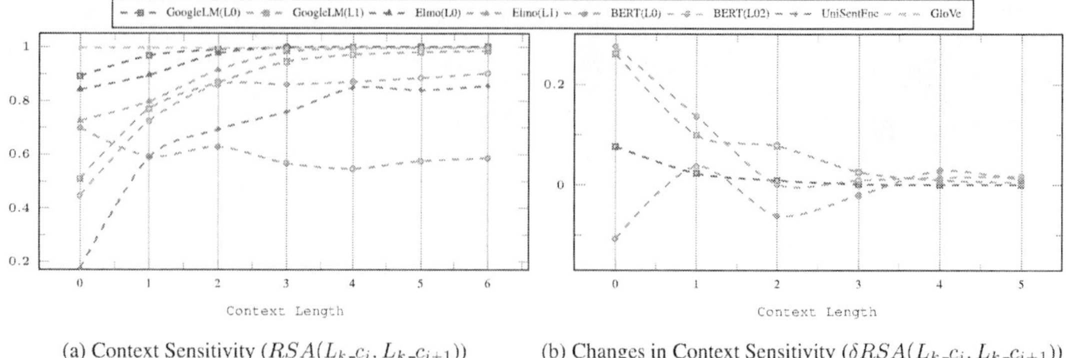

(a) Context Sensitivity ($RSA(L_k\_c_i, L_k\_c_{i+1})$)    (b) Changes in Context Sensitivity ($\delta RSA(L_k\_c_i, L_k\_c_{i+1})$)

Figure 4: Changes in RSA by increasing context length. (a) Shows how the amount of difference in the representational spaces changes by increasing the context length. (b) Shows for all models that we study, regardless of whether and how much their representations change by increasing context length, the amount of difference becomes almost constant after context length of 3 sentences. Note that in (b), we have scaled the plot and removed some of the models to increase the readability.

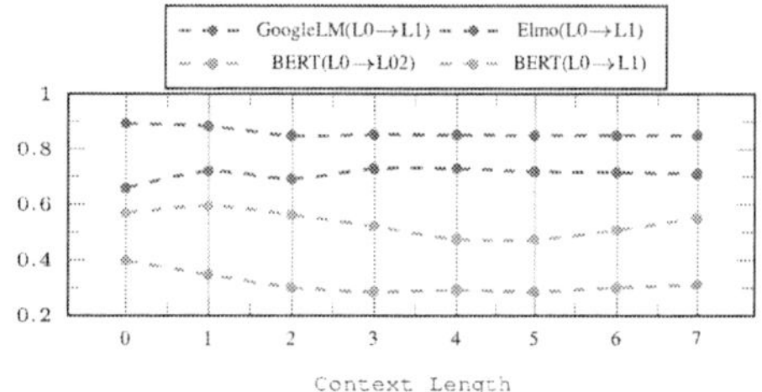

Figure 5: Layer similarities ($RSA(L_k\_c_i, L_{k+1}\_c_i)$. Here we show how increasing context length affects the similarity between different layers of the models.)

layers, the representations correspond to more abstract meanings, and the representational space becomes denser than the lower layers.

## 4.2 RSA across Models

In the second step, we study whether the computational models have learned inherently different representational spaces. According to representational similarity scores, among the models that we study, shown in Figure 3, UniSentEnc seems to learn very different representations from ELMO, GoogleLM and BERT. While BERT and UniSentEnc are both Transformer based models, the representational space of BERT is more similar to the representations from ELMO and GoogleLM that are LSTM based models. This can be due to the fact that ELMO, GoogleLM and BERT are trained with language modelling objectives, while UniSentEnc is trained on skip-thought and classification tasks and this could indicate the effect of the training objective on the representational spaces.

## 5 The Relation between the Models and the Activity Patterns in Human Brains

Figure 7 shows the similarity of different computational representation spaces with brain representations, with respect to different amounts of context provided to the models, averaged over all human subjects. Due to the hemodynamic response delay, we expect to see the peak in similarities after about 4s delay. As we can see in Figure 6, the highest RSA for all models is at $Delay = 4s$, the ranking of the models based on their similarities with brain representations is the same for all amounts of delay. Interestingly, the performances of these models on the NLP tasks are not correlated with their similarity with the brain representations (but note the overall low correlations). The representations learned by LSTM based models are most similar to the brain data, and for both ELMO and GoogleLM the representations from lower layers, $L0$, have higher similarity scores compared to the higher layers, $L1$. Interestingly, for UniSentEnc, BERT($L11$) and also GoogleLM($L1$), increasing the context length, which usually boosts the performance of language encoding models in language understanding tasks (Wang and Cho, 2016), leads to lower similarity with brain representations. It seems that the way these models integrate the context information, pushes the representation further away from the brain representations. This could mean: (1) These models are doing fairly well at encoding the local context, but not at a more global level. Alternatively, (2) The information about the more global aspects of the meaning

196

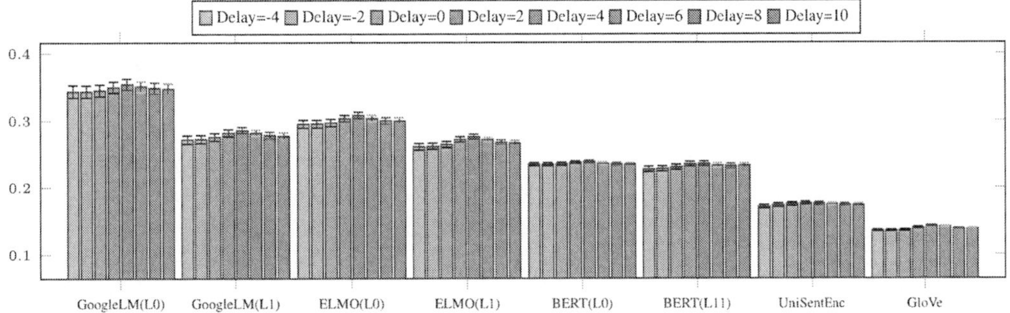

Figure 6: Representational similarity of the models and brains averaged over all subjects and the four blocks at different time delays after the human subjects have read the target words, when the context provided to the models is three sentences. Here the delay is increasing from left to right and the error bars indicate the standard deviation across different blocks.

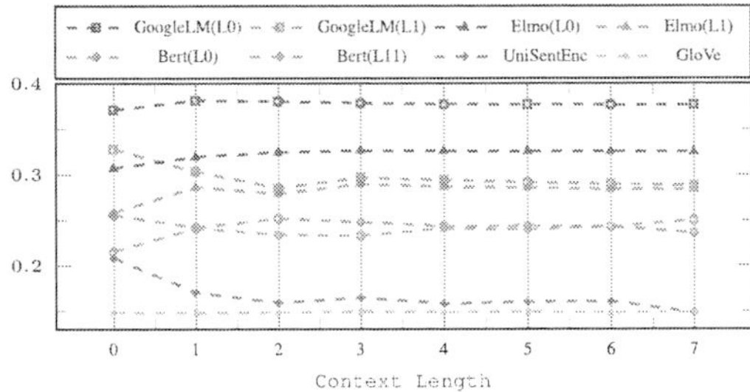

Figure 7: Similarity of the representations from different layers of different models, given different amount of context with brain representations, averaged over all subjects. Note that the average RSA of brains of different human subjects is about 0.55

is not encoded in the brain representations.

**Different Segments of the Story**  If during training the models are only trained on full sentences, it might be the case that the quality of their representations, when given complete sentences, is significantly better than when provided with incomplete sentences. On the other hand, the representation of sentences in the brain might also be more reliable when the full sentence is read. To take this into account, we look at the similarities of each of the models with brain representations, only at the steps in the story where an end of a sentence token is reached. Figure 8a presents the results. We see that in this case, the similarity of all the models with brain representations increases slightly, but this could be because of the reduced dimensionality of the similarity matrix, and we see that the general patterns stay similar.

In Figure 8b we observe that at the story segments where a name of a character is mentioned, the patterns of similarities change a bit, e.g. the

last layer of BERT is less similar to the brain representations compared the first layer of BERT, when an intermediate amount of context is provided to the model. This finding is difficult to interpret, but warrants further research.

**Different Regions of the Brain**  We looked at the similarity scores of the computational representations with the representations at different regions of the brain. This is illustrated in Figure 9 for subject 4 as an example. We observe that the patterns of RSA of different models are very similar across different brain regions, i.e. the scores scale for all regions almost similarly across different models. Despite the low correlations between the models and the brain activation, we find that all the models are consistently best aligned with the regions in the Left Anterior Temporal Lobe (LATL). This region is known for semantic and sometimes syntactic processing of language (Westerlund and Pylkkänen, 2014; Bemis and Pylkkänen, 2011; Leffel et al., 2014). We also find some correlation with the Left Parietal Lobe, which is not known to be responsible for language processing. We also computed the average RSA between different brain regions for the eight subjects, both within and across subjects, and find that the different regions of a single brain are more similar ($RSA = 0.4$) than the same regions of different brains ($RSA = 0.12$). These are counter-intuitive findings that warrant further investigation. If brain functions involved in story comprehension are spatially localized and brains are organized similarly across individuals, we would expect the same regions from different subjects to be more similar than different regions from the same subject.

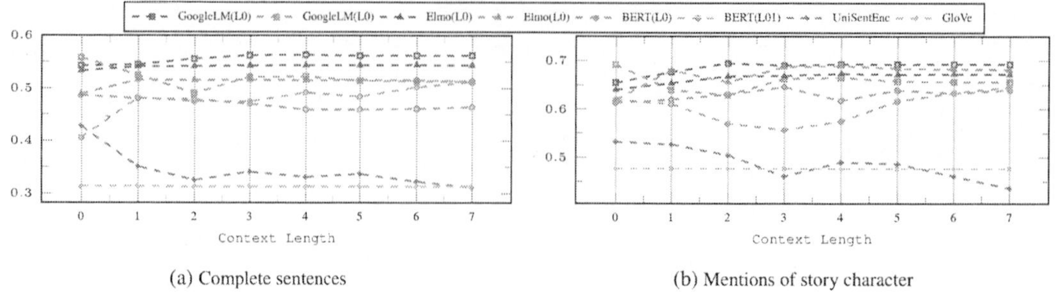

(a) Complete sentences       (b) Mentions of story character

Figure 8: Similarity of the computational representations with brain representations at different segments of the story.

**Predictive Approach** Besides, RSA, we can use a predictive approach to see which regions of the brain are more predictable, given the representations from a computational model. In the predictive approach, we train a linear regression model to predict the brain activity patterns at different steps of the story. This way, we can obtain more fine-grained insights into which parts of the model contribute more to which regions in the brain.

In Figure 10, we show the results of using representations obtained from GoogleLM($L0$) to predict brain activity patterns of different subjects. Similar to the results we obtained from RSA, the effect of hemodynamic response delay is clearly visible here. One of the difficulties of employing a predictive approach is to train a regression model for such high dimensions and with so little data. Hence, if the performance of the prediction is low, it is hard to tell if it is because we are not able to train a good regression model or because there is no correlation between the two models. To overcome this challenge, one solution could be to first use RSA to reduce the search space and then employ predictive modelling to gain more fine-grained insights. We postpone further analysis with the predictive approach to future studies.

## 6 Discussion and Conclusion

In this paper, we employ a representational similarity metric to compare the representations from the language encoding models with the brain activity patterns, i.e. measure the alignment between the brain activation patterns and activations of the internal state of the models. The main advantage of RSA is that it treats both the brain and the model as a blackbox; it does not need to know how brains or models represent objects, words or sentences, but only how similar representations are to each other. For $N$ stimuli considered, the analysis only compares $\frac{1}{2}N(N-1)$ pairs of pairwise similarities (assuming similarities are symmetric), regardless of the dimensionality of two representational spaces. This bottleneck brings many advantages including computational efficiency, reuse of the similarity matrices in multiple comparisons, and not having to worry about how to map representations of very different nature to each other. It also brings important limitations and inevitable information loss, e.g. standard RSA, assumes all features of the representational spaces to have equal contributions.

One of our contributions in this paper is the introduction of ReStA, which uses RSA to measure the stability of the representations from the models when an input condition such as context length is changed. Comparing the representational similarity of different layers of different models, we find that both architectural differences and different training objectives have a noticeable impact on the representations learned by the models and the way they change under different conditions. We see a clear difference in the sensitivity to context size between $L0$ and $L1$ in the LSTM based models. This means, in line with results from previous work using different methods (e.g., Giulianelli et al., 2018), that the $L1$ component integrates information over time steps while $L0$ does not.

Using brain data to evaluate the representations learned at different layers of each of the language encoding models, we find that layers of the LSTM based models achieve higher similarity score with brain data compared to single word representation models like GloVe and the Transformer based models. This observation could show that the learning biases of the LSTM based language models are closer to what happens in the human brain. Zooming into the results, we see that

198

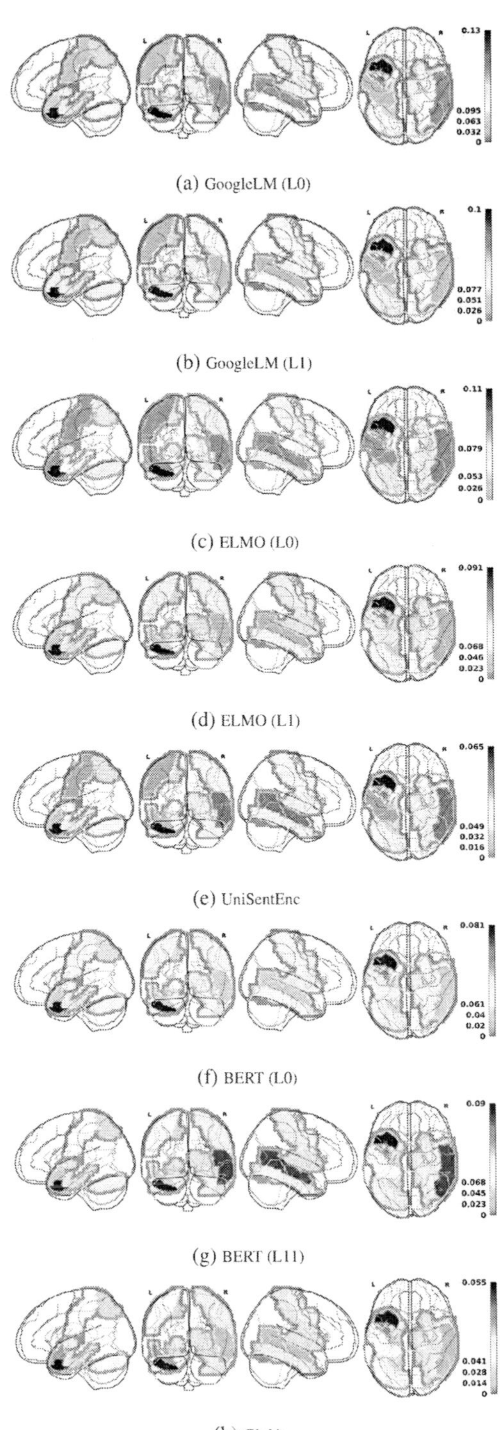

(a) GoogleLM (L0)

(b) GoogleLM (L1)

(c) ELMO (L0)

(d) ELMO (L1)

(e) UniSentEnc

(f) BERT (L0)

(g) BERT (L11)

(h) GloVe

Figure 9: RSA of representations learned at different layers of different models with representations at different regions of Subject4's brain which is chosen randomly (the code accompanying this paper can be used to generate the plots for the other subjects). In order to emphasize the difference of the similarity of each model with different brain regions, the color bar is scaled independently for each model. The darkest region for all models is the Left Anterior Temporal Lobe.

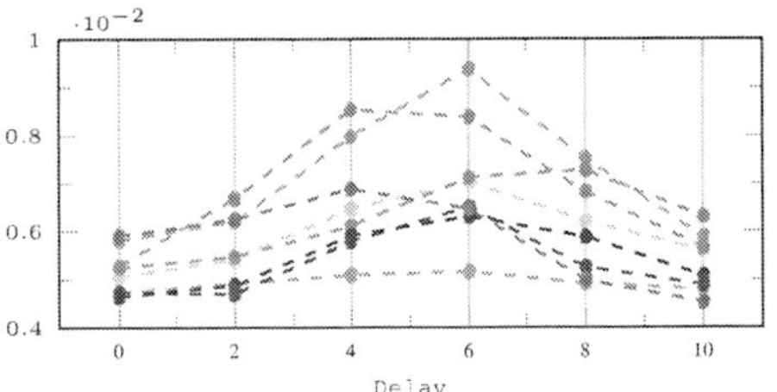


Figure 10: Predictive power of representations learned by Google LM (L0_Cinf) for brain representations in terms of explained variance (each subject in a different color).

while changing the conditions of the inputs to the models has a significant impact on the representations they compute and their performance on NLP tasks (Khandelwal et al., 2018), these changes do not get reflected in their alignment with the brain representations.

Finally, evaluating computational models of language processing with brain imaging data for a task such as "story reading" is hard, because of the inherent issues in the brain data and also the complexity of the task (Beinborn et al., 2019). Both the RSA framework and the predictive modelling approach make it possible to make a bridge between these black boxes, neural network models for language processing on the one hand and the human brain on the other. And while each of these approaches has its benefits and limitations, they might provide us with complementary information. Hence, it is invaluable to look at both.

In our experiments, we observe more similarities between representations learned by some architectures and brain representations. However, caution is required when interpreting these results, as the representational similarity between all models and the brain images remains very low. We plan to perform further analysis on various (bigger) datasets to get a better interpretation of what is happening in both the brain and these computational models.

## Acknowledgement


We thank Dieuwke Hupkes, Arnold Kochari, the Language in Interaction BQ1 team, and the anonymous reviewers for useful comments on the research described here and earlier versions of this paper. The work presented here was funded by the Netherlands Organization for Scientific Research (NWO), through a Gravitation Grant 024.001.006 to the Language in Interaction Consortium.

# References

Samira Abnar, Rasyan Ahmed, Max Mijnheer, and Willem Zuidema. 2018. Experiential, distributional and dependency-based word embeddings have complementary roles in decoding brain activity. In *Proceedings of the 8th Workshop on Cognitive Modeling and Computational Linguistics (CMCL 2018)*, pages 57–66. Association for Computational Linguistics.

Alexandre Abraham, Fabian Pedregosa, Michael Eickenberg, Philippe Gervais, Andreas Mueller, Jean Kossaifi, Alexandre Gramfort, Bertrand Thirion, and Gaël Varoquaux. 2014. Machine learning for neuroimaging with scikit-learn. *Frontiers in neuroinformatics*, 8:14.

David Alvarez-Melis and Tommi Jaakkola. 2018. Gromov-Wasserstein alignment of word embedding spaces. In *Proceedings of the 2018 Conference on Empirical Methods in Natural Language Processing*, pages 1881–1890, Brussels, Belgium. Association for Computational Linguistics.

Lisa Beinborn, Samira Abnar, and Rochelle Choenni. 2019. Robust evaluation of language-brain encoding experiments. *International Journal of Computational Linguistics and Applications*, to appear.

Douglas K Bemis and Liina Pylkkänen. 2011. Simple composition: A magnetoencephalography investigation into the comprehension of minimal linguistic phrases. *Journal of Neuroscience*, 31(8):2801–2814.

Joachim Bingel, Maria Barrett, and Anders Søgaard. 2016. Extracting token-level signals of syntactic processing from fMRI - with an application to PoS induction. In *Proceedings of the 54th Annual Meeting of the Association for Computational Linguistics (Volume 1: Long Papers)*, pages 747–755. Association for Computational Linguistics.

Randy L Buckner. 1998. Event-related fMRI and the hemodynamic response. *Human brain mapping*, 6(5-6):373–377.

Luana Bulat, Stephen Clark, and Ekaterina Shutova. 2017. Speaking, seeing, understanding: Correlating semantic models with conceptual representation in the brain. In *Proceedings of the 2017 Conference on Empirical Methods in Natural Language Processing (EMNLP)*, pages 1081–1091. Association for Computational Linguistics.

Daniel Cer, Yinfei Yang, Sheng-yi Kong, Nan Hua, Nicole Limtiaco, Rhomni St. John, Noah Constant, Mario Guajardo-Cespedes, Steve Yuan, Chris Tar, Brian Strope, and Ray Kurzweil. 2018. Universal sentence encoder for english. In *Proceedings of the 2018 Conference on Empirical Methods in Natural Language Processing, EMNLP 2018: System Demonstrations, Brussels, Belgium, October 31 - November 4, 2018*, pages 169–174.

Grzegorz Chrupała and Afra Alishahi. 2019. Correlating neural and symbolic representations of language. In *Proceedings of the Annual Meeting of the Association for Computational Linguistics (ACL 2019)*.

Jacob Devlin, Ming-Wei Chang, Kenton Lee, and Kristina Toutanova. 2019. Bert: Pre-training of deep bidirectional transformers for language understanding. In *Proceedings of Conference of the North American Chapter of the Association for Computational Linguistics - Human Language Technologies (NAACL HLT 2019)*.

Dhanush Dharmaretnam and Alona Fyshe. 2018. The emergence of semantics in neural network representations of visual information. In *Proceedings of Conference of the North American Chapter of the Association for Computational Linguistics - Human Language Technologies (NAACL HLT 2018)*.

Alona Fyshe, Partha P Talukdar, Brian Murphy, and Tom M Mitchell. 2014. Interpretable semantic vectors from a joint model of brain-and text-based meaning. In *Proceedings of the conference. Association for Computational Linguistics. Meeting (ACL 2014)*, volume 2014, page 489. NIH Public Access.

Mario Giulianelli, Jack Harding, Florian Mohnert, Dieuwke Hupkes, and Willem Zuidema. 2018. Under the hood: Using diagnostic classifiers to investigate and improve how language models track agreement information. In *1st BlackBoxNLP workshop at Conference on Empirical Methods in Natural Language Processing (EMNLP 2019)*.

Alexander G Huth, Wendy A de Heer, Thomas L Griffiths, Frédéric E Theunissen, and Jack L Gallant. 2016. Natural speech reveals the semantic maps that tile human cerebral cortex. *Nature*, 532(7600):453.

Shailee Jain and Alexander G. Huth. 2018. Incorporating context into language encoding models for fMRI. In *Proceedings of the 32Nd International Conference on Neural Information Processing Systems*, NIPS'18, pages 6629–6638, USA. Curran Associates Inc.

Rafal Jozefowicz, Oriol Vinyals, Mike Schuster, Noam Shazeer, and Yonghui Wu. 2016. Exploring the limits of language modeling. *CoRR*.

Urvashi Khandelwal, He He, Peng Qi, and Dan Jurafsky. 2018. Sharp nearby, fuzzy far away: How neural language models use context. In *Proceedings of the 56th Annual Meeting of the Association for Computational Linguistics, ACL 2018, Melbourne, Australia, July 15-20, 2018, Volume 1: Long Papers*, pages 284–294.

Nikolaus Kriegeskorte, Marieke Mur, and Peter A Bandettini. 2008. Representational similarity analysis-connecting the branches of systems neuroscience. *Frontiers in systems neuroscience*, 2:4.

Aarre Laakso and Garrison Cottrell. 2000. Content and cluster analysis: assessing representational similarity in neural systems. *Philosophical psychology*, 13(1):47–76.

Timothy Leffel, Miriam Lauter, Masha Westerlund, and Liina Pylkkänen. 2014. Restrictive vs. non-restrictive composition: a magnetoencephalography study. *Language, cognition and neuroscience*, 29(10):1191–1204.

Tom M Mitchell, Svetlana V Shinkareva, Andrew Carlson, Kai-Min Chang, Vicente L Malave, Robert A Mason, and Marcel Adam Just. 2008. Predicting human brain activity associated with the meanings of nouns. *science*, 320(5880):1191–1195.

Brian Murphy, Partha Talukdar, and Tom Mitchell. 2012. Selecting corpus-semantic models for neurolinguistic decoding. In *Proceedings of the First Joint Conference on Lexical and Computational Semantics*, SemEval '12, pages 114–123, Stroudsburg, PA, USA. Association for Computational Linguistics.

Jeffrey Pennington, Richard Socher, and Christopher Manning. 2014. Glove: Global vectors for word representation. In *Proceedings of the conference on empirical methods in natural language processing (EMNLP 2014)*, pages 1532–1543.

Francisco Pereira, Bin Lou, Brianna Pritchett, Samuel Ritter, Samuel J Gershman, Nancy Kanwisher, Matthew Botvinick, and Evelina Fedorenko. 2018. Toward a universal decoder of linguistic meaning from brain activation. *Nature communications*, 9(1):963.

Matthew E. Peters, Mark Neumann, Mohit Iyyer, Matt Gardner, Christopher Clark, Kenton Lee, and Luke Zettlemoyer. 2018. Deep contextualized word representations. In *Proceedings of the 2018 Conference of the North American Chapter of the Association for Computational Linguistics: Human Language Technologies, NAACL HLT 2018*, pages 2227–2237.

Peng Qian, Xipeng Qiu, and Xuanjing Huang. 2016. Bridging lstm architecture and the neural dynamics during reading. In *Proceedings of International Joint Conferences on Artificial Intelligence Organization (IJCAI 2016)*.

J. K. Rowling. 1998. *Harry Potter And the Sorcerer's Stone*. Arthur A. Levine Books.

Yu-Ping Ruan, Zhen-Hua Ling, and Yu Hu. 2016. Exploring semantic representation in brain activity using word embeddings. In *Proceedings of the 2016 Conference on Empirical Methods in Natural Language Processing (EMNLP 2016)*, pages 669–679.

Anders Søgaard. 2016. Evaluating word embeddings with fMRI and eye-tracking. In *Proceedings of the 1st Workshop on Evaluating Vector-Space Representations for NLP*, pages 116–121. Association for Computational Linguistics.

Liwei Wang, Lunjia Hu, Jiayuan Gu, Zhiqiang Hu, Yue Wu, Kun He, and John Hopcroft. 2018. Towards understanding learning representations: To what extent do different neural networks learn the same representation. In *Advances in Neural Information Processing Systems*, pages 9606–9615.

Tian Wang and Kyunghyun Cho. 2016. Larger-context language modelling with recurrent neural network. In *Proceedings of the 54th Annual Meeting of the Association for Computational Linguistics, ACL 2016*.

Leila Wehbe, Brian Murphy, Partha Talukdar, Alona Fyshe, Aaditya Ramdas, and Tom Mitchell. 2014a. Simultaneously uncovering the patterns of brain regions involved in different story reading subprocesses. *in press.*

Leila Wehbe, Ashish Vaswani, Kevin Knight, and Tom M. Mitchell. 2014b. Aligning context-based statistical models of language with brain activity during reading. In *Proceedings of the 2014 conference on empirical methods in natural language processing (EMNLP 2014)*.

Masha Westerlund and Liina Pylkkänen. 2014. The role of the left anterior temporal lobe in semantic composition vs. semantic memory. *Neuropsychologia*, 57:59–70.

Haoyan Xu, Brian Murphy, and Alona Fyshe. 2016. Brainbench: A brain-image test suite for distributional semantic models. In *Proceedings of the 2016 Conference on Empirical Methods in Natural Language Processing (EMNLP 2016)*, pages 2017–2021.

# A  Appendices

## A.1  Representational Similarity Across Different Layers of Different Models

Figure 11 shows the representational similarity across different layers of the models given different amount of context.

## A.2  Preprocessing Brain Images

Besides the cognitive process of interest, other factors like the physiological processes in the bodies of the human subjects or technical features of the MRI-machine and scanning environment may influence the fMRI measurements. An important issue is therefore how to preprocess the data to filter out those irrelevant effects adequately.

**Detrending.**  We normalise the brain activations in two steps: we scale the activation values by subtracting the per-voxel mean activation. We also experiment with a more elaborate preprocessing procedure, implemented in the `nilearn.signal.clean` Python library. Detrending is a popular strategy in cognitive neuroscience (Abraham et al., 2014), that removes the linear trend, applies a high pass filtering with 0.005 Hz, and standardises the vectors.

**Voxel selection.**  To reduce the noise and remove the voxels which their activation is not related to the story reading task, we apply two steps for selecting the voxels. In the first step, we remove all the constant voxels. These are the brain regions in which the activation does not change at all during the scanning experiment. Next, we compare the similarity of different regions of the brain for all eight subjects and select those regions that their activations over the different segments of the story are most similar among the different subjects. To do this, we rank the regions based on the average of the similarity scores and then selected the top 16 regions. After applying this voxel selection strategy, we have approximately 10000 voxels for each subject.

In our experiments, we do not model the spatial dependency of the voxels. Thus, after the preprocessing steps, we flatten the 3D fMRI images into vectors with the size of the total number of the voxels.

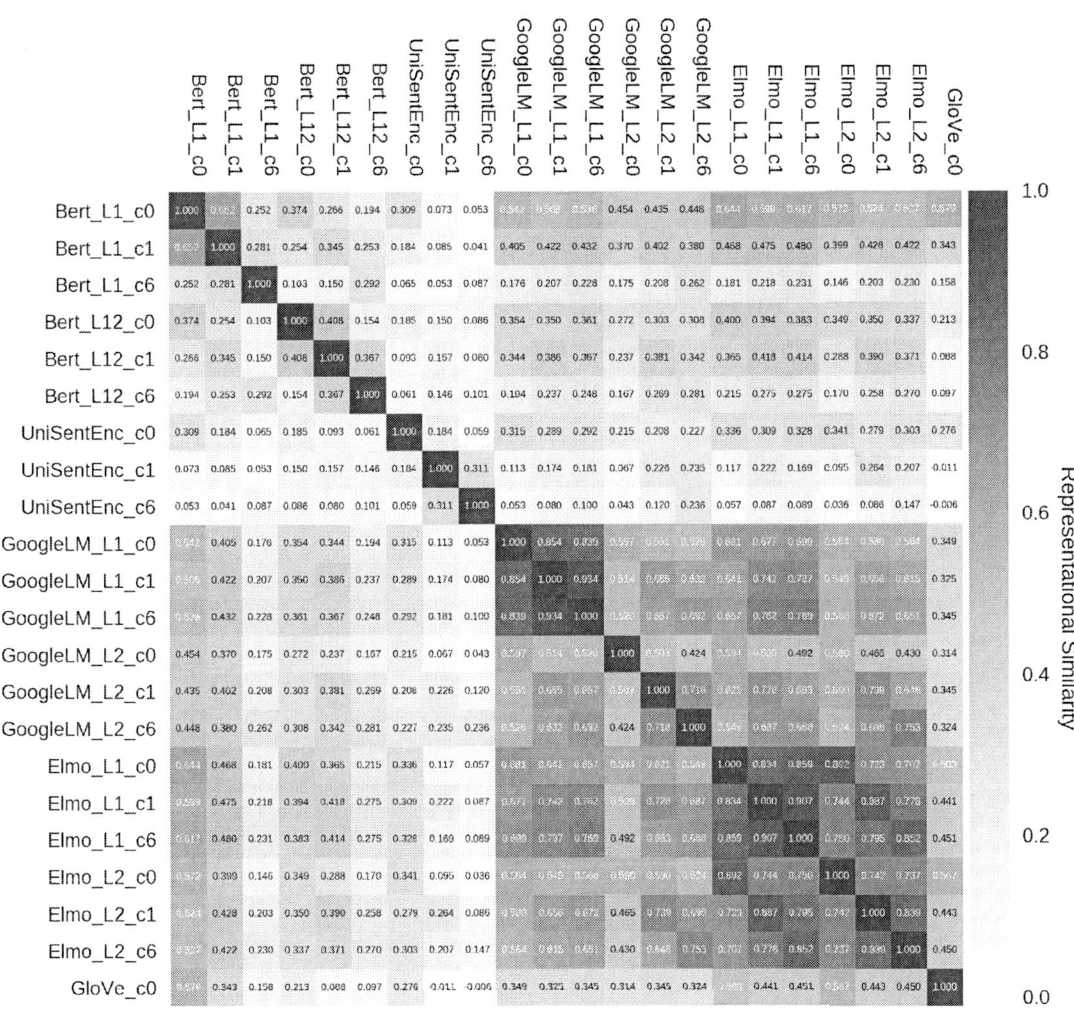

Figure 11: RSA of different layers of different models for different context length. In this plot, for example ELMO_1_c1 means representation from layer 1 of ELMO, when the context length is 1 sentences.

# An LSTM adaptation study of (un)grammaticality

**Shammur Absar Chowdhury and Roberto Zamparelli**
CIMeC: Center for Mind/Brain Sciences
University of Trento
{shammur.chowdhury, roberto.zamparelli}@unitn.it

## Abstract

We propose a novel approach to the study of how artificial neural network perceive the distinction between *grammatical* and *ungrammatical* sentences, a crucial task in the growing field of *synthetic linguistics*. The method is based on performance measures of language models trained on corpora and fine-tuned with either grammatical or ungrammatical sentences, then applied to (different types of) grammatical or ungrammatical sentences. The results show that both in the difficult and highly symmetrical task of detecting *subject islands* and in the more open CoLA dataset, grammatical sentences give rise to better scores than ungrammatical ones, possibly because they can be better integrated within the body of linguistic structural knowledge that the language model has accumulated.

## 1 Introduction

As the language modeling abilities of Artificial Neural Network (ANN) expand, a growing number of studies have started to address a network's ability to distinguish sentences contain various types of syntactic errors from minimally different correct sentences, thus providing the equivalent of human *grammaticality judgments*, one of the cornerstones of theoretical linguistics since Chomsky (1957). These studies are important for at least two reasons: they can shed light on the type and amount of information which can be learned from pure linguistic data without any specialized language-learning device (thus contributing to the debate on human Universal Grammar,

Chomsky 1986; Lasnik and Lidz. 2015; Chowdhury and Zamparelli 2018), and they can be used as probes on the ANNs themselves, investigating whether models which are apparently proficient at language modeling are actually sensitive to the same syntactic and semantic cues humans use.

The ANNs used in this area of research (often LSTMs, Hochreiter and Schmidhuber 1997, but recently also transformer-based ANN, Vaswani *et al.* 2017, all trained on large datasets of normal text) are tested on a mix of grammatical or ungrammatical sentences. The latter are obtained either by altering naturally occurring sentences (semi-randomly, as in Lau *et al.* 2017, or systematically, Linzen *et al.* 2016; Gulordava *et al.* 2018), by collecting examples from the published linguistic literature (Warstadt *et al.*, 2018) or by creating minimal pairs by hand (individually, Wilcox *et al.* 2018, or with sentence-schemata, as in Chowdhury and Zamparelli 2018).[1]

Once test data have been acquired, the literature has threaded between two very different approaches: treating grammaticality as a *classification* problem (i.e. feeding grammatical/-ungrammatical sentences to a classifier and asking it to discriminate, cf. the first experiment in Linzen *et al.* 2016), or feeding the test sentences to a Language Model (**LM**) pretrained on normal language and measuring the perplexity accumulated by the LM as it traverses the sentence.[2]

The classification approach works somewhat better, and can tell us if the possibility to spot un-

---

This work was funded by the Italian 2015 PRIN Grant "TREiL", and is licensed under a Creative Commons Attribution 4.0 International License. License details: `http://creativecommons.org/licenses/by/4.0/`

[1]Most studies except Lau *et al.* (2017) take the simplifying assumption that judgments can be treated as binary (e.g. *acceptable/non-acceptable*). This position is not entirely satisfactory, theoretically, but we believe that it won't do much harm at this early stage of research.

[2]Intermediate methods are possible: Warstadt *et al.* (2018) and Warstadt and Bowman (2019) train a classifier on sentence vectors produced by various types of language models.



*Proceedings of the Second BlackboxNLP Workshop on Analyzing and Interpreting Neural Networks for NLP*, pages 204–212
Florence, Italy, August 1, 2019. ©2019 Association for Computational Linguistics

grammaticality can *in principle* be learned from the data, but is not directly comparable with the human ability to detect ungrammaticality, since explicit syntactic judgments play a negligible role in language acquisition.

The approach which reads (un)grammaticality from the performance of a LM starts from a more naturalistic task—predicting what's coming (van Berkum, 2010)—and can thus be more directly compared to human performances, but the probability assigned by a LM to the words reflects many factors (sentence complexity, level of embedding, semantic coherence, etc.), making it difficult to tease apart 'grammaticality' from a more general notion of 'acceptability' or 'processing load'.

In this paper we propose a third approach to measuring grammaticality, derived from the LM method. In this approach, we utilized our in-house pre-trained LSTM LM and *adapt* the model via *fine-tuning* (Pan and Yang, 2010; Li, 2012) on variations of the test sentences.

Grammaticality is then treated as a comparative measure of coherence: to what extent the new (un)grammatical input can be integrated with what the ANN has learned so far, and to what extent it can improve similar grammatical or ungrammatical constructions. We test this method with a large number of artificially generated examples, focusing on a particularly difficult contrast, the case of subject vs. object subextraction[3]. We then apply the method to a more general scenario, the CoLA dataset, tuning a LM with either *grammatical* or *ungrammatical* CoLA sentences and measuring its performance in various testing scenarios.[4]

In the following sections, we first present a detailed task description, in Section 2, followed by a brief overview of the methodology and datasets used for the study (Section 3). In Section 4, we formalize our hypothesis of how the model should behave and report the results and observation of the network behavior in Section 5; we then discuss our observation and conclude the study with future directions in Section 6.

---

[3]The expanded test sets for each task can be found in `https://github.com/LiCo-TREiL/Computational-Ungrammaticality/tree/master/blackboxnlp2019`.

[4]See Warstadt *et al.* (2018). Every sentence in the corpus, which can be found at `https://nyu-mll.github.io/CoLA/`, is marked as grammatical or ungrammatical. The values are drawn from the published literature, see Warstadt *et al.* (2018, Tab.2) for details.

## 2 Task Description

It has been noted since Ross (1967) that while Wh-questions and relatives clauses (RC) can give raise to gaps at unbounded distance (as in *Who did Mary say that John saw __* and *The boy that Mary thinks that John adopted __*), gaps in certain positions (e.g. inside relative clauses, individual conjuncts, or certain adjuncts) are perceived as degraded. Ross coined the term *syntactic islands* for these environments, which have been the focus of a huge amount of research in theoretical linguistics (see e.g. Szabolcsi and den Dikken 1999). Studies on ANNs' sensitivity to grammaticality have tried to model certain types of islands, with varying degree of success (Lau *et al.*, 2017; Wilcox *et al.*, 2018, 2019; Jumelet and Hupkes, 2018). In this paper, we address *subject islands*, i.e. the difference between (1a) and (b) for Wh-interrogatives, and between (2a) and (b) for RCs.

(1) a.   Which people did activists love [fighting for __]?

    b.   *Which people did [fighting for __] appeal to activists?

(2) a.   the causes that Mary feared [fighting against __]

    b.   *the causes that [fighting against __] scared Mary

Subject islands are an interesting domain for various reasons: (i) extractions from subjects and object can contain nearly the same words (like above), and there are no lexical cues which signal one or the other type (e.g. both cases in (1) require *do*-support); (ii) while (1) and (2) share the extraction phenomenon, they have completely different discourse functions and distributions: is not obvious that a model that learns relative clauses should boost its processing of Wh-questions, or vice-versa; (iii) extractions out of PPs inside nominals are rare in naturally occurring data, so they stand as a challenging test of the ANN's generalization abilities.

Embedded Wh extractions out of PPs (*I know who the painting by __ fetched a high price at auction.*) were one of the violations studied in Wilcox *et al.* (2018), using Google's LM and the model from Gulordava *et al.* (2018). Neither LMs managed to model extractions out of PPs, treating the PP either as a possible extraction domain (Google's LM) or an island in both subject and

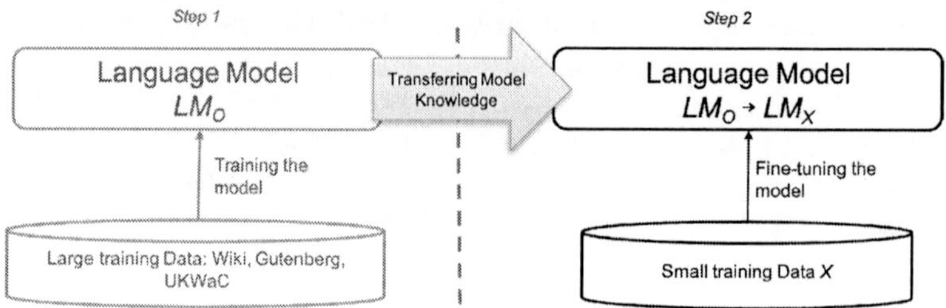


Figure 1: Experimental Pipeline.

object position (Gulorodova's). The study didn't address RCs like (2). This case thus presents an interesting challenge for our technique: combined with the sentence schemata method described in Section 3, it gives a highly controlled environment; however, this comes at the cost of a high lexical overlap (after fine-tuning, the ANN is tested on structures which contain many words it has already practiced with). To try a different and more open testing environment we applied the same method to the 5 test sets of the CoLA dataset (see Section 3 for details) . In this case, we fine-tuned the ANN on grammatical or ungrammatical sentences from the CoLA training set, and tested it on *different* CoLA test-phenomena sentences, checking the interactions. Since this part of CoLA is categorized by topic this gives a sense of which types of phenomena improve with this method.

## 3  Methodology

In this section, we describe our pipeline, including details of the datasets used in each steps. In addition, we present the evaluation measure used to validate the effects (if any) of the fine-tuning method on our tasks.

Figure 1 shows the pipeline we propose for exploring the effect of rehearsing new (un)grammatical input on a trained LSTM language model.

**LM Architecture:**  The first step (Step 1 in Fig. 1) is to train a language model ($LM_O$) using a large text corpus.  For the study, we used a left-to-right long-short term memory (LSTM) language model (Hochreiter and Schmidhuber, 1997), trained with $500$ hidden units in each layer ($layers = 2$) and an embedding dimension of $256$. The model was trained using a PyTorch RNN implementation with dropout regularization technique applied in different layers of the architecture, along with SGD optimizer using a fixed batch

| Corpus | Style | % |
|---|---|---|
| Wiki-103 | Encyclopedic data | 12.15 |
| Gutenberg[6] Dataset | Narrative style: includes collection of English books | 36.58 |
| UKWaC | Mixed, crawled from .uk domain | 51.27 |

Table 1: Composition of the training set and style of training data.

size of 80. We have not tuned the models for different dropouts or learning rate parameters, among other parameters.

**Datasets for Training LM:**  To train the LSTM model, we used different English corpora — for stylistic variety — extracted from Wikipedia, the Gutenberg Dataset (Lahiri, 2014) and UKWaC (Ferraresi *et al.*, 2008), as shown in Table 1. We then tokenized the input sentences, removing URLs, email addresses, emoticons and text enclosed in any form of brackets ({.},(.), [.]). We replaced rare words (tokens with frequency $< 20$)[5] with $<UNK>$ token along with its signatures (e.g. *-ed, -ing, -ly* etc.) to represent every possible out-of-vocabulary (OOV) words.  We also replaced numbers (exponential, comma separated etc) with a $<NUM>$ tag. We removed the sentences from UKWaC with OOV tags. Therefore, to train LM we used a training set consisted of $\approx 0.7B$ words in $\approx 31M$ sentences, with a vocabulary of size $|V| = 0.1M$.

**Adaptation via fine-tuning:**  The trained $LM_0$ was used to initialize the weights of the new LSTM $LM_X$, so as to transfer the knowledge

---

[5] For preparing the vocabulary set $V$, we only considered tokens presents in WikiText and Gutenberg dataset.

[6] We intentionally removed the stories that overlapped with the test and dev set of Childrens Book Test (CBT) (Hill *et al.*, 2015), for training purpose.

$LM_0$ has acquired so far (Step 2 Fig. 1). To adapt the models $LM_X$ to new (un)grammatical structures, we fine-tuned the models by feeding the sentences from our small training data sets, with batch size of 20 and epoch e ($e = \{3, 10\}$). All other parameters remained unchanged with respect to the original $LM_0$. In this paper, for brevity, we only report the results after 3 epochs.

**Datasets for Adaptation:** LMs can be quite sensitive to the specific content words used. To minimize this effect and focus on structure, we used the 'sentence schemata' method from Chowdhury and Zamparelli (2018): starting from a schema such as (3), a script automatically generates sentences containing all the possible combinations of the bracketed expressions. The schema in (3) (tagged **Aff**(irmatives with complex) **Obj**(ects)) gives 160 affirmative sentences (e.g. *Activists hated fighting for these laws*); we also constructed schemata for affirmatives with the gerund in subject position (**AffSubj**, e.g. *fighting for these causes scares politicians*), as well as for the corresponding root Wh-clauses (**WhSubj**, **WhObj**, as in (1a)/(1b), and relatives (**RelSubj**, **RelObj**, as in (2a)/(2b)).[7] In total, we have 6 train/test sets, see Table 2 for details.

(3) [ John Mary politicians activists governments ] [ feared loved hated thought_about ] fighting [ for against ] these [ causes movements people laws ] .

Apart from exploring adaptation of subject islands, we also explored the effect of adaptation in an open testing environment (as mentioned in Section 2). For this setting, our training and testing data is less likely to have a substantial lexical overlap. For the adaptation part, we split the CoLA training set in two parts—one consisting of grammatical sentences ($CoLA_G$), the other one of ungrammatical sentences ($CoLA_{UG}$), both covering different linguistic phenomena such as islands, passives, coordination, negative polarity, etc. As test sets, we used different CoLA-test phenomena.[8] They are:

- Subject-Verb-Object (**SVO**): The test set consists of utterances, generated using different permutation of subject (S), verb (V) and object (O). The set contains 10 subjects, 2 verbs and 5 objects.

- Wh-Extraction (**WhExt**): This set tests the ability to note that a Wh- must correspond to a gap, with pairs such as *What did John fry? / *What did John fry the potato?* (cf. Wilcox *et al.* 2018, Sec.2.3, Chowdhury and Zamparelli 2018, Task B).

- Causative-Inchoative Alternation (**CausAlt**): Based on verbs that do or do not undergo the alternation (*Kelly popped/blew the bubble.* vs. *The bubble popped/*blew.*).

- Subject-Verb Agreement (**SVAgr**): A set based on number agreement mismatch, such as *the child (that was accompanied by his parents) has/*have left.* This is the task used in Linzen *et al.* (2016); Gulordava *et al.* (2018).

- Reflexive-Antecedent Agreement (**ReflAgr**): A test on whether reflexive pronouns have appropriate local antecedents (cf. *I amused myself / *yourself / *herself / *him- self / *ourselves / *themselves*).

**Evaluation Measure:** To track the performance of our LSTM on the test sets, we adopted the popular acceptability measure *Syntactic log-odds ratio* ($SLOR$), introduced in this domain by Lau *et al.* (2017) and shown in Equation 1.

$$SLOR(\varepsilon) = \frac{log(p_m(\varepsilon)) - log(p_u(\varepsilon))}{|\varepsilon|} \quad (1)$$

where $\varepsilon$ represents the sentence; $p_m(.)$ is the probability of the $\varepsilon$ given by the model, calculated by multiplying probabilities of each target words, present in the sentence; $p_u(.)$ is the unigram probability of the $\varepsilon$ and $|\varepsilon|$ represent the length of the sentence.

The measure considers the structure and position of the words, subtracting out the unigram log-probability so that sentences that use rare words are not penalized, and is normalized by sentence length, thus removing (positive or negative) biases due to long sentences. Higher SLOR values correspond to 'better' (i.e. more predictable/acceptable) sentences.

---

[7] For training, we merged AffObj and AffSubj to create a general set of affirmatives, Aff.

[8] Please check Warstadt *et al.* (2018, Tab. 2) for details.

| Sets | # inst. | Used for | Sets | # inst. | Used for |
|---|---|---|---|---|---|
| Close Environment Testing | | | Open Environment Testing | | |
| **AffObj**: *X likes [ fighting for Y ]* | 160 | test | CoLA$_G$ | 6029 | train |
| **AffSubj**: *[ fighting for Y ] pleases X* | 160 | test | CoLA$_{UG}$ | 2532 | train |
| **Aff**: AffSubj∪AffObj | 320 | train | SVO | 500 | test |
| **RelObj**: *the Y that X likes [ fighting for __]* | 160 | train/test | WhExt | 520 | test |
| **RelSubj**: *the Y that [ fighting for __] pleases X* | 120 | train/test | CausAlt | 182 | test |
| **WhObj**: *What did X like [ fighting for __]?* | 200 | train/test | SVAgr | 676 | test |
| **WhSubj**: *What did [ fighting for __] please X ?* | 150 | train/test | RiflAgr | 144 | test |

Table 2: Detailed information of the training/testing set for the adaptation experiments. inst. represent instances

## 4 Our Hypothesis

We expect the adapted LM to improve in proportion to the similarity between the tasks, but also in proportion to how well the material presented in the fine-tuning learning phase is consistent with what the ANN already knows about language structures.

Our expectations are that retraining with ungrammatical sentences should be harder to incorporate into previous knowledge, thus leading to worse performances in terms of generalization. Note that improvements when the ANN is trained on Wh and tested on RC or vice-versa can be attributed in part to lexical familiarity (the training contained most of the words seen in the testing), in part to the model's ability to note the common element in the two constructions, i.e. the extraction. We can mitigate the lexical overlap problem by subtracting the scores of a LM fine-tuned on the affirmative cases (i.e. the sentences generated from (3)) from those obtained from the corresponding extraction cases (RC and Wh), since our affirmative cases already contain most of the lexicon found in the RC/Wh sentences.

In the second experiment, where we tested on CoLA, there is no reason to expect a very high lexical overlap, so any effect found there can be attributed purely to the structures.

## 5 Results

**Subject/Object Extraction** Figure 2 gives an overview of the SLOR values of our LSTM tuned for 3 epochs just on the affirmative sentences (LM$_X$, left), compared to the original (LM$_O$, right). Unsurprisingly, the LM$_X$ shows a large improvement in the AffSubj/AffObj cases, but also an improvement in Wh case and especially in relative clauses. Note that after fine-tuning, all conditions (Aff,Rel and Wh) show a significant preference for the object case (present in Aff/Wh even in the original run). This effect emerged also in Chowdhury and Zamparelli (2018) (and in work of ours, under review, which specifically addresses this phenomenon). Since it is also present in affirmatives, it cannot obviously be attributed to a sensitivity to islands, but can probably be put down to a general preference of LSTM LMs for having complex structures in object position. This effect seems to overcome an effect found in Chowdhury and Zamparelli (2018) (Task A, which however uses different measures), where subject relatives scored better than object relatives (while both being grammatical), in line with human parsing preferences widely discussed in the psycholinguistic literature (Gibson, 1998; Gordon *et al.*, 2001; Friedmann *et al.*, 2009). The general lower score for RCs, compared to Wh cases, could also be attributed to the fact that in the testing phase the LM receives an End-of-Input signal before the sentence is over (i.e. RC are sentence fragments).

Figure 3 shows the effect of fine-tuning the original LM on different parts of the test set and testing it on the others. At a global level, if we compare the scores with the affirmative baseline (the performance of the model fine-tuned with affirmatives only, as in Figure 2, left), we see that on average adding Wh-clauses significantly boosts RCs (+0.64) and vice-versa, though not as strongly (+0.39). Next, tuning with *grammatical* material gives a larger overall boost than tuning on *ungrammatical* material. This can be seen from the Total in Table 3 (using the notation ARelObj(RelObj-Aff(RelObj)) to mean "SLOR of LM$_O$ fine-tuned with Aff+RelObj (ARelObj) and applied to Relatives with OBJect subextraction minus the SLOR of the test set using model adapted by Aff)"). Within construction, tuning with Aff plus Obj extractions boosts other object cases (green cells)

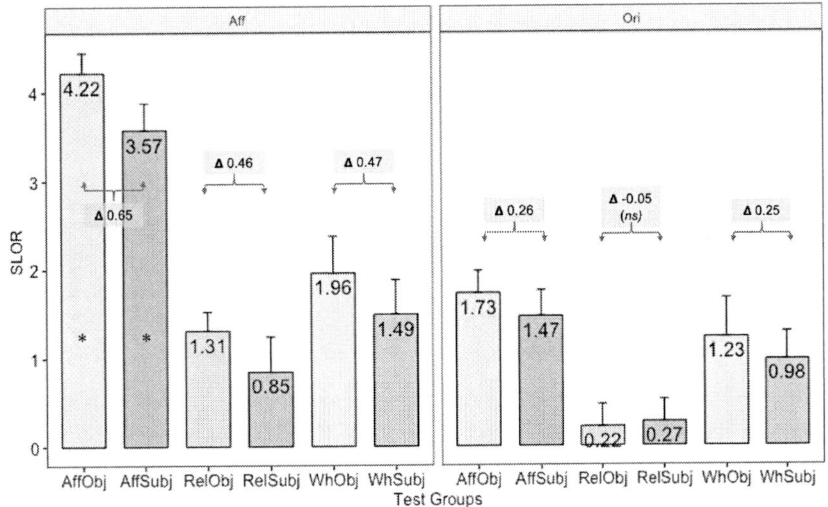

Figure 2: Variation of SLOR measure for different test groups using the model adapted on affirmative sentences (Aff, both AffSubj and AffObj) and the original $LM_0$ (Ori) model. Higher is better. The blue arrows with the $\Delta$ values represents the difference in SLOR between grammatical and ungrammatical sentences. * warns that the same testset is used to adapt the respective model. *ns* indicates that the results are not significantly different from each other.

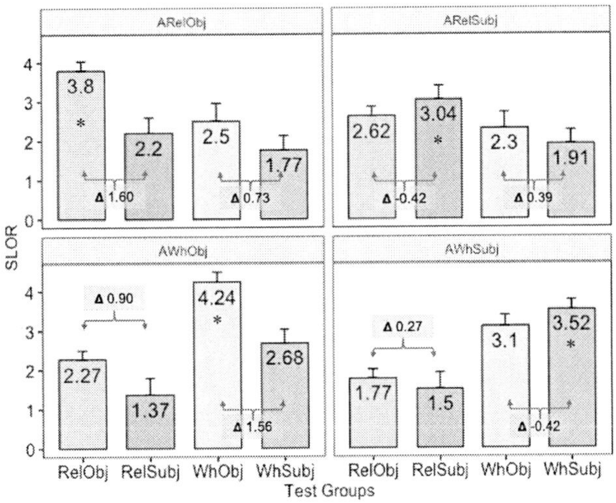

Figure 3: Variation of SLOR measure for different test groups using models adapted on: relative clause-object (ARelObj); relative clause-subject (ARelSubj); wh-object (AWhObj); wh-subject (AWhSubj). All the models are initially adapted on affirmative sentences, hence the presence of A in **A**RelObj and all other models. The blue arrows with the $\Delta$ values represents the difference between the SLOR of grammatical correct sentences with ungrammatical sentences. The * warns when the same testset was used to adapt the corresponding model.

more than tuning on Aff plus Subj extractions boosts other Subj cases (pink cells); across construction, Aff+WhObj tuning boosts RelObj and even RelSub and, to a lesser extent, Aff+RelObj tuning boosts WhObj more than Aff+RelSubj boosts WhSubj.

**CoLA results** Figure 4 shows the results on the 5 test sets for the original model ($LM_O$) and the LM fine-tuned with the CoLA grammatical and ungrammatical sentences, respectively. The first thing to note is that $LM_O$ is already able to significantly distinguish, on average, the two classes, with the worst performances coming from the Causative-Inchoative Alternation, a construc-

| | Testing scores | Fine-tuned with | | | |
|---|---|---|---|---|---|
| | | ARelObj | ARelSubj | AWhObj | AWhSubj |
| a. | **RelSubj–Aff(RelSubj)** | 1.35 | 2.19 | 0.52 | 0.65 |
| b. | **RelObj–Aff(RelObj)** | 2.49 | 1.31 | 0.96 | 0.46 |
| c. | **WhSubj–Aff(WhSubj)** | 0.28 | 0.42 | 1.19 | 2.03 |
| d. | **WhObj–Aff(WhObj)** | 0.54 | 0.34 | 2.28 | 1.14 |
| e. | **Total:** | 4.66 | 4.26 | 4.95 | 4.28 |

Table 3: Effect of fine-tuning. **A**X represent the models tuned with affirmatives followed by **X**. **Y**-Aff(**Y**) represent the test scores (SLOR) using the particular model minus the SLOR of the model adapted on affirmatives (Aff) for the Y test set. $X, Y \in \{RelObj, RelSubj, WhObj, WhSubj\}$.

tion linked to the lexical semantics of a class of verbs which are not likely to be encountered in many other examples. As in the previous experiment, fine-tuning improves the SLOR scores of all cases, ungrammatical ones included. In keeping with the previous experiment, we verify whether the switch from $CoLA_G$ to $CoLA_{UG}$ has a significant effect on the improvements (esp. CoLA-G(G) vs. CoLA-UG(UG), keeping in mind that here, unlike in the previous experiment, the training can contain at most a small dose of the lexicon and the phenomena in the testing set). Given the results in the Subj/Obj island task, our expectations are that tuning on $CoLA_G$ should work better than tuning on $CoLA_{UG}$. The difference turns out not to be significant with Subject-Verb Agreement cases (SVArg, Figure 4a), significant but with ungrammatical cases coming out best for the Subject-Verb-Object permutation cases (SVO, Figure 4b), significantly bigger with grammatical tuning in the remaining cases (see 4f for the overall picture). The case of SVArg might be due to the fact that the contrastive examples found in the syntactic literature might not cover something as basic as wrong subject-verb agreement. The behavior of SVO remains unclear.

## 6 Discussions and Conclusions

The results of ours first experiment suggest that, even though the contrast between subject and object subextraction is one of the hardest for ANNs to detect (see Wilcox *et al.* 2018), fine-tuning a language model with one of the two conditions does not give the same effect: above and beyond the effect of assertions (see Figure 3), tuning with grammatical extractions (i.e. object cases) yields a larger boost for the construction used for tuning than tuning with the ungrammatical cases. In small measure, the boost extends to the related construction (Wh to RC, and partially vice-versa).

The same effect is found with the much less controlled CoLA dataset, at least for some of the constructions we tested.

The results are consistent with the hypothesis that grammatical cases are somehow easier to integrate into what the ANN has already discovered about linguistic structures. Of course, positive examples of grammatical extractions like WhObj and RelOBj also boost the ungrammatical cases, but possibly this is because they apply to parts of the sentence different from the extraction site (indeed, ungrammatical cases boost grammatical and ungrammatical cases almost to the same degree). This suggests that the methodology we are proposing could be a useful addition to the toolbox of this research area.

An obvious question, at this point, is whether the fine-tuning approach could be turned into a *classification* method. One could for instance imagine classifying a sentence as grammatical or ungrammatical on the basis of its SLOR difference across LMs tuned with grammatical/ungrammatical sets (e.g. $CoLA_G$ and $CoLA_{UG}$ conditions). Recall however that SLOR is sensitive to a variety of factors which have nothing to do with grammaticality (e.g. collocations, pragmatic plausibility), and that it has been used to study grammaticality only with carefully constructed minimal pairs. While not impossible, we suspect that a classification experiment could not be done with relatively open data like CoLA, though it is possible that with more balanced materials such an experiment might become possible. Probably a better use for the technique proposed here would be to study similarity across constructions *as seen by the network*. Using the more fine-grained classification of the CoLA data given in Warstadt and Bowman (2019), it might be possible to selectively fine-tune a model with one construction, test it with all the others and discover

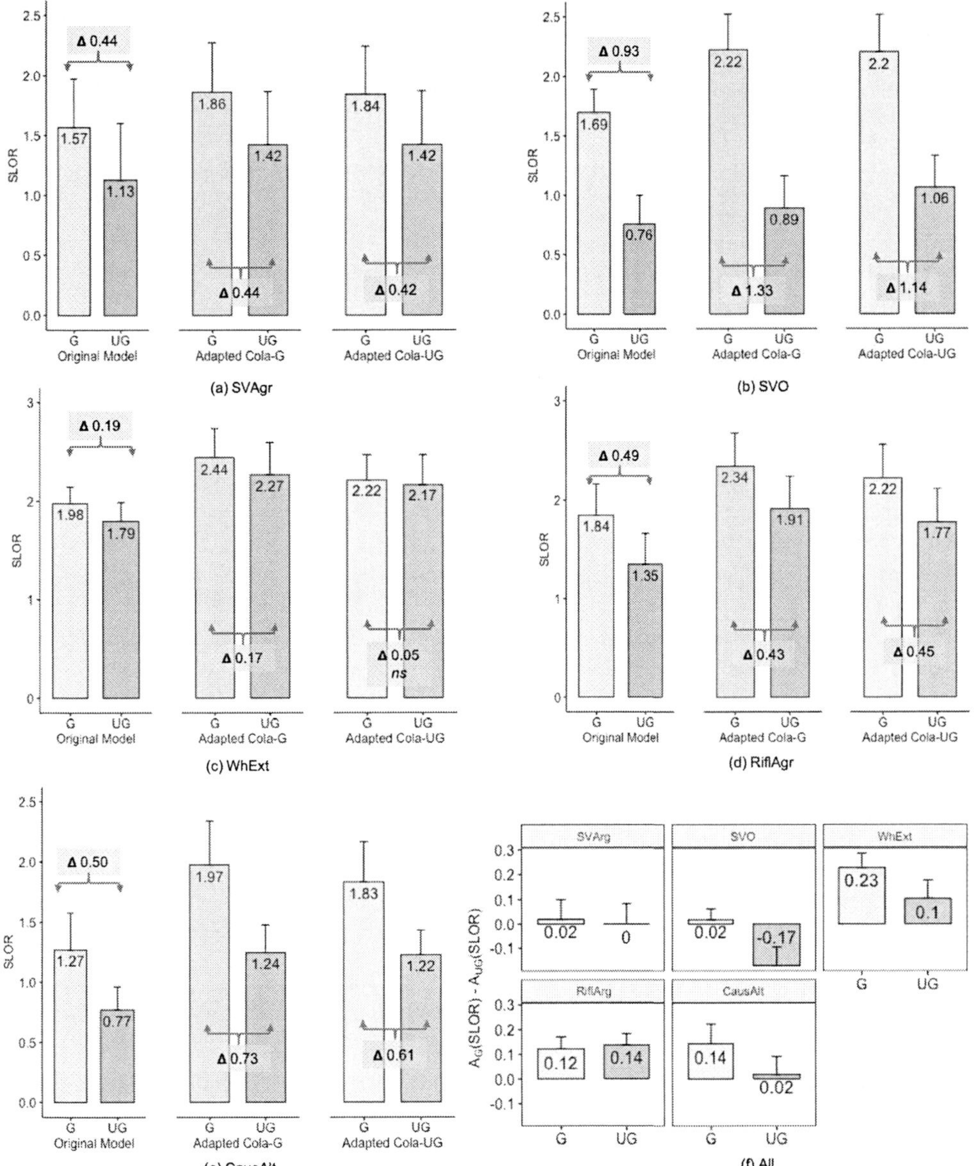

Figure 4: Variation of global SLOR measure for: Figure 4a - Subject-Verb Agreement (SVAgr); In Figure 4b - Subject-Verb-Object (SVO); In Figure 4c - Wh-Extraction (WhExt); In Figure 4d - Reflexive-Antecedent Agreement (RiflAgr); Figure 4e - Causative-Inchoative Alternation (CausAlt). For all Figure 4 a-e, Original model is un-adapted LM model, where as Adapted Cola-G(UG) represent the results from the model which is adapted on CoLA train grammatical (ungrammatical) instances. Figure 4f represents the difference in the measure of SLOR value, for grammatical (G) and ungrammatical (UG) examples, between Cola-G and Cola-UG model, i.e. $A_G(SLOR) - A_{UG}(SLOR)$ for all the above test cases (a-e), where $A_G$ represents result from Cola-G model and similarly $A_{UG}$ represents result from Cola-UG. The blue arrows with the $\Delta$ values represents the difference between the SLOR of grammatical correct sentences with ungrammatical sentences. *ns* indicates that the results are not significantly different from each other.

from the variations in a performance measure like SLOR how the ANN 'sees' the relation between different linguistic cases.

## References


Chomsky, N. (1957). *Syntactic Structures*. Mouton, The Hague.

Chomsky, N. (1986). *Knowledge of Language: Its Nature, Origins and Use*. Praeger, New York.

Chowdhury, S. A. and Zamparelli, R. (2018). RNN simulations of grammaticality judgments on long-distance dependencies. In *Proceedings of the 27th International Conference on Computational Linguistics*, pages 133–144. Association for Computational Linguistics.

Ferraresi, A., Zanchetta, E., Baroni, M., and Bernardini, S. (2008). Introducing and evaluating ukWaC, a very large web-derived corpus of English. In *Proceedings of the 4th Web as Corpus Workshop WAC4*, pages 47–54.

Friedmann, N., Belletti, A., and Rizzi, L. (2009). Relativized relatives: types of intervention in the acquisition of a-bar dependencies. *Lingua*, **119**(1), 67–88.

Gibson, E. (1998). Linguistic complexity: locality of syntactic dependencies. *Cognition*, **68**, 1–76.

Gordon, P., Randall, H., and Marcus, J. (2001). Memory interference during language processing. *J. Exp. Psychol. Learn. Mem. Cogn.*, **27**, 1411–1423.

Gulordava, K., Bojanowski, P., Grave, E., Linzen, T., and Baroni, M. (2018). Colorless green recurrent networks dream hierarchically. In *Proceedings of NAACL*.

Hill, F., Bordes, A., Chopra, S., and Weston, J. (2015). The goldilocks principle: Reading children's books with explicit memory representations. *arXiv preprint arXiv:1511.02301*.

Hochreiter, S. and Schmidhuber, J. (1997). Long short-term memory. *Neural computation*, **9**(8), 1735–1780.

Jumelet, J. and Hupkes, D. (2018). Do language models understand anything? on the ability of lstms to understand negative polarity items. In *Proceedings of the 2018 EMNLP Workshop BlackboxNLP: Analyzing and Interpreting Neural Networks for NLP*, pages 222–231, Brussels, Belgium.

Lahiri, S. (2014). Complexity of Word Collocation Networks: A Preliminary Structural Analysis. In *Proceedings of the Student Research Workshop at the 14th Conference of the European Chapter of the Association for Computational Linguistics*, pages 96–105, Gothenburg, Sweden. Association for Computational Linguistics.

Lasnik, H. and Lidz., J. (2015). The argument from the poverty of the stimulus. In I. Roberts, editor, *Oxford Handbook of Universal Grammar*, pages 221–248. Oxford University Press.

Lau, J. H., Clark, A., and Lappin, S. (2017). Grammaticality, acceptability, and probability: A probabilistic view of linguistic knowledge. *Cognitive Science*, **41**(5), 1202–1241.

Li, Q. (2012). Literature survey: domain adaptation algorithms for natural language processing. *Department of Computer Science The Graduate Center, The City University of New York*, pages 8–10.

Linzen, T., Dupoux, E., and Goldberg, Y. (2016). Assessing the ability of LSTMs to learn syntax-sensitive dependencies. In *Transactions of the Association for Computational Linguistics*, volume 4, pages 521–535.

Pan, S. J. and Yang, Q. (2010). A survey on transfer learning. *IEEE Transactions on knowledge and data engineering*, **22**(10), 1345–1359.

Ross, J. R. (1967). *Constraints on Variables in Syntax*. Indiana University Linguistics Club, Bloomington.

Szabolcsi, A. and den Dikken, M. (1999). Islands. *GLOT Internationaal*, **4**(6), 3–8.

van Berkum, J. J. A. (2010). The brain is a prediction machine that cares about good and bad – any implications for neuropragmatics? *Italian Journal of Linguistics*, **22**.

Vaswani, A., Shazeer, N., Parmar, N., Uszkoreit, J., Jones, L., Gomez, A. N., Kaiser, Ł., and Polosukhin, I. (2017). Attention is all you need. In *Advances in neural information processing systems*, pages 5998–6008.

Warstadt, A. and Bowman, S. R. (2019). Grammatical analysis of pretrained sentence encoders with acceptability judgments.

Warstadt, A., Singh, A., and Bowman, S. R. (2018). Neural network acceptability judgments. https://arxiv.org/abs/1805.12471.

Wilcox, E., Levy, R., Morita, T., and Futrell, R. (2018). What do RNN language models learn about filler-gap dependencies? In *Proceedings of the 2018 EMNLP Workshop BlackboxNLP: Analyzing and Interpreting Neural Networks for NLP*, pages 211–221, Brussels. ACL.

Wilcox, E., Qian, P., Futrell, R., Ballesteros, M., and Levy, R. (2019). Structural supervision improves learning of non-local grammatical dependencies.

# An Analysis of Source-Side Grammatical Errors in NMT

**Antonios Anastasopoulos**
Language Technologies Institute
Carnegie Mellon University
aanastas@cs.cmu.edu

## Abstract

The quality of Neural Machine Translation (NMT) has been shown to significantly degrade when confronted with source-side noise. We present the first large-scale study of state-of-the-art English-to-German NMT on real grammatical noise, by evaluating on several Grammar Correction corpora. We present methods for evaluating NMT robustness without true references, and we use them for extensive analysis of the effects that different grammatical errors have on the NMT output. We also introduce a technique for visualizing the divergence distribution caused by a source-side error, which allows for additional insights.

## 1 Introduction

Neural Machine Translation (NMT) has become the *de facto* option for industrial systems in high-resource settings (Wu et al., 2016; Hassan Awadalla et al., 2018; Crego et al., 2016) while dominating public benchmarks (Bojar et al., 2018). However, as several works have shown, it has a notable shortcoming (among others, see Koehn and Knowles (2017) for relevant discussion) in dealing with source-side noise, during both training and inference.

Heigold et al. (2018) as well as Belinkov and Bisk (2018) pointed out the degraded performance of character- and subword-level NMT models when confronted with synthetic character-level noise –like swaps and scrambling– on French, German, and Czech to English MT. Belinkov and Bisk (2018) and Cheng et al. (2018) also studied synthetic errors from word swaps extracted from Wikipedia edits. Anastasopoulos et al. (2019) focused on a small subset of grammatical errors (article, preposition, noun number, and subject-verb agreement) and evaluated on English-to-Spanish synthetic and natural data.

However, no previous work has extensively studied the behavior of a state-of-the-art (SOTA) model on natural occurring data. Belinkov and Bisk (2018) only trained their systems on about 200K parallel instances, while Heigold et al. (2018) and Anastasopoulos et al. (2019) trained on about 2M parallel sentences from the WMT'16 data. Importantly, though, none of them utilized vast monolingual resources through back-translation, a technique that has been consistently shown to lead to impressively better results (Sennrich et al., 2016a).

In this work, we perform an extensive analysis of the performance of a *state-of-the-art* English-German NMT system, with regards to its robustness against real grammatical noise. We propose a method for robustness evaluation without gold-standard translation references, and perform experiments and extensive analysis on all available English Grammar Error Correction (GEC) corpora. Finally, we introduce a visualization technique for performing further analysis.

## 2 Data and Experimental Settings

To our knowledge, there are six publicly available corpora of non-native or erroneous English that are annotated with corrections and which have been widely used for research in GEC.

The NUS Corpus of Learner English (NUCLE) contains essays written by students at the National University of Singapore (Dahlmeier et al., 2013). It has become the main benchmark for GEC, as it was used in the CoNLL GEC Shared Tasks (Ng et al., 2013, 2014). The Cambridge Learner Corpus First Certificate in English FCE corpus[1] (Yannakoudakis et al., 2011) consists of essays collected from learners taking the Cambridge Assessment's English as a Second or Other Language

---

[1] We use the publicly available portion.



*Proceedings of the Second BlackboxNLP Workshop on Analyzing and Interpreting Neural Networks for NLP*, pages 213–223
Florence, Italy, August 1, 2019. ©2019 Association for Computational Linguistics

(ESOL) exams.[2] The LANG-8 corpus (Tajiri et al., 2012) was harvested from user-provided corrections in an online learner forum. Both have also been widely used for the GEC Shared Tasks. Another small corpus developed for evaluation purposes is the JHU FLuency-Extended GUG corpus (JFLEG) (Napoles et al., 2017) with correction annotations that include extended fluency edits rather than just minimal grammatical ones. The Cambridge English Write & Improve (W&I) corpus (Andersen et al., 2013) is collected from an online platform where English learners submit text and professional annotators correct them, also assigning a CEFR level of proficiency (of Europe. Council for Cultural Co-operation. Education Committee. Modern Languages Division, 2001). Lastly, we use a portion of the LOCNESS corpus,[3] a collection of essays written by *native* English speakers. 50 essays from LOCNESS were annotated by W&I annotators for grammatical errors, so we will jointly refer to these two corpora as WI+LOC.

All datasets were consistently annotated for errors with ERRANT (Bryant et al., 2017), an automatic tool that categorizes correction edits.[3] This allows us to consistently aggregate results and analysis across all datasets.

### 2.1 Notation and Experimental Settings

Throughout this work, we use the following notations:

- $x$: the original, noisy, potentially ungrammatical English sentence. Its tokens will be denoted as $x_i$.
- $\tilde{x}$: the English sentence with the correction annotations applied to the original sentence $x$, which is deemed fluent and grammatical. Again, its tokens will be denoted as $\tilde{x}_i$.
- $y$: the output of the NMT system when $x$ is provided as input (tokens: $y_j$).
- $\tilde{y}$: the output of the NMT system when $\tilde{x}$ is provided as input (tokens: $\tilde{y}_j$).

For the sake of readability, we use the terms grammatical errors, noise, or edits interchangeably. In the context of this work, they will all denote the annotated grammatical errors in the source sentences ($x$). We also define the number of errors, or the amount of noise in the source, to

be equivalent to the number of annotated necessary edits that the source $x$ requires to be deemed grammatical ($\tilde{x}$), as per standard GEC literature.

The main focus of our work is the performance analysis of the NMT system, so our experimental design is fairly simple. We use the SOTA NMT system of Edunov et al. (2018) for translating both the original and the corrected English sentences for all our GEC corpora.[4] The system achieved the best performance in the WMT 2018 evaluation campaign, using an ensemble of 6 deep transformer models trained with slightly different back-translated data.[5]

## 3 Evaluating NMT Robustness without References

When not using human judgments on output fluency and adequacy, Machine Translation is typically evaluated against gold-standard reference translations with automated metrics like BLEU (Papineni et al., 2002) or METEOR (Banerjee and Lavie, 2005). However, in the case of GEC corpora, we do not have access to translations – only monolingual data (potentially with ungrammaticalities) and correction annotations.[6] Quality Estimation for MT also operates in a reference-less setting (see Specia et al. (2018) for definitions and an overview of the field) and is hence very related to our work, but is more aimed towards towards *predicting* the quality of the translation. Our goal instead, is to analyze the behavior of the MT system when confronted with ungrammatical input. Reference-less evaluation has also been proposed for text simplification (Martin et al., 2018) and GEC (Napoles et al., 2016), while the grammaticality of MT systems' outputs has been evaluated with target-side contrastive pairs (Sennrich, 2017).

In this work, the core of our evaluation of a system's robustness lies in the following observation: **a perfectly robust-to-noise MT system would produce the exact same output for the clean and erroneous versions of the same input sentence.**

---

[2] https://www.cambridgeenglish.org/

[3] NUCLE, LANG8, FCE, and WI+LOC are pre-annotated with ERRANT for the BEA 2019 GEC Shared Task. We also annotated JFLEG.

[4] We use all data, concatenating train, dev, and test splits. We sample 150K sentences from LANG8.

[5] Refer to (Edunov et al., 2018) for further system details.

[6] The ideal way to potentially obtain such references of noisy text is debatable, and the extent to which humans are able to translate ungrammatical text is unknown. A well-crafted investigation could ideally elicit translations of both original and (the multiple versions of) corrected texts from multiple translators in order to study this issue. Although we highly encourage such a study, we could not conduct one due to budgetary constraints.

Denoting a perfect MT system as a function $\text{MT}^{perfect}(\cdot)$ over input sentences to the correct output sentences $\hat{\mathbf{y}}$, then both input sentences $\mathbf{x}$ and $\tilde{\mathbf{x}}$ would yield the same output:

$$\hat{\mathbf{y}} = \text{MT}^{perfect}(\mathbf{x}) = \text{MT}^{perfect}(\tilde{\mathbf{x}}).$$

In our case, $\hat{\mathbf{y}}$ is unknown and we only have access to a very good (but still imperfect) system $\text{MT}^{actual}(\cdot)$. We propose, therefore, to treat the system's output of the cleaned input ($\tilde{\mathbf{y}}$) as reference. Our assumption is that $\tilde{\mathbf{y}}$ is a good approximation of the correct translation $\hat{\mathbf{y}}$:

$$\hat{\mathbf{y}} \approx \text{MT}^{actual}(\tilde{\mathbf{x}}) = \tilde{\mathbf{y}}.$$

Under this assumption, we can now evaluate our system's robustness by comparing $\mathbf{y}$ and $\tilde{\mathbf{y}}$ using automated metrics at the corpus or sentence level. Here we list the metrics that we use and briefly discuss their potential shortcomings.

**Robustness Percentage (RB):**  Given a GEC corpus $\{X, \tilde{X}\}$, this corpus-level metric evaluates the percentage at which the system outputs agree at the sentence level:

$$RB = \frac{\sum_{\mathbf{x},\tilde{\mathbf{x}}\in\{X,\tilde{X}\}} c_{agree}(\text{MT}(\mathbf{x}), \text{MT}(\tilde{\mathbf{x}}))}{|X|},$$

$$c_{agree}(\mathbf{y}, \tilde{\mathbf{y}}) = \begin{cases} 1 & \text{if } \mathbf{y} = \tilde{\mathbf{y}}, \\ 0 & \text{otherwise.} \end{cases}$$

**f-BLEU:**  BLEU is the most standard MT evaluation metric, combining n-gram overlap accuracy with a brevity penalty. We calculate sentence- and corpus-level BLEU-4 scores for every $\mathbf{y}$ with $\tilde{\mathbf{y}}$ as the reference. Note that the BLEU scores that we obtain in our experiments are not comparable with any previous work (as we do not use real references) so we denote our metric as faux BLEU (f-BLEU) to avoid confusion.[7]

**f-METEOR:**  Same as above, we define faux-METEOR using the METEOR MT metric (Denkowski and Lavie, 2014) which is more semantically nuanced than BLEU.

**Target-Source Noise Ratio (NR):**  A notable drawback of all the previously discussed metrics is that they do not take into account the source sentences $\mathbf{x}$ and $\tilde{\mathbf{x}}$ or their distance. However, it is expected that minimal perturbations of the input (e.g. some missing punctuation) will also be minimally reflected in the difference of the outputs, while more distant inputs (which means higher levels of noise in the uncorrected source) would lead to more divergent outputs. To account for this observation, we propose Target-Source Noise Ratio (NR) which factors the distance of the two source sentences into a metric. The distance of two sentences can be measured by any metric like BLEU, METEOR, etc. We simply use BLEU:

$$\text{NR}(\mathbf{x}, \tilde{\mathbf{x}}, \mathbf{y}, \tilde{\mathbf{y}}) = \frac{d(\mathbf{y}, \tilde{\mathbf{y}})}{d(\mathbf{x}, \tilde{\mathbf{x}})} = \frac{100 - \text{BLEU}(\mathbf{y}, \tilde{\mathbf{y}})}{100 - \text{BLEU}(\mathbf{x}, \tilde{\mathbf{x}})}.$$

If the average (corpus-level) Noise Ratio score is smaller than 1 ($\text{NR}(X, \tilde{X}, Y, \tilde{Y}) < 1$) then we can infer that the MT system reduces the relative amount of noise, as there is higher relative n-gram overlap between the outputs than the inputs. On the other hand, if it is larger than 1, then the MT system must have introduced even more noise.[8]

Recently, Michel et al. (2019) proposed a criterion for evaluating adversarial attacks, which requires also having access to the correct translation $\hat{\mathbf{y}}$. Using a similarity function $s(\cdot)$, they declare an adversarial attack to be successful when:

$$s(\mathbf{x}, \tilde{\mathbf{x}}) + \frac{s(\mathbf{y}, \hat{\mathbf{y}}) - s(\tilde{\mathbf{y}}, \hat{\mathbf{y}})}{s(\mathbf{y}, \hat{\mathbf{y}})} > 1$$

In our reference-less setting, assuming $\hat{\mathbf{y}} \approx \tilde{\mathbf{y}}$ leads to $s(\tilde{\mathbf{y}}, \hat{\mathbf{y}}) = 1$. Finally, representing the similarity function with a distance function $s(\cdot) = 1 - d(\cdot)$ and simple equation manipulation, the criterion becomes exactly our Target-Source Noise Ratio. We have, hence, arrived at a reference-less criterion for evaluating any kind of adversarial attacks.[9]

## 4   Analysis

We first review the aggregate results across all datasets (§4.1) and with all metrics. We also

---

[7]In absolute numbers, we obtain higher scores than the scores of a MT system compared against actual references: the best English-German system from the WMT 2018 evaluation (Edunov et al., 2018) obtained a BLEU score of 46.5; our f-BLEU scores are in the [37-65] range, but we consider them informative only when viewed relative to other f-BLEU scores.

[8]As presented, the NR metric assumes that the length of the input and target sentences are comparable. In the English-German case, this is more or less correct. A more general implementation could include a discount term based on the average sentence length ratio of the two languages.

[9]Indeed, grammatical noise is nothing more than natural occurring adversarial noise.

| dataset | | number of sentences | average #corr/sent. | RB | over non-robust sent | | NR |
|---|---|---|---|---|---|---|---|
| | | | | | f-BLEU | f-METEOR | |
| WI+LOC | A | 9K | 3.4 | 17.77 | 46.75 | 65.29 | 2.12 |
| | B | 10K | 2.6 | 21.17 | 54.72 | 70.80 | 2.39 |
| | C | 5.9K | 1.8 | 29.07 | 63.46 | 76.63 | 2.73 |
| | N | 500 | 1.8 | 28.80 | 64.79 | 77.35 | 3.23 |
| NUCLE | | 21.3K | 2.0 | 20.69 | 59.97 | 74.6 | 2.92 |
| FCE | | 20.7K | 2.4 | 20.48 | 50.45 | 67.49 | 2.43 |
| JFLEG | | 1.3K | 3.8 | 12.42 | 42.05 | 61.99 | 2.18 |
| LANG8 | | 149.5K | 2.4 | 16.06 | 37.15 | 58.89 | 2.20 |
| ALL\LANG8 | | 69K | 2.4 | 20.94 | 54.65 | 70.64 | 2.55 |
| ALL | | 218.5K | 2.4 | 17.60 | 42.65 | 62.59 | 2.55 |

Table 1: Aggregate results across all datasets. As expected, the NMT system's performance deteriorates as input noise increases. For all metrics except NR, higher scores are better.

present findings based on sentence-level analysis (§4.2). We investigate the specific types of errors that contribute to robustness as well as those that increase undesired behavior in §4.3. Finally, in Section §4.4 we introduce the more fine-grained notion of divergence that allows us to perform interesting analysis and visualizations over the datasets.

## 4.1 Aggregate Results

Table 1 presents the general picture of our experiments, summarizing the translation robustness across all datasets with all the metrics that we examined, and also providing basic dataset statistics. Note that the aggregate f-BLEU and f-METEOR scores in Table 1 are calculated excluding sentences where the system exhibits robustness. We made this choice in order to tease apart the differences across the datasets by focusing on the problematic instances; having between 17% and 29% of the scores be perfect 100 f-BLEU points would obscure the analysis. We also report average scores across all datasets (last row) as well as scores without including LANG8, since the LANG8 dataset is significantly larger than the others.

**Takeaway 1: Increased amounts of noise in the source degrade translation performance.** The first takeaway confirms the previous results in the literature (Belinkov and Bisk, 2018; Anastasopoulos et al., 2019). The average number of corrections per sentence and the robustness percentage (RB) column have a Pearson's correlation coefficient $\rho = -0.82$, while both f-BLEU and f-

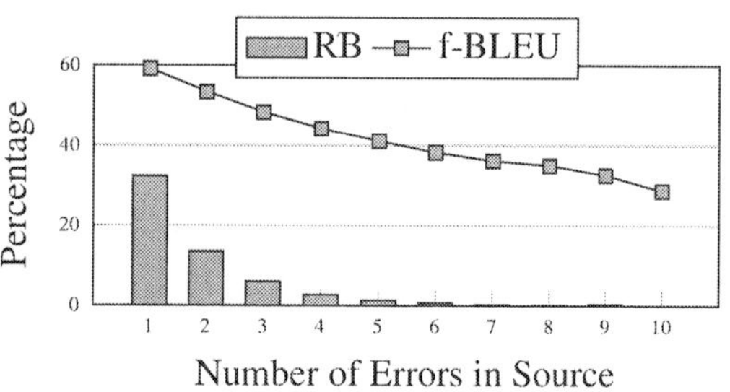



Figure 1: Effect of the number of errors on robustness. Robustness Percentage more than halves for each additional input sentence error, while f-BLEU on the non-robust sentences reduces linearly.

METEOR have lower $\rho = -0.71$.

This is further outlined by the results on the WI+LOC datasets. The English proficiency of the students increases from the A to B to C subsets, and the N subset is written by native English speakers. An increase in English proficiency manifests as a lower number of errors, higher robustness percentage, and larger f-BLEU scores.

**Takeaway 2: The MT system generally magnifies the input noise.** This is denoted by the NR column which is larger than 1 across the board. This means that the MT system exacerbated the input noise by a factor of about 2.5. This effect is more visible when the source noise levels are low, as in the WI+LOC C and N or the NUCLE datasets.

## 4.2 Sentence-level Findings

We continue our analysis focusing on instance or sentence-level factors, presenting results combining all datasets.

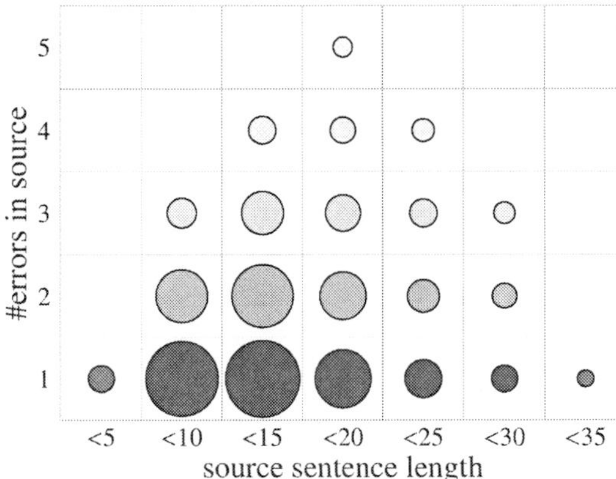

Figure 2: Robustness Percentage broken down by sentence length and number of source errors. The radius of each circle is proportional to the number of sentences and the opacity corresponds to RB score (darkest: RB=33%, lowest: RB≈2%). The model is more robust with few errors regardless of sentence length.

| Recoverable | | Non-recoverable | |
| --- | --- | --- | --- |
| Error | RB | Error | EB |
| VERB-INFL | 22% | CONJ | 3% |
| VERB-SVA | 22% | OTHER | 5% |
| ORTH | 19% | NOUN | 6% |
| VERB-FORM | 17% | ADV | 7% |
| WO | 17% | VERB | 7% |

Table 2: Some errors are easier to translate correctly than others. The average error has an RB score of 11%. We present the errors that fall out of the $[\mu \pm 2\sigma]$ range.

**Effect of the input number of errors:** Figure 1 clearly shows the compounding effect of source side errors. Each additional error reduces overall robustness by more than 50%: from robust behavior in about 32% of the 1-error instances, to 13% for the 2-errors instances, to 6% on instances with 3 errors; and so forth, to the point that the model is robust in less than 1% of instances with more than 5 source-side errors. The robustness drop when computed with f-BLEU is practically linear, starting from about 59 f-BLEU points when a single error is present, falling to about 28 when the source has more than 9 errors.

**Effect of input length:** One factor related to the number of input errors is the effect of the source sentence length. We find that there is a negative correlation between the input length and the model's robustness. This is to be expected, as input length and the number of errors are also correlated: longer sentences are more likely to more errors, and inversely, short sentences cannot have a large number of errors.

Figure 2 presents the RB score across these two factors. We bin the input sentences based on their sentence lengths and based on the number of errors in the source. We only plot bins that have a RB score of more than 1% (reflected in the opacity of the plot). It is clear that more errors in a source sentence lead to reduced robustness, while the sentence length is not as significant a factor.

A closer look at sentences with a single error

reveals that the system is robust about 30% of the time regardless of their length, with a slight increase in accuracy as the length increases. Longer sentences provide more context, which presumably aids in dealing with the source noise. This pattern is similar across all rows in Figure 2.

### 4.3 Error-level Analysis

In this section we aim to study and identify the error types from which the NMT system is able to recover, or not. To avoid the compounding effects of multiple source-side errors, we restrict this analysis to sentences that have a single error.

We have already discussed in Section 4.1 how the NMT system is robust on about 20% of the instances across all corpora. By selecting those instances and computing basic error statistics on them, we find that the average error is recoverable about 11% of the time ($\mu = 0.11$). Table 2 presents the errors that are harder or easier to translate correctly. We choose to present the errors that are at the bottom and top, respectively, of the ranking of the errors, based on the average RB score that their corresponding test instances receive.

The non-recoverable errors on the right side of Table 2 are mostly semantic in nature: all five of them correspond to instances where a semantically wrong *word* was used.[10] Correcting and even identifying these types of errors is difficult even in a monolingual setting as world knowledge and/or larger (document/discourse) context is needed. One could argue, in fact, that such errors are not *grammatical*, i.e. the source sentence is fluent. Furthermore, one could form a solid argument for not wanting/expecting an *MT* system to alter the semantics of the source. The MT system's job is exactly to accurately convey the semantics of the

---

[10]We refer the reader to Bryant et al. (2017) for a complete list of the error type abbreviations.

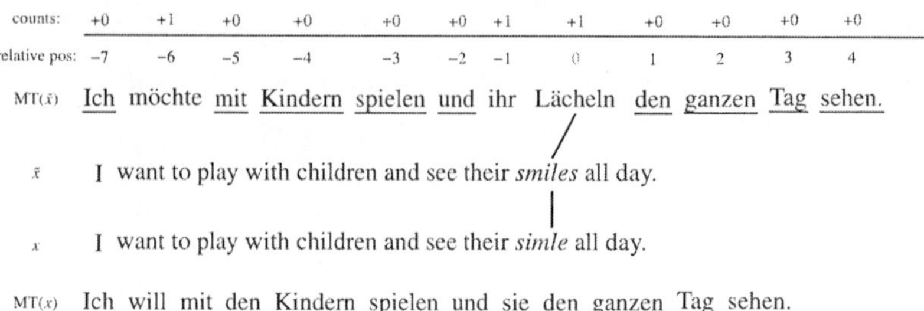



Figure 3: The procedure of computing *divergence* over a quadruple $(\mathbf{x}, \mathbf{y}, \tilde{\mathbf{x}}, \tilde{\mathbf{y}})$. Each token in output $y$ not in the desired output $\tilde{y}$ is considered a divergent token (underlined=matching). The x-axis is centered around the token $\tilde{y}_k$ that aligns to the edit $x_i^* \rightarrow \tilde{x}_j$. The counts describe the caused divergence relative to the expected error's position.

source sentence in the target language.

However, there are errors where the intended meaning is clear but ungrammatically executed, as in Table 2's left-side errors. There are three plausible (likely orthogonal, but we leave such analysis for future work) reasons why these errors are easier than average to correctly translate:

**1. Self-attention.** The encoder's final representations are computed through multiple self-attention layers, resulting in a representation heavily informed by the whole source context. The VERB-INFL, VERB-SVA, and VERB-FORM error categories (all related to morphology and syntactic constraints) apply to edits that subword modeling combined with self-attention would alleviate. Consider the example of the verb inflection (VERB-INFL) error *danceing*/dancing*. The segmentation in the erroneous and the corrected version is *dance|ing* and *danc|ing* respectively. In both cases, the morpheme that denotes the inflection is the same. Verb form (VERB-FORM) errors, on the other hand, typically involve infinitive, to-infinitive, gerund, or participle forms. It seems that in those cases the self-attention component is able to use the context to recover, especially because, as in the VERB-INFL example, the stem of the verb will most likely be the same.

Also, apart from the positional embeddings, no other explicit word order information is encoded by the architecture (unlike recurrent architectures focused on by all previous work, which by construction keep track of word order). We suggest that the self-attention architecture makes word order errors (WO errors are strictly defined as exact match tokens wrongly ordered, e.g. *know already*/already know*) easier to recover from.

**2. The extensive use of back-translation.** The SOTA model that we use has been trained on mas-

sive amounts of back-translated data, where German monolingual data have been translated into English. The integral part is that English sources were *sampled* from the De-En model, instead of using beam-search to generate the most likely output. This means that the model was already trained on a fair amount of source-side noise, which would make it more robust to such perturbations (Belinkov and Bisk, 2018; Anastasopoulos et al., 2019; Singh et al., 2019).

Although we do not have access to the back-translated parallel data that Edunov et al. (2018) used, we suspect that translation errors are fairly common and therefore more prevalent in the final training bitext, making the model more robust to such noise. Current English-to-German SOTA systems might not have issues with translating noun phrases, coordinated verbs, or pronoun number, but they still struggle with compound generation, coreference, and verb-future generation (Bojar et al., 2018).

**3. Data preprocessing and subword-level modeling.** It is worth noting that ERRANT limits the orthography (ORTH) error category to refer to edits involving casing (lower↔upper) and whitespace changes. Our model, as most of the SOTA NMT models, is trained and operates at the subword level, using heuristic segmentation algorithms like Byte Pair Encoding (BPE) (Sennrich et al., 2016b), that are learned on clean truecased data. Truecasing is also a standard preprocessing step at inference time, hence dealing with casing errors. The BPE segmentation also has the capacity to deal with whitespace errors. For example, the incorrect token "weatherrelated" gets segmented to *we|a|ther|related*. Although imperfect (the segment's segmentation with proper whitespacing is *we|a|ther related*), the two segmentations agree for 3/4 tokens. Most previous work e.g. (Belinkov and Bisk, 2018) has focused on character-level modeling using compositional functions across characters to represent tokens, which are by construction more vulnerable to such errors.

### 4.4 Divergence

We introduce a method for computing a *divergence distribution*. Computing *divergence* requires a quadruple of $(\mathbf{x}, \tilde{\mathbf{x}}, \mathbf{y}, \tilde{\mathbf{y}})$. We will focus on instances where $\mathbf{x}$ and $\tilde{\mathbf{x}}$ differ only with a single edit, as a simple working example.

**Process:** Given a source side sentence pair $\mathbf{x}$ and $\tilde{\mathbf{x}}$ with a single grammatical error, it is trivial to identify the position $i^*$ of the correction in $\tilde{\mathbf{x}}$, since we work on corpora pre-annotated with grammatical edits at the token level. Also, using traditional methods like the IBM Models (Brown et al., 1993) and the GIZA++ tool, makes it easy to obtain an alignment between $\mathbf{x}$ and $\mathbf{y}$, as well as between $\tilde{\mathbf{x}}$ and $\tilde{\mathbf{y}}$. We use the alignment variable $\alpha_j = i$ to denote that the target word $y_j$ is aligned to source position $i$, and equivalently the variables $\tilde{\alpha}$ for the corrected source pair. We denote as $k^*$ the target position that aligns to the source-side correction, such that $\tilde{\alpha}_{k^*} = i^*$.

We define the set of divergent tokens $\mathcal{Y}_*$ as the set of tokens of $\mathbf{y}$ that do not appear in $\tilde{\mathbf{y}}$:

$$\mathcal{Y}^* = \{y_j \mid y_j \notin \tilde{\mathbf{y}}\}.$$

Now, we use all the previous definitions to define the set $\mathcal{P}$ of target divergent positions for a quadruple $(\mathbf{x}, \tilde{\mathbf{x}}, \mathbf{y}, \tilde{\mathbf{y}})$ as the set of target-side positions of the tokens that are different between $\mathbf{y}$ and $\tilde{\mathbf{y}}$, but *relative* to the position of the target-side token that aligns to the source-side correction:

$$\mathcal{P}(\mathbf{x}, \tilde{\mathbf{x}}, \mathbf{y}, \tilde{\mathbf{y}}) = \{j - k*, \forall y_j \in \mathcal{Y}^*\}.$$

We provide an illustration of this process for a single-error example in Figure 3. The correction *simle*/smiles* is aligned to the word $y_7$ (Lächeln) in the reference target, so the center of the distribution is moved to $k^* = 7$. For the rest of the positions in the target reference $\tilde{\mathbf{y}}$, we simply update the counts based on whether the word $\tilde{y}_j$ is present in $\mathbf{y}$. The final step is collecting counts across all instances for all the relative divergent positions and analyzing the effect of a source-side error on the target sentence.

Essentially, we expect some source-side errors to have a very local effect on the translation output, which would translate in divergence distributions with low variance (since we center the distribution around $k^*$). Other source-side errors might cause larger divergence as they might affect the whole structure of the target sentence.

In the Figure 3 example, the only difference between $\mathbf{x}$ and $\tilde{\mathbf{x}}$ is a single word towards the end of the sentence, but the outputs $\mathbf{y}$ and $\tilde{\mathbf{y}}$ diverge on three words. One of them is 6 words away (before) from where we would have expected the divergence to happen (in relative position 0).

After collecting divergence counts for each instance, we can visualize their distribution and compute their descriptive statistics. We focus on the mean $\mu$, standard deviation $\sigma$, and the skewness of the distribution as measured by Pearson's definition, using the third standardised moment, defined as:

$$\gamma_1 = \mathbb{E}\left[\left(\frac{X - \mu}{\sigma}\right)^3\right].$$

Across all datasets and errors, the distribution of the divergence caused by single errors in the source has a mean $\mu_{all}{=}0.7$, standard deviation $\sigma_{all}{=}5.1$, and a slight positive skewness with $\gamma_{1_{all}}{=}0.8$. This means that the average error affects its general right context, in a $\pm 5$ word neighborhood.

In Figure 4 we present several of the errors with the most interesting divergence statistics. Some errors heavily affect their left (e.g. R:ORTH) or right context (U:CONJ). Also, some errors affect a small translation neighborhood as denoted by the low variance of their divergence distribution (e.g. U:CONTR). On the other hand, verb form errors (M:VERB:FORM) have the potential to affect a larger neighborhood: this is expected because English auxiliary verb constructions (e.g. "have eaten X") often get translated to German V2 constructions with an auxiliary verb separated from a final, non-finite main verb (e.g. "habe X gegessen").

In Figure 5 we present the divergence distributions across the sentence quartiles where the error appears. We find that errors in the sentence beginning (1st quartile) severely affect their right context. Errors towards the end of the sentence (4th quartile) affect their left context. Interestingly, we observe that mid-sentence errors (2nd, 3rd quartiles) exhibit much lower divergence variance than errors towards the sentence's edges.

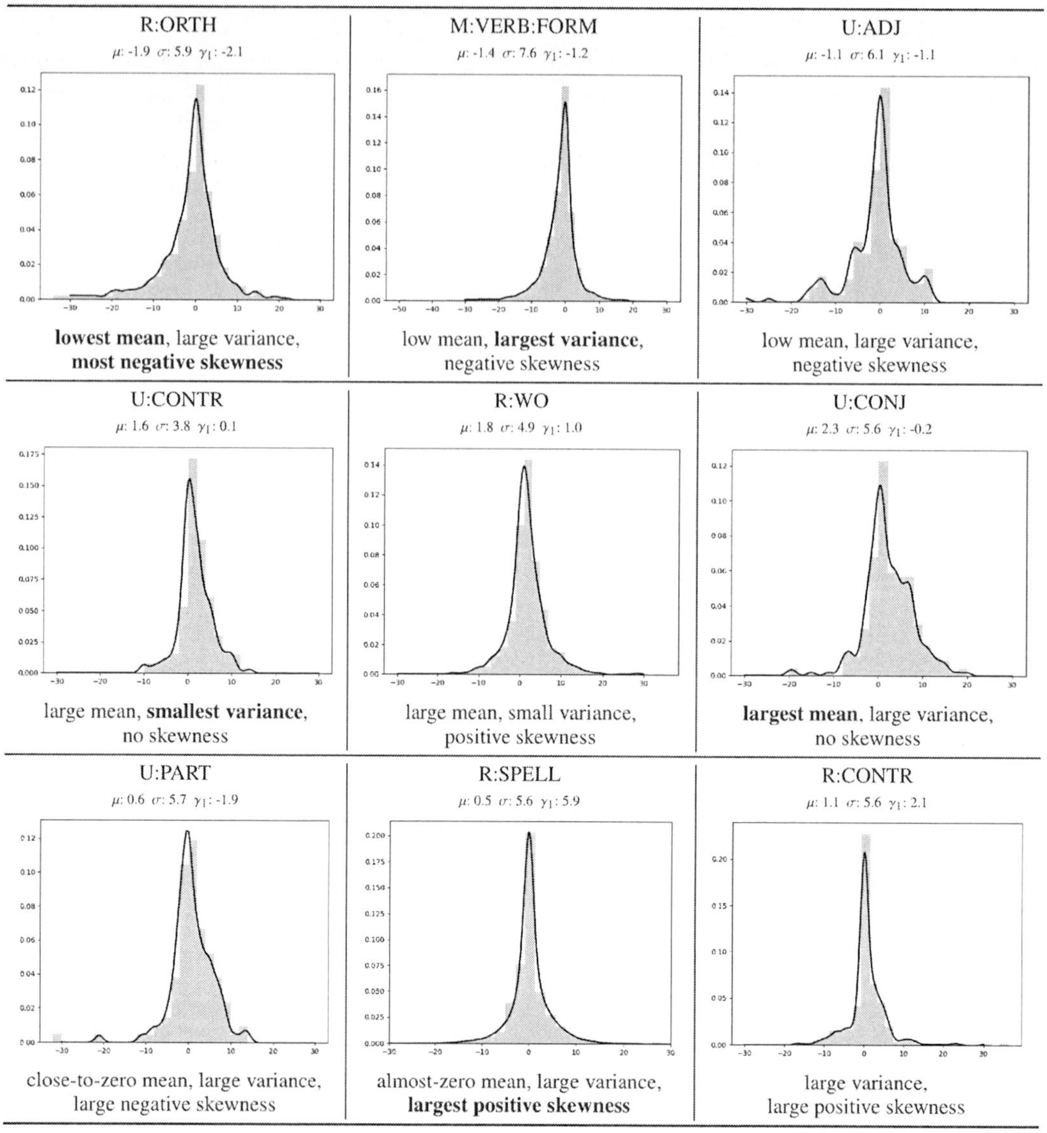

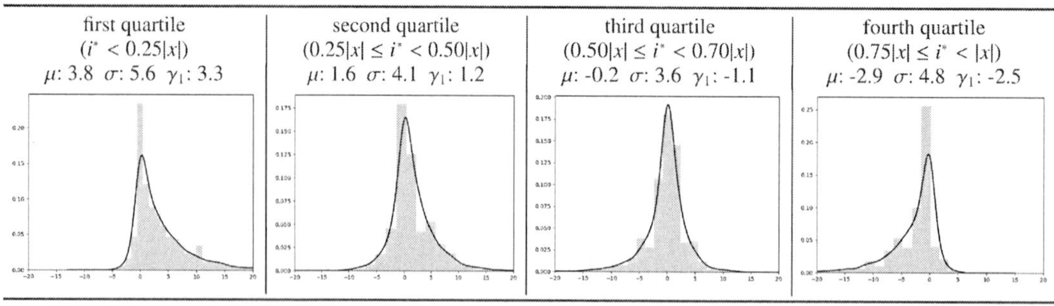

Figure 4: Some interesting errors with statistics on their *divergence distribution*. Some errors (negative mean and skewness: R:ORTH, M:VERB:FORM, U:ADJ) affect the left context of their translation more, while others affect their right translation context (positive mean and skewness R:WO, U:CONJ). Errors might affect a small neighborhood (low variance: U:CONTR, R:WO) or a larger part of the translation (high variance: M:VERB:FORM, U:ADJ, R:CONTR).

Figure 5: Divergence Distributions for single source error instances per the error's location quartile.

## 5   Limitations and Extensions

A major limitation of our analysis is the narrow scope of our experiments. We solely focused on a single language pair using a single MT system. Whether different neural architectures over other languages would lead to different conclusions remains an open question. The necessary resources for answering these questions at scale, however, are not yet available. We were limited to English as our source side language, as the majority of the datasets and research works in GEC are entirely English-centric. Perhaps small-scale GEC datasets in Estonian (Rummo and Praakli, 2017) and Latvian (Deksne and Skadina, 2014) could provide a non-English testbed. One would then need error labels for the grammatical edits, so if such annotations are not available, an extension of a tool like ERRANT to these languages would also be required. One should also be careful in the decision of what (N)MT system to test, as using a low-quality translation system would not produce meaningful insights.

Another limitation is that our metrics do not capture whether the changes in the output are actually grammatical errors or not. In the example in Figure 3: the German words "möchte" and "will" that we identified as divergent are practically interchangeable. Therefore, the NMT model is technically not wrong outputting either of them and it is indeed generally possible that differences between $y$ and $\tilde{y}$ are just surface-level ones. The inclusion of f-METEOR as a robustness metric could partially deal with this issue, as it would not penalize such differences. We do believe it is still interesting, though, that a single source error can cause large perturbations in the output, as in the case of errors with large variance in their divergence distribution. Nevertheless, an extension of our study focusing on the grammatical qualities of the MT output would be exciting and automated tools for such analysis would be invaluable (i.e. MT error labeling and analysis tools extending the works of Zeman et al. (2011), Logacheva et al. (2016), Popović (2018), or Neubig et al. (2019)).

A natural next research direction is investigating how to use our reference-less evaluation metrics in order to create a more robust MT system. For instance, one could optimize for f-BLEU or any of the other reference-less measures that we proposed, in the same way that an MT system is optimized for BLEU (either by explicitly using their scores through reinforcement learning or by simply using the metric as an early stopping criterion over a development set). Cheng et al. (2018) recently proposed an approach for training more robust MT systems, albeit in a supervised setting where noise is injected on parallel data, and the proposed solutions of Belinkov and Bisk (2018) and Anastasopoulos et al. (2019) fall within the same category. However, no approach has, to our knowledge, used GEC corpora for training MT systems robust to grammatical errors. In any case, special care should be taken so that any improvements on translating ungrammatical data do not worsen performance on clean ones.

## 6   Conclusion

In this work, we studied the effects of grammatical errors in NMT. We expanded on findings from previous work, performing analysis on real data with grammatical errors using a SOTA system. With our analysis we were able to identify classes of grammatical errors that are recoverable or irrecoverable. Additionally, we presented ways to evaluate a MT system's robustness to noise without access to gold references, as well as a method for visualizing the effect of source-side errors to the output translation. Finally, we discussed the limitations of our study and outlined avenues for further investigations towards building more robust NMT systems.

## Acknowledgements

The author is grateful to the anonymous reviewers, Kenton Murray, and Graham Neubig for their constructive and insightful comments, as well as to Gabriela Weigel for her invaluable help with editing and proofreading the final version of this paper. This material is based upon work generously supported by the National Science Foundation under grant 1761548.

## References

Antonios Anastasopoulos, Alison Lui, Toan Q. Nguyen, and David Chiang. 2019. Neural machine translation of text from non-native speakers. *Proc. NAACL-HLT*.

Øistein E Andersen, Helen Yannakoudakis, Fiona Barker, and Tim Parish. 2013. Developing and testing a self-assessment and tutoring system. In *Proc. BEA-NLP*.

Satanjeev Banerjee and Alon Lavie. 2005. Meteor: An automatic metric for mt evaluation with improved correlation with human judgments. In *Proceedings of the acl workshop on intrinsic and extrinsic evaluation measures for machine translation and/or summarization*.

Yonatan Belinkov and Yonatan Bisk. 2018. Synthetic and natural noise both break neural machine translation. In *Proc. ICLR*.

Ondřej Bojar, Rajen Chatterjee, Christian Federmann, Mark Fishel, Yvette Graham, Barry Haddow, Matthias Huck, Antonio Jimeno Yepes, Philipp Koehn, Christof Monz, et al. 2018. Proceedings of the third conference on machine translation. In *Proc. WMT*.

Peter F. Brown, Vincent J. Della Pietra, Stephen A. Della Pietra, and Robert L. Mercer. 1993. The mathematics of statistical machine translation: Parameter estimation. *Computational Linguistics*, 19(2):263–311.

Christopher Bryant, Mariano Felice, and Ted Briscoe. 2017. Automatic annotation and evaluation of error types for grammatical error correction. In *Proc. ACL*.

Yong Cheng, Zhaopeng Tu, Fandong Meng, Junjie Zhai, and Yang Liu. 2018. Towards robust neural machine translation. In *Proc. ACL*.

Josep Crego, Jungi Kim, Guillaume Klein, Anabel Rebollo, Kathy Yang, Jean Senellart, Egor Akhanov, Patrice Brunelle, Aurelien Coquard, Yongchao Deng, et al. 2016. Systran's pure neural machine translation systems. arXiv:1610.05540.

Daniel Dahlmeier, Hwee Tou Ng, and Siew Mei Wu. 2013. Building a large annotated corpus of learner english: The nus corpus of learner english. In *Proc. BEA-NLP*.

Daiga Deksne and Inguna Skadina. 2014. Error-annotated corpus of latvian. In *Proc. Baltic HLT*.

Michael Denkowski and Alon Lavie. 2014. Meteor universal: Language specific translation evaluation for any target language. In *Proc. WMT*.

Council of Europe. Council for Cultural Co-operation. Education Committee. Modern Languages Division. 2001. *Common European Framework of Reference for Languages: learning, teaching, assessment*. Cambridge University Press.

Sergey Edunov, Myle Ott, Michael Auli, and David Grangier. 2018. Understanding back-translation at scale. In *Proc. EMNLP*.

Hany Hassan Awadalla, Anthony Aue, Chang Chen, Vishal Chowdhary, Jonathan Clark, Christian Federmann, Xuedong Huang, Marcin Junczys-Dowmunt, Will Lewis, Mu Li, Shujie Liu, Tie-Yan Liu, Renqian Luo, Arul Menezes, Tao Qin, Frank Seide,

Xu Tan, Fei Tian, Lijun Wu, Shuangzhi Wu, Yingce Xia, Dongdong Zhang, Zhirui Zhang, and Ming Zhou. 2018. Achieving human parity on automatic chinese to english news translation.

Georg Heigold, Stalin Varanasi, Günter Neumann, and Josef Genabith. 2018. How robust are character-based word embeddings in tagging and mt against wrod scramlbing or randdm nouse? In *Proc. AMTA*.

Philipp Koehn and Rebecca Knowles. 2017. Six challenges for neural machine translation. In *Proc. WNMT*.

Varvara Logacheva, Chris Hokamp, and Lucia Specia. 2016. Marmot: A toolkit for translation quality estimation at the word level. In *Proc. LREC*.

Louis Martin, Samuel Humeau, Pierre-Emmanuel Mazaré, Éric De La Clergerie, Antoine Bordes, and Benoît Sagot. 2018. Reference-less quality estimation of text simplification systems. In *Proc. ATA*.

Paul Michel, Xian Li, Graham Neubig, and Juan Miguel Pino. 2019. On evaluation of adversarial perturbations for sequence-to-sequence models. In *Proc. NAACL-HLT*.

Courtney Napoles, Keisuke Sakaguchi, and Joel Tetreault. 2016. There's no comparison: Reference-less evaluation metrics in grammatical error correction. In *Proc. EMNLP*.

Courtney Napoles, Keisuke Sakaguchi, and Joel Tetreault. 2017. Jfleg: A fluency corpus and benchmark for grammatical error correction. In *Proc. EACL*, Valencia, Spain.

Graham Neubig, Zi-Yi Dou, Junjie Hu, Paul Michel, Danish Pruthi, and Xinyi Wang. 2019. compare-mt: A tool for holistic comparison of language generation systems. In *Proc. NAACL-HLT*.

Hwee Tou Ng, Siew Mei Wu, Ted Briscoe, Christian Hadiwinoto, Raymond Hendy Susanto, and Christopher Bryant. 2014. The conll-2014 shared task on grammatical error correction. In *Proc. CoNLL*.

Hwee Tou Ng, Siew Mei Wu, Yuanbin Wu, Christian Hadiwinoto, and Joel Tetreault. 2013. The conll-2013 shared task on grammatical error correction. In *Proc. CoNLL*.

Kishore Papineni, Salim Roukos, Todd Ward, and Wei-Jing Zhu. 2002. Bleu: a method for automatic evaluation of machine translation. In *Proc. ACL*.

Maja Popović. 2018. Error classification and analysis for machine translation quality assessment. In *Translation Quality Assessment*, pages 129–158. Springer.

Ingrid Rummo and Kristiina Praakli. 2017. TÜ eesti keele (võõrkeelena) osakonna õppijakeele tekstikorpus [the language learners corpus of the department of estonian language of the university of tartu]. In *Proc EAAL*.

Rico Sennrich. 2017. How grammatical is character-level neural machine translation? assessing mt quality with contrastive translation pairs. In *Proc. EACL*.

Rico Sennrich, Barry Haddow, and Alexandra Birch. 2016a. Improving neural machine translation models with monolingual data. In *Proc. ACL*.

Rico Sennrich, Barry Haddow, and Alexandra Birch. 2016b. Neural machine translation of rare words with subword units. In *Proc. ACL*.

Sumeet Singh, Craig Stewart, Graham Neubig, et al. 2019. Improving robustness of machine translation with synthetic noise. arXiv:1902.09508.

Lucia Specia, Carolina Scarton, and Gustavo Henrique Paetzold. 2018. Quality estimation for machine translation. *Synthesis Lectures on Human Language Technologies*, 11(1):1–162.

Toshikazu Tajiri, Mamoru Komachi, and Yuji Matsumoto. 2012. Tense and aspect error correction for esl learners using global context. In *Proc. ACL*.

Yonghui Wu, Mike Schuster, Zhifeng Chen, Quoc V. Le, Mohammad Norouzi, Wolfgang Macherey, Maxim Krikun, Yuan Cao, Qin Gao, Klaus Macherey, et al. 2016. Google's neural machine translation system: Bridging the gap between human and machine translation. arXiv:1609.08144.

Helen Yannakoudakis, Ted Briscoe, and Ben Medlock. 2011. A new dataset and method for automatically grading esol texts. In *Proc. ACL-HLT*.

Daniel Zeman, Mark Fishel, Jan Berka, and Ondřej Bojar. 2011. Addicter: what is wrong with my translations? *The Prague Bulletin of Mathematical Linguistics*, 96:79–88.

# Finding Syntactic Representations in Neural Stacks

**William Merrill,**[*][†] **Lenny Khazan,**[†] **Noah Amsel,**[†]
**Yiding Hao,**[†] **Simon Mendelsohn,**[†] and **Robert Frank**[†]
[†] Yale University, New Haven, CT, USA
[*] Allen Institute for Artificial Intelligence, Seattle, WA, USA
`firstname.lastname@yale.edu`



## Abstract

Neural network architectures have been augmented with differentiable stacks in order to introduce a bias toward learning hierarchy-sensitive regularities. It has, however, proven difficult to assess the degree to which such a bias is effective, as the operation of the differentiable stack is not always interpretable. In this paper, we attempt to detect the presence of latent representations of hierarchical structure through an exploration of the unsupervised learning of constituency structure. Using a technique due to Shen et al. (2018a,b), we extract syntactic trees from the pushing behavior of stack RNNs trained on language modeling and classification objectives. We find that our models produce parses that reflect natural language syntactic constituencies, demonstrating that stack RNNs do indeed infer linguistically relevant hierarchical structure.


## 1 Introduction

Sequential models such as long short-term memory networks (LSTMs; Hochreiter and Schmidhuber, 1997) have been proven capable of exhibiting qualitative behavior that reflects a sensitivity to regularities that are structurally conditioned, such as subject–verb agreement (Linzen et al., 2016; Gulordava et al., 2018). However, detailed analysis of such models has shown that this apparent sensitivity to structure does not always generalize to inputs with a high degree of syntactic complexity (Marvin and Linzen, 2018). These observations suggest that sequential models may not in fact be representing sentences in the kind of hierarchically organized representations that we might expect.

Stack-structured recurrent memory units (Joulin and Mikolov, 2015; Grefenstette et al., 2015; Yo-

gatama et al., 2018; and others) offer a possible method for explicitly biasing neural networks to construct hierarchical representations and make use of them in their computation. Since syntactic structures can often be modeled in a context-free manner (Chomsky, 1956, 1957), the correspondence between pushdown automata and context-free grammars (Chomsky, 1962) makes stacks a natural data structure for the computation of hierarchical relations. Recently, Hao et al. (2018) have shown that stack-augmented RNNs (henceforth *stack RNNs*) have the ability to learn classical stack-based algorithms for computing context-free transductions such as string reversal. However, they also find that such algorithms can be difficult for stack RNNs to learn. For many context-free tasks such as parenthesis matching, the stack RNN models they consider instead learn heuristic "push-only" strategies that essentially reduce the stack to unstructured recurrent memory. Thus, even if stacks allow hierarchical regularities to be expressed, the bias that stack RNNs introduce does not guarantee that the networks will detect them.

The current paper aims to move beyond the work of Hao et al. (2018) in two ways. While that work was based on artificially generated formal languages, this paper considers the ability of stack RNNs to succeed on tasks over natural language data. Specifically, we train such networks on two objectives: language modeling and the *number prediction task*, a classification task proposed by Linzen et al. (2016) to determine whether or not a model can capture structure-sensitive grammatical dependencies. Further, in addition to using visualizations of the pushing and popping actions of the stack RNN to assess its hierarchical sensitivity, we use a technique proposed by Shen et al. (2018a,b) to assess the presence of implicitly-represented hierarchically-organized structure through the task

---

[*] Work completed while the author was at Yale University.




*Proceedings of the Second BlackboxNLP Workshop on Analyzing and Interpreting Neural Networks for NLP*, pages 224–232
Florence, Italy, August 1, 2019. ©2019 Association for Computational Linguistics

of unsupervised parsing. We extract syntactic constituency trees from our models and find that they produce parses that broadly reflect phrasal groupings of words in the input sentences, suggesting that our models utilize the stack in a way that reflects the syntactic structures of input sentences.

This paper is organized as follows. Section 2 introduces the architecture of our stack models, which extends the architecture of Grefenstette et al. (2015) by allowing multiple items to be pushed to, popped from, or read from the stack at each computational step. Section 3 then describes our training procedure and reports results on language modeling and agreement classification. Section 4 investigates the behavior of the stack RNNs trained on these tasks by visualizing their pushing behavior. Building on this, Section 5 describes how we adapt Shen et al.'s (2018a; 2018b) unsupervised parsing algorithm to stack RNNs and evaluates the degree to which the resulting parses reveal structural representations in stack RNNs. Section 6 discusses our observations, and Section 7 concludes.

## 2   Network Architecture

In a stack RNN (Grefenstette et al., 2015; Hao et al., 2018), a neural network adhering to a standard recurrent architecture, known as a *controller*, is enhanced with a non-parameterized *stack*. At each time step, the controller network receives an input vector $\mathbf{x}_t$ and a recurrent state vector $\mathbf{h}_{t-1}$ provided by the controller architecture, along with a *read vector* $\mathbf{r}_{t-1}$ summarizing the top elements on the stack. The controller interfaces with the stack by computing continuous values that serve as instructions for how the stack should be modified. These instructions consist of $\mathbf{v}_t$, a vector that is pushed to the top of the stack; $d_t$, a number representing the *strength* of the newly pushed vector $\mathbf{v}_t$; $u_t$, the number of items to pop from the stack; and $r_t$, the number of items to read from the top of the stack. The instructions $\langle \mathbf{v}_t, u_t, d_t, r_t \rangle$ are produced by the controller as output and presented to the stack. The stack then computes the next read vector $\mathbf{r}_t$, which is given to the controller at the next time step. This general architecture is portrayed in Figure 1. In the next two subsections, we describe how the stack computes $\mathbf{r}_t$ using the instructions $\langle \mathbf{v}_t, u_t, d_t, r_t \rangle$ and how the controller computes the stack instructions.

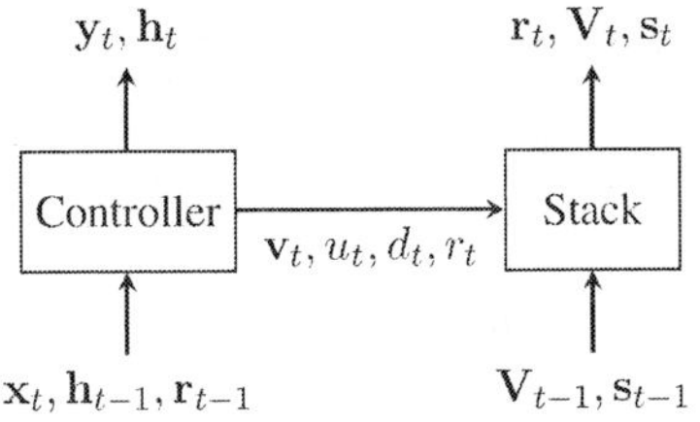


Figure 1: The neural stack architecture.

### 2.1   Stack Actions

A stack at time $t$ consists of a sequence of vectors $\langle \mathbf{V}_t[1], \mathbf{V}_t[2], \ldots, \mathbf{V}_t[t] \rangle$, organized into a matrix $\mathbf{V}_t$ whose $i$th row is $\mathbf{V}_t[i]$. By convention, $\mathbf{V}_t[t]$ is the "top" element of the stack, while $\mathbf{V}_t[1]$ is the "bottom" element. Each element $\mathbf{V}_t[i]$ of the stack is associated with a *strength* $\mathbf{s}_t[i] \geq 0$. The strength of a vector $\mathbf{V}_t[i]$ represents the degree to which the vector is on the stack: a strength of 1 means that the vector is "fully" on the stack, while a strength of 0 means that the vector has been popped from the stack. The strengths are organized into a vector $\mathbf{s}_t = \langle \mathbf{s}_t[1], \mathbf{s}_t[2], \ldots, \mathbf{s}_t[t] \rangle$. At time $t$, the stack receives a set of instructions $\langle \mathbf{v}_t, u_t, d_t, r_t \rangle$ and performs three operations: *popping*, *pushing*, and *reading*, in that order.

The popping operation is implemented by reducing the strength of each item on the stack by a number $\mathbf{u}_t[i]$, ensuring that the strength of each item can never fall below 0.

$$\mathbf{s}_t[i] = \mathrm{ReLU}\left(\mathbf{s}_{t-1}[i] - \mathbf{u}_t[i]\right)$$

The $\mathbf{u}_t[i]$s are computed as follows. The total amount of strength to be reduced is the *pop strength* $u_t$. Popping begins by attempting to reduce the strength $\mathbf{s}_t[t-1]$ of the top item on the stack by the full pop strength $u_t$. Thus, as shown below, $\mathbf{u}_t[t-1] = u_t$. For each $i$, if $\mathbf{s}_{t-1}[i] < \mathbf{u}_t[i]$, then the $i$th item has been fully popped from the stack, "consuming" a portion of the pop strength of magnitude $\mathbf{s}_{t-1}[i]$. The strength of the next item is then reduced by an amount $\mathbf{u}_t[i-1]$ given by the "remaining" pop strength $\mathbf{u}_t[i] - \mathbf{s}_{t-1}[i]$.

$$\mathbf{u}_t[i] =$$
$$\begin{cases} u_t, & i = t-1 \\ \mathrm{ReLU}(\mathbf{u}_t[i+1] - \mathbf{s}_{t-1}[i+1]), & i < t-1 \end{cases}$$

The pushing operation simply places the vector $\mathbf{v}_t$ at the top of the stack with strength $d_t$. Thus,

$\mathbf{V}_t$ and $\mathbf{s}_t[t]$ are updated as follows.

$$\mathbf{s}_t[t] = d_t \qquad \mathbf{V}_t[i] = \begin{cases} \mathbf{v}_t, & i = t \\ \mathbf{V}_{t-1}[i], & i < t \end{cases}$$

Note that $\mathbf{s}_t[1]$, $\mathbf{s}_t[2]$, ..., $\mathbf{s}_t[t-1]$ have already been updated during the popping step.

Finally, the reading operation produces a "summary" of the top of the stack by computing a weighted sum of all the vectors on the stack.

$$\mathbf{r}_t = \sum_{i=1}^{t} \min\left(\mathbf{s}_t[i], \rho_t[i]\right) \cdot \mathbf{V}_t[i]$$

The weights $\rho_t[i]$ are computed in a manner similar to the $\mathbf{u}_t[i]$s. The sum should include the top elements of the stack whose strengths add up to the *read strength* $r_t$. The weight $\rho_t[t]$ assigned to the top item is initialized to the full read strength $r_t$, while the weights $\rho_t[i]$ assigned to lower items are based on the "remaining" read strength $\rho_t[i+1] - \mathbf{s}_t[i+1]$ after strength has been assigned to higher items.

$$\rho_t[i] = \begin{cases} r_t, & i = t \\ \mathrm{ReLU}\left(\rho_t[i+1] - \mathbf{s}_t[i+1]\right) & i < t \end{cases}$$

## 2.2 Stack Interface

The architecture of Grefenstette et al. (2015) assumes that the controller is a neural network of the form

$$\langle \mathbf{o}_t, \mathbf{h}_t \rangle = C(\mathbf{x}_t, \mathbf{h}_{t-1}, \mathbf{r}_{t-1})$$

where $\mathbf{h}_t$ is its state at time $t$, $\mathbf{x}_t$ is its input, $\mathbf{r}_t$ is the vector read from the stack at the previous step, and $\mathbf{o}_t$ is an output vector used to produce the network output $\mathbf{y}_t$ and the stack instructions $\langle \mathbf{v}_t, u_t, d_t, r_t \rangle$.

The stack instructions $\langle \mathbf{v}_t, u_t, d_t, r_t \rangle$ are computed as follows. The read strength $r_t$ is fixed to 1. The other values are determined by passing $\mathbf{o}_t$ to specialized layers. The vectors $\mathbf{y}_t$ and $\mathbf{v}_t$ are computed using a tanh layer, while the scalar values $u_t$ and $d_t$ are obtained from a sigmoid layer. Thus, the push and pop strengths are constrained to values between 0 and 1.

$$\begin{aligned}
\mathbf{y}_t &= \mathrm{softmax}\left(\mathbf{W}^y \mathbf{o}_t + \mathbf{b}^y\right) \\
\mathbf{v}_t &= \tanh\left(\mathbf{W}^v \mathbf{o}_t + \mathbf{b}^v\right) \\
u_t &= \sigma\left(\mathbf{W}^u \mathbf{o}_t + b_u\right) \\
d_t &= \sigma\left(\mathbf{W}^d \mathbf{o}_t + b_d\right) \\
r_t &= 1
\end{aligned} \qquad (1)$$

This paper departs from Grefenstette et al.'s architecture by allowing for push, pop, and read operations to be executed with variable strength greater than 1. We achieve this by using an enhanced control interface inspired by Yogatama et al.'s (2018) Multipop Adaptive Computation Stack architecture. In that model, the controller determines how much weight to pop from the stack at each time step by computing a distribution $\mathbb{P}[u]$ describing the probability of popping $u$ units from the stack. The next stack state $\mathbf{V}$ is computed as a superposition of the possible stack states $\mathbf{V}^u$ resulting from popping $u$ units from the stack, weighted by $\mathbb{P}[u]$. Our model follows Yogatama et al. in computing probability distributions over possible values of $u_t$, $d_t$, and $r_t$. However, instead of superimposing stack states, which may hinder interpretability, we simply set the value of each instruction to be the expected value of its associated distribution. For a distribution vector $\mathbf{p}$, define the operator $\mathbb{E}[\mathbf{p}]$ as follows:

$$\mathbb{E}[\mathbf{p}] = \sum_{i=0}^{k} i\mathbf{p}[i+1]$$

$\mathbb{E}[\mathbf{p}]$ denotes the expected value of $\mathbf{p}$ if we treat it as a distribution over $\{0, 1, \ldots, k\}$. The maximum value $k$ is fixed in advance as a hyperparameter of our model. The output $\mathbf{y}_t$ and instructions $\mathbf{v}_t$, $u_t$, $d_t$, and $r_t$ are then computed as follows:

$$\begin{aligned}
\mathbf{y}_t &= \mathrm{softmax}\left(\mathbf{W}^y \mathbf{o}_t + \mathbf{b}^y\right) \\
\mathbf{v}_t &= \tanh\left(\mathbf{W}^v \mathbf{o}_t + \mathbf{b}^v\right) \\
u_t &= \mathbb{E}\left[\mathrm{softmax}\left(\mathbf{W}^u \mathbf{o}_t + b^u\right)\right] \\
d_t &= \mathbb{E}\left[\mathrm{softmax}\left(\mathbf{W}^d \mathbf{o}_t + b^u\right)\right] \\
r_t &= \mathbb{E}\left[\mathrm{softmax}\left(\mathbf{W}^r \mathbf{o}_t + b^r\right)\right]
\end{aligned}$$

The full architecture that we used for language modeling and agreement classification is a controller network which, at time $t$, reads the word $\mathbf{x}_t$ as well as the previous stack summary $\mathbf{r}_{t-1}$. These vectors are passed through an LSTM layer to produce the vector $\mathbf{o}_t$. Then, instructions for the stack are computed from $\mathbf{o}_t$ according to the equations above. Finally, these instructions are executed to modify the stack state and produce the next stack summary vector $\mathbf{r}_t$. In our experiments, the size of the LSTM layer was 100, and the size of each stack vector was 16.

## 3 Model Training

This paper considers models trained on a language modeling objective and a classification objective. On each objective, we train several neural stack models along with an LSTM baseline.[1] This section describes the procedure used to train our models and presents the perplexity and classification values they attain on their training objectives.

### 3.1 Data and Training

Our models are trained using the *Wikipedia corpus*, a subset of the English Wikipedia used by Linzen et al. (2016) for their experiments. The classification task we consider is the *number prediction task*, proposed by Linzen et al. (2016) as a diagnostic for assessing whether or not LSTMs can infer grammatical dependencies sensitive to syntactic structure. In this task, the network is shown a sequence of words forming the beginning of a sentence from the Wikipedia corpus. The next word in the sentence is always a verb, and the network must predict whether the verb is singular (SG) or plural (PL). For example, on input *The cats on the boat*, the network must predict PL to match *cats*. We train and evaluate our models on the number prediction task using Linzen et al.'s (2016) *simple dependency dataset*, which contains 141,948 training examples, 15,772 validation examples, and 1,419,491 testing examples.

We used a model with very few parameters and basic setting of hyperparameters. The LSTM hidden state was fixed to a size of 100, while the vectors placed on the stack had size 16. Including the embedding layer, the Wikipedia model had 1,584,255 parameters. We used the Adam optimizer (Kingma and Ba, 2015) with a learning rate of 0.001. The language models were trained for five epochs, while the agreement classifiers used an early stopping criterion. In addition to the LSTM baseline, for each task, we trained a stack RNN in which $u_t$ is fixed to 1 and $d_t$ ranges from 0 to $k = 4$, as well as a stack RNN in which $d_t$ fixed to 1 and $u_t$ ranges from 0 to $k = 4$. Additionally, for the classification task we trained a stack RNN in which $u_t$ ranges from 0 to $k = 4$ and $d_t$ is computed as in Equation 1.

---



|  | Stack ($u_t = 1$) | Stack ($d_t = 1$) | LSTM |
|---|---|---|---|
| Perp | 92.81 | 128.28 | **91.69** |
| Agree | 93.59 | 92.28 | **93.95** |

Table 1: Results for language models trained on the Wikipedia dataset.

### 3.2 Evaluation

Our language models are evaluated according to two metrics. Firstly, we reserve 10% of the Wikipedia corpus for evaluating test perplexity of the trained language models. Secondly, as a simple diagnostic of sensitivity to syntactic structure, we evaluate the performance of our Wikipedia-trained language models on *number agreement prediction* (Linzen et al., 2016). Under this evaluation regime, we use our language model to simulate the number prediction task and compute the resulting classification accuracy. We do this by presenting the model with an input for the number prediction task and comparing the probabilities assigned to the verb that follows the input in the Wikipedia corpus. For example, if *The cats on the boat purr* appears in the Wikipedia corpus, then we present *The cats on the boat* to the language model and compare the probabilities assigned to the singular and plural forms *purrs* and *purr*, respectively. We consider the language model to make a correct prediction if the form of the next lexical item with the correct grammatical number (SG or PL) is predicted with greater probability than the alternative.

The number prediction classifiers we trained are evaluated according to classification accuracy. For each input sentence, we define the *attractors* of the input to be the nouns intervening between the subject and the verb whose number is being classified. For example, in the input *The cat on the boat*, *cat* is the subject of the following verb, while *boat* is an attractor. We compute the accuracy of our classifiers on the full testing set of the simple dependency data set as well as subsets of the testing set consisting of sentences with a fixed number of attractors.

### 3.3 Training Results

Table 1 shows the quantitative results for our language models. The stack RNN is comparable to our LSTM baseline in terms of language modeling perplexity and agreement prediction accuracy when $u_t$ is fixed to 1, though the latter per-

| Number of Attractors | Stack ($u_t = 1$) | Stack ($d_t = 1$) | Stack | LSTM |
|---|---|---|---|---|
| Overall | **98.89** | 98.88 | 98.88 | **98.89** |
| 0 | **99.29** | 99.23 | 99.24 | 99.26 |
| 1 | 94.75 | **95.43** | 95.18 | 95.27 |
| 2 | 89.85 | 91.70 | **91.86** | 90.15 |
| 3 | 83.42 | 86.59 | **87.47** | 84.30 |
| 4 | 79.50 | 84.14 | **85.56** | 78.61 |
| 5 | 71.07 | 71.70 | **77.99** | 74.21 |

Table 2: Number prediction accuracies attained by the three stack RNN classifiers and the LSTM baseline.

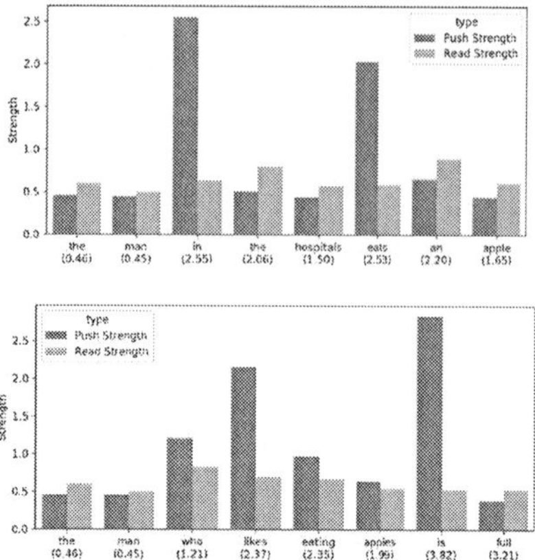

Figure 2: Push and read strengths computed by the $u_t = 1$ language model. Values underneath each word show the total strength remaining on the stack at that step.

forms slightly better according to both metrics. The stack RNN attains a significantly worse perplexity when $d_t$ is fixed to 1, and its agreement prediction accuracy is worse than both the LSTM baseline and the stack RNN with $u_t = 1$.

Table 2 shows test accuracies attained by classifiers trained on the number prediction task. While the stack classifier with $u_t$ fixed to 1 and the LSTM baseline achieve the best overall accuracy, the stack with unrestricted $u_t$ and sigmoid $d_t$ and the stack with $d_t$ fixed to 1 exceed the baseline on sentences with at least 2 attractors. We take this to suggest that the hierarchical bias provided by the stack can improve performance on syntactically complex cases.

## 4 Interpreting Stack Usage

The results presented in Subsection 3.3 show that the $u_t = 1$ stack RNNs perform comparably to LSTMs in terms of quantitative evaluation metrics. The goal of this section is to assess whether or not stack RNNs achieve this level of perfor-

mance in an interpretable manner. We do this by visualizing the push and read strengths computed by the $u_t = 1$ language model when processing two example sentences. These visualizations are shown in Figure 2 and Figure 3. Notice that the push strength tends to spike following words with subcategorization requirements. For example, the preposition *in* and the transitive verbs *eat* and *is* both require NP objects, and accordingly the model assigns a high push strength to these words. This suggests that the model is using the stack to capture hierarchical dependencies by keeping track of words that predictably introduce various kinds of phrases.

Figure 4 shows push strengths computed by the $u_t = 1$ language model, aggregated across the entire Wikipedia corpus. We see that push strengths differ systematically based on part of speech. The distribution of push strengths computed by the network upon seeing a noun is tightly concentrated around $0.5$, whereas the push strength upon seeing a verb tends to be greater—usually more than $2.5$. This phenomenon reflects the fact that verbs typically take objects while nouns do not.

We also find that push strengths assigned to verbs depend on their transitivity. The right panel of Figure 4 shows push strength distributions for a collection of common transitive and intransitive verbs. The model distinguishes between these two types of verbs by assigning high push strengths to transitive verbs and low push strengths to intransitive verbs. We make similar observations for other parts of speech: prepositions, which take objects, typically receive higher push strengths, while determiners and adjectives, which do not take phrasal complements, receive lower push strengths.

## 5 Inference of Syntactic Structure

Section 4 has shown that the push strengths $d_t$ computed by the $u_t = 1$ language model reflect the subcategorization requirements of the words encountered by the network. Based on this phenomenon, we may interpret the stack to be keeping track of phrases that are "in progress." A high push strength induced by a transitive verb, for example, may be thought to indicate that a verb phrase has begun, and that this phrase ends when the object of the verb is seen. We thus hypothesize that for each time step $t$, $d_t$ represents the size of the phrase that begins with the word read by the network at time

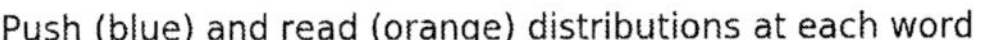


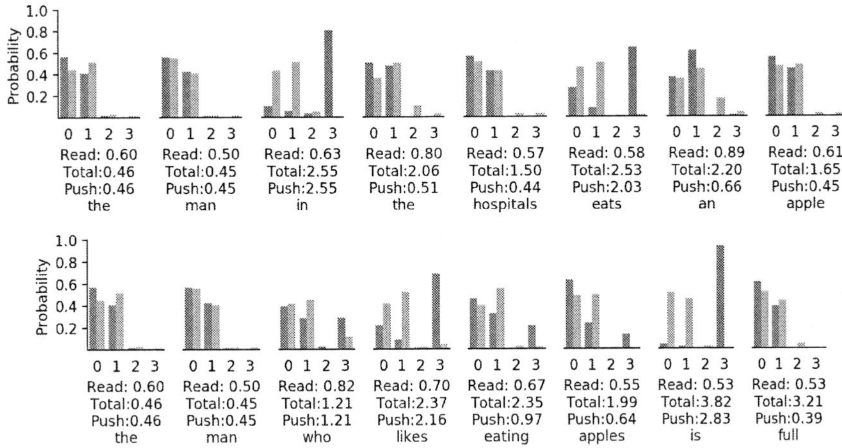


Figure 3: Distributions for push and read strengths at each step of processing example sentences. For example, the push strength chosen after processing *the* (0.46) is the expected value of the blue distribution in the far left plot.

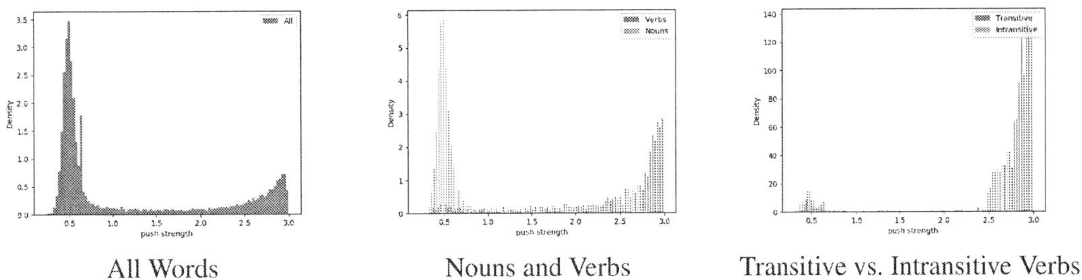


Figure 4: Distributions of $d_t$ for the $u_t = 1$ language model over all test sentences. The center panel shows the distributions of $d_t$ for nouns and verbs, and the right panel shows the distributions for selected transitive and intransitive verbs.

$t$. If $d_t$ is low, then this phrase consists of a single word; if it is high, then this is a complex phrase consisting of multiple words.

A similar intuition underlies the unsupervised parsing framework of Shen et al. (2018a,b). Under this framework, constituency structure is induced from a sequence of words by computing a *syntactic distance* between every two adjacent words. Intuitively, the syntactic distance between two words measures the distance from the lowest common parent node of the two words to the bottom of the tree. If two words have a low syntactic distance, then they are likely siblings in a small constituent; if they have a high syntactic distance, then they probably belong to different phrases. Whereas Figure 2 and Figure 3 allow us identify specific time steps at which the stack recognizes the beginning of a phrase, the unsupervised parsing framework allows us to explicitly visualize the phrasal

organization of input sequences induced by our interpretation of the push strengths.

Given an input sequence $\mathbf{x}_1, \mathbf{x}_2, \ldots, \mathbf{x}_n$, we define the syntactic distance between each $\mathbf{x}_t$ and $\mathbf{x}_{t-1}$ for our $u_t = 1$ model to be the push strength $d_t$ computed by the controller during time $t$. If the current word does not open any new constituents, then it belongs to the same constituent as the previous word, and therefore should be assigned a low syntactic distance. On the other hand, if the current word opens a complex constituent, then it is lower in the parse tree than the previous word, and therefore should be assigned a high syntactic distance. Similarly, for our $d_t = 1$ model, we let $u_t$ be the syntactic distance between $\mathbf{x}_t$ and $\mathbf{x}_{t+1}$. Under this interpretation, the pop strength estimates the complexity of the constituents that the current word closes. If the current word closes many complex constituents, then the next word appears at a higher level in the parse tree, and is therefore syntactically distant from the current word.

**Algorithm 1** (Shen et al., 2018a,b)

---
1: **procedure** MAKETREE($\mathbf{X}, \mathbf{d}$)
2:     **if** $\mathbf{X}$ has at most one word **then**
3:         **return** $\mathbf{X}$
4:     **else**
5:         $i \leftarrow \mathrm{argmax}_j\, \mathbf{d}_j$
6:         $l \leftarrow$ MAKETREE($\mathbf{X}[:i-1], \mathbf{d}[:i-1]$)
7:         $r \leftarrow$ MAKETREE($\mathbf{X}[i+1:], \mathbf{d}[i+1:]$)
8:         **if** $l$ and $r$ are not empty **then**
9:             **return** $\mathrm{Tree}[l, \mathrm{Tree}[\mathbf{X}[i], r]]$
10:        **else if** $l$ is empty **then**
11:            **return** $\mathrm{Tree}[\mathbf{X}[i], r]$
12:        **else**
13:            **return** $\mathrm{Tree}[l, \mathbf{X}[i]]$
---

Algorithm 1 shows our procedure for constructing trees. The algorithm takes as input a sequence of words arranged into a matrix $\mathbf{X}$ and a vector $\mathbf{d}$ containing the syntactic distance between each word and the previous word. Following Shen et al. (2018a,b), we recursively split $\mathbf{X}$ into binary constituents. At each recursion level, we greedily choose the word with the highest syntactic distance as the split point. The final output is a binary tree spanning the full sentence.

### 5.1 Evaluation

We compute F1 scores for the parses obtained from our Wikipedia language models by comparing against parses from Section 23 of the Penn Treebank's Wall Street Journal corpus (WSJ23, Marcus et al., 1994). Since Algorithm 1 produces unlabeled binary trees, our evaluation uses the gold standard of Htut et al. (2018), which consists of unlabeled, binarized versions of the WSJ23 trees. We also decapitalize the first word of every sentence for compatibility with our training data.

As a baseline, we the F1 scores attained by our models to those computed for purely right- and left-branching trees. A right-branching parse is equivalent to the output of Algorithm 1 on a sequence of equal syntactic distances. Thus, the difference between the right-branching F1 score and our models' scores is a measure of the amount of syntactic information encoded by the push and pop strength sequences. We also compare our

| Model | Parsing F1 |
|---|---|
| Stack ($u_t = 1$) | 31.2 |
| Stack ($d_t = 1$) | 16.0 |
| Right Branching | 13.1 |
| Left Branching | 7.3 |
| Best PRPN-UP (Htut et al., 2018) | 26.3 |
| Best PRPN-LM (Htut et al., 2018) | 37.4 |

Table 3: Unsupervised parsing performance evaluated on the WSJ23 dataset, attained by our stack models (top), the right- and left-branching baselines (middle), and the PRPN models (bottom).

F1 scores to the results of Htut et al.'s (2018) replication study for the *parsing–reading–predict network* models (PRPN-LM and PRPN-UP), the two syntactic-distance-based unsupervised parsers originally proposed by Shen et al. (2018a).

### 5.2 Results

The F1 evaluation (see Table 3) shows that our Wikipedia model with $u_t = 1$ significantly outperforms the baseline on the Penn Treebank, while our model with $d_t = 1$ performs slightly better than the baseline. This is evidence that the types of hierarchical structures produced by Algorithm 1 resemble expert-annotated constituency parses.

Our results do not exceed those of Htut et al.'s (2018) replication study. It is worth noting that our right- and left-branching baseline scores are somewhat lower than theirs. This suggests that differences in data processing or implementation might make our evaluation more difficult. Regardless, we consider our results to still be somewhat competitive, given that our language models were trained on out-of-domain data with few parameters and minimal hyperparameter tuning.

We provide example parses extracted from the stack RNN language models with $u_t = 1$ in Figure 5. Overall, our unsupervised parses tend to resemble the gold-standard parses with some differences. Periods in our parses systematically attach lower in the structure in our extracted parses than in the gold-standard trees. High attachment would require a high syntactic distance (i.e., high push strength) between the period and the remainder of the sentence. However, the period inherently does not have any subcategorization requirements, so it induces a low push strength. In contrast, prepositional phrases attach higher in our structures than in the gold parses. This may be the result of fixed subcategorization-associated push strengths for prepositions that give rise to fairly high esti-

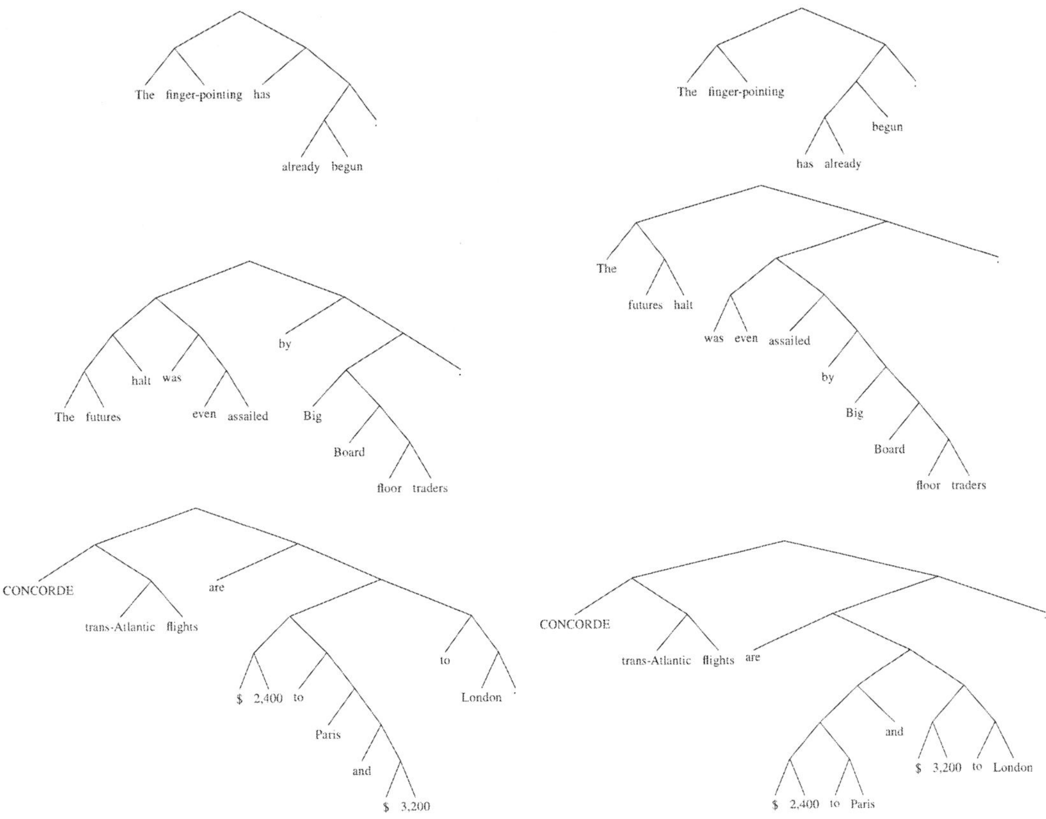

Figure 5: Sample parses obtained from our stack RNN language model with $u_t = 1$ (left), compared to Htut et al.'s (2018) gold-standard parses (right).

mates of syntactic distance.

## 6 Discussion

Overall, our stack language models show no improvement over the LSTM baseline in terms of perplexity and classification accuracy. Although the $u_t = 1$ language model is comparable to the LSTM on these metrics, it ultimately achieves worse scores than the baseline. However, we have now seen that the pushing behavior of the model reflects subcategorization properties of lexical items that play an important role in determining their syntactic behavior, and that these properties allow reasonable parses to be extracted from this model. These observations show that the $u_t = 1$ model has learned to encode structural representations using the stack. Quantitatively, the importance of this structural information for the training objectives can be seen in Table 2, where the stack at least partially alleviates the difficulty experienced by the LSTM classifier in handling syntactically complex inputs.

While our stack language models do not exceed the LSTM baseline in terms of perplexity and agreement accuracy, Yogatama et al. (2018) find that their Multipop Adaptive Computation Stack architecture substantially outperforms a bare LSTM on these metrics. Compared to their models, we use fewer parameters and minimal hyperparameter tuning. Thus, it is possible that increasing the number of parameters in our controller may lead to similar increases in performance in addition to the structural interpretability that we have observed.

## 7 Conclusion

The results reported here point to the conclusion that stack RNNs trained on corpora of natural language text do in fact learn to encode sentences in a hierarchically organized fashion. We show that the sequence of stack operations used in the processing of a sentence lets us uncover a syntactic structure that matches standardly assigned structure reasonably well, even if the addition of the stack does not improve the stack RNN's performance over the LSTM baseline in terms of the language modeling objective. We also find that using the stack RNN to predict the grammatical number of a verb results in better hierarchical generalizations in syntactically complex cases than is possible with stackless models. Taken together, these results suggest that the stack RNN model yields comparable performance to other architectures, while producing structural representations that are easier to interpret and that show signs of being linguistically natural.

## References


Noam Chomsky. 1956. Three models for the description of language. *IRE Transactions on Information Theory*, 2(3):113–124.

Noam Chomsky. 1957. *Syntactic Structures*, 1 edition. Mouton, The Hague, Netherlands.

Noam Chomsky. 1962. Context-free grammars and pushdown storage. Technical Report 65, MIT Research Laboratory for Electronics, Cambridge, MA.

Edward Grefenstette, Karl Moritz Hermann, Mustafa Suleyman, and Phil Blunsom. 2015. Learning to Transduce with Unbounded Memory. *Computing Research Repository*, arXiv:1506.02516v3.

Kristina Gulordava, Piotr Bojanowski, Edouard Grave, Tal Linzen, and Marco Baroni. 2018. Colorless Green Recurrent Networks Dream Hierarchically. In *Proceedings of the 2018 Conference of the North American Chapter of the Association for Computational Linguistics: Human Language Technologies*, volume 1, pages 1195–1205, New Orleans, LA. Association for Computational Linguistics.

Yiding Hao, William Merrill, Dana Angluin, Robert Frank, Noah Amsel, Andrew Benz, and Simon Mendelsohn. 2018. Context-free transductions with neural stacks. In *Proceedings of the 2018 EMNLP Workshop BlackboxNLP: Analyzing and Interpreting Neural Networks for NLP*, pages 306–315, Brussels, Belgium. Association for Computational Linguistics.

Sepp Hochreiter and Jürgen Schmidhuber. 1997. Long short-term memory. *Neural Computation*, 9(8):1735–1780.

Phu Mon Htut, Kyunghyun Cho, and Samuel Bowman. 2018. Grammar induction with neural language models: An unusual replication. In *Proceedings of the 2018 EMNLP Workshop BlackboxNLP: Analyzing and Interpreting Neural Networks for NLP*, pages 371–373, Brussels, Belgium. Association for Computational Linguistics.

Armand Joulin and Tomas Mikolov. 2015. Inferring Algorithmic Patterns with Stack-Augmented Recurrent Nets. In *Advances in Neural Information Processing Systems 28*, pages 190–198, Montreal, Canada. Curran Associates, Inc.

Diederik P. Kingma and Jimmy Lei Ba. 2015. Adam: A Method for Stochastic Optimization. In *ICLR 2015 Conference Track*, San Diego, CA. arXiv.

Tal Linzen, Emmanuel Dupoux, and Yoav Goldberg. 2016. Assessing the Ability of LSTMs to Learn Syntax-Sensitive Dependencies. *Transactions of the Association for Computational Linguistics*, 4(0):521–535.

Mitchell Marcus, Grace Kim, Mary Ann Marcinkiewicz, Robert MacIntyre, Ann Bies, Mark Ferguson, Karen Katz, and Britta Schasberger. 1994. The Penn Treebank: Annotating Predicate Argument Structure. In *Proceedings of the Workshop on Human Language Technology*, pages 114–119, Plainsboro, NJ. Association for Computational Linguistics.

Rebecca Marvin and Tal Linzen. 2018. Targeted Syntactic Evaluation of Language Models. In *Proceedings of the 2018 Conference on Empirical Methods in Natural Language Processing*, pages 1192–1202, Brussels, Belgium. Association for Computational Linguistics.

Yikang Shen, Zhouhan Lin, Chin-wei Huang, and Aaron Courville. 2018a. Neural Language Modeling by Jointly Learning Syntax and Lexicon. In *ICLR 2018 Conference Track*, Vancouver, Canada. OpenReview.

Yikang Shen, Zhouhan Lin, Athul Paul Jacob, Alessandro Sordoni, Aaron Courville, and Yoshua Bengio. 2018b. Straight to the Tree: Constituency Parsing with Neural Syntactic Distance. In *Proceedings of the 56th Annual Meeting of the Association for Computational Linguistics*, volume 1: Long Papers, pages 1171–1180, Melbourne, Australia. Association for Computational Linguistics.

Dani Yogatama, Yishu Miao, Gabor Melis, Wang Ling, Adhiguna Kuncoro, Chris Dyer, and Phil Blunsom. 2018. Memory Architectures in Recurrent Neural Network Language Models. In *ICLR 2018 Conference Track*, Vancouver, Canada. OpenReview.

# Adversarial Attack on Sentiment Classification


**Alicia Yi-Ting Tsai**
aliciatsai@berkeley.edu

**Tobey Yang**
minchu.yang@berkeley.edu

**Erica Chen**
hanyu_chen@berkeley.edu



## Abstract

In this paper, we propose a white-box attack algorithm called "Global Search" method and compare it with a simple misspelling noise and a more sophisticated and common white-box attack approach called "Greedy Search". The attack methods are evaluated on the Convolutional Neural Network (CNN) sentiment classifier trained on the IMDB movie review dataset. The attack success rate is used to evaluate the effectiveness of the attack methods and the perplexity of the sentences is used to measure the degree of distortion of the generated adversarial examples. The experiment results show that the proposed "Global Search" method generates more powerful adversarial examples with less distortion or less modification to the source text.


## 1 Introduction

In the past few decades, machine learning and deep learning techniques have been successful in several applications. However, these techniques developed so far are proven to be vulnerable given some manipulated inputs, which are called adversarial examples, that human can easily distinguish but algorithms can not (Szegedy et al., 2014; Goodfellow et al., 2015).

Current research have shown successful results in producing adversarial images that cause the algorithms to completely fail in computer vision (Kurakin et al., 2016). Studies of adversarial examples in the applications of natural language processing such as sentiment analysis, fake news detection and machine translation remain relatively low. Nonetheless, it is an emerging field that is worth exploring and has increased attention re-

cently due to the success of adversarial learning in images. When generating an adversarial example, if the adversary does not have knowledge of the classifier or the training data, we call this a black-box setting. On the other hand, if the adversary has full knowledge of the classifier and the training data, we call this a white-box setting.

In a black-box setting, Belinkov and Bisk introduces a simple attack method by randomly replacing characters with their nearby key on the keyboard, which is similar to keyboard typos, to attack a machine translation system (Belinkov and Bisk, 2017). Similar idea can be found in the work of Hosseini et al., the authors generate adversaries that deceive Google Perspective API by misspelling the abusive words or adding punctuation to the letters (Hosseini et al., 2017). Another work from Alzantot et al. attempts to generate semantically and syntactically similar adversarial examples by word replacement (Alzantot et al., 2018). They develop an genetic algorithm that uses population-based gradient-free optimization, inspired by the process of natural selection. In the black-box setting, the adversary tries different perturbations and evaluates the quality of perturbations by querying the model to get the classification result or the output score. The adversary continues to altered the sentence until the model fails or until score reduces significantly.

In the white-box setting, the adversary has access to the model and thus is capable of generating more sophisticated adversarial examples. Ebrahimi et al. show that adversarial examples generated in a white-box setting achieve a higher success rate than examples generated in a black-box setting. The authors introduce a white-box adversary against differentiable classifiers that substitutes characters ("flips") in a sentence. When operating in a white-box setting, the adversary has full access to the gradients of the classifier, giv-




*Proceedings of the Second BlackboxNLP Workshop on Analyzing and Interpreting Neural Networks for NLP*, pages 233–240
Florence, Italy, August 1, 2019. ©2019 Association for Computational Linguistics

ing the adversary important information to find the classifier's weak points. Because white-box adversary has access to the gradients of the model, the adversary does not have to query the output score from the classifier every time. Using the gradients as a surrogate loss, the white-box adversary can efficiently find the best changes that maximize the surrogate loss simply by backpropagation.

Other white-box adversary includes word-level substitution. Kuleshov et al. try to replace 10-30% of words in the source text by solving an optimization problem that maximizes a surrogate loss subject using a greedy approach, which is similar to the "Greedy Search" baseline used in the experiment. A similar idea can be found in Samanta and Mehta where the authors apply different rules (insertion, replacement and deletion of words) to generate adversarial examples. Liang et al. later combine the strategies above and try to avoid introducing excessive modification or insertion to the original source text.

In this paper, we consider the task of white-box attack where the adversary has full knowledge of the model under attack. We propose a "Global Search" attack method that mitigates some of the problems faced in the commonly used greedy approach. A very simple misspelling noise baseline is also reported to show the effectiveness of the 2 white-box attack methods in the experiment.

## 2  Attack Method

### 2.1  Misspelling Noise

We first consider a very simple case by swapping two characters in a word (eg. perfect → pefrect), which is similar to keyboard typos or misspelling. To maintain the readability of source text, the noise is only applied to word of length longer than 3 and 50% of the words in the source text are randomly swapped.

### 2.2  Greedy Search Approach

We follow a similar greedy optimization strategy in (Kuleshov et al., 2018) for constructing adversarial examples for sentiment classification. At each iteration, the algorithm considers $k$ nearest neighbors of each word in the word embedding space. It then picks the one among the $k$ neighbors that has the greatest impact on the prediction result. Consider a sentiment classifier $f$, the greedy approach forms the adversarial example by replacing the original word $w$ with the candidates $w'$. If

the label is positive, then the final sigmoid layer of the model should output a value $\sigma$ greater than 0.5. The algorithm then replaces the original word $w$ with each candidate $w'$ among the $k$ neighbors and see if the sigmoid value of the adversary $x'$ is less than $\sigma$, indicating that replacing $w$ with $w'$ can contribute to flipping the prediction result to negative. The candidate $w'$ that results in the maximum difference is then chosen to be the final replacement, i.e. smallest $\sigma'$ for positive class (1) and the largest $\sigma'$ for the negative class (0).

$$\arg\min_{w'} f_{\text{sigmoid}}(x')$$
$$\text{s.t. } f_{\text{sigmoid}}(x') < f_{\text{sigmoid}}(x) \quad \text{if positive class}$$

$$\arg\max_{w'} f_{\text{sigmoid}}(x')$$
$$\text{s.t. } f_{\text{sigmoid}}(x') > f_{\text{sigmoid}}(x) \quad \text{if negative class}$$

Algorithm 1 summarizes the "Greedy Search" approach. Although the objective of the algorithm is to fool the sentiment classifier, the grammar, semantic and sentiment should not be altered. Thus, some constraints are imposed in order to maintain the similarity between the original source text and the adversarial example.

---

**Algorithm 1** Generate adversarial example via greedy search

---

1: $\sigma \leftarrow f_{\text{sigmoid}}(x)$
2: Initialize $x' \leftarrow x$, *count* $\leftarrow 0$
3: **for** $w$ in $x'$ **do**
4:     *candidates* $\leftarrow$ $k$ nearest neighbors of $w$ within distance $d$ and have the same POS tag as $w$
5:     $\Sigma \leftarrow \emptyset$
6:     **for** $w'$ in *candidates* **do**
7:         $\bar{x} \leftarrow$ replace $w$ with $w'$
8:         $\sigma' \leftarrow f_{\text{sigmoid}}(\bar{x})$
9:         $\Sigma \leftarrow \Sigma$ append $\sigma'$
10:     **if** positive and $\min \Sigma < \sigma$ **then**
11:         $x' \leftarrow \text{argmin}_{\bar{x}} \Sigma$
12:         *count* $\leftarrow$ *count* $+1$
13:     **else if** negative and $\max \Sigma > \sigma$ **then**
14:         $x' \leftarrow \text{argmax}_{\bar{x}} \Sigma$
15:         *count* $\leftarrow$ *count* $+1$
16:     $\sigma \leftarrow f_{\text{sigmoid}}(x')$
17:     **if** positive and $\sigma < 0.5$ **then return** $x'$
18:     **if** negative and $\sigma > 0.5$ **then return** $x'$
19:     **if** $count/\text{len}(x) > r$ **then return** *None*

---

**Word Choice.** When picking the word candidates in each iteration, we consider the top $k$ nearest neighbors in the word embedding space. The nearest neighbors in GloVE word embedding space usually appear in the same context as the original word. Thus, by picking nearest neighbors in GloVE vectors, we can ensure semantic similarity after word replacement. Although word embedding helps to find words that are used in similar context, it does not guarantee that the part of speech (POS) will remain the same after replacement. Therefore, we examine the part of speech of the original word and ensure the selected candidates have the same part of speech as the original word.

**Hyper-parameters.** There are 3 hyperparameters, $k$, $d$, and $r$, used in Algorithm 1 to maintain the semantic similarity of the sentences. The first parameter $k$ is used to decide how many nearest neighbors should be considered in the first place. When $k$ is too small, there might not be enough candidates to successfully form an adversarial example. $d$ represents the maximum distance allowed between the candidate words and the original word in the word embedding space. When $d$ is large, the meaning of the altered sentence is generally farther from the original one. When $d$ gets too small, the chance of generating a successful attack decreases. The last hyperparameter, $r$, stands for the percentage of replacement allowed in the sentence. When the threshold $r$ is too low, the chance of generating a successful adversarial example decreases. Similarly, when $r$ is too large, too many words will be replaced and thus the generated sentence will be very dissimilar to the original one.

## 2.3 Global Search Approach

The greedy approach proposed above does not guarantee to produce the optimal results and is sometimes time consuming because the algorithm needs to search the candidate words for every iteration. To mitigate the problem, we propose to search for the candidates globally by computing a small perturbation, $\delta$.

To learn the perturbation, $\delta$, we define an objective function $J(\delta)$. The objective function tries to maximize the difference between the sigmoid value of the original input $x$ and that of perturbed input $x + \delta$. Furthermore, we add two regularization terms in the objective function. The first

regularization penalizes large perturbations and is controlled via the hyperparameters $\lambda_1$. The second regularization penalizes large distance between original word embedding and perturbed word embedding and is controlled by the hyperparameters $\lambda_2$. The two regularization terms are added to help keep the semantic of chosen words.

$$
\begin{aligned}
\mathcal{J}(\delta) = & (f_{\text{sigmoid}}(E_x) - f_{\text{sigmoid}}(E_x + \delta))^2 \\
& + \lambda_1 \cdot \|\delta\|_2 \\
& + \lambda_2 \cdot \|(E_x - (E_x + \delta))\|_2
\end{aligned}
$$

The attack algorithm is described in Algorithm 2. We first initialize the perturbation $\delta$ to be 0. Here, the original input embedding is denoated as $E_x$ and the perturbed embedding is denoted as $E'_x = E_x + \delta$. For each iteration, the algorithm computes the gradient, $\nabla_\delta$, of the objective function $J(\delta)$ with respect to the perturbation $\delta$, and update the perturbation $\delta$ via backpropagation. We then form a perturbed embedding $E'_x$. The perturbed embedding $E'_x$ is a matrix and each row of $E'_x$ is the perturbed word embedding for each word, denoted as $e$, in the source text. The perturbed embedding $e$ usually does not have a actual word that can be mapped back to. Thus, we find the candidate words $w'$ in the embedding space that is the closest to the perturbed word embedding $e$ and record the $w'$ in the candidate list $k_e$. The candidate words for replacement are recorded in another list $W'$. After computing the perturbed embedding, and record the candidate words, the algorithm checks if the current perturbed embedding $E'_x$ flips the prediction result. The algorithm continues to compute new $E'_x$ and record the candidate words if the previous $E'_x$ fails to fool the model, otherwise, the algorithm returns the candidate words and the perturbation.

Next, we can use the generated candidate words list and the perturbation to generate the adversarial example. The algorithm is described in algorithm 3. The algorithm sorts the magnitude of the perturbation and replaces words in the positions that have higher perturbation magnitude. A higher perturbation magnitude indicates that the classifier is more sensitive to changes of the original word. Here, we have a hyperparameter $d$ that controls the threshold for word distance. If the last candidate $w'_n$ in the candidate words list is too far away from the original word, then the algorithm rejects the candidate $w'_n$ and move to the previous candidate $w'_{n-1}$ in the list. The hyperparameter $r$ controls

**Algorithm 2** Global Search Attack Function

---

1: $y \leftarrow Round(f_{\text{sigmoid}}(x))$
2: Initialize $\delta \leftarrow 0$, $success = False$
3: $E_x \leftarrow$ input embedding
4: $W' \leftarrow \varnothing$
5: **for** $e$ in $E'_x$ **do**
6:      $k_e \leftarrow \varnothing$        $\triangleright$ Empty candidate list
7:      $W' \leftarrow W'$ append $k_e$
8: **while** not $success$ **do**
9:      $\nabla_\delta \leftarrow$ via $back\text{-}propagation$
10:     $\delta \leftarrow \delta - \epsilon \cdot \nabla_\delta$
11:     $E'_x \leftarrow E_x + \delta$     $\triangleright$ perturbed embedding
12:     **for** $e$ in $E'_x$ **do**
13:         $k_e \leftarrow k_e$ append $\text{argmin}_{w'} \|e - E_{w'}\|_2$
14:     $\hat{y} \leftarrow Round(f_{\text{sigmoid}}(E'_x))$
15:     $W' \leftarrow W' \cup \{k_e\}$
16:     **if** $\hat{y} \neq y$ **then**
17:         **return** $W', \delta$

---

the percentage of changes allowed as the described earlier.

**Algorithm 3** Global Search Generate Adversary Function

---

1: $y \leftarrow Round(f_{\text{sigmoid}}(x))$
2: $positions \leftarrow reversed(\text{argsort } \|\delta\|_2)$
3: Initialize $success = False$
4: **for** $i$ in $positions$ **do**
5:      $w \leftarrow i$-th word in the source text $x$
6:      $candidates \leftarrow W'_i$
7:      $candidates \leftarrow reversed(candidates)$
8:      **for** $w'$ in $candidates$ **do**
9:         **if** $\|e_w - e_{w'}\|_2 < d$ **then**
10:        $E'_i \leftarrow e_{w'}$     $\triangleright$ replace embedding
11:        break
12:      $x'_i \leftarrow w'$        $\triangleright$ replace word
13:      $\hat{y} \leftarrow Round(f_{\text{sigmoid}}(E'_x))$
14:      **if** $\hat{y} \neq y$ **then**
15:        $success = True$
16:        **return** $x'$
17:      **if** $\frac{i}{\text{len}(x)} > r$ **then**
18:        **return** $None$

---

## 3 Experiment

### 3.1 Dataset

We use a dataset of 25,000 informal movie reviews from the Internet Movie Database (IMDB) (Maas et al., 2011) and randomly select 80% of the dataset to include in the training set, and 20% in the testing set [1].

### 3.1.1 CNN Sentiment Classifier

In this experiment, we used the convolutional neural network classifier (Kim, 2014) as the target model to be attacked. We replicated the architecture of the CNN model from Kim work. In the CNN model, an embedding of a fixed dictionary and size serves as the very first layer. Convolutional layers with filter widths of 3, 4, 5 and 100 are added with a max-over-time pooling layer and a fully connected layer with dropout rate of 0.5. We trained the model with 20,000 reviews and tested it with another 5,000 reviews with batch size of 64, reaching testing accuracy of 0.9. The result is summarized in Table 1.

### 3.2 Evaluation

### 3.2.1 Success Rate

The end goal of the attack algorithms is to trick the model to make wrong prediction by manipulating the input. To access the effectiveness of the attack models, we select 500 examples that are correctly classified from the test set, so that the accuracy of the classifiers does not affect the evaluation. We then input these source text into the attack algorithms to generate adversarial examples. The adversarial examples are then fed into the CNN classifier to get the final prediction. The success rate of the attack algorithm is defined as the percentage of wrong prediction by the CNN classifier. Higher success rate means that the attack algorithm can generate more powerful adversaries that can cause the CNN classifier to misbehave. The experiment result in Table 2 shows that Global Search approach has 72% success rate while Greedy Search approach has 65%. Compared with the Global Search method, it generally requires higher percentage of words replacement for Greedy Search to successfully generate an adversary. Because of the greedy nature, the algorithm replaces words as long as changing the words can help confuse the classifier; hence, the algorithm can replace sub-optimal words in a earlier position that do not contribute the most to the end goal. Another limitation of the Greedy Search approach is that word replacements tend to locate in a close area of the sentence, especially in an earlier position. This greatly reduce the readability of

---



236

| Accuracy | Training | Testing |
| --- | --- | --- |
| CNN | 0.99 | 0.90 |

Table 1: Sentiment Classifier Result

the sentences and can destroy the semantic meaning of the source text.

### 3.2.2 Hyper-parameters Choice

As mentioned above, there are 3 hyper-parameters in the greedy approach, which are $k$, the number of candidates to be considered; $d$, the maximum distance allowed between the original word and the candidate; $r$, the ratio of word changes allowed with respect to the length of the sentence. The global search algorithm also includes the hyper-parameters $d$ and $r$. In our experiment of the greedy approach, $k$ is set to 20. This parameter does not affect much since the maximum word distance allowed and the limitation of picking words with the same part-of-speech tag help to maintain similarity. The parameter is used to reduce the run-time complexity of the algorithm by limiting the number of candidates. As for $d$, we run the algorithm for a few different values, we decide to set $d$ to 20 to reach a high success rate while not picking words too far from the original one. There exists a trade-off between similarity and success rate in choosing the value for $d$. While allowing words farther from the original word, the success rate increases but similarity decreases as a penalty. The threshold $r$ controls how many words are allowed to change in a sentence; it is also shared by the two approaches. In greedy approach, $r$ should be at least set to 0.2 to achieve a good result. When $r$ is set to 0.1, the success rate is merely 0.18; when $r$ is 0.2, the success rate increases to 0.65. So we decide to set the threshold $r$ to 0.2 for greedy approach in the following experiment. On the other hand, the global search algorithm can reach a pretty good result when $r$ is set to 0.1. In our experiment, we found that global search algorithm is more effective than the greedy approach since the global search algorithm looks for the word that contributes most to classification result while greedy algorithm swap words with any degree of contribution.

### 3.2.3 Perplexity

In order to evaluate the adversarial examples generated from our models, we decide to measure the perplexity, which is widely used in assessing

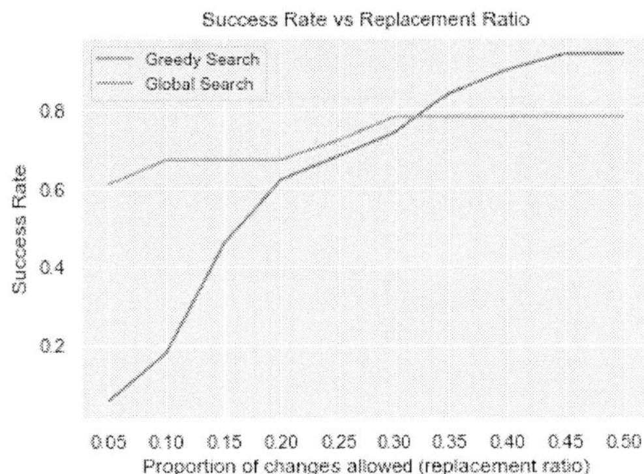


Figure 1: Success Rate vs Replacement Ratio

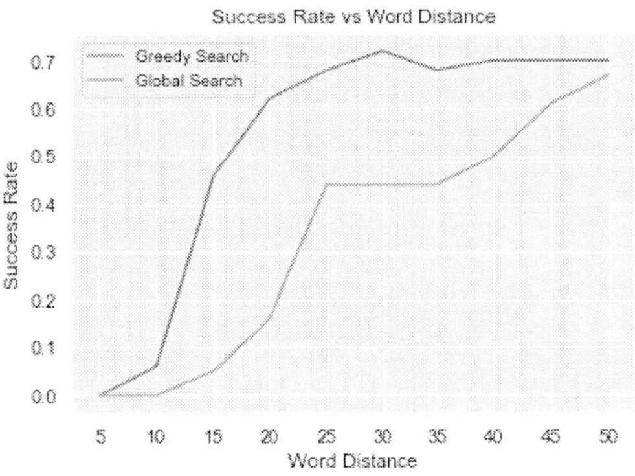


Figure 2: Success Rate vs Word Distance

| Misspelling Noise | Greedy Search | Global Search |
| --- | --- | --- |
| 6% | 65% | 72% |

Table 2: Success rate of attacking methods

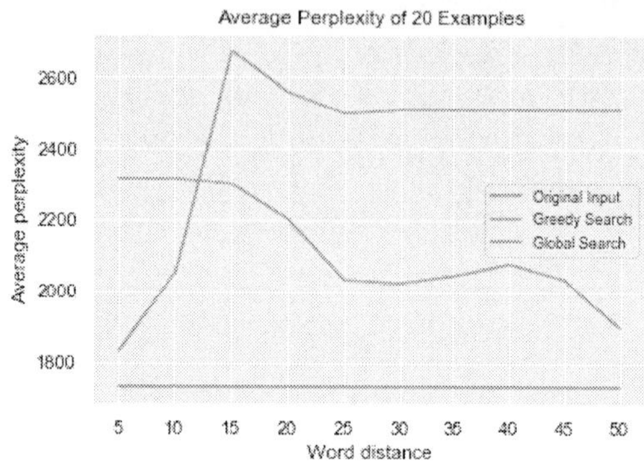

Figure 3: Average Perplexity vs Word Distance

Figure 4: Average Perplexity vs Replacement Ratio

language models, of 20 examples with different hyper-parameters. As Figure 3 shows, the perplexity increases as the word distance increases in the greedy approach, meaning that the generated examples are less likely to occur in the corpus. However, in the global search approach, it is the opposite. It might be that the number of change decreases while allowing larger word distance. We also calculate the perplexity with different values of proportion of changes. The perplexity increases as the proportion of changes allowed in both attacking models. See result in Figure 4. When comparing the perplexity of the two attacking models, the global search approach generally does better than the greedy one. Since the greedy algorithm usually requires more changes than the global search approach even though we have set the threshold for the replacement rate.

### 3.2.4 Human Evaluation

We conduct a survey and propose two criteria to measure the performance of the adversarial examples from three attack methods. The first criteria is the sentiment classification accuracy of the adversarial examples which is predicted by human, and the second is the similarity between the adversarial examples and the original sentence.

**Human Prediction Accuracy.** Unlike adversarial examples in the context of image classification, natural language perturbation is generally perceptible since words are deleted, added, or replaced. Thus, we need to redefine imperceptibility in the context of natural language. Since we are crafting adversarial example to fool the sentiment classifier, we define it as imperceptible if human can still correctly classify without being fooled by the perturbation. Therefore, we ask some volunteers to evaluate adversarial examples and look at the percentage of responses that match the original classification.

**Sentence Similarity.** In addition to classification accuracy, we also care about how similar the generated adversaries examples are to the original unaltered sentences. we ask volunteers to rate the similarity, from 1 to 5, which means less similar to very similar between the adversarial sentence and original sentence.

We choose two sentences which originally classified as positive comment and negative comment, and then flipped to opposite sentiment result after applying three attack methods. After asking 15 volunteers and analyzing the survey data, we found that the adversarial example from Global Search is most similar to the original sentence, with an average similarity of 4.4, while the example from Greedy Search is less similar, with the score of 2.9.

Refer to human prediction accuracy, Global Search method also reaches the highest accuracy, which is 0.83. It means that although sentiment classifier make the wrong prediction on the Global

Search adversarial examples, human could still classify sentiment correctly. However, greedy search only has 0.30 accuracy because it alter too many words to fool the sentiment classifier. In this survey, some of the volunteers feel that the adversarial sentences from Greedy Search are hard to read and can not tell the sentiment of the senetence.

| Examples of adversarial text generated |
| --- |
| **Original reviews:** as long as you go into this movie knowing that it 's terrible : bad acting , bad " effects , " bad story , bad ... everything , then you 'll love it . this is one of my favorite " goof on " movies ; watch it as a comedy and have a dozen good laughs ! |
| **Global Search:** as long as you go into this movie knowing that it 's terrible : worse acting , bad " effects , " bad story , bad ... everything , then you 'll love it . this is one of my favorite " goof on " movies ; watch it as a comedy and have a dozen good laughs yes |
| **Greedy Search:** as long as you leave into this blockbuster telling whether it 's horrendous : bad acting , bad " effects , " bad story , bad ... everything , then you 'll love it . this is one of my favorite " goof on " movies ; watch it as ... |
| **Misspelling Noise:** as lnog as you go into this mvoie knowing that it's terirble : bad aicing , bad " effects , " bad sotry , bad ... everything , then you 'll lvoe it . this is one of my favorite " goof on " movies ; watch it as a comedy and hvae a dzoen good laguhs ! |

## 4  Conclusion and Future Work

In this experiment, we generalize the concept of adversarial examples to the context of sentiment classification in natural language. We prove that some machine learning algorithms are vulnerable to adversarial examples. Some works have been done using the greedy approach and have proved the method to be effective; however, the global search algorithm is proved to be much more powerful than the greedy approach. The global search method requires less change to the original sentence and maintain a higher level of similarity in terms of both human evaluation and perplexity measure.

Both of the greedy and global search algorithms are operating in a white-box scenario; they are not as powerful as the black-box algorithms. The black-box character swapping algorithm could be further applied to CNN model with character-level embedding. Other word-level attacking models operating in black-box scenarios can be a way to improve the limitation of white-box models.

By far, we developed some successful strategies to attack the sentiment classifiers. Further studies can be done to strengthen the classifiers. By training the classifiers with generated adversarial examples, we hope to help defend the classifier against adversarial attack and improve the model accuracy.

## References


Moustafa Alzantot, Yash Sharma, Ahmed Elgohary, Bo-Jhang Ho, Mani Srivastava, and Kai-Wei Chang. 2018. Generating natural language adversarial examples.

Yonatan Belinkov and Yonatan Bisk. 2017. Synthetic and natural noise both break neural machine translation. *CoRR*, abs/1711.02173.

Javid Ebrahimi, Anyi Rao, Daniel Lowd, and Dejing Dou. 2017. Hotflip: White-box adversarial examples for NLP. *CoRR*, abs/1712.06751.

Ian Goodfellow, Jonathon Shlens, and Christian Szegedy. 2015. Explaining and harnessing adversarial examples. In *International Conference on Learning Representations*.

Hossein Hosseini, Sreeram Kannan, Baosen Zhang, and Radha Poovendran. 2017. Deceiving google's perspective API built for detecting toxic comments. *CoRR*, abs/1702.08138.

Yoon Kim. 2014. Convolutional neural networks for sentence classification. In *Proceedings of the 2014 Conference on Empirical Methods in Natural Language Processing (EMNLP)*.

Volodymyr Kuleshov, Shantanu Thakoor, Tingfung Lau, and Stefano Ermon. 2018. Adversarial examples for natural language classification problems.

Alexey Kurakin, Ian J. Goodfellow, and Samy Bengio. 2016. Adversarial examples in the physical world. *CoRR*, abs/1607.02533.

|                                    | Misspelling Noise | Greedy Search | Global Search |
| ---------------------------------- | ----------------- | ------------- | ------------- |
| Semantic Similarity (Scale: 1-5)   | 3.8               | 2.9           | 4.4           |
| Human Prediction Accuracy          | 0.70              | 0.30          | 0.83          |

Table 3: Human Evaluation Survey Results


Bin Liang, Hongcheng Li, Miaoqiang Su, Pan Bian, Xirong Li, and Wenchang Shi. 2018. Deep text classification can be fooled. *Proceedings of the Twenty-Seventh International Joint Conference on Artificial Intelligence.*

Andrew L. Maas, Raymond E. Daly, Peter T. Pham, Dan Huang, Andrew Y. Ng, and Christopher Potts. 2011. Learning word vectors for sentiment analysis. In *Proceedings of the 49th Annual Meeting of the Association for Computational Linguistics: Human Language Technologies*, pages 142–150, Portland, Oregon, USA. Association for Computational Linguistics.

S. Samanta and S. Mehta. 2017. Towards Crafting Text Adversarial Samples. *ArXiv e-prints.*

Christian Szegedy, Wojciech Zaremba, Ilya Sutskever, Joan Bruna, Dumitru Erhan, Ian Goodfellow, and Rob Fergus. 2014. Intriguing properties of neural networks. In *International Conference on Learning Representations.*

# Open Sesame: Getting Inside BERT's Linguistic Knowledge

**Yongjie Lin**[a,*] and **Yi Chern Tan**[a,*] and **Robert Frank**[b]
[a]Department of Computer Science, Yale University
[b]Department of Linguistics, Yale University
{yongjie.lin, yichern.tan, robert.frank}@yale.edu

## Abstract

How and to what extent does BERT encode syntactically-sensitive hierarchical information or positionally-sensitive linear information? Recent work has shown that contextual representations like BERT perform well on tasks that require sensitivity to linguistic structure. We present here two studies which aim to provide a better understanding of the nature of BERT's representations. The first of these focuses on the identification of structurally-defined elements using diagnostic classifiers, while the second explores BERT's representation of subject-verb agreement and anaphor-antecedent dependencies through a quantitative assessment of self-attention vectors. In both cases, we find that BERT encodes positional information about word tokens well on its lower layers, but switches to a hierarchically-oriented encoding on higher layers. We conclude then that BERT's representations do indeed model linguistically relevant aspects of hierarchical structure, though they do not appear to show the sharp sensitivity to hierarchical structure that is found in human processing of reflexive anaphora.[1]

## 1 Introduction

Word embeddings have become an important cornerstone in any NLP pipeline. Although such embeddings traditionally involve context-free distributed representations of words (Mikolov et al., 2013; Pennington et al., 2014), recent successes with contextualized representations (Howard and Ruder, 2018; Peters et al., 2018; Radford et al., 2019) have led to a paradigm shift. One prominent architecture is BERT (Devlin et al., 2018), a Transformer-based model that learns bidirectional encoder representations for words, on the basis of

a masked language model and sentence adjacency training objective. Simply using BERT's representations in place of traditional embeddings has resulted in state-of-the-art performance on a range of downstream tasks including summarization (Liu, 2019), question answering and textual entailment (Devlin et al., 2018). It is still, however, unclear why BERT representations perform well.

A flurry of recent work (Linzen et al., 2016; Gulordava et al., 2018; Marvin and Linzen, 2018; Lakretz et al., 2019) has explored how recurrent neural language models perform in cases that require sensitivity to hierarchical syntactic structure, and study how they do so, particularly in the domain of agreement. In these studies, a pre-trained language model is asked to predict the next word in a sentence (a verb in the target sentence) following a sequence that may include other intervening nouns with different grammatical features (e.g., "the **bear** by the <u>trees</u> *eats*..."). The predicted verb should agree with the subject noun (**bear**) and not the attractors (<u>trees</u>), in spite of the latter's recency. Such analyses have revealed that LSTMs exhibit state tracking and explicit notions of word order for modeling long term dependencies, although this effect is diluted when sequential and structural information in a sentence conflict. Further work by Gulordava et al. (2018) and others (Linzen and Leonard, 2018; Giulianelli et al., 2018) argues that RNNs acquire grammatical competence in agreement that is more abstract than word collocations, although language model performance that requires sensitivity to the phenomena such as reflexive anaphora, non-local agreement and negative polarity remains low (Marvin and Linzen, 2018). Meanwhile, studies evaluating *which* linguistic phenomena are encoded by contextualized representations (Goldberg, 2019; Wolf, 2019; Tenney et al., 2019) successfully demonstrate that purely self-attentive architectures like BERT can

---

*Equal contribution.

[1]The code is available at https://github.com/yongjie-lin/bert-opensesame.

241

*Proceedings of the Second BlackboxNLP Workshop on Analyzing and Interpreting Neural Networks for NLP*, pages 241–253
Florence, Italy, August 1, 2019. ©2019 Association for Computational Linguistics

capture hierarchy-sensitive, syntactic dependencies, and even support the extraction of dependency parses (Hewitt and Manning, 2019). However, the way in which BERT does this has been less studied. In this paper, we investigate how and where the representations produced by pre-trained BERT models (Devlin et al., 2018) express the hierarchical organization of a sentence.

We proceed in two ways. The first involves the use of diagnostic classifiers (Hupkes et al., 2018) to probe the presence of hierarchical and linear properties in the representations of words. However, unlike past work, we train these classifiers using a "poverty of the stimulus" paradigm, where the training data admit both linear and hierarchical solutions that can be distinguished by an enriched generalization set. This method allows us to identify what kinds of information are represented most robustly and transparently in the BERT embeddings. We find that as we use embeddings from higher layers, the prevalence of linear/sequential information decreases, while the availability of on hierarchical information increases, suggesting that with each layer, BERT phases out positional information in favor of hierarchical features of increasing complexity.

In the second set of experiments, we explore a novel approach to the study of BERT's self-attention vectors. Past explorations of attention mechanisms, whether in the domain of vision (Olah et al., 2018; Carter et al., 2019) or NLP (Bahdanau et al., 2015; Karpathy et al., 2015; Young et al., 2018; Voita et al., 2018), have largely involved a range of visualization techniques or the study of the general distribution of attention. Our work takes a quantitative approach to the study of attention and its encoding of syntactic dependencies. Specifically, we consider the relationships between verbs and the subjects with which they agree, and reflexive anaphors and their antecedents. Building on past work in psycholinguistics, we consider the influence of distractor noun phrases on the identification of these dependencies. We propose a simple attention-based metric called the *confusion score* that captures BERT's response to syntactic distortions in an input sentence. This score provides a novel *quantitative* method of evaluating BERT's syntactic knowledge as encoded in its attention vectors. We find that BERT does indeed leverage syntactic relationships between words to preferentially attend

to the "correct" noun phrase for the purposes of agreement and anaphora, though syntactic structure does not show the strong categorical effects we sometimes find in natural language. This result again points to a representation of syntactically-relevant hierarchical information in BERT, this time through attention weightings.

Our analysis thus provides evidence that BERT's self-attention layers compose increasingly abstract representations of linguistic structure without explicit word order information, and that structural information is expressly favored over linear information. This explains why BERT can perform well on downstream NLP tasks, which typically require complex modeling of structural relationships.

## 2 Diagnostic Classification

For our first exploration of the kind of linguistic information captured in BERT's embeddings, we apply diagnostic classifiers to 3 tasks: identifying whether a given word is the sentence's **main auxiliary**, the sentence's **subject noun**, and the sentence's $n^{th}$**-token**. In each task, we assess how well BERT's embeddings encode information about a given linguistic property via the ability of a simple diagnostic classifier to correctly recover the presence of that property from the embeddings of a single word. The three tasks focus on different sorts of information: identifying the main auxiliary and the subject noun requires sensitivity to hierarchical or syntactic information, while the $n^{th}$-token requires linear information.

For each token in a given sentence, its input representation to BERT is a sum of its token, segment and positional embeddings (Devlin et al., 2018). We refer to these inputs as **pre-embeddings**. Note that by construction, a) the pre-embeddings contain linear but not hierarchical information, and b) BERT cannot generate new linear information that is not already in the input. Thus, any linear information in BERT's embeddings ultimately stems from the pre-embeddings, while any hierarchical information must be constructed by BERT itself.

### 2.1 Poverty of the stimulus

To classify an embedding as a sentence's main auxiliary or subject noun, the network needs to have represented structural information about a word's role in the sentence. In many cases, such structural information can be approximated lin-

|  | Main auxiliary task | Subject noun task |
| --- | --- | --- |
| Training, Development | the cat <u>will</u> sleep<br>the cat <u>will</u> eat the fish that can swim | the <u>bee</u> can sting<br>the <u>bee</u> can sting the boy |
| Generalization | the cat that *can* meow <u>will</u> sleep<br>the cat that *can* meow <u>will</u> eat the fish that can swim | (compound noun) the *queen* <u>bee</u> can sting<br>(possessive) the *queen*'s <u>bee</u> can sting |

Table 1: Representative sentences from the main auxiliary and subject noun tasks. For the latter, the generalization set contains two types of sentences, compound nouns and possessives, which are evaluated on separately. In each example, the correct token is underlined, while the distractor (consistent with the incorrect linear rule) is italicized.

early: the main auxiliary or subject noun could be identified as the first auxiliary or noun in a sentence. Though such a linear generalization may be falsified if given certain complex examples, it will succeed over a large range of simple sentences. Chomsky (1980) argues that the relevant distinguishing examples may be very rare for the case of identifying the main auxiliary (a property that is necessary in order to form questions), and hence this is an instance of the "poverty of the stimulus" that motivates the hypothesis of innate bias toward hierarchical generalizations. However, it seems clear that distinguishing examples are plentiful for the subject noun case. The question we are interested in, then, is whether and how BERT's embeddings, which result from training on a massive dataset, encode hierarchical information.

Pursuing the idea of poverty of the stimulus training (McCoy et al., 2018), we train diagnostic classifiers only on sentences in which the relevant property (main auxiliary or subject noun) is stateable in either hierarchical or sequential terms, i.e., the linearly first auxiliary or noun (cf. Section 2.2). The classifiers are then tested on sentences of greater complexity in which the hierarchical and linear generalizations can be distinguished. Since our classifier is a simple perceptron that can access only one embedding at a time, it cannot compute complex contingencies among the representations of multiple words, and cannot succeed unless such information is already encoded in the individual embeddings. Thus, success on these tasks would indicate that BERT robustly represents the words of a sentence using a feature space where the identification of hierarchical generalizations is easy.

## 2.2 Dataset

The main auxiliary and subject noun tasks use synthetic datasets generated from context-free grammars (cf. Appendix A.1) that were designed to isolate the relevant syntactic property for a poverty of the stimulus setup. Typical sentences are highlighted in Table 1. In both tasks, the training, development and generalization sets contained 40000, 10000, and 10000 examples respectively.

**Main auxiliary**  In the training and development sets, the main auxiliary (<u>will</u> in Table 1) is always the first auxiliary in the sentence. A classifier that learns the naive linear rule of identifying the first linearly occurring auxiliary instead of the correct hierarchical (syntactic) rule still performs well during training. However, in the generalization set, the subject of each sentence is modified by a relative clause that contains an intervening auxiliary (that *can* meow). Since the main auxiliary is never the first auxiliary in this case, learning the hierarchical rule becomes imperative.

**Subject noun**  In the training and development sets, the subject noun (<u>bee</u> in Table 1) is always the first noun in the sentence. A classifier that learns the linear rule of identifying the first linearly occurring noun does well during training, but only the hierarchical rule gives the right answer at test time. In the generalization set (both compound nouns & possessives cases), the subject noun is the head of the construction (<u>bee</u>) and not the dependent (*queen*). In the possessives case, we note that subword tokenization always produces *'s* as a standalone token, e.g. *queen's* is tokenized into *[queen] ['s]*. Also, we allow sentences to chain an arbitrary number of possessives via nesting.

$n^{th}$-**token**  For this experiment, we use sentences from the Penn Treebank WSJ corpus. Following the setup of Collins (2002) and filtering for sentences between 10 to 30 tokens BERT tokenization, we obtained training, development and generalization sets of sentences of sizes 21142, 3017 and 2999. We only consider $2 \leq n \leq 9$. In particular, we ignore $n = 1$ since the first token produced by BERT is always trivially [CLS].

### 2.3 Methods

**BERT models** In our experiments, we consider two of Google AI's pre-trained BERT models *bert-base-uncased* (**bbu**) and *bert-large-uncased* (**blu**) from a PyTorch implementation.[2] bbu has 12 layers, 12 attention heads and embedding width 768, while blu has 24 layers, 16 attention heads and embedding width 1024.

**Training** For each task, we train a simple perceptron with a sigmoid output to perform binary classification on individual token embeddings of a sentence, based on whether the underlying token possesses the property relevant to the task. This is similar to the concept of diagnostic classification by Hupkes et al. (2018); Giulianelli et al. (2018).

$$
\begin{array}{ccccc}
 & \text{the} & \text{cat} & \text{will} & \text{sleep} \\
\text{(BERT)} & \downarrow & \downarrow & \downarrow & \downarrow \\
 & e_1 & e_2 & e_3 & e_4 \\
\text{(Classifier)} & \downarrow & \downarrow & \downarrow & \downarrow \\
 & \widehat{y}_1 & \widehat{y}_2 & \widehat{y}_3 & \widehat{y}_4
\end{array}
$$

Each input sentence is tokenized and processed by BERT, and the resulting embeddings $\{e_i\}$ are individually passed to the classifier $f_\theta$ to produce a sequence of logits $\{\widehat{y}_i\}$. Supervision is provided via a one-hot vector of indicators $\{y_i\}$ for the specified property. For example, in the main auxiliary task, the above example would have $y_1 = y_2 = y_4 = 0$ and $y_3 = 1$, since the third word is the main auxiliary. The contribution of each example to the total cross-entropy loss is:

$$
\mathcal{L}_\theta = - \sum_i \left( y_i \log \widehat{y}_i + (1 - y_i) \log(1 - \widehat{y}_i) \right) \quad (1)
$$

Each classifier is trained for a single epoch using the Adam optimizer (Kingma and Ba, 2014) with hyperparameters $lr = 0.001, \beta_1 = 0.9, \beta_2 = 0.999$. We freeze BERT's weights throughout training, which allows us to take good classification performance as evidence that the information relevant to the task is being encoded in BERT's embeddings in a salient, easily retrievable manner.

**Evaluation** For each example at test time, after computing the logits we obtain the index of the classifier's most confident guess within the sentence:

$$
i^* = \arg\max_i \widehat{y}_i \quad (2)
$$

The average $y_{i^*}$ across the test set is reported as the classification accuracy.

[2]https://github.com/huggingface/
pytorch-pretrained-BERT

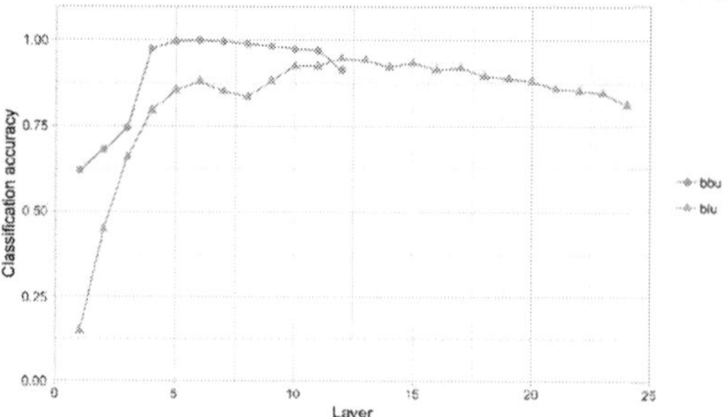

Figure 1: Layerwise accuracy of diagnostic classifiers on the generalization set of the main auxiliary task.

**Layerwise diagnosis** One key aspect of our experiments is the training of layer-specific classifiers for *all* layers. This yields a *layerwise* diagnosis of the information content in BERT's embeddings, providing a glimpse into how BERT internally manipulates and composes linguistic information. We also train classifiers on the pre-embeddings, which can be considered as the "zero-th" layer of BERT and hence act as useful baselines for content present in the input.

### 2.4 Results

**Main auxiliary** Classifiers for both models achieved near-perfect accuracy across all layers on the development set. In Figure 1, we observe that on the generalization set, the classifiers for both models can identify the main auxiliary with over 85% accuracy past layer 5, and bbu in particular obtains near-perfect accuracy from layers 4 to 11.

As discussed in Section 2.2, the classifiers were only given training examples where the main auxiliary was also the first auxiliary in the sentence. Although the linear rule "pick the first auxiliary" is compatible with the training data, the classifier nonetheless learns the more complex but correct hierarchical rule "pick the auxiliary of the main clause". By our argument from Section 2.1, this suggests that BERT embeddings encode syntactic information relevant to whether a token is the main auxiliary, as a feature salient enough to be recoverable by our simple diagnostic classifier.

We found that almost all instances of classification errors involved the misidentification of the linearly first auxiliary (within the relative clause) as the main auxiliary, e.g. *can* instead of <u>will</u> in Table 1. We believe that this stems from the significance of part-of-speech information for language modeling. As a result, any word of a different POS will not be chosen by the classifier.

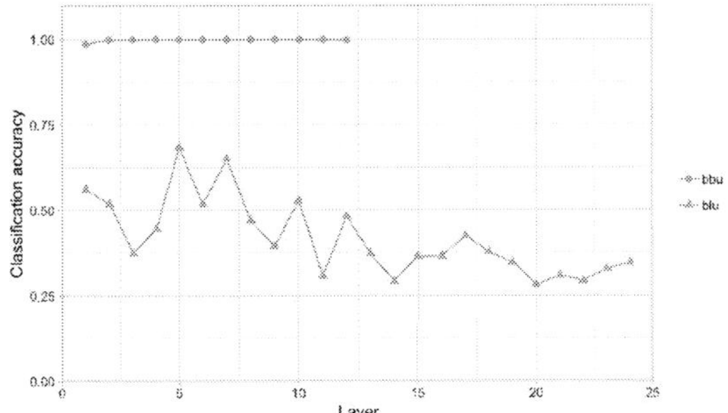

Figure 2: Layerwise accuracy of diagnostic classifiers on the compound noun generalization set of the subject noun task.

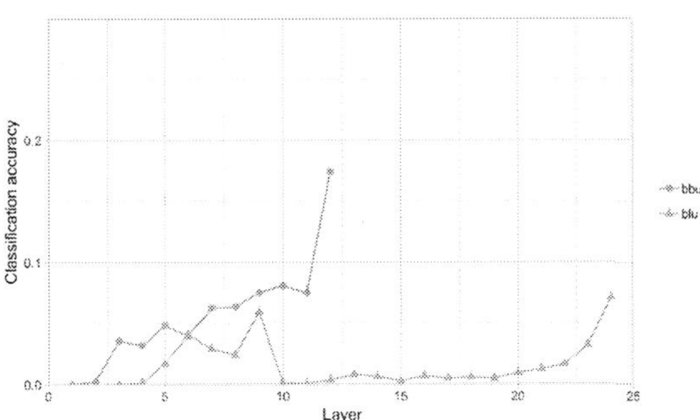

Figure 3: Layerwise accuracy of diagnostic classifiers on the possessive generalization set of the subject noun task.

**Subject noun** As with the previous task, classifiers for both models achieved near-perfect accuracy across all layers on the development set. On the compound noun generalization set (Figure 2), while bbu achieved near-perfect accuracy in later layers, blu consistently performed poorly. bbu's performance suggests that in the classifier successfully learns a generalization that excludes the first noun of a compound, as opposed to the naive linear rule "pick the first noun". As before, this suggests that BERT encodes syntactic information in its embeddings. However, blu's performance is unexpected: it consistently predicts the object noun when it makes errors. In contrast, on the possessive generalization set (Figure 3), both models perform poorly. We offer an explanation for this distinctive performance in Section 2.5.

$n^{th}$ **token** Since this property is entirely determined by the linear position of a word in a sentence, it directly measures the amount of positional information encoded in the embeddings. Here we have two baselines characterizing both extremes: the normal pre-embeddings (denoted pE) and a variant (pE − pos) where we exclude the

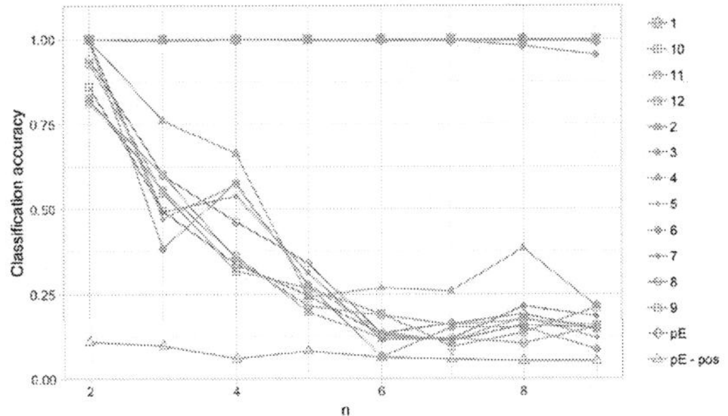

Figure 4: Layerwise accuracy of diagnostic classifiers on the generalization set of the $n^{th}$ token task, for the bbu model only. Note that each line corresponds to a particular layer's embeddings as we vary $2 \leq n \leq 9$. pE denotes pre-embeddings and pE − pos denotes pre-embeddings without the positional component.

positional component from its construction. Since BERT cannot introduce any new positional information, we expect these two to represent upper and lower bounds on the amount of positional information present in BERT's embeddings.

In Figure 4, we see a dramatic difference in performance on pE (one of the topmost lines) compared to pE − pos (bottommost line). We note that performances across all 12 layers fall between these two extremes, confirming our intuitions from earlier. Specifically, the classifiers for layers $1 - 3$ have near-perfect accuracy on identifying an arbitrary $n^{th}$ token ($2 \leq n \leq 9$). However, from layer 4 onwards, the accuracy drops sharply as $n$ increases. This suggests that the positional component of pre-embeddings is the primary source of positional information in BERT, and BERT (bbu) discards a significant amount of positional information between layers 3 and 4, possibly in favor of hierarchical information.

### 2.5 Further Analysis

**Main auxiliary** In Figure 1, we observe that classification accuracy increases sharply in the first 4 layers, then plateaus before slowly decreasing. This mirrors a similar layerwise trend observed by Hewitt and Manning (2019). We postulate that the embeddings reach their "optimal level of abstraction" with respect to their ability to predict the main auxiliary halfway through BERT (about layer 6 for bbu, 12 for blu). At layer 1, the embedding for each token is a highly localized representation that contains insufficient sentential context to determine whether it is the main auxiliary of the sentence. As layer depth increases,

BERT composes increasingly abstract representations via self-attention, which allows it to extract information from other tokens in the sentence. At some point, the representation becomes abstract enough to represent the hierarchical concept of a "main auxiliary", causing an early increase in classification accuracy. However, as depth increases further, the representations become so abstract that finer linguistic features are increasingly difficult to recover, e.g., a token embedding at the sentence-vector level of abstraction may longer be capable of identifying itself as the main auxiliary, accounting for the slowly deteriorating performance towards later layers.

**Subject noun** Given the similarity of the main auxiliary and the subject noun classification tasks, we might expect them to exhibit similar trends in performance. In Figure 2, we observe a similar early increase in diagnostic classification accuracy for the bbu embeddings. The lack of significant performance decay on higher layers possibly reflects the salience of the subject noun feature even at the sentence-vector level of abstraction. Strangely, blu performed poorly, even worse than chance (50%). We are unable to explain why this happens and leave this for future research.

On the possessive generalization set, the poor performance of both models seems to contradict the hypothesis that BERT has learned an abstract hierarchical generalization to classify subject nouns. We conjecture that BERT's issues in the possessive case stem from the ambiguity of the *'s* token, which can function either as a possessive marker or as a contracted auxiliary verb (e.g."She's sleeping"). If BERT takes a possessive occurrence of *'s* as the auxiliary verb, the immediately preceding noun can be (incorrectly) analyzed as the subject. If so, this would suggest that BERT does not represent the syntactic structure of the entire sentence in a unified fashion, but instead uses local cues to constituency. In Figure 3, the gradually increasing but still poor performance towards later layers in both models suggests that the embeddings might be trending toward a more abstract representation, but do not ultimately achieve it.

$n^{th}$ **token** For each layer $k \geq 3$, Figure 4 shows an asymmetry where the classifier for layer $k$ performs worse at identifying the $n^{th}$ token as $n$ increases. We believe that this may be an artifact of the distributional properties of natural language:

the distribution of words that occur at the start of a sentence tends to be concentrated on a small class of parts of speech that can occur near the beginning of constituents that can begin a sentence. As $n$ increases, the class of possible parts is no longer a function of the beginning of the sentence, and as a result becomes more uniform. As a result, it is easier for a classifier to predict whether a given word is the $n^{th}$ token when $n$ is small, since it can make use of easily accessible part-of-speech information in the embeddings to limit its options to only the tokens likely to occur in a given position.

## 3 Diagnostic Attention

Our second exploration of BERT's syntactic knowledge focuses on the encoding of grammatical relationships instead of the identification of elements with specific structural properties. We consider two phenomena: **reflexive anaphora** and **subject-verb agreement**. For each, we determine the extent to which BERT attends to linguistically relevant elements via the self-attention mechanism. This gives us further information about *how* hierarchy-sensitive syntactic information is encoded.

### 3.1 Quantifying intrusion effects via attention

Subject-verb and antecedent-anaphor dependencies both involve a dependent element, which we call the *target* (the verb or the anaphor) and the element on which it depends, which we call the *trigger* (the subject or the antecedent that provides the interpretation). A considerable body of work in psycholinguistics has explored how humans process such dependencies in the presence of elements that are not in relevant structural positions but which linearly intervene between the trigger and target. Dillon et al. (2013) aim to quantify this intrusion effect in human reading for the two dependencies we explore here. Under the assumption that higher reading time and eye movement regressions indicate an intrusion effect, they conclude that intruding noun-phrases have a substantial effect on the processing of subject-verb agreement, but not antecedent-anaphor relations.

We adapt this idea in measuring intrusion effects in BERT. We propose a simple and novel metric we term the "confusion score" for quantifying intrusion effects using attention. This quantita-

| Subject-Verb Agreement | | | | |
| --- | --- | --- | --- | --- |
| **Condition** | **Relative Clause** | **DN Number Match** | **Example Sentence** | **Mean Confusion Score** |
| A1 | ✗ | ✓ | the cat near *the dog* does sleep | 0.97 |
| A2 | ✗ | ✗ | the cat near *the dogs* does sleep | 0.93 |
| A3 | ✓ | ✓ | the cat that can comfort *the dog* does sleep | 0.85 |
| A4 | ✓ | ✗ | the cat that can comfort *the dogs* does sleep | 0.81 |

| Reflexive Anaphora | | | | | |
| --- | --- | --- | --- | --- | --- |
| **Condition** | **Relative Clause** | **DN$_o$ Gender Match** | **DN$_r$ Gender Match** | **Example Sentence** | **Mean Confusion Score** |
| R1 | ✗ | ✓ | NA | the lord could comfort *the wizard* by himself | 1.01 |
| R2 | ✗ | ✗ | NA | the lord could comfort *the witch* by himself | 0.92 |
| R3 | ✓ | NA | ✓ | the lord that can hurt *the prince* could comfort himself | 0.99 |
| R4 | ✓ | NA | ✗ | the lord that can hurt *the princess* could comfort himself | 0.89 |
| R5 | ✓ | ✓ | ✓ | the lord that can hurt *the prince* could comfort *the wizard* by himself | 1.57 |
| R6 | ✓ | ✓ | ✗ | the lord that can hurt *the princess* could comfort *the wizard* by himself | 1.52 |
| R7 | ✓ | ✗ | ✓ | the lord that can hurt *the prince* could comfort *the witch* by himself | 1.49 |
| R8 | ✓ | ✗ | ✗ | the lord that can hurt *the princess* could comfort *the witch* by himself | 1.39 |

Table 2: Representative sentences from the subject-verb agreement and reflexive anaphora datasets for each condition, and corresponding mean confusion scores. DN$_o$: distractor noun as object. DN$_r$: distractor noun in relative clause.

tive metric allows us to measure the preferable attention of transformer-based self-attention on one entity as opposed to another. Formally, suppose $X = \{x_i\}_{i=1}^{n}$ are linguistic units of interest, i.e. candidate triggers for the dependency, and $Y$ is the dependency target. For each layer $l$ and attention head $a$, we sum the self-attention weights from the indices of $x_i$ (since each $x_i$ may consist of multiple words) on attention head $a$ of layer $l - 1$ to $Y$ on layer $l$, and take the mean over $A$ attention heads:

$$\text{attn}_l(x_i, Y) = \frac{1}{A} \sum_{a=1}^{A} \sum_{x_{ij} \in x_i} \text{attn}_{la}(x_{ij}, Y) \quad (3)$$

We finally define the **confusion score** on layer $l$ as the binary cross entropy of the normalized attention distribution between $\{x_i\}$ given $Y$ as follows:

$$\text{conf}_l(X, Y) = -\log \frac{\text{attn}_l(x_1, Y)}{\sum_{i=1}^{n} \text{attn}_l(x_i, Y)} \quad (4)$$

Note that this equation assumes that each dependency has a unique trigger $x_1$: verbs agree with a single subject, and anaphors take a single noun phrase as their antecedent.

Our study focuses on the examples of the forms shown in Table 2. For subject-verb agreement, there are two types of examples: with the distractor within a PP (A1 and A2) and with the distractor within a RC (A3 and A4). Past psycholinguistic work has shown that distractor noun phrases within PPs give rise to greater processing difficulty than distractors within RCs (Bock and Cutting, 1992). For each type, we compare confusion in the case of distractors that share features with the subject, the true trigger of agreement, (A1 and A3) with those that do not (A2 and A4). Our expectation is that distractors that do not share features with the target of agreement will yield less confusion.

For reflexive anaphora, because of the possibility of ambiguity, we also consider sentences that include a noun phrase that is a structurally possible antecedent. For example, condition R1 has the subject *the lord* as its antecedent, but the object noun phrase *the wizard* is also grammatically possible. In contrast, for R2, the mismatch in gender features prevents the object from serving as an antecedent, which should lead to lower confusion. Sentences R3 and R4 include a distractor noun phrase within a RC. Since this noun phrase does not c-command the anaphor, it is grammatically inaccessible and should therefore contribute less, if at all, to confusion. Sentence types R5 through R8 include both the relative modifier and the object noun phrase, and systematically vary the agreement properties of the two distractors.

We hypothesize that attention weights on each linguistic unit indicate the relative importance of that entity as a trigger of a linguistic dependency. As a result, the ideal attention distribution should put all of the probability mass on the antecedent noun phrase for reflexive anaphora or on the subject noun phrase for agreement, and zero on the distractor noun phrases. As a baseline, a uniform distribution over two noun phrases, one the actual target and the other a distractor, would lead to a confusion score of $-\log \frac{1}{2} = 1$; with two distractors, the uniform probability baseline would be $-\log \frac{1}{3} = 1.6$.

### 3.2 Dataset

We construct synthetic datasets using context-free grammars (shown in Appendix A.1) for both subject-verb agreement and reflexive anaphora and compute mean confusion scores across multiple sentences. This allows us to control for semantic effects on the confusion score. All datasets for each condition contain 10000 examples.

In the subject-verb agreement datasets, we vary 1) the type of subordinate clause (prepositional phrase, PP; or relative clause, RC), and 2) the number on the distractor noun phrase. All conditions should be unambiguous, since only the head noun phrase can agree with the auxiliary.

In the reflexive anaphora datasets, we vary 1) the presence of a RC, 2) the gender match between the RC's noun phrase and the reflexive 3) the presence of an object noun phrase, and 4) the gender match between the object noun and the reflexive. All nouns are singular. Conditions R1, R5, R6 are ambiguous conditions, as they include an object noun phrase that matches the reflexive in gender. In other conditions, only the head noun phrase is the possible antecedent: the object mismatches in features and the noun phrase within the RC is grammatically inaccessible.

### 3.3 Methods

We use Equation 4 to compute the confusion score on each layer for the target in each sentence in our dataset. As in Section 2.3, this yields a *layerwise* diagnosis of confusion in BERT's self-attention mechanism. We also compute the mean confusion score across all layers.[3] In our experiments, we compute confusion scores using bbu only.

Note that in conditions R1, R5 and R6, there are two possible antecedents of the reflexive. We nonetheless use Equation 4 to calculate confusion scores relative to a single antecedent (the subject).

To compute the significance of the presence of different types of distractors and of feature mis-

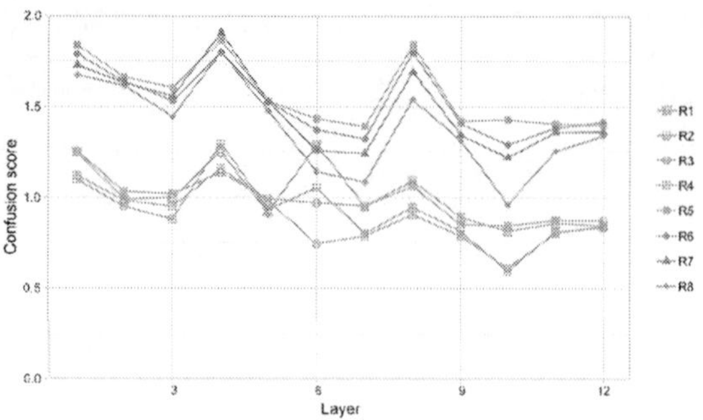

Figure 5: Layerwise confusion scores for each reflexive anaphora condition listed in Table 2. Conditions R1 to R4 have one distractor noun phrase, but conditions R5 to R8 have two distractor noun phrases.

| Coefficient | Estimate | p-value |
|---|---|---|
| Subject-Verb Agreement | | |
| Intercept | $1.33 \pm 1.32\mathrm{e}{-3}$ | $< 2\mathrm{e}{-16}$ |
| Relative Clause | $-0.12 \pm 1.03\mathrm{e}{-3}$ | $< 2\mathrm{e}{-16}$ |
| $DN_r$ Number Match | $0.03 \pm 1.03\mathrm{e}{-3}$ | $< 2\mathrm{e}{-16}$ |
| Layer | $-0.06 \pm 1.50\mathrm{e}{-4}$ | $< 2\mathrm{e}{-16}$ |
| Reflexive Anaphora | | |
| Intercept | $0.63 \pm 1.24\mathrm{e}{-3}$ | $< 2\mathrm{e}{-16}$ |
| $DN_o$ Gender Match | $0.60 \pm 9.09\mathrm{e}{-4}$ | $< 2\mathrm{e}{-16}$ |
| $DN_o$ Gender Mismatch | $0.50 \pm 9.09\mathrm{e}{-4}$ | $< 2\mathrm{e}{-16}$ |
| $DN_r$ Gender Match | $0.57 \pm 9.09\mathrm{e}{-4}$ | $< 2\mathrm{e}{-16}$ |
| $DN_r$ Gender Mismatch | $0.49 \pm 9.09\mathrm{e}{-4}$ | $< 2\mathrm{e}{-16}$ |
| Layer | $-0.03 \pm 9.72\mathrm{e}{-5}$ | $< 2\mathrm{e}{-16}$ |

Table 3: Regression estimates and p-values for the coefficient effects under reflexive anaphora and subject-verb agreement. All effects are statistically significant.

match of the distractors, we run a linear regression to predict confusion score. For subject-verb agreement, the baseline value is the confusion at layer 1 of a sentence with a PP and a mismatch in number on the distractor noun (condition A2 in Table 2). For reflexive anaphora, the baseline is the confusion at layer 1 of a sentence with no RC and no object noun (e.g. "the lord comforts himself").

### 3.4 Results

**Subject-verb agreement** Since sentence types A1 to A4 are all unambiguous, ideal confusion scores should be zero. However, Table 2 indicates that the mean confusion scores are instead closer to the uniform probability baseline confusion score of 1, suggesting that BERT's self-attention mechanism is far from able to perfectly model syntactically-sensitive hierarchical information. Nonetheless, from Table 3, we see that BERT's attention mechanism is in fact sensitive

---

[3]We built on Vig (2019)'s BERT attention visualization library https://github.com/jessevig/bertviz to implement the attention-based confusion score.

to subtleties of linguistic structure: a distractor within a PP causes more confusion than one within a relative clause (i.e., the presence of the relative has a negative coefficient in the linear model), in agreement with past psycholinguistic work (Bock and Cutting, 1992). Moreover, the presence of matching distractors has a significant positive effect on confusion scores. These findings therefore suggest that BERT representations are sensitive to different types of syntactic embedding as well as the values of number features in computing subject-verb agreement dependencies.

**Reflexive anaphora** From Table 2, we see the major effect of the number of distractor noun phrases: mean confusion scores for conditions with one distractor (R1-R4) are lower than those with two distractors (R5-R8). If BERT were perfectly exploiting grammatical structure, we should expect the presence of a grammatically inaccessible distractor noun within a relative clause not to add to confusion. Thus, we might expect R5 and R6 to have mean confusion scores comparable to R1, as both include single grammatically viable distractor. However, they both have higher mean confusion scores than R1 (the same is true for R7/R8 vs. R2). Moreover, conditions R2 to R4 and R7 to R8 should have confusion scores of zero, since the head noun phrase is the only grammatically possible antecedent. This, however, is not so. Taken together, we might conclude that BERT attends unnecessarily to grammatically inaccessible or grammatically mismatched distractor noun phrases, suggesting that it does not accurately model reflexive dependencies.

Nonetheless, if we look more closely at the effects of the different factors through the linear model reported in Table 3, we once again find evidence for a sensitivity to both syntactic structure and grammatical features: the presence of grammatically accessible distractors has a (slightly) larger effect on confusion than grammatically inaccessible distractors (i.e., $DN_o$ vs. $DN_r$), particularly when the distractor matches in features with the actual antecedent.

### 3.5 Further Analysis

**Layerwise diagnosis** Figure 5 and Table 3 show that confusion is negatively correlated with layer depth for reflexive anaphora. Confusion scores for subject-verb agreement exhibit a similar trend. This provides additional evidence for our con-
jecture that BERT composes increasingly abstract representations containing hierarchical information, with an optimal level of abstraction. Notably, the observed sensitivity of BERT's self-attention values to grammatical distortions suggests that BERT's syntactic knowledge is in fact encoded in its attention matrices. Finally, it is worth noting that confusion for both reflexives and subject-verb agreement showed an increase at layer 4. Strikingly, this was the level at which linear information was found, through diagnostic classifiers, to be degraded. We leave for the future an understanding of the connection between these.

## 4  Conclusion

In this paper, we investigated how and to what extent BERT representations encode syntactically-sensitive hierarchical information, as opposed to linear information. Through diagnostic classification, we find that positional information is encoded in BERT from the pre-embedding level up through lower layers of the model. At higher layers, information becomes less positional and more hierarchical, and BERT encodes increasingly complex representations of sentence units.

We propose a simple and novel method of observing, for a given syntactic phenomenon, the intrusion effects of distractors on BERT's self-attention mechanism. Through such diagnostic attention, we find that BERT does encode aspects of syntactic structure that are relevant for subject-verb agreement and reflexive dependencies through attention weights, and that this information is represented more accurately on higher layers. We also find evidence that BERT is responsive to matching of grammatical features such as gender and number. However, BERT's attention is only incompletely modulated by structural and featural properties, and attention is sometimes spread across grammatically irrelevant elements.

We conclude that BERT composes increasingly abstract hierarchical representations of linguistic structure using its self-attention mechanism. To further understand BERT's syntactic knowledge, further work can be done to (1) investigate or visualize layer-on-layer changes in BERT's structural and positional information, particularly between layers 3 and 4 when positional information is largely phased out, and (2) retrieve the increasingly hierarchical representations of BERT across layers via the self-attention mechanism.

## References

Dzmitry Bahdanau, Kyunghyun Cho, and Yoshua Bengio. 2015. Neural machine translation by jointly learning to align and translate. In *International Conference for Learning Representations*.

Kathryn Bock and J. Cooper Cutting. 1992. Regulating mental energy: Performance units in language production. *Journal of Memory and Language*, 31(1):99–127.

Shan Carter, Zan Armstrong, Ludwig Schubert, Ian Johnson, and Chris Olah. 2019. Activation atlas. `https://distill.pub/2019/activation-atlas` [Accessed: 19 Apr 2019].

Noam Chomsky. 1980. Rules and representations. *Behavioral and Brain Sciences*, 3(1):1–15.

Michael Collins. 2002. Discriminative training methods for hidden Markov models: Theory and experiments with perceptron algorithms. In *Proceedings of the 2002 Conference on Empirical Methods in Natural Language Processing*, pages 1–8. Association for Computational Linguistics.

Jacob Devlin, Ming-Wei Chang, Kenton Lee, and Kristina Toutanova. 2018. BERT: Pre-training of deep bidirectional transformers for language understanding. *Computing Research Repository*, abs/1810.04805.

Brian Dillon, Alan Mishler, Shayne Sloggett, and Colin Phillips. 2013. Contrasting intrusion profiles for agreement and anaphora: Experimental and modeling evidence. *Journal of Memory and Language*, 69(2):85–103.

Mario Giulianelli, Jack Harding, Florian Mohnert, Dieuwke Hupkes, and Willem Zuidema. 2018. Under the hood: Using diagnostic classifiers to investigate and improve how language models track agreement information. In *Proceedings of the 2018 EMNLP Workshop BlackboxNLP: Analyzing and Interpreting Neural Networks for NLP*, pages 240–248, Brussels, Belgium. Association for Computational Linguistics.

Yoav Goldberg. 2019. Assessing BERT's syntactic abilities. *Computing Research Repository*, abs/1901.05287.

Kristina Gulordava, Piotr Bojanowski, Edouard Grave, Tal Linzen, and Marco Baroni. 2018. Colorless green recurrent networks dream hierarchically. In *Proceedings of the 2018 Conference of the North American Chapter of the Association for Computational Linguistics: Human Language Technologies, Volume 1 (Long Papers)*, pages 1195–1205, New Orleans, Louisiana. Association for Computational Linguistics.

John Hewitt and Christopher Manning. 2019. A structural probe for finding syntax in word representations. In *International Conference for Learning Representations*.

Jeremy Howard and Sebastian Ruder. 2018. Universal language model fine-tuning for text classification. In *Proceedings of the 56th Annual Meeting of the Association for Computational Linguistics (Volume 1: Long Papers)*, pages 328–339, Melbourne, Australia. Association for Computational Linguistics.

Dieuwke Hupkes, Sara Veldhoen, and Willem Zuidema. 2018. Visualisation and diagnostic classifiers reveal how recurrent and recursive neural networks process hierarchical structure. *Journal of Artificial Intelligence Research*, 61:907926.

Andrej Karpathy, Justin Johnson, and Li Fei-Fei. 2015. Visualizing and understanding recurrent networks. *Computing Research Repository*, abs/1506.02078.

Diederik P Kingma and Jimmy Ba. 2014. Adam: A method for stochastic optimization. *Computing Research Repository*, abs/1412.6980.

Yair Lakretz, German Kruszewski, Theo Desbordes, Dieuwke Hupkes, Stanislas Dehaene, and Marco Baroni. 2019. The emergence of number and syntax units in LSTM language models. *Computing Research Repository*, abs/1903.07435.

Tal Linzen, Emmanuel Dupoux, and Yoav Goldberg. 2016. Assessing the ability of LSTMs to learn syntax-sensitive dependencies. *Transactions of the Association for Computational Linguistics*, 4:521–535.

Tal Linzen and Brian Leonard. 2018. Distinct patterns of syntactic agreement errors in recurrent networks and humans. In *Proceedings of the 40th Annual Conference of the Cognitive Science Society*, pages 690–695.

Yang Liu. 2019. Fine-tune BERT for extractive summarization. In *Computing Research Repository*, volume abs/1903.10318.

Rebecca Marvin and Tal Linzen. 2018. Targeted syntactic evaluation of language models. In *Proceedings of the 2018 Conference on Empirical Methods in Natural Language Processing*, pages 1192–1202, Brussels, Belgium. Association for Computational Linguistics.

R Thomas McCoy, Robert Frank, and Tal Linzen. 2018. Revisiting the poverty of the stimulus: hierarchical generalization without a hierarchical bias in recurrent neural networks. In *Proceedings of the 40th Annual Conference of the Cognitive Science Society*, pages 2093–2098.

Tomas Mikolov, Ilya Sutskever, Kai Chen, Greg S Corrado, and Jeff Dean. 2013. Distributed representations of words and phrases and their compositionality. In *Advances in Neural Information Processing Systems*, pages 3111–3119.

Chris Olah, Arvind Satyanarayan, Ian Johnson, Shan Carter, Ludwig Schubert, Katherine Ye, and Alexander Mordvintsev. 2018. The building blocks of interpretability. https://distill.pub/2018/building-blocks [Accessed: 19 Apr 2019].

Jeffrey Pennington, Richard Socher, and Christopher Manning. 2014. GloVe: Global vectors for word representation. In *Proceedings of the 2014 Conference on Empirical Methods in Natural Language Processing*, pages 1532–1543.

Matthew E Peters, Mark Neumann, Mohit Iyyer, Matt Gardner, Christopher Clark, Kenton Lee, and Luke Zettlemoyer. 2018. Deep contextualized word representations. *Computing Research Repository*, abs/1802.05365.

Alec Radford, Jeffrey Wu, Rewon Child, David Luan, Dario Amodei, and Ilya Sutskever. 2019. Language models are unsupervised multitask learners. https://d4mucfpksywv.cloudfront.net/better-language-models/language-models.pdf [Accessed: 19 Apr 2019].

Ian Tenney, Patrick Xia, Berlin Chen, Alex Wang, Adam Poliak, R Thomas McCoy, Najoung Kim, Benjamin Van Durme, Samuel R Bowman, Dipanjan Das, et al. 2019. What do you learn from context? probing for sentence structure in contextualized word representations. In *International Conference on Learning Representations*.

Jesse Vig. 2019. Visualizing attention in transformer-based language models. *Computing Research Repository*, abs/1904.02679.

Elena Voita, Pavel Serdyukov, Rico Sennrich, and Ivan Titov. 2018. Context-aware neural machine translation learns anaphora resolution. In *Proceedings of the 56th Annual Meeting of the Association for Computational Linguistics (Volume 1: Long Papers)*, pages 1264–1274, Melbourne, Australia. Association for Computational Linguistics.

Thomas Wolf. 2019. Some additional experiments extending the tech report "Assessing BERT's Syntactic Abilities" by Yoav Goldberg. https://huggingface.co/bert-syntax/extending-bert-syntax.pdf [Accessed: 19 Apr 2019].

Tom Young, Devamanyu Hazarika, Soujanya Poria, and Erik Cambria. 2018. Recent trends in deep learning based natural language processing. *IEEE Computational Intelligence Magazine*, 13(3):55–75.

# A  Appendix

## A.1  Context-free grammars for dataset generation

| S | $\rightarrow$ | NP$_M$ VP$_M$ |
|---|---|---|
| NP$_M$ | $\rightarrow$ | Det N \| Det N Prep Det Nom \| Det N RC |
| NP$_O$ | $\rightarrow$ | Det Nom \| Det Nom Prep Det Nom \| Det Nom RC |
| VP$_M$ | $\rightarrow$ | Aux VI \| Aux VT NP$_O$ |
| RC | $\rightarrow$ | Rel Aux VI \| Rel Det Nom Aux VT \| Rel Aux VT Det Nom |
| Nom | $\rightarrow$ | N \| JJ Nom |
| Det | $\rightarrow$ | the \| some \| my \| your \| our \| her |
| N | $\rightarrow$ | bird \| bee \| ant \| duck \| lion \| dog \| tiger \| worm \| horse \| cat \| fish \| bear \| wolf \| birds \| bees \| ants \| ducks \| lions \| dogs \| tigers \| worms \| horses \| cats \| fish \| bears \| wolves |
| VI | $\rightarrow$ | cry \| smile \| sleep \| swim \| wait \| move \| change \| read \| eat |
| VT | $\rightarrow$ | dress \| kick \| hit \| hurt \| clean \| love \| accept \| remember \| comfort |
| Aux | $\rightarrow$ | can \| will \| would \| could |
| Prep | $\rightarrow$ | around \| near \| with \| upon \| by \| behind \| above \| below |
| Rel | $\rightarrow$ | who \| that |
| JJ | $\rightarrow$ | small \| little \| big \| hot \| cold \| good \| bad \| new \| old \| young |

Figure 6: Context-free grammar for the main auxiliary dataset.

| S | $\rightarrow$ | NP$_M$ VP |
|---|---|---|
| NP$_M$ | $\rightarrow$ | Det MNom \| Det MNom Prep Det Nom \| Det MNom RC |
| NP$_O$ | $\rightarrow$ | Det Nom \| Det Nom Prep Det Nom \| Det Nom RC |
| VP | $\rightarrow$ | Aux VI \| Aux VT NP$_O$ |
| RC | $\rightarrow$ | Rel Aux VI \| Rel Det Nom Aux VT \| Rel Aux VT Det Nom |
| Nom | $\rightarrow$ | N \| JJ Nom |
| MNom | $\rightarrow$ | MNom1 \| MNom2 |
| MNom1 | $\rightarrow$ | N \| JJ MNom1 |
| MNom2 | $\rightarrow$ | N \| JJ MNom2 \| NS Poss MNom2 \| Nadj+MN |
| Det | $\rightarrow$ | the \| some \| my \| your \| our \| her |
| Poss | $\rightarrow$ | 's |
| NS | $\rightarrow$ | bird \| bee \| ant \| duck \| lion \| dog \| tiger \| worm \| horse \| cat \| fish \| bear \| wolf |
| N | $\rightarrow$ | bird \| bee \| ant \| duck \| lion \| dog \| tiger \| worm \| horse \| cat \| fish \| bear \| wolf \| birds \| bees \| ants \| ducks \| lions \| dogs \| tigers \| worms \| horses \| cats \| fish \| bears \| wolves |
| Nadj+MN | $\rightarrow$ | worker bee \| worker ant \| race horse \| queen bee \| german dog \| house cat |
| VI | $\rightarrow$ | cry \| smile \| sleep \| swim \| wait \| move \| change \| read \| eat |
| VT | $\rightarrow$ | dress \| kick \| hit \| hurt \| clean \| love \| accept \| remember \| comfort |
| Aux | $\rightarrow$ | can \| will \| would \| could |
| Prep | $\rightarrow$ | around \| near \| with \| upon \| by \| behind \| above \| below |
| Rel | $\rightarrow$ | who \| that |
| JJ | $\rightarrow$ | small \| little \| big \| hot \| cold \| good \| bad \| new \| old \| young |

Figure 7: Context-free grammar for the subject noun dataset.

| S | $\rightarrow$ | NP$_{sg_Agr}$ Aux$_{sg}$ VI \| NP$_{pl_Agr}$ Aux$_{pl}$ VI |
|---|---|---|
| NP$_{sg_Agr}$ | $\rightarrow$ | Det N$_{sg}$ \| Det N$_{sg}$ Prep Det N \| Det N$_{sg}$ Prep RC$_{sg}$ |
| NP$_{pl_Agr}$ | $\rightarrow$ | Det N$_{pl}$ \| Det N$_{pl}$ Prep Det N \| Det N$_{pl}$ Prep RC$_{pl}$ |
| RC$_{sg}$ | $\rightarrow$ | Rel Aux$_{sg}$ VI \| Rel Aux$_{sg}$ VT Det N \| Rel Det N$_{sg}$ Aux$_{sg}$ VT \| Rel Det N$_{pl}$ Aux$_{pl}$ VT |
| N | $\rightarrow$ | N$_{sg}$ \| N$_{pl}$ |
| RC$_{pl}$ | $\rightarrow$ | Rel Aux$_{pl}$ VI \| Rel Aux$_{pl}$ VT Det N \| Rel Det N$_{sg}$ Aux$_{sg}$ VT \| Rel Det N$_{pl}$ Aux$_{pl}$ VT |
| Aux$_{sg}$ | $\rightarrow$ | does \| Modal |
| Aux$_{pl}$ | $\rightarrow$ | do \| Modal |
| Det | $\rightarrow$ | the \| some \| my \| your \| our \| her |
| N$_{sg}$ | $\rightarrow$ | bird \| bee \| ant \| duck \| lion \| dog \| tiger \| worm \| horse \| cat \| fish \| bear \| wolf |
| N$_{pl}$ | $\rightarrow$ | birds \| bees \| ants \| ducks \| lions \| dogs \| tigers \| worms \| horses \| cats \| fish \| bears \| wolves |
| VI | $\rightarrow$ | cry \| smile \| sleep \| swim \| wait \| move \| change \| read \| eat |
| VT | $\rightarrow$ | dress \| kick \| hit \| hurt \| clean \| love \| accept \| remember \| comfort |
| VS | $\rightarrow$ | think \| say \| hope \| know |
| VD | $\rightarrow$ | tell \| convince \| persuade \| inform |
| Modal | $\rightarrow$ | can \| will \| would \| could |
| Prep | $\rightarrow$ | around \| near \| with \| upon \| by \| behind \| above \| below |
| Rel | $\rightarrow$ | who \| that |

Figure 8: Context-free grammar for the subject-verb agreement dataset.

| S | $\rightarrow$ | NP$_{M_Ant}$ Aux VT Refl$_M$ \| NP$_{F_Ant}$ Aux VT Refl$_F$ \|<br>NP$_{M_Ant}$ Aux VT Det N$_F$ by Refl$_M$ \| NP$_{F_Ant}$ Aux VT Det N$_M$ by Refl$_F$ \|<br>NP$_{M_Ant}$ Aux VT Det N$_M$ by Refl$_M$ \| NP$_{F_Ant}$ Aux VT Det N$_F$ by Refl$_F$ |
|---|---|---|
| NP$_{M_Ant}$ | $\rightarrow$ | Det N$_M$ \| Det N$_M$ RC |
| NP$_{F_Ant}$ | $\rightarrow$ | Det N$_F$ \| Det N$_F$ RC |
| N | $\rightarrow$ | N$_M$ \| N$_F$ |
| RC | $\rightarrow$ | Rel Aux VI \| Rel Det N Aux VT \| Rel Aux VT Det N |
| Refl$_M$ | $\rightarrow$ | himself |
| Refl$_F$ | $\rightarrow$ | herself |
| Det | $\rightarrow$ | the \| some \| my \| your \| our \| her |
| N$_F$ | $\rightarrow$ | girl \| woman \| queen \| actress \| sister \| wife \| mother \| princess \| aunt \| lady \| witch \| niece \| nun |
| N$_M$ | $\rightarrow$ | boy \| man \| king \| actor \| brother \| husband \| father \| prince \| uncle \| lord \| wizard \| nephew \| monk |
| VI | $\rightarrow$ | cry \| smile \| sleep \| swim \| wait \| move \| change \| read \| eat |
| VT | $\rightarrow$ | dress \| kick \| hit \| hurt \| clean \| love \| accept \| remember \| comfort |
| VS | $\rightarrow$ | think \| say \| hope \| know |
| VD | $\rightarrow$ | tell \| convince \| persuade \| inform |
| Aux | $\rightarrow$ | can \| will \| would \| could |
| Prep | $\rightarrow$ | around \| near \| with \| upon \| by \| behind \| above \| below |
| Rel | $\rightarrow$ | who \| that |

Figure 9: Context-free grammar for the reflexive anaphora dataset.

# GEval: Tool for Debugging NLP Datasets and Models


**Filip Graliński**[†,§] and **Anna Wróblewska**[†,‡] and **Tomasz Stanisławek**[†,‡]

[†]Applica.ai, Warszawa, Poland

`firstname.lastname@applica.ai`

**Kamil Grabowski**[†,‡] and **Tomasz Górecki**[§]

[‡]Faculty of Mathematics and Information Science, Warsaw University of Technology

[§]Faculty of Mathematics and Computer Science, Adam Mickiewicz University, Poznań



## Abstract

This paper presents a simple but general and effective method to debug the output of machine learning (ML) supervised models, including neural networks. The algorithm looks for features that lower the evaluation metric in such a way that it cannot be ascribed to chance (as measured by their p-values). Using this method – implemented as GEval tool – you can find: (1) anomalies in test sets, (2) issues in preprocessing, (3) problems in the ML model itself. It can give you an insight into what can be improved in the datasets and/or the model. The same method can be used to compare ML models or different versions of the same model. We present the tool, the theory behind it and use cases for text-based models of various types.


## 1 Introduction

Currently, given the burden of big data and possibilities to build a wide variety of deep learning models, the need to understand datasets, intrinsic parameters and model behavior is growing. These problems are part of the interpretability trend in the state-of-the-art research, the good example being publications at NeurIPS 2018 conference and its Interpretability and Robustness in Audio, Speech, and Language Workshop.[1]

The problem of interpretability is also crucial in terms of using ML models in business cases and applications. Every day, data scientists analyze large amounts of data, build models and sometimes they just do not understand: why the models work in a certain way. Thus, we need fast and efficient tools to look into models in their various aspects, e.g. by analyzing train and test data, the way in which models influence their results, and how their internal features interact with each other. Consequently, the aim of our research and paper is to present a tool to help data scientists understand the model and find issues in order to improve the process. The tool will be show-cased on a number of NLP challenges.

There are a few extended reviews on interpretability techniques and their types available at (Guidotti et al., 2018; Adadi and Berrada, 2018; Du et al., 2018). The authors also introduce purposes of interpretability research: justify models, control them and their changes in time (model debugging), improve their robustness and efficiency (model validation), discover weak features (new knowledge discovery). The explanations can be given as: (1) other models easier to understand (e.g. linear regression), (2) sets of rules, (3) lists of strong and weak input features or even (4) textual summaries accessible for humans.

The interpretability techniques are categorized into global or local methods. "Global" stands for techniques that can explain/interpret a model as a whole, whereas "local" stands for methods and models that can be interpreted around any chosen neighborhood. Another dimensions of the interpretability categorization are: (1) intrinsic interpretable methods, i.e. models that approximate the more difficult ones and are also easy to understand for humans or (2) post-hoc explanations that are derived after training models. Hence, explanations can be model-specific or model-agnostic, i.e. needing (or not) the knowledge about the model itself.

As far as model-agnostic (black-box) methods are concerned, one of the breakthroughs in the domain was the LIME method (Local Interpretable Model-Agnostic Explanations) (Tulio Ribeiro et al., 2016). LIME requires access to a model and it changes the analyzed dataset many times (doing perturbations) by removing some features from input samples and measuring changes in the model output. The idea has two main drawbacks. The first is that it requires access to the model to know

---

[1]`https://irasl.gitlab.io/`

254


*Proceedings of the Second BlackboxNLP Workshop on Analyzing and Interpreting Neural Networks for NLP*, pages 254–262

Florence, Italy, August 1, 2019. ©2019 Association for Computational Linguistics

the model output for perturbed samples. The other disadvantage is that it takes a very long time to process big datasets, which makes the method unfeasible in case of really large datasets, e.g. several millions of text documents.

Other interpretability methods concern the internal model structure in a white-box manner, e.g. L2X (Chen et al., 2018), which instruments a deep learning model with an extra unit (layer) and the analyzed model is trained with this unit jointly.

We introduce an automatic, easy to use and a model-agnostic method that does not require access to models. The only requirement is access to the dataset, i.e. input sample data points, model results and gold standard labels. The method (and a command-line tool), called GEval,[2] is based on statistical hypothesis testing and measuring the significance of each feature. GEval finds global features that "influence" the model evaluation score in a bad way and worsen its results.

Moreover, we present the work of GEval using examples from various text-based model types, i.e. named entity recognition, classification and translation.

In the following sections we introduce the idea to use p-value and hypotheses testing to debug ML models (Section 2), describe the algorithm behind GEval (Section 3), and then show some use cases for state-of-the-art ML models (Section 4).

## 2 Using p-values for debugging ML Models – general idea

Creating an ML model is not a one-off act, but a whole continuous process, in which data scientist or ML engineer should analyze what are the weakest points of a model and try to improve the results by fixing the pre- or post-processing modules or by changing the model hyperparameters or the model type itself. Moreover, regression checks are needed for new releases of a model and its companion software, because, even if the overall result is better, some specific regressions might creep in (some of them for trivial reasons) and be left unnoticed in the face of the general improvement otherwise. Thus, one may look for features, in a broad sense, in the test data and, during the ML engineering process, focus on the ones for which the evaluation metric

significantly goes down below the general average (in absolute terms or when compared with another model) as they might reveal a bug somewhere in the ML pipeline.

Which features are suspicious? We should look for either the ones for which evaluation metric decreases abruptly (even if they are infrequent) or the ones which are very frequent and which influence the evaluation metric in a negative manner, even if just slightly (or the ones which are somewhere in between these two extremes). We will show (in Section 4) that natural language processing (NLP) tasks are particularly amenable to this, as words and their combinations can be treated as features. Consider, for example, a binary text classification task. If you have an ML model for this task, you could run it on a test set, sort all words (or bigrams, trigrams, or other types of features) using a chi-squared statistical test to confront the feature (or its lack) against the failure or success (using a $2 \times 2$ contingency table) of the classification model and look at the top of the list, i.e. at words with the highest value of $\chi^2$ statistics, or, equivalently, the lowest p-value. P-value might be easier to interpret for humans and they are comparable across statistical tests. As we are not interested in p-values as such (in contrast to hypothesis testing), but rather in comparing them to rank features, there is no need to use procedures for correcting p-values for multiple experiments, such as Bonferroni correction.

See, for instance, Table 1, where we presented the results of such an experiment for a specific classifier in the Twitter sentiment classification task. The average accuracy for the tweets with the word "know" is higher than for the ones containing the word "reading"; still, the accuracy for "know" is more significant (as it was more frequent). Thus, when debugging this ML model, more focus should be given to "know", and even more to "though", for which lower average accuracy and p-value was found (this is, of course, related to the fact that this conjunct connects contrastive clauses, which are hard to handle in sentiment analysis).

| WORD | COUNT | + | − | ACC | $\chi^2$ | P-VALUE |
|---|---|---|---|---|---|---|
| THOUGH | 343 | 254 | 89 | 0.7405 | 35.2501 | 0.00000 |
| KNOW | 767 | 619 | 148 | 0.8070 | 13.4284 | 0.00025 |
| READING | 72 | 57 | 15 | 0.7917 | 2.226 | 0.1357 |

Table 1: Example of words from Twitter classification (see Section 4) task with their statistical properties

---

[2] `https://gonito.net/gitlist/geval.git/`; see also (Graliński et al., 2016) for a discussion of a companion Web application

This kind of analysis is clearly not white-box debugging (it does not depend on the internals of the models), but even calling it black-box is not accurate, as the model is not re-run. What is needed is just the input and the actual and expected output of the system. Hence, the most appropriate name for this technique should be "no-box" debugging.

## 2.1 Evaluating ML models for NLP

Counting successes and failures (accuracy) is just the simplest evaluation metrics used in NLP and there are actually many more: for the classification itself, a soft metric such as cross-entropy could be used, for other tasks we have metrics such as F1 (sequence labeling tasks), BLEU (machine translation), WER (ASR) or even more specialized metrics, e.g. GLEU for grammatical error correction (Napoles et al., 2015). For such non-binary evaluation schemes using chi-square test is not enough, a more general statistical test is needed.

Let us introduce some notation first. A test set $T = (X, Y)$ is given, where $X = (X_1, \ldots, X_p), X_1, \ldots, X_p \in \mathfrak{X}$ are inputs and $Y = (Y_1, \ldots, Y_p), Y_1, \ldots, Y_p \in \mathfrak{Y}$ — corresponding expected outputs (i.e. $T$ consists of $p$ items or data points and their expected labels). There are no assumptions as to what $X_i$ and $Y_i$ are, they could be numbers, strings, vectors of numbers/strings, etc. Also, actual outputs $\hat{Y} = (\hat{Y}_1, \ldots, \hat{Y}_p), \hat{Y}_1, \ldots, \hat{Y}_p \in \mathfrak{Y}$ from the analyzed ML system are given. An evaluation metric

$$Z : \mathfrak{X}^p \times \mathfrak{Y}^p \times \hat{\mathfrak{Y}}^p \to \mathbb{R},$$

is assumed and defined for any $p$.

No assumption is made for $Z$ here, it does need to be differentiable, its values does not have to be interpretable on an interval or ratio scale. All that is assumed is that higher values of $Z$ represent a "better" outcome. $Z$ is a the-higher-the-better metric, a loss function $L$ would need to be turned into $Z$ as: $Z = -L(X, Y, \hat{Y})$.

The evaluation metric $Z$ is usually run for the whole test set to get one number, the overall value summing up the quality of the system.

For the purposes of "no-box" debugging, however, we are going to use it in a non-standard manner: the evaluation score $Z$ is going to be calculated for each item *separately* to learn which items are "hard" and which items are "easy" for an ML model in question. For a classification tasks, it means simply partitioning the items, e.g. sentences, into successes and failures, but in the case of more "gradual" evaluation schemes, the items will be ranked more "smoothly" – from items for which the system output was perfect, through nearly perfect, partially wrong to completely incorrect. Building on this, we will be able to compare the distribution of evaluation scores (or rather their ranks) within the subset of items *with* a given feature against the subset of items *without* it (see Section 2.3).

In other words, a vector $\zeta = (\zeta_1, \ldots, \zeta_p)$ of evaluation scores, one score for each data point will be calculated:

$$\zeta_i = Z((X_i), (Y_i), (\hat{Y}_i)).$$

This approach is natural for some evaluation schemes, especially the ones for which the evaluation metric for the whole test set is calculated as a simple aggregate, e.g. as the mean:

$$Z(X, Y, \hat{Y}) \;=\; \frac{1}{p} \sum_{i=1}^{p} Z((X_i), (Y_i), (\hat{Y}_i))$$

$$\;=\; \frac{1}{p} \sum_{i=1}^{p} \zeta_i.$$

The examples of metrics having the above property are accuracy and cross-entropy. There exist, however, evaluation metrics for which the equality like this would not hold. For instance, BLEU evaluation metric, widely used in machine translation, is based on precision of n-grams calculated for the *whole* dataset (Papineni et al., 2002). BLEU is not recommended to be used for *single* utterances, as many translations will be scored at 0 in isolation, even when their quality is not that low (if no 4-gram from the gold standard is retrieved, BLEU scores to zero, which is a problem for isolated sentences, but not when the whole corpus is considered). In other words, it is not a good idea to use BLEU to compare sentences (to know which one was hardest to translate), as many bad and not-so-bad translations are indistinguishable if BLEU $\zeta_i$ values were considered. Still, when looking for words which are "troublesome" for a specific machine translation system, BLEU $\zeta_i$ value might have enough signal to be useful. Alternatively, one could switch to a similar metric, which has better properties for per sentence evaluation, e.g. to Google GLEU for machine translation (Wu et al., 2016).

In exploratory data analysis, only sets of $X$ and $Y$ are usually considered. What we are going to do is to treat the output of an ML model ($\hat{Y}$) and evaluation results ($\zeta$) as additional columns in a data frame and explore such extended dataset to find anomalies. It could be viewed as a blend of machine learning and data science.

## 2.2 Feature extraction

We are interested in "features", i.e. factors that might or might not occur in a data point (features or "metafeatures" as these are taken not only from the inputs, but also from the actual and expected outputs). In the case of textual data, it is words that could be treated as features to be ranked with p-value with our approach, so for NLP tasks, after tokenization (and possibly some normalization), one could obtain features such as: "input contains the word 'der'", "expected output contains the word 'but'", "actual output contains the word 'though'".

In general, we need a set of possible features $\mathfrak{F}$ and a function $\phi$ to extract features from a data point:

$$\phi : \mathfrak{X} \times \mathfrak{Y} \times \hat{\mathfrak{Y}} \to 2^{\mathfrak{F}}.$$

Note that in this general form, a feature might be a combination of simpler features, e.g.: "input contains the word 'ein' and expected output contains the word 'an'".

## 2.3 Using the Mann-Whitney test

The main idea for "no-box" debugging is taken from hypotheses testing, just as assessing different methods for medical treatments or in A/B testing schedule: we assume that we have two datasets – the results of working procedures (Biau et al., 2010; Kohavi and Longbotham, 2017). The datasets are treated as distinct results of different procedures and compared. In our case, one "dataset" is the subset $(X, Y, \hat{Y})^{+f}$ of items with a chosen particular feature $f \in \mathfrak{F}$ and the other one – $(X, Y, \hat{Y})^{-f}$ – the data points without the feature $f$.

We rank the whole dataset $(X, Y, \hat{Y})$ and then check if the distributions of data points from the two subdatasets $((X, Y, \hat{Y})^{+f}$ against $(X, Y, \hat{Y})^{-f})$ are similar or not. Checking is carried out using the Mann-Whitney rank $U$ test. If the p-value is very low, we may suspect that the difference in metric is not accidental. Thus, we can draw the conclusion that the feature reduces the evaluation score of our model and should be looked at.

The (Wilcoxon-)Mann-Whitney signed-ranks (Wilcoxon, 1945) test is a non-parametric equivalent of the paired t-test when the population might not be assumed to be normally distributed. It is most commonly used to test for a difference in the mean (or median) of paired observations.

The Mann-Whitney test makes important assumptions: (1) the two samples need to be dependent observations of the cases, (2) the paired observations are randomly and independently drawn, (3) data are measured on at least an ordinal scale. The assumptions are fulfilled in our non-standard (from the point of view of hypothesis testing) case. One-tailed test will be used, as we want to separate the "hardest" features from the "easiest" ones.

## 2.4 Aren't p-values an abomination?

The p-value is the probability for a given statistical model that, when the null hypothesis is true, the statistical summary would be greater than or equal to the observed value. The use of p-values in hypothesis testing is common in many fields of science. Criticisms of p-values are as old as the measures themselves. There is a widespread thinking that p-values are often misused and misinterpreted. There are many critical articles concerning these problems (Briggs, 2019). In particular, fixed significance level ($\alpha$) is often criticized. The significance level for a study is chosen before data collection, and typically set to 5%. One practice that has been particularly criticized is rejecting the null hypothesis for any p-value less than 5% without other supporting evidence. The p-value does not, in itself, support reasoning about the probabilities of hypotheses but is only an additional tool for deciding whether to reject the null hypothesis or not. Based on this concept we use p-values only to select the most promising features. We do not use significance level but only raw p-values, so that we could generate a ranked list of features.

Instead of p-value, the "expected improvement" (how the evaluation score would improve if we fixed the problem, i.e. the average score were the same as for the items without it?) could be calculated for a feature $f$:

$$Z((X, Y, \hat{Y})^{-f}) - Z(X, Y, \hat{Y}).$$

P-values have, however, some advantages. They can be calculated for numerical features, not just binary factors (such as words), using Kendall's $\tau$. For instance, in the context of NLP we might be interested in questions like: are longer sentences harder to translate? are shorter utterances harder to classify? are named entities harder to find in older texts?

Kendall's $\tau$ coefficient (Kendall, 1938), is a statistic used to measure the ordinal association between two measured quantities. It evaluates the degree of similarity between two sets of ranks given to a same set of objects. This coefficient depends upon the number of inversions of pairs of objects which would be needed to transform one rank order into the other. It is known that when one of the variables is binary and the other is ordered, with or without tied values, the Mann-Whitney test is equivalent to Kendall's $\tau$ test (Burr, 1960). This means that it is sound to rank numerical features against 0/1 features such as words. All p-values reported in the following sections are according to the Mann–Whitney/Kendall test.

### 2.5 Most worsening features

Instead of calculating feature p-values for a single model, one could *compare* the results of two models by looking at the difference in their evaluation scores rather than at the absolute value. Let us assume that two models $M$ and $M'$ are to be compared and their outputs, respectively $\hat{Y}$ and $\hat{Y}'$, are known, hence evaluation scores $\zeta$ and $\zeta'$ can be calculated. Now, we could apply the Mann-Whitney test for $\delta_i = \zeta_i - \zeta_i'$ rather than for $\zeta_i$ or $\zeta_i'$. This way, features that worsen the results (when switching from $M$ to $M'$) can be tracked, e.g. whenever a new version of a model or a processing pipeline is released. This could be viewed as a form of regression testing for ML models.

Note that for some evaluation metrics, other methods for comparing scores (e.g. $\zeta_i/\zeta_i'$ rather than $\zeta_i - \zeta_i'$) may be more sound. Still, simple difference should give you at least a general direction for each feature.

## 3 Implementation

GEval was implemented in Haskell as a command-line tool. First of all, it is a general evaluator for a wide variety of tasks, i.e. it simply calculates the total score for a number of evaluation metrics. On top of this basic functionality, more advanced modes are available in GEval, e.g. one can evaluate the test set item by item (basically calculate $\zeta_i$) and sort the items starting from the ones with the worst score. Calculating p-values for features is a step even further. Fortunately, this can be done in an effective manner even for a very large number of features simply by accumulating feature ranks, as the sum of the ranks could be easily turned into Mann-Whitney $U$ and, then, the final p-value.

As the item-by-item (or "line-by-line") mode or calculating p-values can be done for any evaluation metric in GEval, whenever a new metric, even an exotic or complicated one, is implemented in GEval, such advanced options for data analysis are available and ready to use.

This stands in contrast to specialized evaluation tools, e.g. SacreBLEU for Machine Translation (Post, 2018). Moreover, GEval processed very large datasets in minutes in contrast to popular model-agnostic interpretability tool LIME (Tulio Ribeiro et al., 2016) that works about 14 s per one data point (tests made at GPU DGX machine). Thus, LIME method is not efficient for very large datasets.

### 3.1 Features

First of all, we need to understand the output of GEval analysis and what is meant as a feature.

Features are combined from the inputs, model outputs and expected results (i.e. gold standard), identified respectively as "in:", "out:", "exp:". There might be an additional index, mainly for the input data, e.g. "in<number>" indicates the index of a column in the file.

A feature generated in GEval listing is of the following form:

- a token from the input/output/expected output, e.g. *in<1>:though,*

- a bigram from the input/output/expected output, e.g. *out:even ++ better,*

- a word shape based on regular expressions, e.g. *in<1>:SHAPE:99* for two-digit numbers, *in<1>:SHAPE:A+* for acronyms,

- a Cartesian feature – two features occurring together in one item, but not needing to stand side by side to each other, e.g. *exp:1 ~in<1>:sad* being a combination of class 1 in the expected output and "sad" occurring in the input text.

## 4 Case studies

We analyzed 3 different types of text-based models – for classification, machine translation and named entities recognition. We tested models on common open-source datasets. Finally, we observed if our tool can help us understand model problems and their causes. In the following we show a few tips how the tool can help to find solutions to improve models, get some important findings or post-process model results to improve final predictions.

### 4.1 The GEval workflow

At the very beginning we should know the overall metric for our validation or development set, GEval should be run for this as:

```
geval —metric Multilabel—F1 —i in.tsv —
    o out.tsv —e expected.tsv
```

Then we analyze GEval listing obtained with the `--worst-features` option (even more features can be derived using extra options such as `--bigrams`, `--word-shapes`, `--cartesians`) and look for interesting features, i.e. features with very low p-value and the metric value much smaller than the metric value for overall test set. These features should have considerably high coverage in the dataset.

When we get the interesting feature listing, we may specific analyze data points from input dataset (GEval options: `--line-by-line` and `--filter`) to understand why there is a problem with those features.

### 4.2 Sentiment analysis

We tested text classification tasks on the "Twitter" data set (Go et al., 2009). The models are fitted using ULMFiT library (Howard and Ruder, 2018).

Results of Twitter sentiment analysis with ULMFiT are shown in Table 2. What is worth to note that the model has a problem with positive tweets that contain words of negation or words expressing sadness or anger by their own (not in a longer context), e.g. "can't", "doesn't". Examples of such hard cases are: "Don't hate physics. it is lovely.", "It doesn't mean I am angry with him.".

We performed an additional test with the ULMFiT model: We trained the model using half of the training set (774,998 text samples) and then found interesting/suspicious features. We added a set of samples (of size 18,009) with *"though"* word, then trained a new model (though-model). Additionally, we combine preliminary set with the same additional number (18,009) of random

| FEATURE | COUNT | ACC | P-VALUE |
|---|---|---|---|
| *in<1>:though* | 343 | 0.74 | 0.00004 |
| *in<1>:no++idea* | 21 | 0.48 | 0.001 |
| *in<1>:yeah* | 227 | 0.76 | 0.003 |
| *in<1>:know* | 767 | 0.81 | 0.004 |
| *in<1>:which* | 98 | 0.71 | 0.006 |
| *in<1>:wouldn't* | 38 | 0.68 | 0.029 |
| *exp:1 ~in<1>:sad* | 13 | 0.38 | 0.001 |
| *exp:1 ~in<1>:though* | 72 | 0.67 | 0.002 |
| *exp:1 ~in<1>:can't* | 160 | 0.73 | 0.002 |
| *exp:1 ~in<1>:never* | 81 | 0.67 | 0.001 |
| *exp:1 ~in<1>:but* | 549 | 0.73 | 0.0000 |
| *exp:1 ~in<1>:not* | 395 | 0.71 | 0.0000 |
| *exp:0 ~in<1>:you* | 958 | 0.77 | 0.0000 |
| *exp:0 ~in<1>:haha* | 73 | 0.63 | 0.0002 |

Table 2: GEval feature listing for classification for sentiment analysis on Twitter dataset. We used output from model ULMFiT with 0.86 total accuracy on the chosen validation set. "Acc" stands for the average accuracy for tweets with a given feature. Labels for positive sentiment are "1", i.e. in feature names "exp:1", and for negative sentiment – "0".

samples (random-model). The "though"-model achieved better accuracy of 85.704% than random and preliminary ones (respectively: 85.383% and 85.558%).

In Figure 1, we show the result of LIME method for one data point (sentence) which contains hard features gotten from GEval.

Figure 1: LIME visualisation of influence of tokens on final results. The sentence is marked as positive in gold annotations. GEval hard feature are "FAIL" and "which" that generate drop in F1 for the whole test dataset (down to 59% and 71% respectively). They also contributes negatively into this sample.

### 4.3 Machine translation

We tested machine translation tasks on a German-to-English challenge WMT-2017 (WMT). We compared two models: LIUM (García-Martínez et al., 2017) (BLEU score of 30.10) and the best UEDin (Sennrich et al., 2016) (BLEU 35.12). We checked cases when UEDin is worse than LIUM, using the method described in Section 2.5. In other words, we were looking the specific features for which the best model behaves badly when compared with an inferior model. The interesting features worsening UEDin in comparison with LIUM are shown in Table 3. Inspecting specific sentences we can see a problem that euro currency is translated to pounds, which can be a critical bug in an industry translation system. Obviously, it is very easy to repair with post-processing. However the point is not to overlook the source of model problems, that can be easily and efficiently achieved with GEval.

Other examples of translation problems are "be" which is a very difficult word to translate in various contexts or words like "people" and "Menschen" that meanings varies in different contexts.

| FEATURE | COUNT | DROP IN BLEU | P-VAL |
| --- | --- | --- | --- |
| *exp:euros* | 31 | -0.0647 | 0.0000 |
| *in<1>:Euro* | 31 | -0.0534 | 0.0000 |
| *exp:be* | 296 | 0.0206 | 0.0004 |
| *exp:Federal* | 12 | -0.0529 | 0.0004 |
| *exp:small* | 21 | -0.0288 | 0.0008 |
| *out:$* | 36 | -0.0193 | 0.0012 |

Table 3: Comparison of machine translation models: LIUM and UEDin – features worsening UEDin (WMT-17 new task test data).

### 4.4 Named entity recognition

We tested known NER (named entities recognition) models with GEval. Here we report results with FLAIR (Akbik et al., 2018) on CoNLL 2003 dataset (Tjong Kim Sang and De Meulder, 2003). We achieved 93.06% F1 score[3].

Our test procedure is as follows. We generated GEval listing. Below we explain the findings – GEval features and we show results in Table 4. A few input samples and outputs for the chosen features are presented in Table 5. To understand the results we need to bear in mind that output results and annotations (gold standard) are encoded in CoNLL 2003 files as upper-cased named entity class (i.e. LOC, PER, ORG, MISC) and the index in the input sentence, e.g. "LOC:0 PER:7,8".

___
[3] Results reported in authors publication for NER models on original CoNLL 2003 test set is 93.07%. This result was not achieved with the current version of the library. See the discussion at (Flair, 2018).

A few of our finding are presented here (in the Table 4, the relevant rows are listed in the same order):

• upper-cased texts are difficult for the model, e.g. features: *in<1>:SHAPE:A+ ~in<1>:SHAPE:.* (word written in upper case combined with a punctuation mark, i.e. not a header);

• there is a problem when named entity is expected at the beginning of sentence, e.g. *exp:0 ~out:0,1* or *exp:1,2++PER*. It means that a named entity was expected just for the first word, but was wrongly marked by the ML model for the first two words);

• there is a problem with MISC class, especially in upper-cased texts and at the beginning of texts, e.g. features: *out:MISC ~in<1>:SHAPE:A+*; *out:MISC++0,1*; *out:MISC++0,1 ~in<1>:SHAPE:A+*;

• localization and organization classes are quite often mixed, e.g. *exp:LOC++: ~out:ORG++:*;

• a role of a person is sometimes mixed with the person name and in such cases there is a problem with annotation consistency between train and test dataset, e.g. *in<1>:Pope*;

• also part of organization names that also are common words are sometimes misannotated or not recognized by the model, e.g. *in<1>:League*; *in<1>:National*; *in<1>:DIVISION*;

• numbers are hard for the model – numbers for dates, e.g. *in<1>:/ ~in<1>:SHAPE:9.999*; *exp:ORG ~in<1>:SHAPE:99.99*.

• and there are many particular cases that are worth looking into, e.g. country names that are might be adjectives as well: *in<1>:German*; *in<1>:Czech*.

## 5 Conclusions

Interpretability of machine learning models is a very active field of research. We presented GEval tool to analyze datasets and ML models. GEval is a post-hoc model agnostic technique that do not require any access to the model. The tool is very efficient so it can be particularly useful for very big text datasets that are difficult to process using perturbation-based interpretability methods, e.g. LIME. We also showed use cases to explain what kind of conclusions we can drive from the GEval analysis.

| FEATURE | COUNT | F1 | P-VAL |
|---|---|---|---|
| *in<1>:SHAPE:. ~~in<1>:SHAPE:A+* | 399 | 0.828 | 0.000 |
| *exp:0 ~~out:0,1* | 17 | 0.484 | 0.000 |
| *exp:1,2++PER* | 10 | 0.767 | 0.002 |
| *exp:MISC* | 563 | 0.849 | 0.000 |
| *out:MISC ~~in<1>:SHAPE:A+* | 176 | 0.639 | 0.000 |
| *out:MISC++0,1* | 45 | 0.289 | 0.000 |
| *out:MISC++0,1 ~~in<1>:SHAPE:A+* | 35 | 0.100 | 0.000 |
| *exp:LOC++: ~~out:ORG++:* | 29 | 0.704 | 0.000 |
| *in<1>:Pope* | 4 | 0.748 | 0.003 |
| *in<1>:DIVISION* | 35 | 0.495 | 0.000 |
| *in<1>:League* | 17 | 0.548 | 0.000 |
| *in<1>:National* | 25 | 0.615 | 0.000 |
| *in<1>:/ ~~in<1>:SHAPE:9.999* | 15 | 0.800 | 0.000 |
| *exp:ORG ~~in<1>:SHAPE:99.99* | 13 | 0.752 | 0.000 |
| *in<1>:German* | 15 | 0.709 | 0.001 |
| *in<1>:Czech* | 14 | 0.693 | 0.000 |
| *in<1>:Santa* | 19 | 0.727 | 0.001 |

Table 4: Named entity recognition on CoNLL 2003 test dataset with FLAIR model (92.36% for the whole test set).

| FEATURE & EXAMPLES | GOLD STANDARD ANNOTATIONS & MODEL OUTPUTS |
|---|---|
| *in<1>:National* | |
| *Peters left a meeting between NZ First and National negotiators...* | GOLD: ORG:*NZ First*, ORG:*National*; OUTPUT: ORG:*NZ First and National* |
| *in<1>:SHAPE:(* | |
| *1. United States III ( Brian Shimer , ... ) one;* | GOLD: ORG:*United States III*; OUTPUT: LOC:*United States* |
| *in<1>:Santa* | |
| *German Santa in bank nearly gets arrested .* | GOLD: MISC:*German* PER:*Santa*; OUTPUT: MISC:*German Santa* |

Table 5: Named entity recognition on CoNLL 2003 – items from the dataset for features extracted and shown in Table 4.

## Acknowledgements

The authors would like to acknowledge the support the project conducted by Applica.ai has received as being co-financed by the European Regional Development Fund (POIR.01.01.01-00-0144/17-00).

## References

Shared task: Machine translation of news, emnlp wmt 2017.

A. Adadi and M. Berrada. 2018. Peeking inside the black-box: A survey on explainable artificial intelligence (xai). *IEEE Access*, 6:52138–52160.

Alan Akbik, Duncan Blythe, and Roland Vollgraf. 2018. Contextual string embeddings for sequence labeling. In *COLING 2018, 27th International Conference on Computational Linguistics*, pages 1638–1649.

David Jean Biau, Brigitte M. Jolles, and Raphaël Porcher. 2010. P value and the theory of hypothesis testing: An explanation for new researchers. 468(3):885 – 892.

William M. Briggs. 2019. Everything wrong with p-values under one roof. In *Beyond Traditional*

*Probabilistic Methods in Economics*, volume 809 of *Studies in Computational Intelligence*, pages 22–44. Springer International Publishing.

Edmund. J. Burr. 1960. The distribution of Kendall's score S for a pair of tied rankings. *Biometrika*, 47(1-2):151–171.

Jianbo Chen, Le Song, Martin J Wainwright, and Michael I Jordan. 2018. Learning to explain: An information-theoretic perspective on model interpretation.

Mengnan Du, Ninghao Liu, and Xia Hu. 2018. Techniques for interpretable machine learning. *CoRR*, abs/1808.00033.

Flair. 2018. Flair repository (issue 206 and 390).

Mercedes García-Martínez, Ozan Caglayan, Walid Aransa, Adrien Bardet, Fethi Bougares, and Loïc Barrault. 2017. Lium machine translation systems for wmt17 news translation task. In *Proceedings of the Second Conference on Machine Translation*, pages 288–295. Association for Computational Linguistics.

A. Go, R. Bhayani, and L. Huang. 2009. Twitter sentiment classification using distant supervision.

Filip Graliński, Rafał Jaworski, Łukasz Borchmann, and Piotr Wierzchoń. 2016. Gonito.net - Open Platform for Research Competition, Cooperation and Reproducibility. In *Proceedings of the 4REAL Workshop*, pages 13–20.

Riccardo Guidotti, Anna Monreale, Salvatore Ruggieri, Franco Turini, Fosca Giannotti, and Dino Pedreschi. 2018. A survey of methods for explaining black box models. *ACM Comput. Surv.*, 51(5):93:1–93:42.

Jeremy Howard and Sebastian Ruder. 2018. Universal language model fine-tuning for text classification.

Maurice G. Kendall. 1938. A new measure of rank correlation. *Biometrika*, 30(1/2):81–93.

Ron Kohavi and Roger Longbotham. 2017. *Online Controlled Experiments and A/B Testing*, pages 922–929. Springer US, Boston, MA.

Courtney Napoles, Keisuke Sakaguchi, Matt Post, and Joel Tetreault. 2015. Ground truth for grammatical error correction metrics. In *Proceedings of the 53rd Annual Meeting of the Association for Computational Linguistics and the 7th International Joint Conference on Natural Language Processing (Volume 2: Short Papers)*, volume 2, pages 588–593.

Kishore Papineni, Salim Roukos, Todd Ward, and Wei-Jing Zhu. 2002. Bleu: a method for automatic evaluation of machine translation. In *Proceedings of the 40th annual meeting on association for computational linguistics*, pages 311–318. Association for Computational Linguistics.

Matt Post. 2018. A call for clarity in reporting BLEU scores. *CoRR*, abs/1804.08771.

Rico Sennrich, Barry Haddow, and Alexandra Birch. 2016. Edinburgh neural machine translation systems for wmt 16. In *Proceedings of the First Conference on Machine Translation: Volume 2, Shared Task Papers*, pages 371–376. Association for Computational Linguistics.

Erik F. Tjong Kim Sang and Fien De Meulder. 2003. Introduction to the conll-2003 shared task: Language-independent named entity recognition. In *Proceedings of the Seventh Conference on Natural Language Learning at HLT-NAACL 2003 - Volume 4*, CONLL '03, pages 142–147, Stroudsburg, PA, USA. Association for Computational Linguistics.

Marco Tulio Ribeiro, Sameer Singh, and Carlos Guestri. 2016. Model-agnostic interpretability of machine learning. In *Proceedings of the International Conference on Machine Learning, Workshop on Human Interpretability in Machine Learning (WHI / ICML 2016)*, Stanford, CA. Morgan Kaufmann.

Frank Wilcoxon. 1945. Individual comparisons by ranking methods. *Biometrics Bulletin*, 1(6):80–83.

Yonghui Wu, Mike Schuster, Zhifeng Chen, Quoc V Le, Mohammad Norouzi, Wolfgang Macherey, Maxim Krikun, Yuan Cao, Qin Gao, Klaus Macherey, et al. 2016. Google's neural machine translation system: Bridging the gap between human and machine translation. *arXiv preprint arXiv:1609.08144*.

# From Balustrades to Pierre Vinken:
## Looking for Syntax in Transformer Self-Attentions


**David Mareček** and **Rudolf Rosa**

Charles University, Faculty of Mathematics and Physics
Institute of Formal and Applied Linguistics
Malostranské náměstí 25, 118 00 Prague, Czech Republic
`{marecek, rosa}@ufal.mff.cuni.cz`



## Abstract

We inspect the multi-head self-attention in Transformer NMT encoders for three source languages, looking for patterns that could have a syntactic interpretation. In many of the attention heads, we frequently find sequences of consecutive states attending to the same position, which resemble syntactic phrases. We propose a transparent deterministic method of quantifying the amount of syntactic information present in the self-attentions, based on automatically building and evaluating phrase-structure trees from the phrase-like sequences. We compare the resulting trees to existing constituency treebanks, both manually and by computing precision and recall.


## 1 Introduction

The classical approach to Natural Language Processing used to be complex pipelines, e.g. (Popel and Žabokrtský, 2010; Manning et al., 2014; Forcada et al., 2011), consisting of multiple steps of linguistically motivated analyses, such as part-of-speech tagging or syntactic parsing, using explicit intermediate representations (e.g. dependency trees) to abstract over the underlying texts.

In recent years, this has changed with the introduction of deep neural end-to-end models, which take raw text as input and produce the desired output directly. Any intermediate representations of the text may emerge during the training of the neural network, and are hidden to us.

We focus on the encoder part of the Transformer architecture (Vaswani et al., 2017), applied to neural machine translation (NMT), as visualizations presented by the authors suggest that its attention heads capture various phenomena such as syntax, semantic roles or anaphora links.

In this work, we analyze the syntactic properties of the self-attention heads both qualitatively and quantitatively. For the quantitative evaluation, we devise a new technique that quantifies the amount of syntactic information by explicitly building constituency trees from the attentions and comparing them with the standard syntactic trees.

Section 3 briefly describes the Transformer encoder architecture and the way we visualize the self-attention matrices using heatmaps. In Section 4, we present our findings from an extensive manual inspection of the heatmaps, identifying several common patterns, including the baluster-like structures which seem to resemble syntactic phrases. To avoid confirmation bias, we proceed by devising a linguistically uninformed tree extraction algorithm (Section 5), which builds a constituency tree based solely on the assumption that the balusters correspond to syntactic phrases. We analyze the resulting parse trees and compare them with standard syntactic trees, both manually and via automatic evaluation. In Section 6, we follow the hypothesis that only some of the attention heads are "syntactic", and try to identify them.

## 2 Related Work

Initial analyses of syntax captured by neural networks focused on RNNs. Shi et al. (2016) examine how much syntax is learned by RNN encoder by freezing its weights and using a decoder to predict syntactic trees. Adi et al. (2016) examine sentence vector representations by training auxiliary classifiers to take sentence encodings and predict attributes like word order. Linzen et al. (2016) assess the ability of LSTMs to learn syntax by predicting verbal numbers. Blevins et al. (2018) measure the amount of syntax in RNNs by predicting part-of-speech tags and constituent labels.

In the last year, related studies appeared also for the Transformer architecture. Tang et al. (2018) show the Transformer networks perform better




*Proceedings of the Second BlackboxNLP Workshop on Analyzing and Interpreting Neural Networks for NLP*, pages 263–275
Florence, Italy, August 1, 2019. ©2019 Association for Computational Linguistics

than RNNs on word sense disambiguation. Zhang and Bowman (2018) show that language models use more syntactic and morphological information than translation models.

Recently, Hewitt and Manning (2019) tried to find syntactic structures in contextual word representations by training simple models on annotated parse trees, concluding that syntactic trees are embedded both in BERT (Devlin et al., 2018) and ELMo (Peters et al., 2018) models. This is also supported by Liu et al. (2019), who successfully trained probes to extract linguistic structures, including syntactic dependencies, from various trained neural networks.

Most existing works train probing models on annotated data (e.g. treebanks). However, such a model may learn to predict the linguistic structure not because it is captured by the network, but because it can be predicted from features preserved from the input, as has been already noted e.g. by Belinkov and Glass (2018). In our work, we try to avoid that risk by not using annotated data for the predictions, but rather looking for structures explicitly present in the network representations.

In a study closely related to ours, Raganato and Tiedemann (2018) also observe syntax-like patterns in Transformer encoder self-attentions, and try to extract syntactic trees without using annotated data (except for taking the root node from the gold annotation). However, they construct dependency trees, while we observe phrase-like rather than dependency-like structures. Moreover, their findings are somewhat inconclusive, as the accuracy of the resulting trees is close to the baseline, while our results are clearly positive. A similar approach was already suggested (but not evaluated) in (Mareček and Rosa, 2018).

## 3 Transformer NMT Encoder

In the Transformer architecture, Vaswani et al. (2017) came up with several important improvements over the classical attention, including *multi-headed* attention. It features a set of independent attention heads, each deciding on its own to which states to attend. This allows each of the heads to specialize to provide a different type of information or feature (similarly e.g. to CNN filters). The encoder typically uses six multi-head self-attention sub-layers. Each state on a given layer (*output state*) is computed from a concatenation of the result of applying a set of attention heads to the states on the previous layer (*input states*), passed through a feed-forward layer. This may allow the encoder to do more advanced multi-step processing, such as aggregating the information about several subwords into one position and then attending to this position on the higher layers.

Another notable feature of the Transformer encoder is the use of residual connections, which transport the source subword embeddings forward, bypassing the self-attention mechanism, and get averaged with the outputs of the self-attention. This ensures that the *output state* at each position retains a significant amount of the corresponding source subword embedding, supporting the usual shortcut of assuming that the hidden states can be thought of as representations of the underlying subwords (in the context of the sentence).

### 3.1 Encoder Self-Attention Visualization

We focus on exploring multi-head self-attentions of the encoder. We use a natural visualization of self-attention heads using square matrix heatmaps (Figure 1), going from black (attention weight = 0) to white (attention weight = 1). The subwords that correspond to the rows and columns are printed alongside the matrix. The rows correspond to *output states*, and the columns to *input states*; as the *output states* attend to *input states*, the softmaxed attention weights on each row sum to 1.

Note that the visualizations may be deceiving in several aspects. It is important to understand that the fact that a given head at a given position on a given layer attends to a position of a specific subword does *not* mean that the resulting hidden state will simply contain the representation of that subword, for several reasons:

- The input to the self attention is the output of the previous layer, i.e. a hidden state, presumably but not necessarily representing the subword at this position to some extent, and usually mixing in information about other subwords in the sentence.
- The hidden states emitted from each layer are the outputs of a feed forward network that takes a concatenation of outputs from all of the heads on that layer as input, and can thus mix them, ignore them, only use parts of them, etc.

### 3.2 Experiment Setup

We analyze the Transformer NMT encoders for the following three languages: English (en),

| en-de | 33.5 | en-fr | 45.2 | fr-de | 24.3 |
| de-en | 39.8 | fr-en | 42.1 | de-fr | 32.9 |

Table 1: BLEU scores measured on the test data.

French (fr), and German (de). We selected those particular languages because they are available in the Europarl corpus[1] (Koehn, 2005) comprising large high-quality multiparallel data, and because constituency syntax parse trees can be obtained for them by the Stanford parser (Klein and Manning, 2003) out-of-the-box.[2]

As we want to explore a state-of-the-art setup, we use the Transformer model (Vaswani et al., 2017) as reimplemented by Helcl et al. (2018) in the Neural Monkey framework[3] in standard setting: 6 encoder and decoder layers, 16 attention heads, embedding size of 512, hidden-layers' size of 4096, dropout 0.9, and batch size 30.

We train the translator for all 6 source-target language pairs (en-fr, en-de, fr-en, fr-de, de-en, de-fr).[4] From the Europarl corpus, we take first 1,000 sentences as development data, last 1,000 sentences as evaluation data, and the remaining 486,272 sentences for training. Table 1 lists the BLEU scores of the systems. All inspections and evaluations, both manual and automatic, have been performed on the evaluation data.

The data are tokenized by the Stanford Tokenizer[5] to make the tokens consistent with the constituency trees with which we will compare our results. We then build a shared dictionary of 100,000 BPE subword units (Sennrich et al., 2016) on the concatenated training data of all three languages, append an EOS symbol to each sentence, and train the translation model.

## 4 Manual Analysis of Attention Matrices

On a small sample of 10 sentences and for each language pair, we created the heatmaps for all 16 attention heads of all 6 encoder layers. Six heatmaps for one sentence from the en→de encoder are shown in Figure 1; all 96 of them are

enclosed in the Appendix.

A general observation is that the attentions are nearly always very peaked. Even though the attention mechanism was designed as soft, most attention heads concentrate nearly all of the attention at each *output state* onto just one *input state*.

In the following subsections, we list all of the distinctive patterns that we have identified.[6] An important thing to note is that typically, a head behaves consistently across all sentences, i.e., for a given head on a given layer of a given trained Transformer encoder, we typically see the same attention patterns across all sentences.

### 4.1 Diagonals

Especially at the first encoder layer, there often appear various simple *diagonal* heads.

Typically, each *output state* attends to the *input state* at the same position. This may serve to pass the subword information to the higher layers.

In some cases, most of the *output states* attend to the corresponding *input states*, but some of them attend elsewhere. The role of such *partial diagonal* may be looking for a specific phenomenon that only occurs for some of the *output states*.

Often, individual *output states* attend to preceding or following *input states*, forming a *parallel diagonal* (Figure 1b). Sometimes the heads attend further, e.g. to the "pre-previous" *input state*.

### 4.2 Balustrades

The most frequent pattern, appearing in about 2/3 of the attention heads, are *balustrades* – a series of vertical bars, typically placed at the diagonal, which resemble the balusters of a staircase railing. Examples of such balustrades are shown in Figure 1c,d,e. The balustrades are often placed upwards or downwards from the main diagonal.

We observe that different heads contain balusters of different lengths. For longer balusters, the *input state* that they attend to often corresponds to a punctuation or a conjunction; often there are also heads that attend exclusively or almost exclusively to the sentence-final punctuation.

We have noticed that in many cases, the sequence of subwords spanned by a baluster may be understood as a syntactic phrase (e.g. a noun and its determiner, or a syntactic clause between

---



[4] We intersect the English-German and English-French parallel corpora using English as pivoting language.



[6] We observe all patterns which Raganato and Tiedemann (2018) identified, i.e. diagonals and attending to the end of the sentence, but also other patterns which they did not observe.

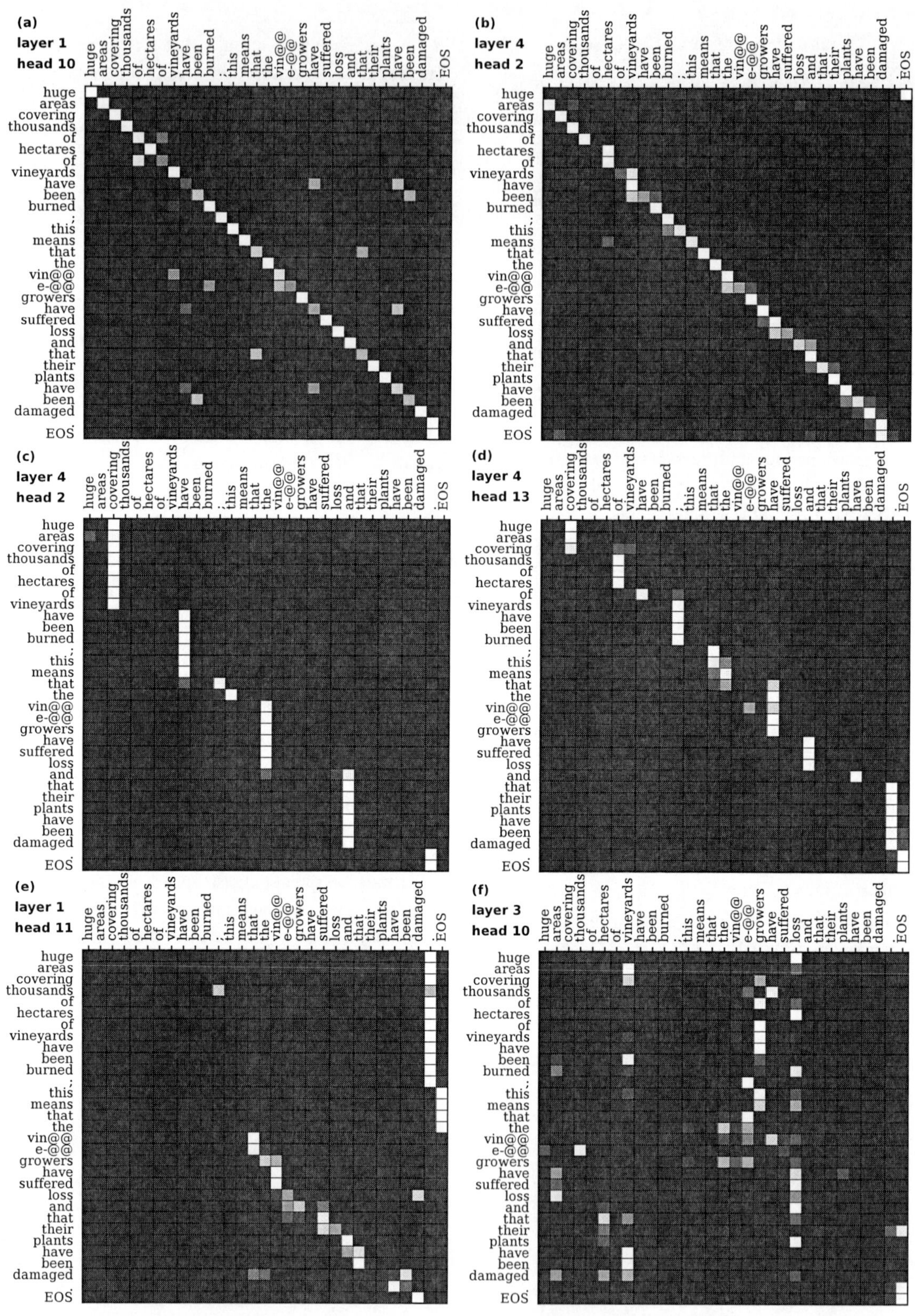

Figure 1: Heatmaps of selected attention heads showing different patterns. There are *diagonal* patterns in (a) and (b), *balustrades* in (c) and (d), a combination in (e), and rather scattered attention in (f).

two commas). Furthermore, by looking at multiple attention heads at once, we can interpret the balusters of various lengths spanning the same subwords as shorter phrases nested within longer phrases. This leads us to the idea of constructing a constituency tree from the nested phrases, and comparing it with classical syntactic constituency trees (see Section 5).

### 4.3 Equal or Similar Subwords

There is typically one or two heads where each *output state* attends to all instances of the same subword, usually with a more or less uniform distribution (see the subwords "of", "have" and "that" in Figure 1a).   We have also seen these heads to sometimes attend to very similar but not identical subwords (e.g. singular and plural).

### 4.4 The Rest

Admittedly, for about 1/5 of the attention heads, we have not identified any clear pattern, and thus have no hypothesis as for the function of such heads. Sometimes, the head shows some of the behaviours only for some of the *output states*; sometimes we do not see even such partial patterns (Figure 1f).

## 5 Extracting Constituency Trees

Our aim is to analyze whether syntactic structures seem to be captured by Transformer self-attentions, to what extent, and of what kind. As explained in the previous section, we often observe balusters of various lengths in the attention heatmaps, which can be interpreted as nested syntactic phrases. In this section, we try to measure to which extent this interpretation seems to be valid.

For this purpose, we devise a linguistically uninformed transparent deterministic algorithm to extract binary constituency trees from the balusters (Section 5.1). We automatically evaluate the results by comparing them with classical syntactic trees, generated by a standard syntactic parser (Section 5.2), to see whether the observed structures seem to capture syntax as we know it. We discuss the results in Section 5.3.

### 5.1 Tree Extraction Algorithm

We now explain how we construct constituency trees from the balusters in the attention matrices.

Our goal is not to optimize our algorithm towards producing good syntactic trees. Rather, we try to keep our algorithm linguistically uninformed, to reveal only what really is captured by the self-attentions. Therefore, we:

- build binary constituency trees, as this is quite a basic way to represent nested phrases,
- use information from all attention heads, not only those which seem to capture syntax,
- keep the number of other hyperparameters minimal and set them to the most uninformed values, rather than tuning them,
- do not train or tune the tree extraction in any way (unlike most related work).

The first step is to identify the balusters. We have previously described a baluster as a sequence of *output states* attending to a single *input state*. The attentions are typically very peaked, with nearly all of the attention mass concentrated onto one *input state*. However, as the attentions are soft, each of the *output states* in fact attends to all of the *input states* to some extent. We thus "harden" the soft attention matrix $A'$ by only keeping the maximal attention weight on each row of the attention matrix, setting all the other weights to 0:

$$A_{o,i} = \begin{cases} A'_{o,i} & \text{if } A'_{o,i} = \max_{j \in [1,N]} A'_{o,j} \\ 0 & \text{otherwise} \end{cases} \quad (1)$$

where $i$ is the *input state* index, $o$ is the *output state* index, and $N$ is the sentence length.

Next, we extract candidate phrases from the balusters and weight them. From each baluster, we extract only the candidate phrase corresponding to the full length of the baluster. The weight of the phrase corresponds to the average attention that *output states* in the phrase give to the common *input state* they attend to (i.e. the average brightness of the points in the baluster). If the same phrase appears in multiple attention matrices, their scores are summed together. The weight of the phrase spanning the $a$-th to $b$-th subwords thus is:

$$w'_{a,b} = \sum_{h \in H_{a,b}} \frac{\sum_{o \in [a,b]} A^h_{o,i_h}}{b - a + 1} \quad (2)$$

where $H_{a,b}$ is the set of attention heads containing a baluster spanning the *output states* $a$ to $b$, $A^h$ is the hardened attention matrix for head $h$, and $i_h$ is the *input state* attended by the baluster in head $h$.

The weights defined in this way are unbalanced, giving more importance to shorter phrases, as they are more frequent in the attention matrices.

We thus equalize the weights so that the average weight of all phrases of the same length equals 1:

$$w_{a,b} = \frac{w'_{a,b} \cdot |P^{b-a+1}|}{\sum_{(c,d)\in P^{b-a+1}} w'_{c,d}} \quad (3)$$

where $P^k$ is the index pair set of all extracted phrases of length $k$.

To construct the constituency tree from the phrases, we use the CKY dynamic programming algorithm (Ney, 1991), which searches for the highest scoring constituency tree in $O(n^3)$.

For each tree spanning the $a$-th to $b$-th subword, we define its score $s_{a,b}$ recursively by finding a separator $k$, $a \leq k < b$, that maximizes the average of scores and weights of the two subtrees with spans $(a, k)$ and $(k+1, b)$:

$$s_{a,b} = \max_k \frac{s_{a,k} + s_{k+1,b} + w_{a,k} + w_{k+1,b}}{4}. \quad (4)$$

The initial scores for single-subword subtrees are set to 1. The averaging then keeps the scores equalized – subtrees then have the same power regardless of the size of their spans.

The CKY algorithm works bottom up, starting with the trivial single-subword trees, and then iteratively computing the values of larger subtrees based on the values precomputed in previous steps. Together with the score of each tree, the algorithm also stores the $k$ from Equation 4, which defines the highest scoring pair of subtrees covering the same span. Once the algorithm reaches the tree covering the whole sentence, it recursively returns the highest scoring tree based on the stored values of the highest scoring subtrees.

### 5.2 Automatic Evaluation

To evaluate the syntacticity of the Transformer self-attentive encoder, we extract the constituency trees using our tree extraction algorithm for the 1,000 sentences of our evaluation set; we will refer to these as *extracted trees*.

We then induce syntactic trees for these sentences with the Stanford Parser. We use the factored lexicalized parsing models distributed together with the parser, which had been trained on standard constituency treebanks of the languages – English Penn Treebank (Marcus et al., 1993), German Negra Corpus (Skut et al., 1999), and French Treebank (Abeillé et al., 2003). We post-process the trees in the following way:

1. remove phrase labels

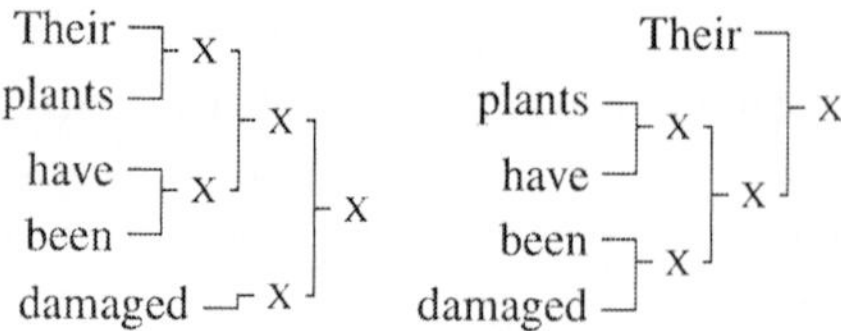

Figure 2: Left (*lbal*) and right (*rbal*) balanced binary tree baselines.

2. wrap each word into a single-word phrase
3. split words into subwords
4. flatten phrases containing only one immediate subphrase or only one subword

We show an example of applying this procedure:

0. (S (VP vinegrowers suffer) )
1. ( (vinegrowers suffer) )
2. ( ( (vinegrowers) (suffer) ) )
3. ( ( (vin- e- growers) (suffer) ) )
4. ( (vin- e- growers) suffer)

We will refer to the resulting trees as *parse trees*.

We compare the extracted trees with the parse trees, assuming that the more similar they are, the more syntactic the Transformer encoder is.

We calculate the *precision* of the extracted tree as the proportion of its phrases that are "correct" in the sense that they are consistent with the parse tree, not crossing any of its phrases. (For the sake of this analysis, we only consider one possible way of capturing syntax, as defined in the respective treebanks; we discuss that in Section 5.3.)

Let $P$ be the parse tree, an extracted phrase $e$ is correct if and only if:

$$\forall p \in P : (p \cap e = \emptyset) \vee (p \subseteq e) \vee (e \subseteq p). \quad (5)$$

*Recall* is computed inversely, as the proportion of phrases in the parse tree that are consistent with the extracted tree. We compute the total precision and recall as an average over all extracted phrases in all the trees, and also report their harmonic mean (*F1*).

The results of the evaluations for all three source languages are shown in Table 2. To put them into perspective, we also report scores for several uninformed parsing baselines:

1. *rbal*: balanced binary tree aligned right
2. *lbal*: balanced binary tree aligned left
3. *rand.init*: our proposed algorithm using randomly initialized Transformer weights

Examples of the *lbal* and *rbal* baselines are shown in Figure 2.

English

| system | precision | recall | F1 score |
|---|---|---|---|
| rbal | 30.1% | 24.3% | 26.8% |
| lbal | 27.8% | 20.8% | 23.8% |
| rand.init | 25.1% | 20.0% | 22.3% |
| en → de | 35.4% | 30.6% | 32.8% |
| en → fr | 35.4% | 30.2% | 32.6% |

German

| system | precision | recall | F1 score |
|---|---|---|---|
| rbal | 39.1% | 31.3% | 34.8% |
| lbal | 38.1% | 27.6% | 32.0% |
| rand.init | 33.7% | 25.9% | 29.3% |
| de → en | 46.1% | 39.6% | 42.6% |
| de → fr | 46.7% | 40.9% | 43.6% |

French

| system | precision | recall | F1 score |
|---|---|---|---|
| rbal | 34.3% | 28.7% | 31.3% |
| lbal | 32.5% | 25.4% | 28.5% |
| rand.init | 26.1% | 24.4% | 25.3% |
| fr → en | 44.4% | 39.7% | 41.9% |
| fr → de | 46.9% | 41.7% | 44.2% |

Table 2: Scores of baseline trees and our extracted trees using all attention heads, evaluated against standard syntactic parse trees.

## 5.3 Discussion of Results

The F1 scores of the trees extracted from the attention matrices are 6 to 13 percentage points higher than the best baselines, showing that some syntax is indeed captured by the Transformer encoder.

For English, the scores are notably lower than for the other languages. Manual inspection has shown that this is mostly due to the English parse trees being strongly right-branching, while the other treebanks use flatter, more balanced trees, mainly due to different annotation styles of the treebanks. The trees extracted from the attention matrices are similar for all of the languages, and resemble the German or French parse trees more than the English ones. However, a part of the score differences may also be due to a differing syntacticity of the individual encoders, as can be seen from the differing scores for fr→en and fr→de.

Figure 3 shows an example of a tree extracted from the en→de encoder (the sentence is the same as in Figure 1). We can see that many of the subtrees seem to make sense syntactically, both smaller ones, such as "[have been] damaged", as well as larger ones, such as the tree spanning "huge…vineyards". Some are questionable, but

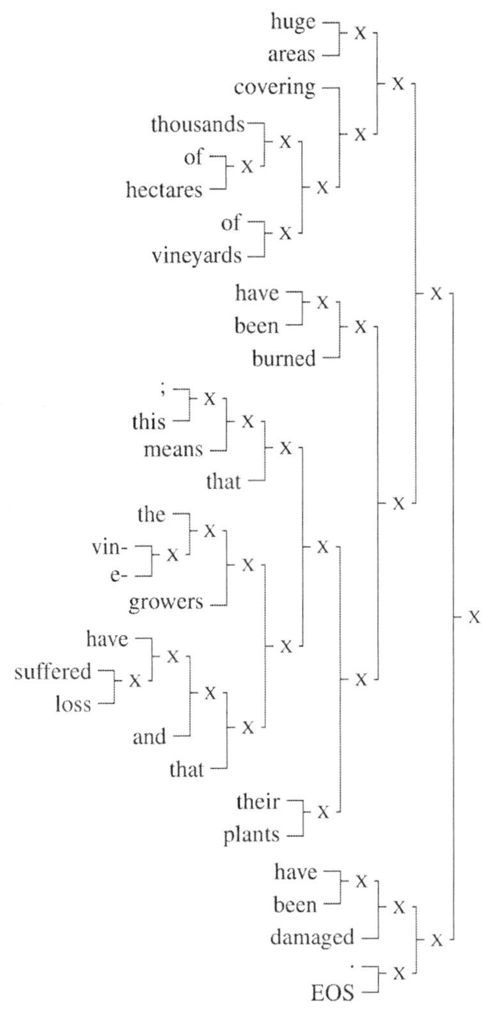

Figure 3: A constituency tree generated by our tree extraction algorithm from the attention matrices of the en-de encoder for the 4th sentence of the evaluation set.

not necessarily wrong, e.g. "[the vine-] growers".

A clear limitation of our automatic evaluation method is that it only evaluates whether the structures match those of the syntactic formalism of the standard treebank, but it cannot appreciate alternative structures that also make sense syntactically. However, this issue is hard to solve without a significant amount of manual work.

Nevertheless, some structures clearly do not correspond to the syntactic structure of the sentence, regardless of the syntactic formalism that we adhere to. E.g. the phrases "their plants" and "have been damaged" belong together, but they are separated in the extracted tree all the way to the root. The reason we find these incorrect structures in the extracted trees may be that we are using all

269

the encoder attention matrices in the extraction algorithm, even though not all of the attention heads seem to behave syntactically; we investigate this to some extent in the next section. However, it is also quite likely that the encoder only captures some parts of the syntactic structure of the sentence, not a full syntactic tree – especially given the fact that the model is trained to do machine translation, and may thus have no reason to capture structures irrelevant for this task. Moreover, classical syntactic trees are by far not the only possible way of capturing syntax, and it is quite likely that the syntax captured by the self-attentive encoder should be understood differently.[7]

## 6  Selecting Syntactic Heads

As we have discussed in Section 4, there is a range of different types of attention heads. In our interpretation, some of them, especially the *balustrades*, seem to capture syntactic structures, while others seem not to do so. A logical step thus is to try to identify the syntactic heads, and only use those for the tree extraction.[8]

We propose to use the automatic evaluation as the criterion for selecting the "syntactic" heads. We suggest two greedy approaches: *head addition*, and *head ablation*.

In the *head addition* approach, we start with an empty set of heads and then iteratively add the heads one by one, maximizing the precision of the extracted trees in each step, until we have the set of all heads. We then identify the highest scoring head combination that we encountered.

The *head ablation* approach is the logical inverse; we start with all the heads and iteratively remove them until we end up with only one head.

We ran the selection algorithms using only the first 100 sentences. The setups selected as best by the algorithm were then evaluated on the full evaluation set. As the *head addition* consistently outperformed *head ablation* by approximately 2 percentage points, we only report the evaluation of

---

[7] For example, the syntactic structure could be quite flat, with shorter phrases or treelets joined into a linked list, rather than a complex tree structure with long-distance relations. Also, we have noted that connectors, such as punctuation and conjunctions, often seem to be part of both of their neighbouring phrases, which could lead to a formalism using partially overlapping phrases. We intend to investigate this in future.

[8] However, once we start subselecting only some of the heads, we are clearly introducing our expectations about the syntactic structures to be found into the process – we are now contaminating the so far linguistically uninformed approach with our notion of "good" or "syntactic" phrases.

|         | improvement in | | |
| system | precision | recall | F1 score |
|---|---|---|---|
| en → de | +9.48% | +7.01% | +8.10% |
| en → fr | +8.43% | +6.23% | +7.19% |
| de → en | +4.60% | +2.06% | +3.13% |
| de → fr | +5.96% | +1.76% | +3.52% |
| fr → en | +11.58% | +8.54% | +9.91% |
| fr → de | +12.16% | +8.63% | +10.20% |

Table 3: Evaluation of syntactic heads subselection. Score gains over the base tree extraction as reported in Table 2, in percentage points.

| L | 1 | 2 | 3 | 4 | 5 | 6 |
|---|---|---|---|---|---|---|
| P | 36% | 3% | 10% | 10% | 19% | 21% |

Table 4: Average proportion of attention head layers in the best subselection setups for all language pairs. $L$ is the number of the layer, $P$ is the proportion of the selected heads that come from the given layer.

the *head addition* in Table 3.

We can see improvements in F1 ranging from 3 to 10 percentage points, showing that better syntactic trees can be extracted by subselecting the heads. However, we are perhaps overtuning the setup, and the reported numbers are thus probably somewhat inflated. Therefore, we are reluctant to draw any strong conclusions from the results.

Nevertheless, the meta-analysis of the heads selected as syntactic is of interest. For each of the language pairs, between 18 and 32 heads of the total 96 were selected. However, these are not evenly distributed across the layers. As we show in Table 4, on average, one third of the selected heads come from the first layer, which mostly contains diagonals and short balusters; the last two layers, which contain a lot of balusters of varied lengths, each contributes one fifth of the heads.

## 7  Conclusion

We analyzed the Transformer encoder self-attention, identifying baluster structures resembling syntactic phrases. We devised a transparent linguistically uninformed algorithm for extracting constituency trees from the balusters, compared the resulting trees with standard syntactic parse trees, and showed that syntax is indeed captured.

## Acknowledgments

This work has been supported by the grant 18-02196S of the Czech Science Foundation.

# References

Anne Abeillé, Lionel Clément, and François Toussenel. 2003. Building a treebank for french. In *Treebanks*, pages 165–187. Springer.

Yossi Adi, Einat Kermany, Yonatan Belinkov, Ofer Lavi, and Yoav Goldberg. 2016. Fine-grained analysis of sentence embeddings using auxiliary prediction tasks. *CoRR*, abs/1608.04207.

Yonatan Belinkov and James Glass. 2018. Analysis methods in neural language processing: A survey. *CoRR*, abs/1812.08951.

Terra Blevins, Omer Levy, and Luke Zettlemoyer. 2018. Deep RNNs encode soft hierarchical syntax. In *Proceedings of the 56th Annual Meeting of the Association for Computational Linguistics (Volume 2: Short Papers)*, pages 14–19, Melbourne, Australia. Association for Computational Linguistics.

Jacob Devlin, Ming-Wei Chang, Kenton Lee, and Kristina Toutanova. 2018. BERT: pre-training of deep bidirectional transformers for language understanding. *CoRR*, abs/1810.04805.

Mikel L. Forcada, Mireia Ginestí-Rosell, Jacob Nordfalk, Jim O'Regan, Sergio Ortiz-Rojas, Juan Antonio Pérez-Ortiz, Felipe Sánchez-Martínez, Gema Ramírez-Sánchez, and Francis M. Tyers. 2011. Apertium: a free/open-source platform for rule-based machine translation. *Machine Translation*, 25(2):127–144.

Jindřich Helcl, Jindřich Libovický, Tom Kocmi, Tomáš Musil, Ondřej Cífka, Dušan Variš, and Ondřej Bojar. 2018. Neural monkey: The current state and beyond. In *The 13th Conference of The Association for Machine Translation in the Americas, Vol. 1: MT Researchers' Track*, pages 168–176, Stroudsburg, PA, USA. The Association for Machine Translation in the Americas, The Association for Machine Translation in the Americas.

John Hewitt and Christopher D. Manning. 2019. Structural Probe for Finding Syntax in Word Representations. In *Proceedings of NAACL 2019*.

Dan Klein and Christopher D Manning. 2003. Fast exact inference with a factored model for natural language parsing. In *Advances in neural information processing systems*, pages 3–10.

Philipp Koehn. 2005. Europarl: A Parallel Corpus for Statistical Machine Translation. In *Conference Proceedings: the tenth Machine Translation Summit*, pages 79–86, Phuket, Thailand. AAMT, AAMT.

Tal Linzen, Emmanuel Dupoux, and Yoav Goldberg. 2016. Assessing the ability of LSTMs to learn syntax-sensitive dependencies. *Transactions of the Association for Computational Linguistics*, 4:521–535.

Nelson F. Liu, Matt Gardner, Yonatan Belinkov, Matthew Peters, and Noah A. Smith. 2019. Linguistic knowledge and transferability of contextual representations. *CoRR*, abs/1903.08855.

Christopher D. Manning, Mihai Surdeanu, John Bauer, Jenny Finkel, Steven J. Bethard, and David McClosky. 2014. The Stanford CoreNLP natural language processing toolkit. In *Association for Computational Linguistics (ACL) System Demonstrations*, pages 55–60.

Mitchell P Marcus, Mary Ann Marcinkiewicz, and Beatrice Santorini. 1993. Building a large annotated corpus of english: The penn treebank. *Computational linguistics*, 19(2):313–330.

David Mareček and Rudolf Rosa. 2018. Extracting syntactic trees from transformer encoder self-attentions. In *Proceedings of the First Workshop on Analyzing and Interpreting Neural Networks for NLP*, pages 347–349, Stroudsburg, PA, USA. The Assotiation of Computational Linguistics.

Hermann Ney. 1991. Dynamic programming parsing for context-free grammars in continuous speech recognition. *Trans. Sig. Proc.*, 39(2):336–340.

Matthew E Peters, Mark Neumann, Mohit Iyyer, Matt Gardner, Christopher Clark, Kenton Lee, and Luke Zettlemoyer. 2018. Deep contextualized word representations. *arXiv preprint arXiv:1802.05365*.

Martin Popel and Zdeněk Žabokrtský. 2010. TectoMT: Modular NLP framework. In *Lecture Notes in Artificial Intelligence, Proceedings of the 7th International Conference on Advances in Natural Language Processing (IceTAL 2010)*, volume 6233 of *Lecture Notes in Computer Science*, pages 293–304, Berlin / Heidelberg. Iceland Centre for Language Technology (ICLT), Springer.

Alessandro Raganato and Jörg Tiedemann. 2018. An analysis of encoder representations in transformer-based machine translation. In *Proceedings of the 2018 EMNLP Workshop BlackboxNLP: Analyzing and Interpreting Neural Networks for NLP*, pages 287–297. Association for Computational Linguistics.

Rico Sennrich, Barry Haddow, and Alexandra Birch. 2016. Neural machine translation of rare words with subword units. In *Proceedings of the 54th Annual Meeting of the Association for Computational Linguistics (Volume 1: Long Papers)*, pages 1715–1725. Association for Computational Linguistics.

Xing Shi, Inkit Padhi, and Kevin Knight. 2016. Does string-based neural MT learn source syntax? In *EMNLP*, pages 1526–1534.

Wojciech Skut, Hans Uszkoreit, and Thorsten Brants. 1999. Syntactic annotation of a german newspaper corpus. In *ATALA sur le Corpus Annotés pour la Syntaxe Treebanks, June 18-19*, pages 69–76, Paris, France. o.A.

Gongbo Tang, Mathias Müller, Annette Rios, and Rico Sennrich. 2018. Why self-attention? a targeted evaluation of neural machine translation architectures. In *Proceedings of the 2018 Conference on Empirical Methods in Natural Language Processing*, pages 4263–4272. Association for Computational Linguistics.

Ashish Vaswani, Noam Shazeer, Niki Parmar, Jakob Uszkoreit, Llion Jones, Aidan N Gomez, Lukasz Kaiser, and Illia Polosukhin. 2017. Attention is all you need. In I. Guyon, U. V. Luxburg, S. Bengio, H. Wallach, R. Fergus, S. Vishwanathan, and R. Garnett, editors, *Advances in Neural Information Processing Systems 30*, pages 6000–6010. Curran Associates, Inc.

Kelly W. Zhang and Samuel R. Bowman. 2018. Language modeling teaches you more syntax than translation does: Lessons learned through auxiliary task analysis. *CoRR*, abs/1809.10040.

# Appendix: Visualization of all attention heads

We provide visualisations of encoder's self-attention heads for English source sentence *"Huge areas covering thousands of hectares of vineyards have been burned; this means that the vin@@ e-@@ growers have suffered loss and that their plants have been damaged."*, when translating into German.

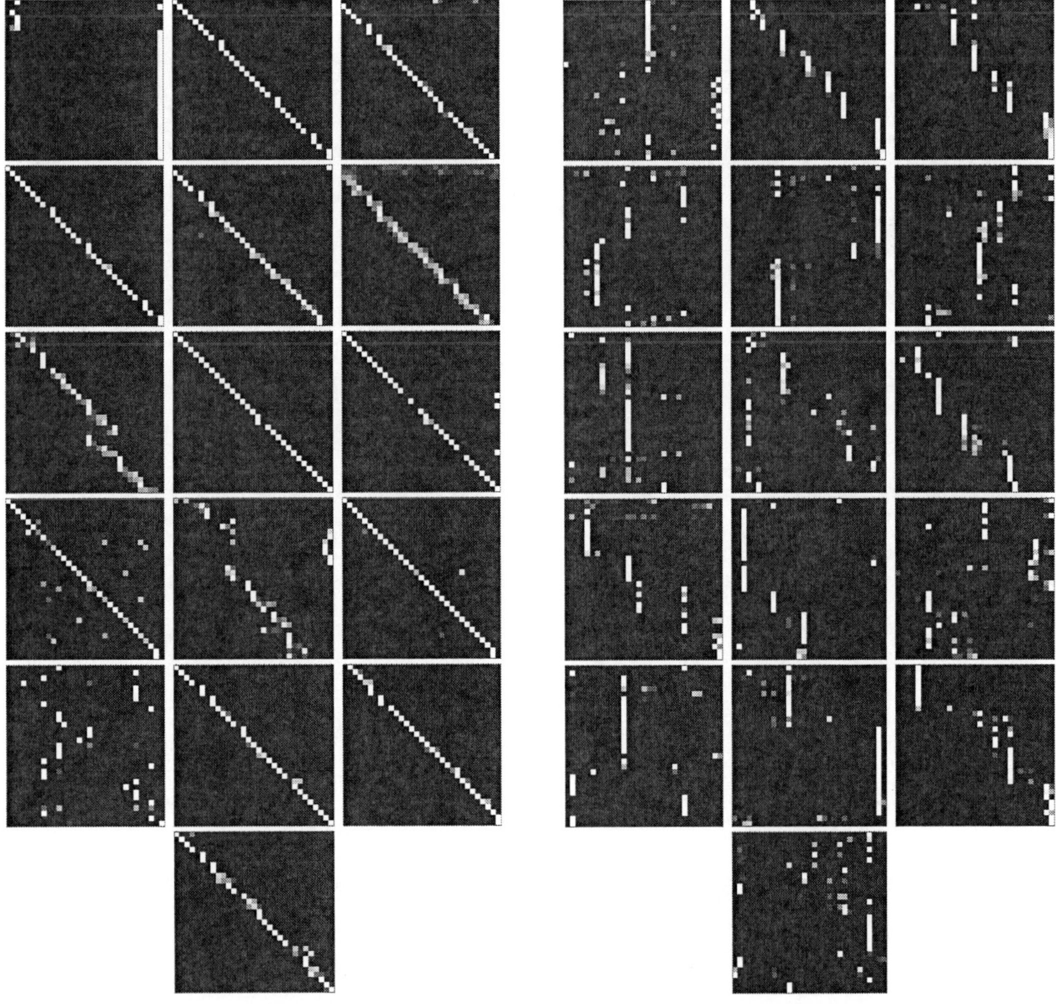

Figure 4: Layer 1

Figure 5: Layer 2

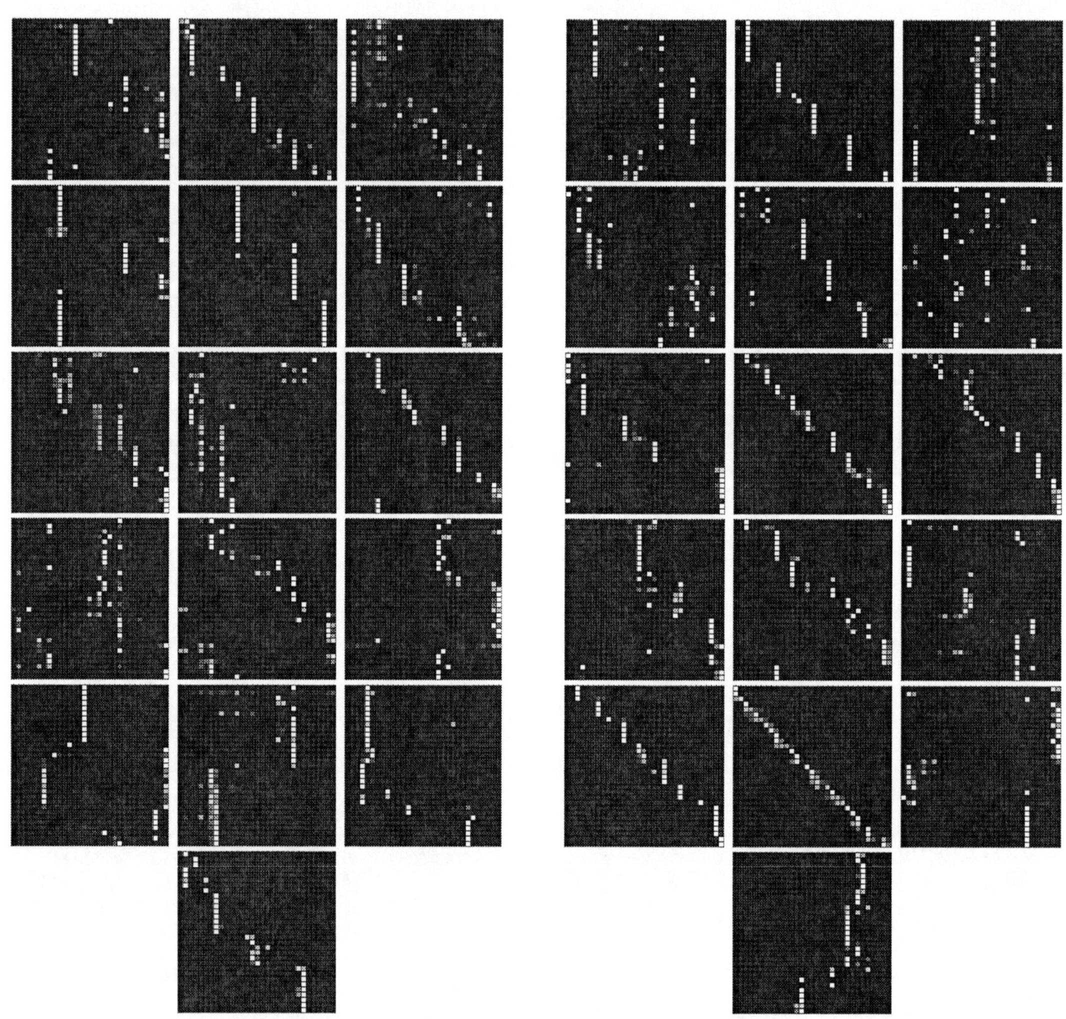

Figure 6: Layer 3                    Figure 7: Layer 4

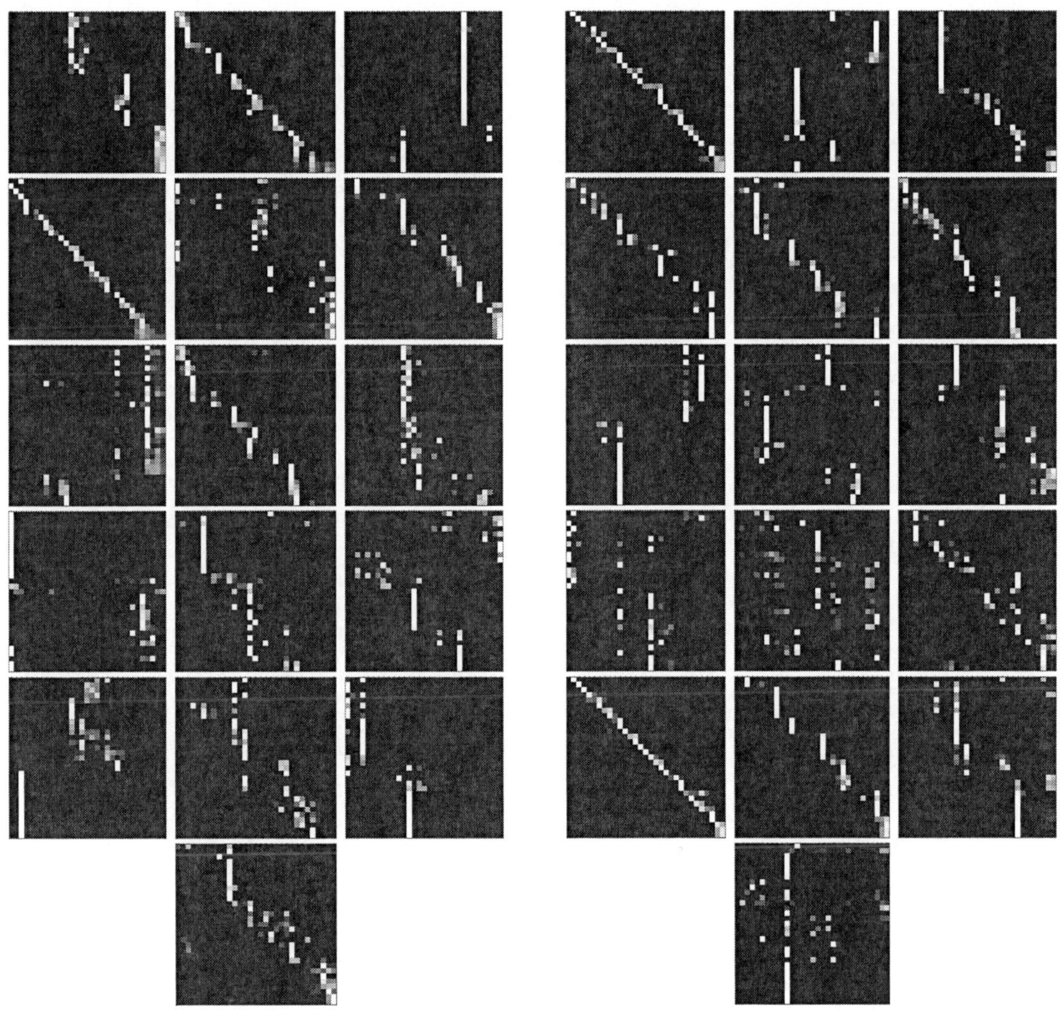

Figure 8: Layer 5            Figure 9: Layer 6

# What does BERT look at?
# An Analysis of BERT's Attention


**Kevin Clark**[†]  **Urvashi Khandelwal**[†]  **Omer Levy**[‡]  **Christopher D. Manning**[†]

[†]Computer Science Department, Stanford University

[‡]Facebook AI Research

`{kevclark,urvashik,manning}@cs.stanford.edu`

`omerlevy@fb.com`



## Abstract

Large pre-trained neural networks such as BERT have had great recent success in NLP, motivating a growing body of research investigating what aspects of language they are able to learn from unlabeled data. Most recent analysis has focused on model outputs (e.g., language model surprisal) or internal vector representations (e.g., probing classifiers). Complementary to these works, we propose methods for analyzing the attention mechanisms of pre-trained models and apply them to BERT. BERT's attention heads exhibit patterns such as attending to delimiter tokens, specific positional offsets, or broadly attending over the whole sentence, with heads in the same layer often exhibiting similar behaviors. We further show that certain attention heads correspond well to linguistic notions of syntax and coreference. For example, we find heads that attend to the direct objects of verbs, determiners of nouns, objects of prepositions, and coreferent mentions with remarkably high accuracy. Lastly, we propose an attention-based probing classifier and use it to further demonstrate that substantial syntactic information is captured in BERT's attention.


## 1 Introduction

Large pre-trained language models achieve very high accuracy when fine-tuned on supervised tasks (Dai and Le, 2015; Peters et al., 2018; Radford et al., 2018), but it is not fully understood why. The strong results suggest pre-training teaches the models about the structure of language, but what specific linguistic features do they learn?

Recent work has investigated this question by examining the *outputs* of language models on carefully chosen input sentences (Linzen et al., 2016) or examining the internal *vector representations* of the model through methods such as probing classifiers (Adi et al., 2017; Belinkov et al., 2017). Complementary to these approaches, we

study[1] the *attention maps* of a pre-trained model. Attention (Bahdanau et al., 2015) has been a highly successful neural network component. It is naturally interpretable because an attention weight has a clear meaning: how much a particular word will be weighted when computing the next representation for the current word. Our analysis focuses on the 144 attention heads in BERT (Devlin et al., 2019), a large pre-trained Transformer (Vaswani et al., 2017) network that has demonstrated excellent performance on many tasks.

We first explore generally how the attention heads behave. We find that there are common patterns in their behavior, such as attending to fixed positional offsets or attending broadly over the whole sentence. A surprisingly large amount of BERT's attention focuses on the deliminator token [SEP], which we argue is used by the model as a sort of no-op. Generally we find that attention heads in the same layer tend to behave similarly.

We next probe each attention head for linguistic phenomena. In particular, we treat each attention head as a simple no-training-required classifier that, given a word as input, outputs the most-attended-to other word. We then evaluate the ability of the heads to classify various syntactic relations. While no single head performs well at many relations, we find that particular heads correspond remarkably well to particular relations. For example, we find heads that find direct objects of verbs, determiners of nouns, objects of prepositions, and objects of possesive pronouns with >75% accuracy. We perform a similar analysis for coreference resolution, also finding a BERT head that performs quite well. These results are intriguing because the behavior of the attention heads emerges purely from self-supervised training on unlabeled data, without explicit supervision for syntax or coreference.

---

[1]Code will be released at `https://github.com/clarkkev/attention-analysis`.




*Proceedings of the Second BlackboxNLP Workshop on Analyzing and Interpreting Neural Networks for NLP*, pages 276–286

Florence, Italy, August 1, 2019. ©2019 Association for Computational Linguistics

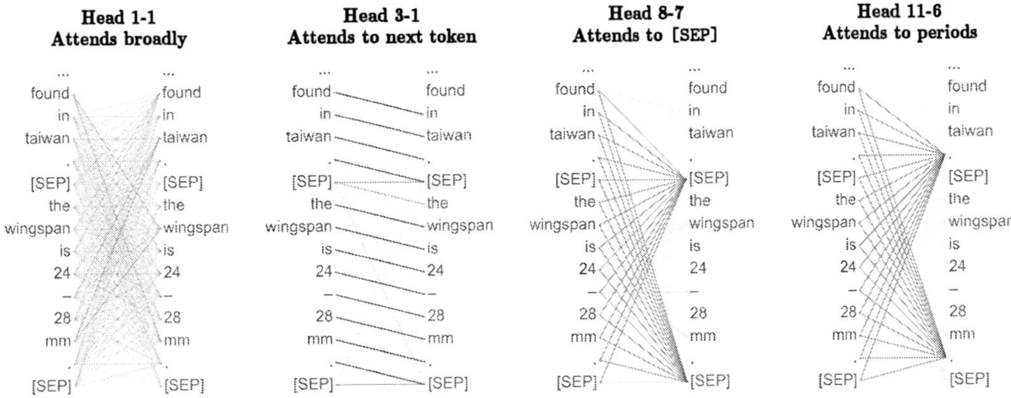



Figure 1: Examples of heads exhibiting the patterns discussed in Section 3. The darkness of a line indicates the strength of the attention weight (some attention weights are so low they are invisible).

Our findings show that particular heads specialize to specific aspects of syntax. To get a more overall measure of the attention heads' syntactic ability, we propose an attention-based probing classifier that takes attention maps as input. The classifier achieves 77 UAS at dependency parsing, showing BERT's attention captures a substantial amount about syntax. Several recent works have proposed incorporating syntactic information to improve attention (Eriguchi et al., 2016; Chen et al., 2018; Strubell et al., 2018). Our work suggests that to an extent this kind of syntax-aware attention already exists in BERT, which may be one of the reason for its success.

## 2 Background: Transformers and BERT

Although our analysis methods are applicable to any model that uses an attention mechanism, in this paper we analyze BERT (Devlin et al., 2019), a large Transformer (Vaswani et al., 2017) network. Transformers consist of multiple layers where each layer contains multiple attention heads. An attention head takes as input a sequence of vectors $h = [h_1, ..., h_n]$ corresponding to the $n$ tokens of the input sentence. Each vector $h_i$ is transformed into query, key, and value vectors $q_i, k_i, v_i$ through separate linear transformations. The head computes attention weights $\alpha$ between all pairs of words as softmax-normalized dot products between the query and key vectors. The output $o$ of the attention head is a weighted sum of the value vectors.

$$\alpha_{ij} = \frac{\exp\left(q_i^T k_j\right)}{\sum_{l=1}^{n} \exp\left(q_i^T k_l\right)} \qquad o_i = \sum_{j=1}^{n} \alpha_{ij} v_j$$

Attention weights can be viewed as governing how "important" every other token is when producing the next representation for the current token.

BERT is pre-trained on 3.3 billion tokens of unlabeled text to perform two tasks. In the "masked language modeling" task, the model predicts the identities of words that have been masked-out of the input text. In the "next sentence prediction" task, the model predicts whether the second half of the input follows the first half of the input in the corpus, or is a completely separate random text segment. Further training the model on supervised data results in impressive performance across a variety of tasks ranging from sentiment analysis to question answering. An important detail of BERT is the preprocessing used for the input text. A special token [CLS] is added to the beginning of the text and another token [SEP] is added to the end. If the input consists of multiple separate texts (e.g., a reading comprehension example consists of a separate question and context), [SEP] tokens are also used to separate them. As we show in the next section, these special tokens play an important role in BERT's attention. We use the "base" sized BERT model, which has 12 layers containing 12 attention heads each. We use <layer>-<head_number> to denote a particular attention head.

## 3 Surface-Level Patterns in Attention

Before looking at specific linguistic phenomena, we first perform an analysis of surface-level patterns in how BERT's attention heads behave. Examples of heads exhibiting these patterns are shown in Figure 1.

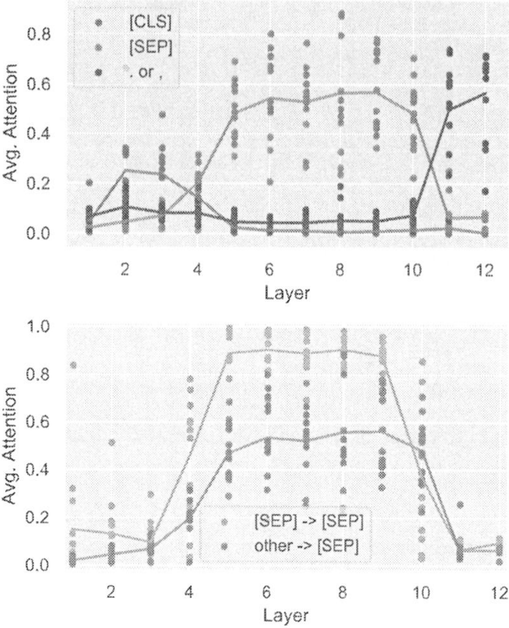

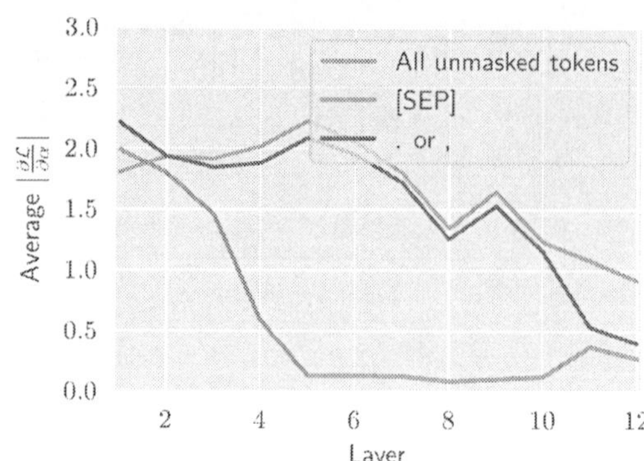

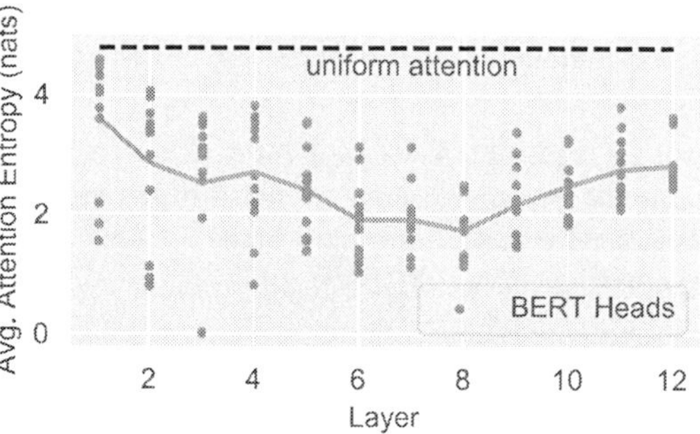

Figure 2: Each point corresponds to the average attention a particular BERT attention head puts toward a token type. Above: heads often attend to "special" tokens. Early heads attend to [CLS], middle heads attend to [SEP], and deep heads attend to periods and commas. Often more than half of a head's total attention is to these tokens. Below: heads attend to [SEP] tokens even more when the current token is [SEP] itself.

Figure 3: Gradient-based feature importance estimates for attention to [SEP], periods/commas, and other tokens.

Figure 4: Entropies of attention distributions. In the first layer there are particularly high-entropy heads that produce bag-of-vector-like representations.

**Setup.** We extract the attention maps from BERT-base over 1000 Wikipedia segments. We follow the setup used for pre-training BERT where each segment consists of at most 128 tokens corresponding to two consecutive paragraphs of Wikipedia. The input presented to the model is [CLS]<paragraph-1>[SEP]<paragraph-2>[SEP].

### 3.1 Relative Position

First, we compute how often BERT attention heads attend to the current token, the previous token, or the next token. We find that most heads put little attention on the current token. However, there are heads that specialize to attending heavily on the next or previous token, especially in earlier layers of the network. In particular four attention heads (in layers 2, 4, 7, and 8) on average put >50% of their attention on the previous token and five attention heads (in layers 1, 2, 2, 3, and 6) put >50% of their attention on the next token.

### 3.2 Attending to Separator Tokens

Interestingly, we found that a substantial amount of BERT's attention focuses on a few tokens (see Figure 2). For example, over half of BERT's attention in layers 6-10 focuses on [SEP]. To put this in context, since most of our segments are 128 tokens long, the average attention for a token occurring twice in a segments like [SEP] would normally be 1/64. [SEP] and [CLS] are guaranteed to be present and are never masked out, while periods and commas are the most common tokens in the data excluding "the," which might be why the model treats these tokens differently. A similar pattern occurs for the uncased BERT model, suggesting there is a systematic reason for the attention to special tokens rather than it being an artifact of stochastic training.

One possible explanation is that [SEP] is used to aggregate segment-level information which can then be read by other heads. However, further analysis makes us doubtful this is the case. If this hypothesis were true, we would expect attention heads processing [SEP] to attend broadly over the whole segment to build up these representations. However, they instead almost entirely (more than 90%; see bottom of Figure 2) attend to themselves and the other [SEP] token. Furthermore, qualitative analysis (see Figure 5) shows that heads with specific functions attend to [SEP] when the function is not called for. For example, in head 8-10 direct objects attend to their verbs. For this head, non-nouns mostly attend to [SEP]. Therefore, we speculate that attention over these special tokens might be used as a sort of "no-op" when the attention head's function is not applicable.

To further investigate this hypothesis, we apply gradient-based measures of feature importance (Sundararajan et al., 2017). In particular, we compute the magnitude of the gradient of the loss from BERT's masked language modeling task with respect to each attention weight. Intuitively, this value measures how much changing the attention to a token will change BERT's outputs. Results are shown in Figure 3. We find that starting in layer 5 – the same layer where attention to [SEP] becomes high – the gradients for attention to [SEP] become small. This indicates that attending more or less to [SEP] does not substantially change BERT's outputs, supporting the theory that attention to [SEP] is used as a no-op for attention heads.

### 3.3 Focused vs Broad Attention

Lastly, we measure whether attention heads focus on a few words or attend broadly over many words. To do this, we compute the average entropy of each head's attention distribution (see Figure 4). We find that some attention heads, especially in lower layers, have very broad attention. These high-entropy attention heads typically spend at most 10% of their attention mass on any single word. The output of these heads is roughly a bag-of-vectors representation of the sentence.

We also measured entropies for all attention heads from only the [CLS] token. While the average entropies from [CLS] for most layers are very close to the ones shown in Figure 4, the last layer has a high entropy from [CLS] of 3.89 nats, indicating very broad attention. This finding makes sense given that the representation for the [CLS] token is used as input for the "next sentence prediction" task during pre-training, so it attends broadly to aggregate a representation for the whole input in the last layer.

## 4 Probing Individual Attention Heads

Next, we investigate individual attention heads to probe what aspects of language they have learned. In particular, we evaluate attention heads on labeled datasets for tasks like dependency parsing. An overview of our results is shown in Figure 5.

### 4.1 Method

We wish to evaluate attention heads at word-level tasks, but BERT uses byte-pair tokenization (Sennrich et al., 2016), which means some words (∼8% in our data) are split up into multiple tokens. We therefore convert token-token attention maps to word-word attention maps. For attention *to* a split-up word, we sum up the attention weights over its tokens. For attention *from* a split-up word, we take the mean of the attention weights over its tokens. These transformations preserve the property that the attention from each word sums to 1. For a given attention head and word, we take whichever other word receives the most attention weight as that model's prediction[2]

### 4.2 Dependency Syntax

**Setup.** We extract attention maps from BERT on the Wall Street Journal portion of the Penn Treebank (Marcus et al., 1993) annotated with Stanford Dependencies. We evaluate both "directions" of prediction for each attention head: the head word attending to the dependent and the dependent attending to the head word. Some dependency relations are simpler to predict than others: for example a noun's determiner is often the immediately preceding word. Therefore as a point of comparison, we show predictions from a simple fixed-offset baseline. For example, a fixed offset of -2 means the word two positions to the left of the dependent is always considered to be the head.

**Results.** Table 1 shows that there is no single attention head that does well at syntax "overall"; the best head gets 34.5 UAS, which is not much better than the right-branching baseline, which gets 26.3 UAS. This finding is similar to the one reported by Raganato and Tiedemann (2018), who also evaluate individual attention heads for syntax.

However, we do find that certain attention heads specialize to specific dependency relations, some-

---

[2]We ignore [SEP] and [CLS], although in practice this does not significantly change the accuracies for most heads.

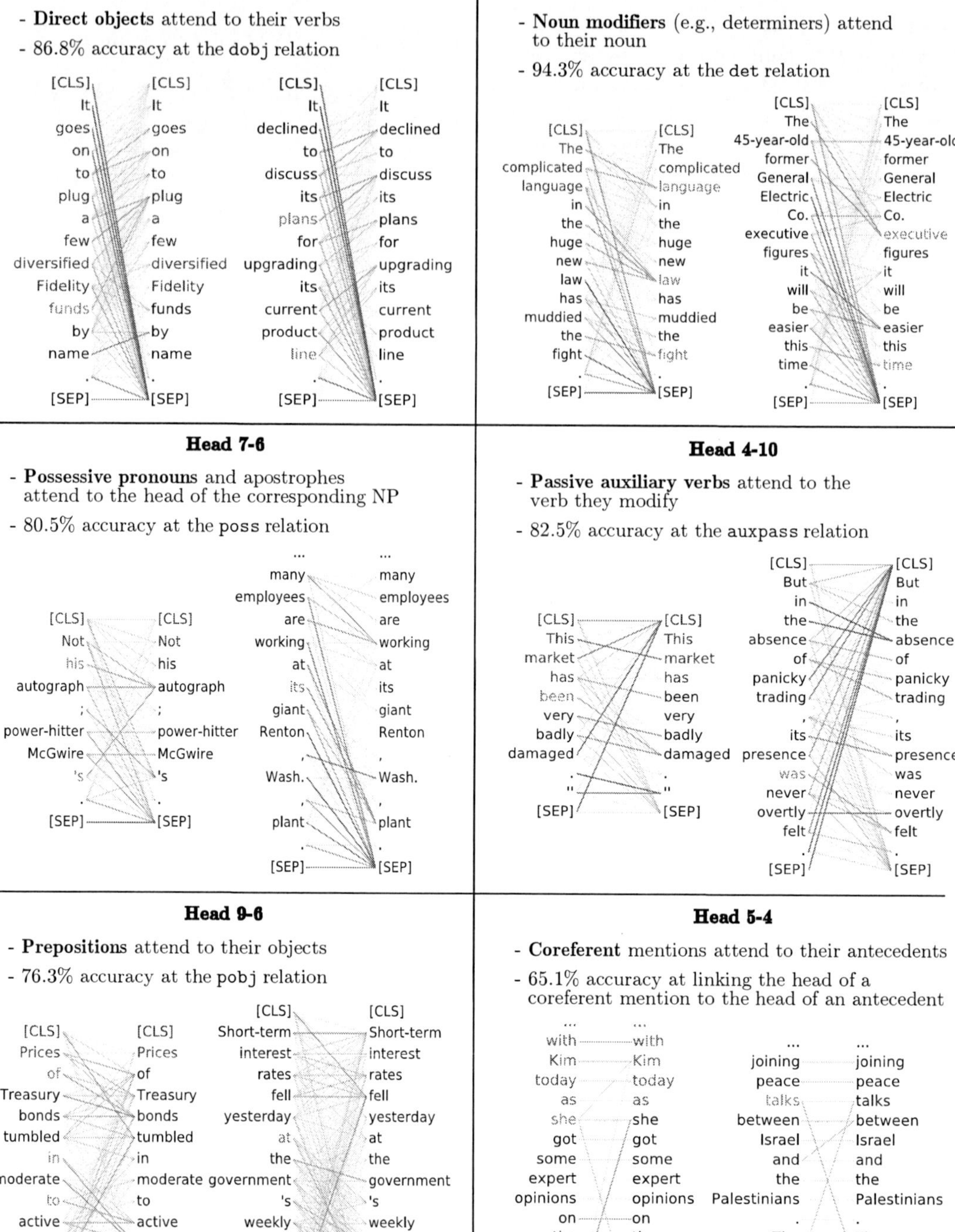


Figure 5: BERT attention heads that correspond to linguistic phenomena. In the example attention maps, the darkness of a line indicates the strength of the attention weight. All attention to/from red words is colored red; these colors are there to highlight certain parts of the attention heads' behaviors. For Head 9-6, we don't show attention to [SEP] for clarity. Despite not being explicitly trained on these tasks, BERT's attention heads perform remarkably well, illustrating how syntax-sensitive behavior can emerge from self-supervised training alone.

| Relation | Head | Accuracy | Baseline |
|---|---|---|---|
| All | 7-6 | 34.5 | 26.3 (1) |
| prep | 7-4 | 66.7 | 61.8 (-1) |
| pobj | 9-6 | **76.3** | 34.6 (-2) |
| det | 8-11 | **94.3** | 51.7 (1) |
| nn | 4-10 | 70.4 | 70.2 (1) |
| nsubj | 8-2 | 58.5 | 45.5 (1) |
| amod | 4-10 | 75.6 | 68.3 (1) |
| dobj | 8-10 | **86.8** | 40.0 (-2) |
| advmod | 7-6 | 48.8 | 40.2 (1) |
| aux | 4-10 | 81.1 | 71.5 (1) |
| poss | 7-6 | **80.5** | 47.7 (1) |
| auxpass | 4-10 | **82.5** | 40.5 (1) |
| ccomp | 8-1 | **48.8** | 12.4 (-2) |
| mark | 8-2 | **50.7** | 14.5 (2) |
| prt | 6-7 | **99.1** | 91.4 (-1) |

Table 1: The best performing attentions heads of BERT on WSJ dependency parsing by dependency type. Numbers after baseline accuracies show the best offset found (e.g., (1) means the word to the right is predicted as the head). We show the 10 most common relations as well as 5 other ones attention heads did well on. Bold highlights particularly effective heads.

times achieving high accuracy and substantially outperforming the fixed-offset baseline. We find that for all relations in Table 1 except pobj, the dependent attends to the head word rather than the other way around, likely because each dependent has exactly one head but heads have multiple dependents. We also note heads can disagree with standard annotation conventions while still performing syntactic behavior. For example, head 7-6 marks 's as the dependent for the poss relation, while gold-standard labels mark the complement of an 's as the dependent (the accuracy in Table 1 counts 's as correct). Such disagreements highlight how these syntactic behaviors in BERT are learned as a by-product of self-supervised training, not by copying a human design.

Figure 5 shows some examples of the attention behavior. While the similarity between learned attention weights and human-defined syntactic relations are striking, we note these are relations for which attention heads do particularly well on. There are many relations for which BERT only slightly improves over the simple baseline, so we would not say individual attention heads capture dependency structure as a whole.

### 4.3 Coreference Resolution

Having shown BERT attention heads reflect certain aspects of syntax, we now explore using attention heads for the more challenging semantic task of coreference resolution. Coreference links are usually longer than syntactic dependencies and state-of-the-art systems generally perform much worse at coreference compared to parsing.

**Setup.** We evaluate the attention heads on coreference resolution using the CoNLL-2012 dataset[3] (Pradhan et al., 2012). In particular, we compute antecedent selection accuracy: what percent of the time does the head word of a coreferent mention most attend to the head of one of that mention's antecedents. We compare against three baselines for selecting an antecedent:

- Picking the nearest other mention.

- Picking the nearest other mention with the same head word as the current mention.

- A simple rule-based system inspired by Lee et al. (2011). It proceeds through 4 sieves: (1) full string match, (2) head word match, (3) number/gender/person match, (4) all other mentions. The nearest mention satisfying the earliest sieve is returned.

We also show the performance of a recent neural coreference system from (Wiseman et al., 2015).

**Results.** Results are shown in Table 2. We find that one of BERT's attention heads achieves decent coreference resolution performance, improving by over 10 accuracy points on the string-matching baseline and performing close to the rule-based system. It is particularly good with nominal mentions, perhaps because it is capable of fuzzy matching between synonyms as seen in the bottom right of Figure 5.

## 5 Probing Attention Head Combinations

Since individual attention heads specialize to particular aspects of syntax, the model's overall "knowledge" about syntax is distributed across multiple attention heads. We now measure this overall ability by proposing a novel family of attention-based probing classifiers and applying them to dependency parsing. For these classifiers we treat the BERT attention outputs as fixed, i.e.,

---

[3]We truncate documents to 128 tokens long to keep memory usage manageable.

| Model | All | Pronoun | Proper | Nominal |
|---|---|---|---|---|
| Nearest | 27 | 29 | 29 | 19 |
| Head-word match | 52 | 47 | 67 | 40 |
| Rule-based | 69 | 70 | 77 | 60 |
| Neural coref | 83* | – | – | – |
| Head 5-4 | 65 | 64 | 73 | 58 |

*Only roughly comparable because on non-truncated documents and with different mention detection.

Table 2: Accuracies (%) for different mention types of systems selecting a correct antecedent given a coreferent mention in the CoNLL-2012 data. One of BERT's attention heads performs fairly well at coreference.

we do not back-propagate into BERT and only train a small number of parameters.

The probing classifiers are basically graph-based dependency parsers. Given an input word, the classifier produces a probability distribution over other words in the sentence indicating how likely each other word is to be the syntactic head of the current one.

**Attention-Only Probe.** Our first probe learns a simple linear combination of attention weights.

$$p(i|j) \propto \exp\left( \sum_{k=1}^{n} w_k \alpha_{ij}^k + u_k \alpha_{ji}^k \right)$$

where $p(i|j)$ is the probability of word $i$ being word $j$'s syntactic head, $\alpha_{ij}^k$ is the attention weight from word $i$ to word $j$ produced by head $k$, and $n$ is the number of attention heads. We include both directions of attention: candidate head to dependent as well as dependent to candidate head. The weight vectors $w$ and $u$ are trained using standard supervised learning on the train set.

**Attention-and-Words Probe.** Given our finding that heads specialize to particular syntactic relations, we believe probing classifiers should benefit from having information about the input words. In particular, we build a model that sets the weights of the attention heads based on the GloVe (Pennington et al., 2014) embeddings for the input words. Intuitively, if the dependent and candidate head are "the" and "cat," the probing classifier should learn to assign most of the weight to the head 8-11, which achieves excellent performance at the determiner relation. The attention-and-words probing classifier assigns the probabil-

ity of word $i$ being word $j$'s head as

$$p(i|j) \propto \exp\left( \sum_{k=1}^{n} W_{k,:}(v_i \oplus v_j)\alpha_{ij}^k + \right.$$

$$\left. U_{k,:}(v_i \oplus v_j)\alpha_{ji}^k \right)$$

Where $v$ denotes GloVe embeddings and $\oplus$ denotes concatenation. The GloVe embeddings are held fixed in training, so only the two weight matrices $W$ and $U$ are learned. The dot product $W_{k,:}(v_i \oplus v_j)$ produces a word-sensitive weight for the particular attention head.

**Results.** We evaluate our methods on the Penn Treebank dev set annotated with Stanford dependencies. We compare against three baselines:

- A right-branching baseline that always predicts the head is to the dependent's right.

- A simple one-hidden-layer network that takes as input the GloVe embeddings for the dependent and candidate head as well as a set of features indicating the distances between the two words.[4]

- Our attention-and-words probe, but with attention maps from a BERT network with pre-trained word/positional embeddings but randomly initialized other weights. This kind of baseline is surprisingly strong at other probing tasks (Conneau et al., 2018).

Results are shown in Table 3. We find the Attn + GloVe probing classifier substantially outperforms our baselines and achieves a decent UAS of 77, suggesting BERT's attention maps have a fairly thorough representation of English syntax. As a rough comparison, we also report results from the structural probe from Hewitt and Manning (2019), which builds a probing classifier on top of BERT's vector representations rather than attention. The scores are not directly comparable because the structural probe only uses a single layer of BERT, produces undirected rather than directed parse trees, and is trained to produce the syntactic distance between words rather than directly predicting the tree structure. Nevertheless, the similarity in score to our Attn + Glove probing classifier suggests there is not much more syntactic information in BERT's vector representations compared to its attention maps.

---

[4]indicator features for short distances as well as continuous distance features, with distance ahead/behind treated separately to capture word order

| Model | UAS |
| --- | --- |
| Right-branching | 26 |
| Distances + GloVe | 58 |
| Random Init Attn + GloVe | 30 |
| Attn | 61 |
| Attn + GloVe | 77 |
| Structural probe (Hewitt and Manning, 2019) | 80 UUAS* |

Table 3: Results of attention-based probing tasks on dependency parsing. A simple model taking BERT attention maps and GloVe word embeddings as input performs quite well at dependency parsing. *Not directly comparable to our numbers; see text.

Overall, our results from probing both individual and combinations of attention heads suggest that BERT learns some aspects syntax purely as a by-product of self-supervised training. Other work has drawn a similar conclusions from examining BERT's predictions on agreement tasks (Goldberg, 2019) or internal vector representations (Hewitt and Manning, 2019; Liu et al., 2019). Traditionally, syntax-aware models have been developed through architecture design (e.g., recursive neural networks) or from direct supervision from human-curated treebanks. Our findings are part of a growing body of work indicating that indirect supervision from rich pre-training tasks like language modeling can also produce models sensitive to language's hierarchical structure.

## 6   Clustering Attention Heads

Are attention heads in the same layer similar to each other or different? In general, can attention heads be clearly grouped by behavior? We investigate these questions by computing the distances between all pairs of attention heads. Formally, we measure the distance between two heads $H_i$ and $H_j$ as:

$$\sum_{\text{token} \in \text{data}} JS(H_i(\text{token}), H_j(\text{token}))$$

Where $JS$ is the Jensen-Shannon Divergence between attention distributions. Using these distances, we visualize the attention heads by applying multidimensional scaling (Kruskal, 1964) to embed each head in two dimensions such that the euclidean distance between embeddings reflects the Jensen-Shannon distance between the corresponding heads as closely as possible.

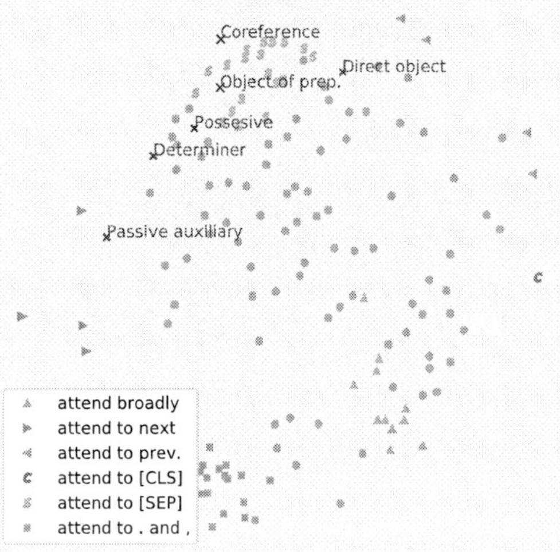


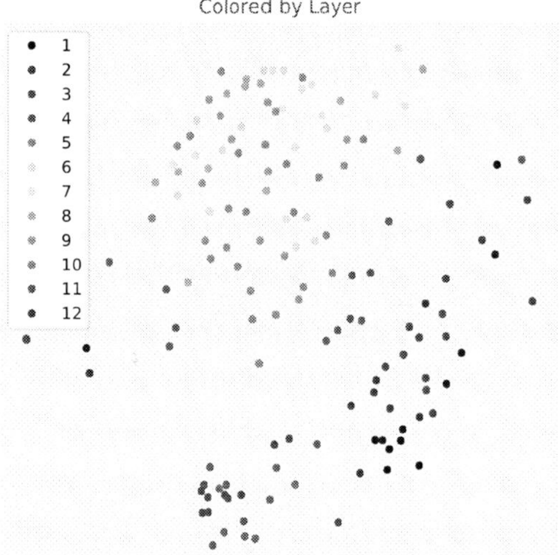


Figure 6: BERT attention heads embedded in two-dimensional space. Distance between points approximately matches the average Jensen-Shannon divergences between the outputs of the corresponding heads. Heads in the same layer tend to be close together. Attention head "behavior" was found through the analysis methods discussed throughout this paper.

Results are shown in Figure 6. We find that there are several clear clusters of heads that behave similarly, often corresponding to behaviors we have already discussed in this paper. Heads within the same layer are often fairly close to each other, meaning that heads within the layer have similar attention distributions. This finding is a bit surprising given that Tu et al. (2018) show that encouraging attention heads to have different behaviors can improve Transformer performance at machine translation. One possibility for the apparent redundancy in BERT's attention heads is the use of attention dropout, which causes some attention weights to be zeroed-out during training.

## 7 Related Work

There has been substantial recent work performing analysis to better understand what neural networks learn, especially from language model pre-training. One line of research examines the *outputs* of language models on carefully chosen input sentences (Linzen et al., 2016; Khandelwal et al., 2018; Gulordava et al., 2018; Marvin and Linzen, 2018). For example, the model's performance at subject-verb agreement (generating the correct number of a verb far away from its subject) provides a measure of the model's syntactic ability, although it does not reveal *how* that ability is captured by the network.

Another line of work investigates the internal *vector representations* of the model (Adi et al., 2017; Giulianelli et al., 2018; Zhang and Bowman, 2018), often using probing classifiers. Probing classifiers are simple neural networks that take the internal vector representations of a pre-trained model as input. They are trained to do a supervised task (e.g., part-of-speech tagging). If a probing classifier achieves high accuracy, it suggests that the vector representations reflect the corresponding aspect of language (e.g., low-level syntax). Like our work, some of these studies have also demonstrated neural networks capturing aspects of syntactic structures (Shi et al., 2016; Blevins et al., 2018) or coreference (Tenney et al., 2018, 2019) without explicitly being trained for the tasks.

With regards to analyzing attention, Vig (2019) builds a visualization tool for the BERT's attention and reports observations about some of the heads' behaviors, but does not perform any quantitative analysis. Burns et al. (2018) analyze the attention of memory networks to understand model performance on a question answering dataset; we instead aim to understand linguistic information captured in pre-trained models. There has also been some initial work in correlating attention with syntax. Raganato and Tiedemann (2018) evaluate the attention heads of a machine translation model on dependency parsing, but only report overall UAS scores instead of investigating heads for specific syntactic relations or using probing classifiers. Marecek and Rosa (2018) propose heuristic ways of converting attention scores to syntactic trees, but do not quantitatively evaluate their approach.

Concurrently with our work Voita et al. (2019) identify syntactic, positional, and rare-word-sensitive attention heads in machine translation models. They also demonstrate that many attention heads can be pruned away without substantially hurting model performance. Interestingly, the important attention heads that remain after pruning tend to be ones with identified behaviors. Michel et al. (2019) similarly show that many of BERT's attention heads can be pruned. Although our analysis in this paper only found interpretable behaviors in a subset of BERT's attention heads, these recent works suggest that there might not be much to explain for some attention heads because they have little effect on model perfomance.

Jain and Wallace (2019) argue that attention often does not "explain" model predictions. They show that attention weights frequently do not correlate with other measures of feature importance. Furthermore, attention weights can often be substantially changed without altering model predictions. However, our motivation for looking at attention is different: rather than explaining model predictions, we are seeking to understand information learned by the models. For example, if a particular attention head learns a syntactic relation, we consider that an important finding from an analysis perspective even if that head is not always used when making predictions for some downstream task.

## 8 Conclusion

We have proposed a series of analysis methods for understanding the attention mechanisms of models and applied them to BERT. While most recent work on model analysis for NLP has focused on probing vector representations or model outputs, we have shown that a substantial amount of linguistic knowledge can be found not only in the hidden states, but also in the attention maps. We think probing attention maps complements these other model analysis techniques, and should be part of the toolkit used by researchers to understand what neural networks learn about language.

### Acknowledgements

We thank the anonymous reviews for their thoughtful comments and suggestions. Kevin is supported by a Google PhD Fellowship.

## References

Yossi Adi, Einat Kermany, Yonatan Belinkov, Ofer Lavi, and Yoav Goldberg. 2017. Fine-grained analysis of sentence embeddings using auxiliary prediction tasks. In *ICLR*.

Dzmitry Bahdanau, Kyunghyun Cho, and Yoshua Bengio. 2015. Neural machine translation by jointly learning to align and translate. In *ICLR*.

Yonatan Belinkov, Nadir Durrani, Fahim Dalvi, Hassan Sajjad, and James R. Glass. 2017. What do neural machine translation models learn about morphology? In *ACL*.

Terra Blevins, Omer Levy, and Luke S. Zettlemoyer. 2018. Deep rnns encode soft hierarchical syntax. In *ACL*.

Kaylee Burns, Aida Nematzadeh, Alison Gopnik, and Thomas L. Griffiths. 2018. Exploiting attention to reveal shortcomings in memory models. In *BlackboxNLP@EMNLP*.

Kehai Chen, Rui Wang, Masao Utiyama, Eiichiro Sumita, and Tiejun Zhao. 2018. Syntax-directed attention for neural machine translation. In *AAAI*.

Alexis Conneau, Germán Kruszewski, Guillaume Lample, Loïc Barrault, and Marco Baroni. 2018. What you can cram into a single $&!#* vector: Probing sentence embeddings for linguistic properties. In *ACL*.

Andrew M Dai and Quoc V Le. 2015. Semi-supervised sequence learning. In *NIPS*.

Jacob Devlin, Ming-Wei Chang, Kenton Lee, and Kristina Toutanova. 2019. BERT: Pre-training of deep bidirectional transformers for language understanding. In *NAACL-HLT*.

Akiko Eriguchi, Kazuma Hashimoto, and Yoshimasa Tsuruoka. 2016. Tree-to-sequence attentional neural machine translation. In *ACL*.

Mario Giulianelli, Jack Harding, Florian Mohnert, Dieuwke Hupkes, and Willem H. Zuidema. 2018. Under the hood: Using diagnostic classifiers to investigate and improve how language models track agreement information. In *BlackboxNLP@EMNLP*.

Yoav Goldberg. 2019. Assessing BERT's syntactic abilities. *arXiv preprint arXiv:1901.05287*.

Kristina Gulordava, Piotr Bojanowski, Edouard Grave, Tal Linzen, and Marco Baroni. 2018. Colorless green recurrent networks dream hierarchically. In *NAACL-HLT*.

John Hewitt and Christopher D. Manning. 2019. Finding syntax with structural probes. In *NAACL-HLT*.

Sarthak Jain and Byron C. Wallace. 2019. Attention is not explanation. *arXiv preprint arXiv:1902.10186*.

Urvashi Khandelwal, He He, Peng Qi, and Daniel Jurafsky. 2018. Sharp nearby, fuzzy far away: How neural language models use context. In *ACL*.

Joseph B Kruskal. 1964. Multidimensional scaling by optimizing goodness of fit to a nonmetric hypothesis. *Psychometrika*, 29(1):1–27.

Heeyoung Lee, Yves Peirsman, Angel Chang, Nathanael Chambers, Mihai Surdeanu, and Dan Jurafsky. 2011. Stanford's multi-pass sieve coreference resolution system at the conll-2011 shared task. In *CoNLL*.

Tal Linzen, Emmanuel Dupoux, and Yoav Goldberg. 2016. Assessing the ability of lstms to learn syntax-sensitive dependencies. *TACL*.

Nelson F. Liu, Matt Gardner, Yonatan Belinkov, M. Peters, and Noah A. Smith. 2019. Linguistic knowledge and transferability of contextual representations. In *NAACL-HLT*.

Mitchell P Marcus, Mary Ann Marcinkiewicz, and Beatrice Santorini. 1993. Building a large annotated corpus of english: The Penn treebank. *Computational linguistics*, 19(2):313–330.

David Marecek and Rudolf Rosa. 2018. Extracting syntactic trees from transformer encoder self-attentions. In *BlackboxNLP@EMNLP*.

Rebecca Marvin and Tal Linzen. 2018. Targeted syntactic evaluation of language models. In *EMNLP*.

Paul Michel, Omer Levy, and Graham Neubig. 2019. Are sixteen heads really better than one? *arXiv preprint arXiv:1905.10650*.

Jeffrey Pennington, Richard Socher, and Christopher Manning. 2014. Glove: Global vectors for word representation. In *EMNLP*.

Matthew E Peters, Mark Neumann, Mohit Iyyer, Matt Gardner, Christopher Clark, Kenton Lee, and Luke Zettlemoyer. 2018. Deep contextualized word representations. In *NAACL-HLT*.

Sameer Pradhan, Alessandro Moschitti, Nianwen Xue, Olga Uryupina, and Yuchen Zhang. 2012. Conll-2012 shared task: Modeling multilingual unrestricted coreference in ontonotes. In *Joint Conference on EMNLP and CoNLL-Shared Task*.

Alec Radford, Karthik Narasimhan, Tim Salimans, and Ilya Sutskever. 2018. Improving language understanding by generative pre-training. *https://blog.openai.com/language-unsupervised*.

Alessandro Raganato and Jörg Tiedemann. 2018. An analysis of encoder representations in transformer-based machine translation. In *BlackboxNLP@EMNLP*.

Rico Sennrich, Barry Haddow, and Alexandra Birch. 2016. Neural machine translation of rare words with subword units. In *ACL*.

Xing Shi, Inkit Padhi, and Kevin Knight. 2016. Does string-based neural mt learn source syntax? In *EMNLP*.

Emma Strubell, Patrick Verga, Daniel Andor, David I Weiss, and Andrew McCallum. 2018. Linguistically-informed self-attention for semantic role labeling. In *EMNLP*.

Mukund Sundararajan, Ankur Taly, and Qiqi Yan. 2017. Axiomatic attribution for deep networks. In *ICML*.

Ian Tenney, Dipanjan Das, and Ellie Pavlick. 2019. Bert rediscovers the classical nlp pipeline. *arXiv preprint arXiv:1905.05950*.

Ian Tenney, Patrick Xia, Berlin Chen, Alex Wang, Adam Poliak, R Thomas McCoy, Najoung Kim, Benjamin Van Durme, Samuel R Bowman, Dipanjan Das, et al. 2018. What do you learn from context? probing for sentence structure in contextualized word representations. In *ICLR*.

Zhaopeng Tu, Baosong Yang, Michael R. Lyu, and Tong Zhang. 2018. Multi-head attention with disagreement regularization. In *EMNLP*.

Ashish Vaswani, Noam Shazeer, Niki Parmar, Jakob Uszkoreit, Llion Jones, Aidan N. Gomez, Lukasz Kaiser, and Illia Polosukhin. 2017. Attention is all you need. In *NIPS*.

Jesse Vig. 2019. Visualizing attention in transformer-based language models. *arXiv preprint arXiv:1904.02679*.

Elena Voita, David Talbot, Fedor Moiseev, Rico Sennrich, and Ivan Titov. 2019. Analyzing multi-head self-attention: Specialized heads do the heavy lifting, the rest can be pruned. *arXiv preprint arXiv:1905.09418*.

Sam Joshua Wiseman, Alexander Matthew Rush, Stuart Merrill Shieber, and Jason Weston. 2015. Learning anaphoricity and antecedent ranking features for coreference resolution. In *ACL*.

Kelly W. Zhang and Samuel R. Bowman. 2018. Language modeling teaches you more syntax than translation does: Lessons learned through auxiliary task analysis. In *BlackboxNLP@EMNLP*.

# Author Index